ROBERT A. HEINLEIN

IN DIALOGUE WITH HIS CENTURY

ROBERT A. HEINLEIN

IN DIALOGUE WITH HIS CENTURY

VOLUME 1

1907–1948
LEARNING CURVE

WILLIAM H. PATTERSON, JR.

TOR®

A TOM DOHERTY ASSOCIATES BOOK · NEW YORK

ROBERT A. HEINLEIN: IN DIALOGUE WITH HIS CENTURY:
VOLUME 1, 1907–1948: LEARNING CURVE

A Tor Book
Published by Tom Doherty Associates, LLC
175 Fifth Avenue
New York, NY 10010

www.tor-forge.com

Tor® is a registered trademark of Tom Doherty Associates, LLC.

Library of Congress Cataloging-in-Publication Data

Patterson, William H., 1951–
    Robert A. Heinlein / William H. Patterson.—1st ed.
      p. cm.
    "A Tom Doherty Associates book."
    Includes bibliographical references.
    Contents: v. 1. 1907–1948, learning curve
    ISBN 978-0-7653-1960-9
    1. Heinlein, Robert A. (Robert Anson), 1907–1988. 2. Heinlein,
Robert A. (Robert Anson), 1907–1988—Political and social views.
3. Authors, American—20th century—Biography. 4. Science fiction—
Authorship. I. Title.
PS3515.E288Z82   2010
813'.54—dc22
[B]
                                                 2009041202

First Edition: August 2010

Printed in the United States of America

0 9 8 7 6 5 4 3 2 1

To be overwise is to ossify; and the scruple-monger ends by standing stock-still. Now the man who has his heart on his sleeve, and a good whirling weathercock of a brain, who reckons his life as a thing to be dashingly used and cheerfully hazarded . . . keeps all his pulses going true and fast, and gathers impetus as he runs, until, if he be running towards anything better than wildfire, he may shoot up and become a constellation in the end. . . .

Every heart that has beat strong and cheerfully has left a hopeful impulse behind it in the world, and bettered the tradition of mankind. . . . The noise of mallet and chisel is scarcely quenched, the trumpets are hardly done blowing, when, trailing with him clouds of glory, this happy-starred, full-blooded spirit shoots into the spiritual land.

ROBERT LOUIS STEVENSON, "Aes Triplex"

CONTENTS

Introduction   11

1. The Heinleins of Butler, Missouri   17
2. Growing Up, Kansas City   24
3. A Jazz Age Teenager   33
4. Plebe Summer   48
5. Plebe Year   61
6. Youngster Year   74
7. Second Class Year   87
8. First Classman   97
9. Frying Pan and Fire   110
10. New York State of Mind   121
11. Robert and Uncle Ernie   126
12. Leslyn MacDonald   144
13. Swallowing the Anchor   158
14. Baptism of Fire   173
15. Party and Shadow Party   185
16. Party Animal   201
17. The Next Thing   214
18. And the Next   224
19. Not Quite Done with Politics   236
20. Out and About: The Long, Strange Trip   252
21. Expanding Horizons   271
22. "And put aside childish things . . ."   293

23. "Do with thy heart what thy hands find to do . . ."   306

24. Keeping On—   324

25. Stabilizing, Somewhat   338

26. Dangerous New World   352

27. Settling In   371

28. Writing Factory   393

29. Separation. Anxiety.   411

30. Also on the Road . . .   433

31. Once More, Dear Friends . . .   448

32. Fresh Starts   458

     Acknowledgments   475

     Appendix A: Family Background   479

     Appendix B: Campaign Biography   493

     Notes   495

     Index   595

ROBERT A. HEINLEIN

IN DIALOGUE WITH HIS CENTURY

INTRODUCTION

What were you doing when . . . ?

Life-defining events come in all sizes. Everyone experiences the big, public ones together:

- the assassinations of John F. Kennedy, Martin Luther King, and Bobby Kennedy
- the first Moon landing
- the *Challenger* disaster
- the morning of September 11, 2001.

The small-scale, personal events are shared by ones and twos:

- your first kiss and the song that was playing on the radio, your first dance
- the day your father or mother died.

For hundreds of thousands of people around the world, Sunday afternoon, May 8, 1988, was one of those life-defining moments. Phone trees formed spontaneously, friend calling friend: "Have you heard the news?" Robert Anson Heinlein died that morning.

The wake of grief widened and circled the globe several times that day, as it had when Mark Twain died—to Germany, and to France and to Italy. On it went, to Yugoslavia (a country itself now gone) and to the Soviet Union, to Shanghai and on to Japan; north, to Greenland, Canada, Alaska, and south where the scientists at McMurdo Sound in the Antarctic had gathered around him a few years before, to shake his hand.

Heinlein's hard-core un-common sense, dosed out mostly as entertainment, had given the parentless generations of the mid-twentieth century something of what previous generations had gotten, in quiet moments one-on-one with their fathers and their tribe's wise men: their portion, all they could take, of life wisdom. They counted Heinlein their "intellectual father," as an earlier generation regarded Mark Twain, and now "his" boys—and girls—were grown to responsible maturity, hands on the tiller. They had needed, sometimes desperately, to hear what he had to say—not slogans, but tools:

> What are the facts? Again and again and again—what are the *facts*? Shun wishful thinking, ignore divine revelation, forget "what the stars foretell," avoid opinion, care not what the neighbors think, never mind the unguessable "verdict of history"—what are the facts, and to how many decimal places? You pilot always into an unknown future; facts are your single clue.[1]

The story of Robert A. Heinlein is the story of America in the twentieth century, and the issues he concerned himself with—and the methods by which he grappled with them—were cutting-edge for his time. When Heinlein began writing, science fiction was in a struggle to lift itself and its readers out of Victorian notions, and he was immediately recognized as a leader in that Modernist struggle. After World War II he took on "propaganda purposes," as he styled them, that required him to reframe science fiction again, to talk, not just to excited genre readers and editors, but to the general public, who could use the intellectual tools science fiction had created before the war to grasp and manage their increasingly technology-dominated future.

It is a truism of literature that the prestige forms of one era grow out of the subliterary forms of a prior era, and Heinlein's writing career spans the transformation of a subliterary pulp genre into a significant dialogue partner at the interface of science and public policy—a transformation for which he is in no small degree responsible.

Like his mentors, H. G. Wells and Mark Twain, Heinlein became a public moralist, sure that what his readers *really* needed to know was how the world actually worked—dangerous knowledge and subversive, especially in his influential novels for young readers.

Robert A. Heinlein was not a "public" figure in the usual sense: he had won people's hearts and minds on a retail basis, one by one, in the close community of a reader and a book.

What he meant to his readers grew slowly over the years. The nervous teenager who stood in the shade of the Gate House of the United States Naval Academy and took the midshipman's oath on June 16, 1925, was a rustic by the standards of the society he was moving into, all raw potential.

In 1947 he became a public figure when he pioneered science fiction into the prestige general-fiction magazines with four moving stories in *The Saturday Evening Post*. In 1949 he was pioneering again, into a truly mass-entertainment form—the motion pictures, the *first* modern science-fiction film, *Destination Moon*. A local television station filmed a forty-seven-minute featurette on the making of the film, and Heinlein assured Mr. and Mrs. John Q. Public that what they were about to see they could make happen anytime they were ready to open their pocketbooks—twenty years at a guess.[2]

And twenty years later, Heinlein sat in a makeshift CBS studio in Downey, California. It was July 20, 1969, and *Eagle* had landed. Walter Cronkite and Arthur C. Clarke were talking heads on the studio monitor . . . and they wanted him there for commentary, when he was too excited, almost, to talk at all.

Heinlein had yearned for the Moon for most of his life, and he had done what he could to make it happen—in aeronautical engineering in the Navy, then writing about it, making it real to readers after the Navy chewed him up and spit him out in 1934. *Destination Moon* was released in 1950 and caused a national sensation by visualizing for the people of the world the first trip to the Moon. Heinlein got on with his real work, teaching people how to live in the future. Now, in 1969, he was a celebrity again, his big satire on hypocrisy, *Stranger in a Strange Land,* still picking up steam, though almost nobody seemed to understand it was not a book of answers, but a book of questions.

Heinlein grew up in the horse-and-buggy Midwest of Kansas City. He lived through the Jazz Age and the tearing poverty of the Great Depression. He churned out bucketfuls of pulp, and this is where it brought him. He had hit it almost on the dot: his fictional lunar landing in "The Man Who Sold the Moon" was set in 1970, and it was happening only five months early.

"This is the great day," Heinlein would tell Cronkite:

This is the greatest event in all the history of the human race, up to this time. This is—today is New Year's Day of the Year One. If we don't change the calendar, historians will do so. The human race—this is our change, our puberty rite, bar mitzvah, confirmation, from the change from infancy into adulthood for the human race. And we are going to go on out, not only to the Moon, to the stars: we're going to spread. I don't know that the United States is going to do it; I hope so. I have—I'm an American

myself; I want it to be done by us. But in any case, the human race is going to do it, it's utterly inevitable: we're going to spread through the entire
universe.[3]

The Moon landing came and went, but Heinlein endured, always framing
the hard questions. So successful was this writerly mission that Heinlein was
increasingly sought out as a guru—a position he rejected. At almost the same
time *Stranger* was speaking to the spiritual life of a new generation, so, too,
The Moon Is a Harsh Mistress was galvanizing another movement of young
people coming together. The movement has suffered many ups and downs,
but well into the twenty-first century, libertarianism is with us still, still field-
ing presidential candidates, and still holding out Heinlein's vision of what an
untrammeled society might look like.

And on and on it would go, for nearly twenty years more, putting into
words what people—his kind of people—thought and felt, telling the hard
truths, the ones that needed to be told, the ones that *all* people needed to hear.
And for that grandfatherly kindness he was given what can only be called love.

And in the selvages of his time and energy, in the chinks of time he had
left between the books, "do with thy heart what thy hands find to do." He
helped change blood collection services over to an all-volunteer donor force,
and then went to work on the new great project, ending Mutual Assured
Destruction.

Just months after his death, the Cold War ended: its great symbol, the
Berlin Wall, was taken down, and the Soviet Union collapsed, unable to move
into the future Robert Heinlein had laid out for us.

For all that the world of the twenty-first century is troubled by the breakup
of the Soviet bloc and its aftereffects, the disappearance of whole nations devoted to the systematic brutalization of their citizens was something Robert
Heinlein was proud to participate in.

In death he moved on to the next frontier: his and his wife's entire estate
was devoted to founding the Heinlein Prize for Accomplishments in Commercial Space Activities, the essential next step in establishing humanity in
the cosmos. "It's raining soup," Heinlein once said of the benefits of space
and its limitless resources, "grab a bucket!"—words as true now as when he
wrote them first, decades ago.

For almost fifty years Heinlein conducted a dialogue with his culture, a dialogue that, once started, continues in his works—still asking the hard questions (and undercutting any answers you might think you have found!). And
people responded to what they could sense of this greater dialogue, even if

they didn't always have the words to talk about it. The story of his public influence is almost unique in American letters, grouping him among a select company of American writers who had found "tipping points" of social crux and galvanized social change of some kind:

- Upton Sinclair's *The Jungle* (1906) portrayed labor conditions in the Chicago meatpacking industry and galvanized support for Theodore Roosevelt's Pure Food and Drug Act, thereby ushering in the twentieth century's regulatory and legislative style;
- Edward Bellamy's *Looking Backward* (1888) inspired the National Club movement, a wave of radical political action that was the precursor to the Populist movement, now largely forgotten but enormously influential in the last years of the nineteenth century;
- Harriet Beecher Stowe's melodrama *Uncle Tom's Cabin* (1852) galvanized the Abolition movement around its portrayal of cruelty, abandonment, abuse;
- Thomas Paine and *Common Sense* (1776) provided the statement of the plain sense of the American cause and unified the colonies in the Revolutionary War.

And even among this select group of writers-*cum*-culture-figures, Heinlein is unique. He galvanized not one, but *four* social movements of his century: science fiction and its stepchild, the policy think tank, the counterculture, the libertarian movement, and the commercial space movement.

Robert Heinlein spent his life—and his fortune—pushing and pulling us into our future, in a continuing contest for the human mind, in a dialogue with everything in the twentieth century that deadened the human spirit. His books remain in print—every one of them—more than twenty years after his death (a commercial fact that puts him in a very select group of American writers) because they continue to speak to the indomitable human spirit.

Ultimately, this should not be surprising. He grew up immersed in the radical liberal movements of the late nineteenth and early twentieth century, and almost the whole of the concerns that characterize his later writing are rooted in this tradition. His extraordinary fame, literary longevity, and cultural impact—in art forms, in cultural movements, and in political movements—rest on his strong affirmation, first to last, of the liberal-progressive values he held crucial—values Americans continue to hold important.

Was he a science-fiction writer? He was—and yet the category simply will not contain him. He did not float on the currents of the current; he continued to grapple with the hard issues throughout his long life. His life is a witness: in showing us how he "did" a concerned, substantial human being, he showed us how we might do it, as well—different in the details, because every human life is different from every other, but always the same in substance.

Heinlein's job, as he conceived it, was to keep before us those perennial values, those essentially American values that belong even more to the world and to the future. Robert A. Heinlein was our bridge to the future, no less now, twenty years after his death, than during his life, begun so very long ago. Early in the last century, during that time of unimaginable ferment that was the Roaring Twenties, he collected hard questions for himself. His books and stories are interim reports on what he learned. His importance for us is that he learned better, he learned how to stand outside the box of assumptions that preoccupy us all.

The first phase of his education on the hard questions took him nearly half his life, the period I have designated his "learning curve."

THE HEINLEINS OF BUTLER, MISSOURI

Butler, Missouri, has been the county seat and market town for Bates County since the resettlement of the "dark and bloody ground" after the Civil War. Eighty miles southeast of Kansas City, in 1907 it was in its third decade of sustained growth and had achieved a kind of stability that let its residents—most of them—enjoy what is now seen as a golden age of America, though in October of that year they were in for another depression, as debilitating as the savage depression of 1893.

Both the Heinlein and Lyle families were well established in Butler. Rex Ivar Heinlein and Bam Lyle Heinlein grew up there (though Rex's father, Samuel Edward Heinlein, was a traveling salesman working out of Kansas City), and they began dating when both were attending Butler's Academy (the local equivalent of a college). Rex enlisted for the Spanish-American War, and when he came back, sick and "on a shutter," as family lore has it,[1] they were married in November 1899.

The couple immediately moved into Bam's parents' house—a common practice in the days before installment credit contracts brought the purchase of a house within the range of newlyweds. Extended families were the rule, and houses were built to accommodate generations living under the same roof. Even so, the Lyle ménage must have been crowded: Bam's six-year-old brother, Park, was living at home, and when her older sister, Anna, was widowed, leaving her to support her daughter, Thelma, by teaching, she, too, had gone back home to Butler and to her father's house.

Fortunately, Dr. Lyle's horse-and-buggy medical practice was flourishing; even with the additional people in residence, he was able to indulge in trotting races as a hobby, running a fashionable sulky—a light cart with only a driver's seat—in the annual Bates County Fair, drawn by a half-brother of the famous Dan Patch.

In 1899 Rex Ivar had prospects: he was working as a clerk and bookkeeper in his uncle Oscar Heinlein's dry goods store in Butler, a kind of combination hardware and general store. Uncle Oscar, in his mid-thirties, was unmarried and childless; it was understood that, if he applied himself and worked hard, Rex Ivar might inherit O. A. Heinlein Mercantile one day.[2]

Rex Ivar and Bam started a family: their first child, a boy, was born on August 15, 1900. They named him Lawrence Lyle Heinlein, honoring grandparents on both sides of the family. On March 25, 1905, another boy was born. They named him Rex Ivar, after his father. A year later, Bam Heinlein became pregnant again.

On July 7, 1907, not-quite-seven-year-old Larry Heinlein was delegated to keep his two-year-old brother, Rex, under control, at least till his father got home from work.[3] Bam Lyle Heinlein was upstairs for her lying-in, attended by her father's office partner, Dr. Chastain, since it would have been improper for Dr. Lyle to attend his own daughter. Shortly after 3 p.m., she delivered a fine baby boy. They named him Robert Anson, after her great-grandparents Robert Lyle and Anson S. Wood.

But by 1907 Rex Ivar's prospects in Butler no longer seemed quite so rosy. Like the biblical Jacob, he had served his uncle for seven years, and that was enough. The October stock market crash and Panic of 1907 threw the country into a depression. That winter Rex Ivar decided to give up on Butler and joined his father and uncles (plus aunt Jessie) in Kansas City.

Rex Ivar's father, Samuel Edward Heinlein, had been in Kansas City for some years, working as a traveling salesman for the Kansas-Moline Plow Company. In 1903 he moved to the Midland Manufacturing Company, where his brothers Harvey and Lawrence also got work as salesmen and his sister Jessie was a clerk. In 1906 Samuel Edward was promoted from traveling salesman and assistant manager to full manager for Midland Manufacturing (soon to become Midland Implements, Jobbers of Implements & Vehicles), and with the attendant raise he bought a larger house. In December 1907 Rex and Bam and the three boys moved into his father's house. Rex Ivar, too, started out as a traveling salesman for Midland, and Robert remembered being taken several times by his mother to the train station at the foot of Wyandotte (building torn down in 1914) to meet his father returning home from his sales route.[4] Soon, however, Midlands promoted him to clerk and cashier, and he was able to rent a small house of his own at 2605 Cleveland.[5] Now Rex and Bam felt truly launched in Kansas City.[6] They would work hard and strive— and have many more children.

Robert Anson was an easy baby for his mother. She later said he gave no trouble and always entertained himself.[7] Robert later recalled that he was fed on Eagle Brand condensed and sweetened milk, rather than breastfed like the rest of the children.[8] No explanation for this has survived. Sometimes it just happens that lactation does not start.

Robert's infancy cannot have been easy for him, though: a middle child, between the older boys and the new babies that came one by one, he was out-competed for his mother's attention. He said on several occasions that he was a stammerer as a young man, and stammering is often associated with family disturbances during the time when a child is learning to speak, roughly from about ages two through five—for Robert, that was from 1909 through 1912.[9] Bam seems to have preferred her father's day-to-day care during her pregnancies (there are no records of perinatal doctoring or midwifery), and she spent a great deal of time in her father's house in the early days.

A baby girl, Louise, arrived on February 27, 1909. In 1910 Midland failed and went out of business. In 1911 brothers Samuel and Harvey Wallace Heinlein put the Heinlein family's expertise to work and set up their own company—Heinlein Brothers, Agricultural Implements—across the street from the old Midlands site. Rex Ivar was their clerk-cashier.[10]

He was thirty-one years old; he was also sickly and had a series of operations during Robert's childhood. Work, church, and politics left very little time to spend with the family. When Bobby was five years old, he noticed unusual tension in the house; he later found out his father had received word from a local doctor that he had only three months to live—a false alarm, it turned out.[11]

The children shared two bedrooms, with the smallest children in a crib in the parents' bedroom. Nor were there enough beds to go around. Heinlein recalled as an adult that he slept on a pallet on the floor for years, in a constant state of amiable warfare with baby sister Louise, "a notorious pillow-swiper (with nine in the family, pillows were at a premium) clear back when she pronounced the word *pillow* as 'pidduh.'"[12]

As is common in large families, the older children had to help raise the younger. Bobby adored his oldest brother, Lawrence, but not brother Rex. Rex was only two years older, but gave himself privileges Bobby did not appreciate. A family anecdote from about 1911 or 1912 illustrates the problem: Rex came running in to their mother complaining—tattling—that Bobby was standing by the curb and saying hello to everybody who came along, and Rex didn't approve of that.[13] Rex continued trying to raise his brother for a very long time, and this was a source of strain between them as they grew older.

On September 10, 1912, another boy was born, Jesse (later called "Jay")

Clare, named for his Aunt Jessie. Then Rose Elizabeth on July 23, 1918, named apparently for the paternal and maternal grandmothers, Rose Adelia Wood and Elizabeth Johnson (much as Robert Anson had been named for the grandfathers). Mary Jean, arriving on Christmas Day in 1920, rounded out the family at seven children. Bam Heinlein was forty-one years old.

Until 1914 Bam and the children went by train to live with Dr. Lyle in Butler during summers and holidays. There she and the children could get out from under many of the pressures and privations of their life in Kansas City and Bam could let the children run (relatively) free in the cleaner, rural environment. Rex Ivar was bound to his desk in Kansas City, joining them when he could get away—weekends occasionally; a full week when possible. (In 1909 he had taken a temporary job with a bank in Butler while Bam was pregnant with Louise.)[14]

Young Bobby seems to have been a particular favorite of Dr. Lyle's, and the affection was certainly reciprocated; Dr. Lyle built a special seat in his sulky for the boy, so he could accompany him on his medical rounds. Dr. Lyle did not shield the realities from the boy: outside the very largest and most advanced hospitals, medical practice consisted of iodine and aspirin, and encouraging people to heal themselves.[15] Years later, Robert remembered seeing Dr. Lyle burn and bury his instruments after an infectious disease case, possibly anthrax.[16]

Dr. Lyle also taught Bobby to play chess at age four. As Dr. Lyle died in August 1914, when his grandson had just turned seven years old, these incidents must have made a very deep impression on him. Heinlein was to take Dr. Lyle as his pattern for all the American frontier virtues of intellectual range and toughness, patriotism, and pragmatic morality in his fictional portrait of Lazarus Long's grandfather, Dr. Ira Johnson, in *Time Enough for Love* (1973) and *To Sail Beyond the Sunset* (1987).

But Kansas City was home, more and more. The Heinleins had an almost proprietary, family interest in Swope Park, since an uncle Ira (who had married Bobby's Aunt Jessie) worked for the city, and he drew for his own amusement a detailed map locating every rock and shrub in the park (he also achieved renown for collecting a large ball of twine).[17] Later, Heinlein recalled stripping and playing naked in the park, before World War I, pretending he was Tarzan.[18] Nakedness became an important sensual experience for him. Years later, for fictional purposes, he recalled:

When I was a boy, ages and ages ago, it got unbearably hot in July and August where we lived—the sidewalks used to burn my bare feet. Houses were bake ovens even at night—no air conditioning. An electric fan was a luxury most people did not have. Nights when I couldn't sleep because of heat I used to sneak quiet as a mouse and bare as a frog out the back door, being oh so careful not to let my parents hear, and walked naked in the dark, with grass cool on my feet and the soft night breeze velvet on my skin. Heavenly![19]

For recreation, the Heinleins had books, family Bible readings, Sunday school, morning church, evening church, prayer meeting, and church socials and entertainments. Bam was a strict churchgoer, and Rex Ivar was a deacon, very serious about his ecclesiastical duties.[20] Most of his friends were drawn from church rather than from his business activities. At the age of three, Bobby was already enrolled in the Cradle Roll of the Grand Avenue Methodist Episcopal Church, as a surviving birthday card attests.

The Methodist Episcopal Church (MEC) is not the same as the Missouri Synod Methodist churches more familiar in the rest of the country—or in the rest of Missouri, for that matter. Neither the Missouri Synod Lutherans, commonplace elsewhere, nor Catholics were present in any sizable numbers in Bates County, where Bam had grown up. The predominant sects were the Christian Church (Disciples of Christ), Baptists, and the MEC, in two synods, the other denominating itself as MEC South. The congregation had split in the Civil War along Abolitionist/pro-slavery lines and had never merged back together. Abolition was a minority sentiment in Missouri, a slave state because of the Missouri Compromise of 1820, but that was the side the Lyles and the Heinleins were on.

The Heinleins stayed with the Methodist Episcopal Church, moving their membership from Grand Avenue to the Phoenix Park MEC when they moved to 2605 Cleveland in 1910. Early in 1914 the family moved again, and took their church membership to the Martha Slavens Memorial MEC for most of Bobby's youth. He was thus, as he had remarked on several occasions, raised Methodist, in the strict 1904 Discipline—though he also called himself an "outstanding failure" of Martha Slavens Memorial Church, which he characterized (sardonically) as a "soul-saving institution."[21] But it was a success in at least one way: the family's MEC was Abolitionist and antiracist, and so was he.

In addition to church, the Heinleins were also active in local politics. They were a "mixed marriage," as Bam was Republican while Rex Ivar was a Democrat, but their political activities were Democrat, at a time when Democratic Party politics in Kansas City almost necessarily meant the Pendergast political machine.

Jim Pendergast had been alderman of the city's river-bottom First Ward since 1892, and in the second decade of the new century was one of the principal controllers of the city's political machine, which could be characterized as a relatively benign version of New York's Tammany Hall.[22]

Alderman Jim Pendergast died in 1911, leaving his organization in the hands of his much younger brother, Tom. Rex Ivar was one of Tom Pendergast's *Joe Doakes*es, who helped administer the organization. By 1927 Rex worked his way up to the minor patronage job of Collector (a low-level city office).

Most people remember only fragments and images of their life before the emotional watershed of puberty, but Heinlein's recollections of his early childhood were sharp and thoughtful. His continuous stream of memory starts at the age of five, in 1912. He remembered that year playing the part of Captain Miles Standish in a school pageant—undoubtedly Sunday school— and "thot it was dreadful to have to carry a musket to church."[23] He recalled with great pleasure his first ride in an automobile—at a breathtaking seventeen miles per hour. His fascination with the stars had started even earlier: his brother Lawrence took him out in the yard one night to see the 1910 apparition of Halley's Comet.[24] Bobby was three years old. Heinlein remembered Lawrence patiently explaining a lunar eclipse to him in 1912,[25] and the understanding—at the age of five—gave him his first of what, by inference from his later remarks on the subject, must have been an epiphany—an emotion of awe and wonder and intellectual exaltation.

That same year he remembered the *Titanic* incident (1912) as aweinspiring: "I remember so sharply the extras about it, and my own awe and lack of understanding—I had never seen water bigger than the Missouri River."[26] A little while later, he saw one of the last performances of Buffalo Bill's traveling circus. "He looked like Mark Twain with a goatee,"[27] Robert remembered.

An incident witnessed on a family outing in Swope Park in 1912 stayed with him for the rest of his life. He would take it out of memory and turn it over in his mind again and again, examining it with wonder:

A young couple was walking along a set of railroad tracks that cut through the park in those days when the woman got her heel caught in a switch—a nuisance, until they heard a train whistle approaching at speed. Another young man—the newspapers later said he was a tramp—stopped to help them get free. As the train bore down on them, the husband and the tramp struggled to get the woman free and were struck, all of them. The wife and the tramp were killed instantly, the husband seriously injured.

Why did he do it? Not the husband, who was, after all, simply (simply!) doing his duty by his wife—but the tramp, who had no personal stake in their welfare and could have jumped aside, even at the last minute, to save himself. *Why did he do it?* wondered little Bobby and then adolescent Bobby—and so, repeatedly, did Midshipman Bob and politician Bob and adult Robert, understanding a bit more, a bit differently, every time he looked at it.

An artist works in images and articulates images even when he can't necessarily articulate the meaning. This incident became a core image for him, one that showed him in a way beyond words what it means to be a human being. At the end he still could not articulate it. All he could say about it was: "This is how a man dies. This is how a *man* lives!"[28] And that was enough. It was in images Heinlein worked, and while we can recognize that unnamed tramp most obviously in the end sequences of "Gulf" and *Starship Troopers,* his example formed the core of Heinlein's understanding of what it meant to be a self-responsible being, giving back to those around you, and thus was a shaping influence on *Starship Troopers, Stranger in a Strange Land,* and *The Moon Is a Harsh Mistress*—three books that transcended genre and gave Heinlein an important place in the lives of his readers.

2

GROWING UP, KANSAS CITY

Heinlein Brothers, Agricultural Implements, failed in 1912. Samuel Edward, Rex Ivar, and Uncle Harvey found work at the Elite Post Card Co.—his uncles as traveling salesmen, Rex Ivar as bookkeeper, setting up their chart of accounts. He picked up extra work—moonlighting—doing bookkeeping and accounting odd jobs until he found steady employment as a cashier for International Harvester. One moonlighting job he did for neighbors who lived around the corner from the Heinleins. They had formed a new company, Hall Brothers Lithography, and Rex Ivar set up their books for them. They were so pleased with his work that they invited him to take over as treasurer of the new company. It was tempting: his Uncle Harvey was already traveling for them as the West Coast sales manager, but they couldn't guarantee as large a salary as International Harvester was paying him, and he had to turn down the opportunity: he had a growing family to support.[1]

Hall Brothers eventually became Hallmark Cards.

Early in 1914, the Heinleins found a larger house in the same neighborhood, at 1617 East Thirty-seventh Street. The older boys were enrolled in the relatively new Horace Mann Elementary School a few blocks away, and Bobby was placed in the Greenwood Grammar School.

First grade was heaven for Bobby: there were sixty-three others in the class, many from the deeply impoverished orphanage in the neighborhood, but he was surrounded by books. He already owned several books of his own, given him as gifts starting in 1912: a copy of L. Frank Baum's *Sky Island* (1912) and another book illustrated by John R. Neill, who later moved on to the Oz books. Sister Louise "inherited" a number of Robert's childhood books, including *The Water Babies,* over his strenuous objections (his protests continued for at least sixty years). He remembered reading two books of Roy Rockwood's Great Marvel series—*Through Space to Mars* (1910) and *Lost on the Moon* (1911)—shortly after they were published.[2]

That first year, though, was the last time for many years he had the luxury of a full day of school; overcrowding caused the district to go into split sessions, holding the classroom size to about forty. One of the students at Greenwood Grammar School, three years older than Bobby, was Billie (Harriet Helen Gould) Beck, who was later to be world-renowned under her stage name of Sally Rand. She could not have been in Kansas City very long, as she fulfilled every child's dream by running away with a carnival as a teenager.

All the Heinlein children were bright and all worked hard. The family expected high marks, and Rex Ivar enforced his expectations with nearly every means at his disposal. "I don't know what might have happened if one of us had brought home a D," Heinlein once wrote. "I don't think he would have been whipped, but he might have been prayed over; indolence was definitely classed as a sin."[3]

A grade of B might cause a raised eyebrow and an invitation to discuss anything that might be wrong. Once—just once—one of the children brought home a C in Spanish, and this was cause for consternation. "Could we have raised a stupid child?" Rex wondered to Bam.[4] (This was the child—Clare—who later became a doctor of political science.)

Bobby was already an unusual sort of boy. His intelligence was obvious, and he was resourceful, as well, but he hid the most startling evidence of his personal uniqueness: he was having what we would now call mystical experiences—and, what is more unusual, understanding what they meant. Most of these mystical experiences were past-life recollections that stopped in adolescence—a common-enough pattern recorded in *Twenty Cases Suggestive of Reincarnation*.[5] But he did not forget them. Like the train incident in Swope Park, they colored his internal life with the conviction of personal immortality.

This conviction did not take the form of a belief in reincarnation so much as something that threads through his works and looks superficially—but not strictly correctly—like a kind of solipsism:[6] "I have had a dirty suspicion since I was about six that all consciousness is one and that all the actors I see around me . . . are myself, at different points in the record's grooves."[7] Later, he found this idea articulated in the essays, very widely read then, of Ralph Waldo Emerson, as the "Over-Soul." Even later he encountered it again in Hindu sacred writing: *Tat tvam asi,* translated variously as Thou art That, Thou art Brahma, or Thou art God. But as a small child, his experience was direct and personal:

I had a very curious, entirely personal emotional experience in grammar school. Do you know the story about the earthworm who fell in love and declared his love to the object of his affections, whom he had encountered underground? The "other" worm answered, "Don't be silly—I'm your other end." Never mind the impossible biology; the story is pertinent—One day I was looking at another boy in school, across the classroom, looking at him with loathing. I had been having trouble with him, he was bigger than myself and had been bullying me at every recess for some time. I used to lie awake and try to figure out ways to do him in without getting caught. That day, while looking at him, I suddenly thought of him as my "other end"; I had a curious and possibly illogical feeling that if only I could come wide awake I would find that he and I were the same person.[8]

He didn't talk about these experiences then, but he thought about them. There was something wrong with the way the adults were acting. They must be hiding something from him—from children in general, possibly, but from him specifically. The flares of emotions, the incomprehensible and irrational sets of likes and dislikes, the mind-numbing daily routine, and, most of all, the sheer inability to *make contact*—surely that was a sham, an act put on to deceive him?[9] It was completely incompatible with those glimpses he had of the unity of everything—the "other-endness" of others. This separation, this feeling that he was different and unique—and isolated—could not be the truth of things.

But he kept this to himself and got on with the business of being a boy. He had measles in 1914, but remembered fondly his birthday that year: his mother threw a big birthday party, with a score of children, and pink lemonade and a big white cake with pink candles. "That was also the summer that the collie dog in the house diagonally across from us bit me. Later that summer I heard my first 'wireless' and saw my first 'aeroplane,' a Curtiss pusher biplane."[10]

The Great War broke out in Europe that year—the "Guns of August"—"Horrible German Atrocities in Belgium." In August, too, his Grandfather Lyle died, and life changed for the family, not for the better. The summers in Butler ceased, and Bobby was moved to Horace Mann Elementary School for the second grade.

By the age of eight (1915), Bobby realized that his family was poor and was going to stay that way.[11] His father's income was never quite enough (even though he advanced at International Harvester until he retired in 1937). The family always outgrew Rex Ivar's earning capability. Any money Bobby ever had, he would have to earn.

So, in third grade, Bobby got a job. His older brothers were already working. Lawrence had been driving every day for his job since he was twelve.

In 1916, few states had anything like child labor laws. In Missouri, a twelve-year-old could get a full work permit if he or she had completed—or been expelled from—grammar school. At age nine, Bobby got a limited work permit so he could be a "PJG Boy," selling subscriptions door-to-door to the sister magazines *The Saturday Evening Post, Ladies' Home Journal,* and *The Country Gentleman.*[12] By 1916 he was earning the money for his own clothing, working at a series of odd jobs—delivery boy, office boy, distributor of handbills—whatever he could pick up. He raised silkworms in the piano case—ordered from the back pages of a magazine. In fourth grade (1917) he had his first part-time job during the school year, and he worked full-time during the summers thereafter. He had a job selling soda pop and dodgers (hot dogs) for a theater, which allowed him to see movies (he was a fan of cowboy star William S. Hart).[13]

He and a pal rented an electric vacuum cleaner in the days before "suck-brooms" became widely distributed, and sold vacuum-cleaning services door-to-door.[14] One winter (1917–18) he got up at 4:00 A.M. every day to deliver *The Kansas City Star* to his neighbors in the snow, in minus-twenty-degree weather, dragging a sled piled high with folded papers.

Bobby started earning his own way just in time: in about 1917 Rex Ivar co-signed a loan for a friend who was worse off than the Heinleins. The friend defaulted on the note, and Rex Ivar had to pay it off. It was all he could do to put food on the table—and there was one stretch of three months when the family subsisted on potato soup. Bobby's earnings paid for his clothing and for all his incidental expenses—school lunches, carfare, schoolbooks, everything.

By 1923, at the age of fifteen, he was completely self-supporting, even though he had to overcome some opposition to make that happen. Working twenty-two hours a week, he didn't have time to study, except for the street-car rides to and from school, ten hours a week. Fortunately, that was all he needed to master the material: he had learned in grammar school to read while walking, without lifting his eyes from the pages. But that wasn't quite enough leisure time for nonessential work. His American History teacher objected because he wasn't keeping one of the project notebooks he had been assigned. That called for a serious compromise conference, with the principal ruling on the pragmatics, in Bobby's favor. (He got through the course with an A grade anyway.)

This sounds rather grim—and perhaps it was, as he later remarked that he knew at first hand what it was to work in sweatshop conditions—but

Bobby's life was by no means all Dickensian drudgery. He fondly recalled a pair of roller skates he owned in 1915 and a Bluebird bicycle that he received for Christmas in 1916. He had a home workshop and was good with his hands: one Christmas, about 1920, Santa Claus presented Bobby's younger brother, Clare (as Jesse Clare was called in the family), with a set of half-sized woodworking tools. Bobby made the tool chest for it; the paint was so fresh that it collected the glitter that dropped off the Christmas tree's branches.[15]

The basement held more than the workshop; it was also an indoor shooting gallery—the holes in the rafters remained for decades and became family legend—and an experimental chemical laboratory. His youngest sister, Mary Jean, wryly remarked that her mother never knew when the house might explode. Once in his childhood, Bobby put out a household fire by himself, without calling the local fire department.[16]

Bobby was fascinated by stage magic. On one glorious occasion, he was taken to see Thurston the Magician.[17] One of Thurston's tricks was threading needles with one hand, but the trick wasn't well adapted to the stage: the audience couldn't see it, so he had observers from the audience go on the stage and watch to see that there was no hanky-panky. Bobby volunteered and was chosen to go up onstage: he watched the trick close-up, very dutifully and very carefully. For this mark of distinction, he received the unusual privilege (in a low Protestant family) of owning a deck of cards so that he could study card tricks and prestidigitation. He practiced covertly, even in church, whiling away the long sermons.

And he was so taken with the swordplay in a stage performance of *The Tales of Hoffmann* that he talked a neighbor and his own younger brother, Clare, into taking up fencing with him, with homemade swords and screen wire helmets.[18] No doubt that gave him many bad habits to overcome when he took up fencing as a sport.

When the United States entered the Great War, in 1917, Bobby followed the war news avidly, tracing troop movements on maps of Europe and observing the various meatless and sweetless days, gathering peach pits for charcoal to make gas masks for the troops.[19] The Liberty Bell toured the country by rail, to drum up support for the first Liberty Loan, and Bobby was taken to the train depot at the foot of Wyandotte to see it. In the yards around the depot, an open flatcar held the bell, and the crowd was so dense that the ten-year-old was nearly trampled.[20]

On March 26, 1918, five months before his eighteenth birthday, Lawrence Lyle Heinlein enlisted with the Machine Gun Company, 7th Regiment.

Uncle Park, age twenty-five, was serving as a bugler with Company B of the 2nd Missouri. Rex Ivar, at the age of forty, also volunteered but was turned down, since he had a wife and six children to support. Lawrence was discharged in October 1918. What with boot camp and special machine gun training, his active duty in World War I amounted to two months.

In the winter of 1918–1919, the angel of death passed twice over America, and Bobby Heinlein heard the rustle of his wings: in addition to the war deaths, the great Spanish influenza epidemic killed nearly half a million Americans—twice as many as war casualties. The Heinlein family seems to have escaped losing any of its members—though Bobby suffered with the flu and also with a case of typhoid fever—but one of his teachers died in a way that shocked him: one day she was at school, at work, and the next day she was dead.[21]

While Lawrence was in the Army, the family's finances had drawn even tighter. On one occasion Bobby accidentally overheard a discussion between his father and mother that came down to whether they should use their scant resources to buy a winter coat for Bobby or riding boots for Rex. Bam, incredibly, sided with Rex and the riding boots. This was shattering to ten-year-old Bobby. Rex was the favorite son in that household, and Bobby was . . . somewhere down the list. For most of his youth, he would be competing with Rex.

It was probably at that moment that Bobby lost whatever hold on mother love he had been able to retain through a not notable degree of nurturing. It might have gone into depression; instead, it encouraged his tendency to independence and made the necessity of self-reliance into a virtue. If, as H. G. Wells remarked, "A cared-for child cannot conceive that there is a fundamental insecurity of life,"[22] Bobby was already too familiar with the fundamental insecurity of life: he was never neglected, precisely, but he never had the sense of being cared for. "Home was a place to eat and to sleep; anything beyond that was up to each of us."[23]

Independence it certainly gave him: he was growing up and had girls on his mind continuously from the age of eleven (1918), though he said he was laughed at whenever he tried to make a pass at a girl[24]—and in any case he was much too busy with work and the many school activities he maintained to get into much trouble.

And always there was reading, best of all occupations. The whole Heinlein family were readers—"garbage paper readers" they called themselves after Clare was found sitting on the sidewalk and unpeeling the newspaper in which the family garbage was wrapped, so he could follow a story. But Robert was more voracious than any of them, reading under the covers with a candle[25]—a feat that speaks equally to his appetites and the care and discretion with which he satisfied them. He sweet-talked (and doubtless found ways to bribe) his sisters and brothers into lending him the use of their public library cards so that he could get more books than children were usually allowed. He later was to identify the public library as one of his several "homes."[26]

His earliest exposure, to Baum and the Oz books, had given Bobby a taste for the fantastic. At the age of eight, his favorite book was *Alice in Wonderland,* which led naturally, by a concatenation not obvious but nevertheless common enough, to science reading. He worked for seven months delivering *The Kansas City Journal* in order to buy his own set of *The Book of Knowledge,* a popular encyclopedia for young readers. He read through all the science books in the library, particularly those that dealt with astronomy and space flight. The astronomy he used as material for the paid lectures he gave around town (another way to earn pocket money); the space flight fed his soul (he had made a bet with a high school friend in 1918 that man would be on the Moon before his fortieth birthday).[27]

Like all his friends, he read the Rover Boys series and all the Horatio Alger books[28]—and all of Kipling, borrowing some of the collected works from a neighbor who owned the set.[29] But science-adventure and marvelous invention stories he particularly loved. He graduated from the Tom Swift and Motor Boys series to Jules Verne and to Edgar Rice Burroughs's wonderful and exotic Mars books as they came out—*A Princess of Mars* in 1917, *The Gods of Mars* in 1918, and *Warlord of Mars* in 1919 (Tarzan, of course, was already a particular favorite). He loved the Mars books because of their careful and imaginative use of Percival Lowell's scientific discoveries about the Red Planet made in the 1890s and the high, romantic coloration Burroughs brought to the science. "For that period," Heinlein later noted judiciously, "E.R.B. was correct, and his imaginative extrapolations were magnificent."[30]

Soon he found that some of the pulp magazines—*Argosy* and *All-Story* and Hugo Gernsback's *Electrical Experimenter*—published these stories occasionally. The pulps had come into existence only recently, as part of a movement to democratize science and literature for the newly literate masses. They were the early-twentieth-century equivalent of PBS television, designed to entertain as they educated. What made the pulps distinct was originally their all-fiction format, but as the field developed commercially and magazine "chains" came into existence, nonfiction pulps emerged, too, devoted to the new technology of radio transmission, or to aviation. They were lumped together as a genre of "science and invention pulps" (which might, nevertheless, publish some fiction among the articles about radio or aviation). Hugo Gernsback, an émigré-inventor-turned-pulp-editor, was developing an explicit theory about science stories he would carry over when he created the first science-fiction pulp, *Amazing Stories,* in 1926. This kind of story was good training for boys, sugarcoating science teaching.

By 1917 Robert had discovered Mark Twain, and his current favorite book was The *Adventures of Huckleberry Finn.* This was not particularly unusual, as all the boys in his neighborhood had virtually memorized the book and played at Tom Sawyer and Huck Finn the way later generations would play at cowboys and Indians or superhero and supervillain.

> I remember a violent argument I got into with several other boys in my neighborhood, over which one of us could identify the largest number of single sentences in the book, tell what came before and after any given sentence read at random. We never settled it—because we *all* could identify *anything* in it. Oh we read "Tom Swift" too and the Alger books, and the Motor Boys. But Huck Finn we practically memorized—it had everything.[31]

He read everything of Twain's he could find and was profoundly affected by *What Is Man?* (1906) and *The Mysterious Stranger* (1916). His admiration of Twain became a lifelong passion.

He worked through the Harvard Classics set at the same time he was absorbing the Horatio Alger books. He liked the Sherlock Holmes stories of Sir Arthur Conan Doyle and the wry humor of Jerome K. Jerome's *Three Men in a Boat.* He read *everything,* in fact, except the usual run of nauseating Victorian children's literature. "What most people call a 'juvenile,'" he said, "made my flesh creep."[32] He wanted "tough books, chewy books—not pap."[33] Jack London's Yukon adventure books led him to Edward Bellamy's *Looking Backward, 2000–1887* and *Equality.* Bobby Heinlein was absorbing progressivism.

By 1919 he had a new favorite: H. G. Wells. Wells—particularly *When the Sleeper Wakes*—had the same appetite for flying, and for space travel and for the stars.[34] But Wells had much more to offer Bobby: Wells's knife-edge intellectual balancing act between Victorian materialism and an awareness of the nonmaterial dimension of life—secular but spiritual—echoed Bobby's own "balancing act," living in a highly religious family. But he was also drawn to Wells because of the "utopian socialist" idealism with which Wells burned.[35]

Wells's socialism was highly compatible with the other side of socialism that had flourished in the United States throughout the nineteenth century and flourished now in the Freethought wing of the Democratic Party. Wells gave Heinlein a framework for his own social-progressive ideas, and he came to value Wells's appreciation of the technical dimensions of what would come to be called "social engineering."

Robert was also deeply affected by the essays of T. H. Huxley and, most of all, Charles Darwin.[36] In 1920 he read both *On the Origin of Species* and *The Descent of Man*. He was already prepared by that time, by reading Wells, to view Darwinian natural selection without the irrelevant burden of teleology that the old-fashioned Victorian Social Darwinists had brought to the subject. He could see the apparent purposiveness in biological events as the kind of pattern-making the human mind does routinely when it tells itself stories about things that happen—the shapes of clouds, patterns of cracks in a wall— and not that of a master story imposed by a master storyteller in the sky.

Robert Heinlein began to become an adult when he began to understand what Wells and Darwin had to say to the modern world.

3

A JAZZ AGE TEENAGER

On March 1, 1919, Samuel Edward Heinlein passed away. There is no record of a bequest, but later that year Rex Ivar bought a house at 2102 East Thirty-sixth Street, for $2,000. The house had only two bedrooms for the eight of them, but it was their own home, for the first time. Bam was pregnant with Mary Jean at the time, so a ninth was on the way. The sleeping arrangements were already a little crowded: the older children doubled up, and the baby, Rose Elizabeth, slept in a crib in her parents' room.

They talked occasionally of installing a bed or beds in the living room, but that seemed somewhat beneath their social position—it would leave Rex Ivar no place to discuss Sunday school matters with the other deacons, and Bam no place to receive the Ladies Aid Society. Robert slept for three years on a pallet on the floor of the living room, bedding put away in a closet during the day.[1]

Robert's transition from elementary to high school in 1919 was somewhat eased by Horace Mann's experimental junior high program, amalgamating Robert's eighth grade with the freshman class at Central High School. His world had been expanding steadily as he was thrown into contact with different social worlds. At Greenwood Grammar School, most of his classmates had come from the orphanage down the street, children visibly poorer than the Heinleins. Throughout his teen years, Robert lived in a racially and culturally mixed neighborhood, just a few blocks from the edge of Darktown. Robert's family—intellectually conservative but not necessarily rigid or doctrinaire—fit easily into the multicultural mix, not sharing a number of the racial and religious prejudices that were commonplace early in the century. His best friends in the neighborhood were Jewish twins Saul and Solomon—and Jack, a Catholic boy. His first enlightenment thus was not about religion, but about race: "I got it through my head that human beings must never be judged by categories, but only as individuals."[2]

That year, Robert was twelve, and he began to be treated by his family more or less as an adult. Rex Ivar had some rigid ideas about the perquisites that went along with taking on adult responsibilities and earning your own way. Robert was no longer required to attend church services—impractical in any case because of his erratic work schedule.

Nor was he any longer disciplined around the house. While the Heinlein children were in grammar school, the house rule was that if they received discipline at the school (typically a whipping or some other form of corporal punishment, such as feruling),[3] they would be disciplined a second time at home—"twice as hard." Bobby was never put to this indignity, as one of his brothers had already "explored the territory" and Bobby had no wish to recapitulate the experience. As his mother put it later, spanking Rex Ivar was enough to keep Bobby in line for two weeks.[4] Bam's peach switch was "middle justice" in the house, and the "high justice"[5] of his father's razor strop was an effective motivational tool. Bobby learned the boundaries and came later to value the whole system of social and moral values this taught him. His father, he came to see, was doing his best in a difficult situation:

> My father did much more for me with his razor strop than he ever did with his Bible reading. . . . He taught me to keep my commitments on time, always pay my bills no matter what happened, and to sweep in the dark corners as thoroughly as out in the open when it shows.[6]

Parental discipline was being replaced by self-discipline. Scouting and the Horatio Alger books, with their emphasis on instilling self-discipline, made a deep impression on him, for much the same reason.

Junior high school also brought Robert's first opportunity to follow in the Heinlein family tradition of military service. His high school yearbook[7] shows him a member of the Rifle Club and of the junior ROTC (Reserve Officers' Training Corps) company. It was expected that all the (male) family members would take up arms, if not as a profession, then at least as their patriotic duty. His older brother Rex (now called Ivar, or sometimes Ike, to distinguish him from his father) was already a member.

High school was very demanding. For the first time, Robert was not within walking distance of the school. He had an hour-long trolley ride each way, and that was when he studied; between household chores and money-earning work, there was no other time available. His academic coursework was fairly heavy: Latin and French, geometry, algebra, and a series of history courses advancing from ancient to medieval to modern European to American history. In addition to the course work, he took in a wide range of extracurricular activities. His life-drawing class was taught by one of Maxfield Parrish's teachers, and Robert did some paid modeling for the class, as well. He kept up modeling throughout his youth, even, in 1928, professionally, for Coca-Cola ads.[8]

He also acted in a number of school plays, and he was a member of two science clubs. The school's Kelvin Club was oriented toward physics, but some of the boys, including Ivar, had organized their own Newton Club, where they could pool their resources and do more interesting activities, out from under the thumb of Central's administration. They sold toy soldiers to raise extra money. The Newton Club was much more to Robert's liking, even though he was the youngest of its members. He built the club's telescope in his basement shop—and since he had the keeping of the scope, he was able to observe from the roof of his home or from the tops of billboards in the neighborhoods. When the weather was promising, he would sacrifice a few hours' sleep and carry the scope the ten blocks or so to the local park, where the seeing was closer to the horizon.[9]

As a matter of policy, Robert took every public-speaking course offered at Central, hoping to cure, or at least mitigate, his stammering.[10] He was invited to join the Shakespeare Club—the school's most prestigious literary society—for its public-speaking competition (and eventually became its president). He also worked into the Forensics (debate) squad and eventually became captain of the squad and of the Negative Debate Team.

All these activities kept him very busy, but his real education was taking place outside the school. In 1920 he left Bible Belt fundamentalism behind when he read Darwin's *On the Origin of Species* and *The Descent of Man*. By 1921, his apostasy was complete. At about this time, Heinlein recalled, his best friend in junior high school (and a Russian Jew), Isidore Horoshem, "laughed at me and asked me if I *really* believed in all that crap about Jesus."[11] Still a believer, he was shocked—but not enough to bust up the friendship. What set the final seal on his apostasy, though, was his discovery of T. H. Huxley's essays. Reading Huxley, he began to appreciate how far an unfettered mind could go in self-analysis. Huxley's kind of critical thinking gave him a model for what he should be doing for himself.

He was developing other unorthodox ideas, as well. Although Heinlein was later to portray the figure drawn from his Grandfather Lyle (Ira Johnson,

M.D.) as a freethinker, there is no definite evidence that anyone in Robert Heinlein's family held any views outside what might loosely be called the mainstream. It is more likely that Heinlein came by his progressive inclinations the hard way. At one point, he said he probably became a socialist (of the utopian, rather than the Marxist, type) in reaction to his poverty-stricken up-bringing. How could it be, he wondered, that an intelligent, hardworking person such as his father could struggle so hard and yet just barely manage to scrape along?[12] He searched for clues in Jack London, Upton Sinclair, Karl Marx, and Edward Bellamy, writers who thought there was something basi-cally wrong with the whole economic setup. There were bits and pieces that seemed to add up to an answer: Edward Bellamy's *Looking Backward* seemed to have a chunk of it; Henry George's *Progress and Poverty* (1879) had a bit of it, too—Robert was fascinated by the Single Tax idea—though there seemed to be something a little wrong with it, too. For the most part, the adults he knew wouldn't talk about the subject at all.[13]

In 1919, Robert "heard William Jennings Bryan before he got too old and . . . heard Woodrow Wilson when he was killing himself trying to sell the League of Nations."[14] At thirteen, Robert vigorously supported the League of Nations, an idea H. G. Wells portrayed as the first magnificent step toward utopia. America would thus, Wells assured us, lead the world into the twen-tieth century.[15]

And so it seemed to be: on August 18, 1920, the Tennessee legislature rat-ified the Nineteenth Amendment, guaranteeing women the vote. President Wilson's principled progressive and individualist "New Freedoms" inspired Robert at the age of eleven—enough to overlook Wilson's enormously de-structive racism. He described himself as a "world-stater from way back."[16] He learned to read and speak Esperanto because it was going to be the lan-guage of the unified, American-led world.

He did not think of his military interests as being in conflict with his so-cialist ideals. To American socialists steeped in the tradition of Noyes and Fourier and Owens—and now Wells—socialism and patriotism might go arm in arm, and did in Robert Heinlein: socialism was how he *did* his patriotism.

Nor was socialism the only shaping force he was taking from his reading, which had long since gone beyond the bounds of "boys' books." His astro-nomical reading was expanding his universe. The size and distance of some of those fuzzy nebulae barely visible through a telescope had recently (1917) been determined, and the scale of creation was suddenly staggering. The universe of his Victorian-trained teachers, of the generation that still domi-nated science in the new world of radiation and relativity, had been a stately pavane; the new picture of the universe was a whirling, dynamic immensity, shocking to his teachers' ordered sensibilities.

And he found material to shock his own sensibilities: in 1920 he ran across an old book, *From Nebula to Nebula* (G. H. Lepper, 1912), which described an old and deep conspiracy, known only to the professional ballisticians who calculated orbits: they had known for centuries that Newton's mechanics were wrong, and they had quietly agreed to use a fudge factor to make the calculations come out even with the observations. Robert found that shocking. The adults *were* keeping secrets from him![17] That's where Huxley's critical thinking came in: you had to examine every assumption, all the time, and see the world—and even yourself—with a kind of doubled vision, alert to the reality as well as the assumptions. Hypocrisy was not just a religious thing, after all.

Robert's personal universe was expanding in other ways, as well: Electric Park, on the edge of the city, was the temple and exhibition of the wonders of science and technology—"heaven on earth for kids at that time."[18] He went frequently, drawn by another sort of electric marvel: Billie Beck, one of the girls he knew at Central High, had gone to work as a dancer at Electric Park Follies, a judicious lie increasing her age from fifteen to eighteen. This was long before she changed her name and became famous as nude (or faux-nude) dancer Sally Rand. Robert had hit puberty the year before (1918),[19] and his hormones were raging.

It is hard for us, nearly a hundred years later, to imagine how frustrating it was to be a teenager then. There was nothing like sex education for a high schooler: for Robert, such information as there was came from his grandfather's antique medical textbooks. The scandalous sexology books of Havelock Ellis were just beginning to be published in England—very hard to come by in any case. Experience was the best teacher, of course, but even harder to come by: male and female high school students were not even permitted to touch. Nevertheless,

> my high school had quite a lot of friendly and/or frantic fornication in it. I never managed to get in on it but it was not from lack of trying. . . . But youth, inexperience, lack of money and an automobile—and just being too damned busy—kept me out of the game, in high school.[20]

That was not an exaggeration: between household chores and work to support himself and all the extracurricular activities, he was fully committed.

Robert did make some time for homemade entertainments—plays and reviews, which could also be moneymaking ventures. One of the more luxe productions had a typed program, which Robert pasted into one of his scrapbooks:[21]

PROGRAM

Shadowgraphs

Amusing and Interesting Scenes in the Land of Shadow

Magic

Act I

Slips and Sleights with Silks and Cottons

Act II

Capricious Cards

Act III

1. Oriental Liquids

2. Never Say "Die"

3. A Boarding School Favorite

4. Finale

Magicians:	A. W. Felt
	R. I. Heinlein
Shadowgrapher:	Robert Heinlein

Other productions were on a smaller scale—eye still on the cash register. One of the Heinlein family's neighbors, Don Johnstone, recalled attending one of these extravaganzas in 1920:

A few days after we moved in, a cardboard sign with crayon lettering appeared on the porch railing of a house across the street. *Shakespearean drama,* it read: *Today at 2. Admission 2 cents.* Mother and I went, she figuring it would be an easy way to begin getting acquainted. The play was something called *King of the Cannibal Isles,* and the relation to Shakespeare never became clear. The acts were short—about two minutes each—and the props were simple, a fly-swatter serving as a broadsword. The actors were three: Clare, 8 years old; Louise, more or less my twin; and Bob, two or three years older. I think Bob was author and producer as well as director and actor.[22]

It was necessary to make even the entertainments pay for themselves. The country was in another depression, with farm prices falling in 1920 by as much as 40 percent. Robert worked, briefly, shelling pecans for a wholesaler, then moved to a job lighting gas streetlamps. In between, he made his personal amusements pay their way by giving paid lectures for adult audiences on astronomical subjects.

Through 1920 and 1921, Robert worked at a succession of pickup jobs, doing whatever came to hand. His oldest brother, Larry, occasionally loaned his car and some money, and taught Robert how to use a Thompson submachine gun—the Tommy gun, the favorite weapon of J. Edgar Hoover's agents at the Bureau of Investigation, as the FBI was called at the time. (Larry was later loaned by the Army to the Bureau, to teach them how to shoot Tommy guns. "He's the best Tommychopper in the USA," Robert boasted.[23])

After Christmas 1922, Robert took a steady job, working part-time and evenings as a page in the Reference Room of the Kansas City Public Library, where he earned the munificent sum of $9.50 for his twenty-nine hours a week and considered himself "quite prosperous."[24] When he was not helping the librarian answer reference calls—usually fetching books—he could hole up in the stacks, surrounded by the Kansas City Public Library's astonishing half a million books, and read to his heart's content.[25]

[T]hat gave me time to plow through Fiske,[26] Schopenhauer, Darwin, Plato, and other books we did not have at home, and to dabble in Einstein and Freud, both just becoming much talked about, and to read some *very* interesting books in the locked shelves . . . [27]

By 1923, Heinlein was taking in all this material and trying to integrate it. In 1922 he had acquired his own personal copy of H. G. Wells's *Outline of History,* and he was soon to hear—he says "study under"[28]—socialist intellectual Will Durant.

A notorious freethinker, Durant had scandalized New York by marrying his thirteen-year-old student, Ariel, and then consorting with anarchists at the Ferrer Schools as he toured the nation, lecturing. Kansas City was on his lecture circuit every year. In February and March 1923 he was back in Kansas City, delivering his usual mix of art and history and economics and philosophy and political subjects—infotainment in the last days of the Chautauqua circuit.[29] Durant was very explicit about his socialist ideas, and he put them in the context of a total view of science and economics and philosophy and art. This was just exactly what Robert needed to bring cohesion to the material he was reading in the library, and it excited him.[30]

He also wanted to travel and unsuccessfully entered a *National Geographic* contest for a prize trip to India, to see the Taj Mahal.

He did manage to take one trip to Colorado, to spend the entire month of July 1923 hiking with his friend Stanley Moise—the first time, at age sixteen, he had been away from home for any substantial length of time.

The boys took the *Colorado Flyer* from Kansas City, arriving in Colorado Springs on the first of July. That day Robert saw the Garden of the Gods. On July 2, he went to Manitou Springs and visited the Cave of the Winds, Ute Canyon Pass (which he spelled in his itinerary "Yute Canon"), and Green Mountain Falls. Coming from flat country, he was awed by the Rockies. Pikes Peak and Longs Peaks "were the greatest emotional experience in my life up to that time."[31]

He had a lot to think about that summer. Larry had gotten married in April and set up housekeeping elsewhere with his new bride. His father had pulled in all the political favors owed him and obtained an appointment for Ivar to the United States Naval Academy at Annapolis. Ivar had left early in June, accompanied by articles in the local newspaper about the Kansas City boy off to Annapolis. The matter of Robert's own future had suddenly become an immediate concern.

While in Denver on the way home, he saw the August 1923 "All Scientific Fiction" issue of the science-and-technology pulp *Science and Invention* on a newsstand. For years, Heinlein had been searching out all the science fiction and fantasy he could find. He used half of his remaining fifty cents to buy it. He spent the rest on a dozen doughnuts and made them last until he got home. But he thought both good investments: "food for the body, food for the soul."[32]

He was about to start his junior year at Central High—time to start planning for college. College would be an uphill struggle without some kind of financial help, which would not be forthcoming from the family. If he could obtain an appointment for himself to one of the U.S. military academies, it would effectively be a scholarship. He could use them as stepping-stones into professional astronomy: both the Army and the Navy used astronomers—in fact, the United States Naval Observatory was one of the most prestigious astronomical facilities in the world at that time. But it would take a lot of work, particularly since Ivar was already at Annapolis. It was not common (though not completely unknown) to have two people from the same generation of the same family at Annapolis at the same time.

His father advised against it: he and Bam wanted Robert to become a doctor, though Robert knew he was not temperamentally suited to medicine.[33]

Perhaps, too, his father did not relish the thought of going back to his political contacts for a second favor so soon after the first. In any case, he did not volunteer to make the effort.

It is apparent that, by this time, Robert had accepted the hard truth that Ivar was his parents' favorite. But he must also have known that what Ivar could do with his parents' help he could often do on his own. His father might have expended his political capital on Ivar—but to Robert, that only meant an appointment was something *possible* to achieve. The appointments to the military academies—he would take either one, West Point or Annapolis—were patronage held by congressmen; local politics was a machine, and the example of others seems to have taught him that he could work the levers for his own benefit. Bright, promising high school students had their own entrées.

He resigned his job with the Kansas City Public Library's Reference Room on July 30, 1923, to take a night job. On August 1, 1923, he wrote to the Navy Department's Bureau of Navigation (BuNav) and the War Department's Adjutant General's Office asking about vacancies at Annapolis and West Point. The initial results were discouraging: there were no local appointments to Annapolis opening up until 1927, after Ivar graduated. West Point, too, was filled. But there were other congressmen and other appointments open. Over the next two years he wrote dozens of letters, submitting applications, exploring loopholes in the law, and seeking recommendations to both Annapolis and West Point from the local businessmen he had been brought into contact with as an astronomy lecturer. He even inquired about gaining admission as an enlisted man, instead of by appointment, but was informed his chances were no better that way.[34] He did, however, have one avenue of preferment open to him: Robert went off to the Civilian Military Training Camp at Fort Leavenworth, Kansas, at the end of August 1923, and worked the system.

The CMTC concept—gathering college-age men together for the purpose of "military and citizenship training"—had been proposed during Theodore Roosevelt's first term, and the first camps were held in 1913. CMTC grew into a movement. After World War I, Congress formally incorporated the CMTC into the National Defense Act of 1920, and the program continued to grow. The participants paid their own way, and it was a significant commitment of Robert's savings (even though travel expenses were reimbursed by the CMTC). He did well and made sure that his supervisors noticed his superlative performance. Then and in 1924, he tapped them for letters of recommendation.

The first appointment that came up happened to be in his backyard: his own senator James A. Reed had a vacant appointment to the U.S. Naval Academy.

Reed was a Pendergast man and former mayor of Kansas City. Politics in the Kansas City of the Pendergast era was a matter of personal contacts. Robert could create personal contacts.

There was a certain amount of irony in Robert having to court Senator Reed, because Reed had helped kill Congressional approval of the League of Nations five years earlier. Robert could not be expected to like having to go through him—but the way to the military academies was through Reed, and that was how he had to go. It was an early and important lesson in practical politics.

Machine politics was an odd mixture of very good and very bad. The ward system meant that there was personal contact with every individual voter. It was Pendergast policy that nobody in need was turned away empty-handed—irrespective of affiliation, background, religion, or race. Tolerance was good politics.

While Robert was growing up in Kansas City, the Pendergast machine paid strict attention to the superficial civilities, yet it was to become as rapacious as any corrupt political machine in the country.[35] Heinlein as a young man got a worm's-eye view of how it worked, and he had a practical demonstration that year of how the local and the national merged into each other: when the Teapot Dome scandal erupted in the news, the quality of the local corruption was echoed on the national stage.[36] Robert's first real exposure to the Pendergast machine came just at the time the Teapot Dome scandal erupted in the national news. Although Robert was always to insist on the need to work in practical politics, he also developed a permanent disgust for hypocrisy.

His efforts paid off: early in 1924, he was formally notified by the Senate Judiciary Committee that Senator Reed had nominated him to Annapolis. If all went well, he might be there by July. He later found out that there had been fifty-one applicants for the one appointment Senator James Reed had not yet made to the military academies. Fifty candidates had each sent a single letter of recommendation with their application. Robert had sent in fifty for himself.[37] Robert began a course of self-treatment to strengthen his eyesight—myopia ran in his family—using the method described in William Horatio Bates's *Cure of Imperfect Sight Without Treatment by Glasses* (1920).[38]

And the preparation and hard work paid off: he continued to drill in the

Central High School ROTC and was promoted to major on February 14, 1924. *The Kansas City Star* reported the promotion, noting that he had been in service for only six months when he was jumped ahead of two-year men.[39]

Robert's rapid advancement in ROTC was not universally admired. He had driven his "men" unmercifully, and he received what was probably his first anonymous hate mail—a sarcastic note signed "Very Respectfully, Mr. Major," saying he had stolen the credit from the people in his regiment who actually did the work. The note was illustrated with a stick figure saluting in the stiff-armed "Sieg—Heil!" mode, limp penis dripping.

His commanding officer, Sergeant Frank Bowling, PMST at Central High, received a petition signed by every member of his regiment protesting Robert's strenuous drillmastering and asking that he be relieved of command as a "detriment to the morale of the unit."[40] But the CO left Robert just as he was. Two months later, on May 13, Robert was advanced to Lieutenant Colonel of ROTC—the same rank Ivar had held. But Ivar had gotten his honors easily and was liked by his men. By working very hard Robert could recapitulate Ivar's successes, but no matter what he did, he didn't have that knack of being liked.

Robert could not have been easy to live with. Like Tom Sawyer, he was invested in the romance of the military. The late-nineteenth-century idealization of the medieval in which Twain had so gloried left an indelible mark on Heinlein's personality, and he was to celebrate gallantry for the remainder of his life. Along with them went a boyish love of ceremony and ritual, and adolescent punctilio. His appearance in the Central Officers' Club group portrait in his senior class yearbook for 1924 conveys a little of this in his ramrod-straight posture, shoulders thrown back, flanked by the civilian Sponsor-Major Kathleen Carey and by his CO, PMST Sergeant Frank Bowling.

Adolescents respond to outsiders like sharks to the smell of blood. Many of his contemporaries probably saw Robert as brilliant, undeniably—possibly even as brilliant as he thought himself—but a wart nonetheless, and an outsider. It takes an unusual moral strength to survive the ordeal of high school in such circumstances—particularly since the appointment to Annapolis did not come through that spring.

Robert graduated from high school in June 1924. The school yearbook, *The Centralian,* had collected its final information between February and May 1924 and listed his activities as:

National Honor Society, 23–24; Major, R.O.T.C.; President, Central Officers' Club; Captain, Negative Debate Team; President, Central Shakespeare

Club; Student Council; Inter-Society Council; Boy's High School Club; Kelvin Club; Central Classics Club; Rifle Club.[41]

He had entered the school's literary competition each year but without conspicuous successes; this year, he was given an Honorable Mention in the yearbook for his entry in the thirty-ninth Annual Inter-Society Contest:

The Last Adventure

Why stand ye here with lagging feet when ye can go beyond?
Why say 'tis cowardly to defeat your fate as Death's poor pawn?
It seems to me to take oneself out of the Three's cold hands
Were better far than let life ebb and leave you on the sands.

The craven thing that rates the flesh above romance to come
May gain a little hour of life but lose the greater sum.
But the brave soul that pledges all on one cast of the die
Gains the adventure of his life and learns all reasons why!

And whoso says a man's a fool to call his death his own
Lacks the courage to depart as soon he must—Alone!
Let then each man who's lived his life and wishes to be free
Set then his feet in freedom's path and taking courage—Be!

The yearbook entries reveal how Robert Heinlein appeared to his classmates—accepted, barely; an outsider. He was designated the class's "Worst Boy Grind," and his tagline said, "He thinks in terms of the fifth dimension, never stopping at the fourth."[42] He must have been considered particularly memorable in his class, as he is noted twice in the Retrospectives section of his graduating yearbook—on page 287 as expected to grace the cover of *Scientific American* magazine, and quoted on page 301 under the "Practiced Proverbs" heading: "A man of understanding holdeth his peace."

He was remembered as "the sweetest boy in his graduation class" by another of the girls in the Shakespeare Club[43]—though possibly it was a sweet-and-hot with some deviltry involved: his very first date had been, very proper, with the "queen of the campus," a former neighbor; but of another girl at Central in the same years he reminisced: "I'll go to my grave regretting one little 16-yr.-old in high school. She was a lecherous little honey—and I was too young and too chicken."[44]

And directly under Robert's picture in *The Centralian* for 1924 is that of Alice Catherine McBee—a pretty, swan-necked girl he had met in the Shakespeare Club. He felt quite sentimental about Alice McBee: her Christmas card from later that year, addressed to "Bobby," is preserved in his scrapbook. He would stay in touch with Alice McBee.

A ticket from Stripes, the annual ROTC ball for 1925, suggests he was casually dating someone else—one Elinor Curry. They had attended the same grammar school, but Elinor had gone to the new Westport High when it opened. They got reacquainted through their respective schools' debate squads: Curry was the captain of her debate squad and captain also of the Negative Debate Team at Westport High, as Robert was captain of the Negative Debate Team at Central. In 1924 and 1925 the schools in Kansas City had debated whether the United States should recognize Lenin's Russia—though Elinor and Robert probably had not squared off on that topic in the main competition that year: not only were boys and girls segregated by teams, but the Westport Negative Team debated Manual High—and lost. Clippings from *The Kansas City Times* spell her name variously as "Elinor" and Elanor."[45]

Robert's brother Larry joined the Missouri National Guard on June 8, 1924. Robert had already enlisted, by lying about his age, and by this time had been promoted to corporal—a move he received with mixed emotions since it would mean losing one of the two specialist ratings (surveyor and draftsman) he had held as a private first class—and consequently taking a cut in pay of $1.31 per drill. But: "I didn't mind: I was terribly proud of those two chevrons."[46]

Robert was deeply affected by the feeling he was a part of something greater than one person and living through history. If the family was a unit tiled against the outside world, so, too, was the military. There was something almost magical about the visceral way these things affected him: "Did I ever tell you of the first time I heard 'to Arms'? I had never heard it before, didn't know it, but I came bursting out of my tent with rifle and cartridge belt. *And most of the other recruits did so too.*"[47] Even more: he learned at first hand that Army "chicken shit" was only part of the story. There were always petty individuals who abused the hierarchical structure, but there were also thought-provoking counterexamples:

When I was a Pfc. in the 35th division, our company latrine at Camp Clark got plugged up. My captain, Captain Clifford Marchant, remarked that he had never yet asked a man to do anything he was not willing to do—rolled up his sleeve, stuck his arm down into the filth, and cleared it out with his fingers.[48]

The Civilian Military Training Camp in Fort Leavenworth, Kansas, took up the full month of August in 1924. Robert was enrolled in Company H, and he mentioned being a drill instructor that year and leader of a company of "incredibly raw recruits."[49] The training was designed to give the young men a broad exposure to military subjects. He recalled taking equitation and musketry under Captain Hobart "Hap" Gay (later General Patton's chief of staff). Robert soaked up anecdotes and personal history from the older men, as well as military technique. He began to rise in rank, and his company commander in the 110th Engineers wrote to Robert, forwarding recommendations for the Annapolis appointment and declaring himself "mighty proud of the reputation you have gained up at Leavenworth. It is not only a boost for yourself, but also for the company."[50] Major George B. Duncan, commanding the Seventh Corps Area, visited and Robert, as "student brigadier general," was commanding officer for Major Duncan's review. In the final standings, he was named "Best Drillmaster" and awarded a silver loving-cup trophy by the commander of the CMTC, World War I hero Brigadier General Harry A. Smith.

So his hard work had paid off—and the lesson he learned was that faith in himself was justified.

If he had not been able to get in on any of the "friendly and/or frantic" fornication at his high school, he was able, finally, to remedy that situation. There is only one reference to the occasion in his later correspondence, and that reference says only that he lost his virginity during the Coolidge Administration (1923–1929) to a grandmother (which, given the early marriage and childbirth common at the time, might mean only a woman in her mid- to late thirties).[51]

In the fall of 1924, Robert enrolled in the engineering program at Kansas City Junior College, which was accredited as a junior college of the University of Missouri–Columbia.[52] He later recalled, in defense of his later aggressive policy of inclusiveness, that his teacher of advanced calculus was a woman, and he was tutored by a Negro.[53] He continued working full-time, at night, using the time until the appointment should come through to save up for the expense of moving to Annapolis—someday.

On November 9, 1924, Robert was mustered with the rest of National Guard Company C for the ceremonial laying of the cornerstone of the Liberty

Memorial—the war memorial that had been in preparation since 1919. President Coolidge, recently reelected, attended the ceremonies.

December came, and Robert was hired as a temporary "non-certified clerk in the Railway Mail Service at the Kansas City Terminal," where Elinor Curry's father was a clerk. He was paid $5.25 a day for sorting Parcel Post mail for the Christmas rush season.

Once the postal rush was over, Robert had too much time for reflection that Christmastime of 1924. He had been waiting on the appointment to the Naval Academy for nearly a year, since Senator Reed had nominated him. He continued his Bates exercises to strengthen his eyesight. Waiting on the process, he took stock of himself. A list of his jobs was preserved in his scrapbook. Not all of them can be dated with any certainty, and some of the jobs he later talked about in letters are not included on this list (movie theater usher, for example):

Janitor
Insurance (salesman for Aetna Life Insurance Company)
Magazine salesman [presumably the PJG route]
Nutcracker [shelling pecans by hand]
Bum
Roadhouse hoofer [professional tap or soft-shoe dancer for saloons on a
    road between cities]
Navy
Pre-medic
Engineer stewdent [sic] [presumably at Kansas City Junior College]
Art stewdent
Taught mathematics, yeah? [no doubt tutoring]
Railway mail clerk
Artist's model, no foolin!
Librarian [the recent page position for the Kansas City Public Library]
Telephone operator—PBX
Sap.

And that was Robert Heinlein's preparation for a career in the U.S. Navy.

PLEBE SUMMER

On January 7, 1925, Heinlein received a telegram from the secretary of the Senate Judiciary Committee notifying him that Senator Reed's appointment to a midshipman slot at Annapolis had finally come through. He telegraphed his acceptance, and the appointment was announced in *The Kansas City Star* on February 18, 1925. His two-year campaign had paid off.

This incoming Class of 1929 was the first under a new admission system that required each candidate to pass a series of examinations "to prove his fitness A. and B. -neck (above and below)."[1] In February, Heinlein gave the Bureau of Navigation, which handles personnel matters for the Navy, a certification they accepted as a substitute for the psychological examination.

The new competitive examination for academic subjects was not a problem, though it took some time to get through channels. On May 16, 1925, Ivar sent Robert a telegram from Annapolis: "Congratulations. Your name posted today as having posted [passed?] examinations."[2] The official notification was dated May 20, 1925, just three weeks before he had to be at the Academy, and he had a thousand minor details to attend to. Clothing (shirts and a travel suit), books, and train tickets to Annapolis by way of Chicago, where he had a third hurdle to get over: a physical and athletic skills examination at the Great Lakes Naval Training Station near Chicago. This exam might pose a problem for him: his health was good, but he was quite underweight.

Heinlein was formally discharged from the 110th Engineers, Company C of the Missouri National Guard, with a purely nominal bump from buck sergeant to staff sergeant. Another man stood down long enough for Heinlein to take the promotion with him to the Academy.[3]

Heinlein's formal enrollment in the U.S. Naval Academy was processed *in absentia* on June 5, 1925. Three days later he left Kansas City by train after a farewell dinner at the Muehlebach Hotel. He arranged a five-day stopover in Chicago for his physical exam, one entire day of which was spent at the Great Lakes Naval facility. On June 10, he was able to wire his family that he had passed the physical. He had weighed in at six feet tall and 118 pounds. He later remarked wryly of his Medical Department photograph that "it is living proof that a skeleton can walk."[4]

Heinlein spent the rest of his time in Chicago sightseeing and left for Annapolis on Saturday, June 13, arriving on Monday, June 15. He was awed, as many westerners still are, to see and even touch the living legacy of his country's history. One of his earliest and sharpest memories of Annapolis was the sight of "a tattered and shot-torn homemade flag occupying the central position of honor in Memorial Hall which reads: 'DON'T GIVE UP THE SHIP!' "[5]

The Class of '29 had 409 boys arriving over a two-week period, and Heinlein's quarters were not yet ready. He was given the name of some hotels in Annapolis and told to find someone to bunk with and let the school know at 9 A.M. the following day. Roommates were usually left to the discretion of the students, and could be changed each year. If he didn't have any preferences, they would try to match him up with another singleton.

He stayed that night just outside the Academy grounds, at Carvel Hall. A number of arriving candidates were staying there until their quarters were ready. Heinlein was not impressed with the rest of the incoming Plebes:

> I have met a lot of my classmates and have kept my mouth discreetly shut. But I don't see how some people can be that ignorant and live. One of them thinks he is going to be a cadet [cadets are students at the West Point, the *Army* Academy]. And he isn't the worst of the lot.[6]

One of the incoming Plebes he met—presumably not the one who thought he was going to be a cadet—was Frank Novak, of Elizabeth, New Jersey, and they agreed to request room assignment together for their Plebe year. Novak was described by a later roommate as quiet and unassuming, with a sense of humor—athletic and interested in "ac"[academics].[7]

On the morning of June 16, 1925, the candidates who had arrived assembled in the shade of the gatehouse. A clerk came out of the administration building and spoke briefly to them—a ceremony that would be repeated many times as Plebe candidates arrived on campus. At 9 A.M. Robert Anson Heinlein took the oath and was sworn in as a midshipman at the United States Naval Academy.

First order of business was the endless issue lines for the Plebes' traditional work clothes, consisting of white cotton trousers, T-shirts, and pullover sailors' blouses, always in the traditional sizes of too large and too small, and a shapeless soft cap with a blue band around the forehead. They had been measured for white and blue dress uniforms, but the formal clothing would not be ready until September. They would live in their issue cotton, marked with their names in permanent India ink.

In the battalion office, the bewildered Plebes were deluged with instructions given in the arcane jargon of the Academy: "formations, late blasts, roll-calls, study hours, pap-sheets and various other odds and ends of vernacular . . ."[8] Unless, like Heinlein, they had an older brother who had already been through it, there was nothing to help them sort out the barrage of jargon until their student manual, *The Lighthouse,* came out in the fall.

Then to Bancroft Hall, the Academy's residence building, where they could settle in. Most rooms were designed for two students, with simple furniture—one desk/table, two beds, a sink, a wardrobe, chairs—and bathrooms down the hall. Water for personal uses—drinking and washing—was carried in milk cans from enormous butts (casks), with locked spigots, and measured out, a bucket a day. The corner rooms on each floor had 4-sets with a common room. There they found an assigned Mate of the Deck who had a podium seat to watch over the activity of his deck (floor) and maintain order. The midshipmen would rotate mate-of-the-deck duty a certain number of days of the year. Every day a commissioned officer—usually a lieutenant—would come in for inspection, rapping on a door. By custom the Middies jumped to attention, saying, "Welcome aboard, sir." In addition, the Plebes rotated duty in the main office.

Heinlein looked at his half of the wardrobe and knew immediately that he couldn't keep his civilian clothing, so he expressed it all home that day, except for one suit, which he left at the tailor's, to be cleaned and stored in mothballs.[9]

The United States Naval Academy was unlike anything Heinlein had ever encountered before, a step into a new way of life, strange and new and wonderful and foreign and overwhelming. Even the dining hall was enormous and intimidating, large enough to seat four thousand. The tables were served with exotic foods like scrapple and grits and fried green tomatoes—and oysters (legendarily oysters for lunch on Saturdays). Nothing tells you you're not in Kansas—or Missouri!—anymore like the odd and unlikely things outlanders eat.

One of the trials of Plebedom surfaced immediately: at meals, the upperclassmen who supervised each table of Plebes kept snapping questions so the Plebes could hardly eat—"How many ships in the China Station,

Mister?"—and Heinlein had not yet developed ways to compensate for the interruptions. In the first week he lost ten pounds he could hardly afford to lose. He went to bed those first nights more homesick than he thought he could ever be.[10]

Although the lowest form of naval life, a midshipman—even a raw Plebe—is an officer in the U.S. Navy (by a peculiarity of the law, a West Point cadet is not an Army officer). The Naval Academy used the Army system for its Table of Organization: the Corps of Midshipmen was divided up into regiments by classes, with officers of grades going from Third Class to Second Class to First Class. On graduation, a midshipman would be commissioned with the lowest rating in the Naval table of organization, the ensign.[11] When the bell rang for the Class of 1929's first formation, Second Classmen (the equivalent of juniors in college) who for some reason did not go on the practice cruise that year formed them up into two battalions of two companies each—two called "French" and two "Spanish." (The boys would be encouraged to speak these languages among themselves, and this would help satisfy the Academy's modern languages requirement, called "Dago.") This would be their permanent organization during their four years at the Naval Academy. Heinlein was in one of the French companies.

The Second Classmen who had charge of the Plebes were brusque and businesslike but not particularly oppressive—a class history recalls their most common remarks to the Plebes as "Brace up, Mister," "Just what do you think you rate, anyway?" and the ever-popular "You're on the pap!"[12]—that is, reported for demerits. Heinlein was an old hand at drill, but most of the Plebes had no exposure to military ways.

The summer was traditionally given over to the initial training of the incoming class of Plebes. A daily schedule for Heinlein's Plebe Summer is preserved in his scrapbooks:

ROUTINE, MONTHS OF JUNE, JULY, & AUGUST, 1925

reveille. . . . . 6:30 A.M.
Assembly for morning roll call. . . . . 7:00 A.M.
Morning roll call late bell . . . . 7:03 A.M.
     Publish conduct report and orders
     March to breakfast
Inspection of rooms by Midshipman in Charge . . . . 7:40 A.M.
     Prayers immediately after breakfast
Sick Call . . . . 7:40 A.M.

Call to first drill period . . . . 8:00 A.M.
Late bell . . . . 8:03 A.M.
       March to drill
Recall from first drill period . . . . 9:30 A.M.
Assembly for second drill period . . . . 10:00 A.M.
Late bell . . . . 10:03 A.M.
       March to drill
Recall from second period . . . . 11:30 A.M.
Assembly for Midday roll call . . . . 12:30 P.M.
Late bell . . . . .12:33 P.M.
       Publish orders. March to midday meal.
Assembly for third drill period . . . . 1:30 P.M.
Late bell . . . . 1:33 P.M.
       March to drill
Recall from third period . . . . 3:00 P.M.
Assembly for fourth period . . . . 3:15 P.M.
Late bell . . . . .3:18 P.M.
       March to drill
Recall from fourth period . . . . 4:30 P.M.
Sick call . . . . .5:30 P.M.
Assembly for evening roll call. . . . . 6:45 P.M.
Evening roll call, late bell. . . . . 6:48 P.M.
       Publish orders. March to evening meal.
Call to rooms . . . . 7:45 P.M.
Release from rooms . . . . 9:30 P.M.
Tattoo . . . . 9:55 P.M.
Taps-inspection by Midshipman in Charge of Floors . . . . 10:00 P.M.

"Study" he penciled in wherever he had a half hour to spare in the schedule (he took a break in the fifteen minutes between third and fourth drill periods); athletics took place between fourth drill period and evening Sick Call, and he penciled in "letters—2 a day" before "Call to rooms"—with care of uniform, shaving, and washing up to take place after.

But Plebe Summer was mostly reserved for drilling. The midshipmen went everywhere in formation. Drill was the Academy's principal tool to introduce them to the proper order and discipline that would be utterly necessary in overcrowded conditions when the full complement of midshipmen got back in September.[13]

There was method in the exhausting drill and labor the Plebes underwent: in addition to teaching the Academy's regulations and necessary self-discipline, it gave them a chance to develop personal skills they would need to survive when the academic year started and the pace racheted up. Between drills, the Plebes were lectured by anyone handy, on subjects nautical and military. And between lectures, they drilled.

In the remaining time they also got their first exposure to the academic departments of the school. *All* the upperclassmen helped to "raise" the Plebes: there was an enormous amount of naval lore to be learned, and it wasn't covered in the classwork or the drill. The routine hazing gave the Plebes a very unpleasant incentive to pick up the lore and be able to spout it back without hesitation.

They sailed on the Severn and learned the etiquette of the water and other matters of basic small-craft seamanship. Heinlein loved ship handling and went sport sailing as often as possible.[14] They got a brief exposure, too, to naval ordnance, once with an inspection tour of the armory. Heinlein was enthusiastic about the airplane motors he studied in the Department of Engineering and Aeronautics. He had an ambition to become a naval aviator.

In addition to drill and study, the Plebes were required to go out for one of the school's sports, and Heinlein first tried track-and-field, where the coach thought he had potential as a high jumper. But it didn't really attract him—in any case he never followed up an initial positive evaluation.[15] There were two mandatory-pass tests for sports requirements, boxing and wrestling. He hated both.[16] He did go out for soccer and was, for a short time, the manager of the two Plebe lacrosse teams. Perhaps he wangled this position to get out of the line of fire, for he says of it: "There are more ways of killing a cat than choking it to death with butter."[17] Although he continued with lacrosse through Plebe Summer and into the academic year, he decided he didn't like any of the body-contact sports.[18] He passed his qualifying tests and then went to the other end of the gym, where he took up "dirty fighting"—*la savate*, judo, cane fighting, and rough-and-tumble under its various names.[19] For his required sport, he finally settled on fencing.

In a sense, it was almost inevitable that Heinlein would choose fencing as his sport: he had been playing at fencing for years, ever since he saw the stage play of *The Tales of Hoffmann* in about 1915. Fencing was the Academy's oldest sport and was followed with interest by many of the midshipmen for that reason.[20] His fencing master was a real French swordsman with a mystery in his past. *Capitaine* Deladrier gave instruction in épée, fleuret (foil or small-sword), and saber. Heinlein decided to specialize in épée: it was the closest you could get to real swordplay without (usually) serious bloodshed.[21] Fencing was a good choice for him: it gave him a chance to use his speed and reflexes without a great deal of knocking about.

Heinlein's weaknesses were in swimming and rifle. He was one of those rare, naturally buoyant persons who cannot sink in water[22] and so had never really worked at swimming. He was placed on the "weak squad" for remedial work until his swimming skills were considered up to standard.

Heinlein also did not do as well as he knew he could on the rifle range. He was a little exasperated because of the poor shooting conditions—and because there was nothing he could do to improve them.[23] While he was shooting on the rifle team, his coach saw that he was really too light for the shooting, so he put a sandbag across Robert's shoulders to help with the recoil.[24] He qualified as a marksman on July 24.

In the evenings and on weekends, during the weeks before their first leave to go into Annapolis, the Plebes had little relatively free time to themselves—except for Sunday afternoons, when they were expected to write letters to their family and spend at least two hours in athletics. They had no access to cars or even to newspapers and radios (for which reason Heinlein missed the Scopes trial that July, the first trial ever to be broadcast on the radio). Most evenings Plebes would gather in "Smoke Park" and shoot the breeze.[25] Heinlein wrote home frequently—short and sometimes awkward notes:

> I found out as Ivar predicted that this place isn't much fun. But I shall stick it out and manage somehow to enjoy it. I like it even now fairly well. And I know the training is wonderful; I wouldn't miss it for anything. Just the same I'm looking forward to my first leave. . . . We are well into the swing of the drills now. I am getting along satisfactorily but not brilliantly. I can see a long hard pull ahead if I distinguish myself in anything.[26]

The family knew just what he needed from home, based on Ivar's two years at Annapolis. For his eighteenth birthday on July 7, they sent a package with letters and hometown newspapers, which made him even more homesick, and cookies and candy that he shared with his "wife" (Academy slang for roommate). Heinlein thanked them profusely for the treats. "I get awfully hungry between meals and it surely helps to have some thing around."[27]

Homesickness was making him reflective. About two hours every afternoon he felt homesick (though he could not account for the regularity of the experience).[28] In a pocket notebook he carried all through his years at the Academy, he tallied all the letters (and packages) received from family and friends in his Plebe Summer (along with a "Hate List" of five names, with one name checked off and noted "settled!").[29] In a letter written on July 7, his eighteenth birthday, he opened up to his mother:

> I know, mother, we didn't always think alike, but I nearly always see your viewpoint in the long run. The same way with dad. He's generally right but I can't always see it at the time. But then in some of the things you didn't approve of, you weren't in a position to see the pressure I was under.[30]

His mother's birthday was exactly a week later, and he continues in much the same vein:

> Dearest Mother, I hope this gets to you by your birthday. Many happy returns of the day and all the love in the world.
> I wish I could see you now. I never knew till I left home, Mother, just how much I loved you and Dad and the rest, too, but you two especially. I never have been as good a son as I might have but I've always tried.[31]

By that time he had received one set of his dress whites and had a photo taken for his family. He sent it along with birthday greetings (July 23) for his favorite—Rose Elizabeth. (He always said that he had two girlfriends: his "big girl friend" was his "drag" at the Academy, and the other was Rose Betty, his "little girl friend.") The family had recently sent him a sixteen-page memory book, with a whole roll of photographs of the family (plus one of a downtown street scene, to use up the last picture in the roll) and a crayon picture Rose Betty had made for him, of the house with lawn and trees.

Throughout his life, Heinlein was easily roused to emotions of all kinds, and so he gradually developed ways of coping with his excitability. But this early, he had few psychological tools to deal with his feelings. He was finding that he was the outlander at Annapolis, the rustic from the Wild West plunked down among eastern "sophisticates." His easily aroused emotions of wonder and his strong sense of dedication were unfashionable and déclassé in the crowd of mostly privileged, mostly white, mostly Protestant young men who nevertheless thought of themselves as "rainbow spectra, collected from the corners of the sky."[32] Once he decided to abandon his policy of keeping his mouth discreetly shut, his first overtures were not met with easy acceptance. This may have been one of those defects-of-his-virtues things: he had been made platoon leader early on—the battalion officers were often chosen from ROTC men, and Heinlein was a natural candidate on that ground—but he was probably not very gracious in sharing his ampler knowledge of procedure. Toward the end of Plebe Summer, he complained to his brother Larry:

> I can't write letters like I should any more. I was just interrupted to explain to my dear company commander the intricacies of company drill. The drill competition for the summer occurs Saturday [August 22?] and he hadn't studied it as yet. Ignorance is annoying. We are going to be beaten and there is little I can do about it. I am the only plebe striper in the company that knows the D.R. and there are half a dozen former cadet officers *in the ranks,* colonels and on down.
>   It's a great life,
>
>   Bob[33]

Word got around about his rank of brigadier general at the Civilian Military Training Camp and the 1924 General Smith trophy for Best Drillmaster, and he was nicknamed "the Boy General"—a very cutting nickname to carry through a military school.

Although he never talked about it explicitly, Heinlein must never before in his life have felt more like a square peg in a round hole than in those first months at the Naval Academy. That sense of being misfitted is probably at the root of his determination to persevere and work through, and he did refine there an important tool of self-presentation (which must have been already familiar to an atheist teenager in a religious home): to maintain a public face that will protect and conceal the private reality. He had no buffer of camaraderie to ease the pangs of homesickness (even Ivar was off on a practice cruise that summer), and he later said that the experience forced him to grow:

> I was very homesick, as I had never been so far away from my home and my parents and brothers and sisters and friends. But eventually that feeling wore off and I began to behave like an adult, able to stand on my own feet and no longer needing the emotional support of others. The transition from child to adult is not easy, but it is necessary.[34]

In his pocket notebook he made a list of principles, with "keep your mouth shut" repeated on different pages. Controlling his tongue was his biggest personality problem.

The book is full of excellent advice for himself:

Worldly Wisdom
from
The Old Master

Speaking of the Ladies
 I. Don't force the issue.
 II. No matter who she is, or how low she is, treat her like a lady, they always fall for it, no matter how low.
 III. Humor them.
 IV. Don't, above all things, force the issue.
 V. When likely to go bad, read one of Bljdf's[35] letters.

 I. Say what you've got to say in as few words as possible.
 II. Keep your mouth shut and soldier.
 III. It isn't what you believe, it's how you act.
 IV. Don't expect a square deal.
 V. (a) Make all the acquaintances you can.
  (b) Make all the friends you can.
  (c) Never miss a chance to meet anyone.
  (d) Never drop an acquaintance.
  (e) But don't be greasy.
 XI. When in Rome shoot Roman Candles.
 XII. When discouraged by the start anyone has on me remember my first year in military; dogged persistence will overcome any lead.
 XIII. And don't do anything rash. Your judgment is bad in emergencies.—Captain Kearney.
 VI. "Bob would go over big if he'd just keep his mouth shut."—Jap.
 VII. Never pet for amusement.
 VIII. (a) When in doubt keep still.
  (b) Never talk without something to say.
  (c) Never open your mouth unless there is some purpose to be served by doing so.
 IX. They who play the victrola must buy the records.
 X. *Don't be greasy*

    (a) go slow on salutes, etc.

    (b) go slow on sirs.

    (c) go slow on etc.

  XI. "If you can make a man sit down, you've got him."—Booth Tark-
ington.

  XII. *Success breeds Success.*

 XIII. Keep your word (in particular to men under you).

 XIV. Be impartial.

  XV. Don't talk fight unless you mean fight, then *don't talk, fight!*

By August of Plebe Summer, when the Plebe intercompany competition
started, things were beginning to settle into a routine. His second set of dress
white service arrived, and his blue service, too, so his kit was finally complete—
just as well, as his cash reserves had dwindled to $3.50. Occasional "expense
account" money from home helped, as did the $2.00 per month midshipmen
received as their stipend. That wasn't a lot, even in 1925, and out of his stipend
he was supposed to save, by the end of four years, $1,000 for his graduation
kit—formal uniforms including cocked hat and swords. It could not be done,
of course: even though the monthly stipend increased throughout the four
years, the total came to something less than $300. But that was a problem to
be dealt with later.

He got along well enough with Frank Novak, but they didn't really "connect," so he decided to request a new roommate assignment in September.
He did not give a reason in his letters, but there is one brief protest of a demerit for a disorderly room, during a day when Frank was supposed to be in
charge of tidying up.[36] Heinlein settled on Seraphin Bach Perreault, another
Kansas City boy who had also been to the Civilian Military Training Camp
in Fort Leavenworth (though there is no evidence they knew each other at
that time). Perreault—"Perry"—was also on the lacrosse and fencing squads.
They agreed and requested a rooming reassignment in September.

Heinlein still had trouble with his physical requirements. Late in August
he wrote that he had pulled the weak squad the day before—that is, he was
placed with others who couldn't make the physical requirements—but he
was making rapid improvement: "We had some instruction in life saving
last week. I believe I could save a person now under reasonably favorable
conditions, say from a swimming pool or the Blue River. It is interesting
work."[37]

If the hazing and social distancing and the constant overwork and lack of
food had been unrelieved, the Academy would have been an unbearable

place, and we would have in the United States something comparable to the British genre of memoirs detailing the horrors of the British public school system (the American public schools have their own horror stories). But the Academy had been functioning for a very long time, and there were relief valves built into the system. Some of the relief valves gave the boys something to focus on other than their emotions—friendly competition between French and Spanish companies, for instance. Or Superintendent Nulton's regular Saturday afternoon garden parties and lunches for apparently randomly selected Midshipmen. Nor was the discipline in Bancroft Hall completely restrictive:

> We had a broom fight last night between this deck and the one above. More fun! The Midshipman officer of the Watch, a first classman got beat up in the rush.
>
> I got soaked with a pitcher of water in addition to touched with a broom.[38]

Such customs allowed the steam to bleed off harmlessly.

Late in August 1925, they had a bit of excitement: fire broke out in Isherwood Hall. The incident is remembered in the class history, but Heinlein's firsthand telling, for his family, is better. He never did panic in a crisis—a trait he says he inherited from both sides of the family (though he might come down with the shakes afterward)—and he managed to enjoy this crisis, in some detail:

> We had the first fire in several years here yesterday. It sadly interfered with me serving extra duty. . . .[39]
>
> As I was dressing for the Com's party, the gong sounded and the M.C. yelled, "Outside fire drill! All hands turn out!" I chased over to my station in the Fourth Wing and was ready for action before I knew it was an actual fire. I forgot to say, I am a fire chief. Oh, yes, a hose truck and sixteen doughty firemen.[40] Only three of them were there when I arrived but we went anyway. We hauled out the truck and went hooting and yelling down officers row in front of the Admiral's house.
>
> The Admiral came out as we passed and wanted to know where the fire was. I told him it was in Sherwood Hall (Steam bldg.) He didn't deign to come with us but followed in a Packard. It was some fire. The insides looked like a furnace. My hose happened to be the only one that got any real action. I didn't get much as I was outside passing the word and trying to stop a leak.

A couple of fellows up on the roof with a hose had a hose turned on them and were nearly knocked down into a blazing mass. Several fellows were slightly hurt by falling glass. The Admiral was drenched and knocked over a couple of times in the rush. After the fire was put out, it took me some time to sort out the defective hose in my lot. Consequently we were the last truck to leave. As we were leaving we were called back to attend to another truck that was deserted. We were about an hour late coming in. A first classman on duty attempted to get some of us excused from extra duty. He succeeded in getting excused from that period of which there was about an hour to go but we served instead a later period of full two hours. Such is life! Heroes are never appreciated. I think I'll quit being one. Not even a word of praise from the Supe and me yelling my lungs hoarse all afternoon. 'Twas ever thus.

Yours,
Bob[41]

And with that, Heinlein's introduction to life at the Academy was complete. His brother and the rest of the midshipmen would be returning from practice cruise the following week, only to leave immediately for a month's leave in September while the Plebes formally commenced their academic year. Heinlein became so pressed for time that he could not keep up his correspondence with his family: the September 3, 1925, crash of the helium-filled dirigible airship *Shenandoah,* launched from nearby Lakehurst, New Jersey, was not mentioned in correspondence, though it must have rattled around Bancroft Hall as much as did the fire.

He was doing reasonably well—well begun, though not half done. He had regained the weight he had lost in that first nerve-racking week, plus another eleven pounds of muscle. He had made up most of his physical deficiencies and had enough money for his limited needs (at least, until leave on September 7). Except for the minor annoyance of eyestrain that needed attention, all was well.

True, he had accumulated a few demerits for "room out of order" and had had "a couple of encounters with an overzealous Midshipman Officer of the Watch on the subject of dust,"[42] but this just gave him enough material to complain about for his spiritual health:

I'm like the Toonerville trolley that meets all the trains. I'm the plebe that walks all the punishment periods. . . . "And lo! Blessed is he that has tried hard to be good, for he shall be papped." It doesn't worry me.[42]

PLEBE YEAR

By early August 1925, the incoming Plebes were ready to tackle their first big class project: in October, they would be required to put out a special edition of the Academy's weekly news magazine, *The Log*—the first of the school year and the first opportunity for the incoming Plebe class to show their stuff.

The Log was an important publication at the Academy. Issued every Friday, it was the semiofficial voice of the institution, carefully supervised by officers, though actually produced by the midshipmen. The contents were usually in three sections. The first section was devoted to military humor and cartoons, the second section to current events, and the third section to sports. Every week, 6,500 copies of *The Log* went out to midshipmen and their families and "drag" (girlfriends). *The Plebe Log*'s humor section usually dealt with the events of Plebe Summer.

The Log's regular staff was away on practice cruise during Plebe Summer. Robert's brother Ivar (nicknamed "Ike" at the Academy) was working on the business end of *The Log*, soliciting advertising and so forth. Robert decided to get into the creative end of the venture. He knew as early as the beginning of August what he wanted to do, and he hit the mark on the first shot: his cartoon was chosen for the cover of the 1925 *Plebe Log*, proudly signed "—R. A. Heinlein—'29," his first published work. He shows a barefoot and smudged Plebe, frustrated and dismayed, in characteristic T-shirt and white trousers, making a mess of the labels he is writing on his clothing. The name on the blotted sailor's blouse he holds is "Joe Gish" (though a fold in the fabric makes it look like "Fish," appropriate for the new-caught Plebes), that Plebe archetype, "one of the 10% Who Never Gets the Word and all five of the Three Stooges."[1] He is memorialized in *The Lighthouse* for 1929 as "[a]n international character. The best-known Middie in the world."

Shortly before the end of August, the Plebes shuffled their temporary

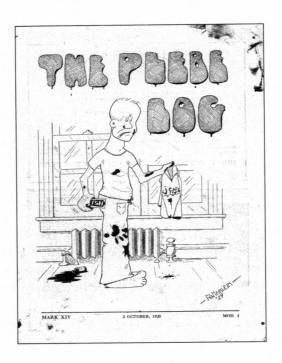

room assignments around, and Heinlein settled in with Seraphin Bach Perreault.

Life at the Academy changed drastically in the last week of August, when
the practice cruises ended and the rest of the older midshipmen came back to
campus. The Practice Squadron sailed up the Severn in the early evening of
August 28 and anchored off Greenbury Point overnight. At five o'clock the
next morning, all the upperclassmen were released at the same time, and they
came flooding into Bancroft Hall, waking all the Plebes (an hour and a half
before their usual reveille) and taking over the showers. Most of the returning
midshipmen left immediately for a month of "September leave," but Robert's
brother Ivar stayed overnight, just long enough to collect his civilian clothes,
and left again for Kansas City on the following Sunday. The Plebes got a brief
leave—their first—on September 7, just enough time to wander around Annapolis a bit and perhaps pick up some sundries they couldn't get at the com-
missary. And then back to the grind. The Plebes were kept on a very tight
leash, and their academic year started a month before everyone else's.

They couldn't have gone very far in any case. In 1925, Plebes were not
even permitted to ride in an automobile except while on extended leave—and
in any case the automobile was not yet a common accessory. Most travel was
difficult and expensive. For longer-distance travel, the train was the only op-

tion, and it was not always comfortable or convenient: except in the longest leaves, boys from the West Coast could not get back to see their families at all.

Most of the Plebe year course work was taken up by the foundation disciplines for engineering: principles of boilers and mathematics. Naval officers were expected to know the applied mathematics needed in their trade—at a minimum, "spherical trigonometry, partial triple differentials, ballistics both for ordnance and for celestial mechanics, solution of empiricals by brute-force numerical integration, etc."[2]—a tough course for kids who had previously had little exposure to mathematics. "Juice"—electricity—was an important course for all midshipmen. Mechanical drawing was particularly important because much of the instruction midshipmen would receive over the next five years would consist of making engineering diagrams of ships' systems. There was language and history, as well, and light touches of other subjects—four books on astronomy, for instance, in one week during Plebe year, though as Heinlein noted, all were significantly out-of-date: a textbook by F. R. Moulton, the head of the Department of Astronomy at the University of Chicago, published as recently as 1922, did not even mention the ongoing measurements of the speed of light, which Michelson had started at the Naval Academy in 1886.[3]

The teaching staff at the Academy was a very mixed bag. Usually the Superintendent was an elderly and distinguished figure who did not participate in the teaching but served as a father figure and might have little feel for the academic life of the institution.[4] There was a hard core of professional teachers— some very good—and then a cadre of officers assigned to the Academy, about half the size of the core of professionals, who might or might not have any aptitude for instruction. The general opinion of the midshipmen was that those officers had been assigned to the Academy for reasons of punishment or discipline. Their opinion was that the Academy in those days was a kind of dumping ground for the Navy's odds and sods[5]—not entirely reasonable considering the number of top men in their field who have been associated with the Academy.

In Heinlein's day, however, most of the teachers didn't try to be more than a referee between the midshipman and his books,[6] and *The Lighthouse* defined "Prof" as "the referee in our struggle." In the most egregious cases, it was noticed, the professor was simply timing the number of problems and solutions that could be put up on the board during the class period. Nevertheless, there was generally a good relationship between the Mids[7] and their instructors.

Academy education was just a beginning. This was never made explicit, but it gradually dawned on most of the midshipmen that "education" would be something they did themselves, later.[8] They were being given the fundamentals and exposures to this and that, rather than an education in depth. Except for the Seaman classification, every job in the Navy is specialized—sometimes highly specialized—and the Academy couldn't do more than touch lightly on some of the specializations during this basic course work, leaving it for later instruction to develop the more highly specialized skills.

Instead, the Academy concentrated on developing a generalized engineering background, which would serve as the fundamentals to learn anything else. The humanities, except for the modern languages requirement, were brushed over lightly. The Plebe Summer and Plebe Year curriculum concentrated on composition and literature. The English Department, which also supervised the history curriculum, encouraged library research for the Plebes and wide reading—self-disciplines that stood Heinlein in good stead all his life.

More emphasis was given to customs and etiquette, especially the dances they would need to know; there were one-hour sessions with an instructor to talk the midshipmen through the basics—waltz, fox-trot, and so on—so they wouldn't disgrace the Academy when they began to be invited out by the townspeople of Annapolis. Heinlein probably needed this instruction, despite claiming on his scrapbook list of miscellaneous jobs to have worked as a "roadhouse hoofer," since his family was strictly raised under the Methodist discipline, and dancing—particularly of this recreational sort—was not allowed at home. But dances were the main social activities midshipmen could expect to participate in, and one of the few opportunities to associate with girls.

The Academy made out monthly report cards and sent them home to his father. The cards showed both a grade point for each subject, on a descending scale from 4.0 ("Distinction") to 2.49 or lower ("Failing"), and a class standing. The academics were not in themselves a problem for Heinlein—all his marks were in the "Distinction" range—but his class standing varies from subject to subject, and class standing with respect to conduct is given as 91 on his first report card, for the month of October 1925. He has three demerits. He would stay at three demerits until nearly the end of the academic year.

The monthly report cards also note the size of the class, which was already losing members. From a starting size of 478, the Plebe class had dropped to 403 in November. In December it fell to 400, and the number continued to fall until it stabilized at 316 late in 1926. It would fall to 240 by the end of the four years.

Midshipmen left the Academy for all sorts of reasons. Most common were failures in academics, but the physical requirements also accounted for some of the attrition in the early years. Some couldn't cut the athletics. There were some discipline problems. Medical problems cropped up, too: one of Heinlein's best friends—a healthy-looking boy named Art Stiles, broad-shouldered and athletic, went in for his end-of-Plebe-Summer physical, and the doctors discovered a heart murmur. Stiles was given *congé*—leave to go. Myopia, too, was a big problem, as the Navy then and for decades thereafter continued to require all its officers to have perfect, uncorrected vision. That was troubling to Heinlein, who had passed his own physical: nearsightedness ran in his family, and during the summer he had begun to experience some eyestrain.

Some midshipmen left for other reasons: the economic boom was starting, and they may have been offered other opportunities more congenial. That was the case with Heinlein's friend Woody Teague, who resigned in 1926 to go into banking.[9] A few may have washed out because of the hazing.

Hazing is always a problem at closed institutions. At the Academy, it was officially forbidden but by long tradition unofficially tolerated. The hazing welded the Plebes into a community with a common enemy: every other midshipman in the Academy, but particularly the outgoing First Classmen.

Hazing varied in degree from time to time and from person to person. Heinlein left a more or less accurate portrait[10] of the hazing at the Academy in his fictional reminiscence of classmate Delos Wait in "The Man Who Was Too Lazy to Fail," a segment of *Time Enough for Love*:

But the unceasing barrage of questions did not bother [him] save for the possibility of starving to death at meal times—and he learned to shovel it in fast while sitting rigidly at attention and still answer all questions flung at him. Some were trick questions, such as, "Mister, are you a virgin?" Either way a plebe answered he was in trouble—if he gave a straight answer. In those days some importance was placed on virginity or the lack of it; I can't say why.

But trick questions called for trick answers; [he] found that an acceptable answer to that one was: "Yes *sir*!—in my left ear." Or possibly his belly button.

But most trick questions were intended to trap a plebe into giving a meek answer—and meekness was a mortal sin. Say a first classman said, "Mister, would you say I was handsome?"—an acceptable answer would be, "Perhaps

your mother would say so, sir—but not *me*." Or, "Sir, you are the hand-
somest man I ever saw who was intended to be an ape."

Such answers were chancy—they might flick a first classman on the
raw—but they were safer than meek answers.[11]

When the Plebe gave the wrong answer—"wrong" defined by the First Classman in his sole discretion—he would be told: "Mister, report to my room after dinner!" and often, "Bring your own broom!" When the hapless Plebe
arrived in the First Classman's room he would be told to "bend over and
assume the attitude," and then a variable number of whacks would be administered. Physical abuse of the Plebes was expressly forbidden—though,
again, unofficially tolerated so long as kept within recognized and traditional
bounds.

As this recollection suggests, the Plebes were not expected to be entirely
passive: Heinlein brought down the wrath of one of the school's graduating
star football players, Royce Flippin (Class of 1926), on himself with one act
of defiance. Years later, Heinlein's close friend Cal Laning called the incident
to mind in a letter to Virginia Heinlein:

> Re the little sketch in my last letter, suggesting you show it to Bob and see
> if he remembers it. Can't blame for forgetting. He has risen high since
> chalking that on his plebe or youngster year room door in the Fourth Bat-
> talion wing. Ask again, if he remembers his penaltude under Royce Flip-
> pin, our Batt. Commander. Bob expressed his revolting mood in that
> secret hieroglyph—two balls suspended with prick rampant over four hor-
> izontal stripes, latter stripes symbolizing Flippin's rank. "Fagin, youse is a
> prick."[12]

Beating with a broom handle was the traditional limit of physical punishment, though if the First Classman did not feel inclined for the salutary
exercise of administering the beating, the Plebe could be required to do
push-ups or some other form of exercise until he amusingly gave out. For
most of the upperclassmen it was a mild and sublimated but publicly acceptable form of sadism. Sometimes the invisible and undefined line would be
crossed:

> But no matter how carefully a plebe tried to meet impossible standards,
> about once a week some first classman would decide that he needed
> punishment—arbitrary punishment without trial. This could run from

mild, such as exercises repeated to physical collapse . . . up to paddling on the buttocks. . . . I'm not speaking of paddling children sometimes receive. These beatings were delivered with the flat of a sword or with a worn-out broom that amounted to a long, heavy club. Three blows delivered by a grown man in perfect health would leave the victim's bottom a mass of purple bruises and blood blisters, accompanied by excruciating pain.[13]

That was under the best of circumstances—the dark side of institutionalized "good clean fun." The fact that it was institutionalized, and that there were therefore unwritten but understood limits, was the only slender protection the Plebes enjoyed.

For some midshipmen, the sadism was not so sublimated. Heinlein attracted the attention of one of these, First Classman "Marsh"—Marshall Barton—Gurney, Class of '26.[14]

Heinlein had undoubtedly called attention to himself during Plebe Summer with the kind of mental arithmetic tricks he outlined for David Lamb in *Time Enough for Love*.[15] Perhaps also he slipped and let out the kind of indiscreet remarks found in his letters home about the "insufficiencies" he encountered that he never expected to see at the Academy (certainly there are admonitions to himself about keeping his mouth shut in his personal notes).[16] This would have made him a smart-ass Plebe likely to be targeted for taking down a peg—or several pegs—by the First Classmen returning from September leave.

Gurney may not have been quite stable to begin with: once, at mess, he had been offended by a remark made by one of the Plebes, and he sprayed the entire table with a handy bottle of ketchup. Heinlein found that particularly offensive, as he hated to be caught with less-than-perfect kit.[17] Any display of irritation by a Plebe would, of course, be cause for swats—with wooden coat hangers in Gurney's case—much more painful and potentially damaging. Gurney's 1926 *Lucky Bag* portrait lists a Black N with *five* asterisks. Gurney seemed to have had an unusual degree of trouble with authority.[18]

Gurney had a wicked imagination, exercised to its fullest extent in inventing special torments for Heinlein—within the lines, mostly, but highly unusual nonetheless. During the summer, the Plebes had learned to eat at attention and field the upperclassmen's trick questions. Gurney gave this a twist: Heinlein had to get *under* the table. He took his plate with him and managed to keep from starving.[19] Barely. This went on for some time. Gurney was just getting warmed up.

Probably he figured out that some of Heinlein's answers involved memorization, so he thought up memorization hazing schemes and made Heinlein learn the entirety of Rudyard Kipling's 1894 poem "Mary Gloster,"[20] a 380-line ballad of forty-seven eight-line stanzas, in a difficult meter combining iambic and anapestic feet, in a difficult rhyme scheme. The poem is about a bitter Victorian industrialist who wants to be buried at sea, where he buried his wife decades before, but does not trust his son to carry out his last wishes and decides to take the heir down with him—not one of Kipling's more pleasant efforts. And then the twist: Gurney required Heinlein to recite it *upside down, in the shower.*[21]

When "Mary Gloster" palled, Gurney switched the game: Heinlein would have to memorize something even less appealing: fifty five-place logarithms each day.[22] After a while, Gurney lost interest, but logarithms are very useful for engineers: Heinlein kept up the project for his own uses. He added this autobiographical flourish to his description of David Lamb's hazing in *Time Enough for Love*:

> The first classman grew tired of the matter when [he] had completed only the first six hundred figures—but [he] kept at it another three weeks through the first thousand—which gave him the first ten thousand figures by interpolation and made him independent of log tables, a skill that was of enormous use to him from then on, computers being effectively unknown in those days.[23]

The extracurricular hazing undoubtedly had an adverse impact on his schoolwork and may account for the drop in his grades during the last quarter of 1925. But as spring came on the First Classmen became preoccupied with their own pregraduation rituals, and things let up on him a bit.

Nor was that his only salvation: not all the upperclassmen entered into hazing so enthusiastically—and there was the traditional, if unacknowledged, relief valve of "spooning," as well. Usually on the basis of some personal connection—family or friends of friends or perhaps a romantic interest in a sister or sometimes just coming from the same area of the country—an upperclassman would take one or more Plebes under his wing and "spoon on" them. Almost everybody was spooned on by someone for some reason,[24] so the Plebes had a little relief from the strict discipline; they could go to the upperclassman's room and gripe or otherwise let down their hair.

Although Heinlein never mentioned a spooner in letters home, there were a number of minor personal connections that would have made such spooning possible—a number of upperclassmen from Kansas City, for instance, or friends of Ivar's two years ahead of the Plebes. By coincidence, there were five Kansas Citians each in the '27 and '29 classes. One of the '27 boys, Albert Scoles, known at the Academy as "Buddy" (nearly everyone had a nickname at the Academy; Heinlein's was the pedestrian "Bob"), was a friend to both Ivar and Robert for the rest of their lives, and it's quite likely he and Ivar both spooned on Robert to some degree—probably Buddy Scoles more than Ivar, for Robert and he shared a fanatical belief in rocketry and spaceflight, so they had a great deal of common ground. Continuing from the family setting into the Academy, Robert's relationship with Ivar was one of rivalry, trying to catch up or recapitulate the achievements Ivar seemed to pull off without effort. Many of Ivar's achievements Robert was able to duplicate, but it was a good many years before he could start being himself instead of a surrogate Ivar.

With the competitive season coming on, Heinlein was enjoying the fencing. It was a sport that relied on quickness and agility rather than strength and bulk, and it suited him well, as he had extraordinarily fast reflexes.[25] He might have gone in for gymnastics as well—he admired his roommate's progress with rings and trapeze and tumbling (and later regretted not taking them up himself)[26]—but he would have had to give up sword, since they were both winter sports. He stayed with épée.

Fencing was doing all right for him. A local (Annapolis) newspaper clipping in his scrapbook, undated but apparently from December 1925, praises the Plebe fencing team and mentions him:

> The Plebe fencers won their third straight meet by decisively defeating Forest Park High, of Baltimore. . . . The Plebes presented a strong aggressive team, from which the Forest Park aggregation could not take a single match. . . . Besides the full team of Wait, Heinlein and Stewart, the Plebes have two sabre men and one epee man, all of whom should furnish valuable reserve strength for next year's varsity.

That December, he was able to make it home (though not in time for Christmas, as leave started on December 23 and ended on January 3, with three-day train trips on either end, leaving not much time to spend with family). His father gifted him with $100 he later confessed he could ill afford. But on the whole it was a happy occasion. His brother Larry, in a letter Robert found waiting for him when he got back to Annapolis, told him he had acquitted himself well: "[Y]ou did just fine on your leave and are about the finest brother a man could have." Larry added words of support and encouragement that show Robert's affection for him was reciprocated:

> Keep ever before you a picture of the kind of a man your Mother thinks you will be and try hard to be like it. . . .
>
> If [Alice and I] didn't give you all the time and attention you felt we should please realize that we were kept busy by circumstances over which we had no control.[27]

In closing, Larry said his note was "Not much of a letter, but it means a lot." It did mean a lot: Heinlein kept this letter among his personal papers for the rest of his life.

Back at Annapolis, Heinlein's grades gradually pulled up, as did his class standing, which was recalculated afresh for each monthly report card. He maintained his first-in-class for deportment through spring, but he had other things to occupy his attention, as well. He mentioned having a "harem" of girls interested in him[28]—a welcome change from high school.

He was also acting a bit: he had a role in that year's Gymkhana, a kind of combined cabaret and exhibition presented in the spring each year until it was discontinued in 1928. "I am a Paris swell who gets in a duel over a girl in a café, and kill[s] the other guy."[29] At that, he was lucky—Plebes were usually assigned the "girl" roles in the Academy's theatricals. He kept a studio photo of the production in his scrapbook, but he is also pictured in the 1927 *The Lucky Bag* in his "Paris swell" moustache.

He listed his activities in his pocket notebook:

1. Log
1. Lucky Bag [*sic* the numbering]
2. Masqueraders
3. Gymn-khana
4. Christmas Card [Committee]
5. Hop Com[mittee]
6. Class Ring
7. Juice [Electricity] gang
8. Reef Points [the Academy's little blue guidebook to local customs and jargon]

He left numbered lines for three more activities, never filled in.

Spring was not all jollity, though: he had a second set of Dark Days[30] that year as preparations—expensive preparations—for the upcoming summer practice cruise forced him to confront the fact that he was already running a permanent financial deficit (or close to it). In one page of his pocket notebook, he instructed himself:

VI
Live within my means
a. Don't accumulate grad debts.
b. Don't try to come home Christmas at all.

He had to do something to cope with the flood of expenses, major and minor, that were beyond his experience. He drafted a letter to his father:

Now about money matters. I hate to bring them up but I don't know what to do. As it appears now I will only have enuf in Sept, to pay my fare both ways, clean up my authorized Sept. Debts (*Lucky Bag,* Log, etc.) and perhaps have $25 left. What am I to do? I am promised to pay you $50 and then I won't have anything for Sept. leave expenses and I have to have shoes, hat, and a couple of shirts. My amt. available was knocked $40 this month when I had to order a new suit of service and that was something I wasn't figuring on. Also you sent me $10 and I owe $5 around here (I had to buy a cruise suitcase, some other clothes I forgot to requisition, etc.). Also I am buying a raincoat from a 1st classman which takes another $5 as we are going back to the old style in raincoats and a new one would cost me $18 in Oct. Dad, what am I to do? I can't ask you for money for I know you are doing all you can for me, but what else can I do? I am starting on a cruise of ten thousand miles broke and have the prospect of another broke leave ahead of me. Isn't there some way I can borrow some money to make me able to enjoy life up here, so I can reciprocate when some of the fellows give me a treat, or so I don't have to save for a month in order to go to a picture show? According to agreement I haven't dragged[31] since Xmas, but it won't be any better next year for our monthly money is always used up for assessments, collections, etc. Sometimes I feel tempted to resign and come home and get a job and live decently in a way we can afford instead of trying to keep up a false position up here. I'm about thru. And if my eyes hurt me much more I know I am. Tell me what to do, Dad, for I am pretty far down in the dumps, but at the same time not low enuf to accept money when I know it means denial on your part. Can't we work out some plan? Each time I figure to get by something else comes up. Like that telegram the other day. I wanted to send it but didn't have the money. Young Hines was with me and suggested we telegraph. I told him I didn't have the cash so he paid for it as he insisted I send. Naturally I'll pay him back but you can see how it goes when I am with boys who have always had plenty of money.

When I hold back on acct. of funds they'll treat and I'll have to manage to repay it somehow.

Well, I've unburdened myself considerably but I know you'll understand how I feel. My Dad always does.

Love,
Bob

And a brave P.S.:

Remember I said I'd accept no more money like the "denial" $20 of last July and the $100 of Xmas.[32]

This was the last time he would unburden himself to his father. He got through his cruise, and Larry was able to help out with $8 a month, starting in July.

The last month of spring and the last graded month of the academic year was May; the term was to end on May 26 that year. After that came the rituals of June Week and the (welcomed) departure of the graduating First Class. By tradition, the Plebe class assumed command for one day, the "hundredth night" before graduation.

Heinlein was doing well: he had pulled all his grades back into the "Distinction" range, and his standing in all subjects was in the top 15 percent of the class.

A few days before the end of term, on May 22, Heinlein received devastating news: his sister Rose Elizabeth had fallen out of the family's touring car and was crushed under its wheels.[33] She was seven years old and Robert's favorite among his brothers and sisters. He must have taken it very badly: he received five demerits. That same day, Robert and Ivar were granted emergency leave.

When they got to the hospital, Rose Betty was in critical condition. She recognized him and spoke to him. Soon after, she died. His "little girlfriend" was gone. Robert was devastated—but it was, if anything, harder on his father.

Rex Senior had been driving, and he was in a state of complete emotional collapse, beyond mere grief. Rose Elizabeth's death struck him in his deepest beliefs, and he would never recover:

> The emotional dilemma created in him by trying to reconcile this with the benevolent, personal God he prayed to and had served seven days a week for a lifetime was too much for him. He flipped and was never normal again. . . . A personal God is a pretty cozy thing to have around, and I sometimes miss no longer having Him—but any caring that He does cannot be translated into human values. So don't stake your sanity on it.[34]

There was no time for mourning; both Robert and Ivar had to be back in Annapolis for their respective practice cruises. They hurried back to the Academy and packed their gear into the wooden crates called "cruise boxes."

At the graduation ceremonies in June that year, Heinlein received the Award of the Fourth Class Fencing Team—though he would not officially become a Fourth Classman until the ceremonies concluded. Following the graduation ceremonies, the Plebes traditionally turned their jackets inside out and climbed the monuments on the campus to put a cap on the top. Over the years, this ritual has become restricted to the tallest, the Herndon Monument, and the ritual is known as "the Herndon." Tradition had it that the Plebe who got his cap atop the Herndon Monument would be the class's first to make Admiral. The incoming class would then lose their Plebe status (to the equally traditional shout "There are no more Plebes!") and become 4/C—Fourth Classmen—for a few days, until the commissions began to arrive for the departing First Class. Then they would become Youngsters—though some hard-liners hold that the Youngster year actually began with the return from their first practice cruise.

The three vessels that served as the Academy's practice cruise ships—the *Utah,* the *Arkansas,* and the *Florida*—anchored at the mouth of the Severn, and on June 4, 1926, the Plebes trickled, then flooded toward *Utah* for embarkation. There were 389 left in the class. Eighty-nine had washed out before going to sea—but Heinlein had not.

6

YOUNGSTER YEAR

The formal class history speaks lightly of the 1926 practice cruise on board *Utah*, but it must have been something of a shock, and then shock piled upon shock. All three of the Practice Squadron vessels were considered "antiquated," coal-burners surviving into the age of oil, eking out their dotage training midshipmen.

Utah (BB-31) was a battleship of about twenty-two thousand tons, commissioned in 1909. This year, in addition to its normal complement of one thousand it carried nearly four hundred midshipmen as supercargo (passengers, essentially). The ship was unbelievably overcrowded. Heinlein was billeted in a huge compartment below the waterline, scheduled to sleep 120. He was one of the lucky ones: he got a hammock, so close to the next that he concluded, "If I fell out I would probably fall into the next hammock—but if I did manage to fall through, I still would not hit the steel deck, but human bodies spread solidly on that deck."[1]

As soon as they stowed their kit, the Youngsters were formed up on the deck. They worked to exhaustion for the next sixty days, shoveling coal to feed *Utah*'s insatiable boilers. They were the last class to have a coal-burning Youngster cruise: *Utah* was scheduled to be converted to oil burning immediately after that year's practice cruise.

Typically the first practice cruise would go to northern Europe,[2] and the second went to the Caribbean, but for reasons not recorded, this cruise wandered up and down the Atlantic seaboard, making only fifteen to twenty knots (twenty knots being its top speed), dawdling until August, when they would take part in battle exercises at Guantánamo Bay in Cuba. In the meantime, they hit Newport, then Marblehead, Portland, Charleston, and New York by the beginning of July.

In addition to the "neophitic ordeals of coaling and other forms of sea-drudgery,"[3] these supercargo were taken in hand by the regular crew and taught about actual operations at sea. The mids were broken into groups, and the groups would rotate from department to department of the ship, learning the basics from the people who performed the actual work. As many as could crowd into the compartment would gather around the Chief and hear the Word.

There was a lot to learn all over the ship. Navigation was on the deck, and that was less crowded. The navigator, for example, would patiently show them how to use a sextant to figure the ship's position, an essential skill for anyone on the bridge. Each rotation lasted about a week, then the groups would move on to something else—boilers or gunnery or engineers and machinery spaces—doing the same work the sailors did. The practice cruise was a series of quick courses on ship operations, interlarded with backbreaking physical labor. Every Friday on a practice cruise crew and mids would Holystone the deck on hands and knees, for Captain's inspection on Saturday. The Holystone is a large, heavy block of pumice muscled around the deck to reduce splinters and remove stains and detritus, creating a smooth surface.

But they did have fresh air, refrigeration, and plenty of fresh water for laundry and bathing, and that was a welcomed change from the strict rations and locked water butts at the Academy. *Utah* had evaporators and could produce as much fresh water as they wanted.

The main variation in the ship's routine was their ports of call. Their time in port was often taken up by parades and receptions, though the regular crewmen got shore leave. After a week in New York over the Fourth of July— at which, for a change, they did *not* take part in a parade—they made for Newport again, on Heinlein's nineteenth birthday, July 7, 1926. When they had put in there in June, they found the place deserted. Now the summer season—the exact time and place of Thornton Wilder's *Theophilus North*— was in full swing. For a week, the midshipmen were invited to dances and teas with Newport luminaries, including one memorable tea with Cornelius Vanderbilt.[4]

Then they went to Philadelphia during the sesquicentennial celebration of the city's founding. The whole sky was aglow, reflecting the city's commemorative lighting. The midshipmen were fêted, and the whole complement of midshipmen toured the Naval Aircraft Factory and the Westinghouse Works.[5]

Utah then steamed north, standing off the coast of Maine, where Heinlein got thoroughly chilled one fog watch—"the coldest I recall being in my life"[6]—then south to Guantánamo Bay. As they headed into tropical waters, the temperature climbed to one hundred degrees and stayed there.

Storage space was at such a premium (because of the overcrowding) that the potatoes had been stored in canvas bags in the ship's open cage mast. They rotted in the heat and the damp, with a smell so powerful and so penetrating that they had to be dumped overboard—which left the crew short of mess supplies. Toward the middle of August, the entire ship's complement broke out in boils simultaneously, the first symptoms of scurvy. The potatoes had been their only source of vitamin C.

Scurvy is a very unpleasant—as well as sometimes fatal—disease caused by vitamin C deficiency. As soon as they came into harbor at Haiti, Heinlein bought limes from a bumboat, and his boils disappeared immediately.

They worked through the scurvy. Mornings were filled up with gunnery drills. The midshipmen were placed all over the ship—station and phone, voice tube and telescope—but the most important drill was for loading ammunition in a smooth, uninterrupted flow.

Sometimes in the afternoons they were allowed free time at Hicaal Beach, where they organized baseball teams or broke out the crew gear and practiced rowing for the Battenberg Cup race. Some simply went swimming.

One morning they steamed over to Gonaïves, and to the target range. While standing off Haiti, they had their eagerly anticipated SRBP (Short Range Battle Practice). The midshipmen gathered on the deck and were instructed to stuff cotton into their ears to protect their hearing. This was Heinlein's first exposure to the firepower of an oceangoing vessel. The pounding of the big guns comes shaking up through the legs and is a sensation as much as a sound: proximity to that much raw power was awe-inspiring, sublime— "the voice of the War God to whom we had pledged our future," the class history says of the experience.[7]

After the exercise, *Utah* headed back to the Academy, making landfall on August 26. The midshipmen gathered up their scattered belongings and spent a sleepless night. Early the next morning, they were released all at the same time, to stream up the beach and over Farragut Field to Bancroft Hall. The building shook as the returning midshipmen ran for their cruise boxes, which had been delivered to their assigned rooms. The Plebes were comically startled and peered pillow-haired out their doors—just as Heinlein and his classmates had done a year ago. Now the Youngsters were inside the establishment: they put aside the Plebe whites they had lived in for a year. Their new kit included a mackintosh raincoat and a blouse with a gold diagonal stripe on the left sleeve. Now they would spend most of their time in blues instead of whites—and now they would assume the role of tormenters-of-Plebes.

Robert and Perreault—"Bob" and "Perry"—had gotten on well together, and neither sought a change in bunkmate assignments. They had compatible personal habits and inclinations—or, more exactly, *dis*inclinations to involve themselves in the social doings of the Academy. They also appear to have admired each other's athletics: Perry changed his sports specialization each year. As a Youngster he went out for fencing—though he was on to lacrosse, gym, and soccer the next year.

Robert and Ivar were going back to Kansas City for their September leave, and this trip would be an adventure. Very quietly, Ivar and his friend Buddy Scoles had organized a car trip—strictly against regulations, since midshipmen were not permitted either to own or to drive automobiles in 1926 (though they might ride in one during leaves). Scoles had been on *Utah* for the practice cruise this summer. Now he clubbed together with Ivar and Robert and two other Kansas City boys to buy an old car in Annapolis for $75 and drive it out directly to Kansas City.[8] The roads were primitive, and service stations few and far between in 1926. The car broke down continuously, so these budding engineers mended it with whatever was at hand—toilet paper in one instance,[9] to wrap around burned insulation—and kept going.[10] When they got to Kansas City, they sold the car for $50, so the entire trip cost them only $5 apiece, plus the cost of gasoline.[11]

Things were probably not very comfortable around the Heinlein house in September of 1926: his father was psychologically shattered by his part in Rose Betty's death only four months earlier. But it would have been uncomfortable for Robert even without that additional stress. In his later, fictional retelling of the Academy experience, *Space Cadet,* the reaction he gives his protagonist must surely be an echo of his own experience: the house would seem to have shrunk; the ceilings lower and the furniture more frayed and more frowsty than he remembered it. In Robert's case, the madhouse of a large family would have been much the same—frazzled mother and a mob of bright, growing children going every which way, and mostly somewhere else that didn't really include him anymore. His pallet and books would have been moved into storage (except for the ones Louise took). The new arrangements were sensible, reasonable—and firmly conveyed the message: Robert didn't live here anymore.

The boys were invited out for a round of family dinners, and all the assorted aunts and uncles asked him about the Academy—but they had heard most of it already. It was a subject that always left him in Ivar's shadow. Robert was treated well by the Pendergast people while he was home from

Annapolis, and, interestingly, Ivar is never mentioned in this context. He did not have to be in Ivar's shadow with the boys downtown.[12]

This was the machine's period of greatest prestige in Kansas City, but all was not well for the Pendergast machine: over the summer, while Heinlein was away on his practice cruise, a newcomer, Johnny Lazia, forcibly took over Kansas City's Little Italy, on the promise that he would be able to keep Al Capone out.[13]

Many of Heinlein's high school friends were still in Kansas City, and his gold-braided white uniform would have given him cachet he never had before. One old high school acquaintance he particularly enjoyed renewing was with Alice McBee. There had been something—some spark or the something that might become a spark—between them in high school. Now he was a little more experienced, and they must, by later evidence, have dated while he was on leave. She was a pretty girl, with soft brown hair and blue eyes, a perfect figure, and a cheerful disposition he found perfectly simpatico. She had a sunny quality that made him feel good.[14] Perhaps now they had their first kiss—something to take back with him to the Academy and the start of the academic year in October.

After September leave, Heinlein had to buckle down to work. In the second year, the class took up naval history and the study of important naval engagements—the Russo-Japanese War and the first Korean war. They were also required to write one rather lengthy paper (like a master's thesis) during the four years and shorter papers on narrower subjects.

One of the more interesting and thought-provoking courses given at the Academy was the class in writing orders—the most useful English Department course Heinlein ever got. Each midshipman was given a tactical situation for which he had to write an operations order. Then everyone in the class would pick it apart, trying to find a way to misunderstand the order. This process was called "Major-Browning," after an officer in General Ulysses S. Grant's Civil War staff, whose sole duty was to misunderstand Grant's orders. If the order got by Major Brown, Grant okayed it for release. At Annapolis, the Major-Brown test was pass-fail: if anyone could colorably misunderstand the order, the midshipman got a zero mark for the day. This process, with its panic-making incentive, "gave me a life-time respect for exact meaning of words and clarity of construction of sentences."[15]

Heinlein had no particular trouble with his academics, consistently placing in the "Distinction" range (grade point averages of 3.4 to 4.0) or occasionally dipping into the high end of the "With Credit" range (3.39 to 3.0). His class standing was particularly high in engineering and aeronautics, ranging from first in the class to twelfth or thirteenth (with one notable lapse in early 1927 to a scandalous fifty-eighth place—just barely in the "Distinction" range). In English and modern languages—French in his case—he consistently placed in the top 10 percent, circling over and under the division between "Distinction" and "With Credit"—that is, a B+/A- student. His "Executive" grades ("aptitude for the Service") at the start of the 1927 academic year were consistently in the "With Credit" range. He was doing well on all fronts, though not in the absolute first rank in anything except engineering and aeronautics. Possibly this was a matter of policy on his part: the first-ranked scholars were viewed with suspicion because they so often washed out for one reason or another or did not necessarily make good naval officers.[16]

The Youngsters had far more privileges than they had enjoyed as Plebes. They were, for example, no longer required to march in the center of corridors, and they no longer went everywhere in strict formation. There were still classes, drills, and the usual extra duty, but the Youngsters were considered as broken to the saddle by now. Heinlein received five demerits in October (perhaps he was not quite broken to the saddle yet), and his class standing in "conduct" fell to 184 out of 316, but he received no more for the remainder of the academic year, and his report cards consistently show him as number one in his class thereafter.

They had a visit that year from Japanese midshipmen on their own practice cruise and a state visit by Queen Marie of Romania and her family, Princess Ileana and Prince Carol. It rained that day, and they paraded and double-timed in full dress in Worden Field and stood at parade in the rain, holding their fingers over the muzzles of their rifles so that they would not fill with rainwater. There was also a Hollywood movie filmed on campus that year—though its name was not recorded in any of the yearbooks—probably *Annapolis,* released in 1928, starring Johnny Mack Brown.

Heinlein was concentrating on his fencing and making a very good showing. His record for 1927 was 1-2 and 2-0 (up from 1-2 in 1926), and his published intercollegiate varsity records is only 5-6.[17] Nevertheless, his skill was noticed.

Apparently, the fencers were allowed considerable latitude in developing their own personal style, for Heinlein later remarked that he elected not to use the heavy protective clothing. This was something of a risk, because épée fencing, unlike foil, was as close to real sword work as one could get without courting serious damage. "Serious" was a relative term:

"Serious"—I once laid open the back of a Cornell man for 18' *avec points d'árrete*[18] and I still carry some lesser scars myself, because I preferred freedom of movement to heavy canvas. But the blood a little point can raise is certainly not serious.[19]

Sport and competition occupied more of their attention than usual that year, since the entire Academy was on a major winning streak coinciding with the unusually large Class of '27 (574 students) and the unusually small Class of '28 (173 students). When the entire First Class went to Philadelphia to see the Penn game, the Second Class could not fill out all the officer ratings for the Academy, so the Executive Department gave some of the Class of '29 temporary rank as midshipmen officers—their first time in full charge. Heinlein's name is not on the list of temporary midshipmen officers.

About 250 were expected to graduate in the Class of '29, so they were in the middle—but what they lacked in numbers they made up for in enthusiasm, proficiency, grit, and determination. They won the interclass competition and were given the Harvard Shield award for general athletic excellence.

But it was football that excited the most attention. The new football coach, Bill Ingram, had taken over a failing team (Navy had won only seven games in the preceding two years). As the annual Army-Navy game approached, Navy was undefeated, 9–0.

This Army-Navy game—held over the 1926 Thanksgiving weekend—was anticipated with special excitement because the game had been moved to Chicago and would take place in conjunction with the rededication of Soldier Field. The entire Brigade of Midshipmen was going.

It was very unusual for the Army-Navy game to be held so far from both academies, but Chicago had lobbied very hard for the privilege. At the Academy, they treated the trip as a mobilization exercise or war game.[20] As the day approached, yells of "Beat Army!" echoed nonstop in Bancroft Hall—otherwise a pap offense, but forgiven for the Cause. The upperclassmen would be required to carry swords, so they drilled constantly in the weeks before the trip.

After lunch on Thanksgiving Day, the entire Brigade of Midshipmen marched out the Main Gate and boarded chartered trains for Chicago. That evening on board the train they had the first of many Thanksgiving dinners—turkey with all the trimmings. When they arrived in Chicago the next day, they marched up Michigan Avenue in formation, in a snowstorm, to the Palmer House and then to Marshall Field's where they shared another turkey dinner—with all the trimmings—with the entire West Point Corps of Cadets. They marched back down Michigan Avenue (again in the snow) for a parade.

That evening, Chicago threw them a series of parties called in the program the "Army-Navy Frolics." There were dinners—more turkey with all the trimmings—theatrical parties, and dances that went on the entire night. Heinlein was a guest at the Drake Dinner Dance for cadets and midshipmen only. He had apparently been developing some moves: he talked one of the girls out of her dance card filled with autographs (his own not among them).[21]

The next day, the midshipmen and cadets were treated to a buffet luncheon at the Field Museum adjoining Soldier Field. Heinlein had tried unsuccessfully to get seating for some of the family and wrote suggesting they drop Lawrence's Army rank—"Lieutenant Heinlein"—to get into the reserved seating. "This is well worth trying. Rex is trying to get you tickets, but probably can't."[22] Indeed, Soldier Field was filled beyond its newly expanded capacity— 110,000 people in a stadium designed for 100,000.

It snowed again during the parade march to Soldier Field, and the temperature stuck at ten degrees Fahrenheit. The mids were exultant, their *esprit* at peak. Just before 2:30 P.M., they marched onto the field for the dedication ceremonies, in columns of companies. Many of them had lost their rubber overshoes in the slush, but they continued to march in place as the Corps of Cadets marched onto the field and took charge of the opposite side of the stadium.

The dedication ceremonies consisted of speeches—speech after speech. Vice President Dawes spoke for three minutes and sat down with the Army side. The governor of Illinois spoke for seven minutes. The temperature dropped below zero, and it began to sleet.

The mayor of Chicago spoke for ten minutes, and then the chairman of the South Park Board, in whose jurisdiction Soldier Field was, spoke for an hour and a half.

The midshipmen stood at parade rest throughout the ceremony. Several of them fainted and were propped up in place. They would not allow themselves to sit until the South Park Board chairman finished his oration.[23]

The Army-Navy game that year was "the greatest of its time and . . . a national spectacle," in the words of James Harrison, a sportswriter who had been reporting the event for *The New York Times* for three days.[24] Going into the game, Army was favored 6 to 5, but at the halftime, Navy led 14–0.

The halftime show was a mock battle between a tank and a twenty-foot dreadnaught (models built much like parade floats). Navy won that, too, driving the "mutilated tank" off the field. The Army representatives solemnly escorted Vice President Dawes to the center of the field, and the Navy representatives just as solemnly escorted the vice president to the Navy side of the field, where he remained for the rest of the game.

In the second half, Army rallied to tie 21–21, but the judges named Navy the national champion.[25]

The midshipmen were jubilant, but also determined to display their superior discipline: at dusk Assembly sounded, and the midshipmen formed up into companies and silently marched away.

Christmas leave was less than a month away.

Heinlein did not go home that year; nor, apparently, did he leave Annapolis. He may have stayed over in Bancroft Hall, though he might equally have spent the holiday with some of the Annapolis civilian locals. But Heinlein, like so many people raised in poverty, never came to enjoy Christmas. This year, he had the minor dilemma of two girlfriends who would each expect time and attention—and, of course, the expense of two Christmas presents. He resolved his dilemma by writing each an intimate letter, then switching the envelopes, so that each girl got the letter intended for the other—and that was the end of his dilemma.[26] There was always another potential drag around the corner—particularly when the rest of the class was away, home, and he was so available.

Alice McBee sent him a portrait with one of her calling cards: "With lots of love and wishing you were here this Christmas time." They had, apparently, progressed to a relationship of some sort, though no letters or comments bearing on the subject survive.

Some of his time that holiday season was spent "babysitting" Buddy Scoles, at Ivar's request, keeping him out of trouble[27] (though Robert liked Scoles and would have helped out in any case). Scoles was a brilliant scholar and would have stood number one in his class if demerits were not factored into his class standing. But he had somehow managed to accumulate 149 demerits for the academic year, which was just three months old. He had six months to go before graduation, but the cutoff point was 150 demerits. If he accumulated even one more demerit, he would be expelled from the Academy and could not graduate.

Demerits were inevitable and unavoidable, and everybody accumulated them by ones and twos for technical infractions of the academy rules: dust found on the top of a door at inspection; the bed found unmade, even minutes after reveille—that sort of thing. For more serious offenses, demerits were handed out in much larger chunks. "Frenching out"—academy slang for going AWOL (from the Revolutionary War slang of "French leave" for deserting under fire)—would earn thirty demerits. Being caught with a forbidden radio would earn about the same. Dereliction of duty might merit a hundred or more. Being caught drunk on the Academy grounds might get you more than demerits; you might be expelled. Whatever Scoles had done to earn 149 demerits has not been recorded.

It was next to impossible to get *no* demerits for six months.

But Scoles was very popular with his classmates—and he was also one of the aviators, which made him a member of an elite within the elite of the midshipmen. The Class of '27 decided jointly they would protect him.

This, too, was a technical infraction of the Academy's honor system, but it was done—one of those matters sanctioned by custom. The midshipmen often found it expedient (or sometimes necessary) to get married, and it was customary for their classmates to turn their collective heads about that sort of thing. In this case, their intervention had to be a bit more active. Scoles pledged to be on his best behavior, and the others positioned themselves so they could take on themselves any demerits that came his way.

Ivar's relationship with Scoles was a stroke of good fortune for Robert. They were compatible personalities, Heinlein's steadiness complementing Scoles's more outgoing nature. Possibly it was Scoles who jollied Heinlein into the Gymkhana skits and acting with the Maskeraders. They both shared the unusual passion for rocketry and spaceflight, and Heinlein wanted to strike for the aviation squad. He had been mad for the romance of flying as long as he could remember:[28] he yearned to be a pilot—and probably had since he first read H. G. Wells's *When the Sleeper Wakes* a few years earlier.

He was able to help babysit Scoles without taking any demerits himself, though he was probably spending a little too much time talking aviation and aeronautical engineering with someone who was on the inside of it, long before the course work would bring him into anything more than fleeting contact with naval aviation. In his pocket notebook, he exhorted himself: "I. Keep fit for Aviation" and worried about increasing his Stoop Falls.

In January 1927, Captain William F. Halsey was assigned to the Academy to take charge of the Academy's flight squadron and turn it into a permanent aviation detail, flying and servicing seaplanes on the Severn River. His headquarters for the aviation squad were to be in the Academy's brig, the captured Spanish-American War ship *Reina Mercedes*. Halsey would be at the Academy for less than three years, but this assignment changed his career and also changed history, for he went on to become Fleet Admiral "Bull" Halsey in charge of the Third Fleet (Pacific) during World War II as a result of his role in developing naval aviation.

Halsey's stint at the Academy could only have made naval aviation more desirable to Heinlein. Halsey was a crusty old salt who said he didn't trust a man who didn't smoke and drink.

"Admiral Halsey's strongest point," wrote a staff officer, "was his superb leadership. While always the true professional and exacting professional performance from all subordinates, he had a charismatic effect on them which was like being touched by a magic wand. Anyone so touched was determined to excel."[29]

This was exactly what resonated with Heinlein and what he wanted for himself: a demanding, exciting specialization and a truly superior officer to work with.[30] There was another factor he probably wasn't yet fully aware of: Heinlein had begun to collect special friendships with older, seasoned, professional men—a kind of hero worship within the bounds of friendship that would go with him for the rest of his life.

He had already built some similar relationships—in his childhood with J. U. Young, an older man (probably in his twenties at the time) in Kansas City, with Hap Gay at the Civilian Military Training Camp, and with his swordmaster, M. Deladrier—and if things had gone the way he wanted, he might have had the same kind of relationship with Captain Halsey.

When he came to take the qualifying examinations for the flight squad, his reflexes were fast enough, but the test involved a long gadget operated by strings, which he had to bring together in the middle of a lot of disorienting noise and distractions, and he couldn't get them together. His stereoscopic vision just wasn't good enough. He took the test over again, whenever they would allow him to, but he always failed on depth perception and, as time went on, visual acuity.[31]

This was more than frustrating for Heinlein: he had been able to approach the physical problems of being underweight when he matriculated, and of being deficient in swimming, with the attitude that hard work would overcome those defects—and in any case, neither deficiency was important to his self-image. But flying *was* important to him. And you cannot work hard to overcome a defect in depth perception.

Flying would remain an unfulfilled longing for the rest of his life. It forced him to confront his own limitations in a way that is generally foreign to nineteen-year-olds.

There are two ways you can take such a confrontation: you can shrug it off and go on, trying to think about it as little as possible. After a while you have it covered over with emotional scar tissue, and you can pretend it never happened, it wasn't important in the first place. Or you can acknowledge the pain and make the experience part of your character. Heinlein chose the second way:

> I compensated somewhat by putting in most of my service in the nonflying end of aviation. But every pilot remains to me the symbol of what I wanted to be and never could be.[32]

The Navy gained an aeronautical engineer at a time when aviation engineering was in its infancy—and science fiction eventually gained a number of highly evocative stories based on that unfulfilled longing.

As early as 1926 and 1927, visual acuity was becoming a concern for Heinlein, as well. The most arbitrary hurdle the midshipmen had to jump was the Navy's requirement for uncorrected 20/20 vision in the entire officer corps. Eye examinations became a regular part of the school year. Robert was still passing those exams, thanks to the Bates exercises he had done in 1924 and 1925, though Ivar must have been having trouble already. It was becoming unlikely that he would be commissioned after graduation because of his eyesight.[33]

Heinlein's immediate problem, though, was to get through the school year. His graduating yearbook shows him participating in the 1927 Gymkhana in April. No role is recorded for him, but he is included in the Gymkhana portrait of the fencing team, with a fake moustache that makes him look, as he wrote in another context, "made up for amateur theatricals."[34] The fencing page in the 1927 *Lucky Bag* lists him as a "promising substitute" on the épée team. He always taped a small ivory elephant to his wrist when he competed. "No, I don't believe in sympathetic magic but it doesn't hurt to be Kosher about such things."[35]

The class began the first steps in putting together its own yearbook, traditionally called *Lucky Bag*—the locker on board a ship for storing any miscellaneous stray property found on deck. Heinlein worked as art editor that year,[36] though he did not stay with it long enough to be included in the final staff listing.

And the rough edges continued to be polished. Heinlein learned to dance the customary dances—fox-trot and waltz and box step and a few others—and to conduct himself as a gentleman. Everybody got this kind of quick-and-dirty social polish, because the midshipmen came from all manner of social and economic backgrounds, but they must all come out of the process as Officers and Gentlemen, by decree of the United States Congress.

Certainly he was also working hard at his academics, consistently ranking in the top 8 to 10 percent of his class in every subject except modern languages (still French), though his grade point average, ranging from 3.46 to 3.58, kept him comfortably in the "Distinction" category of an A student. He had a little trouble with "Juice" that spring—electrical engineering and physics. He swotted and by the end of the academic year pulled his class standing up to fifth in the class, comfortably in the "Distinction" range of grade point average.

The academic year ended in May, and June Week came on and Ivar's graduation—a gargantuan affair. Even with a high nongraduation rate as Midshipmen went into business or married or otherwise disqualified themselves, the Class of '27 was, at 574, the largest class in the Academy's history.

The Kansas City Star was able to list both Rex Ivar Heinlein and Buddy Scoles among six Kansas City graduates that year. Scoles had been on his best behavior for six excruciating months, and the heroic efforts of the entire class paid off: on graduation day, his pap sheet stood at 149—he had (*they* had) performed the minor miracle of accumulating *no* further demerits.

The traditional Farewell Ball held in Dahlgren Hall drew fifteen thousand, including Rex Ivar and Bam, who traveled to Annapolis to see their favorite graduate, even though it was definite by now that Ivar would not be commissioned, despite a "brilliant" performance,[37] because of his eyesight.

Rex Ivar and Bam had some reason to cheer Robert, too: the Secretary of the Navy presented the athletic awards at the graduation, and Robert received the 1927 Epée Medal for dueling sword championship—which made him, *ipso facto,* a champion fencer.

Under ordinary circumstances, Heinlein would have stayed in the Yard for the summer of 1927. Normally, a class will have two summer practice cruises, one at the end of the Plebe year (Fourth Class) and another at the end of the Second Class year. The summer between the cruises the class stayed on the Yard and took the incoming Plebe class in hand.[38] Heinlein was spared taking part in the routine hazing of Plebe Summer: in 1927, for reasons not recorded, there was an extra practice cruise. That year he would be going through the Panama Canal and to the West Coast.[39] The midshipmen's Practice Squadron consisted of two ships that year, USS *Oklahoma* and USS *Nevada.* He packed up his cruise box and boarded the *Okie* the day after graduation.

Ivar went back to Kansas City.

SECOND CLASS YEAR

The USS *Oklahoma* (BB-37) was fifteen years old and had already converted to oil from coal (for which Heinlein and all the midshipmen must have been profoundly grateful). *Okie* was due for further modernization in the fall and would be out of commission for practice cruises until the summer of 1929, so this cruise to the West Coast was her last voyage before refitting. She was larger than the *Utah* and had a ship's complement of 864. What with attrition in the class, things were a lot less crowded this year. She had a larger battery, too—ten 14-inch guns and twenty 5-inch guns—but only four 21-inch torpedo tubes, compared to *Utah*'s twenty-one.

Okie's top speed was 20.5 knots, so she "lackadaisically lumbered," as the class history has it,[1] from the Severn to Colón in Panama, skirting Guantánamo Bay and dropping south to the Canal Zone in eight days. In addition to the teaching drill, which was essentially the same as last year's (crowding into compartments and hearing the Chief lecture for the departments), there was a new twist this year: this was their "engineering" cruise, and the really important part of the tuition this year was their sketchbooks. They clambered throughout the ship, tracing each of the ship's systems from stem to stern, and then produced sketches of every element from hatch covers to the most complicated reducing valves. Their sketchbooks were then graded by the officers. Some of the engineering systems they had already encountered, but this year they had the fuel oil systems to deal with, which *Utah* had not been able to offer them.

This was a form of teaching that would follow them long after they left Annapolis, since they would be expected to memorize the entire engineering apparatus of each ship they were stationed on, by the same procedure of tracing engineering systems and diagramming them in sketchbooks.

The midshipmen were actually allowed and required to stand watches this year, in the overheated engine rooms, "gather[ing] many crum[b]s of black gang lore."[2] So they felt less like supercargo and more like something that might someday become a naval officer. "The Old Okie [is] . . . a person to me. I've sketched her fuel lines down in her bilges. I was turret captain of her number two turret. I have been in her main battery fire control party when her big guns were talking."[3]

Colón, at the foot of the San Blas range of mountains, was the Atlantic terminus (as Panama City is the Pacific terminus) of the fifty-mile-long Panama Canal, a series of engineered canals connecting natural lakes and drowned valleys that had been completed only in 1914 and was known informally shipboard as the "Big Ditch."

After a few days in Colón, *Okie* headed into the Canal and the midshipmen had a chance to marvel at the gigantic and intricate engineering work of the locks. It was a passage Heinlein was to make many times later, but it never lost its fascination for him. He got badly sunburned leaning on the rail watching the waters boil up under the ship in the deep concrete box of the Gatun Lock. He was burning—bad enough to leave permanent scars—but could not tear himself away from the stupendous sight.[4]

Three days in the canal, and twelve days after leaving Colón, they anchored at San Diego, a major naval installation, for a week. There they were greeted by tremendous crowds of people—some sightseers, to be sure, but mostly vendors local and from as far away as Tijuana.

After four days in port, they went north and east up the Pacific Coast, retracing the route of the Spanish explorers in the sixteenth and seventeenth centuries, and just about as slow as the old sailing ships: they averaged about ten knots. After three days—on July 3, 1927—they rumbled through the still open Golden Gate (this was nearly ten years before the Golden Gate Bridge was built) and anchored in the Port of San Francisco for nine days. Heinlein was footloose and on his own in San Francisco for his twentieth birthday.

The midshipmen had traditional side trips to the naval station on Mare Island, and to Mount Tamalpais. But Heinlein found his own diversions, too. The cable cars were free for the midshipmen, and San Francisco was notoriously inventive in entertaining sailors with dissipations, then more than now. The Barbary Coast still lived, a little faded and a little tattered, bordered by the Chinatown which had only recently acquired the look that has since become world famous: when the earthquake and fire of 1906 leveled Chinatown, it happened that the Chinoiserie architectural style was in vogue, so that's how it was rebuilt, in haste and almost all in wood, before the city fathers could ordinance it out of existence to seize the land for their own uses.

The rapid rebuilding of Chinatown was not a unique occasion; San Francisco had recovered from the earthquake and fire of 1906 with extraordinary energy, hosting a world's fair, the Panama Pacific International Exhibition, in 1915. The Fair had revitalized the city's flagging economy, but it had also put San Francisco's local politics in the national and international eye. The Barbary Coast was infamous throughout the world, so the city council had been cracking down on the area since 1919. Heinlein caught the tail end of some of the sights Mark Twain had seen when he was a newspaper reporter in San Francisco more than fifty years earlier.

The wharf area on the bay side of the city had enough dissipations for seamen ashore, and if he had not yet sampled drink and marijuana (he clearly implies in a late essay[5] that he was familiar with the local connections in Kansas City in 1924), now was the time.[6] Somehow he got into a fistfight—the last time that was to happen in his life—and broke his opponent's nose.[7]

Oklahoma weighed anchor on July 12 and headed back down the West Coast, with more braising engine-room heat and engineering diagrams and gun practice shaking the ship for days on end. She made harbor at San Pedro on July 14 for four days before heading farther south, back to Panama City for a two-week layover before crossing to the Atlantic side and making for Guantánamo Bay and three weeks of target practice. The mids could be blasé about the Canal this time, on their second trip through.

Heinlein's girl back home, Alice McBee, was in a serious automobile accident about this time. This was a stroke of upsetting news for him: he was probably already planning to ask her to marry him when he got back home on leave the next month.[8]

On the day *Oklahoma* cast off to go back through the Canal, Heinlein was caught absent without leave—"Frenching Out," as it is recorded in the discipline section of his permanent record dossier (called his "jacket" at the Academy)—and given seventy-five demerits. This was unprecedented for him—but the circumstances were unprecedented, too.

Very late in the evening, just before their liberty was to expire at midnight, he had boarded a shuttle boat back to *Oklahoma*, filled, as it happened, with First Classmen. For one reason or another, the boat did not get to *Oklahoma* until just after midnight. Liberty had expired, and everybody would be put on report.

But the Midshipman Officer of the Deck was First Classman Joseph

Finnegan, and in the Academy ethos, loyalty to one's class comes before even proper military discipline. The First Classmen knew they would get off, and they did: Heinlein was the one passenger on the boat not a First Classman— and the only passenger on that boat who was placed on report for Frenching Out.

Frenching Out was regarded as a Class A offense, comparable to drinking or gambling, for which the penalty was a certain number of demerits plus being confined to the Academy's brig ship, the *Reina Mercedes,* for a period up to sixty days. In this case, Heinlein was also penalized two weeks of his September leave, from August 26 to September 10 that year. That left only thirteen days of September leave. The *Oklahoma*'s dittoed "Radio Press" dated August 25, 1927, published Navy Department's Orders to Midshipmen, ordering Heinlein to "two weeks (extra) duty, U.S. Naval Academy." Although the jacket does not say so specifically, he must have been in the brig for at least one week this time. He would also have a public record of dishonor in his jacket, the Black N.

The Black N mirrors the Academy's Gold N (for "Navy"), given for conspicuous public honor—usually athletic achievement. Heinlein was to receive a Gold N of his own, yellow felt on a larger black felt diamond, later in the year. The Black N itself represented a week of confinement in the *Reina Mercedes.* For second (and subsequent) confinements, the Academy's yearbook record would show asterisks.[9]

The gross injustice of the Frenching Out incident was offensive— particularly that the older were picking on the younger. This was a grave injustice to him, and one he never forgot.[10]

Somehow he got through the next three weeks—a three-day passage back through the locks and lakes of the Panama Canal. Three days to Guantánamo Bay, followed by two weeks of target practice, then what must have been an excruciatingly leisurely passage of five days back up the Atlantic Coast, to anchor at the Academy on August 25. Early that morning, the midshipmen were released. Heinlein, however, was met by a discipline detail and marched directly into hack at the *Reina Mercedes.* It must have felt like every eye was on him as he was branded with shame.

The *Reina Mercedes* was a place of temporary detention for midshipmen, rather than a true brig. A wooden sailing vessel, she had been captured in the Spanish-American War in 1898 and then, declared unfit for modern warfare, anchored at Annapolis to accommodate the Academy's problem children and all the school's floating gear except racing shells.[11] It was the Brig, but it was not durance vile: the midshipmen under hack would spend nights and weekends there, foregoing any special privileges that might be given the rest of the Corps of midshipmen and sleeping in hammocks that had to be lashed and stowed away every morning. Heinlein was used to stowing his sleeping gear in a closet each day.

They ate the common seamen's mess and were formed up and marched to and from classes during the academic year, or to the extra duty they would be liberally assigned. They were allowed no visitors other than parents (not a possibility in Heinlein's case, anyway), and they were not allowed to participate in sports and other extracurricular activities. This last was not particularly onerous for Heinlein, as his school year had not yet started.

And there was layer after layer, Pelion upon Ossa, of bitterness in this particular confinement for Heinlein: the *Reina* was under the command of Captain Halsey, and much of his extra-duty punishment must have involved scut work for the flight squadron—cleaning up after the service-and-repair operations and hauling the light, canvas-winged planes back into proper orientation for takeoffs on the Severn. Having washed out of piloting, he was condemned to scullery work for the ground crew of his flight squadron. And the eyes of the man who might have become a mentor—if he noticed Heinlein at all—saw only a bilger in midshipman blues.

Flouting Academy discipline was a routine pastime of the more rebellious-minded midshipmen, a kind of exercise in how much you could get away with—or not get away with, as the case might be. It was a way of counting coup on the establishment that oppressed, "getting back" some of your own—showing your classmates that you were not broken in spirit. In a later, more liberal time, disciplined midshipmen would wear their Black Ns as bad-boy badges, like scarlet letters on T-shirts and sweatshirts.

This punishment was particularly arbitrary, and Heinlein made a vow with himself to "go over the wall" (French Out) of the Academy grounds, usually after lights-out, once for each day he was in hack. It suited his sense of justice.[12]

On September 10, he was released from the *Reina* and had a few days on the campus, deserted except for the Plebes boning their ac. As a Second Classman he was expected to participate in the routine hazing of the Plebes. He did, and he may have visited some of Marsh Gurney's aberrant practices on Plebes and Youngsters alike—the only time anything like this would happen.[13] Some of them exacted revenge the next year when his cousin Oscar Allen Heinlein, Jr., came to Annapolis as a Plebe: "I well remember in 1928 Youngsters and Second classmen that you had been rough on, would come over from the 4th to the 2nd Batt. just to beat my rear."[14] (On the other hand, another Plebe that same year remembered Heinlein and the entire Class of 1929 as protecting them somewhat from the unusually sadistic Class of 1930—the Second Classmen Oscar referenced).[15]

Heinlein seems to have disgusted himself:

> I hated the hazing that went on at the Naval Academy and never indulged in it as an upperclassman. My only real political ambition for office was someday to be Undersecretary of the Navy and thereby to have the N.A. under my thumb so that I could stamp it out.[16]

Under the circumstances, this was the best use that could be made of a bad experience. This time in his life undoubtedly fed the insight, written out decades later, of one of his protagonists, who realizes what it means to be human when he sees a monkey beaten by a bigger one that takes out his frustration on the smaller and weaker.[17]

Knowing you are brilliant does not entirely compensate for knowing you are odd, and Heinlein knew he was inescapably not like the "normal" boys around him. And his self-esteem had been taking a beating recently. This early, this young, he had only rudimentary tools to deal with his pain. He could only experience it as rage. He managed to get through his confinement to the Academy without raising official notice. And he made time for a lightning trip home.

Heinlein's record of land trips from this period shows the travel of September 1927 as "Annapolis–St. Louis–Kansas City–Carrollton, Missouri–Kansas City–St. Louis–Annapolis."[18] He could not have left before September 10, and he had to report back at 10 A.M. on September 23. Three days each way by train to and from Annapolis left only a few days for family and that side trip to Carrollton, fifty-eight miles east-northeast of Kansas City, where Alice McBee was probably recuperating. His high school pal, Sammy Roberts, had a car, so it is possible that they made the trip together.

In the Second Class academic year, the preparatory subjects were now out of the way, and the midshipmen were expected to find an area of specialization and work toward it. They boned "professional theory and practice," adding intensive courses in electricity, engineering, and navigation, while the Academy arranged for special activities in the major specializations. Early the next year, for example, a submarine came to the Academy for an exposure trip up the Chesapeake Bay, and the midshipmen got a crash course in submarine operations, including a lecture on salvage by Captain Donald R. Osborn. At the midterm their mathematics requirement—"the ogre of artistic minds," according to the class history[19]—ended, and the midshipmen celebrated with appropriate burial ceremony. Ordnance and seamanship replaced mathematics in their academic schedules. They would also be introduced to the difficult subjects of military organization and theory of discipline in the Navy. Mastering these subjects was essential for advancement in their final year at the Academy.

Heinlein had seemed destined for the extra stripes of honor rank, but he had a hard time getting back into the grind. Any slippage in academics was minor, though on his October 1927 report card class standing dropped to 145 out of 251. This is remarkable, as it means that, even with the Class A offense for Frenching Out on his record, about half the class had more demerits than he. Possibly this reflects his hard work avoiding demerits in prior years. His Executive marks remained high: 3.69 and fortieth in class.

He continued with sword work, competing with distinction in the Intercollegiate Fencing Championships in New York City—the occasion of a Navy Gold N for athletic excellence. So he had a matching set for his collection. On one occasion, his swordmaster, *Capitaine* Deladrier, arranged a match with a Heidelberg épée fencer. He had the aristocratic manner affected by the Heidelberg *Studentenkorps,* which Robert had expected from Mark Twain's *A Tramp Abroad* (1880), and a face so marked with schläger dueling scars Heinlein later said he looked like a checkerboard. But his swordsmanship backed up his affectations: "He utterly outclassed me."[20]

Heinlein accumulated three more demerits during the month of October, but that was inconsequential. More serious was a series of small medical problems. His wrist hurt sometimes, and his vision was beginning to blur—an alarming development in view of Ivar's eyesight problems. Robert began to be in and out of sick bay, trying to keep in shape. His October report card shows incompletes in engineering and electrical classes. But he was still maintaining. When the entire First Class left the campus at the end of October to attend the Navy-Pennsylvania game in Philadelphia, an Executive Department Regimental Order dated 28 October 1927 named Heinlein CPO (Chief Petty Officer) of the regiment.[21]

They normally had only enough officers for drill, and the unusually small size of the Class of 1928 gave the Class of 1929 some special opportunities to assume regimental offices temporarily—circumstances unusual enough to be remarked upon in the official class history in the 1929 *Lucky Bag.* This is the first occasion on which the honor of regimental office is recorded for Heinlein.

November brought two more demerits (eighty for the year), but his class standing rose to 129. Navy lost the Army-Navy football game over

Thanksgiving weekend in New York—the last Army-Navy game until President Hoover reinstated it in 1930.

In December there were five more demerits. Heinlein was inching toward serious attitude problems: his Executive marks in the end-of-term report cards were in the ignominious "Fair and Passing" range (in other words, a C) and ranked him 225 out of 266.

That Christmas—set by Special Order 102-27 to start after midday meal formation on Friday, December 23 and to end at evening roll call on January 2, 1928—he could again not get back to Kansas City. He was in Annapolis part of the time and then went to Washington, D.C., for the last ten days of his leave, as a guest of Dr. Philip B. Matz (not otherwise identified). The City Club of Washington, D.C., extended membership privileges to Heinlein as a visiting midshipman.[22] Perhaps Dr. Matz was his sponsor on this occasion—a common enough practice.

Over the holidays, Robert received a letter from his brother Ivar, important enough for him to keep in his scrapbook. Back in Kansas City, Ivar had surveyed his options and taken an appointment in the Army—in Robert's old unit, in fact. The Army did not require 20/20 vision of its line officers. He became second lieutenant for the 110th Engineers, where Larry was first lieutenant of the headquarters.

Ivar looked back on his experience at the Naval Academy. "Treasure this unique opportunity," he advised Robert: "You are enjoying now probably the best time that you'll ever love in your life, so make every moment full of pleasure."[23]

It was good advice—and possibly just what Heinlein needed to turn himself around. There were no more demerits in January or February 1928.

In January 1928 he had a telegram from home: Alice McBee had died suddenly, of appendicitis.[24]

> I think this was the only time in my life that I ever felt suicidal. Alice was a lovely girl, just turned twenty-one, blue eyes, brown hair, beautiful face, perfect figure—and with a merry, happy disposition to match. We were simpatico in every way, and all my hopes and plans were tied up in her. With Alice gone, all that remained seemed pointless. "Despair" is the word and I shan't elaborate. . . . Oh, I remember every detail of the bad times; the shock when I got the telegram, the painful interview with the Commandant when I tried to get leave and was refused (I was crying and midshipmen aren't supposed to do that, certainly not where it can be seen). I remember the grim, zombie days that followed, the utter despair.[25]

Another disaster followed. He had been experiencing eyestrain for weeks. Whatever benefit he had gained from the Bates exercises the winter before coming to the Naval Academy was gone. In mid-January 1928 his vision was found to be 20/70 in the right eye and 20/50 in the left eye, with occasional flashes of 20/20 without correction. On January 18, 1928, he was admitted to the U.S. Naval Academy Hospital, where the myopia was diagnosed hopefully as "ciliary spasm." He was sent to consult a specialist in Washington, D.C., on January 21, and again on February 3. Dr. Carl Henning recommended to the Academy's Chief Medical Officer, Edward H. H. Old, a course of treatment with atropine, 1 percent solution three times a day, to relax the eye muscles, probably for a week to ten days (though it might take six to eight weeks).

He was released from the hospital on February 13, after less than a month, so the treatment was more rapidly successful than originally anticipated. But he had taken incompletes in all academic subjects, to be made up later. A psychologist might note that his eyes had disgraced him not too long before, weeping in front of the Commandant of the Academy.

He was able to return to school, where the pace of life was picking up for the Class of 1929, after the Dark Days of late winter—baseball, lacrosse, crew, the Masqueraders, and weekend dances. That spring was the last Gymkhana at the Academy—that "quaint combination of tournament and Mardi Gras" went out "[i]n a gorgeous pageantry of music, dramatics, and acrobatics."[26] Heinlein did not participate in the skits or other entertainment, but he did participate in the fencing exhibition; the fencing team had a bout with the Princeton team the night of the Gymkhana, winning 11–6.[27]

But something was happening to his wrist, and he was losing speed and flexibility. By the end of the season, he had to withdraw from the épée team. "The loss of Heinlien [sic] was regrettable," The Lucky Bag noted that year. He certainly regretted it. This may also account for some of the additional demerits he accumulated in March and April, bringing his total for the year up to ninety-three. He retired the tiny ivory elephant charm he had always taped to the inside of his wrist for matches, though he always kept it with him.[28]

Heinlein's series of hard knocks that year must have turned him a little in on himself; he no longer threw himself into the activities of his class, except for the Ring Committee he had joined as a Youngster.[29] Although mathematics was no longer required, he continued his personal studies. He discovered C. H. Hinton's A New Era of Thought (1888) in 1928, with its fascinating method of using n-dimensional geometry to introduce esoteric philosophy. He was ready to start a more systematic search for this kind of thing and talked over finds like this with some other midshipmen who shared such interests. Caleb Barrett Laning, another Kansas City boy, was one of them. Allan "Gus" Gray was another.[30]

By the end of the year, Heinlein had regained some of his lost ground. His end-of-term report card grades in May 1928 showed him well within the top 5 or 10 percent of his class in every subject, though his Executive aptitude was graded at 193 out of 251 in the class. His grades in ordnance and gunnery were particularly good—he had decided to specialize in these mathematics-using disciplines and would be working ordnance on the up-coming summer practice cruise.

On June 5, immediately after the June Week graduation exercises, he qualified as Expert Rifleman. The USS *Arkansas* docked at the Academy to take on midshipmen for the summer practice cruise. This year he would have something real to do, something substantial: in his First Class cruise he would be a working fire-control man for a joint Army-Navy exercise.

FIRST CLASSMAN

The USS *Arkansas* (BB-33) was a Wyoming-class battleship, sixteen years old, but she had been modernized and converted to burn oil in 1925. She was about the same size as the *Oklahoma,* but less crowded. Heinlein was in fire control this trip—a real, working seaman—so he was especially interested in her armament: twelve 12-inch guns, twenty-one 5-inch guns, and two 21-inch torpedo tubes.

Her itinerary for this practice cruise is given in the *Navy Register*:

Annapolis from 6/8 (Joint Army and Navy exercise June 13–14) to Newport RI (6/14–21), New York (6/30–7/6), Boston (7/18–24), Portland ME (7/26–8/2), Guantanamo Bay (8/8–23), returning to Annapolis on August 28.

The joint Army-Navy exercises in North Atlantic waters were a good shakedown for the midshipmen who were getting used to a higher level of responsibility as mates of the deck, squad leaders, and midshipmen aides to the ship's Executive Officers.

They had learned enough of the mechanics of the ships to be seamen, but the seasoned officers made it clear to them that their grasp of the "philosophy of command" was nonexistent. In addition to the usual bull-session topics of girls, complaints about the Academy, girls, grease, girls, the current state of their velvet, girls, food, and, for a change, their current and prospective drags, debate on policy became momentarily urgent, and the First Classmen hammered out a coherent command philosophy. They introduced some minor innovations for mail delivery and established courts of justice that earned the class a commendation.[1]

After week in Newport and almost a week in New York, *Arkansas* was at sea, on her way to Boston, on Heinlein's twenty-first birthday. Kansas City was in the news that summer: in June the Republican National Convention was held in the Kansas City Convention Hall, nominating Herbert Hoover for President and Charles Curtis, a Kansas native, for Vice President.

Over the last few years Heinlein had developed something of a love-hate relationship with his rustic origins and had begun to distance himself from his life before the Navy.[2] He had already started using "Bob" instead of "Bobby," and possibly this was due as much to his separation from all that as to the simple transition he was making from boy to man.

That summer, he was in a foul temper. He was, in fact, moping, resentful, and in a sink of self-pity. Perhaps it was on this occasion that he got an object lesson in the continuing importance of formal courtesy. On one occasion visiting *en famille,* he called his hostess by her first name, forgetting that he had not dotted the proper i's by first getting her husband's approval of this familiarity. "I was always a sucker for a right hook; he led with his left and one-twoed me."[3] The experience was valuable—but it cost him an upper left molar. It was undoubtedly a relief to get back to Boston and the Practice Squadron for the jog up to Portland, Maine.

On August 2, exactly one year after getting caught Frenching Out, and coincidentally the day *Arkansas* pulled out of Portland to make for Guantánamo Bay, Heinlein was awarded thirty demerits for "shirking," Academy slang for malingering.

Although it is hard to find time and opportunity to slack off on a practice cruise, it can be accomplished by a combination of cleverness, steady nerves, boldness, good prior planning, and smooth execution of the opportunity when it rises. Heinlein didn't make the effort. Accompanying the demerits was another week in the *Reina Mercedes,* though his Academy jacket does not note time lost from his September leave this year. There was no possibility of blaming anyone but himself this time.

Anniversaries of traumas can often be traumatic themselves.

At Guantánamo Bay, the Practice Squadron's main task was, as in previous years, to prepare and conduct target practice. This year Heinlein was Assistant Fire Control Officer and got to direct the battery in practice, experiencing that gut-shaking, bone-shaking, satisfyingly soul-shaking firing of the battery from the fire-control station itself.

The Practice Squadron got back to Annapolis on August 28, and Heinlein took off on his September leave immediately—stopping only at the Annapolis magazine shop, probably to get something to read on the train. The current issue of *Amazing Stories* had a serial novel by a couple of authors whose names he didn't recognize, Smith and Hawkins. He found himself shelling out a quarter from his carefully hoarded pocket change—but it was a good investment: *The Skylark of Space* started a lifelong admiration for E. E. "Doc" Smith.[4]

He had a complicated itinerary planned for this year's September leave. He reached Kansas City by way of St. Louis, then went on to Denver (possibly to visit another mid), back to Kansas City, and on to New York by way of Chicago. Since Heinlein in later life always made an opportunity to meet up with his old grade-school friend and lust object Sally Rand when they were in the same city, perhaps they met in Chicago.[5] She had just moved there from Los Angeles, where she had been working for several years in vaudeville. Sally Rand got her first break when Eddie Cantor did a turn at the Orpheum Theatre in Los Angeles. She was featured walking across the stage to embellish Cantor's rendition of the new Ager-Yellen hit "Ain't She Sweet." She had even begun to do some film work, but sound film—"the talkies"—was coming in, and she had a pronounced lisp. Sally Rand was one of the many casualties of the talkies.

Back at Annapolis,[6] Heinlein settled into the academic year, again rooming with Perreault. They had gotten on well together for the past three years and saw no particular reason to change the arrangement now. Perreault was made 1PO (Petty Officer, First Class) for his company, and Heinlein was given a permanent rating of Midshipman 2PO (Petty Officer, Second Class) on September 28, 1928. The 1PO carried the platoon's flag within the regiment,[7] and the duty of the 2PO was to muster everybody in the platoon. In addition, Heinlein was asked to teach rifle and pistol to the lower classmen.

This last year at Annapolis, he had made one new friend in Barrett Laning (Caleb Barrett Laning, but he went by his middle name at the Academy), another Kansas City boy, though they seem never to have met there, since Barrett went to Westport High and spent his free time immersing himself in jazz music, "hanging out in the balcony of nigro [*sic*] highschool gyms . . . when the local black gangs, like Benny Moten, played" and once sitting in for Coon-Sanders for five minutes, before Sanders's men threw him out.[8]

But they connected at the Academy when they found out they had a mutual interest in Mark Twain and in what one of Heinlein's high school teachers-cum-mentors called "foolosphy."[9] Laning was interested in anything mystical and out-of-the-way—and so was Heinlein. It was the basis for a lifelong friendship.

The last year at the Academy was in many ways the most crucial. Heinlein buckled down and "boned grease,"[10] bringing both academics and the administration's opinion of his Executive (aptitude for the service) up to the

"Distinction" range. And no more demerits of any kind.[11] His report cards show that he started out the year ranked 71st in Executive—within the top third of his class—and his previous good record had earned him a gold eagle for the sleeve of his jackets, in addition to the usual First Classman's gold band surmounted by a star. By December, his class standing in Executive was 45th—in the top 20 percent of his class.

In addition to the regular course work in naval subjects, the First Classmen did practicums in various specialties, and the Navy provided some rather unusual briefings. One day Heinlein was summoned to a closed-meeting brief and found a senior official of the State Department talking about the geopolitical relations of Japan and the United States. The death of the old emperor the preceding January and accession of the young emperor, Hirohito, had Japan in the news at that time. Heinlein was particularly interested in this subject because his grandfather Lyle had told him before World War I that the United States would have to go to war with Japan one day.[12] No such war was on the horizon—in fact, the last several classes had reconciled themselves to peacetime Navy careers, and the Class of 1929 had even chosen "The Navy in Peacetime" as the theme for its production of *The Lucky Bag* graduating yearbook. But this official was telling them straight out that the war with Japan was inevitable—one day—because of geography and economic factors (and possibly sooner rather than later because the young emperor's advisers were known to be markedly militarist).

Heinlein was also expected to take charge of some Plebes and shape them up by the usual hazing (without Marsh Gurney's sadistic refinements), but he decided he would opt out of that game and instead treated his Plebes in a firm but reasonably humane manner.[13]

Still, discipline must be maintained, and the older raise the younger. The barrage of questions was a comparatively light martyrdom, hallowed by tradition. The favorite hazing question of the graduating class was, "What's that song, Mister?"—to which the only correct answer was: " 'No More Rivers,' Sir!" "No More Rivers to Cross" was the traditional First Class song, and it suddenly became a sentimental favorite.

With some of the Plebes—Dick Mandelkorn, for example—he remained friends for the rest of their respective lives. Frank Wigelius, Class of '32, recalled that late in March that year Heinlein put him on the pap (that is, cited him for demerits) and told him to report to his room—normally a prelude to a ritual beating with a broomstick on the buttocks. Instead, Heinlein let him

off the hook when he discovered the Plebe had learned to fly in the Navy
Reserve at Sand Point, Seattle, and had his own private pilot's license as a student Navy Reserve aviator chief AP instructor.[14]

Heinlein no longer had fencing to distract him, and his attention to the
football season—characterized even in the 1929 *Lucky Bag* as "mediocre"—
was perfunctory. Heinlein had a personal interest in the rifle and pistol teams,
since he taught general classes in those subjects to the less proficient. That year,
"his boys" on the Second Class team actually outshot the varsity squad, and the
incoming Plebes had an undefeated season in the small-bore competition.

But athletics were no longer quite so important for class cohesion. The
Class of 1929 had started to pull together socially over the summer practice
cruise—but the sudden sentimental fellow-feeling did not, apparently, much
include Heinlein. He had a small circle of friends, half a dozen or so,[15] but
he was not popular—and even his demerits did not make him a regular guy:
malingering, the offense for which he had received his latest (and last) large
batch of demerits, was not "cool."

His lack of connectedness must have become painfully obvious to him
when one of his classmates, Delos Wait (the captain of the foil fencing team),
secretly married, and the rest of the class quietly agreed to look the other way.
It was against the Academy rules and could get Wait expelled on the very eve
of his graduation.

Wait was well liked despite a sometimes shocking directness. An Arkansas
boy, Wait had made the aviation squad and grown into a man's man—able
to mingle well and give and receive help, just the things that came hardest to
Heinlein. Wait's graduating portrait caption in *The Lucky Bag* tries to account for his popularity: " 'To have friends, be one.' Perhaps this accounts for
the popularity of Delos. A shipmate and a classmate, and—to show he plays
no favorites in his affections—a snake—by habit, disposition, and circumstances."[16]

Wait was frank in bull sessions about his rationalizations for every decision:
minimize risk to his precious skin and keep from having to go back to honest
work—defined as contemplating the south end of a northbound mule from
the vantage of the furrow.[17]

The entire class colluded in keeping Wait's marriage secret—just as Heinlein had helped keep Buddy Scoles out of trouble in 1927. Whether the same
kind of protection might be given him was questionable.

Heinlein was unbending a bit: during the academic season he had managed
a team under P. V. H. Weems, who was, unbeknownst to the midshipmen,

one of the Navy's great navigators. "Daddy Weems" impressed them more "by his most unusual skill at the tango" and because he took part in amateur theatricals. One of Weems's memorable comic turns as a butler[18] may have helped inspire Heinlein to join the Naval Academy's drama society, the Maskeraders.

That year's play was a departure from the usual formula mystery. *The Devil in the Cheese* was a successful Broadway play that combined some of the elements of Shakespearean comedy with drawing-room farce. Heinlein had a role in the performance, and in some of the other skits. And he did some amateur theatricals of his own: in the last semester, he and Barrett Laning did a barracks-room performance of Mark Twain's Elizabethan fart-comedy, *1601.*

Barrett Laning, who later gave up using his middle name and went by "Cal," quickly became one of Heinlein's best friends. In various bull sessions, Heinlein had shared with him his suspicion that there was a Big Secret of some kind that the adults were hiding from them—things just *couldn't* be as messy as real life or as irrational as the explanations he was handed. The two of them and classmate Gus Gray thought it would be a fine idea to pass to each other any clue they discovered to the Big Secret. They called this The Quest.[19]

All sorts of things went into The Quest—anything that might bear on the real reality. In their last semester at the Academy, Laning gave Heinlein a book that was to have a major shaping influence on his life, *Jurgen: A Comedy of Justice,* by James Branch Cabell.

Jurgen had been an international scandal and a *cause célèbre* since its initial publication in 1919, when the New York Society for the Suppression of Vice brought suit against Cabell and his publisher for violating the 1873 Comstock censorship laws. There was, indeed, an ample supply of indelicacies in the book, drawn, Cabell said, from an uncle's library of improper books, but they were also concealed by some of the most delicately ironic and satiric prose ever written in American English. Literary figures throughout the world came to Cabell's defense, and this case broke the power of the Comstock organizations. By 1929, Cabell was still thought of as the leading writer of this generation. By 1930 he was *passé.*

Perhaps Heinlein learned from Cabell something about himself—why he was so drawn to the idea of gallantry. Cabell's Gallant, of which Jurgen was the first example, knew the traditions of his society but stood outside them. It gave him an unusual degree of freedom, but it also placed him outside the emotional framework that could express effortlessly the workings of God and society. That certainly described Heinlein—and it suggested, also, the potential power of the "hypocrisy" of the Navy's designating its officers as gentlemen and according them privileges not given citizens or even ordinary seamen, so long as the customs were followed. That was something they all knew, even if they didn't talk about it.

While Heinlein was reading *Jurgen* (and then the rest of Cabell), he brought C. H. Hinton's *A New Era of Thought* (1888) to Laning.[20] H. G. Wells had mentioned Hinton in his new book that year, *The Way the World Is Going*. The main part of Hinton's book was about visualizing geometric forms in higher dimensions, but it had some mystical tinges to it, too: this visualization trick was supposed to be the key to esoteric powers of mind and so forth—just the sort of thing Laning was interested in. Wells had also mentioned J. W. Dunne, another philosopher of time and multiple dimensions. Dunne had published in 1927 *An Experiment with Time,* a book that was provoking a lot of discussion among physicists about the nature of time. These subjects were fodder for The Quest.

In turnabout, Laning then taught Heinlein how to hypnotize people—a useful and entertaining trick for impressing dates.[21]

Heinlein did feel personally connected to Laning, who had never snubbed him[22]—and this was a tie to his origins he could feel comfortable with. Laning's active interest in mystical matters probably allowed Heinlein to reconnect with his own mystical experiences as a child, experiences that had been covered up with getting and spending (and boning grease that year).

First Class year expenses were enormous. Graduating midshipmen were expected to have $1,000 saved up—a year's salary for a working man—for their officer's full kit of work and dress uniforms—including officer's sword, cocked hat, and the dressy frock coat with gold braid used only for the most formal occasions (such as a visit and inspection by the President of the United States). These items would be shipped in wooden boxes to the officers' first billet. And there were other expenses—boat cloaks, the drag for graduation ceremonies, and so forth. The Academy ring was also extra. A typical plain ring was solid gold (at $65 in the days of the $20 per ounce specie price), but they could be ordered with a variety of stones, for extra amounts. Heinlein decided to splurge on his ring, ordering a green nonprecious stone called "New Zealand Jade" in the catalog. It came inscribed with his name and class on the inside of the band.

There wasn't much left of his monthly stipend from the Academy—but there hadn't been much to start with, so the difference would have to be made up from his savings from his pre-Plebe earnings and the periodic gifts he had received from his father and brothers over the years. In addition to his job with International Harvester, Rex Ivar had been promoted to Collector, a patronage office in Kansas City's local political structure. With two other wage earners in the immediate family, things were no longer as tight as once they were, but Lawrence had a family of his own to support now and could not have contributed much on an Army lieutenant's pay. His brother Ivar gifted Robert with his own graduating sword.

Heinlein did not go home that Christmas, and used the time principally to refocus his priorities. He was invited to Westport, Connecticut, again, where he did some life-modeling for an artist-friend.[23] He had modeled, for one reason or another, for years ("artist's model" is on his pre-Academy list of miscellaneous jobs he had held). That year (1928), he mentioned modeling for Coca-Cola ads (though none of these ads have been identified).[24]

His first priority was to raise his class standing and particularly his standing in Executive. True to his resolve, he had not another demerit. His class standing for the last year was 44 out of 243, but his four-year average Order of General Merit was twentieth in his class, and that was the number that counted. His numbers in all the subjects were mostly on the border between grades of B and A. Interestingly, he did not stand particularly high in English (90th in the class), though his marks in engineering and aeronautics put him back into the top 10 percent of his class.

He was promoted to Midshipman 1PO (Petty Officer, First Class) on January 29, 1929. Now he would carry the regimental flag. The comments for the graduates' portraits in *The Lucky Bag* must already have been written by that time, as his rating is still shown there as 2PO. In his graduate portrait, he begins to look familiar—an obviously handsome young man, but with a narrower jaw than we are accustomed to seeing.

It was the custom for roommates to write the tribute to each other, to appear as captions to the photo portraits on facing pages in their graduating *Lucky Bag*; Heinlein's write-up of his roommate, Seraphin Bach Perreault, is the first surviving sample of his writing for public consumption:

> Perry may be expected to do the unexpected. No known rules appear to govern his conduct. His friends are often surprised, occasionally shocked, but frequently amused at his actions. He was born in Kansas of French and Scottish parents and educated in the public schools of Kansas City. A month spent at the Citizens Military Training Camp at Leavenworth resulted in military ambitions and an appointment to Annapolis. While here he has been a sport-a-season man, four years a member of varsity squads.

An unsuspected tendency towards the non-regulation kept him from stripes.

Superficially a social recluse, rarely seen at hops, Perry has been a constant source of wonder to his roommate because of his ability to keep from six to ten girls interested at once. He has entirely too big a heart to be restricted to one. In spite of his weakness for the ladies, he has the enviable record of never having given away a pin or miniature. His undoubted ability, his willingness to work, and his cheerful disposition should stand him in good stead in the fleet.[25]

By comparison to the sometimes empurpled prose of the class history in *The Lucky Bag*, Heinlein's writing is already clear, direct, relatively unornamented—serviceable. Perry's prose portrait of Heinlein reveals a glimpse of the person:

The stellar rise of our Bob has been exemplified by his promotion from the "boy general" to 2 P.O. But this indicates little of his true self. Starring for the course of four years is by no means a trifle, and his prowess as a fencer is established for he was the recipient of the 1927 epee medal. He does have uncanny ability to do those things which to others seem impossible.

Oftentimes Bob has stumbled into the room, cheeks aglow, eyes flashing, and in a quavering voice would say, "Well, boys, I've reformed. I'm in love again." Then just as night follows day or ebb follows flood he would resume his previous ways. "Repentance oft I swore—but was I sober when I swore?"

Memories of the cruise give to us our fondest dreams, but Bob disagrees. Too many teas and receptions aboard to suit him. Instead, he would rather stay below and study engineering. Moonlight canoe rides and cruises in an admiral's barge, chaperoned by a coxswain, are not included in his aversion to life afloat.

We hope Bob will stay in the Navy, for if he goes in the construction corps, as he threatens, some of us will probably crash in the planes he will design. "I consider any plane which I design a success if it rises high enough to crash."

Very Wet Stuff of him.

That spring, Heinlein's small circle of friends was diminished even further, when Elwood "Woody" Teague left the Academy before graduation, to take up a career in the stock market. The world of 1929 was thoroughly

modern and buzzing on a caffeine high, and there were many things a
bright young man might do rather than hide himself away in a ship. In the
jubilee year of the lightbulb, Henry Ford sponsored a celebration in Edison's honor. Philip Francis Nowlan introduced the first science-fiction
comic strip, *Buck Rogers*. The dirigible airship *Graf Zeppelin* circled the
world. The postwar economic depression was long over, and the stock market was soaring.

But the Naval Academy was not a complete backwater: the Fox Film
Corporation had arranged to film an Army-Navy football rivalry film—
Salute!—on the U.S. Naval Academy campus that spring (despite the dis-
continuation of the Army-Navy game). Director John Ford brought popular
star George O'Brien as the Army cadet hero, and the entire USC football
team to play the Army and Navy teams. This film launched the film careers
of two Trojan football players, Ward Bond and Marion Morrison (better
known by his stage name, John Wayne). In 1929 films began to talk. The
film was released in a silent version and a talking version—neither to great
success.

Heinlein had migrated into fire control as his area of specialization, and
his overnight trip to the naval shipyards in Norfolk, Virginia, in May of that
year[26] may have been a practicum for advanced instruction.

One thing new this year was the news that the Naval Academy would be
eligible for the Rhodes Scholarship for the first time, starting the next year.
Heinlein was to be considered for the first Rhodes Scholarship given at the
Naval Academy.

The Rhodes Scholarships are the legacy of Cecil John Rhodes, a
nineteenth-century British statesman and colonial pioneer, particularly of
South Africa, who left the bulk of his estate, when he died in 1902, to establish scholarships sending colonials overseas to Oxford for two years (with the
possibility of renewal for a third year), where they would get breadth and develop their abilities.

The terms of Rhodes's will specified that the scholarship trust should seek
out scholars of exceptional ability, without regard to need, race, or religion,
but "not . . . merely bookworms": the selection criteria included literary and
scholastic attainments; qualities of maturity, truthfulness, courage, devotion
to duty, sympathy for and protection of the weak, kindliness, unselfishness,
and fellowship; athletic attainments, or at least physical vigor demonstrated
by a fondness for outdoor activities; and moral vigor, as shown by involvement in public duties. In 1929 each state nominated its own candidates for
the scholarships, after a series of interviews. The entire process usually in-

volved about three hundred applications for the thirty-two available scholarships. The selection would be made at a meeting of the selection committee in early December, six months after graduation.

Heinlein never recorded his thinking about the Rhodes Scholarship—in fact, he never mentioned it at all, and all that is known about the matter is in his naval records. But it is easy to see the opportunity it might represent for Heinlein to get back on track for astronomy. Astronomy was a kind of intellectual intoxication for him.

There was very little real astronomy done in the Navy in 1929—but there was the U.S. Naval Observatory, a very prestigious billet, even though most of the astronomical work done there had to do with standards of weight and length measurement. Still, modern physics and modern astronomy—in fact, all of twentieth-century science—had started at the Academy in the 1870s. Albert Michelson was in the news again in 1929, announcing a new series of measurements of the speed of light—the same experiments he had started right there on the banks of the Severn fifty years earier. Ironically, Heinlein's astronomy textbook that year, *The Elements of Astronomy* by E. A. Fath, was incredibly out-of-date, even though it had been published just three years earlier, in 1926. It discussed the luminiferous ether—a concept already all but completely discarded—but did not even mention Einstein's Special Relativity or the Michelson-Morley experiments:

> I find it sardonically amusing that I was required to study Fath's book at the school where Michelson graduated in 1873, and to recite from Fath's book a few feet—less than a hundred yards—from the spot where Michelson performed his *first* famous experiment in 1878.[27]

Heinlein asked the Superintendent of the Academy to apply on his behalf for the first Rhodes Scholarship to be given at the Academy. It was a good gamble: it would be two years of fully paid study at Oxford, and after that, he could credibly apply to the Naval Observatory or for some other mathematical or astronomical job.

He had nothing to lose and everything to gain.

There was some doubt as to whether Heinlein should apply from Missouri, his state of residence, or from Maryland, the location of the Academy—or from wherever he was stationed. It would have to be finalized when he received his first billet. In extremely formal language the Superintendent drafted a letter postdated to 1 August 1929, when the selection process for the 1930 scholarships would commence, recommending him to the selection committee of whatever state Heinlein would ultimately apply from:

> Dear Sir:
> Robert Anson Heinlein has been selected to represent the United States Naval Academy in the competition for a Rhodes Scholarship from the State of _____.
>
> > /s/ S. S. Robinson
> > Rear Admiral, U.S. Navy,
> > Superintendent.
>
> Secretary, Committee of Selection,
> State of _____ [28]

What Heinlein had going for him was that the selection committee in the U.S. favored institutions that had never had a successful candidate before. What he had going against him was that his academic credentials were not absolutely top-notch. He stood fifth in academics in his class, though the disciplinary actions brought his overall standing down to twentieth. And the Naval Academy was not well regarded at that time as an academic institution—it didn't even issue a graduating degree in engineering, though the Rhodes selection committee waived the formal requirement of a bachelor's degree in this case.

And then June Week and graduation was upon him. June Week encompassed a number of arcane rituals at the Academy: on the last day of classes, the Firsts would go about with uniforms in deliberate disarray and hold a mock funeral for their academic career at the foot of the statue of Tecumseh in the forecourt of Bancroft Hall. The last athletics of the year were a series of Army-Navy competitions, with the cadets of West Point coming to the Annapolis campus for lacrosse, track, and baseball competitions that in 1929 drew "the largest crowds ever assembled on Navy fields."[29]

Heinlein elected to cut the formal social events—the Ring Dance and the graduation ceremony itself—and left for Kansas City by train on June 3, to spend some time with family and friends before reporting to his first billet on the USS *Lexington* at San Pedro Naval Station. He was assigned a Navy service number, 0-62624, on graduation, the first of any official identifiers for him, since Missouri did not keep vital statistics in that time before Social Security.

Before he left, he and Gus Gray and Barrett Laning made a pact: if any of them were killed, they would visit at least one of the others from the astral plane, or whatever lay beyond death. That way, they would have personal proof of life after death. That was a major point of The Quest, and it would continue after the Naval Academy—though Heinlein thought Laning was more serious about The Quest than he was.[30]

Heinlein was still on a train headed for Kansas City on Thursday, June 6, 1929—the last day as midshipmen for the Class of 1929, concluding with the actual graduation ceremonies. His name was listed alphabetically among the rest of the midshipmen graduating as ensigns.

Commissioning and assignment of first billet followed within a week. Most—205 of the 240—were to be commissioned ensigns in regular line. Heinlein received his commission dated June 6. Nineteen of his classmates were commissioned Second Lieutenants of Marines and four others were commissioned to the Supply Corps. Eleven were disqualified because of physical defects and would not receive commissions. Instead, they would re-sign. Heinlein's eyesight was still holding up. He had escaped his brother's fate.

FRYING PAN AND FIRE

Leaving the campus early in June Week, Heinlein cut himself off from the social activities of his class—partly because of the expense, to be sure, but possibly also because of the gush of sentimental fellow-feeling.

At this stage, Heinlein was part of the way into any personal goals he might have set for himself going into the Naval Academy: he had succeeded in bootstrapping a career for himself on very little money. With hard work and a little luck—always luck!—he might get the Rhodes Scholarship, and that would open up more possibilities for him.

Back in Annapolis, immediately following the graduation ceremony which took place on Thursday, June 6, the graduating midshipmen traditionally gathered in Tecumseh Court and tossed their white caps into the air to celebrate their release—a ceremony immediately followed by a number of weddings at the chapel in the Yard, far the most important of all the social events.

Instead of celebrating release and freedom—and marriage!—Heinlein went directly to work. From Kansas City he would travel to San Pedro, California, to report by June 23 to his billet, the USS *Lexington*. That could only have been exciting: these new aircraft carriers were the high tech of the 1920s—as close as you could get to living science fiction in 1929.

On the train home, Heinlein noticed a pretty twenty-year-old with a major bust, definitely interesting—and interested.[1] Mary Briggs was engaged to be married—she was, in fact, meeting her fiancé in St. Louis. But as that Friday evening came on she surprised Heinlein by seizing an opportunity for a kiss, and that kiss was an unmistakable invitation. Late that night, he decided to risk it: he dropped down to Lower Berth 7 and hesitantly parted the curtain. She was waiting for him, excited and happy, and things moved faster than he was quite prepared for. There was no seduction, no elaborate protestations of "love," no having to talk her into bed. They fell into sex without even thinking about the condoms he was carrying.

Heinlein was completely unprepared for this. She was the first woman he had ever known, he said, who was a mature human being—"with warmth and depth and outflowing matur[ity,] years and years beyond her contemporaries."[2] She made him feel inexperienced and clumsy, as if sex without complications and concessions to Victorian notions of propriety and hypocrisy was a completely new thing to him—as, indeed, it was, an undiscovered territory opening up before him.

This changed everything. Suddenly he saw all the girls he had slept with before as "unfinished human beings, usually narcissistic."[3] He was frankly overwhelmed. Decades later, he told her: "Mary, you put a mark on me that never wore off . . . to the benefit of every girl or woman I ever knew thereafter, in or out of bed. You oriented me, in major and important respects."[4]

He had missed the formal graduation on Thursday, but his real graduation—into adulthood—happened on Friday, June 7, 1929. From Mary Briggs, Heinlein got the adult vision, of sex as more than a dance of seduction, of reflexes and the mechanics of mucous membranes in friction. She was exactly the tonic Robert Heinlein needed at that moment in his life.

He came to stay with her at her home in East St. Louis that weekend. The sex was wonderful by itself, but he was half—more than half—in love with her. "If you had said to me 'I'm not going to marry him'—well, I suspect that we would have married before I ever left East St. Louis."[5] But they both had appointments to keep, and they did separate.

This relationship was a true enlightenment for him, and he kept changing internally. In releasing himself from the sexual rules and mores of his upbringing, he liberated himself from *all* the Bible Belt Christianity he disbelieved but had nonetheless held on to since childhood. This may be the first moment that Robert Heinlein ceased to be just another bright young man in search of a career like so many other bright young men in 1929.

Kansas City had changed. Tom Pendergast had removed his main rival, Joe Shannon, by kicking him upstairs, to the U.S. House of Representatives. The campaign was starting up as Heinlein got into town, and Tom Pendergast and his seven hundred "Joe Doakes" precinct captains were finally in complete control of Kansas City. Senator Reed, now retired, made a big fuss over him— the first (and last!) of his appointments to the military academies ever to graduate—and Robert was treated to an adult's introduction to the wide-open nightlife of Kansas City. Heinlein was in his element. "I was spoiled by Kansas City under the Pendergast machine," he later remarked: "The Merchant's Lunch at the Chesterfield Club included five strippers to the buff. Very nice buff, too."[6]

Heinlein didn't spend *all* his time with the machine hangers-on. At some time, probably during this period, he must have looked into joining the Masons—one of his friends at the Academy had him about talked into it—but decided his interest in the matter had faded.[7] Heinlein family life seems not to have occupied his thoughts in 1929. Things must have been very different with so many of the children away, and his older brothers in the Army. He spent much of his leave away from home.

Some of his time he spent with the boys from the Academy who returned home one by one after the graduating ceremonies in Annapolis. There were six of them that year. Cal Laning had been assigned to the USS *Oklahoma* and would be going back east in July to join the ship at the Philadelphia Navy Yard. Bob Clark was visiting Kansas City, as well, though Heinlein later said he did not meet and become friends with Clark until they were both stationed on *Lexington*.[8] Laning undoubtedly widened their acquaintance with the jazz clubs on the wrong side of the tracks.[9]

Part of the time Heinlein spent catching up with his high school friends. Sammy Roberts was the keeper from that group, a buddy from the ROTC rifle team. Sammy had a lifelong love affair with rifles and was interested in things military, so their relationship wore better than some other high school friendships. Sammy also owned a car, and this could have let them escape out of the stifling city and into the countryside (still hot and even more humid—but not so unbearable).[10]

Heinlein also renewed his acquaintance with Elinor Leah Curry.

Elinor and Robert had met a few times since high school, when she captained the girls' Negative Debate Team at Westport High, while he captained the corresponding boys' team at Central. He knew her father slightly, a postmaster on the railway (one of his last jobs before he left for Annapolis had been sorting mail in the same department). Elinor's mother had died when she was a child. After high school, Elinor had gone to William Jewell College and then Kansas University. In 1927, she went to work for the Southwestern Bell Telephone Company as a clerk, renting a room in a respectable neighborhood on Sixty-eighth Street, in the home of a local businessman.[11]

Since high school, they had dated occasionally,[12] but there was no suggestion of any special attraction at that time. Now, however, it is possible that the epiphany of Mary Briggs bore on him that he really wanted—needed—to be married. If things had gone as planned, he would have married Alice McBee immediately after graduation, and possibly in the Academy's chapel with others of his graduating class.

Heinlein's sentimental streak got the better of him, and he did a foolish thing. On Friday, June 21, 1929, he took a road trip with Elinor, Cal Laning, and Sammy Roberts to Platte City, about sixty miles northwest of Kansas City, and got married:

This certifies that Robert Anson Heinlein of Kansas City, State of Missouri, and Elinor Leah Curry of Kansas City, State of Missouri, were united in Holy Matrimony at Platte City on the 21st day of June A.D. 1929, by authority of a License bearing date the 21st day of June A.D. 1929, and issued by the Recorder of Deeds of Platte County, Missouri. Witness my signature.

> Walter M. Mundell, minister, Christian Church.
> Witnesses: S. J. Roberts, Mrs. W. M. Mundell.[13]

Sammy Roberts signed the marriage certificate as a witness.[14]

They had a brief honeymoon in Elinor's rented room. Heinlein did not tell his family he had married.[15]

Of Elinor Curry, Heinlein's only remarks were that she had very fair hair—almost albino[16]—and was "sexually adventurous."[17] In the Roaring Twenties, there was a sexual revolution going on, and her sexual openness must have reminded him tantalizingly of Mary Briggs. Perhaps also he—or both of them—were under the influence of Judge Lindsey's radical book, *Companionate Marriage* (1927) (or the film of the book that came out in 1928). Judge Lindsey was the voice of the sexual revolution of the 1920s.

Robert took over Elinor's room-rental agreement in his name and made arrangements to have a telephone installed.[18] They would have to make plans for more permanent arrangements later. Robert was due to report to *Lexington* in San Pedro, California, in less than two weeks.

But problems emerged almost immediately: Elinor didn't want to take his name[19]—and there was no question of her quitting her job. She absolutely refused to move to California. It remains an open question why she wanted to get married at all.

Perhaps naïvely—these are not "differences to be settled"—Heinlein was determined to make this work, even if it had to be by long distance. But even before he left to take up his billet, he was unfashionably shocked that Elinor slept with someone else[20] while they were still on their honeymoon: he was "shaken by the fact that she had committed adultery just days after their marriage."[21]

It wasn't the infidelity that bothered him:[22] he knew his Elinor and he knew himself, and if it was anything like a "companionate marriage," this kind of thing was going to happen, on both sides.[23] But his reaction indicates that Heinlein had certain expectations of what marriage should be: he had expected the marriage to mean something special to her, as it did to him. Sexual infidelity should not impair the emotional bond—they should still cleave together as man and wife, support and helpmeet each for the other.

Heinlein mentioned this matter only once, in a letter to Laning the next year.[24] Something Laning had said or done set Elinor off into an astonishing bout of hysteria (Laning had probably mentioned—casually, in the way talking about sex was *de rigueur* in the twenties, and especially among the flaming youths—"double dating in bed" with Heinlein, a phrase he was later to use in conversation).[25] Heinlein was not angry with Laning—except at his insensitivity in setting Elinor off.

Early in July, Robert left Elinor, and his family, and Kansas City, issues unresolved. Robert didn't know it at the time, but he was finally leaving home.

The USS *Lexington*—nicknamed the Lady Lex—had started out in 1921 as a battle cruiser, but the arms limitation provisions in the Washington Naval Treaty halted construction, and she was redesigned as an aircraft carrier, designated CV-2. When launched in 1925, she was the largest ship then afloat.

In her early years, the Lady Lex filled a very important role for the Navy: only the second large aircraft carrier ever built, *Lexington* would pioneer aircraft-carrier methods and techniques (and more important, strategy and tactics) during a period when the Navy was not yet completely convinced of the usefulness of airpower and might prefer to put its money into battleships. Her captain at that time was F. D. Berrien. She was a floating city, with a crew of 3,373 and eighty-one canvas-winged airplanes, including Martin T4M torpedo bombers and Boeing F4B fighters, the last wooden-winged biplane fighters produced by Boeing.

Lexington had new-minted ensigns stacked up like cordwood because of the relatively large sizes of several recent graduating classes. Aside from Bob Clark, Heinlein found several other classmates also reporting in. In one sense, it is not surprising that so many recent graduates would gravitate toward the new aircraft carriers: they represented the cutting edge of this technology, and the cutting edge is always where the best and the brightest like to start. This best and brightest found himself billeted in a stateroom that had a rack of canisters for fulminate of mercury—an unstable explosive that had to be stored separately from the ammunition.

Because of the surplus of ensigns, each would get a short rotation in the various departments of the ship, while taking on various administrative tasks. Instruction would continue—more notebooks sketching the ship's systems in detail. At least it was familiar work. But young naval officers live and die by their quarterly fitness reports—more report cards, but these affect their career in an "up or out" organization.

On July 13, just a week after reporting to *Lexington,* Heinlein received a letter from the Academy asking how he wanted the application for the Rhodes Scholarship to read. The nomination could not be submitted until he chose the location he would apply from—Maryland, Missouri, or California.[26] The letter was dated June 24, 1929—just three days after he had gotten married.

Rhodes Scholars could not be married: they were supposed to spend two years (or possibly three, since the scholarship could be extended) at Oxford University in England. He had put himself out of the running for the first Rhodes Scholarship to be given at the United States Naval Academy.[27] His short reply, saying simply that he was no longer eligible "by reason of marriage," was sent off the same day.

On August 2, 1929—the very day the application process would have been started—the Superintendent's secretary penciled "canceled" across the carbon copy of his nomination letter. That closed his file at the Academy and closed a door on his first career ambition. Astronomy would not be possible now. He would have to make his career in the line of the Navy.

Heinlein immediately applied again for flight training. On July 31, 1929, he took his examination—and washed out again, "because of Defective Visual Acuity. Defective Depth Perception. Low angle of convergence."[28]

Doors were closing for him, right and left.

Heinlein's first administrative assignment was to take charge of the ship's office and act as aide to the ship's Executive Officer, John H. Hoover. Heinlein shortly learned that Hoover had the habit of dressing down his department heads in front of their juniors—"unpleasant to witness and humiliating to the victim."[29]

But he could be fair. One day, Hoover sent for him and told him that some of the ship's liberty cards (permissions to be somewhere other than at work at one's post) had been stolen—and what did he know about it?

Heinlein felt sick.[30] In order to take over managing the ship's office, Heinlein had to practically memorize the BuNav manual—"the Book"—and had given only cursory attention to the printed forms and other expendable supplies that his Chief Yeoman had told him were stored in an unlocked safe. Chief Schmidt pulled any forms he needed, and bossed four yeomen under him. Heinlein was utterly dependent on the Chief.

The liberty cards, it turned out, were stored in an unmarked stationery box in the safe, and Heinlein had been caught in the easiest infraction for an incoming officer to make: signing for supplies without inventorying them personally. The problem was compounded by other regulations not followed; yeomen were left unattended in the office—two of them slept in the office.

Heinlein girded up his mental and moral loins and reported back, taking sole responsibility. Hoover looked at him without expression for an endless moment. "Correct the situation," he said, and turned his head away. That ended it. Later, Heinlein figured out that Hoover might have dressed him down if he had tried to pin blame on the Chief, but owning up to a mistake was the ideal Navy way—the *only* way—to handle that kind of situation.[31]

Heinlein's "boot makee-learnee"[32] rotations, each about three months, were in gunnery, engineering, and communications. He would be given weekly or biweekly assignments to describe and understand the various operating parts of the ship's systems. His engineering sketches would be graded by an officer senior to him. Heinlein's sketchbooks are filled with a mixture of laudatory and exasperated remarks from his supervising officers, including Hoover.

Heinlein's rotation in Communications meant that he had to get in some time in the air, which suited him just fine. Most of *Lexington*'s radio traffic was with the flight squadrons when they were off the deck, and Heinlein used two radio sets, depending on which station he was covering: the pilots had primitive dot-dash equipment using Morse code; the guard planes had regular voice-communication gear and could talk to the ship via the radio compass. Heinlein had to be familiar with both sets of equipment, from both ends. On one occasion in the air, the squadron turned into its homing vector and found only empty water. No sign of the Lex. The radio equipment at the time used the loop antenna, which fixed the position of the signal by turning a coil of antenna wire until the signal was at maximum strength or minimum strength, estimated by ear. That could give two answers, 180 degrees apart. In this case, the vector was definitely "apart." They got back safely that time.

Even with all the miscellaneous work, there was time for reading, and

Heinlein continued to read all the science fiction he could get his hands on, even though the cost of a pulp magazine—there were no less than *three* science-fiction pulps on the market now that Hugo Gernsback had launched a series of science-fiction and adventure pulps with "Wonder" in the title— meant a real financial sacrifice, since most of his pay was going to Elinor in Kansas City. The 1930 Census shows "Elinor Heinlein" living with her parents and brother—and reflects that she has no occupation, so Heinlein must have won some of the battles, at least: she had apparently given up her job with the telephone company. Married women were not encouraged to work, as it took a job away from a man who had a family to support.

Heinlein was at sea on October 29, 1929—Black Tuesday—when the stock market crashed and the Great Depression began. Thirty billion dollars in paper assets disappeared—at a time when a nickel bought a piece of pie.[33] Nobody yet knew that this wasn't just another business-cycle adjustment like the Panics of 1893 or 1907.

As a naval officer, Heinlein would be somewhat insulated from the worst effects of the Depression. He fell into a comfortable shipboard routine and improved his idle hours learning—"somewhat expensively" he said[34]—that poker is not a game of chance.

San Pedro is Los Angeles's port, and the officers had entrée to the social life in Hollywood. Heinlein fell in with a number of stars, staff, and directors at Columbia and was often on the Columbia lot. He recalled knowing Barbara Stanwyck in 1929 and 1930.[35] That home port also gave Heinlein greater access to a part of his family he actually enjoyed, his paternal uncle Lawrence Ray Heinlein and Ray's wife, Kitty.[36] Heinlein's relationship with Ray and Kitty was welcoming and familial, and he sometimes brought shipboard pals along with him on visits. On one of these visits, one of his friends, Ron Steward, sat for Heinlein, who was sculpting in clay.[37]

Heinlein became exceptionally close to Ray and Kitty's son, Ray—Edward Ray Heinlein. They were partners, Ray had said, and shared everything. He died young, a loss Robert never really got over. Decades later, he remembered this time in his life in a letter to his uncle Ray:

I could have turned a corner and found Ray and Bunny and a pinochle deck and played a few hands while slandering each other, with Kitty tossing in an occasional trimmer-downer remark of her own. You two taught me how to ace up to things then, how to accept what had to be, if not with happiness, then with gallantry.

I learned some other things from you at that time [Ray's death], too—what had to be done, those grim inescapable chores, that seemingly endless list of details which must be attended to.[38]

Early in December 1929, *Lexington* received instructions to go to Tacoma, Washington: the city's power grid was collapsing. Most of Tacoma's electricity—most of the electricity for western Washington—came from hydroelectric plants, and the preceding winter had been unusually dry. Tacoma's Lake Cushman was far below its normal level, and the Nisqually River power plants, operating at full capacity, were not able to supply the demand.[39] *Lexington*'s four monstrous electric generators could, in theory, supplement the local power sources and put the power grid back on a stable footing. It had never been done before, but it was feasible on paper.

Lexington came into Commencement Bay on December 16, 1929, and was towed into Tacoma's Baker Dock, where Seattle City Power had installed transmission facilities. The lines were installed overnight, and the following day *Lexington* began running one engine at half-power for a month—time enough for everybody to settle in.

The JO (Junior Officer) Mess clubbed together to rent a house for a month. As adjutant of the *Lexington*'s landing force—a mixed battalion of Marines and bluejackets—he had duties as Range Officer at Fort Lewis each annual overhaul period. A little early this year, he joined up with the rifle team there and had some shooting matches using rifle, pistols, and small arms of all sorts.

For Christmas that year, his father sent him a single-volume collection of Rudyard Kipling's verse. That was touching. Heinlein had been reading and rereading Kipling's poetry for more than ten years: the stories he had read only once, in 1921, but he came back to the verse over and over; not even Marsh Gurney and the "Mary Gloster" could spoil Kipling for him. The rhythms and verbal patterns were intoxicating: "That collection caused me to become acutely conscious of the sound and shape of every word I wrote."[40]

At that time, he did his first fiction writing, a 2,540-word mystery set at the U.S. Naval Academy, titled "Weekend Watch," for a ship's literary contest, typed on *Lexington* onionskin stationery. A First Class midshipman Frenching Out accidentally intercepts a spy trying to steal a piece of advanced, classified equipment—a revolutionary new torpedo design that is on campus for secret demonstrations. He foils the attempt, barely surviving the fight that ensues (in which he performs prodigies of heroism and endurance, of course).

Things look grim for the hero: he may not be permitted to graduate. The Navy fixes it up, however, so that he takes his punishment for Frenching Out and then receives a commendation for valor. This is a very peculiar arrangement that occurs over and over in naval history, and one with which Heinlein was particularly fascinated.

"Weekend Watch" is very poorly written, barely competent at the most basic narrative functions of prose. It did not win the contest, and the manuscript does not show any indication that he attempted to market it at that time.

On January 16, 1930, *Lexington* disconnected from Tacoma's power grid and lifted anchor. They would be back many times to Bremerton and Tacoma. In fact, they were at Tacoma in March when the Lex was ordered to Guantánamo for fleet exercises—just as the start of the new quarter brought Heinlein to a rotation in navigation. He served as Supernumerary Assistant Navigator—spare part—under Merrill Comstock, a very different officer from John Hoover, though both were equally competent and equally mean. But Comstock was a superb navigator and, like Hoover, "a military, taut son of a bitch."[41] Heinlein learned a lot from him, and did "navigator's 'day work'"—maintaining the chart and fixing ship's position—while standing communication watches.

One evening, he took his sextant to measure ship's position by triangulating the stars, as navigators have been doing for thousands of years, but the sky was partly cloudy, and he couldn't use the standard stars.

> . . . so I shot Vega, Jupiter, and the upper limb of the moon, worked it, and got a point fix—to my surprise as I had never shot the upper limb of the moon before (or even the easier lower limb) and it had been over two years since I had worked one in class. I handed my work to Comstock. He looked at it, increased his habitual frown, started to speak—did not and checked my work very carefully.
>
> Then he erased his own fix (an excellent small triangle), and cut my fix in, in place of it—never said a word, ignored me. So I left, feeling as if I had just had a medal pinned on me.[42]

That was the Navy way!

This trip through the Big Ditch would be something of an adventure for everyone: *Lexington* would be the first aircraft carrier ever to go through the Panama Canal. Some of the Canal's locks were barely large enough, on the numbers, to accommodate her.

An aircraft carrier is designed to have a lot of freeboard deck (the top surface of a vessel) in proportion to her freeboard (the measurement from the freeboard deck to the waterline), so as to give the aircraft storage space and runway. In one lock, the ship was positioned a little off-center, and when *Lexington* began to move out of the lock, the overhanging sweep of her freeboard deck scraped all the standard lights off the sides—embarrassing but memorable. They were moved back when rebuilt.

10

New York State of Mind

Heinlein's in-ship battle station was at the main battery. When they were finished with the spring exercises at Guantánamo, he was detached for temporary duty to Long Island City to attend the Ford Instrument Company school from May 3 to June 17, 1930, to learn how to run the electromechanical "computers" that coordinated the ship's main battery—the Mark XVIII Director and Mark III Range Keeper. After a four-day leave to visit Rex at Fort Humphreys, Virginia, he left *Lexington* at the Norfolk Yards and traveled overland to New York City.[1]

New York City in 1930 was an exhilarating place to be. Just seven months after the stock market crash, New Yorkers had not yet completely recovered from the reports of bankers and brokers leaping out the windows of skyscrapers. But the can-do spirit was still very strong. Less than a month after the crash that ushered in the Great Depression, architect William Van Alen had turned the unfinished Chrysler Building into the tallest building in the world by having its seven-story, stainless-steel spire secretly constructed inside the tower and raised through a hole in the roof, the whole process taking only an hour and a half. The building was completed and opened in the spring of 1930.

But the Chrysler Building was not long to hold the record. As Heinlein came to New York, Shreve, Lamb & Harmon were pushing construction of the Empire State Building at the rate of four and a half stories *per week*. When it was finished, it was going to be tall enough, at 102 stories (compared to the Chrysler Building's 77 stories), to moor dirigibles to a specially designed mast.

The Ballistic Computer School was the least of Heinlein's concerns. He headed straight for Greenwich Village, which already had a reputation for bohemianism, and found an apartment one block south of Washington Square. His high school intellectual hero, Will Durant, was headquartered there, at the Labor Temple—but it was not for Durant and philosophy he came. Nor, strictly speaking, for the speakeasies and the bathtub gin (they were just a side benefit). He wanted to get back into art—not just the drawing he had kept up with (or the cartooning he had not kept up): something more substantial . . . painting or sculpture.[2] In his apartment he had some space and set up a studio for himself.

Heinlein began looking around and was immediately immersed in Greenwich Village in the Jazz Age. It was like stepping on a live wire and being jolted to sudden life.

Heinlein had nearly eleven weeks in New York, and Elinor would not join him there, either, so he made the best use he could of this opportunity. He was bright, young (just turning twenty-two), handsome, talented, and not obviously "taken": he was under no obligation to maintain any inconvenient sexual fidelity. "I was the most eligible bachelor in Strunsky's Love Stables simply because *my* studio had a bath tub—and the prospect of a sit-down hot bath was even better bait than a 75-cent bottle of muscatel (the standard bait)."[3]

His natural entrée was with artists' models and their hangouts[4]—and that led to meeting painters and other sculptors and from thence to poets and writers and their ilk, and that would have led by natural degrees into being exposed to everything *à la mode*.

Nightlife of the Village bohemians of this period is reasonably well portrayed in memoirs and histories of this, the *Youngblood Hawke* period. If Heinlein's experience was typical for his endowments, once he became known around the various arts circles in Greenwich Village, he could not have missed being taken to the studio of the doyen of the Greenwich Village art scene, Gertrude Whitney Vanderbilt.[5] He would have been handed around from set to set, meeting everyone (we know he met Dorothy Parker at this time— "With her short stature, big hats, and scared-little-girl voice she reminded me of a frightened toad stool"[6]), reading pretentious "little" magazines (and the new comic strip, just started that year, featuring a sexy flapper, Betty Boop), and attending experimental theater. In those circles, he would naturally also have run into the poet Edna St. Vincent Millay, whose reputation for feminism and open bisexuality—promiscuous affairs with women as well as men—was outstanding even in that outstandingly promiscuous society.

Heinlein's personal inclinations and theoretical model came together very neatly in Greenwich Village in 1930. It was a society polymorphous perverse in theory and in practice (his lesbian models figure in his recollections, though he made no reference to male homosexuals in this period), the logical extension of the marriage-reform movements on the radical-socialist wing of the old American liberal movement.

He was almost immediately an insider in a world where entrepreneurs arranged tours of "artistic" locations for out-of-town tourists and *la vie de bohème* was theater and life at the same time.[7] The practice was not always so idealized: he lost the ivory elephant charm he used to tape to his wrist for fencing to a flapper who wanted it badly enough to make a public scene—she may not actually have wanted the elephant, but she did want the scene, and Heinlein didn't, so abandoning the elephant was the lesser of the two evils.[8]

Heinlein had always thought of himself as a liberal and as a socialist, but opportunities for direct, practical expression were limited at the Naval Academy (though the military was one of the examples cited repeatedly by Edward Bellamy, in *Looking Backward,* of highly organized cooperative structures). Socialism and liberalism were on the anvil, right there, right then. While Heinlein was in New York, John Dewey, "America's philosopher," was running a series of essays in *The New Republic,* about the apparent fragmentation and ferment that was going on, that they were all a part of . . . how it was actually the coming together of a new individualism, an individualism that would go hand in hand with the socialism that was coming, inevitable.[9]

Whether or not Heinlein read Dewey's essays as they came out, he was acting out the social evolution Dewey was sensing: even that back-of-the-mind Quest that Heinlein and Laning and Gray were on might relate to what Dewey identified as fragmentation being part of a larger pattern: the boys were trying to discover for themselves the patterns that tied together this dazzling spectacle of life. The science and technology Heinlein had immersed himself in—from theoretical astronomy to the cams and gears of the Mark IV Ballistic Computer—were parts of the "American mentality," and while the idea that "technique" could be applied to the engineering of society may have been a Bolshevik discovery, it was Americans who were taking the idea all over the world. The new world was going to be "corporated"—just what H. G. Wells had been saying in his social novels published through the 1920s—and Americans were exploring how to do the new corporatedness. "I shall look to America . . . ," Wells was insisting as late as 1926, "for the first installments of the real revolution."[10] If Heinlein did not catch the breathless sense of the excitement of his times from Dewey, he was prepared for it already by reading Wells's social novels.

Some kind of socialism was inevitable—indeed, Heinlein thought, it was already partly here: "Here in the USA, where we have much more socialism than most people appear to believe, we are good at it in some spots, fair in others, lousy in some."[11] Wells and Dewey dovetailed in an exhilarating picture of the evolution that Heinlein himself had an exciting, personal role in advancing. The way to bring about the future, Dewey said, was to deal, without preconceptions, with the realities that one confronts in the here and now, using the scientific method applied to life situations, bringing oneself into harmony with the conditions of the new, coming world.

So, being right here, right now, doing just what he was doing, put Robert Anson Heinlein, U.S.N., in the vanguard of progress, of the inevitable and irresistible social change that was going to take place. Wells, the utopian socialist social thinker, and Dewey, the American philosopher of Pragmatism, were on the same wavelength—and so was Ralph Waldo Emerson, and so was he.

Heinlein's place in the scheme of things would involve art—specifically, he decided, sculpture. As a child, he had modeled figures of Tarzan and Mowgli in Plasticine, and his favorite toy elephant he considered the perfect sculptural subject—for a five-year-old. His tastes in three-dimensional figures had broadened somewhat in the intervening years; he wanted to sculpt more adult subjects now: life studies of nudes.[12] His models were all local girls, and they seem to have made up his main social life during the weeks he had in New York. They introduced him to other aspects of life in the Village in the thirties, all fascinating to a young man of Robert Heinlein's temperament. But there was more to life in Greenwich Village in 1930 than the time he spent in the sack. There was also time spent out of the sack, in the most wide-open social group he was ever to know.

> . . . when I had a sculpture studio in Greenwich Village, I knew a lot of them [Lesbians] both butch and sweetheart, quite well. My best model was one. I tried with boyish enthusiasm to seduce her (she was not virgin with respect to men, just not interested)—and I got nowhere; she just laughed at me. But we were chums and used to "cruise" together, both hunting the same game—with an agreement that each would respect the other's "point." A lovely girl and she could pose like a rock, as long as I kept her well supplied with wine.[13]

Almost all of Heinlein's correspondence from this period was destroyed in later years, but around this time, Cal Laning and Gus Gray and he must have started their experiments with telepathy,[14] setting up blind trials according to the methods suggested in Upton Sinclair's new (1930) book, *Mental Radio*—a book Heinlein specifically mentions in one of his early stories.

Heinlein knew Sinclair as a socialist editorialist in the journal *Appeal to Reason*, which Heinlein had read as a boy.[15] Sinclair was a famous muckraker who had caused a national scandal in 1906 and 1907 by describing in *The Jungle* labor practices in the Chicago meatpacking industry and was world famous because of that book. *Mental Radio* was a straightforward report of his wife's experiments with telepathy, picking up where Mark Twain had left off in his "Mental Telegraphy" essays, with a series of "case studies"—transmissions of words, messages, and even images, from near and far—and a first pass at statistical analysis of the results. It looked like a thoughtful attempt to put a very firm statistical grounding under the type of "anecdotal evidence" Twain had collected. It stood to become the basis for a scientific investigation of telepathy.[16] More important, Mary Craig Sinclair gave directions for developing telepathic talents. In the introduction to the book, Sinclair had suggested that telepathic ability could be "cultivated deliberately, as any other object of study . . . The essential in this training is an art of mental concentration and autosuggestion, which can be learned."[17] Heinlein was very interested in the idea that special abilities could be learned by mental exercises[18]—and now it appeared that the hypnosis Cal Laning was playing around with might lead in that direction, too.

Heinlein, Gus Gray, and Cal Laning would write to one another, setting times for trials, and then, at the appointed day and hour, they would try to transmit and receive telepathic images and messages. They could exchange the results by mail, too, or in person on the infrequent occasions when they were in the same port.[19]

But Heinlein had other matters to occupy his immediate attention. The Ford Instrument Company school was finally over on June 17, 1930, and he was certified to operate the *Lexington*'s Mark III Range Keeper. This was a theoretical qualification, though: like so many other Navy jobs, the training would have to be finished hands-on, on the job, no practical instruction being available at Long Island City.

He closed down his apartment in Greenwich Village on June 19, a day before he had to leave for Norfolk. There, he found changes in progress: Captain Berrien had given up his command. Heinlein would be coming back to a new captain—Ernest J. King.[20]

11

ROBERT AND UNCLE ERNIE

Heinlein knew King slightly. King and his family had been living in Annapolis while he was at the Academy. Heinlein had dated one of King's daughters and served as usher at the wedding of another. They had gotten along—but captains have literally the power of high and middle justice in their hands, a very different matter from the father of one's drag.

Heinlein was still in Greenwich Village when King took command on June 20, 1930, so he missed the reception that took the place of the formal calls on the captain traditionally made by each officer aboard a naval vessel. *Lexington* had far too many officers for formal calls to be practical. Scuttlebutt had it that things had gotten too lax under Berrien, and King had been sent to get *Lexington* shipshape and military. Discipline was going to be tightened up, and the process had already started. Heinlein heard that at the reception, King had raised and shown everyone a copy of Navy Regulations—The Book by which things are done "by the book"—and stated flatly that they would be obeyed from then on, no ifs, ands, or buts.

Heinlein rapidly worked back into the routine of minor duties and major as *Lexington* cast off on June 30, 1930, for its new home port in Long Beach, California. His Condition "A" battle station was in main battery control above the flag bridge. For the next six months he served as assistant to the Chief Warrant Electrical Gunner. This battle assignment continued no matter what department he was in, since the Gunny was due to be rotated soon, and that would leave him the only officer in the ship with the special schooling needed to program and run the battery. It was a plum assignment for an ensign; he would be de facto fire-control officer. The Chief introduced him to Lieutenant j.g. (junior grade) Sweetser (Annapolis Class of '26), who was currently operating the Mark IV, and they started immediately to teach Heinlein all the practical matters not covered in the Ford Instrument Company's seminar. He learned more from Lieutenant Sweetser than he had learned from the Ford Instrument Company in two months.[1] When Heinlein was ready to operate the Mark IV, Sweetser became Captain King's Secretary, but they stayed drinking buddies.

Heinlein's Condition "B" battle station would depend on the department to which he was assigned. For the present, he was reserve officer of the deck and navigator in the number 2 bridge on the stack housing, under the Executive Officer. At other times he would be on the main bridge four hours on, four hours off.

He soon had a night shift as Junior Officer of the Watch. King had already made some changes in the way things were done. Under Captain Berrien it was sometimes possible for the Junior Officer of the Watch and the Officer on Deck to grab a smoke sitting down in the chart house while pretending to study the chart. But under King you studied the chart before you went forward and reported, "Ready to relieve you, sir," not later than ten minutes before the hour—or else. And King might show up on deck at any moment. On one memorable occasion, the water was quiet. Heinlein was scanning the horizon.

> Out of the darkness behind me, a voice pitched just loud enough for me to hear it said in flat tones, "Get out of my way." I teleported myself bodily about ten feet to starboard.
>
> And I never got in E. J. King's way again.[2]

Later, he realized that what King had was the authentic "voice of command," the flat tone of voice that conveys absolute, convincing conviction that there is no possibility of not being obeyed.[3] Heinlein was immediately intrigued: E. J. King was obviously a very unusual man.

King, Heinlein concluded, was pure Navy, in the best possible sense. He meant what he said about going by the book—so long as it brought about justice tempered with solid common sense. Heinlein didn't know how he did it, but King's personality began to be felt everywhere in the ship, and they all felt themselves straightening out, bracing up, without being quite sure *why*.

They were bound this trip for Guantánamo, for fleet exercises. The ballistic computer was a very complex mechanical calculator, turning three-dimensional cams and pushing mechanical springs to perform four simultaneous integrations and seventeen simultaneous differentiations, in six simultaneous answers to control the first of eight turret guns. "And that was a lot of fun—like playing an organ."[4]

On one occasion, he got the downside of the responsibility: "I suppose my own 'finest hour' was in unloading a 105 mm hangfire after ordering the gun crew away from the gun—I damned near pissed my pants but I really had no choice; it was my battery."[5]

Coming through the Panama Canal that August they "swung around the hook"[6] for three days before entering the Gatun Locks, in the lake that forms part of the Canal. King knew about the embarrassing incident last time through, when Berrien had allowed *Lexington*'s freeboard to scrape the lights off the side of the lock. He had a reputation to protect, as a crack shiphandler. He waited for almost dead calm water to enter and used a Navy tug rather than the usual Canal tug. Hoover was overseeing the starboard wing, Heinlein on duty as Junior Officer of the Watch. Hoover's naturally sour disposition, coupled with the tight transit and the knowledge that King was observing, brought out the worst of his very sharp tongue. He verbally flayed the Chief Boatswain who was skippering the Navy tug. When they were through, King quietly took Hoover's megaphone and invited the tug captain aboard for coffee. Hoover's face flamed red. Heinlein understood what had just happened: quietly and without a reprimand, King had just reminded Hoover that the most senior job on this planet was the captain— any captain—of a vessel under way. Heinlein began to get an inkling of the incredible amount of technique he could learn from King.

When they got to their new home port in Long Beach, the routine changed again. Curiously, although *Lexington* was very stable at sea, she would roll up to thirty degrees in Long Beach Harbor. Her length almost exactly matched the gentle swells in the harbor—the same coincidence of natural period that caused the Tacoma Narrows Bridge—"Galloping Gertie"—to shake itself to pieces in 1940.

King took a house in Long Beach and moved his family there from Annapolis. Elinor had agreed to obtain a divorce, and Heinlein was effectively a bachelor again; he resumed dating one of King's daughters. The fact that she was now his CO's daughter did weigh against her, but she was pretty and vivacious and fun to be around—and Heinlein needed a partner for the demanding social schedule of King's *Lexington*.[7] Ships' officers were expected to participate in the social life of the city, and the ship routinely gave formal balls, as well.

King was a very different person ashore and off-duty than he was on duty. Ashore he was friendly and cordial, with a natural warmth of expansive personality. On duty, he seemed . . . lonely.[8] He obviously chose that for himself, not inviting fraternization—in fact, only once in two years did King ever address a social, rather than business, remark to Heinlein while on duty.

"I think (sheer guesswork) that he judged it to be better for the ship for its commanding officer to hold himself aloof, remote from all those he commanded."[9] If that's what *Lexington* needed to come up to her potential, that was just what he would give her. King had an ironclad sense of duty. It was an inspiring example for a young naval officer who could see it, and King's manner fit exactly with Heinlein's old habits of driving himself more than he drove his subordinates. But King managed to do it, to get 110 percent out of his men, without alienating them. Heinlein had more to learn from King than shipboard procedure and tricks of positioning in formation. He paid close attention to every interaction and spent the next two years studying King as a model and mentor.[10] And with King his real schooling in Navy began—schooling in the management and shaping of men, psychological sculpture of the most delicate and complex kind.

Heinlein also took the opportunity in Long Beach to stock up on reading material—books and magazines. *Amazing Stories* had just started a serial by E. E. "Doc" Smith—"Skylark III"—in August. This was a sequel to "Skylark of Space," which had appeared while Heinlein was still a midshipman. "Skylark III" was even more engrossing. He risked taking the second installment one midwatch and reading it with one eye on the gauges.

He also confided to Cal Laning his decision to divorce Elinor after she would not join him in Greenwich Village. Their personal relationship had gone from bad to worse. Every contact with her was unpleasant, toxic:

> Barrett—I am delighted to hear from you. You may well have wondered at my conduct. It was partially emotional reaction not anger at you, although I cursed your stupidity. Well, Barrett, you remain my one true contact, I think. The truth is, I was attempting to handle a difficult situation with an hysterical woman, and am still concerned with it. I must get rid of Elinor. She is poisonous, like mistletoe. She is the most tumblebug of tumblebugs and desires nothing quite so sincerely. . . .
>
> I shall get rid of her presently and in so doing get rid of my family, Kansas City, and all that that implies.[11]

He had finally accepted that it just wasn't working and wasn't ever going to work. Divorce was the only answer.

As a practical matter, Robert would let Elinor start the proceedings (though he could certainly have sued for divorce on grounds of adultery). A man could more easily bear the loss of reputation that came with a divorce in 1930.

In September, *Lexington* sailed to San Francisco for some time in dry dock at Hunters Point. As they were docking, stem over the sill, Heinlein took a call reporting a fire in one of the ammunition magazines. He sounded the General Alarm and reported it to King, who kept his eyes locked on the bow and simply said to him in an ordinary tone of voice, "Take care of it."

Heinlein was startled and terrified at the responsibility King had suddenly dumped in his lap—but he also knew King was doing the correct thing; his responsibility lay with the docking, and his professional behavior depended on his moral values. They put out the fire, but he also learned a long-term lesson from King: that is how you handled moral conflicts. "It is only necessary to know what your moral standards are, and why, and then have the guts to carry out the answers."[12] When you know what is important, you can make the right choices about what you must attend to and when.

About this time, another of Heinlein's classmates, Clayton McCauley, rejoined *Lexington*'s flight squadron, fresh out of flight school at Pensacola, and all the pilots who had reported in at the same time last June were back together. Heinlein knew them all, of course: Buddy Scoles was his best friend on the ship, except possibly for Bob Clark, and Scoles was the only one who shared Heinlein's passion for rockets and spaceflight. Scoles and he shared the science-fiction magazines and talked about interplanetary rockets on board the Navy's most expensive, most high-tech vessel run by the latest computers— and then Buddy Scoles, Denbo, McCauley, and the rest went out in canvas-winged mosquitoes.

Lexington carried many types of aircraft—typically eighty to ninety at a time, depending on the models that were assigned to her. Some were land-based planes; others were amphibious, charged with rescuing any of the land-based planes that went into the water, as happened occasionally. Very little aircraft research and design was done specifically for the military in those days; the civilian market drove the design, with the military using and adapting civilian designs.

The plane Heinlein was most familiar with was the Martin T4M—a new, canvas-winged Torpedo bomber biplane with a top speed of ninety knots. Landing these planes was tricky at best—Heinlein later called the process a "controlled crash."[13] The basic method involved a pilot standing on the deck with "wigwag" signal flags, telling the pilot his height and pitch of approach. The airborne pilot dropped speed to about twenty knots relative to the deck and came in. A metal hook on the plane caught an "arresting wire" stretched across the deck. Tension in the wire would slow the plane, very smoothly, to a stop with an even, uniform deceleration, and then the wire released as the plane stopped and moved automatically back into its rest position.

If all went well.

Twice while King had *Lexington,* a pilot came in too low and dropped the plane into the sea—or the sea had reached up and grabbed it, which comes to the same thing. The swells could be treacherous. But King lost no pilots. Nor were the pilots reprimanded. There were no instruments at all in the airplanes of 1930, and the ocean swells, which can cut a plane's relative altitude from plus to minus in seconds, often could not be seen from the flight deck. It was a nerve-racking, gut-grabbing, unavoidable hazard of the job. A pilot's first carrier landing was always traumatic, and baby pilots often earned "diaper diplomas" if their bladders cut loose when they discovered they had made it down alive.

Night landings were worse.

During the off-hours, Heinlein was still making engineering sketches of the ship's systems. Over the summer his marks were uniformly good to excellent, but the change of quarter brought him under a new department. Now he was expected to know how to fix the ship's systems he had been sketching and even suggest reengineering improvements. One of his supervising officers, T. B. Thompson, made his first caustic comments in Heinlein's sketchbook on September 16, 1930: "Examined. Perfunctory. Last assignment is not so thorough as the first. Average mark 3.0"—and then below that "seen 22 September 30," signed E.J.K.—Captain King. Heinlein would have to work harder to keep up his marks. He had received a flat 4.0 rating in all respects for his first quarter under King, and he wanted to keep it that way.

Perhaps Heinlein's less-than-perfect study efforts that fall can be attributed to domestic stress at long distance: Elinor had finally filed for divorce in October in the Jackson County (Missouri) Circuit Court, citing abandonment and cruelty.[14] The matter was heard on October 15, 1930, Elinor and her attorney appearing. Robert was at sea, so he was represented only by his attorney from Harding, Murphy & Tucker.[15] The court's minute order dated October 15, 1930, granted Elinor her petition for divorce and returned her maiden name to her. She was assessed the costs of the proceedings—but the court ordered Robert to make the actual payment.[16] There is no indication that this is an interlocutory decree; the whole matter is handled in this one set of documents.[17]

Heinlein pulled up his socks and soldiered on: his engineering sketchbook up to December shows a balance of approving comments by ERJ (otherwise unidentified) and very negative comments by T. B. Thompson, punctuated by "perfunctory" and "disappointing." Thompson's comments gradually improved—grudgingly. King left no comments in the sketchbook—and Heinlein's fitness reports continued a flat 4.0.

Thompson's down on Heinlein might not have been personal; there was trouble on the bridge, and the watchstanders were all tense. Merrill Comstock's tour as *Lexington*'s navigator was up, and King was not satisfied—*very* not satisfied—with Comstock's replacement. When King noticed too much difference (for shiphandling purposes) between the logged positions and the navigator's daily fixes, he quietly began taking some sights himself. Seeing the captain's fixes entered in the log just once would probably send the navigator to his cabin to write the one-line request for "any ship, any station" that would get immediate attention from the Bureau of Naval Personnel (BuPers). This was repeated three times until King was satisfied with his fourth replacement navigator, Commander Deems.

Heinlein was given more and broader miscellaneous duties this quarter. As ship's Aide, he was put in charge of *Lexington*'s internal newspaper, *The Observer*. Exec. Hoover's name was on the masthead as editor, but, Heinlein found, Hoover did not so much "edit" as merely censor the text, to assure that the paper only reported good news.[18] This forced Heinlein to extend his grapevine throughout the ship for enough news to fill the paper. If his grapevine failed, he would have to write uncredited filler. In addition to news items of local (shipboard) interest, Heinlein was assigned to write "The Weekly Retrospect" (sometimes titled "News of the Week"), a continuing "department" of *The Observer* that always contained a few paragraphs summarizing the week's events. For the most part, these regular columns are unremarkable as the early work-product of an accomplished writer—except that they show a self-conscious grappling with the conventions of "society" reporting of the time. Most of the prose is strictly utilitarian, but from time to time a suggestion of Heinlein's later, more polished prose rings out, as in the observation that concludes his August 8, 1931, column, complaining about having to get up early: "In any case a man who arises late will never be shot at sunrise."[19] This earlier column is typical:

"Events of the Week":
This week has been almost exclusively devoted to recreation, recuperation, and rest. We anchored off Panama City early Saturday following the completion of Fleet Problem XII. . . .

The three holidays were put to good use. All hands were rather weary after the strenuous mimic war and a little relaxation was in order. Ashore we found a great many tars and jollies from His Majesty's Ship *Nelson.* The spirit of good fellowship that existed between our own men and those of the Royal Navy was something pleasant to see. Little or no friction was evident whereas mixed groups of Britishers and Americans could be seen chumming together at every corner and every bar. We are very happy to have our cousins with us. For those who did not care for the ephemeral delights of shore-going in the tropics, swimming parties were organized every day this week. . . . For a real thrill equal to parachute jumping or dodging quick tempered husbands, we recommend putting your trust in a rubber tube and going down to see the fishes. . . .

H.M.S. *Nelson* is now at the dock near the fleet landing just beyond the "Texas." She is quite different from our ships in many respects. Her severe box-like lines and clear upper decks combined with her huge size and great free board give her a formidable fortress-like appearance. The unusual arrangement of all turrets forward and the bridge abaft of midships give her an unique silhouette. . . .

Please note again that all the turrets are forward. These Britishers intend to face the enemy, not run.

We have had some fun guessing at the British rating badges. The officers are easy to guess, being about the same as our own. The Petty Officer marks are more complicated. It appears that all petty officers except the most junior, wear that outfit similar to our commissioned officer's white service. The commissioned officers wear a double-breasted coat. Those chevrons on the men in the round hats and square collars signify good conduct not rank. The present writer won't swear to the accuracy of the above paragraph, but he was so informed by a man with twelve years service in the Royal Navy, practically a boot by their standards. Go aboard her. It is well worth the trouble. She has the prettiest and smartest paintwork in the world. She is in every way a trim ship to please the heart of a sailor.[20]

Lexington had her annual repair session in Bremerton, Washington, in December 1930. The ship stopped at San Francisco on the way north for two weeks of R & R, most of which was taken up by an unfortunate incident ashore. At a welcoming party for the *Lexington* officers, the wife of one of the aviators had died during a struggle to avoid rape. The Navy did not have jurisdiction—it was a civilian matter—but Captain King convened a court of inquiry ashore, taking Hoover with him and leaving his new navigator, Commander Deems, wearing three hats: Commanding Officer, Executive Officer, and Navigator. Since Heinlein knew all the ship's routines from his days working in the Executive Office, he would have to stay on board as Deems's Aide. The trial proceeded quietly, and the records were sealed, so Heinlein never did learn how it turned out.

On the approach to Bremerton, Bob Clark quietly passed him the word: if he wanted to see something interesting he should show up on the bridge as they approached the Narrows. This was King's first time through that tricky approach—and apparently his first time in Puget Sound. Curious, Heinlein studied the plot. It was dazzling: the passage was so tight in spots that "our Lady Lex really should have been hinged in the middle."[21]

Heinlein grabbed a spot on the flag bridge where he could see the navigator at about the same angle of view as the Captain had. On this occasion, King took the conn himself; when the ship came through without touching, there was a long sigh—soft but very audible, as it came from so many.

> King did not seem to hear it. He relieved the exec, turned the conn back to the navigator, went to his fold-down seat on the port (flight deck) wing, sat down and simulated a passenger enjoying the pleasant sight of a scenic channel.[22]

Very Wet Stuff of him.

Heinlein had been in Seattle the previous winter, when *Lexington* was supplying power for Tacoma, but now he was going to be there long enough really to get acquainted with the city. The Junior Officer Mess again clubbed together to rent a house and made some interesting alterations: they got a keg of whiskey installed in the attic and replumbed the house so that the liquor flowed in the taps. That was making whoopee, Navy style. He also learned to homebrew beer, which was legal (when done for personal use) even under Prohibition.

He found Seattle as open and bawdy in some ways as Kansas City.

> I recall one occasion, in what was then Seattle's second-best hotel (not the Olympic), when a young lady (who had possibly had a bit to drink) came wandering out of a booth in the dining room dressed in high heels and a sleepy smile. No real fuss was made about it; the waiter just shooed her back into her booth (the "two warm spoons" technique)—nor did the other diners make any fuss. . . . I did recognize her, I had met her socially

on another occasion. Her family was wealthy and lived on the "right" hill in Seattle.[23]

A bit of the Wild West lumber town still clung to Seattle in the 1920s and 1930s, and the cultural shaking up of the country's first sexual revolution of the twentieth century suited it—and suited Heinlein as well:

Shucks, I can testify that at least several of the sorority houses at the University of Washington had each a room on the ground floor where the lights were never lighted, where there were plenty of sofas, and the most the house mother ever did was to come to the door and announce the time at curfew on week nights—not at all on week ends.[24]

With the new year, the Chief Gunner was transferred out of *Lexington,* and Ensign Heinlein became the *de facto* chief Fire Control Officer. He would be transferred formally from the Communications Department to the Gunnery Department in July. In February 1931, though, the fleet held a war game off the coast of Peru and Ecuador, and he shuttled around between departments, at one point even being detached from the ship. On the second day of the exercise, *Lexington* was ordered toward the Galapagos Islands and out of the main action. King was irritated by the diversion—but belowdecks the more experienced sailors were delighted, for this side trip would allow them some unscheduled fun initiating the new guys ("Pollywogs") in a King Neptune's court, a kind of oceangoing Carnivale traditionally held whenever a ship crosses the equator.

Just short of the equator, however, Captain King turned *Lexington* about and back to the fleet. At midday, they received word that an "enemy" carrier—the USS *Langley*—had been spotted to the northeast. Captain King decided to launch everything at once, forty-six ships. Suddenly Heinlein, who was working the—voice—radio contact with his flight squadrons' guard planes, found himself with four squadrons in the air at the same time and under radio silence.

All had to be back before sunset according to fleet regulations, but the scouting squadron had not located any of the flight squadrons by late in the afternoon. Things got a little tense on the bridge as dusk approached. Most of the pilots had not been checked out for night landings, and they *had* to be found before nightfall. King stood to lose thirty-one aircraft on his first big operation.

Three of the squadrons were back when Heinlein finally established radio contact with the fourth. Coincidentally, Buddy Scoles was piloting the guard plane for that squadron. They had somehow fouled up their dead reckoning and were lost. Heinlein recognized the situation immediately: the same thing had happened to him on a training flight near Hawaii. Now Heinlein was on the other end of the radio.

The signal strength indicated they were at least fifty miles over the horizon. Heinlein rotated the loop antenna trying to find a minimum (zero) for the signal strength. But the signal was zero over too wide an arc—twenty or thirty degrees. He gave them the best homing vector he could guess—but they were separated by a lot of ocean: Scoles described the sea conditions as Beaufort Three—whitecaps on the waves. The sea around *Lexington* was almost calm, with gentle swells: they were far enough away to have different weather. Not good—and there was nothing anyone could do about it.

As night fell with tropic suddenness, they got the last transmission from the squadron, preparing to ditch. It was night where the *Lexington* was, but still dusk where the squadron was. That fixed the direction—but it might be too late. Suddenly, the sky lit up with searchlights from every ship in the fleet that carried them—the radio silence had been canceled to save the squadron. The squadron saw the lights and homed in on the fleet. They were coming in with very low fuel reserves, but they all got in safely—"although one did sort of bend his prop around the crash barrier."[25] Buddy Scoles was the last to come in, since he was in a seaplane with pontoon and could land on the water if necessary. His engine coughed and died just as his tailhook caught the wire, and he brought it in dead-stick. He had made it with no margin at all. The commander of the flight squadron reported to King that evening. "Where in the hell have you been?" was all that King said.

At some point during this exercise, Hoover was detached from the ship so he could umpire the fleet problem, Heinlein acting as his assistant. This detachment was a paper transfer; they stayed aboard *Lexington* while they processed the paperwork. This put Heinlein on the bridge virtually all the time for three days in a row, since Hoover allowed him to go below to eat and/or nap only at irregular intervals. King never seemed to leave the bridge for any reason. He probably never slept at all during that problem.

Fleet Problem XII ended close to Panama City. Heinlein raced to bathe, shave, eat, get into civilian clothes, and catch the first boat—but the Captain's gig splashed first and Captain King was first ashore.

Early in the evening, Heinlein saw Captain King in the back lounge of Marie Kelly's Ritz Bar. Four or five hours later he returned and found King still there, at the same table, alone, though his private bottle of Dewar's

White Label was half empty. Captain King looked up, said, "Sit down, Heinlein. What will you have to drink?" Nervous, Heinlein made polite conversation and noted that King invited every officer who looked in to have a drink. Over the course of the evening, he would host nearly every officer ashore that way. After a while, King let him go genially, to stir around a bit and have some fun. They met up again around dawn, when King found Heinlein and Bob Clark waiting for the shuttle back to Lex, and King invited them to ride back with him and the executive in the Captain's gig. King was alert and apparently sober, even though he must have consumed the better part of a bottle of whiskey.

A few days later, Heinlein was again detached from the ship and sent to Fort Clayton in the Panama Canal Zone to compete in fleet rifle and pistol matches. He was a little rusty, so he had a coach for the shooting—a small (roughly 120-pound), wiry Sergeant of Marines named Deacon—"all rawhide and a face suitable to a bible-belt deacon and a manner to match."[26] Deacon taught him things about the rifle that weren't in the book—how to rely on his instincts, his rifle sense. He also taught Heinlein things about handling men that complemented what he was learning from King. No one ever heard Deacon use bad language or raise his voice—"he didn't need to, as he was widely known to be the toughest non-com around—sudden death, armed or unarmed."[27] And he had the same kind of undefinable presence that King had—just being there, he would steady the men he was coaching. The whole team's performance rose from mediocre to exceptional. He kept Heinlein firing in the black all that day.

Heinlein often got back from Panama City to his accommodations at Fort Clayton long after taps. The Navy camp was well separated from the Army regiment stationed there, and the base swimming pool was very inviting. The highly flexible and nuanced view of the rules and regulations he was learning from King and now from Deacon, too, gave him a very pragmatic approach to such things. He knew his team captain didn't care so long as he racked up a high score on the rifle range, and he wasn't responsible to anyone else at Fort Clayton. He stripped naked and swam in the warm water, in the moonlight, until he was completely relaxed and ready for bed.[28]

Lexington must have transited the Panama Canal without him. Sometime after he rejoined the ship, he had a bout of flu and, about ten days later—in late February or early March, though the specific date was not recorded—he noticed the first signs of a urethral infection: a clear drop in the morning that wasn't urine and ought not to be there. In the military, one is always alert to the possibility of venereal disease, but in this case it wasn't: no organisms

were found in the fluid or in a prostate smear. It was just an infection—
"nonspecific urethritis." He was treated with protargol and neosilvol and
some clear astringent, and the problem went away in a couple of months, by
itself.[29]

On the morning of March 31, *Lexington* was standing off Guantánamo
Bay, readying for an admiral's inspection, when they received emergency orders from Washington, D.C.: at 10:10 A.M. an earthquake measuring 5.6 on
the Richter scale struck Managua, Nicaragua. Within seconds, 2,400 people
were killed outright, and several thousand more were injured. Property damage was estimated at $15 million to $30 million in 1931 dollars, and 35,000
were left homeless over ten square kilometers. *Lexington* was to head directly
to Managua and help with the relief efforts. By that time King had the ship
in such a state of readiness that they had the admiral's inspection out of the
way and were under way in less than forty minutes, making no special preparations and leaving their shore parties behind. What the 35,000 homeless
needed most was fresh water. All hands were ordered not to bathe until further notice and to be sparing in use of fresh water for any purpose until the
evaporative condensers could refill the fresh-water tanks.

A month later, in May 1931, Captain King made Heinlein ship's Aide in
charge of the Executive Office—a responsible administrative position. Although nominally under the Executive Officer, Hoover, Heinlein was brought
into nearly daily contact with Captain King and got an insider's view of
King's operating style. King, he found, really *meant* that old chestnut about
the ship being a home as well as a combat vessel and lived by it, taking unusual care for the quality of meals and amenities provided his crew—all of
them, from flight officers to able seamen.[30] And he had the Navy Way deeply
ingrained in him, as his inspection policy demonstrated immediately.

Lexington was too large to be inspected by the Captain once a week. Instead, there were six inspection tours, and when it came time to inspect officers' country, the Captain would discreetly send his orderly to present his
compliments to the President of the Mess and say that he intended to make
an informal inspection in about twenty or thirty minutes. This gave them
time to get embarrassing items out of sight.

And there were embarrassing items. The routine disorder might include
"improper" magazines or even open bottles of liquor—absolutely forbidden
during Prohibition. If any officer had been so indiscreet as to leave a bottle
of liquor out, the Captain would not "see" it during his inspection—but the
matter would be dealt with officer-to-officer.

There were more serious matters to conceal, though, than liquor. The JO smoking room, a large separate compartment in Junior Officer country, was used for gambling that included the ship's Marines and the aviators. Heinlein used to say that his birth date—7/7/7—gave him luck at craps. But poker was his game, and he supplemented his ensign's salary as a card mechanic, teaching aviators with too much money and too little card sense to figure the odds, what poker was all about: "I used a cold-blooded two-pocket system and could count on ca. $100 profit anytime I was willing to lose a night's sleep to get it."[31] What with the legal expenses of his divorce, he must occasionally have needed that extra $100.

King's warning gave the officers time to get all the gambling clutter tidied out of the way. Inspection, too, it seemed, was one of King's tools to tighten up *Lexington*. A ship's readiness is almost entirely made up of small matters concatenated together. Knowing that you are prepared for anything translates from Saturday morning inspection to confidence in the field and in emergency and battle situations. A ship that is not ready at all times is useless to the country, and it was King's first job to get *Lexington* ready for anything, anytime.

Almost the first thing Heinlein discovered as ship's Aide was that Captain King's inspections were not the once-over-lightly thing he had imagined. After each inspection, King would send Hoover a detailed memorandum listing the tiniest details of less-than-perfect ship's housekeeping. Heinlein would break the information down into departments and prepare memoranda from Executive Officer to department heads for Hoover's signature. This confirmed the conclusion Heinlein had reached about King in the Bremerton Narrows incident: King always looked unhurried and unworried, but he worked very hard, anticipating anything that could go wrong and paying attention to every detail—even the ones he seemed not to notice at the time. That was just exactly what Heinlein wanted for himself. King expected perfect performance from his subordinates—and got it: "I find a boss who consistently requires highest performance much easier to work for than one who blows both hot & cold. As for the third sort, who are satisfied always with poor performance—I quit!"[32]

Heinlein learned a great deal about the technique of administration. Both the Executive Officers he worked under tacitly encouraged him to try occasionally to initiate policy. He would prepare paperwork involving a change in policy and then send it up without discussing it first with the Execs. Sometimes it would be signed without discussion (and he would feel smug about it—he was learning the ropes, after all). Sometimes, however, Hoover would send it back with a curt written comment telling him where and how he had erred. The next Executive Officer, V. D. Herbster, would send for him and discuss it more fully in person, explaining things he understood but Heinlein did not.

Discipline worked both ways with King, as Heinlein shortly came to see. As part of his duties as Ship's Aide, he prepared the Captain's daily Mast—effectively the Captain holding court and dispensing justice. In a ship as large as *Lexington,* Captain's Mast would be held daily while in port, two or three times a week while at sea. The Mast would be *very* large after a weekend on R & R—fifty or more cases at a time. In court, King was extremely strict and by-the-book: ten days bread and water, remanded for summary—thirty days' restriction, deck court, maximum of extra duty, and so on. Each sentence would be "accompanied by oral chewing out, each of which was a literary gem. No profanity, no salty slang, all just loud enough to be heard by everyone present, always grammatical, never repetitious—words that cut like strokes of the cat."[33]

As soon as King stood up and left, indicating he was finished for the day, Heinlein went directly to his office. After ten or fifteen minutes, Captain King would call him to send up the various offenders' service records. So predictable was this that Heinlein always had the files ready on his desk, with a messenger standing by. Then he waited—arranging for a late lunch if necessary—until King called him to his cabin, looking ten or fifteen years older. He had made some changes to the sentencing: punishments for first offenders changed to warnings, sentences chopped in half and suspended, and so forth. Publicly he threw the book—and that was the word that got on the grapevine; then privately and singly, and therefore not as quickly on the grapevine, if at all, Captain King handed out extremely gentle sentences, ones that rarely marred a man's official record enough to slow up his promotions. King also used the occasion to review the man's service record, spotting anomalies that might have contributed to the offense. He took an interest in each man as an individual—ordinary seaman just as much as his officers—and had a remarkable memory.

King discouraged overuse of the more formal discipline methods, but serious matters did come up occasionally, and for this purpose officers were assigned to defend the men at court. Heinlein was assigned the extra duty of preparing cases, prosecuting, and defending accused men. Heinlein understood immediately that his job was to mount the most vigorous defense he could think of—and he was very good at thinking of defenses. He was much in demand because he never lost a case while King was in the ship, even when King knew the man was guilty and Heinlein knew the man was guilty, since he made a point to extract the unvarnished truth from his "client," so that he would never be taken by surprise and not be able to defend him properly. The prosecuting officers rarely looked beneath the surface and did not study the rules, particularly those governing evidence. Heinlein did.

Seamen lead notoriously irregular lives, and maritime law to a certain extent treats seamen as if they are irresponsible adolescents—a vicious and self-perpetuating cycle. It was an eye-opening experience for Heinlein, throwing him into direct contact with personal foibles he must have known about only from reading. It threw into high contrast the degree of self-discipline that he had naturally and which was encouraged of Academy graduates and naval officers.

That discipline has to come from inside; it can't be imposed from the outside. In some respects, confinement was worse than useless:

> With respect to . . . locking a man in jail, [my opinion] arose from having sat in all three positions in court—as a prosecutor, as counsel for the defense and as a member of the court. . . . I've never in my life seen a man rehabilitated by putting him in the stockade or the brig.[34]

Heinlein's personal distaste for confinement—honed by his own days in the Academy's brig and its durance comparatively less vile—was very great.

> . . . everything I have seen leads me to believe that confinement, even the mild confinement of the brig, is bad for a man, demoralizing. But, time and again, because of the law, I was forced to sentence a man to brig or prison. I hated it so much that I served as defense counsel whenever I could—and got many a guilty man off, acquitted. Whereupon I would talk to him privately, tell him that if he did not behave himself in the future, I would take him apart with my bare hands . . . which I could do in those days (and could still take a stab at it; skill at dirty fighting does not drop off with age the way skill at boxing does—unexpectedness counts more than endurance).
>
> Quite a few of those boys I did rehabilitate, after getting them acquitted. But if they had been sent to building 46 at Mare Island to break rocks, they would have been ruined for life. One offense, even a serious one (short of rape and murder and the like) does not mean that a man is useless; he may simply be young and foolish, with a poor capacity for liquor. . . . But two years up the river and you might as well have shot him in the first place.

Even thirty days in the brig is likely to ruin him for military service; his vulnerable and utterly necessary pride is damaged.[35]

Effective punishment would ideally be immediate and then over and done with:

I am still convinced today that official punishment is rarely of real service in producing a fighting man and that a report for misconduct points to some neglect or professional flaw in the officer in charge of that man . . . a regulation concerning conduct works best when one does not have to invoke it.[36]

The top-down discipline King had imposed was relatively minor—and the exceptions were more significant than the rule. Everything King had done simply framed the circumstances so that the temptations to relax one's self-discipline, at every level of the ship, were removed or minimized. Once each officer returned to peak performance, then all the other departures from strict regulation were trivial, unimportant—so long as the boys did not think they were getting away with something. That was bad for self-discipline. Discipline does not come from externals and organization—though clarity and appropriateness of organization and externals can help; it comes from within each individual performing his duty as it is given him. Success breeds success.

There is, of course, a downside to the double standard, leaving the Navy officer corps open to charges of elitism and, later, in World War II, of running their own little empire in the Pacific. But the double standard was a custom over the whole country at that time and that place. King made it work by evenhandedly enforcing both sides of the standard. When a cook came to Mast over leave and King found that he had been delayed by a corrupt small-town policeman who claimed a straggler's reward, King rousted out the Federal District Attorney, the county District Attorney, the mayor of that town, and his own court personnel to get the message across that this villainous practice would cease immediately.

Captain's Mast is for rewards as well as punishment, and King consistently praised his men when their job was done to his satisfaction. Heinlein and Chief Schmidt and their Yeoman Second Class, Williams, once received a commendation for processing the hundreds of fleetwide annual examinations without any errors. Heinlein put Schmidt and Williams on the list for Mast the next day—and then had to assure the yeoman that he was not in trouble.

Heinlein tried to emulate King—but practice had not yet made perfect: he was still too heavy-handed about it, as he found out when he overheard his nickname among the crew—"Navy Joe" or "Military Joe" Heinlein.[37]

Several things were coming together in his life. He was filling several respectable and responsible positions in the Navy; he was learning fast under someone he considered a master in all the skills he needed to possess.

In the fall of 1931, after a severe cold, he had a recurrence of that nonspecific urethritis that had bothered him in the spring. This time it was more severe. It was diagnosed as prostate infection of *Myxococcus catarrhalis,* treated with cold serum plus "some syringe-injected drug for a short period, and by prostate massage (continued for four months) . . . sitz baths and diathermy."[38] He also had his tonsils out, to cut down the constant colds and respiratory infections—a minor operation for a child, but at the age of twenty-four, somewhat more serious and debilitating.

By Christmastime his medical problems were pretty much behind him, and he took a quick trip to Kansas City to clean up several outstanding matters. That was the first time he participated in what had become a sad family ritual: before breakfast on Christmas mornings, the family took roses to Rose Elizabeth's grave. Rex Ivar was so deeply affected by her death that the family never owned a car again.[39]

Heinlein canceled the telephone subscription in his name and returned the lease on the room to Elinor. Within a couple of years, Elinor had left the room on Sixty-ninth Street. No trace of her can be found in Kansas City after 1934.[40]

He saw family, of course, while he was there. The Depression had already hit hard. Lawrence told him he was lucky to have a career in the Navy, where he probably would never be called on to fire into a crowd of his neighbors.[41] That was a chilling likelihood with the Army Reserve and the National Guard.

Heinlein returned to San Pedro. That sordid episode of his first marriage was at last over, and he was a free man, only slightly soiled. The *Oklahoma* was ported at San Pedro over the holidays, and he had a chance to look up Cal Laning. This would be Laning's last winter on the Okie, as he was going into submarine work. Laning had some news to report: he had been stirring around, poaching on Heinlein's old stomping ground at Columbia Pictures, and he had come up with a girl Heinlein had missed.

12

LESLYN MACDONALD

Laning was positively aglow about his new girl, Leslyn MacDonald, in January 1932—very unusual for that casual and enthusiastic sex-hound. Heinlein was curious to meet this find of Laning's.

Leslyn MacDonald, Laning told him, was Boston born and California raised, nearly three years older than they, which made her just twenty-six at the start of 1932. She was a very slim, intense dark-brunette with medium complexion, lively and attractive, not quite five feet, one inch tall—which made her just right for Laning, who was on the short side himself. She was an unusual woman—astonishingly intelligent, widely read, and extremely liberal, though a registered Republican. She had taken a master's degree in philosophy in 1930 at the University of Southern California and had high school teaching credentials in history and public speaking. Between her undergraduate degree (also in philosophy, with a minor in drama) and the master's, she had acted in several productions of the 1927 theatrical season of the Pasadena Playhouse and even directed two workshop productions of experimental theater.[1] She was a published writer, with short poems in the *Los Angeles Times* as early as 1920 and 1921.[2] *World Theosophy Magazine*—her mother, Skipper, was a Theosophist[3]—had published a poem of hers, "The Great Mother," in April 1931:

> So I lay dreaming in the grass awhile
> And felt the earth beneath my outstretched hands;
> This was the mother-heart that understands,
> The fertile earth with her unchanging smile.
> I felt her veins go pulsing mile on mile
> Under the fragrant flesh of all her lands,
> Over high-breasted mountains and smooth sands
> As down long limbs of continents they file.

I felt my fingers trembling in the grass,
A burning summer's wind has blown along;
My heart began to beat with that great mass
Of vibrant living, and I burst in song,
Leapt to my feet, and felt my languor pass.
The earth awoke in me and made me strong.[4]

Her most recent placement was, of all things, a football poem for a collection of sports-related poetry to be published in 1933: "Before the Game" appeared in *The Sportsman's Hornbook*, edited by Charles Grayson:

Blue was the autumn sky, and gold the sun,
Color and space and beauty everywhere.
The massive oval shone with living green,
And through the coliseum arches rose
The splendor of a park in bronze and flame.

A blare of music flung the senses high,
Into the limitless reach beyond the rim.
And thrillingly, a-sudden on the field
A score of supermen ran out for play.
Even the opponents gasped a bit for pride
That nature had made men so beautiful.

Suddenly one, more perfect than the rest,
Sprang out alone upon the wedge of green,
Poised like a dancer, swung, and kicked. The ball
Made a great sweeping arc and, curving, fell
Into the arms of a runner on the field.
O, singing harmony of rippling limbs
And power of body perfect for its work.
O, space of walls and height of glorious sky
And white gulls floating over burnished trees.
When all the race are giant-gods like these,
Then will the wings of men beat at the stars.

Leslyn had worked her way up to Assistant Director of the Music Department at Columbia Pictures (and she was rumored to moonlight as a story doctor). That explained why Heinlein had not met her before. Social life in

Los Angeles meant the movie business, but he had been dating mostly starlet and administrative types. Leslyn wasn't in the talent or administrative end of the business.

Surprisingly, given her other accomplishments, she was also skilled with needlework and had supported herself for a year by teaching knitting, crocheting, tatting, and other fancy work.[5]

Laning's description made Leslyn MacDonald sound like a real Renaissance woman. Laning was seriously thinking of proposing marriage to her, after only a few dates, and wanted Heinlein's opinion.[6] Heinlein went with Laning to meet Leslyn and found Laning's report, if anything, understated. She *was* a touch on the dramatic side—she wore costumelike clothing and habitually flung draping cloths over her shoulders in a dramatic gesture—but she was intelligent, highly intelligent, and ahead of him in some respects. She had a better grounding in philosophy than he did—and genuine insight, which can't be faked. Her opinions on communism, for example, were sound (she was against it), and she had good things to say about the usefulness of a military career. She even had mystical leanings.[7] They were very compatible.[8]

Laning left the two of them together, and they wound up in bed together that night—possibly even by prior arrangement with Laning, who may have intended to have a Companionate marriage himself. It was not so surprising, under the circumstances, that he might begin by sharing his wife-to-be with his best friend. What Laning could not have anticipated was that Heinlein would jump the gun on him: Laning joined them the next morning, and Heinlein shocked both of them silly by proposing marriage to Leslyn in front of him.[9]

Heinlein had already formed the pattern of making decisions quickly and acting on them with speed, but this was precipitous even for him. Some of the factors that may have gone into this decision can be guessed at: he must have seen the possibility that this attractive, intelligent woman could make the kind of life with him that he wanted for himself. In this he may have been working out the epiphany he had touched with Mary Briggs three years earlier. His marriage to Elinor Curry—also precipitate—had not worked out well, but Leslyn didn't seem to have the same kind of emotional problems Elinor Curry had. She could be a real companion in life, someone who shared his own interests, and they could grow and develop together.

Leslyn was startled, but she accepted on the spot. Laning was dumbfounded—but he knew Heinlein, and he knew that Heinlein was known to be led about by the little head.[10]

What Leslyn found in him is a little more problematical. She must have found him intensely attractive, for the usual reasons: a handsome man who knows what he wants from a woman can be very persuasive. Also, he was intensely intelligent, possibly the brightest man she had ever met—and he had this undefinable *something* about him. . . .

It also could not have hurt that he obviously looked up to her intellectually and offered her the opportunity to shape him, as willing clay. This may have been wishful thinking on her part (as it almost always is).

But Heinlein had an extra dimension that came out in his relationships with women: sex was, to him, almost a religious rite, a rite of joy: in the secular and materialist twentieth century, he was—intense. Leslyn was, beyond doubt, utterly charmed by him.

Leslyn passed what must have been her first real test when she agreed to go with Robert: he would be going to Bremerton in April for the usual long layover in Washington while *Lexington* was being repaired and outfitted. Leslyn agreed to quit her job with Columbia Pictures and close up her apartment in Los Angeles. They would get something more permanent when *Lexington* returned to home port in Long Beach.

Robert and Leslyn had a brief but intense engagement. She did not drive, but Robert arranged outings when she was not at work—picnics, when the weather was good (not often in January and February in Los Angeles, when rain is often ankle-deep above the drains and punctuated with hail)—and outings to see the construction for the Los Angeles Memorial Coliseum, which was being expanded for the 1932 Olympics. They went also to places like Laguna Beach, where she had friends from college such as Elcy Arnold, wife of the actor Edward Arnold II.

Heinlein read to her the serialization of John Taine's *The Time Stream*, then appearing in four installments (December 1931 through March 1932) in *Science Wonder Stories*. "John Taine" was the pen name of the mathematician Eric Temple Bell, and Heinlein particularly wanted to discuss the theory of time Bell was putting forth, discarding the use of "past" and "present" and "future" except as conveniences of perspective of the observer—a relativistic approach that tried to grapple with this business about space and time and the fourth dimension. Heinlein had been interested in the implications of n-dimensional geometry for everyday life for a very long time.

It was probably Leslyn, out of her background in philosophy, who suggested he look into Ouspensky's *Tertium Organum* to supplement his reading of Dunne and Wells on the subject. Ouspensky had started from Kant's critical idealism in 1912 and went on to Einstein-Minkowski space-time very early on. Ouspensky presented a unification of philosophy and science—and art and religion, too—just the kind of thing Heinlein and Laning and Gus Gray had been looking for in their Quest.[11]

Late in January Heinlein joined the new American Interplanetary Society that had been formed in December 1931 in New York, with fourteen charter members. Heinlein had membership number 22. He told people about it in the Navy—Buddy Scoles, especially—and found that he was considered something of a "goof" because rockets were "crazy Buck Rogers stuff"— toys, at best.[12] The first bulletin he received from the society contained a report of a visit by Robert Esnault-Pelterie, of the Académie Française, saying he thought it might be possible to travel to the Moon and return as soon as fifteen years from now—1946.

That was a stunning thought: men walking on that airless surface within his lifetime. That he was a member of a group preparing the groundwork for it actually to come about could only have reinforced his sense of being among an elite, with special training and special knowledge to make the new world that was coming.

But he had his own part to do to make the new age. And now he would have a proper helpmeet. This time he was going into the marriage with eyes open. Leslyn was "advanced" and this suited her. She reregistered as a Democrat that year.[13]

The wedding would be on March 28, 1932. That would give her time to make arrangements for the formal ceremony she wanted. They couldn't afford anything really fancy, but her friends would pitch in, and he could have the traditional military displays that go along with such things. He left all the arrangements to her.

On February 1, 1932, *Lexington* got under way, up the coast, their eventual destination Hawaii for fleet exercises. Suddenly, the lid clamped down, and they made an unscheduled overnight stop in San Francisco's Hunters Point, under very strict secrecy. No liberty for crew, no shore leave for officers, no telephone calls at all. No mail was left for the ship. Nor did the radio shack accept messages.

They worked all night and into the next morning, unloading target ammunition and practice warheads, and taking aboard war ammunition and extra supplies of all sorts—real warheads. They topped off the oil, water, and aviation fuel and took aboard another squadron of thirty planes, pilots, crews for the planes. They were stocked well over their complement—120 planes instead of 90. There was news coming in by radio, but it went directly to Captain King—and he wasn't sharing it with his crew.

Lexington made full speed for Hawaii as soon as the supplies were aboard, under radio silence and Condition "B" once clear of the Bay. Tension increased throughout the ship. They were supposed to be headed for a fleet exercise, but clearly they were headed into a real fight, not just an exercise. Heinlein found himself demoted to Junior Officer of the Watch again. When they got to Honolulu, they joined the entire Pacific Fleet to take part in the annual Grand Joint Army and Navy Exercises.

Heinlein always thought there was something more to it, something that had never been talked about in print:[14] in February the Japanese had invaded China. This invasion was guarded by naval forces superior to the U.S.'s peacetime force, a clear violation of the Washington Naval Treaty. International tensions had been escalating ever since. President Hoover sent the Imperial Japanese government a warning to stop the invasion—and backed it up by assembling the Pacific Fleet within attack range. The Japanese backed down: they carved the enormous province of Manchuria away from China and installed the puppet Manchukuo regime in power, and there they stopped. That time.[15]

The U.S. Navy's war games continued, the Pacific Fleet splitting into Blue and Black teams[16] to run a simulated Japanese attack on Oahu. The Blacks defended and the Blues invaded. *Lexington* was in the Blue force; her sister aircraft carrier, *Saratoga,* carried the Admiral's flag for aircraft, commanded by Admiral Yarnell.

Japan now had the third-strongest Navy in the world, after the U.S. and Britain. The U.S. Navy had begun reevaluating the shipping and bases in the Pacific. The Naval War College had evolved a war scenario called "Plan Orange"[17] (which must have been the scenario Heinlein was briefed on while still at Annapolis). The Plan Orange scenario was based on the idea of a surprise attack—a favorite Japanese tactic that could produce devastating losses on the enemy. Plan Orange anticipated a surprise attack against Pearl Harbor, launched from aircraft carriers. *Lexington* and *Saratoga* ranged ahead of its battleship support and prepared to launch an air attack against Pearl.

Everyone had assumed the carriers would be detected and "sunk" by Black submarines or land-based planes long before they could get within range to launch their planes, but *Saratoga* evaded the Black patrol planes and came in northeast of Oahu in rain and squally winds. Once they launched their planes, the weather would carry them directly to Oahu; the pilots could roar through the rain clouds and burst into clear, sunny weather over Pearl Harbor . . . on Sunday morning, February 7, 1932.

Heinlein was scheduled to go up with Buck Brandley in a T4M as an observer for the attack. *Lexington* received an order to remain at complete darken ship in launching planes. He was startled when King burst into sulphurous profanity, "in approximately these censored words":

> "Deleted censored blank *blank*! I will *not* allow myself to be forced to have to write to the mother of some blank kid and explain to her how he got his censored head chopped off by a deleted prop of a blank plane he couldn't see in the dark and was too inexperienced to know how to avoid! No, by blank, I will *not!* What in the blank censored did the Admiral think this was? A war? It's a *drill* . . . and I won't have my men killed just for realism in a blank blank blankety drill!"[18]

Completely justified—with the extra flight squadron on board, the flight deck was a tightly packed jungle. All the illumination the flight crews had was the faint blue lights of engine exhaust. Pilots and crew wouldn't even have a chance to see the live propeller before they tripped and blundered into it.

They would be launching two hours before dawn—and Heinlein had no experience at all in nighttime operations.

But orders were orders.

Two hours before dawn, King turned on every floodlight on the flight deck, and kept them on until the last plane was in the air, directly defying Admiral Yarnell's orders from *Saratoga*—and destroying any chance he might have had for promotion to admiral.[19]

Legal orders are orders and must be obeyed—except when they must *not* be obeyed. That was the thorniest problem of the theory of command, one they worried over in bull sessions and class sessions at the Academy. But it could not be reduced to principles; it had to be tested in the contingency of battle.

> I was *proud* of the Old Man that night, he showed his bravery and his basic humanity . . . by taking his finger off his number for his men—with his flag almost in sight.[20]

Brandley and Heinlein's T4M went up in a combined launch of 152 planes from the *Saratoga* and the *Lexington*. An hour later, the planes came out of the storm front over the Koolau Range and into clear air over Pearl Harbor, where they "strafed" lines of planes parked on runways. The dive-bombers dumped twenty tons of theoretical explosives on airfields, ships in the anchorage, the Army headquarters at Fort Shafter, Schofield Barracks, and Hickam Field. It was a complete surprise: not a single fighter plane was launched from Pearl that morning. The aircraft squadron got back to their carriers almost without incident. It was twenty-four hours before the Black group even located them. They got Yarnell's flag a few days later when *Saratoga* was "bombed" from the air and ruled damaged by the Referee, Admiral Schofield.

At the postmortem critique conducted on the Grand Joint Exercise No. 4, on February 18, 1932, Admiral Yarnell argued that the successful attack on Pearl Harbor meant the Navy should reevaluate American naval tactics— but he was voted down by the majority of battleship admirals. The final report's conclusion was exactly the reverse of the actual experience:

> [I]t is doubtful if air attacks can be launched against Oahu in the face of strong defensive aviation without subjecting the attacking carriers to the danger of material damage and consequent great losses in the attack air force.[21]

If the lesson was lost on the U.S. Navy, Japanese observers filed a thorough report of the attack. This report would form the basis for the 1936 recommendation for surprise attack against Pearl Harbor made in the Japan Navy War College's "Study of Strategy and Tactics in Operations Against the United States."[22]

While in transit from Lahaina, all the Class of '29 ensigns received word that they would at last, in April, be given their examinations for promotion to lieutenant. Heinlein's physical examination was scheduled in two weeks. Captain King told him to prepare a book of extracts from confidential Navy circulars to make a study guide in Strategy and Tactics.

They returned to Long Beach, where they found waiting for them orders from the Department of the Navy to cooperate with Fox Movietone News, who wanted fifteen minutes of film of the crew of the *Lexington* at their morning exercises. Fox didn't tell King it would probably take two days to get that much usable film.

Normal ship's routine called for fifteen minutes of exercise in the morning. That would do. Heinlein was on top of the No. 2 turret helping the chief cameraman—he caught the sound camera in his arms once when a sudden roll pitched it off its tripod. They had gotten perhaps three minutes of usable film when Captain King appeared on deck and told the new Executive Officer, Herbster, to stop this "civilian nonsense" and put the men back to work. It was not surprising that the men dispersed, but the location company left without grumbling. Heinlein concluded that *anyone* recognizes the "voice of command" when he hears it.[23]

Leslyn and her best friend, Elcy Arnold, put together a very extravagant wedding—on no budget at all: Elcy loaned Leslyn the sumptuous gown and veil her mother had made for Elcy's own wedding—a white, floor-length, formal gown trimmed with lace, with long, close sleeves that emphasized her slim arms.

Elcy's mother was a caterer, and the cake was her wedding gift to Leslyn— "a 4-tier dream of confection and sentiment."[24] Elcy even corralled her youngest brother into helping out, sending him downtown to the Los Angeles Flower Mart early one morning to get a washtub full of daffodils, which she and Leslyn made into bouquets for the six bridesmaids and matrons, all friends from UCLA, including Elcy, Brita Bowen, and Mrs. Herbert Hayland. Leslyn's cousin Marion Beard was her matron of honor—a very fitting turnabout; Leslyn had helped engineer Marion's marriage, against their parents' wishes, to Chester Beard in 1922, when he was finishing up his chemical engineering degree at the University of Southern California (the MacDonalds had taken Marion in when her father died in 1910 or 1911, and her mother was not able to support her, so the girls had grown up together).[25] The day before the wedding, Elcy surprised Leslyn with two dozen Talisman roses, a gorgeously romantic sunset pink, for her bride's bouquet—a traditional choice of flowers for very formal weddings.[26]

Heinlein turned out the next morning in his most formal uniform, gold-braided Navy frock coat with cocked hat and saber. He had grown a neat Van Dyke beard—except that it was his first beard and had not come in evenly. It had "holidays" in it, areas where the hair had not grown as thick as the rest of the beard. He was accompanied by his closest friends from *Lexington,* also in frock coats and cocked hats. They formed an aisle under an arch of raised sabers for the couple. Dick Downer, an aviator from Davenport, Iowa, who had graduated from the Academy with Ivar, signed the marriage certificate as witness. Robert N. S. Clark, who had become one of Heinlein's best friends, was best man.[27] In the small group snapshot of the wedding party Heinlein put in his scrapbook, a short man in formal Naval uniform stands on his right. This may have been Cal Laning, about to be detached from *Oklahoma.* In later years, even with Laning's personal tendency to dramatize himself, all that was left was the periodic lament: "Robert stole my girl"[28] with a varying spice of irony, depending on how he felt at the time.

The honeymoon had to be short: *Lexington* was due in April for its annual overhaul in Bremerton, so Heinlein could get only six days of leave—and he had to take the medical part of his examination for promotion the day after the wedding. It was to be a working honeymoon, too.

Heinlein arranged to sublet an apartment in Seattle for six weeks. Leslyn would go up by train—she did not drive—and start making their first real home. Heinlein returned to *Lexington,* presumably a very happy man. The "supervisory professional examinations" for promotion took place on April 11, 1932. Heinlein was allowed—required—to handle the approach to the Strait of Juan de Fuca, in dense, nerve-racking fog, with only the slightest input from Captain King, who went belowdecks, leaving him with the conn.[29] His education as a naval officer continued to progress.

The Strategy and Tactics studying he had been doing for the promotion exam got him interested in the subject, and he applied to the War College for a correspondence course. They sent him the first two installments, and he began working on the course in the apartment he and Leslyn sublet for their stay.

All the bachelors of the steerage had again rented a farmhouse far out on the Sound, away from any prying eyes, and furnished it with scrounged furniture. Again they modified the plumbing so that the taps in the kitchen sink dispensed moonshine "cougar milk" from a barrel in the attic. They called it Stone Acres and hung two suggestive coconut shells as their road sign at the gate. Stone Acres was devoted—and "devoted" was just the word—to "drunken brawls"[30] each night, with marathon sessions each weekend. Robert and Leslyn were invited to at least one of those marathon brawls and knew what was going on—but so long as the boys kept the Eleventh Commandment wholly ("Thou Shalt Not Get Caught"), Heinlein would do nothing about it.

These junior officers got caught.

Two Seattle debutantes stayed at Stone Acres for a week or more. They had told their parents they were staying with Robert and Leslyn, a respectable married couple. If the girls had bothered to let Robert or Leslyn in on the secret, they would certainly have been very annoyed—it was at the very least an imposition—but, Robert said, he would nevertheless have rolled with the punch—"and lied to their parents to protect their (frail) reputations and to keep my messmates out of a jam, and I'm sure that [Leslyn] would have lied just as calmly and convincingly."[31]

The honor code forbidding an officer and gentleman to lie, cheat, or steal did not require him to impeach a woman's reputation. He would have preferred simply to stand mute—respectfully refuse to answer and accept the consequences: "I will not lie to a brother officer at any time and I will not lie under oath to anyone. But I can imagine circumstances under which I would refuse to answer."[32]

One of the girls' parents telephoned them while Robert was out, asking for their daughter. Caught off guard, Leslyn simply said that the girls were not staying with them and that she knew nothing about it. One or both sets of parents then hired a private detective to find their daughters—and the whole mess came to light and, more important, to Captain King's very public attention. Probably one of the parents had gone straight to King, as the junior officers' commanding officer.

If Robert and Leslyn had been given a chance to discuss the potential risk, they could have avoided the problem entirely:

[I]f these chuckleheads had warned me, they and the girls would never have been caught—[Leslyn] would have told the inquiring parent that the girls were "out shopping" or some such stall, then would have jumped into a taxi, rushed out to Stone Acres, grabbed the girls, taken them back to town, had them phone home, then seen to it that they caught the next ferry . . . and their silly coverup would have remained intact. Yes, I'm hypothesizing . . . but on other occasions for other girls she had covered matters far more difficult.[33]

On Monday morning when Heinlein reported back to *Lexington,* he found that almost the entirety of Steerage was under hack, except for two or three who, like himself, had wives and apartments in town. Suddenly, it was Heinlein's problem, too, since he was then president of the Junior Officers Mess.

King handled it very quietly. Since Heinlein was not directly involved with the investigation King conducted, he never knew the details, and nobody involved ever spilled the beans, either. But there were no records of orders about the confinement of the Junior Mess. Heinlein was not asked to prepare charges and specifications. The whole matter was handled orally, no reports at all once King ascertained that no serious crime had been committed—no kidnapping or rape—all adults, and the girls had gone there of their own volition, stayed because they wanted to stay, had been free to leave at any time.[34]

At that point, well, it was "damfoolishness all the way around"—youthful indiscretion—but not something that called for official discipline by the

Navy. King kept it from becoming an open scandal; he probably, Heinlein thought,[35] pointed out to the girls' parents that any major punishment to his junior officers would have to be based on sworn and public testimony by their daughters, and that was the end of that. Hack was quietly lifted; nothing was logged, nothing was said. Surprisingly, Heinlein even saw the girls later, at ship's social functions.

On June 6, 1932, exactly three years after his commissioning as ensign, Heinlein was promoted to lieutenant, j.g. (junior grade), and, with the increase in pay, began sending small sums home to his mother in Kansas City. A new assistant gunnery officer had joined *Lexington,* and Heinlein was given the title and responsibility for a turret division. That would look good on his records, as he was due to be rotated to another ship soon. But, with his quarterly fitness report, Heinlein found a recommendation from King that he be retained as *Lexington*'s gunnery officer.[36] That was an extraordinary compliment, but also an eminently sensible recommendation, as Heinlein was one of the very few men in the Navy trained—and very expensively—on the ballistic computer.

Captain King must have sent in a request of his own at about the same time.

In a sense, the Stone Acres crisis must have been the touchstone test for King's command. There was personal slackness involved—lack of good judgment, to be sure—but none of the officers involved had been even slightly derelict in the performance of their duties. He had been brought in to tighten up a slack ship, and within a few months after he took command, the Lady Lex was taut and humming, the fittest, happiest ship in the fleet, and winning fleet competitions of every sort. Morale was high. Captain King's work on *Lexington* was done.

King was relieved by Captain Blakely on June 10, 1932, without ceremony, as he had ordered. Captain Blakely came aboard and relieved him in civilian dress. King shook hands with the new Captain, saluted him, and requested permission to leave the ship. Five minutes or less later, he walked away.

I watched him walking down the dock. He seemed smaller in civilian clothes, older, and slightly stooped. He was carrying an overnight bag and that did not look right, either. He knew that he had just left his last ship . . . and must have known (as we all suspected) that he had tossed away his career, blown his chances for flag, by one act of defiance in refusing to endanger any man of his unnecessarily.[37]

The only recognition King would accept was a large scroll of appreciation for his unprecedented perfect flight-safety record, signed by every aviator who had flown under his care.

The Navy had not taken Captain King's recommendation to retain Heinlein as gunnery officer on *Lexington*. Nor did they grant Heinlein's request for duty in the Asia stations: on June 20, 1932, Heinlein received orders to transfer to the destroyer *Roper,* home ported in San Diego, ninety miles south of San Pedro. He reported in to his new billet on June 23, though he would still spend some weeks on *Lexington* before the transfer would be complete.

Captain Blakely was no King, as Heinlein found out dramatically within two weeks of his taking command of *Lexington*. On June 29, 1932, Dick Downer—the aviator who had witnessed Heinlein's wedding certificate— was killed in a flying accident off Encinitas, California. Heinlein was given the difficult task of notifying Downer's parents.[38] It was even more difficult for him because he had just recently had a run-in with the dead pilot; Downer had given him an order[39] that didn't sound right at all, and Heinlein had fallen back on the CYA (Cover Your Ass) defense of asking for the order in writing. This is not something one does lightly: it is a strong message to one's superior officer that he's heading down a wrong path. Most officers will think twice about putting any order in writing that might be questionable, but Downer had ignored him and given him the written order. As Heinlein had expected, it went wrong. Heinlein was exonerated, leaving Downer to take the brunt of the discipline. It hadn't affected their friendship—Downer was bright enough to know that Heinlein had tried to warn him; he just got carried away and lost his temper and his judgment.

But Downer's good attitude didn't make the loss of Heinlein's friend any easier to take.

King, he heard, was passed over for promotion, as everyone had expected.

And life went on, losing some of its savor every day. Heinlein had a particularly unappetizing legal case to defend before the new captain: "He was a nasty little beast who would have looked well hanged at the yardarm . . . but he was *my* client, and I always gave my clients all I had, no matter how angry it sometimes made the President of the Court."[40]

There were eight specifications in the General Court Martial, and Heinlein got him acquitted of the seven he was actually guilty of, tangling the witnesses up on cross-examination. But the man was convicted on the eighth count—of which he was innocent (a reviewing board later reversed this conviction)—and sentenced to two years in prison.

Representing such defendants was duty Heinlein would rather have avoided,[41] but he didn't really have any way out: if a prisoner requested him for defense, he had to serve. On one occasion, late in his tour, he was with an inspection party that visited the brig. For some reason, he closed the door this time, and on the back he found a list of officers' names, with some stars marked after each name. He asked around and discovered that it was a kind of legal handicap sheet for the prisoners: any time an officer defended a guilty man and got him off, his name would be posted on the inside of that door, and for each additional case in which a guilty man got off, a star would be added. Heinlein had a lot of stars after his name—and that must have accounted for his being tagged so often for defense. He took an eraser and rubbed out his name, and that was the end of his "law practice."

And just in time. He and Leslyn would make a new home near his new station, the *Roper*'s home port of San Diego.

13

SWALLOWING THE ANCHOR

Carrier men looked down on the destroyers and battleships as antiquated, just as battleship men looked down on carriers as flibbertigibbety experiments. When he reported in on June 23, 1932, Heinlein found nothing to shake his prejudices: *Roper* was tied up to a mooring buoy with three other World War I–vintage ships, constituting a "desdiv" (destroyer division). To Heinlein's eyes, fresh from the clean, modern lines of *Lexington*, she must have looked like a piece of junk.

Roper (DD-147) was a Wickes-class destroyer, smaller, faster, and lighter than *Lexington*. *Roper* had been laid down and launched in 1918, but was mothballed in the 1920s and recommissioned in 1930. Her annual schedule was similar to *Lexington*'s, taking part in fleet exercises in Panama, Hawaii, and the Caribbean.

Heinlein would have to learn the ropes all over again in California while the ship went on to Port Angeles, near Seattle—two and a half months of shore duty at North Island, near Coronado, during which he would be carried on *Roper*'s T.O. (Table of Organization) as "Under Instruction B.F. Gunnery School." At the end of the course, he would probably be promoted and assigned as *Roper*'s gunnery officer.

Leslyn found a house in Coronado. They acquired a dog—a mongrel with some basset hound in him—and Heinlein named him Nixie, after the butterfly-chasing mongrel he had owned as a teenager. "American brown democrats, both of them," he said.[1] Once, he accidentally locked Leslyn out of the house for about fifteen minutes. Leslyn was oddly distressed about it; locks seemed to bother her unusually.[2] He shook it off; everybody has quirks. He was much more concerned about how little she ate, how thin she was. "He was always urging her to eat more," Virginia Heinlein later recalled, "and tried to tempt her into doing that, unsuccessfully, usually. And he praised her cooking a lot, although that seemed to me rather ordinary. Nothing special."[3]

At the end of the summer, Heinlein received his promotion from ensign to lieutenant j.g. and returned to *Roper* to take up the Gunnery Officer billet.

Immediately he ran into a serious problem: *Roper* was so small and light that she bounced around on the seas too much for his stomach; he was continuously seasick while they were at sea.

Seasickness is often treated as a comic malady, but it is no joke to the sufferers. The brief respites for shore leave were barely enough to keep him going, but as soon as they cast off, it was back to the rail.[4] There were various remedies that were supposed to allay motion sickness in the days before Dramamine and Bonine—ginger and lemon drops, for example. Nothing helped.

And he couldn't keep food down. He began to have acute stomach pains after meals and lost weight rapidly as he fought the queasiness and the clamminess and sweat—and tried to ignore the imperative signals coming from his brain's vomiting-center.[5] He finished out the gunnery season on December 15, 1932, with a score of 93 percent on Long Range Battle Practice, but he was a walking skeleton at that point and went into the U.S. Naval Hospital in San Diego the next day. X-rays found a spot on his lung: he had contracted pulmonary tuberculosis.

Tuberculosis in the 1930s could still be a death sentence by slow wasting away. Before broad-spectrum antibiotics (and in the 1930s, medical orthodoxy still didn't recognize the possibility of an "internal antiseptic," even though penicillin was already on the market), the only thing the doctors could do was to make you comfortable and hope for a spontaneous cure.

It is not clear whether the seasickness caused the TB or simply masked it: the symptoms are virtually identical—loss of appetite, loss of weight, constant tiredness, clammy skin, and sweating. In healthy people, *Mycobacterium tuberculosis* can be present but inactive: the body's natural defenses put shells—tubercles—around the infection sites. Under stress (thy name is seasickness!) the tubercles break down, and the bacteria spread every time the victim coughs. Robert's brother Ivar had developed TB the year before and was being treated at the Fitzsimmons Army Hospital near Denver, Colorado. Robert developed fevers and a constant cough—and finally coughed up bloody sputum. By the time he was hospitalized, Robert was so weak that bed rest alone was not enough. Attending his brother Larry's wedding to his second wife, Caryl Dart, on December 30, 1932, was out of the question.[6] The U.S. Naval Hospital at San Diego was not set up to treat TB. All the armed services sent their consumption cases to Fitzsimmons Army Hospital in Denver, where Ivar was already under treatment. They were still using the old mechanical treatments at Fitzsimmons. As weakened as Robert was, with secondary medical problems coming on, Fitzsimmons would be a death sentence for him—a slow, drawn-out, and terrible death. He and Leslyn found a progressive sanatorium close to Los Angeles that was getting exceptional results from the new tuberculin treatments. When Dr. Francis Pottenger agreed to accept him as a patient, Heinlein petitioned the Navy to be allowed to pay for his own treatment.

On February 13, 1933, he was detached for a three-month sick leave and moved from San Pedro to Arcadia, California, where Leslyn had found a house close to the Pottenger Clinic in Monrovia. Dr. Pottenger's X-rays showed cloudiness on the upper lobes of both lungs—more on the left than on the right—and scars on the left lower lobe.[7]

In 1932, the sanatorium cure was the gold standard for TB care, but that was really nothing more than rest in the fresh air, in a mild climate, and a reduction of physical stresses. Being away from *Roper,* being able to rest, and undergoing Dr. Pottenger's tuberculin treatments brought about a rapid improvement. Soon Robert was moved to outpatient status, getting his bed rest at home in Arcadia and coming in periodically for tuberculin injections.[8]

Leslyn managed his daily regimen:

7:45	Temp & Pulse
8:00	Breakfast C.L.O.
8:30	Defecation
10:30	Milk or eggnog
10:30–11:30	Rest
11:30	Temp & Pulse
1:00	Lunch—C.L.O.
1:30–1:45	Air Bath
1:45–4:30	Nap period
4:30	Temp & Pulse
4:35	Milk or eggnog
6:00	Dinner C.L.O.
8:30	Temp & Pulse
9:30	Lights Out.[9]

He was not comatose, despite the long daily periods allocated to sleep: the backs of his temperature records have a pencil sketch for a "mechanical shoe blacker" and notations about people to write to. "Feel well for the first time in months," he wrote to his brother on March 10, 1933. Heinlein was optimistic, even though he also had a recurrence of his nonspecific urethritis/prostatitis that seemed to come on anytime his health was stressed.

While he was writing this letter—on March 10, 1933, at 1:54 P.M.[10]—the Long Beach earthquake struck. "This is the most exciting time," he continued. "Another quake—a big one." There had been a sharp foreshock just two days before.

Californians, whether native-born or imports, can become quite blasé about the relatively minor earthquakes that happen every day, but the big ones are a different matter. In a major quake, people freeze and ask themselves, "What was that?" It takes a few seconds, usually, to register that it's an earthquake. At magnitudes over 4.0 there is often a low rumble from the earth, followed by cracking reports from buildings as their foundations shift or the building takes stress in its frames. It is common to see structural damage—cracks in buildings, sidewalks buckling, sinkholes opening up in soft earth or landfill. The Long Beach earthquake was rated 6.4 on the Richter scale, and even sixty miles away from the epicenter of the quake, "it scared the pants off me."[11]

There were deaths—115 people were killed. Property damage to unreinforced masonry structures from Los Angeles to Laguna Beach was later estimated at $40 million in 1933 dollars. Aftershocks strong enough to be felt continued for two months.

In May, when Heinlein's sick leave expired, the Commanding Officer of the San Diego Naval Hospital ordered him to appear in person for evaluation, though he was still confined to bed. Dr. Pottenger's interim evaluation found his symptoms were decreasing on the tuberculin-and-bed-rest regimen. He formally recommended continuing the regimen, gradually decreasing bed rest and adding an exercise regimen. Reluctantly, after initially turning down Heinlein's request for an extension of sick leave, the CO granted another three-month extension.[12]

"I believe in Doctor Pottenger and feel sure that he will very rapidly get me well," Robert wrote to his brother Ivar.[13] Pottenger was a good guy as well as a very competent doctor, charging patients according to their ability to pay. Some patients were paying as much as $1,000 a week for the same treatment others received free of charge.[14] It evened out. That tended to give Heinlein personal confidence in the man as well as the doctor. It put him in mind of his own grandfather Lyle, who used to accept a side of bacon—or nothing, if circumstances warranted—for delivering a baby.[15]

Even though he remained confined to bed much of the time, Heinlein was getting stronger. He took up walking for exercise and was gradually able to add other activities—reading books, writing letters, and talking with Leslyn, who was more than supportive.

He and Leslyn belonged to one of the photography clubs in Southern

California that from time to time hired nude models for their members to shoot. A wife's chaperonage was considered sufficient to keep the men on their best behavior—but in the case of an open marriage like the Heinleins', chaperonage might be a mere formality, and probably was: Leslyn noted that Robert was exercising his extramarital sex privileges within the first year of their marriage[16]—though it is hard to imagine how he could have managed much bed-hopping between TB and bouts of urethritis.

The national news seemed to parallel Heinlein's medical conditions. Franklin Roosevelt had won the 1932 presidential election, when the national economy seemed to be circling the drain. Heinlein had voted for him (and against the Republican incumbent, President Hoover).[17] President Roosevelt was already shaping up: as soon as he took office in March 1933, he closed every bank in the country for ten days, to stop the slow hemorrhage of money being withdrawn from the banking system. He also called Congress into special session to enact his new "alphabet soup" of government agencies that would become the backbone of his New Deal: WPA (Works Progress Administration), CCC (Civilian Conservation Corps), NRA (National Recovery Administration), and PWA (Public Works Administration). At the very least, he was willing to try drastic solutions, and that put him streets ahead of anybody else on the American political landscape.

Heinlein found the Agriculture Adjustment Act that went into effect in May 1933 particularly offensive: the government was going to pay farmers *not* to raise crops, and to plow under ten million acres of cotton fields already planted—and to slaughter farrows and pregnant sows. Heinlein understood the logic—overproduction had to be dealt with somehow (and the bill had come to Roosevelt for signature after spring planting had begun)[18]—but he found it offensive nonetheless.[19]

Heinlein was not the only American who found the farrow slaughter program offensive. It was grotesque enough to generate a series of jokes:

> Under Socialism, if you own two cows, you give one to your neighbor; under Communism, you give both cows to the government and the government gives you back some of the milk; under Fascism, you keep the cows but give the milk to the government, which sells some of it back to you.
>
> And under the New Deal, you shoot both cows and milk the government.[20]

There was personal news that spring: in May, when The Century of Progress World's Fair opened in Chicago, the sensation of the show was not the exhibits or the architecture, but Heinlein's old friend and lust object from Greenwood Grammar School, Sally Rand. Talkies had ended her budding film career in 1928—sound cameras were not lisp-friendly—and she had wound up in Chicago, dancing with a stage revue. When its run ended, she had put together a specialty act that involved a body stocking and two large (seven-foot) pink ostrich feather fans she had found at a secondhand shop. When she performed outside the gates of the fair, the attendees were convinced she was dancing nude beneath the screen of the feathers—a sensation! Her shows were packed, and fans insisted she transcended burlesque: Sally Rand's fan dance was Art. Completely predictably, detractors became indignant, and Sally and other dancers at the fair were brought up on obscenity charges. The press had a field day. A local judge dismissed the case, and the fan dance went on.

Now that Heinlein was up and around, he and Leslyn visited the Elysian Fields nudist camp that had been set up that May near Topanga Canyon. Heinlein had never forgotten the exhilarating feeling he had experienced as a small child, of running naked in Swope Park while playing Tarzan.[21] German immigrants had brought the nudist lifestyle to the U.S., and after a decade of litigation, "naturist" resorts could make a go of it so long as they maintained a very low profile and did not provoke their local jurisdictions.

Elysian Fields was one of the first nudist resorts in the West—and became a leader in the movement later that year when Fox film director Bryan Foy shot a film of Elysian Fields, *Elysia (Valley of the Nude),* which was shown around the country—discreetly without acting or directing credits. Judge Joseph B. David's ruling in the Sally Rand obscenity matter, quoted in the film, fixes the date of filming at around July 20, 1933. The film stresses the health benefits of fresh air and sunshine, and these are elements of the sanatorium cure for tuberculosis. No doubt Heinlein had his mind on his health management.

Heinlein's extended leave was expiring in August. Dr. Pottenger thought he was well on the way to recovery: "I would say that your lesion is quiescent and approaching an arrestment at the present time."[22] He recommended a convalescent regime for the next few months, leading to a resumption of "light duty" in the late fall of 1933, continuing 12–14 hours a day of bed rest over the crucial next two to three years. "Your future should be good. There has been no destruction of lung tissue; consequently you should have a good working capacity." Eventually.

Heinlein reported back to the Naval Hospital in San Diego on August 20 and was immediately readmitted as a patient. Now he was strong enough to be transferred. Leslyn found a room in downtown Denver at the War Mothers' National Memorial Home while Robert reported in to Fitzsimmons, as ordered, on September 2, 1933.

The standards of care were much lower at Fitzsimmons, and the environment was more stressful than at Dr. Pottenger's sanatorium. The previous week, Ivar had been the first of four to get pneumothorax, and he told Robert a grisly story: a new doctor had been assigned to perform pneumothorax, and he had accidentally killed one of the patients after Ivar's procedure.[23]

Part of the treatment for tuberculosis in the 1930s involved artificial pneumothorax—a needle put in the space between the ribs and the wall of the lung to pump the cavity there full of air, collapsing the lung so that it could rest and heal up. It was not a traumatic procedure—usually only a prick as the needle goes in—and it was over in a few minutes, but it had to be done often. The air would gradually be absorbed in the body over a few days. Private TB patients would go two or three times a week to be pumped up again, so that the lung would be immobilized. At Fitzsimmons it was once a week, on Friday mornings.

Artificial pneumothorax is not normally dangerous, but if the needle goes in just a little too far and then somehow forces an air bubble into a blood vessel, the air bubble (embolus) can travel through the bloodstream to the heart and cause a "vapor lock" embolism. That's just what happened to the patient after Ivar. The heart convulses, blood flow stops. Everyone—especially the young doctor—was shaken up, but the next patient calmly hopped up on the table—and died, too. The last of that group calmly took his place on the table and refused a new doctor. This time it went perfectly.

Now, Ivar pointed out, the fourth patient was certainly brave, but he wasn't the bravest of the four, after all: an autopsy showed that the third patient, Josephs, had not died from an embolism: he had died of fright. He had been so terrified that he literally killed himself, but he went ahead anyway, and that was bravery.[24]

Heinlein agreed. It was one of those stories he took out every so often and turned it over in his mind.

Robert did not thrive at Fitzsimmons. Leslyn visited almost every day, but fundamentally hospitals are often not good places to get well in. It wasn't just the TB: starting in October 1933 he had a series of minor colds and, toward the end of November, a severe case of influenza. He was not able to get to his sister Louise's wedding to Wilfred "Bud" Bacchus that October in Kansas City.

The nurses refused to bring his meals to him when he was too weak to get out of bed—would not even see him but simply sent word that he was to get up if he wanted a meal. He was weakening, unable to enjoy the end of Prohibition in December by going out and getting drunk with the rest of the country.

About ten days after the flu cleared up, his nonspecific urethritis came back, and he developed an unpleasant inflammation. This time, it was stronger than ever, with a pussy discharge and a continuous low-grade fever. The Army doctors were so sure it was gonorrhea that they didn't even bother to do the test.[25]

Heinlein was sure he did not have gonorrhea. He continued to weaken. He was worse off, if possible, than when he had checked in to Dr. Pottenger's. In an Army hospital, Leslyn, a civilian and a woman, was helpless as his condition deteriorated through not being able to move enough. Heinlein recalled this period, years later:

> Bothered by bed sores and with every joint aching no matter what position I twisted into, I thought often of the Sybaritic comfort of floating in blood-warm water at night in Panama [at Fort Clayton]—and wished that it could be done for bed patients . . . and eventually figured out how to do it, all details, long before I was well enough to make working drawings.[26]

That is, he engineered the modern conception of the water bed[27] as a thought exercise while he was sick.[28] He couldn't do any real engineering in his condition; he wasn't even really all there. If he did not improve, he might actually die within a few weeks—not from the tuberculosis, but from his organs shutting down because of the infection. The doctors ignored his attempt to tell them about his history of nonspecific urethritis. One went further, telling him to shut up and go away until he had more significant symptoms to report. He even dressed Heinlein down in public for going to the G.U. [Gastrointestinal and Urology] clinic.[29]

The Army doctors at Fitzsimmons were prepared just to let him die, but he wasn't quite ready for that. He made a pest of himself, forcing the issue and getting a prostate smear and test for TB involvement in the urethral infection on December 26. He followed the progress of the lab work anxiously, but it was not reported until ten days later. The infection continued to grow worse; the orders given by the doctors became confusingly contradictory—and he was also reprimanded for reading in the lavatory.

On January 5, 1934, one of the doctors told him the results of the tests were negative. "Few pus cells, no organisms." Heinlein knew immediately that something was wrong: the specimens were mostly pus, and the two reports the doctors had read were identical in wording. He talked the lab clerk into letting him see the actual results: the urethral smear report was "Many pus cells, no gonococci found." The doctor had not even read the report correctly. Nor was there any report for the petri bowl sample he had given for TB involvement in the infection. On that, the doctor had apparently just made it up.

Heinlein asked for a reevaluation, and two days later the doctor blew up at him again, ordering him to stay away from the G.U. clinic. On January 9, he was placed on sick-in-quarters status—outpatient status, essentially chucked out without ever receiving any treatment at all for the urethritis. He took up residence with Leslyn at the War Mothers' National Memorial Home outside the hospital, where the matron turned off the heat—in Denver, in the middle of winter—at 9:30 P.M. "I nearly died," Leslyn said.[30]

Grimly Heinlein started documenting the events for a future naval board of inquiry. He wrote a letter to one of the doctors, placing his request for examination on record—the equivalent of asking for written orders. The doctor's reply admitted that the TB test had never been done, though there had been two reports. Heinlein again asked for permission to see a private specialist. On January 20 his new attending physician, a Captain Smith,[31] gave him the name of a Denver G.U. specialist—Dr. Howard[32]—and Heinlein made an appointment the same day.

This was a definite change: Dr. Howard listened attentively to his history. Even before examining him, he knew what was wrong: bladder cysts. He had Heinlein on the operating table within ten minutes. It was as simple as that. Dr. Howard's report to the Navy on Heinlein's case that same day notes tersely: "EXAMINATION: Cysto-urethascopic showed prostatic urethra filled by large sub-mucous cysts. These were fulgurated."[33] Heinlein was as well as he could be by May.

Heinlein was to have medical problems all his life with his genitourinary tract, not all related to this incident. But now he at least knew how to go about dealing with the problems as they arose. When the Chief of Medical Services at Fitzsimmons sent him a stern note—not quite an order—saying he wanted him back in the hospital to check up on the "bladder condition," Heinlein returned the note with a polite endorsement. "I do not desire to return to Fitzsimmons General Hospital for treatment for my bladder condition. I am perfectly contented with the treatment being administered by an outside specialist."[34] No further issue was made of the matter.

As Heinlein's strength returned, he needed to get out and around. One day at the Denver Athletic Club when he was judging a chess match, he met Robert Cornog, a young physics student; they found they had the same birthday, five years apart (Cornog was born in 1912)—and both had joined the American Rocket Society at about the same time. They became friendly thereafter.[35]

In addition to the more usual kinds of social life, Robert and Leslyn found special social interests in Denver. Undoubtedly the McConville/Elysia nudist group in Los Angeles provided him and Leslyn with an introduction to John and Alice Garrison, the leaders of the local (Denver) group of nudists just as they were in the process of organizing a local nudist association, the Colorado Sunshine Club. Couples were preferred at nudist associations, to cut down on publicity-attracting hanky-panky. Heinlein could continue his fresh-air regimen, though the Colorado Sunshine Club was at that time an "unlanded" group that met in private homes, since they did not have a ranch or retreat to go to. In any case, in the dead of winter, naked outdoor activities were out of the question in Denver.

Heinlein had an unpleasant and depressing fact to face: between the tuberculosis and the damage done by the infection and bladder cysts, it was just a matter of time before a medical review board would force him into early retirement, medical. On March 22, 1934, he received an order from the Navy Department instructing him to report "for examination for retirement."[36] It was small comfort that the Navy awarded him a medal for Expert Rifleman and Expert Pistol Shot ten days later. On April 20, 1934, he reported as ordered. The process began.

The career he had worked toward for half his life was over before it was well begun. He could get a job of some kind, even in the middle of the Great Depression; he was a trained engineer with a background in aeronautical engineering, and trained engineers were always in demand, even without a degree. But punching a time clock didn't appeal to him: his father had done that all his life, and it hadn't gotten him anywhere at all.

What he did not know—could not know—is that his naval career had already made an important impact. His friend Robert N. S. Clark wrote him and Leslyn after World War II: "[T]he Navy suffered a loss of some magnitude when Bob was retired from the Active List." Clark praised Heinlein's keen intellect and command personality. "I always think of him as a perfect model for a Naval officer."[37]

While the paperwork for his forced retirement ground on, Heinlein learned that a Colorado silver mine with proved ore was available, and there might be a financial backer if he would do the legwork.[38] The old

Colorado silver mines had been closed after the Panic of 1893 and the re-
peal of the Coinage Act of 1873, when the price of silver fell below the
level at which the mines could be worked economically. But the price of
silver was rising again. Mining engineering was a little out of his experience, but a base in mechanical engineering could be applied very broadly
to any technical engineering subject. Heinlein could pick it up. It would be
a lot of hard work, learning a new business—but it could also pay off in a
major way.

Heinlein had not been back to Kansas City in years, but Senator Reed
talked him up all the time: he was the first and only one of Reed's appointments to the military academies actually to graduate and serve.[39] And his father's long-standing involvement in Democratic Party politics in Kansas City
might be helpful, as well. He located a financial backer in a blind arrangement with a lawyer[40]—that is, the lawyer represented someone with investment funds, whom he would not identify to Heinlein.

Heinlein never admitted it, but he could not have been unaware of the
likelihood he would be expected to front for a Pendergast investment. That
might not be such a bad thing. Tom (T. J.) Pendergast had uses for honest
men, too: several official functionaries in his organization were well known
for probity and honesty, and this was the environment in which Harry S.
Truman had been flourishing since 1923 as an outstandingly honest Eastern
District Judge of Jackson County, Missouri.[41]

After the end of Prohibition, when rum-running could no longer be done
profitably, Tom Pendergast had begun taking the machine investments legitimate. He had a strong incentive to keep an investment such as this at arm's
length—hence a blind arrangement through the lawyer, 100 percent separated from anything that might smell, either politically or by virtue of racketeering. If this was to be a Pendergast investment, it would be a silent
partner arrangement—a straight money arrangement, with Heinlein two
states away.

These considerations may help explain why Heinlein violated the cardinal
rule of business start-ups and used his own money: he invested his dwindling
savings in the initial investigation, traveling to the Sophie and Shively Lodes
near Denver[42] and having his own assays made of the ore.

The ore was rich; on the numbers, it could be made to pay a very large
profit, so there was initially some question about why it wasn't making money
already. Heinlein found the current operation desperately underfinanced: the
mines would need new equipment, retimbering, a blacksmith shop, a truck . . .
drifting a new tunnel through to the right-of-way—"the overhead stuff before

you start collecting cash profits."[43] With his engineering expertise and the money he could bring in, things looked promising, so he set up a bond-and-lease arrangement.[44] Then in May 1934 he returned to Kansas City to get the money matters settled.

He was feeling relatively strong, and he took the opportunity to catch up on friends and family. His family killed the fatted calf to welcome him and Leslyn: they were given the best room the house had to offer, the best bed, and the best electric fan. Robert was allowed to sleep as late as he could. Leslyn would make breakfast for him separate from the rest of the family, and clear up later. Leslyn was very well liked by the rest of the family.

They were still in Kansas City on his twenty-seventh birthday, in the middle of an extended heat wave. Summers in Missouri are always hot and sticky, with daytime temperatures over a hundred degrees Fahrenheit and relative humidity over 90 percent. The summer of 1934 set records with three months of temperatures near 120 degrees, cooling—sometimes, late at night—to a hundred degrees. There was no letup, no rain except one brief shower in July. He hurt his mother deeply one day by remarking that the room was like the Black Hole of Calcutta. He hadn't meant to be offensive; it was just a general remark, more about the weather than about the room in his parents' house. But tempers fray in the heat, and his father took offense—and never forgot it[45] (and Robert was always, like his family, hypersensitive about implied criticism of his own hospitality). Trying to change a tire one afternoon, Robert stood up too fast and keeled over in a dead faint.[46] He was not even close to being well yet. The mountains in Colorado would be cooler.

> I had an appointment one morning [July 10, 1934] with a lawyer to sign the papers for the new silent partner. When I showed up, bright and cheerful, ready to sign and walk out with a certified check, the lawyer looked sour.
>
> "What's the matter?" says I.
>
> "What's the matter?" he says. "Don't you read the papers? They machine-gunned Johnny last night."[47]

"Johnny," it turned out, was Johnny Lazia. Heinlein undoubtedly knew Lazia slightly, or at the very least knew of him, though he hadn't had dealings with him: Lazia was on the seamier side of the Pendergast business—an outright gangster often mentioned in connection with Chicago's Al Capone, who had just been sent to prison for tax evasion. In 1926, while Heinlein was on his Youngster cruise, Lazia had forced Tom Pendergast's man Ross out of control of the Ninth Ward—Kansas City's "Little Italy"—and struck a deal with T.J.: he would keep the Chicago mob out of Kansas City, and T.J. would give him a share in Kansas City's gambling, racketeering, and liquor—as well as a say in the hiring of Kansas City's police forces. He even had an office at the police headquarters.[48] He also controlled sales of marijuana and heroin in the jazz clubs around 18th and Vine. Johnny Lazia was effectively the crime boss of Kansas City, his domain taking up where T.J.'s milder graft and corruption ended.

Over the years, Lazia had developed a close, personal relationship with T. J. Pendergast. When the machine started to go legitimate after Prohibition, much of Lazia's black market in liquor evaporated, and he probably needed the silver mines to soak up some of the profits. Lazia and his wife had been machine-gunned getting out of a car at 3 A.M. that day, outside the Plaza Central Hotel. Two unknown assailants had been waiting in the dark. He had many enemies.

Heinlein had exhausted his savings: he was effectively destitute, except for his Navy pay.

The medical retirement procedures ground inexorably on. The medical board found that he was "cured," in the sense that he wasn't shedding TB anymore and the existing germs were safely encysted—but he was permanently weakened by the scarring in his lungs; he would never be able to handle a full workload on a naval vessel again. Even if he were allowed to stay in the active Navy, he would have to be kept segregated from the other men, lest he become infectious again. The hearing voted to retire him as of August 1, 1934, "totally and permanently disabled."[49] A forced retirement is not a discharge: he would continue to be carried on the Navy's rolls for the rest of his life.

Heinlein decided to separate himself, make a clean break:

> After retirement I intentionally kept away from the Navy and became as civilian as possible, for I had seen sad, neurotic cases of retired officers who could not or would accept the change emotionally and who became mere zombies, living in the past. Retirement had come as a great disappointment to me; I had expected a lifetime Naval career and had hoped someday to fly my own flag. So I determined to let the dead past bury its dead and made for myself a new life.[50]

His retirement pay would be calculated at two-thirds of his full-service pay, and that would keep him afloat in California, where he would return with Leslyn. He was comfortable in California; the climate is congenial for a lunger. It may have been Leslyn who suggested he could go back to school and take an advanced degree. Leslyn had her master's degree: in a couple of years, he could take a doctorate—he could position himself right where the action was, in physics. Nobody in his family had gone to college: "Herr Professor Doktor Heinlein" must have sounded just fine to him.

By the end of August, they were back in Los Angeles, ensconced in what is now West Hollywood, at 905 La Jolla, close to Santa Monica and Fairfax.[51] Perhaps one of these was the house he later mentioned, that had its own live-in poltergeist, who/which picked up and dropped the end of the bed when he was in it.[52] He did not have a lot of time to make the necessary arrangements to get into college.

He couldn't get into his first choice, Cal Tech, or indeed into any university graduate school because he didn't have a bachelor's degree. The Naval Academy did not issue degrees when Heinlein graduated. In 1933, as a Depression cost-cutting measure, the Navy commissioned only the top half of the graduating class, letting the rest go with a year's pay. In order to make the midshipmen they did not commission competitive, the Class of '33 was issued degrees in engineering. Suddenly, the Naval Academy was in competition with other schools. It had to upgrade its curriculum.

But that didn't help with Heinlein's immediate problem. Given time, he might have been able to talk the Naval Academy into issuing a retroactive degree, but the semester was starting now. He set inquiries in motion with the Naval Academy and went for his second choice, the University of California, Los Angeles.[53]

Without a degree, he could not actually enroll at UCLA. Instead, he must have arranged privately with the professors to sit in on classes in both the physics and mathematics departments—in atomic physics, advanced chemistry, upper-atmosphere physics, and optics. This could not, strictly speaking, be called "auditing" the courses, as auditing is a process normally mediated by the university's administration, and he was still a nonperson so far as they were concerned.[54] Leslyn gave him a scholar's gift to get started—a briefcase for his course work.[55]

There was some interesting material in the courses—and some good and bad teaching. The atomic physics course was concerned with determining the mass of the electron. Heinlein noted that one experimental run did not agree with what theory predicted, so the instructor threw out the results. This is standard pedagogy—science teaching—but bad for *doing* science. "Had he [the teacher] forgotten the other runs, the 'good' ones, we might have jumped ten years ahead in atomic physics. But he didn't, because he knew, from theory, that the run was a 'bad' one."[56] But Heinlein kept his opinion to himself. His professor in the optics class he did approve of—Dr. Joseph Kaplan's teaching he considered "inspiring." Kaplan was a "born teacher."[57] Otherwise, he complained in a letter to Dick Mandelkorn (one of "his" Plebes who was now working at MIT) that the atmosphere at UCLA was "stultifying."[58]

Early in the semester, Heinlein became ill and stopped attending classes for a while, fearing he could have a tubercular relapse at any time. After several "white nights" of the insomnia he started suffering while in the hospital, he was running a slight temperature in the afternoons.[59] Trying to attend classes and be alert after three or four nights of no sleep in a row was no good. Stress can bring on a tubercular relapse, and he had to be careful for the benefit of others as well as himself. Heinlein had already trained himself into some protective habits he was to keep for the rest of his life—always taking out a handkerchief and covering his mouth, for example, when he had to cough. He kept well hydrated and napped whenever he felt tired.

It was probably when he was in bed for a couple of days, to get the fever down (and sleep, if possible), that he took the opportunity to reevaluate his decision. Graduate school might not be possible without a bachelor's degree from the Naval Academy—and it was questionable in any case how much of his "undergraduate" transcript UCLA would accept, since the Naval Academy was not highly regarded as an institution of higher learning.

It could take years—and a great deal of money—to recapitulate the course work necessary to meet UCLA's requirements for an undergraduate degree—not practical. He would have to change direction—again. His second choice of careers had fizzled.

BAPTISM OF FIRE

Just before Heinlein's transfer to Fitzsimmons in August 1933, the Santa Monica Democratic Club had asked Upton Sinclair, the famous muckraker journalist who lived in Pasadena, to draft a reform platform for them and run for governor as a Democrat against Republican incumbent Frank Merriam.[1] This was an extremely odd thing for them to do, because Sinclair had run for governor twice before, in 1926 and 1930, as the *Socialist Party* candidate for governor of California.

But the move from socialist back to Democrat (his original registration, thirty years earlier)[2] was not an unmanageable obstacle for either Sinclair or the Democrats: liberals in the United States had for more than fifty years looked to their socialist radical wing as a source of strategic ideas and as the purest statement of their goals. Marx's class-warfare tradition had taken root in Europe, but class-conflict socialism was never acceptable in the United States, and in fact, Sinclair specifically repudiated Marxist/communist socialism in issue after issue of his campaign newspaper, agreeing with his friend H. G. Wells's broader, more theoretical view of communism and socialism:

> Socialism which was creative is stunned, and Communism, which is the sabotage of civilisation by the disappointed, has usurped its name and inheritance . . . The new Marxist Socialism, therefore, with its confident dogmas, its finality and hardness, its vindictive will, developed an intensity and energy that drowned and almost silenced the broader, more tentative, and scientific initiatives of the older, the legitimate Socialism. Communism, with its class-war obsession, ate up Socialism.[3]

The socialism of Sinclair and Wells was "progressive"—the term means social change by progressive stages of education and gradual political conversion, as opposed to the violent revolutionary change sought by Marxist theory. Progressivism fit very comfortably with the liberal orientation of the Democratic Party platform; Sinclair switched his party affiliation on September 1, 1933,[4] changing his techniques, he said, but not his principles: "I found I was not getting any where as a Socialist," he explained to an unbylined journalist for *Time* magazine, "and so I decided to make progress with one of the two old parties."[5] "What we want and must have is a movement based upon American conditions and speaking the American language."[6] He would campaign on a statewide version of a people's cooperative program advocated by Governor Olson of Minnesota.[7] Sinclair called his program EPIC—"End Poverty in California."

The EPIC plan called for the State of California to use its credit to buy up repossessed and abandoned factories and farms and employ the hundreds of thousands of out-of-work men. Their first job would be to produce the goods they needed to live. Anything they produced over subsistence, they were welcome to sell on the open market. Governor Olson's version would phase out private firms and all production for profit; Sinclair acknowledged that his EPIC Production-for-Use colonies would probably outcompete private production, but he stopped short of open advocacy of replacing capitalism altogether.

Traditional businessmen, already hard-hit by the collapsing economy, hated the idea of state-financed competition. But something had to be done: the problem of "relief" was overwhelming the resources of the state. As the Depression closed down industries all over the country, desperate families pulled up stakes and went west looking for jobs. By 1934 there were a million unemployed in California. Sinclair's EPIC plan would make the relief problem self-liquidating at a start-up cost of $300 million. Sinclair called it "relief to end relief."

The ordinary citizens of California supported EPIC with its sane, commonsensical "Production-for-Use" (and not for profit) motto. Relief to end relief sounded like just the solution California needed. But the newspapers in the state, all loyal to the traditional business interests upon whom they depended for advertising, ignored Sinclair completely; few would even acknowledge EPIC activities.

Sinclair started a newspaper of his own in December 1933 to get his message out. Every week he wrote an editorial for *EPIC News,* and then a series of pamphlets explaining the EPIC program.

The Democratic Party grass roots turned out in 1934 in support of EPIC. Just four years earlier, Republicans had outnumbered Democrats in California by a margin of three to one; Sinclair's EPIC effort registered 330,000 Democrats, bringing the Democratic Party into parity with Republicans for the first time in California history.

And just in time: in July 1934, just as Heinlein's Colorado mining venture was collapsing, California's Governor Frank Merriam called out the National Guard to put down the Maritime Strike in San Francisco after the San Francisco police had intervened against the striking Longshoremen's Union, using clubs, the new tear gas, and even guns. The strikers fought back with guns and clubs of their own and called a (successful) general strike in San Francisco.

The Longshoremen's Union strike made national, and then international, headlines (and eventually made it into the history books). Liberals and progressives were outraged: conservative Republicans were making war on American citizens.

By August 1934, the Heinleins must already have been planning to return to Leslyn's home base in Southern California when his medical retirement came through. They arrived on August 8, three weeks before the Democratic Party primary. Apparently they had not moved their voter registration to Colorado: they were eligible to vote in the primary on August 28, 1934.

The voters surprised everyone: not only was Sinclair nominated for the governorship, there were nearly fifty successful EPIC and EPIC-supported candidates for the state legislature. Sinclair's nine months of outreach to the grass roots had convinced the new Democrat voters—and a good number of Republicans, as well—that he was no wild-eyed radical, but an honest man reasonably trying to find a humane solution to keeping their unfortunate neighbors alive without taxation eating *them* alive. Hundreds of chapters of Sinclair's End Poverty League sprang up throughout California—each an entirely local effort supported and directed by local residents.

In time, there would be two thousand chapters, and the End Poverty League paralleled the Democratic Party's local club apparatus as a shadow organization. *EPIC News* grew a reader base of two million (in a state whose total population at the time was six million).

The morning after the 1934 Democratic primary, the state's major newspapers—all controlled by conservative Republicans—raised an alarm. The *Los Angeles Times* railed against Sinclair's "maggot-like horde of followers."[8] After a statewide radio address explaining the essentials of EPIC to the voters, Sinclair boarded a train to Hyde Park, New York, to get Franklin Roosevelt's endorsement and then on to Washington, D.C., to discuss EPIC and the New Deal with key figures in the administration.

Under ordinary circumstances, the Democratic National Committee would automatically endorse the party's nominee in California—but these were not ordinary times. President Roosevelt had spent a great deal of political capital getting his New Deal program legislated, and he was politically vulnerable at the moment.

When faced with a political hot potato, Roosevelt's personal style was to temporize, do nothing to cut down his options, and let things sort themselves out. He had a pleasant meeting with Sinclair and vaguely suggested he might have something to say to Sinclair's taste in one of his monthly radio talks late in October. Sinclair was not experienced enough to realize that he had been put off: he thought Roosevelt was offering to endorse the EPIC candidacy. He went back to California to face the storm, for the political establishment in California, Democrat as well as Republican, was determined to get Sinclair at all costs. Democrats even set up pro-Merriam organizations within the Democratic Party. And the party fund-raisers stayed away in droves.

EPIC had been self-funded from the grass roots up; it would continue as it had begun. Sinclair charged seventy-five cents for admission to their rallies (the equivalent, in 1934 dollars, of two pounds of butter, a pound of beef, or four gallons of gasoline, or, another way of measuring it: dinner for a family of three or four), and each ticket holder was pledged to bring in ten more. This was something people *wanted*, and they would support it with their Widow's Mites if necessary. Sinclair also passed the hat in audiences gathered to hear live broadcasts of his radio speeches. It was nickels and dimes—but nickels and dimes were the people's voice.

Both Robert and Leslyn were radical liberals who might have gone to work for Uppie (as the newspapers labeled him when they were forced to notice him at all) in any case. But the *unfairness* of the opposition must have rankled. Anybody in downtown Los Angeles, where EPIC had its headquarters, could see "Red Dollars" passed from hand to hand—fake dollar bills printed in commie red ink and labeled "SincLIAR," issued by the "Uppie and Downey Bank" (Sheridan Downey had beat William Jennings Bryan, Jr., for the Lieutenant Governor's race and so was Sinclair's running mate). That might have been amusing in a heavy-handed sort of way, but the film studio heads Jack Warner and Irving Thalberg threatened to move the film industry out of state if Sinclair were elected, and that was obvious foolishness: they had too heavy an investment in land and capital in Southern California to just up and abandon. By mid-September, this was being acknowledged even by studio flacks, who were trying out the alternative notion that the film industry might simply collapse if Sinclair went into competition, making films with the unemployed.

Late in September, the *Los Angeles Times* escalated its attacks on Sinclair: the paper began running a daily front-page bold-outlined box with the most extreme quotations the editors could find from Sinclair's inflammatory writings, sometimes liberally altered or taken out of context, in an effort to discredit him with conservative voters. Many of the quotes were taken from his 1917 diatribe against the Catholic Church, *The Profits of Religion*. At first Sinclair was delighted: there is a saying in the PR game that any publicity is good publicity. But after a few days he got it: "It is impossible," he said on seeing one particularly outrageous quote, "that the voters will elect a man who has written *that*!" It gradually became clear to Sinclair that if he were defeated, the main reason would be that he had written too many books, too sarcastically.

Then, on September 24, EPIC got its first positive press coverage: *The Huntington Park Signal* broke a story about the anti-Sinclair propaganda campaign being mounted by the California Newspaper Publishers Association.

But external enemies was not Sinclair's problem: on a train trip back from a rally in San Francisco, he told reporters he expected half the unemployed in the country to come to California if he won. The *Los Angeles Times* led with the story in the morning editions on September 27: EPIC was going to double the population of the state by attracting bums. Sinclair tried to spin it less damagingly, quipping, "For the first in history the *Los Angeles Times* is willing to state the number of our unemployed, and even to exaggerate it!"[9] He added that what he meant was that the unemployed always came to California in the winter—there was less chance of freezing to death. But it didn't help.

The anti-Sinclair campaign was escalating and getting more vicious: newly settled down in an apartment at 905 North La Jolla in what is now the City of West Hollywood, Robert and Leslyn must have received one of the direct-mail circulars ridiculing the "SEPTIC Plan—Soak Every Possible Taxpayer in California." Robert was probably at home, sick with what he was afraid might be a relapse of TB. If he got out at all, he might have seen for himself anti-Sinclair forces downtown, shoving cards into people's hands printed with a poem titled "The Ipecac Plan: Out of the Moscow Medicine Chest."

That might have been the final straw for Robert Anson Heinlein: he decided to put his socialist principles to work for the faith-of-his-father

Democratic Party. Late in September, he volunteered and wound up at the main Los Angeles office, the headquarters for the entire statewide EPIC campaign.[10]

Heinlein must have caused something of a stir in the always shorthanded EPIC main office: after a short interview, "to my utter amazement and confusion, I found myself in charge of seven precincts."

The dirty anti-Sinclair campaign continued to escalate: on October 4, the California Real Estate Association held its annual convention in Santa Barbara and abandoned its thirty-year tradition of political noninvolvement. H. G. Wells, a few years before, had praised the trend toward these semiprofessional organizations as part of the socialist-progressive "rephrasing of human life."[11] Now, the Realtors' president, Robert A. Swink, declared war on Sinclair. First, he set up a "Merriam for Governor" organization and prepared to print four hundred thousand posters and bulletins as part of a massive campaign of disinformation: "Sinclair will seize homes; warn clients to not look at homes until after November election." The situation was so desperate, Swink told them, that their only option as True Americans was a self-induced real-estate crash—their own Valley Forge. The next morning, the *Los Angeles Times* struck the same pseudopatriotic note in an editorial titled "Stand Up and Be Counted." EPIC, the *Times* said, represented "a threat to Sovietize California." Defeating Sinclair was the plain patriotic duty of every Californian.

Calling on phony patriotism to misrepresent and crush liberals and progressives must have turned Heinlein's stomach—but it may also have given him an idea: there was no reason *he* could not sell real estate.[12] It would be an ideal solution to his job problem: he could work for himself—and it would be at least a minor help to the EPIC campaign to get the truth to prospective buyers.

The trouble with a career in real estate was, of course, the same as everyone's troubles: it was the middle of the Depression, and real estate wasn't moving. With the help of his Navy pension, he and Leslyn could survive while the business was ramping up—and work very, very hard at EPIC. He borrowed money wherever he could and juggled his debts to keep himself and Leslyn afloat.[13]

President Roosevelt's monthly Fireside Chat on September 30, 1934, made no mention of EPIC or Production-for-Use. A nerve-racking textile workers' strike had just been settled, and he called for a truce between Capital and Labor while the New Deal's NRA agency sorted things out.

EPIC needed that endorsement: by the middle of October, United for

California was mailing half a million flyers and brochures targeted by issue to every household in the state and producing radio programs designed by the advertising firm of Lord & Taylor.

Louis B. Mayer at the MGM studios—he was also the state Republican Party chairman—levied a "Merriam Tax" on every studio employee. The big stars were sent a blank check and told to make it out to one of the anti-Sinclair front organizations; the technical and administrative people were simply docked a day's pay.

Not all the stars went along. Katharine Hepburn made the news by resisting (though her father stated in a filmed interview that she would never consider voting for Sinclair). Jean Harlow and James Cagney (who styled himself a "professional againster") refused point-blank. Cagney told EPIC journalist Frank Scully that if Mayer forced the issue, he would donate a *week's* pay to Sinclair.

Merriam himself had almost nothing to do with any of the activities on his behalf: he was regarded even by Republicans as a windbag without any personal charisma, and the anti-Sinclair forces didn't want Merriam anywhere near their carefully crafted campaign. Already Republicans around the state were saying they would "hold their noses and vote for Merriam."

Outside of California, things were not so grim. When the October 17, 1934, issue of *Time* magazine came out, Upton Sinclair was on the cover, dukes up in a boxer's stance. The interior article was more or less fair. The vested interests hate him, *Time* said: "Fact is, Upton Sinclair is as American as pumpkin pie . . . an ordinary old-fashioned socialist who looks like Henry Ford gone slightly fey."[14] On October 22, *EPIC News* was able to lead with an endorsement of Sinclair from President Roosevelt's main political "fixer," James A. Farley. President Roosevelt still hadn't said anything. The next day (October 23, 1934), Heywood Broun, another writer for the Scripps-Howard papers, denounced the dirty tricks and "willful fraud" of the anti-Sinclair forces in *The New York World-Telegram*. *The New York Times* sent Turner Catledge to cover the campaign from California. Catledge could not find a single mention of EPIC events in the *Los Angeles Times* and asked the *Los Angeles Times*'s political editor, Kyle Palmer, why that was. "We don't go in for that kind of crap you have in New York," Palmer told him, "of being obliged to print both sides. We're going to beat this son-of-a-bitch Sinclair any way we can. We're going to kill him."[15]

Heinlein was elected to the West Hollywood Democratic Club's board of directors. West Hollywood was then just a political subdivision—a subdivision of a subdivision, since Hollywood is also just a geographical area in Los

Angeles. His new, higher-profile position put him in contact with local Hollywood celebrities. He had known many stars and studio personalities socially from his days on *Lexington* and was not overwhelmed by celebrity—but trying to run an active political organization was an entirely different matter: people like James Cagney and Dorothy Parker (he had met her in New York four years earlier but did not then come to know her well) were laws unto themselves. Sometimes he must have longed for the simpler certitudes of the merely corrupt Pendergast operation.

United for California was the real powerhouse of the anti-Sinclair forces. It had collected a war chest estimated at $7.5 million—a sum fabulous and almost unbelievable in politics in 1934—and was spending it lavishly, erecting two thousand highway billboards, mailing out millions of pieces of direct-mail advertising targeted to groups as well as individuals, creating and sponsoring radio programs, and mounting lawsuits. United for California filed a lawsuit alleging that huge numbers of the new Democratic voter registrations were fraudulent.

Roosevelt's October Fireside Chat came and went, with no mention of Sinclair or Production-for-Use. Sinclair never got an endorsement from President Roosevelt (since the New Deal was going to go through with or without California's support). James Farley rapidly backpedaled from his endorsement.

Heinlein's hands-on political experience was based in Kansas City's ward system, and his manual of grassroots politicking, *How to Be a Politician*, shows the legacy of Jim Pendergast: the most essential element in a successful political organization, he said, is direct personal contact.[16] EPIC workers should walk the precincts in the district, talking with every single voter in every house. That personal contact could be the tiny nudge that would push an uncommitted voter over to their side. The schedule was multiply redundant where he could manage it, and Heinlein indicates in his advice to aspiring grassroots politicians that he oversaw the canvass himself, from the field, as he knew you can't manage effectively when your people know they have to do the drudge work you are not willing to do yourself. There is no substitute for pushing doorbells.

EPIC's position going into the vote was shaky: Father Coughlin not only withheld an endorsement, he explicitly criticized Sinclair in his weekly radio address.[17] United for California filed a second lawsuit, targeting 35,000 more "fraudulent" voter registrations—all Democrat. So far, 50,000 of the 330,000 new Democrats the EPIC forces had registered were under challenge. Two Assistant Court Commissioners resigned in protest, calling the fraudulent registration suit a "political sham." When the California Supreme Court issued its ruling—on Halloween, appropriately enough, and just seven days before the election—prohibiting the wholesale purging of voters in Los Angeles, the justices confirmed EPIC's position: "It is perfectly clear now that this action is a sham proceeding and a perversion of court process, absolutely void . . . It outrages every principle of justice and fair play."[18]

But it would not be enough. What United for California could not achieve wholesale, it might yet accomplish on a retail level: on election day the Republicans would personally challenge 150,000 voters.

On November 2, airplanes dropped leaflets over downtown Los Angeles. A nonexistent relief committee funded by one of the Merriam groups passed out pamphlets pleading for funding to take care of the 1.5 million bums expected to flood into Southern California when Sinclair was elected. A "Thunder over California" leaflet showed a Russian waving a red flag with hundreds of bums trailing behind. EPIC forces retaliated by pasting Merriam's face over the Russians and had the Governor trampling babies beneath his revolutionary feet on their own leaflet. Raymond Haight, once the leading candidate, now running a distant third, predicted "blood will flow" no matter who wins on Tuesday.[19] Six thousand churchgoers gathered in Shrine Auditorium for an eleventh-hour anti-Sinclair meeting, in which evangelist Aimee Semple McPherson mounted an anticommunist pageant. Nine thousand EPICs rallied at the Pasadena Civic Auditorium. Six thousand more could not get into the auditorium, but a thousand stayed crowded around the steps. Sinclair came out to speak to them, telling them, "For twenty-five years I have been [his friend H. L.] Mencken's prize boob because I believed in you. Now we shall find out which of us is right."[20]

The next evening (November 3, 1934), Sinclair made the last personal appearance of the campaign. The EPIC war chest was empty, but his friend Aline Barnsdall (an oil heiress who had mounted an EPIC billboard facing Hollywood Boulevard on her home, Frank Lloyd Wright's Hollyhock House) contributed $10,000 to rent halls and buy radio time for a statewide, coordinated hookup, linking all the major grassroots rallies up and down the state.

The Los Angeles rally started in Grand Olympic Auditorium, which had recently been set up as a boxing arena. This was the last and biggest event of the campaign, and Robert and Leslyn Heinlein must have been there, representing the West Hollywood Democratic Club.

A huge American flag dominated the stage over the boxing ring where Upton Sinclair would emcee the show.[21] As the broadcast began at 8:30 P.M., the audience sang "The Star-Spangled Banner"—to show EPIC's patriotism—and Sinclair read the Twenty-third Psalm—to show his friendliness to religion. Sinclair then tossed the show to Bakersfield for its grassroots rally, then to Fresno, to Sacramento, and, finally, to San Francisco, where Sinclair's running mate, Sheridan Downey, hosted a rally in the Dreamland Auditorium. Downey handed the show back to Sinclair in Los Angeles for a fifteen-minute talk, only the latest of hundreds in this campaign. "We still have a chance to settle our problems with ballots instead of bullets," Sinclair told them. "It may be the last chance. The issue of this campaign is: can they fool you with their lies, and get you to vote in their interest instead of in your own?"

He ended his speech as he had ended so many others during the campaign: "It's up to you!" Bookmakers were giving Merriam odds of five to one, and the professional politicians were privately calling Merriam the winner.

Without the endorsements that would keep the Democratic Party united, EPIC didn't really have a chance. The EPICs in Olympic Auditorium didn't know that. They were confident Sinclair was going to win. Their own estimates showed a three-to-one margin in favor of Sinclair over Merriam.

On Monday, November 5, 1934, the day before the election, the Registrar of Voters asked the police to be ready to guard the polls in Los Angeles to minimize the bloodshed. EPICs gathered that evening in front of Aimee Semple McPherson's Angelus Temple near downtown Los Angeles and paraded several miles into Hollywood—the biggest parade ever held in Los Angeles.

The polls opened at 6 A.M. on Tuesday, November 6. Thousands were already lined up to vote. United for California concentrated on getting out the vote. The Chamber of Commerce had virtually ordered all member businesses to close that day, and the California Real Estate Association's "Merriam or Moscow" force put all their Realtors' automobiles at the disposal of the United for California group. True to their word, the Republicans challenged about 10 percent of the Democrats registered to vote—but the overwhelming majority qualified and voted. EPIC had "flying wedges" of lawyers to rush to assist wherever Democrats were being harassed by Republicans.

Heinlein was an EPIC poll watcher that day. His experience with the comparatively gentle political machine in Kansas City didn't prepare him for what he found: six thugs who didn't like his count-watching threatened to beat him up. He retreated into the polling place until the lawyers came to rescue him.

> It . . . surprised and shocked me. The polling place was in a prosperous, super-respectable residential neighborhood; it had never occurred to me that there could be any danger—that sort of thing happened only down near the river. And not to me in any case! I was a respectable citizen![22]

But EPIC mutual self-help wasn't always enough: he heard that another poll watcher in the same situation had been beaten and left bleeding on the sidewalk.[23]

The polls closed at 7 P.M. Thousands of people—EPICs and Merriamites alike—gathered in downtown Los Angeles to hear the returns announced over loudspeakers or see them posted on signboards. The tallies began to even up as the night went on, but it was a clear loss for Sinclair and EPIC. By 10:30 P.M., Sinclair's campaign manager, Richard Otto, was beginning to confront the possibility of defeat.

But no matter what the outcome, Sinclair told his EPIC supporters, this election had been a great victory for EPIC against the united opposition of all reactionary forces in the state and piles and piles of money. The final count was 1,100,000 for Merriam; 900,000 for Sinclair; 300,000 for Haight.

But the loss of the governorship race did not mean the campaign was a waste of time: even with dissension in the ranks, Sinclair had gotten twice as many Democratic votes for governor as had ever been cast in California. Of the thirty-eight Democratic State Assemblymen (compared to the Republicans' forty-two), twenty-four were now EPICs, including Augustus Hawkins, who would later go on to become California's first black congressman. In Los Angeles County, EPIC-supported John Anson Ford won a seat on the Board of Supervisors. EPIC was still strong in Los Angeles. Rising liberal politician from the San Dimas area Jerry Voorhis lost his election but predicted EPIC would be "one of those great forces which appear from time to time in human history and actually change the minds and hearts of people until the world is made new."[24]

Culbert Olson, an "earnest and idealistic lawyer,"[25] won a seat to the state senate. He compared the EPIC situation to the founding of the Republican Party in 1856. They didn't make a good showing that year, but in 1860 they elected a president—Abraham Lincoln.[26]

The next morning, Governor Merriam claimed victory in a radio speech and acknowledged his bipartisan support, thanking the Democrats for supporting him. That was a signal that California's opposition to the New Deal was over. Sinclair, too, made a radio speech—not as soft and accommodating as his campaign speeches. "I concede that the election has been stolen." To his campaign workers he expressed his "eternal gratitude" and assured them, "We are the Democratic Party of California." The Democrats who had broken with the party were no longer Democrats.

Sinclair announced that he was going to take a month off to do what he did best: write a companion pamphlet to the EPIC campaign books—an exposé of the campaign, *I, Candidate for Governor, and How I Got Licked.* He would publish it on Merriam's inauguration day, January 7, 1935, offering bargain rates for the serial rights: any magazine or newspaper that wanted it could have it for $1 per thousand copies in circulation.

Sinclair was retiring from active management of the EPIC movement. While he was writing, he told EPICs, follow the leadership of his trusted campaign manager, Richard Otto. They would find new directions for EPIC once he had recovered.

In one of forty letters he wrote on November 7, 1934, Sinclair showed that his ego, at least, was not defeated: "We are far from being licked. The crucifixion of Jesus was looked upon as the greatest failure the world had ever known and now we know it resulted in the greatest victory."[27]

True to his word, Sinclair closeted himself in his Beverly Hills home and began dictating *I, Candidate* three days after the election. Dozens of newspapers and magazines across the country took him up on his serial offer—including, ironically enough, the *Los Angeles Times.*

If politics makes strange bedfellows, the prospect of money makes even stranger: movie censor Will Hays suggested to Louis B. Mayer at MGM that a film on the rise of EPIC might be in order, and Mayer went directly to Sinclair for a proposal. Joe Schenck, who had threatened to move the film industry to Florida, had his studio, Twentieth Century Pictures, ramp up a production of Sinclair's *Depression Island.*

Sinclair had gone down in political defeat and went back to his profession as a working socialist/businessman/writer—and now Robert Heinlein's political work began in earnest.

15

PARTY AND SHADOW PARTY

The day after Thanksgiving 1934, things started to come apart for EPIC: EPIC-elected Senator Olson made a public statement calling for the End Poverty League to dismantle the EPIC movement and merge its local clubs into the statewide Democratic Party apparatus. Richard Otto, now de facto head of the End Poverty League, replied succinctly that EPIC was not a party, it was a movement and would stay as it was. The movement then fractured into two groups with very different aims. The Production-for-Use EPICs wanted to take the movement national—renamed "End Poverty in Civilization"—under Sinclair's continuing leadership. Their aim was to strengthen EPIC's ties to other progressive movements, stressing their independence from party affiliations as a grassroots movement in the American populist tradition. The Democrat-oriented EPICs wanted to rebuild the Democratic Party with EPIC dominating its radical wing and continuing to set the party's agenda. Rube Borough, the managing editor of *EPIC News,* resigned and walked out in the middle of production of the next issue, taking most of the staff with him, to found a regular newspaper, *United Progressive News.*

Although Heinlein stayed with the EPIC Democrats, his subsequent activities suggest he sympathized with both factions and couldn't see why there should even *be* factions. With hundreds of thousands of supporters in California and more coming when EPIC went national, the organization should be pursuing *both* sets of goals—and figuring out some more, too. He was out of the fray for the moment, though: his bad cold turned into influenza and a persistent sinus infection. True to form, his prostatitis recurred. He went to see a private doctor on December 7, 1934, and the treatment this time lasted until July.

But the politics could not wait. Sinclair's retirement left a power vacuum, and the EPIC movement split in January 1935. The head office had managed to get *EPIC News* out for the month of December, but had to find new staff.

The End Poverty League business manager scrambled through the card file on campaign workers with publications experience, and Robert Heinlein's name popped up: he had, after all, edited, written, and published the USS *Lexington*'s paper, *The Observer*. Heinlein was called to the League's offices downtown for an emergency get-out-the-paper effort, and he was given the task of organizing the whole project, almost from the ground up. Upton Sinclair himself and his wife, Mary Craig Sinclair, were there to lend a hand.

This emergency not only thinned out the ranks of upper management—always a good thing for promotions—but it threw Robert and Leslyn into direct contact with Sinclair. Sinclair must have taken a liking to this obviously bright and obviously dedicated young couple. Robert was then just twenty-seven years old, and Leslyn thirty-one.

A little of the luster dimmed for Heinlein, though, when he discovered Sinclair could not do simple arithmetic in his head[1]—even though Sinclair had expected to run an economics-driven bureaucracy.

Sinclair must also have found Heinlein's opinions sound and evolved a use for this newfound tool: Sinclair was going to be turning the California EPIC movement over to the local grassroots management, and that would mean a charter and a revised constitution for the End Poverty League in California. He asked Heinlein to join Saul Klein and Luther Bailey and help write the EPIC constitution.[2] Sinclair had just put him in the position of Thomas Jefferson on the Committee of Five formed by the Second Continental Congress to draft the Declaration of Independence—and not a John Adams or Benjamin Franklin in sight.

Within a few weeks, a regular staff was found for *EPIC News*. Heinlein stayed on as managing editor for the upcoming Los Angeles municipal elections, though his name did not appear on the masthead (only Sinclair and the overall managing editor were credited in *EPIC News*). This emergency was over for the moment—leaving only a few dozen other fires to put out. He had made a couple of friends working with *EPIC News*—particularly Sinclair's secretary, Elma Wentz, and her husband, Roby Wentz, as well as a newspaperman, Cleve Cartmill, who wrote for the paper and for *United Progressive News*. The five of them formed a tight social group.

In mid-February 1935, Robert and Leslyn discovered that they had had a close call that could have ruined any further political ambitions they might develop: on February 19, 1935, the Colorado Sunshine Club they had helped found with the Garrisons was arrested *en masse* and prosecuted for violation of Denver's decency laws. The case was front-page news in *The Denver Post* for months. They had left Colorado just in time.

Early in 1935, the EPIC group received an appeal from James M. Carter in Congressional District 3 (Imperial County) for help with his campaign for city council. Sinclair assigned Heinlein to this task—probably because it would give him some hands-on, one-on-one experience with political campaigns, which would be useful to EPIC in coming years. Leslyn was deputized to keep the home fires burning, and Heinlein loaded up his car and headed south and inland from San Diego. What he saw appalled and outraged him: reactionary vigilantes were carrying on a brutal warfare against agricultural workers, migrant and immigrant.

Out-of-work people were coming to California from all directions, but in early 1935 the outflow from the Oklahoma Dust Bowl had already started. After years of drought, dirt storms, and unexpected, killing deep freeze destroyed Oklahoma's wheat crop in 1933. The record-breaking heat of 1934 finished off the state's economy. "Okies," memorialized a few years later (1939) by John Steinbeck in *The Grapes of Wrath,* flooded toward California along U.S. Route 66, into the San Joaquin and Imperial valleys. The season started near Brawley and El Centro, then they could follow the crops to Santa Barbara, working sixteen-hour days from dawn to dusk, stoop labor that paid them not quite enough to keep body and soul together. Immigration restrictions starting in 1929 had cut off the supply of *braceros* from Mexico. Texans and Oklahomans could pick crops and provide manual labor in place of the 'cans who were no longer available. Max Knepper, a columnist for *EPIC News,* had called the area "semi-feudal" by early 1935 and under the "Fascistic rule" of about a thousand oligarchs, growers and shippers.[3]

Not even California's agriculture could absorb the flood of immigrants that came in 1934 and 1935, however: three hundred thousand migrants were not lucky enough to get jobs. They had no prospects at all—not even state relief until they had been in California for a year. They gathered into squatter camps called "little Oklahomas"—eight thousand of them—beside the roadways. Those down in the Imperial Valley were rated by *Fortune* magazine as "the absolute low for the entire state."[4] Heinlein found the reports were not exaggerated: there was gut-wrenching squalor, tear-raising misery— ten people in one family living in a 1921 Ford, the mother sick with tuberculosis and pellagra, their cooking water coming from the same irrigation ditch that functioned as their toilet.[5]

The growers put pressure on local sheriffs to break up these camps and move them along—though the migrants had nowhere to go. Groups of vigilantes beat up migrants, accusing them of being communists, and burned their shacks to the ground. Heinlein was sickened: this was more class warfare; the reactionary establishment was making brutal war on its own citizens, and at a horrifying social cost. The subject came up years later and was still fresh in both Robert's mind and Leslyn's:

> Leslyn just pointed out that the important point is not that such things are immoral, but that they are *stupid*—by any standards which look toward more than an immediate profit. [Creating an illiterate, inefficient, untrained peasant class in this state] will cost the business men who let it happen more than they made on their "smart deals."[6]

Heinlein could verify the reports that were coming in from every source, national and local. He went back to Los Angeles in early March and prepared to give his findings as a lecture before his local (West Hollywood) Democratic club. He had more or less overcome his self-consciousness about stammering in public; his first public speech, just a few dozen words at a luncheon, had left him white and shaking, "so nervous that I went away without my spectacles,"[7] but by now he was a (nearly) fully blooded reform politician.

The lecture was scheduled for March 16, 1935, but he did not get peace to work on his presentation: a student antiwar strike had been called, worldwide, for Friday, March 12, 1935, to show that young people were alarmed over warlike posturing, particularly in Germany. Fascist governments, it was already clear, meant aggressive, territorial wars, and that was inescapable. The whole world seemed to be on an irreversible drift toward war. In the United States, the increase in military appropriations, taken together with antiradical stunts across the country, caused the editors of *EPIC News* to wonder in print if the military appropriations were not intended to put down an uprising of *U.S. citizens* against their civil masters.[8]

The demonstrations were relatively quiet on most college campuses, with 125,000 students walking out of classes across the country. The Los Angeles Junior College campus was the site of an actual riot. Director Roscoe Ingalls of the campus administration ordered the small crowd of students gathered near the steps of the library to disperse, threatening them with suspension, and then blew a whistle to summon an "anti-Red" squad of plainclothes and uniform policemen provided by L.A. Chief of Police James Davis. According to published reports, one of the "red squad" detectives suddenly and without specific provocation began swinging his nightstick, flailing out at random. One of the uniformed sergeants pulled the girl who was speaking at the time off the library steps and began to beat her with his fists when she resisted. Another coed, Flora Turchinsky, had her nose bloodied by a nightstick.[9] An *Evening News-Standard* photographer caught this moment in a front-page splash, and this was how Heinlein learned of the incident.[10]

On the morning of Heinlein's report to the West Hollywood Democratic Club about the Imperial Valley, the *Hollywood Citizen-News* reported the follow-up to the strike. The *Los Angeles Times* barely noticed the fuss. It wasn't news that "fit" in Harry Chandler's newspaper.[11] "I got mad as a boiled owl," Heinlein reported, "and sat down and wrote a most sarcastic letter to the public forum department of the *Hollywood Citizen-News*," their local progressive paper:[12]

The Plot is Broken. Town Meeting:

Courage, citizens, fear no longer. The great revolutionary plot of 1935 is broken. Once again we are safe from those nasty Rooshians (or was it Japs?) In any case the peril is over. Our doughty Chief of Police and our ever-watchful school board have dealt heroically with the invaders and we are safe. Visions of our heroic traditions pass before our eyes. Finally a crowning touch, 18 year old Flora [Turchinsky] knocked unconscious by our brave guardians.

And Comradski Margaret, she got hers. Director Ingalls blew valiantly on his whistle and the deed was practically done. A few manly right arms, raised in defense of liberty and our American honor, and she was through for the day. The shades of Ethan Allen, Nathan Hale and Paul Revere smiled down from the beautiful California sky.

The school board, acting in its wisdom, wouldn't let Bernice come to the party. She was a menace and must be kept from contaminating our youth. What if she is very young and pretty and dimples when she smiles; just that much more insidious.[13]

But it's all over now and we may sleep in peace. Put away the gas masks. The Chief of Police and the School Board have landed and have the situation well in hand. America is safe again.

—R. A. Heinlein
Lieut., U.S. Navy[14]

That very last line—which may have been added by Leslyn (though Robert took full and sole responsibility for it officially[15])—was to have repercussions.

It made the letter appear to be the statement of a serving officer—and therefore presumably in the line of duty.

The letter would appear in the *Hollywood Citizen-News* the day after his report to his local Democratic club on conditions in the Imperial Valley.

The meeting came too late to get into the week's *EPIC News*, which came out on Tuesday each week—but that Tuesday the *Hollywood Citizen-News* carried the report of Heinlein's presentation to the West Hollywood Democratic Club, quoting his "hook": "Constitutional rights of workers in Imperial Valley have been abrogated by some of the citizens and elected officials in amazing display of vigilante activities." The article continued:

> In a report on a recent investigation trip into Imperial county, Robert A. Heinlein described conditions of the workers and the lawlessness permitted there as reported to the Imperial County Board of Supervisors by Gen. Pelham D. Glassford, investigator for Secretary of Labor Frances Perkins.
>
> Vivid scenes among California's unemployed were shown in the first EPIC newsreel which will be part of the club's bi-monthly programs in the future.[16]

Sinclair and Otto continued to heap work on Heinlein. By the time of the municipal elections in the first week of April 1935, he was a county committeeman, a state committeeman, and a district chairman. Heinlein was also one of fifty Assembly District secretaries who helped make the arrangements for the EPIC organizing convention on May 16–18. His constitution committee had grown to six and was producing two different drafts, a minority constitution as well as a majority constitution. Sinclair appointed a conference committee to meld the two drafts into a single proposed constitution in time to be mimeographed and distributed for the convention.

The EPIC convention started at 10:00 A.M. on May 16, 1935, with four hundred delegates gathered in the Labor Temple in downtown Los Angeles. There was a slight hitch over credentials: the delegates were elected by the chapters of the End Poverty League all up and down the state, and the fractioning of the EPL meant that some chapters had elected two slates of delegates. That had to be sorted our first.

It was hardly possible to recognize what was actually going on at the convention from the newspaper reports. The convention was relatively businesslike, but the *Los Angeles Times* reported riots and underhanded double-dealings. They started the Saturday morning session with the crowd singing

American folk and patriotic songs. During the singing of "Marching Through Georgia," agitators for the Communist United Front dropped leaflets, and that brought the United Front issue up for discussion.

The Communist International had recently proposed that all progressive organizations in the world join with them in a united front against fascism and reaction—which sounded like a good idea, except that it meant in practice that the organizations would have to adopt communist tactics wherever the United Front took them.[17] Heinlein had been elected as a delegate representing the West Hollywood EPIC Club (though he had since resigned from the club when they instructed the delegates to vote for the United Front). He was attending now as a delegate-without-portfolio, freelance, as he later said.[18]

Sinclair opposed having EPIC join the United Front—but he responded by scheduling a formal debate on the question for the Sunday session, after the constitution had been adopted. The communists who were not delegates were then ejected, because Sinclair wouldn't allow their demonstration to block the convention. The *Times* report was of some other EPIC convention, with several dramatic events that never actually happened: they had Sinclair leaping to a chair and declaring, "There are Communists among us."[19]

During the reseating that would allow all the actual delegates to vouch for each other, Jerry Voorhis stood in the center aisle and pled with the delegates not to team up with the communists—the first time Heinlein had seen Voorhis[20]; it made an impression on him, and they thereafter became friendly.

In the Saturday afternoon session, the convention took up the draft constitution, section by section, getting through about a third before adjourning for a banquet and dance at Leighton's Cafeteria. They blanket-approved the rest, except for a single section.

The convention took up the last remaining section of the constitution on Sunday and an ad hoc discussion of the United Front, with debate limited to twenty minutes for and twenty against. The convention caucused and agreed to join any united front with all *democratic* organizations, which let the communists out. The EPIC lamb decided not to lie down with the communist lion and chance not getting up again. Things would only grow more difficult over the next several years as they buckled down to making the Democratic EPIC work.

A letter from the Secretary of the Navy dated May 29, 1935, was forwarded to Heinlein from the Naval District 11 Commandant's office in San Diego. It quoted the sarcastic "Town Meeting" editorial letter he and Leslyn had written, which had been published in the *Hollywood Citizen-News* on

April 17, and asked him to explain himself. On June 8, Heinlein wrote back:
"[S]everal explanatory phrases were removed by the editor, but the letter is
essentially mine." He explained: "I was not sympathetic to the student strike
and urged several of my student acquaintances to refrain from participating
in it." He included several newspaper clippings about the incident, including the shocking and grotesque front-page photograph of a policeman clubbing Flora Turchinsky.

> I felt that an injustice had been done. When I read the report of the young
> girls being clubbed senseless by police officers I became highly indignant.
> As an officer and a gentleman I felt that I could not let the matter pass
> without a protest. I used my rank in conjunction with my signature be-
> cause I thought that the citizens had a right to know that officers of the
> federal military forces do not consider violence to young girls necessary in
> order to insure an adequate national defense.

The Navy was not impressed. Heinlein received a private, written admonition from Admiral Leahy, Secretary of the Navy:

> The letter, signed with your Naval title, which you sent to the Hollywood
> Citizen, and which was published on 17 April 1935, is, in the opinion of
> the Department, neither in good taste nor is it composed in a seemly and
> proper manner [and is therefore in violation of Paragraph four of General
> Order Number 46 of 20 May 1921].
> For this indiscretion you are hereby admonished.[21]

The admonition was a minor, if painful, irritant—then. Heinlein conceded it was correct in essence,[22] but it also could be used to tar him with the
same brush as the communists and their sympathizers, even though he most
decidedly was not.

In the meantime, life went on. Since they landed in Los Angeles in August
1934, they had been living in an apartment in what is now West Hollywood,
on La Jolla a block south of Santa Monica Boulevard,[23] but as early as December 1934, when Heinlein wrote his profile for the upcoming sixth reunion of his Annapolis class,[24] he and Leslyn had found and made a firm
offer on a house in the Laurel Canyon area, almost halfway up the mountains that separate Los Angeles from the San Fernando Valley. By June 1935,
they completed the purchase of the house at 8777 Lookout Mountain, with

a mortgage for $3,000, and moved in permanently.[25] At that time, mortgage payments would have been about $25 to $30 a month—the better part of Heinlein's monthly retired pay.

To be an EPIC Democrat in the mid-1930s was to be in the middle of every progressive movement in the United States, all of them concentrated in Southern California. In July 1935, the Seventh World Congress of the Comintern announced the Popular Front against fascism throughout the world, bizarrely holding up the Nazi government of Germany as "the highest form of capitalism." The success of this peculiar "big lie" would cripple the ability of traditional liberals to resist the growth of totalitarian ideology. They would have to be antifascist and anticommunist and anticapitalist all at the same time. Liberals didn't realize it yet, but traditional—"classical"—liberalism began to collapse as an intellectual movement in the United States from that moment. The entire country was watching the ferment in California. As the largest of the progressive movements, EPIC tried to maintain coalition relationships with the cooperative movement, technocracy, and even the Communist Party in the middle of an internal and very uncivil war precipitated by the United Front.

Probably as a direct result of the investigation and report Heinlein had made of vigilantism in the Imperial Valley in 1936, the newly elected Supervisor for Los Angeles County, John Anson Ford, asked Heinlein to investigate relief activities and the WPA in Los Angeles County. Ford had never actually been a part of the EPIC organization, but he was a reformer very much to Sinclair's liking, and EPIC approved Heinlein's cooperation.

Ford had been elected by a grassroots organization in Los Angeles. He had not taken any stand on the state gubernatorial campaign; he was narrowly focused on Los Angeles County issues and, unlike Sinclair, he was not "too far to the left" for the electorate. Heinlein knew both the Fords well from organizing the *EPIC News* coverage of the municipal elections in 1935.

Ford's issue was waste, profiteering, and graft eating away at the county budget. The county's entrenched bureaucracy stonewalled any inquiry through channels, so Ford began asking knowledgeable outsiders to make informal investigations, a tactic so successful that investigators sometimes found their cars bombed.[26] Heinlein is not mentioned in John Anson Ford's professional autobiography, *Thirty Explosive Years in Los Angeles County*[27]; only Clifford Clinton's work is mentioned in any detail. Perhaps this was because Heinlein's investigation duplicated and confirmed the work of others—but it was grist for Heinlein's political mill and is listed in a campaign biography he wrote in 1938.

The 1936 elections were the next big push for the Democrats, and, as Democratic Party secretary for the 59th Assembly District (Hollywood, West Hollywood, and Laurel Canyon), Heinlein actively campaigned for the still mostly EPIC Democratic slate. He must have stayed with real estate for a while, as a temporary real estate salesman card is preserved in his files licensing him to sell land from February 27 to August 26, 1936, for Vandervort & Teague (possibly his old Naval Academy friend Woody Teague). But it was bare subsistence. Politics was where Heinlein concentrated his energies.

Histories of the EPIC movement—including the comments in Upton Sinclair's autobiography and, of course, Mitchell's *Campaign of the Century*—are largely stories of the 1934 campaign. They give the impression that the movement ceased to exist after Sinclair lost the governorship. But EPIC remained a strong force in California (the national EPIC effort never really got off the ground) until after 1940. The 1936 elections were particularly busy for the Heinleins.

Jerry Voorhis had resigned from the EPIC board of directors in order to keep out of the dissension, and now he was running for the 12th District seat in the U.S. House of Representatives. Robert's State Assemblyman, Charles W. Lyon, was not up for reelection that year, but the congressional district, District 16, was contested, and the Heinleins both campaigned hard for the EPIC candidate in the party's primary election, Ordean Rockey. Rockey was a political science professor at UCLA—and a Rhodes Scholar (1917). His one fault, Heinlein thought, was that he liked too much to be liked:

> Ordean could always be persuaded by any pressure group to back anything, just as long as they made it sound as if it would be "noble" of him to do it. Far from being blunt or forthright, Ordean could occupy any platform for any length of time, win ringing applause—and never say anything which would show up as a positive statement under semantic analysis.[28]

Still, those were assets in a campaigner, and Rockey would need every asset he could come up with to win the Democratic primary from the incumbent, John Dockweiler. The Civic Research League, a citizens group that tried to weed out the most corrupt candidates, recommended Rockey for the 16th District in the Democratic primary, and Leslyn organized a Rockey-for-Congress Ball.[29]

Leslyn and Robert worked together in the campaigns for Rockey and

Harlan Palmer (editor of the *Hollywood Citizen-News*). Palmer had been drafted to run as the Democratic candidate for District Attorney, against incumbent Burton Fitts, whom "no true liberal or progressive can support."[30] They concentrated on precinct work—utterly essential direct contact with the voter that is often neglected because it is hard work, demanding and uncongenial except to that rare person who finds talking amiably with strangers energizing rather than enervating. Neither Robert nor Leslyn fit into that profile: talking one-on-one with strangers did not come easily or naturally to Heinlein. He would often get home from these meetings drained and shaking with nervous exhaustion, even when they went smoothly and relations were cordial. Conflict would leave him shaking, his stomach tied in knots.[31]

Heinlein learned in his life in politics to conceal the drain on his energies from the people he was meeting and glad-handing. He prepared intensely, reading and studying all the issues and movements in which his constituents might have an interest, keeping a set of "issue" scrapbooks starting in 1935 that held newspaper and magazine article clippings. He developed a smooth and polished surface manner that struck most people as refined and even aristocratic. And when prepared, he found he could genuinely enjoy meeting people: nothing could be more fascinating than the endless variation in the personal quirks of individuals. Politics, he concluded, was truly the only game for adults.[32]

For the most part, Heinlein kept his own opinions to himself, nodding agreeably and letting the person he was speaking with assume they were together, shoulder to shoulder. Arguing with someone, he found, was no way to win a vote—and usually produced no good results of any kind. In private, with Leslyn, he would voice his opinions—or in tactical conferences, where his evaluation of the situation was critical to the campaign.[33] Heinlein had the social engineer's attitude: facts—not wishful thinking—were the building blocks of what you could do with what resources you had. "This arrogant independence will get my tires slashed someday. Or worse. But I am no sheep and that just might be a Judas Goat leading the procession. I'll decide for myself—and the mistakes will be mine."[34]

The biggest problem they had was the giant split down the middle of the Democratic Party, with EPICs on one side and the traditional Democrats on the other. Scattered around the fringes were all the one-issue and other radical reformers. Sinclair had taken Democratic registration to parity with the Republicans in 1934; by 1936, the California Democratic Party had a three-to-two voter registration advantage—but if the Democrats were going to keep their edge, they were going to have to pull together. "'Blessed is the peacemaker'—for he shall see his party triumph in November!"[35]

Robert and Leslyn started hosting informal breakfasts Sunday mid-mornings for the workers in their district, to provide a neutral ground where all the different factions could come face-to-face. Differences might not actually be resolved, but these occasions could encourage people to realize that they had common ground politically when they had common ground socially, and that's the first condition to resolving differences. Leslyn Heinlein recorded some thoughts about this process:

> . . . one of the most useful functions which Bob and I performed in our political activities was that of getting people together who were in basic agreement and didn't know it. It is amazing how quickly methods of accomplishing a desired end can be worked out, once two people who have been busy hating each other's guts get the idea that they want to accomplish the same end and have been fighting over *how*. When one can approach a problem agreed as to the end in view and the *motives* of the other, the differences can be *discussed* (instead of fought over) ad seriatum, unemotionally, and a solution satisfactory to both worked out, in most cases.[36]

What worked for a congressional district would work for the larger sections in the Democratic Party. Heinlein was appointed to the state Democratic Central Committee and to the Veterans Division of the National Committee (after being elected to the Los Angeles County Central Committee) in 1936.[37] They began following up Sunday breakfasts with Sunday afternoon teas for which Leslyn made butter cookies with one of the newly popular aluminum cookie presses (both the Heinleins loved gadgets of all kinds: Robert even had a set of glass balls with ice inside, so they could keep iced drinks cold without diluting them as the event wore on). There the members of different factions could communicate across the ideological divides. Nobody wins elections with tea and cookies, Heinlein pointed out, but the lesson of Sinclair's defeat in 1934 was that defections in your own party can kill you deader than the opposition of your enemy. "Party harmony makes a fine hobby for anyone."[38]

Their teamwork was superb, and Robert relied on the support Leslyn gave him. They were working together very closely, and they planned their moves carefully by talking everything over at home. When, in public, Robert would suddenly stop in midsentence and grope for a word or be caught by a stammer about to become obvious, Leslyn could often complete his sentences; and when her attention was diverted, he could complete her sentences.[39] They joked about the Heinlein group mind, and Robert was careful to explain that they were actually working as a team, even though most of the public attention was directed to him.[40] And that was the way Leslyn wanted it: with the opposition focused on Robert, she could maneuver freely behind the scenes.[41] They made a very effective team.

But Robert noticed that some little things weren't quite right with Leslyn anymore. They had been married for more than three years, living in each other's laps for most of that time, and he knew she was changing in some way, not just revealing a new aspect of her personality. Nothing was really definite: unexplained irritations, maybe, and flashes of temper from time to time in private.[42]

Otherwise, things were fine. They were enjoying their political work—and Heinlein found that there were days at a time when he didn't miss the Navy. He was finally getting over "swallowing the anchor."[43] Their biggest problem was that they were scraping by on Heinlein's Navy pension and occasional income from sales jobs. Real estate didn't work out for him. Sinclair's loss in the 1934 election had put the established real-estate brokers back in business and eliminated the market niche he had hoped to exploit. And, at any rate, he found he had no talent for sales. He was even thinking about taking a correspondence course in architecture; he had some ideas about planning single-family housing—just jotted notes at this point, something to play with.[44]

Leslyn wrote a piece for *Rob Wagner's Script* magazine, "Communists Are Religious Fanatics."[45] The communists had faded a little into the background after the EPIC constitutional convention in May 1935, but by September 1935, Sinclair was convinced that the communists had co-opted the EPIC movement in California, and he thereafter distanced himself from EPIC, leaving Richard Otto (and the Heinleins) to struggle with the problem on their own.

Pragmatically, Robert and Leslyn knew that the Democratic Party was rotten with communists. "Communists are *not* villains," he said, but they were very much in the way and insofar as the success of the Democratic Party was concerned, they were divisive to a degree that could not be tolerated—part of the problem and not part of the solution.[46] It was a continuing struggle—and an utterly necessary one, for the party's strength in California was very new and could wither away, leaving the Republicans again in control, if the party were allowed to split. Heinlein was *not* a Popular Front liberal.

For his efforts, he got on the Communist Party's "better dead" list.

> Specifically, I have incurred the ire of any and all communist party members and/or party liners who have become aware of my existence. As a left wing but anti-communist politico a large number of them *have* become aware of my existence. . . . I once achieved the honor of being moved up to spot number four on the black list of the communist party in California.[47]

The dislike was mutual. Individual communists may not be villains, but Heinlein had the then common liberal's abhorrence of communism as an active force in the world:

> Let me go on record that I regard communism as expressed by the U.S.S.R. and its friends here and elsewhere as a grisly horror, a tyranny maintained by force and terror, utterly subversive of human liberty, freedom of thought, and dignity. I regard it as Red fascism, distinguishable from black and brown fascism by differences of no importance to me nor to its victims.[48]

So far as he was concerned, European fascism (Germany and Italy) and Soviet communism were identically evil.[49]

The tension of the 1936 campaigns was relieved from time to time that year by visits to and from Sally Rand.[50] After the Century of Progress exhibition finally closed in Chicago, she had taken her fan- and bubble-dance acts to the California Pacific Exposition in San Diego, by invitation. The Expo organization hoped she could help bolster attendance, which had begun to sag.

She worked hard for the Exposition, though she was literally stoned on April 15, 1936: she was assaulted by rocks thrown from the crowd—for no apparent reason—that left her bleeding and with bruises under her left eye and on her thighs. But Sally Rand was a trouper: when not dancing, she gave wholesome interviews, attended church services, and toured San Diego and environs, playing the role of celebrity. She baked a cake for the Expo's Palace of Better Housing, took part in a balloon blowing contest at the Zone, and gave open lectures to teachers and groups and teachers on "the art of the dance."[51]

The Expo had a competing act, nudist Rosita Royce, who trained white doves to perch strategically on her body. Sally Rand's dance act was not nudism—it was art, she said. But she put on a nude show of her own at the 1936 Frontier Exposition in Fort Worth (and repeated it for the 1939 Golden Gate International Exposition in San Francisco).

In 1936, Heinlein picked up a new book that enchanted him as no book had done since Cal Laning had talked him into reading *Jurgen* in 1929. Vincent McHugh's *Caleb Catlum's America* was about a redheaded boy-man-demigod who leads his family of free spirits and true Americans into a safe place of hiding in a land beyond a cave, until the corrupt and materialistic should pass and it was safe to emerge. The frame story was split up by three hundred pages of tall tales and improbabilities. It was a big and complex book, like nothing except, perhaps, *Tristam Shandy*, and he was enchanted with it. So was Leslyn. They used it as a touchstone, along with Charles G. Finney's 1935 *Circus of Dr. Lao*, to measure the personal compatibility of any new acquaintance. If you liked both books, you were in with the Heinleins.[52]

After the elections that November,[53] Heinlein finally saw the film H. G. Wells had just finished. *Things to Come* was a major cultural event; Wells himself was an international celebrity, and the film has the participation of major artists: Alexander Korda produced it, and the score was written by the "advanced" composer Arthur Bliss.[54]

Wells portrayed the old order destroying itself in the war everyone could sense was coming—was perhaps already under way, if the fighting between royalists and fascists in Spain was any indication—and a new, visionary order coming into being, led by Raymond Massey's aviators of Wings Over the World. It was a documentary of the future, as stylish as Albert Speer's designs for the sixth NSADP congress in Nuremberg the September before, grandly memorialized by Leni Riefenstahl's 1935 propaganda documentary *Triumph of the Will*. Heinlein was delighted with Wells's tale.[55]

Britain was in the news. Like many Americans, Heinlein had been following the troubles of the House of Windsor. In December, the boy king Edward VII had been forced to abdicate because he wanted to marry the American divorcée Wallis Simpson. On May 12, 1937, Heinlein tuned in to hear the new King's international radio address on the evening of King George VII's coronation and was deeply affected by the man's halting tongue: "A corrected stammerer myself, I suffered with him during his first radio speech after becoming king—and triumphed with him at the enormous improvement in his later speeches."[56]

Ten days later, on May 22, 1937, his youngest brother, Jesse Clare, married Dorothy Martin, and Robert and Leslyn traveled back to Kansas City for the occasion, returning on June 20. Almost all of the Heinlein children were married now. Only baby Mary Jean, in high school, was still living at home in Kansas City.

In August 1937, Heinlein resigned from the chairmanship of the 59th District Democratic Party organization. He had just finished working on Supervisor Ford's (unsuccessful) campaign for the mayoralty of Los Angeles—and he had gotten enough experience running things in the background. More background work came along all the time, of course: the Los Angeles County Central Committee drafted him to chair the 59th Assembly District Committee he had just resigned from. He did not refuse the draft. Possibly he considered it was something he could do while he prepared for a bigger challenge: the time had come for him to run for office himself.

PARTY ANIMAL

The 1938 elections were even more critical for the California Democratic Party than the 1936 elections had been. Frank Merriam's reign as Governor-King-Log had disgusted even his reluctant supporters from the 1934 elections, and it was unlikely they would again "hold their nose and vote for Merriam."[1] The Democrats were running a former EPIC, Senator Culbert Olson, to oust Merriam; Olson's campaign was managed by Hollywood actor-activist Melvyn Douglas, and it looked as though Olson had solid support.[2]

But they had to fill the Democratic slate. In the pre-Sinclair days, the extremely weak Democratic Party had often not run candidates in many elections; but now they were strong enough to do so, and do so they must. The party's formal platform was still EPIC, and the shadow organization of EPIC clubs nominally controlled the Democratic Party: it was up to EPIC to do something about it.

In 1938, the 59th Assembly District seat would be up for election. This district—Heinlein's home district—was considered "safe" for the Republican incumbent, Charles W. Lyon, but Lyon had been targeted by EPIC as a particularly reactionary legislator who needed to be removed for the good of the state. *EPIC News* ranked his voting record among the worst in the California State Assembly—seventy-first out of eighty, with sixteen "good," sixty-four "bad," and twenty absences.[3] But "good" and "bad" were a matter of definition; his Republican constituency liked Lyon, and the party leadership didn't think *any* Democrat could win in that thoroughly Republican district that included conservative Hollywood and Beverly Hills.

But nothing charges up an old socialist pol's batteries like an action for the good of the state. Heinlein got the charge: he was going to replace Charlie Lyon and send him back to his Hollywood law practice.

This was the largest and most demanding individual project he had ever taken on: he was going to work harder at this than he had ever worked in his life. And as to the important questions, Why him? Why now? . . .

A seat in the California State Assembly would position him to help out with what H. G. Wells called that progressive task of "unusually clear-headed and obstinate individuals" in opposing "the egoist and the fool in man"; to resist "simplified formulae" and gain experience in handling human affairs. Ultimately, Wells continued, when the time is right, "They will reshape the general conceptions of economic, political and social life."[4] There could be no clearer statement of Robert Heinlein's overarching political goals.

Heinlein's situation was somewhat complicated by family matters. His father, Rex, had been ill off and on for the last dozen years, but he had remained employed in the accounting department of International Harvester. In 1937, at the age of fifty-nine, Rex retired with a small pension. All the spirit seemed to have gone out of him. At first he was listless, but he spiraled down alarmingly into a state of acute depression. Initially, they thought it was senility setting in early, though early senility did not run in the family. The Veterans Administration doctors in Kansas were puzzled over his case and referred him to the veterans' hospital in Los Angeles, where his condition was diagnosed as involutional melancholia—a very serious condition and one that required long-term care.

Bam moved the family, by now reduced to just the two of them and Mary Jean (now aged eighteen years), out to Hollywood in 1938.[5] There is no definite record of the move or the circumstances, but they may have stayed with Robert and Leslyn for at least a time. The Laurel Canyon house would have been crowded with three extra people. Since the family was giving up the house in Kansas City, Robert probably agreed at that time to take some of the extra storage—a trunk for his brother Rex.[6] He could store it in the garage, with the accumulation of leftovers from his political activities.

His father's condition was very disturbing to Robert,[7] though he tried not to show it to his family, to be a support. Rex Ivar had fallen off the edge of the world, he just wasn't there anymore. Involutional melancholia is a psychotic depression that usually appears in late middle age—a period called the "involutional period of middle life" in the older literature: forty to fifty-five years old for women, fifty to sixty-five for men. In 1938, Rex Ivar was just in the middle of the male range. The disease classically includes preoccupation with death and loss; agitation; delusions of ill health, poverty, sin, and sometimes even of the nonexistence of the world (all themes that were to show up later in Robert's writing).[8] Robert thought it was brought on by his father's sense of guilt over his part in Rose Betty's death, twelve years earlier, preying on him all these years, perhaps masking the on-set of the serious illness.[9]

Rex Ivar was not senile—but in 1938 he might as well have been: involu-tional melancholia was something you just didn't recover from. The mind died, and the body continued to function. Doctors had recently (1935 and 1937) been successful in bringing some involutional melancholics around with daily or weekly injections of sex hormones—estrogen for women and testosterone for men. But the therapy was very new and not yet widely available. The clinical trials were to continue through the early 1940s[10]—not the kind of thing that veterans' hospitals usually engage in. Robert and Bam might not even have known about the trials at the time. For them, it was to be a long, slow, agonizing good-bye.

And in the meantime, Heinlein resigned from the chairmanship of the Democratic district organization in preparation for the campaign—but he had promptly been drafted to run committees within the county and statewide party organization anyway. In a questionnaire he filled out for the Navy in January 1938, he listed himself as a member of the Los Angeles County Democratic Central Committee and the California State Central Democratic Committee. Leslyn was temporarily out of commission (presumably with chicken pox or something else equally debilitating and equally temporary) when he had to announce his candidacy,[11] so he asked Roby Wentz to manage his campaign.

Roby and his wife, Elma, had become close friends with the Heinleins through EPIC politics. They had initially met early in 1935, when the Hein-leins were thrown into direct contact with Upton Sinclair. Elma was then Sinclair's personal secretary, so Heinlein wound up dealing with her quite a lot on the California constitution committee. She was a lot of fun—politically compatible, naturally—but she also shared some of Heinlein's in-terest in occult and esoteric matters, with a different slant on the ideas that, judging by his passing mentions of her in correspondence over the years, Heinlein found refreshing. Roby had a B.A. from Stanford in English litera-ture and worked as a a political journalist and screenwriter with a side inter-est in seismology that generated an occasional popular science article. He had also written occasionally for *EPIC News*.

The Heinlein brain trust roughed out a platform that touched all the "hot buttons" of his constituency and put together a press release for his an-nouncement on March 15, 1938—a timing that suggests that Heinlein was running as a Democrat and *not* as an EPIC. They had not timed the an-nouncement to catch the *EPIC News* weekly publication cycle—and, in fact,

EPIC News did not include him for three weeks in the "Straw Ballot" feature it ran for several issues before the paper was suspended in May 1938 due to lack of funds (its chronic condition—and now a fatal one). Heinlein first appears in the "Straw Ballot" on April 4, the only registered Democrat in the district.

> *Heinlein to File for Assembly.* Robert A. Heinlein, a member of the Beverly Hills–Carthay Circle Young Democratic Club, has announced himself as a candidate for the Democratic nomination for the State Assembly in the 59th District. If he receives the nomination he will probably oppose the Republican incumbent, Charles W. Lyon of Beverly Hills, long-time corporation attorney with one of the worst records in the California Legislature.
>
> Candidate Heinlein gives the following as his platform:
> Security from waste.
> Security from disaster by flood, fire and earthquakes.
> Security in our homes and persons, from persecution, crime and police brutality.
> Security in our old age.
> Security for our children.
> Security from lobby-control.
> Security of our natural resources for posterity.
> Security from war.
> Security from unjust taxation.
> Security in our jobs.[12]

By this time, Heinlein probably knew too much about managing campaigns in Los Angeles for his own good: he might be tempted to micromanage his campaign instead of behaving like a candidate. But political campaigns in the post-Sinclair era were a new problem, and two heads are in fact better than one in some cases.

Heinlein and Wentz had learned a lot of tricks to run a campaign. Printing is usually the largest cost item for a campaign—campaign flyers and billboards and posters—followed closely by getting the material distributed. Billboards were costly, so there was little point in employing them—except, of course, for offices that had some regulatory power over billboards. On the other hand, there were lots of ways to get the small community newspapers to cover your campaigns. A little "grease" sometimes went a long way; the campaign managers could place an ad accompanied by a check and a press release, dangling the prospect of future ad placements. Then you were "in the family" and the paper—even the neighborhood throwaway papers—would continue to give you press.

At every election, professional fund-raisers called on all the candidates, offering their services. Typically, they skimmed half the "take." In addition, there were paid vote-getters who supervised a corps of volunteers. Heinlein's campaign was too small to support paid fund-raisers; he had to rely on his own seed capital and whatever his "circle of influence" could raise. Among his campaign contributors, he noted a check from "Lloyd Wright, Sr."—the architect Frank Lloyd Wright, who was at that time living in the district, on Doheny near Sunset, while working on one of his Hollywood projects.[13] He drew a lot of help from his Young Democrats—a young volunteer named Bill Corson came to know him in this campaign and became a lifelong friend, based at least partly on Corson's passion for guns and shooting.[14]

It was going to be a tough campaign. Lyon had the incumbent's advantage in a conservative and traditionally Republican district—and he didn't have a split party to deal with. Lyon was confident that he would win: he took a gigantic gamble and cross-filed, having himself, a Republican, put on the Democratic primary ballot. If he won more votes from Democrats than Heinlein, the Democratic candidate in his district,[15] he would automatically win the election, running unopposed. He was confident of his Republican support—and he gambled that mainstream Democrats in his district wouldn't support a Sinclair Democrat.

On top of everything else, everybody was still jittery over the prospect of war. In Congress, isolationism was becoming a strong political force, and Senator Truman had even raised the specter of "preparedness": "[C]onditions in Europe have developed to a point likely to cause an explosion any time."[16] Everybody was Germany-watching when the Nazis' Gauleiter for the Sudetenland started making international headlines: Konrad Henlein—only one letter difference in the names. Heinlein's district was heavily Jewish. They noticed these things. It was one more hurdle to overcome—for a district the party didn't think it could win at all. But more distressing, the local Communist Party endorsed him, and he had a hard time fending off doubtless sincere, but still deadly, offers of help.[17]

But he knew he had a magic weapon that could crank out votes like magic: he had diamonds on the soles of his shoes. Walking the precincts would do it for him, one handshake at a time and one vote at a time.

The Grass-Roots Campaign has gone out of style in most parts of the country. . . . But the people, the individual Americans, are still interested in their candidates; to have one show up at the front door is as delightful a novelty to most of them as would be a chance to ride a circus elephant. That unreality, the candidate on the platform, on the billboard, or in the newspaper, suddenly becomes warmly human and a little more than life size.[18]

Issues count, certainly—but there is magic in direct personal contact of the candidate with the voter. And to this general lever-that-could-move-the-world was added his personal assets: an extraordinary memory for names and faces—a natural gift developed by cultivating it.[19]

Precinct walking was his key strategy, and it was in his blood from his earliest political days in Kansas City's Pendergast ward system. Already the big parties were backing away from the local person-to-person contact that is the real fundamental in politics. By concentrating on the basics, Heinlein would win this election. He got a copy of the voter rolls for his district from the registrar of voters and cut them into individual names and addresses, which he then pasted on three-by-five-inch cards—six thousand index cards in sorting trays he kept in his home office (a deal table in a corner of the living room). During the months of the campaign, he personally visited every house.

Beverly Hills was in his district, and that sometimes posed a problem: the wealthy Hollywood types were almost all rock-ribbed Republicans. On the other hand, the mansions employed fleets of servants, busing in every day along Santa Monica Boulevard, and they were probably *not* rock-ribbed Republicans. Those were back-door houses. Going from back door to back door, he talked to the servants, rather than the house owners, because they were more likely to be Democrats. It does not seem to have occurred to him that they also probably did not live and vote in his district.[20]

And he kept records of his visits on his three-by-five-inch file cards—just bare notes of when he had been there and whether he had found anyone at home, and anything unusual. At each address, he left a calling card printed with his picture and name: "Robert A. Heinlein—the only Democratic Candidate for Assembly, 59th Dist."

He rang doorbells for three months before the primary, forty hours a week. Personal calls on registered voters were the top priority. Everybody in Heinlein's campaign who could walked the precinct, rang doorbells, and made personal contact with the voters, following the candidate's lead. Everything else was scheduled around the precinct walk. Leslyn—and even his now eighteen-year-old baby sister, Mary Jean—helped out in the campaign.

After the daily precinct walk, Heinlein attended political events, rallies, club meetings. For every political meeting, he led his volunteers in greeting each person who came to the meeting and made sure to get a three-by-five-inch card with at least basic contact information. The cards were piled by the door—ideally they were printed or mimeographed with blanks for the information, though plain blank cards would do in a pinch.

Robert led his volunteer campaign workers by example. He knew exactly what he wanted:

> . . . the best way is to fill out [the cards] yourself . . . while asking them the necessary questions and keeping up a running fire of conversation. Don't say "Name? Address? Any other adults in family? Telephone? Occupation?" Such an approach acts like a cold shower. Say, "Glad to know you, Mr. Brewster. Half a minute and let me get that down in writing. My wife says I can't be trusted to buy a pound of butter unless she writes it down. I wouldn't want you to miss getting an invitation to the Spring Dance through my poor memory. That's 'James A. Brewster,' isn't it? Mrs. Brewster come with you tonight? So? My wife's doing the same thing—we've got two kids, both in grammar school, and they have to be in bed by nine. How old are your youngsters? Maybe some day we can arrange a sort of game room or nursery for the kids and get a lot of folks out who are otherwise chained down. Do you think it would help if we moved up the meeting time half an hour? Is that address right? That's your home address, isn't it? Business address, you say? Oh, of course—that's the same block the Safeway Market is in. It's not the same address is it? Oh—I think that's the same block of offices Dr. Boyer is in. Hey—Fred! Doc! Want you to meet a neighbor of yours—Dr. Boyer, Mr. James Brewster. You know each other already—fine. Doc, see that Mr. Brewster meets some of the folks, will you?"
>
> Sounds corny? it is corny—but it works, and it's not hard to do. You have recorded:
>
> Brewster, James A.
> June 8, 1946—mtg.
> 1232 Oak St. r. tel. Br 4395
> 1010 Tenth Ave. b. tel. Cl 8482
> Insurance business, Bedlow Bldg.
> Married, 3 chil. 13 junior 11 Alice, 2 (?)

Masonic pin in lapel, and VFW. Heavy set, bald, well dressed, manner
of a professional man.
Assign to Doc Boyer? Follow up. Mr. S. Check registration.[21]

This description of the process he used was written eight years later,[22]
when he was a practiced writer, and it shows a perfect data capture from what
seems like nothing more than a warmly human personal contact. His skill as a
writer makes it seem easy, and it is anything but.

Show warmth and welcoming. Establish a connection between your life
and his. Offer him an extended contact that will bind him into your group.
Introduce him to someone who has something else in common they can chat
about and let him become more comfortable with your group. Collect the information you can use to follow up the initial contact and cement the relationship.

Here is a network of personal relationships, not a sociology of ideology,
not a brilliant intellect performing a demonstration. Heinlein obviously
needed to meet people as a human being in a social network, and that is the
reason he believed this strategy would work for him. And it works because it
is not a technique divorced from its human context. No doubt it was in just
this way that Heinlein became friends with Bill Corson—discovering in the
very first interview that Corson was a rifle enthusiast. They had something in
common to talk about, and it led, not just to a vote, but to a campaign
worker, and ultimately to a lifelong, close friendship.

Meetings, stumping, ringing doorbells, and rallies. Heinlein talked with
thousands of individuals in the months before the primary. The nervous strain
began to tell on him, and he found himself exhibiting symptoms he knew too
well from having managed candidates in the past four years.

Candidates are subject to a nervous disorder which I choose to term "Candidatitis" . . . something like measles; persons almost always catch it when
first exposed; one seizure usually gives lifetime immunity; and it is best experienced early in life for the mildest symptoms and the least disastrous
side-effects.

The usual symptoms are these: Extreme nervousness and irritability,
suspiciousness raised almost to the persecution-complex level and usually
directed toward the wrong people, a tendency for the tongue to work independently of the brain, especially in public where it can do the most
harm, and a positively childish aversion to accepting advice and management.[23]

But the momentum was up; the juggernaut was rolling. Sometimes he felt as though he was the one under the wheel.

It is a condition of almost insupportable nervous excitement in the face of this utterly new and tremendously stimulating experience. The candidate talks too loudly, too much, and too loosely, and is constantly amazed at his own brilliance. In fact it *is* intoxication, auto-intoxication brought on by excessive adrenalin stimulation. The victim is stubborn, sure of himself, and contemptuous of advice—just like a drunk. It has a hangover phase, too, in which the candidate in a frenzy of nervous reaction tries to explain the mistakes of yesterday.

Most public figures run the course of the disease and acquire immunity the first time they run for office, as young men running for the legislature or city council. Their asinine mistakes are seen by few and remembered by no one except themselves. (I still have nightmares over mine!)[24]

The big issue of the campaign was a new old-age pension scheme nicknamed "Ham and Eggs." Various kinds of old-age pensions were proposed in the days before Social Security. The Townsend Plan for an old-age pension of $200 a month was making some headway nationally in 1938. The Ham and Eggs plan was a local variation on the Townsend Plan—it would provide retirees $30 a week, an amount that could be supported by a more manageable tax. The name was a colorful PR gimmick to replace its more descriptive (but also more cumbersome) initial slogan of "Thirty Dollars Every Thursday."

Heinlein didn't think much of the Ham and Eggs plan, but his district had a lot of elderly people in it, and he could pick up a lot of votes if he endorsed Ham and Eggs. An endorsement was meaningless, of course—the promise of a politician—but Heinlein stuck to his guns: he was in it to change all that and he wanted at least one politician's campaign promises to mean something. But he also knew it would count against him. He had prior experience canvassing the elderly, and no amount of economic reality meant a thing with that constituency:

I was covering a district which lay, half and half, on the right side and the wrong side of the tracks. I interviewed young and old, rich and poor, men and women. I expected and found certain differences in viewpoint on the two sides of the track, but I was surprised to find an amazing and almost unanimous similarity in viewpoint on the part of the elderly rich and the elderly poor. . . . The elderly poor wanted $200 every month, or some other pension which would pay them more income than they had ever earned while working, and they didn't give a hoot what it did to the country! The elderly rich wanted the highest possible return from mortgages, rents, dividends, or other investment income, and they didn't give a hoot what it did to the country . . . blind and narrow selfishness, short range in nature and quite unconcerned with the welfare and future of their children and their country.[25]

And the welfare and future of the country was all he was interested in: sometimes you just have to take the hit in order to live with your conscience. He didn't endorse Ham and Eggs.

As the campaign came down to the primary on August 25, 1938, Heinlein's already tight schedule got even more intense. His big rally was two weeks before the primary—on August 12—in his Beverly Hills Young Democrat territory, at the Legion Hall at 164 North Robertson Avenue. The program for the rally showed the forces backing him:

This meeting is sponsored by the 59th Assembly District Council of Democratic Clubs composed of the following clubs: Beverly-Wilshire Young Democratic Club, Gus S. Childress, Pres. United Democratic Precinct Workers Club, Tom Sawyer, Pres. 59th AD Democratic club, Leonard H. Bachelis, Pres. Beverly Hills Democratic and Civil Club, Judge Lee Champion, Pres. West Hollywood Democratic Club, Jack Clifford Pres. Motion Picture em. Committee, 59th District, Chas. Page, pres.[26]

Heinlein opened the rally with a brief speech and introduced the candidates for the Sixteenth [U.S.] Congressional District (in which the California 59th Assembly District lay). If his experience was at all typical, by this time he was keyed up and his nerves were singing with exhaustion. In the last weeks of a campaign, after three months of unremitting work, the candidate is not quite sane—but that's all right; his moves are by now ingrained, and nobody really notices.

Just before the primary, Heinlein's campaign organization sent out a postcard to every voter, following up his visits to the household:

I trust you will remember that I called at your home recently to present myself as a candidate for State Assemblyman, 59th District. The Republican incumbent has filed on both tickets in an attempt to capture our Democratic nomination for the Republican party. I need your vote next Tuesday. May I count on it? Sincerely Yours Robert Heinlein.[27]

On the day of the primary, the whole organization got on the streets and spent every last ounce of energy on getting people to vote.

In the Democratic primary, Lyon polled 5,241 to Heinlein's 4,791, having virtually ignored Heinlein throughout the campaign.[28] Heinlein lost by not quite one vote per precinct. Lyon also won the Republican primary, running uncontested, and the Assembly District 59 seat would not even be listed on the November general election ballot. "I once lost an election by less than 400 votes," Heinlein said.

> In the post-mortem I was able to tabulate names of more people than that who were personal acquaintances of mine, had promised me support—but did not vote . . . Forty election-day volunteers could have swung the district.[29]

The party had written off that assembly district, but this loss was especially galling for Heinlein: a reactionary Republican had picked up more votes from his fellow Democrats than he had, even with the most intense, personal, hands-on work.

He turned over the problem with Roby and Cleve Cartmill and his other campaign staff in a postmortem. Maybe Ham and Eggs defeated him; maybe it was the phony Nazi connection with Konrad Henlein.[30]

But maybe he was sunk by hewing too close to the EPIC line. EPIC's strength was waning—*EPIC News* had just ceased publication for lack of support, and the party had never been able to elect a full EPIC slate in any district. Maybe the New Deal was as radical as the Democratic Party would get. Mainstream Democrats wanted to take back control of their party apparatus.

This had been an exhausting—and humiliating—campaign. But life goes on. Politics goes on. And you rarely lose political capital with your party by running in a district locked up by the other party. In the meantime, there was an election to win.

The next item of business was housecleaning for the State Democratic Committee. The EPIC wing of the party was sinking partly because its dead weight of communist infiltrators was becoming a problem in the party organization: "A group of three can often stampede a crowd into some action disastrous to the objectives of the crowd but suited in some devious fashion to

Communist purposes."[31] For just this reason, mainstream Democrats had become wary of trying to work with EPIC clubs.

The Sinclair tactic of keeping the EPIC clubs as a shadow organization of the local Democratic clubs was starting to backfire. The problem had only gotten worse since 1935. Now, there wasn't anybody in the California Democratic Party with Sinclair's prestige to stand up against the communists. It had become another of those factors that made working with the mainstream Democrats an uphill battle. It was getting less and less realistic to stay EPIC and Democrat at the same time.

Heinlein realized that the experience of working with EPIC had changed his political orientation somewhat. He used to think of himself as a "pragmatic socialist," unconcerned with "labels, terminology or fine points of ideology."[32] The Democratic Party had all the stuff it really needed, except the driving *will*—and that, the EPICs could provide.

If the EPICs could clean up their act, they could improve their chances at the next election and the next—and that's what the state committee people were supposed to be working toward, after all. He arranged a meeting with Susie (Florence G. McChesney) Clifton, wife of Robert Clifton.[33]

Susie Clifton was an EPIC Democrat, also on the State Central Committee. Heinlein had worked with the Cliftons in Ordean Rockey's 1936 campaign. He suggested that the communist problem was becoming a public embarrassment to both EPIC and the Democratic Party. A housecleaning was in order, he argued. They needed to conduct a purge and clean up the EPIC image in order to be more effective. The general election was shaping up well for California, but not encouraging for Democrats across the country. There is a rule of thumb, he argued to Clifton, that communists in America flourish where there are real problems that need to be dealt with; EPIC is trying to address certain real problems, and it's going to attract communists, and that's all there is to it. "Unfortunately, we are more prone to ignore the sick spots thus disclosed and content ourselves with calling out more cops."[34] He had direct testimony on this point, and he was not prepared to budge: a "very dear friend (now dead)" had actually been present—and voted!—at

the notorious meeting in the '20s in which the Central Committee of the CPUSA ordered a policy under which clandestine members were to infiltrate the clergy, the teachers, and the newspaper men—and besides that I had had my nose rubbed in the fact that clandestine CP members had (1938) infiltrated the organization of the Calif. Demo. Party, top to bottom, and controlled many key positions.[35]

Clifton was not encouraging: it was nearly impossible under the current laws to purge communists from the party rolls. As far as the Registrar of Voters was concerned, a registered Democrat is a Democrat. End of discussion. In order to do anything at all in the way of housecleaning, Mrs. Clifton pointed out, they would have to raise a major stink—with another campaign about to start. And there was no guarantee they would be successful. It might be more divisive than the results could possibly justify. They just couldn't afford to take the hit.

THE NEXT THING

There is always a great deal of cleanup work to do after a political campaign—more, probably, after a failed campaign than after a successful one: by the end of August, the campaign staff, such as it was, were all dispersing to work for the candidates who still had a chance in the November elections. Like a shark, politics never stops.

Heinlein, too, had some political commitments to perform in the important governor's race, and for local Democratic candidates. But after the intense work over the summer, it was almost like being at loose ends.

He must have spent some time working through the unpleasant implications of his talk with Susie Clifton. If her estimate of the party's strategic situation was right, the handwriting was on the wall for EPIC. EPICs had been saying for years that Americans wouldn't tolerate communists; in his own campaign literature he had been saying that communists were just "Red Fascists," morally no better than Hitler's and Mussolini's "Black Fascists"[1]—and he believed at least part of his problem in this campaign was the endorsement and "help" the local Communist Party wanted to give him—whether sincerely or in an effort to blacken his name with the voters. "I would have retired Charlie Lyon from office . . . if the goddam commies had not insisted on playing footie with me, snuggling up to me, and sitting in my lap."[2]

If it could not get communists out of the EPIC movement without committing public relations suicide, the Democratic Party would have to cut EPIC loose—amputate the infestation. The process was already well advanced.

Mene, mene, tekel, upharsin: "You have been weighed in the balance and found wanting."

That pretty much ended Robert Heinlein's interest in working at a high level in the Democratic Party.

He got into party politics in the first place to make a radical break with business-as-usual—political as well as economic. Power had never really interested him for its own sake; nor did party politics as a game played for its own sake.

He would clean up and get out—finish out the year and then just not take on new jobs in politics.[3]

Getting out of political management meant he would have to get a real job, with no prospects that were not distasteful to him:

> I didn't really want to teach high school physics and regarded the "education" courses required for a permanent certificate as a fate-worse-than-death, etc., ad nauseam with respect to several other possibilities, such as excessively difficult commuting if I took a job with Douglas Aircraft.[4]

The break did give him a chance to catch up on his reading: the magazines had been stacking up unread during the months of the campaign.

Three or four years earlier, Hugo Gernsback's *Wonder Stories* magazine had launched a nationwide consortium of local science-fiction clubs, called the Science-Fiction League. Every month there were a few pages consisting mostly of reports of local chapter activities. Later, Heinlein remembered finding, in the October 1938 issue of *Thrilling Wonder Stories,* a story contest announcement:

> The beginning of 1939 found me flat broke following a disastrous political campaign . . . I "owned" a heavily-mortgaged house. About then *Thrilling Wonder Stories* ran a house ad reading (more or less):
> GIANT PRIZE CONTEST—Amateur Writers !!!!!
> First Prize
> $50 Fifty Dollars $50[5]

But his memory embroidered the details. It wasn't a contest at all: the magazine was just trying to drum up new writers. The Science-Fiction League pages in the October 1938 issue began quietly and reasonably with what could be regarded as a "house ad," an open call for new writers. After a bit of musing on how science-fiction stories should be constructed, it went on:

CAN YOU WRITE A STORY?

Thrilling Wonder Stories is looking for new writers from among its thousands of readers. We want stories from readers who have never written a word for professional publication. And we will pay the same rates for these stories as we do for all our professional writers! It doesn't matter who you are—your story will get the same reception that is accorded to our most famous writers.[6]

All the science-fiction magazines needed new writers all the time. Pulp magazines ate up material at a fierce rate, and science fiction had become a specialized genre since 1930. A pulp writer couldn't just dress up an adventure story anymore . . . well, you *could*, but the readers complained. Back in the July issue, just before Heinlein had gotten totally immersed in precinct walking, *Astounding Science-Fiction* had run a similar editorial (trying to drum up new writers) that debunked the whole idea of pulp-magazine writing contests. According to *Astounding*, those "contests" were just a gimmick: the contest winners just became ordinary professional writers and the "prize" was the penny a word (more or less) that the bottom rung of pulp writers was paid.

> So *Astounding* can announce a contest—a contest for new, good authors, a contest that has neither entry not closing date, nor is it limited to one prize apiece nor one entry per contestant. We've all gained by those past winners; we'll gain, I know, on new winners. Better stories—new ideas. The contest is on—and goes on.[7]

The artful public story Heinlein later concocted to explain how he got his start in writing had no room for the details of the mental processes involved—but some of the elements of his thinking can easily be reconstructed. He was faced with unpalatable choices for a job and a need for ready cash, and undoubtedly he, like many devoted readers of science fiction over the decades, held his nose and declared to himself that he could write better stories than the hackwork, formula crap the pulps were publishing. He could, too—almost certainly: he had accumulated a certain amount of journalistic experience over the years.

Leslyn was supportive of the idea, but Heinlein also had two people in his immediate circle of friends who may have contributed to the idea as it percolated from possiblity to intention: Cleve Cartmill was a professional journalist writing for *United Progressive News*, and Elma Wentz had for years been talking about writing pulp.

The Wentzes and Cleve Cartmill typically came over after dinner Saturday evenings for a sherry party and conversation. They were all very supportive and talked it out with him and Leslyn. At some point, the subject of regular fiction—not science fiction—for a regular book may well have come up. If so, Heinlein must have been intrigued: the last three or four years had piled up a lot of stuff he needed to get off his chest.

Those conversations, though never described in any detail in the surviving correspondence, must have given Heinlein a lot to think about, and he gradually evolved a plan: he would give it a serious try, work at it like a professional—work up some story ideas and follow Sinclair Lewis's advice to apply the seat of the pants to the seat of the chair, working consistently every day. Either that would pay off the mortgage or he would know he had to get a real job before the money ran out.

And as for books, Heinlein dove into his research. He avoided the how-to books, but it may well have been his new preoccupation with wordsmithing that led him to Stuart Chase's *Tyranny of Words,* even before the elections were over.[8] The book itself was a creaking propaganda piece, but Heinlein could conceivably justify carrying the book around with him because he could always pull it out and quote from an appropriate passage of stock propaganda comparing President Roosevelt to a modern physicist who creates new experiments to meet new conditions—and is smothered in an avalanche of bitter protest by the people who don't understand what he is doing—"experiments in democracy," Chase called them.

Whenever he got an idea for a story, Heinlein jotted a note on any scrap of paper that was handy and stuffed it into a file folder he kept in his desk drawer. Mostly what he was getting was not so much ideas as fragments of ideas, disconnected from each other. He didn't yet know how to take those fragments and develop them into stories—just the thing a starting writer *needs* to know, and of course the one thing that books on writing never have anything useful to say about.

Tyranny of Words led him to Ogden and Richards's *The Meaning of Meaning* (1922). If Chase was propaganda fluff, Ogden and Richards's survey of the development of modern semantics was tough going. Fortunately, they started with epistemology and Heinlein's teenage reading of Fiske gave him a little background in the subject. Ogden and Richards had begun to move epistemology out of philosophy and into science—and where there is science, can technology be far behind? A technology of language represented a rare opportunity for understanding the core realities of human nature.[9]

As November came on, and the general elections, the political chores gradually eased up, and Heinlein had a little more free time. The Democrats had not fared well in the national elections—people were getting tired of the New Deal as Roosevelt's various attempts to patch things up weren't working—but the party was thriving in California. That year, they managed to elect an EPIC—or former EPIC—governor, Culbert Olson. And there were finally enough progressives on the Los Angeles County Board of Supervisors to have a real voice in things. With Jerry Voorhis in Congress, too, there was finally a real voice for economic reform in the U.S. government. California Democrats had done well, and the party was in good shape. Heinlein could afford to let other people take over some of the load.

Political chores done for the moment, Leslyn went into the hospital for an appendectomy, leaving Robert with some time on his hands. One day in the middle of November,[10] he sat down at the typewriter to make some sense of the ideas he had been collecting. Slowly, the jumble of fragments and bits had started to shape up into a story of a far future, once the country had gotten out of its current mess. The choices he made can be reconstructed from the story he did finally put down on paper: the country would have to put its economic bookkeeping on a rational footing someday—like the Social Credit line. A book like that might make a lot of people very angry—maybe even angry enough to get off their duffs and do something. It might, in fact, not be commercial at all: "The book was written by a man who was not then a writer, and written primarily as a means of ordering his thoughts on many matters. The book was completed before I considered trying to publish it."[11]

H. G. Wells's film *Things to Come* had made the rounds that year, a very impressive achievement.[12] *Things to Come* had demonstrated one very effective way to dramatize political tracts.

Wells had done utopias—*A Modern Utopia* and *When the Sleeper Wakes*—in reaction to Edward Bellamy's *Looking Backward*. Bellamy's book was the most famous utopia in the English language.

All the various subjects *EPIC News* had been reporting on for years were available for use as currently interesting material.[13] The country was being strangled by private monopolies—like the utility companies, which had been in the papers (including *EPIC News*) since municipal utility ownership had come up for vote in 1935 and 1936. And it was a commonplace of liberal thought in the 1930s that the banking and power monopolies were the main problem—if those could be addressed, the road would be cleared to clean up all the big problems.

EPIC News had run a front-page article about using the sun's power for power applications that January. A cheap source of power might provide the necessary shake-up to get from here to there. . . .

Heinlein must have stirred all these elements together until a plan of approach emerged for his book: a man from the present gets into the far future, when the economic troubles are over. Heinlein came up with a new gimmick to get his modern man into the glorious socialist future. Those odd past-life memories he had had as a kid—fading now into just memories of memories—probably contributed to the device he chose, as did J. W. Dunne's serial-time theories: he could get his hero into a jam in the twentieth century that shocked him out of his personal time track and caused him to wake up in the twenty-second century.

Heinlein was dissatisfied with much of the writing about utopias: they were all too goody-goody. They got dull. Perhaps he learned something specific from the experience of writing this book:

> I *hope* the future is going to be Utopian and believe that we have the potentialities to make it so—but for story purposes, sorry, no can do. Why? Because the basis of drama is tragedy and Utopia aint tragic. In this field you can do *short* stories about minor incidents in an otherwise-Utopian culture, but I defy you to do a story 50,000 words or longer about the *future* and have that future be a Utopia—and sell it![14]

Looking Backward was an idealized presentation of the workings of a Fourierist phalanstery[15] on a national scale—the brand of socialism that had been a virtual craze in the United States, in the middle of the nineteenth century. (Fourier had also written a utopia that Heinlein had apparently read: in his Harmony, people lived twice as long as we do and were sexually active into extreme old age.)

But nobody believed in Fourier's crazed accounting system anymore, though the basic principles of utopian socialism were largely accepted in this country.[16] The problems of bookkeeping in the modern world were a lot more complex.

Of all the economic and political schemes that *EPIC News* had summarized and argued about, the one that apparently fascinated Heinlein most was the Canadian Douglas Plan—known by the title of Douglas's 1924 book as "Social Credit." The 1933 revised edition of *Social Credit* was debated in the United States.[17] *EPIC News* had run a long, multipart, mostly disparaging piece on Social Credit in 1935.

He had gotten interested in Social Credit as early as the 1934 gubernatorial campaign, when he made the acquaintance of Pierre Gordon, who would remain part of his social circle for many years.[18] Perhaps what attracted Heinlein to Social Credit was that Douglas had suggested a way out of the scrip problem built into the EPIC plan—one that Sinclair and the EPICs had not picked up on: the EPIC colonies would use scrip and the rest of the state would use U.S. currency; at the interface of the two economies, scrip would somehow have to be exchanged for currency, and none of the suggested mechanisms looked very satisfactory.

The problem disappeared if you looked at the money supply from a fiscal—Social Credit—perspective. The Douglas Plan took a very fresh and provocative look at the whole problem of money.

Heinlein had enough material to stop thinking about it and start writing—a dramatized Social Credit tract. He would have an educated man from the bad old days (1930s) transported into the bright future, when the struggle to implement Social Credit was long over and done with.

And Heinlein had a title for it, from Abraham Lincoln's Gettysburg Address, a title that said exactly what he thought about the task of political reform (and democracy in economics) that every one of us has got to carry on. Lincoln had focused exactly the sense of dedication to the never-ending task:

> The world will little note nor long remember what we say here, but it can never forget what they did here. It is for us, the living rather to be dedicated here to the unfinished work which they who fought here have thus far so nobly advanced.

Heinlein's first actions as a writer must have been those of hundreds of thousands who had gone before him: a carbon set goes into the typewriter—in this case probably the back of a mimeographed poll-watcher's flyer from the election just over—carbon paper, and a sheet of rough newsprint for the carbon copy.[19] Like many, many others before him, he hunted out his title with two fingers:[20]

-- FOR US, THE LIVING --

And four lines underneath, a subtitle, like those James Branch Cabell had used:

A Comedy of Customs

He must already have decided on doing a love story—the most basic of all stories.

He took a contemporary man—a Navy man—and got him killed here, taking his car over one of those steep cliffs out at Pacific Palisades. Reincarnated in the future, he had an innocent eye. He wouldn't even be able to comprehend the Social Credit system. Various experts would have to explain the details to him, and that would give Heinlein his exposition (just the way Edward Bellamy had handled the problem in *Looking Backward*). At the very beginning of what would become his permanent career as a writer, Heinlein had already learned a thing or two from Wells, a writerly principle he repeated over and over throughout the years: steal from the best, then file off the serial numbers and claim it as your own. He established a link between the girl and the boy: her twentieth-century equivalent was the last thing his boy Perry Nelson saw in this life, in the twentieth century—and the first thing he saw in the twenty-second. He took Sally Rand as his model for the girl: she could be an exotic dancer, named Diana, the *chaste* goddess of the hunt. The name would keep her clean, since she wasn't actually going to do any fooling around to set off Perry's atavistic jealousy. He would just be a jealous fool.

When Heinlein got his plot straight in his mind, he had social frontiers, economic frontiers, and technological frontiers all wrapped up in one neat package. He had even worked up a card game as a teaching device to get people to see how real-world economies worked.

Heinlein worked at his novel every day, from mid-November until after Christmas. When the book was finished, he thought it *might* be commercial—or it might not.[21] The scenes at the end, where Perry was in bed with two women at the same time, were sexy enough to carry the book commercially—might even get it banned in Boston . . . if it could be published at all.

Through all the work, he consulted Leslyn constantly. Later, Leslyn recalled his perching on a stool in the kitchen and bothering her when she was fixing dinner, trying out ideas, "fishing for plot twists and climaxes,"[22] and talking out how anything he did at page 10 would affect the story when he got to page 260. . . . On the evidence of what he did next, Leslyn's overall verdict was that he was being too critical. The bottom line was, it was certainly no *worse* than a lot of stuff that did get published.

By 1938, the Heinlein marriage was well established and comfortable. They had started out six years earlier with what amounted to a "companionate" marriage, whether or not they had explicitly agreed on those terms: they were best friends first, last, and always. Robert was very satisfied with his marriage. Leslyn seemed to agree—most of the time. There were rare instances, starting in about 1936,[23] when she just locked herself into an enraged frame of mind, paranoid and vicious, and could not be talked out of it. But these episodes were very rare and always blew over quickly, and she was back to her sweetly loving and lively self.[24] She just *would not* talk about it afterward.

It was impossible to guess what might cause those episodes, and for the most part Heinlein did not speculate (not having enough material to speculate with). We can look backward, with the dubious advantage of much experience with such psychological issues, and wonder if it might have something to do with family issues. She had always been a daddy's girl—small wonder, given that her mother, Skipper, was such a toxic harridan.[25] Her father, Colin MacDonald, had drunk himself to death, at the rate of a quart of whiskey a day, in 1929.[26] That had been very hard on her.

But her troubles might just as well have come from other sources. Her outbursts might have been her way of coping with her own rejection of the so-called moral values of her upbringing. Leslyn was just as liberal and modern as Robert—in some ways, even more so.[27] She even practiced witchcraft— "white witchcraft," in the old pagan tradition of northern Europe, though she didn't (so far as Robert knew) belong to an actual coven. The essence of The Craft is secrecy—and that was about all Heinlein knew about that subject. Heinlein himself had never any strong calling in that direction—and a strong calling is utterly necessary for practical magic working. His own reading had run to hermetic symbolical philosophy—Freemasonry, Rosicrucianism. Interesting intellectually—but it didn't do anything for him, except to provide interesting story materials . . . Taking up pagan witchery might have been as much a rejection of her mother's Theosophy as of Christianity: you are tied to anything you feel strongly enough about to have to reject.

Leslyn's commitment to sexual freedom was just as strong as his in the theoretical sense. That was the whole basis of their friendship, courtship, marriage. When you came right down to it, she had gone directly from Cal Laning's bed to his, and they had begun as they meant to continue. They had both had extramarital affairs—a few—in the six years since they had gotten married.[28]

At its best, sex is lighthearted recreation, the best game people can play with each other, in all combinations (some of them still theoretical to Robert, but he had an ambition to bust as many of the taboos as he could manage).[29] And extremely spiritual when it was at its most lighthearted—the way you lit up inside, like nothing else. That was true "illumination."[30]

After Christmas and for a couple of weeks in January, Heinlein fiddled with revisions. His typing had been unbelievably bad—there were places where whole lines had been left out. He retyped the manuscript to get a clean copy—an agonizing process, even though his typing was getting better. Heinlein really learned how to type while doing this book. He did a slow hunt-and-peck until he taught himself to touch-type by taping over the letters on the keys and posting a chart above and behind the machine, so he would have to look at the chart to find his next key. Once he could think through his fingers, he found he could take the tape off the keys. He was a touch typist, homegrown.[31] Leslyn helped as much as he would let her.

The various writers' guides said publishers usually took a month or two to make their decisions. Heinlein picked out a few publishing houses that might want to take a chance on the book and submitted it first to the Macmillan Company—a first-rate publishing house in its own right.

Elma Wentz had been doing her own research into the writing business. Around Christmastime 1938, she brought over a book she had just finished reading, Jack Woodford's new edition of *Trial and Error*.[32] Now that he had gotten his own book off, Heinlein had a little time for it and the other books and magazines that had accumulated. He didn't really know anything about the fiction business, but he could do what he always did when confronted by a new field of knowledge he wanted to master: research it into submission. Research was his first impulse for nearly everything. He read his way through the Woodford book and found it a blueprint for a writing career.[33]

Trial and Error turned out to be useful mainly because it didn't try to teach writing, but instead focused on the business end of the writing business— selling your product to editors. Woodford's most important advice was not about technique or the mechanics of marketing; it was about attitude and how to focus your thinking on the market. The commercial writer, Woodford said, thinks of himself as a manufacturer of product for the current market.[34] That was very sane and realistic. Even working in science fiction and fantasy, where a lot of Woodford's other advice wouldn't exactly apply, that kind of advice was useful.

18

AND THE NEXT

Robert's baby sister, Mary Jean, married her high school beau, Andy Lermer, on January 19, 1939, the last to leave her parents' house. Bam must have been feeling a little at loose ends. Robert may have been experiencing the same: he decided to take some of the art classes offered by the WPA[1] and enrolled in one of the life-drawing classes given at Hollywood High, on Highland and Fountain, near Hollywood Boulevard. He found it completely absorbing. "When you draw from the model, you really have to sweat. But it is more fun. . . . could never understand how the time passed so quickly, nor how I had gotten so tired."[2]

The life classes were change-of-pace recreation for him. He found the "pansies, pinkos and instructors who do only complete abstractions" irritating, though he could put up with that. It was the eight-mile drive from Laurel Canyon to Hollywood High, over sometimes icy roads (even in Los Angeles), he could not put up with.[3] Drawing could never be more than a leisure-time activity for him.

A lot of his time was still being taken up by political chores and a new interest: Clarence Streit's "One World" book, *Union Now,* was starting to catch on, and Heinlein considered himself a "world-stater from way back."[4]

But it was not radical politics that drew him any longer: he was becoming absorbed that winter in the research he was doing in semantics. After finishing Ogden and Richards's survey of the state of things in semantics and epistemology up to about 1929, he had moved on to Alfred Korzybski[5] and the monumental *Science and Sanity* (1933). What he found there, despite a very difficult presentation, was exactly what was needed to bring semantics into the modern era: the fundamentals of a *technology of language,* which means a technology of how human beings think.[6] That was incredibly exciting. People had been talking about sociology as "social engineering" for decades—at least since Herbert Spencer—but that was mostly poetry and wishful thinking. The tools didn't exist in sociology to make the tools to make the tools for social engineering. Korzybski, Heinlein thought, was building up the necessary tools out of the raw material of mathematical logic: mining gold out of a recent paradigm shift in science.

Alfred Korzybski was in exactly the right time and place to exploit this particular paradigm shift in this way. A Polish aristocrat (he was often referred to as "Count" Korzybski) trained in chemical engineering, Korzybski was wounded three times in the first year of World War I and then sent to America as an expert in artillery. After the war he met and married an American artist, Mira Edgerly, and decided to stay in the United States while he began studying the work in mathematical symbology that had been done recently by Berrand Russell and Alfred North Whitehead. Running underneath his study was the perpetual question, why did these periodic bloodbaths of wars happen uniquely among humans and not among animals? He came to the conclusion that humans were "time binders": we plan for the future. Each succeeding generation inherits a legacy of physical and information wealth.

And yet time binding was left out of virtually all of the stories we tell ourselves about what is important about who and what we are, most of which picture us as only "clever animals." That could not be true, Korzybski reasoned: time binding made humans qualitatively different. The disparity between our mythologies and our realities created what might be called a "sanity gap."

Korzybski published these ideas in 1921 as *Manhood of Humanity: The Science and Art of Human Engineering*. His idea of the childhood of humanity and the twentieth century as the transitional period from childhood to adulthood struck many thinkers as exactly on target. A few years later, H. G. Wells would make very compatible remarks in his *The World of William Clissold* (1926), looking forward to a coming adulthood of mankind—socialist, of course.[7]

Korzybski continued to develop his ideas, extending them into psychiatry. The old ideas had been set long ago and codified by Aristotle. What was needed was a post-Aristotelian framework of ideas. In 1928 he started to write another book, *Time Binding: The General Theory,* whose thrust would be the application of scientific method to life problems. When the massive book was ready for publication in 1933, he changed the name to *Science and Sanity: An Introduction to Non-Aristotelian Systems and General Semantics.* A correct understanding of the symbolization process, which Korzybski labeled "General Semantics," would give people new ways of thinking, inherently more rational and balanced.

Time binding fascinated Heinlein.[8] It seemed to explain so much about how we have continuity across the many dimensions of experience. Ouspensky had talked about this kind of mental continuity distinguishing human consciousness from animal in *A New Model of the Universe* (sometimes Korzybski reads eerily like a gloss on Ouspensky!), in a way that made it compatible with J. W. Dunne's serial-time theories.

The way Heinlein talked about General Semantics at the time suggests that he was getting from it something more than understanding, something that is usually characterized as "illumination." If Heinlein's experience was typical, this illumination would come about whenever he grasped one of Korzybski's ideas—sometimes difficult, as Korzybski would go on using a crucial term sometimes for four hundred pages or more without defining it: in most cases, that sensation is an emotion, an aesthetic-erotic-religious flooded-with-light feeling and the sensation of things whirling around in the head as a whole view of things reshuffles itself into new configurations, a new way to look at the world.

Looking into the subject more thoroughly—Heinlein's first impulse was always to do some research—he found that Korzybski had just founded the Institute of General Semantics near the University of Chicago—and there was a local Los Angeles chapter. The local chapter of the Institute was hosting a lecture/seminar by Korzybski in June of 1939. Both Robert and Leslyn applied for the seminar, though the $25-per-person registration fee would have put a severe crimp in the domestic budget.

Heinlein could see dozens of applications of the theory to his life—to *their* life. He thought he could use it to communicate better with others and improve his personal relations.[9]

Leslyn had more specific aims: "making adjustments to my environment—particularly my mother—and in keeping house (& contact in political and educational fields)."[10] Leslyn had sailed through *Tyranny of Words,* but she found *The Meaning of Meaning* tough going. She started on *Science and Sanity* and bogged down almost immediately.[11] Her graduate degree in philosophy was oriented to psychology, and probably it was not as natural for her to shift back and forth between linear-language thinking and mathematical thinking as it was for Robert. She had to work harder at it.

Practicing the "semantic pause," Heinlein found, kept him from spiraling into anxiety. He had learned to present a cool and collected front to the world (except for the occasional stammer when he did some public speaking), but it was a conscious effort. Inside he felt he was emotionally unstable, prone to fly off the handle and get excited over things most people took for granted. "I tend to be impetuous, and this has often put me in a bight."[12] General Semantics gave him just the tool he needed to keep a better grip on himself. Just a little pause could give him the edge he needed. He could attend to this business of waiting for word from the publishers with much greater equanimity.

The writers' guides Heinlein had found at the library said two months was the average wait time on a first novel—and it might be longer. They recommended he wait for two months before making a polite inquiry about the status of the manuscript, and then an increasingly insistent series of queries every couple of weeks.

In January 1939, a new science-fiction pulp had appeared, *Startling Stories*. At the end of February another showed up on the newsstands: *Unknown*, a Street & Smith fantasy companion for *Astounding Science-Fiction*, also edited by John W. Campbell, Jr. *Unknown* had a unique take on fantasy. *Weird Tales* had dominated pulp fantasy since its founding in 1922, publishing mainly eerie little tales in the Algernon Blackwood/Lord Dunsany vein (only usually more creepy and less lit'ry). If *Unknown*'s first issue was any indication, it was going to open up a whole new commercial market for fantasy.

The time was only getting riper. If Heinlein was going to give pulp a try, now was the time. He had a whole raft of anecdotes from his military service that would make stories—including that short-short he had written in 1930. There were also some political ideas:

Citizen + Denizens conflict
Farmer *vs* City people possibly. Wells type cities + hydroponics.
City distance *Farm*

and a murder mystery:

Story re murder with Nitrogen. This could and should be worked up.
Would the victim suffer from bends? Would this be the key that would trap the murder[?]

Altogether, he spent nearly a month dithering with these kinds of notes. He began spending a lot of time in the kitchen, pitching ideas to Leslyn and listening to the way she broke them down into stories and beats of stories.

He didn't know why she didn't write herself,[13] except that the *process* of writing didn't interest her the way it did him.[14] She was good-natured about it, too, but it exasperated her when he kept picking at things she said, "fishing for plot twists and climaxes," and dinner was late, and he was cranky because he wanted to write but couldn't.[15]

A lot of his ideas turned on psychological points or points of technique he might not be able to write at all:

> Write a horror story for Unknown in which nothing is described, à la Cabell à la Guardians of the Frontier.

Some of his best story notes—the ones that could actually be developed into *stories*—were the ideas he had already put into *For Us, the Living* as part of the backstory, how we got from here to there.

One of the recent story notes must have piqued his interest:

> Write an "Unknown" story based on what would happen if persons knew when they were to die, but nothing else of the future.
>
> For example, what would Alice McB[ee] [his fiancée, who had died early in 1928] have done?
>
> What would I do?
>
> Denouement must of course be the extinguishing of this knowledge.[16]

This note was more a germ than a story—pregnant with things to think about, but he didn't really have a story to go with it.

It is not clear how Heinlein got from this germ to the story he eventually did (around the beginning of April 1939) write up as his first story, "Life-Line."[17] Switching it from pure fantasy to science fiction may have suggested the pulp gadget-story format, which is typically about the inventor and his invention. Heinlein began in a way that would become characteristic for him—with irony: his inventor was not a mad scientist but the only truly sane man in the story, a rational man who faces facts squarely and without wishful thinking, fairly obviously a model of how Heinlein—as a rational man—hoped he would face that dreadful knowledge, resolutely: make time to enjoy the best things life had to offer him in his remaining time and leave Leslyn provided for, possibly by taking out a big insurance policy—any insurance company would scream bloody murder if it was discovered that he was using some kind of arcane knowledge.

The elements of a science-fiction story—with a fantasy "twist" at the end—took shape, and this was a characteristic, also, of Heinlein's approach to fiction: he was never to be comfortable with formula, and many of his stories challenge the boundaries of science fiction.

Equally characteristically, Heinlein chose a pun for his title (perhaps because he started the typing on April 1, 1939—April Fools' Day): the lifeline is a crease in the palm that fortune-tellers use to tell the length of a person's life. It is also what sailors call the rope they throw to a man overboard, to save his life.

Heinlein gathered up enough paper—he was still using mimeographed precinct-worker instructions from the election in 1938—and began typing. The scenes fell into place like clockwork. He got through a thousand words that first day and more than two thousand the next. Two days later, he was done with the story.

If Leslyn's sense for story structure had been honed in the movies, she might have been surprised at how Robert had used the bits she had suggested.[18] This wasn't a conventional commercial plot, with a single, straight-through story arc. He had twined three story lines together—mature stories, too, not pulp kids' stuff. Even in first draft, this was a professional-quality job. Once he retyped it to get a clean manuscript, it would be ready to send out.

This spate of writing had been prompted by a piece in one of the science-fiction pulps, but the "prize" for *Thrilling Wonder*'s "contest" was less than the prevailing pulp story rates of a penny a word. (The most popular writers could earn a lot more, but there was also a bottom rung of the pulp market that was paid a lot less—half a cent a word or less. *Thrilling Wonder Stories* was on that bottom rung.) Instead, Heinlein sent it to the only editor who had both a fantasy magazine and a science-fiction magazine, John Campbell at *Astounding Science-Fiction* and *Unknown*.[19] Even though Heinlein was by now a touch typist, he was not very accurate. The retyping was a chore. He had thirty-two sheets in his rough draft. He drove down the hill into Hollywood, to a stationery store, and bought just enough good bond paper to retype the story.[20]

It took almost as long to retype the story as it did to write it, but eventually it was done, and he had thirty-two sheets of clean copy and a carbon on newsprint. He packaged the bond copy of the story with another envelope, self-addressed, and stamps enough clipped to it to return the manuscript. On April 10, 1939, he sat down to type his cover letter.

Dear Mr. Campbell:

I am submitting the enclosed short story "LIFE-LINE" for either "Astounding" or "Unknown," because I am not sure which policy it fits the better.

   Stamped self-addressed envelope for return of manuscript is enclosed. I hope you won't need it.

Very truly yours,
Robert A. Heinlein

He took the envelope down to the post office and mailed it the same day.

Heinlein started another story almost immediately—one related to the backstory of *For Us, the Living:* an Okie boy in one of the CCC camps finds a place in his new world. Such a tale would make a perfectly good magazine story for one of the prestige, "slick" magazines (so called because they were printed more expensively than the pulps, on glazed paper), such as *Collier's* or *Blue Book,* except that the New Deal's Civilian Conservation Corps was starting to get a reputation as a boondoggle. Heinlein moved his contemporary story into space for the science-fiction magazines. This story was very Darwinian, very evolutionary: change these kids' environment and things started to change in them, as well. Survival factors in evolution formed themselves out of a pool of characteristics neutral or disused in the old environment.

   For a couple of days Heinlein was preoccupied with his CCC story, juggling bits and pieces of story and character and background. And during this process, this "history of the future" began to take a different shape than the backstory of *For Us, the Living,* a slightly different line of possible futures. He jotted some rough notes about where he could fit some of his stories into this new time line, in relationship to one another, and left the notes by his typewriter for future reference. He would have to write about the critical events that made this time line work.

   The "hook" for this story was natural: a first muster. The story would open with young Andrew Jackson Libby (sometimes "Libbey" in Heinlein's notes) picking up his duffel bag and boarding a spaceship. That let Heinlein use the emotions he recalled from his own first muster at the Naval Academy—anxiety, homesickness, anticipation, and nerves—to give it the oomph a hook should have.

   He was well into his story a few days later, when Leslyn came in, excited, with the morning mail: there was a business letter—*not* a returned manuscript!—from Street & Smith. She hadn't opened it, of course: they had a custom of respecting the privacy of each other's correspondence, and the envelope was addressed to him. She wouldn't have opened it even if it were from mutual friends.[21] Inside there were two sheets, one a form of some kind and the other on Street & Smith letterhead and signed by John W. Campbell, Jr., in a looping hand and blue, broad-nibbed fountain pen:

April 19, 1939

Dear Mr. Heinlein:

The legal obligations under which a publishing company operates require that we ask authors who have not previously sold to our magazine to prepare an affidavit of authorship for us.

I like your story "Life-Line," and plan to take it at our regular rate of 1¢ a word, or $70.00 for your manuscript.

However, before this may be put through for payment, the purchasing department ask that the author sign the accompanying form, and have it witnessed by a notary public.

If you will have this done, the check in payment of your story will be sent at once.

John W. Campbell, Jr.

Campbell was buying "Life-Line"!

A few days later, on April 24, the check arrived from Street & Smith—$70.00, as promised. Heinlein stared at it for a moment.

"How long has this racket been going on?" he demanded rhetorically. "And why didn't anybody tell me about it sooner?"[22]

But one swallow and summers, and all that. Macmillan rejected *For Us, the Living,* but he wasn't ready to give up on it yet. His friend Samuel L. Lewis, who had cowritten a book a few years ago about the California radical and progressive movements, *Glory Roads* (1936), told him the Canadian Social Credit Union had a local chapter in Los Angeles. On April 25, Heinlein framed an inquiry to Gorham Munson, the local chapter's secretary, using all his politician's tact: they have a problem in common, he wrote, popularizing Social Credit ideas. He had been an exponent of Social Credit for years, and he had served as the secretary of the Hollywood New Economics Group. He had written a Social Credit book, he said, and offered to send it to them when he got the manuscript back.

"Cosmic Construction Corps" counted out at 9,652 words, and he had done something odd with the scene-to-narrative balance—possibly to get in all the technical exposition he needed to flesh out the background, since his story was really "about" the world his protagonist Libby was growing up in, rather than about Libby *per se*. He typed a clean copy with carbon sets for his files and mailed it off to John Campbell at Street & Smith on May 1—

—and started another story, a long one, maybe two hundred pages, with minor climaxes every fifty pages or so, "The Captains and the Priests." This one was derived more directly from the backstory of *For Us, the Living*—about the backwoods preacher who won the presidency of the United States and destroyed secular democracy. This would be about the revolution that overthrew Nehemiah Scudder's successors, the Second American Revolution.

But he wasn't quite ready, apparently. After three false starts and only twenty-two pages to show for it, he put away the manuscript and idea file.[23]

Then Heinlein took a few days off to do other chores. The Social Credit people hadn't responded to his letter about *For Us, the Living*, sent three weeks earlier, so he took a chance and let the West Coast sales representative of Random House take the manuscript back with him to New York, on May 14, 1939.[24]

Getting his mind off the writing evidently did him good: he figured out a dodge to get cheap electric power out to the public, where it couldn't be monopolized by private utility companies—one of the critical points in the historical backstory he was composing. He played around with the idea for a few days, changing stray bits and trying new combinations to put a fresh spin on some formula figures. He made some switches, avoiding the science-fiction cliché of the bulging-brain inventor and his beautiful daughter. He made the *daughter* the high-powered scientist, and made the necessary bodyguard into a commercial-development engineer. Then he switched the switch and made the development engineer into the son of an industrialist. That gave him a jazzy young couple with a lot of chemistry to work with—one of the "love stories" Jack Woodford insisted a writer start out with.[25]

Around the middle of the month, Heinlein got impatient with his own process and just sat down to write, figuring out the story as he went along. He gave it a working title, "Prometheus 'Carries the Torch' "—typographically awkward—and started writing. But he had been typing too much recently: after a few pages, his hands cramped up, and he switched to longhand and continued writing.[26]

He was almost finished when a big envelope came in the mail: Campbell was returning "Cosmic Construction Corps." But Campbell had sent along a letter instead of a printed rejection slip.

You've got a good idea in your yarn here and I think you can really make something out of it. I have genuine hope for your work in the future.

The difficulty with the present set up in your story is that you have injected a highly artificial villain who seems highly unnecessary and obtrudes from the story like a sore thumb. I think if you would amputate it you'd have a much better yarn.[27]

This could only have been a disappointment—but that was the life of a writer, the life he had chosen. Heinlein had made a list of submission priorities, second- and third-tier magazines to send stories to if Campbell didn't buy one. *Thrilling Wonder Stories* was next on the list, and Ray Palmer had recently taken over editing *Amazing* and was looking for new material. Then it would go to some of the low-pay/slow-pay markets. But first he would revise it, by "chopping out the villain,"[28] and resubmit it to Campbell.

But before he could work on the revision, he received a letter from Gorham Munson at the L.A. chapter of the Social Credit Union, enthusiastic about his "Social Credit novel" and asking to see *For Us, the Living.* He wrote back immediately saying he had sent it to Random House, but he expected them to reject it and would send it along as soon as the manuscript was returned to him.[29]

He finished "Prometheus" the next day, and bought thirty sheets of good bond for the clean submission copy. He had a few other stories ready to write. But first, he read over "Cosmic Construction Corps" with careful attention to the scenes with his villain, Siciliano. His editing on this, only his second story, was almost surgical: he chopped the character out entirely and found the ends of the scenes on either side of the deletions still fit together coherently, in most places. That first edit shortened the story by about 1,500 words, but some came back when he wrote necessary bridging material to make the ends of the cut sequences fit together more smoothly.[30] When he finished retyping the now villainless version of "Cosmic Construction Corps," it was 8,342 words. He sent the revision to Campbell on May 25.

By the beginning of June, he had finished an odd, wry story at 5,500 words, "Pied Piper," which played around with Robert Browning's "Pied Piper of Hamelin" poem and turned the situation into a "wonderful gadget" story. It wasn't in the historical sequence he had been working with, so he had started off with a pen name, Caleb Saunders. "Caleb" came up because of Caleb Catlum from *Caleb Catlum's America* (1936) by Vincent McHugh— one of his very favorite books—but also, of course, because of Cal—Caleb

Barrett Laning. He had come up with another pseudonym, too: he took his maternal grandfather's family name and his paternal grandmother's family name and joined them together: Lyle Monroe. But he decided he would save the pen names for secondary submissions.[31] For Campbell, he used his own name.

He had also started on a big story about human evolution and psi powers, "Lost Legacy," but, after starting several drafts, put it aside. His extensive notes for this story were more carefully organized than for any of his other early stories and were bound with brads in three-hole punched paper. Perhaps he felt the need to work with his research more and was not yet ready to write the story. Certainly it was a very ambitious effort:

> It was an attempt on my part, only partially successful, to do something as good as *Odd John* [Olaf Stapledon, 1935]. To my way of thinking, science-fictionists have become gadget crazy, and are perfectly willing to accept any improbability as long as the author postulates some sketchily-explained "invention" in the sphere of physics. (I've done it myself!) Here is a story with no gadgets, in which the author has hooked together a lot of the erratic data which orthodox theory rejects, and tried to fit it into a single comprehensive philosophy and history.[32]

Now, though, Heinlein was picking up steam. He went immediately to work on "Patterns of Possibility," taking the *n*-dimensional space-time concepts that were in Dunne's *Experiment with Time* and Ouspensky's *Tertium Organum* and mixing them together with the cross-time material in "The Gostak Distims the Doshes."[33] Dunne's physics was based on the idea that consciousness could become detached from its space-time matrix—which meant that one could go wandering in a near-infinity of different space-times, somewhere else. Elsewhen.

Heinlein had finished "Patterns of Possibility" at 10,051 words, when "Prometheus 'Carries the Torch'" came back from *Astounding*—rejected. But Campbell's long letter was full of encouragement to submit more, which took some of the sting out of rejection. He started off:

> Shoot along all the yarns you do. I'll be glad to see 'em, and I feel you'll make more than a few sales. Your work is good. Even this is good, despite the fact it's bouncing. Main reason: the femme is too good. The science-fiction readers have shown a consistent distaste for science-fiction detective stories and feminine scenery in science-fiction stories. She's much more

nicely handled than the average woman in science-fiction, but I'm still afraid of her. Better lay off, or try her on *Marvel*.[34]

In fact, this was almost not a rejection letter at all: Campbell went on, almost chatty, about the economics and the story about the suppressed "miracle carburetor," concluding pages later: "But be that as it may, let's see more yarns. Shorts, in particular."

That was praising with faint damns: Mary Lou was too good![35] If you have to get rejections, that was the way to take 'em!

But early in June he took a break: the General Semantics seminar they had registered for was only two days away.

19

NOT QUITE DONE WITH POLITICS

The material from the General Semantics seminar was interesting and important, but Korzybski himself gave a real human dimension to it, quirky and fascinating. From the difficult, formal prose and tortured organization of *Science and Sanity,* Heinlein had expected some stiff, professorial type, and Korzybski was anything but: he was the most alive person Heinlein had ever seen. He stumped around the stage, waving his arms and talking with a thick Polish accent. He reminded Heinlein of nothing so much as Professor Challenger without the beard.[1] After the seminar, Heinlein stayed behind with some of the members of the local General Semantics chapter to talk with "A.K.," as they called him. Attention was focused on Heinlein straightaway, because he had put down on his application that he was a "pseudo-science writer." They talked for some time about the problems of popularizing General Semantics, A.K. treating him very flatteringly as a professional with professional expertise in communication. Heinlein may have sensed, too, that A.K. was, or at least had the potential to be, the kind of older adviser or mentor he had been missing for a long time now.

He came away from the seminar charged up, but his own "literary business" needed minding. The day after the seminar, he began by putting "Prometheus 'Carries the Torch'" and "Patterns of Possibility" back into circulation, then sat down at the typewriter to write a whimsical little gimmick story that had come to him, "'My Object All Sublime.'" No notes for this story are preserved in Heinlein's records, but his friend journalist Cleve Cartmill probably served as the model for his journalist-protagonist Cleve Carter who tracks down an invisible skunk-juice squirter dedicated to making the punishment—for "stinking bad" drivers—fit their crimes.[2] In the middle of writing it, he got Campbell's acceptance, and check, for the revision of "Cosmic Construction Corps," which Campbell had retitled "Misfit." With "Life-Line" scheduled for the August issue of *Astounding* and now

"Misfit" in November, another milestone was passed: he was not a one-hit wonder.

Heinlein was now juggling five unsold manuscripts at the same time: *For Us, the Living* came back from Random House very quickly, rejected, as he thought it would be. The Social Credit people wouldn't be expecting to see it so soon, so he gambled and sent it right out again, this time to William Sloane at Henry Holt & Company. Sloane also bounced it rapidly, with a friendly note of rejection—suggesting he try it on *Unknown*!—instead of a coldly impersonal printed rejection slip.[3] This time, he sent the manuscript on to Gorham Munson at the L.A. Social Credit office.

Campbell was rejecting "Patterns of Possibility," but his rejection letters were almost not rejections—friendly and chatty, inviting a longer correspondence. Heinlein relished this kind of wide-ranging conversation, and letters like that were almost as good as table talk.[4] This was meaningful to him because he was not getting much encouragement otherwise: *Thrilling Wonder Stories* returned "Prometheus 'Carries the Torch' " with an uninformative rejection slip. He changed the title to a biblical quotation everybody would feel familiar with—" 'Let There Be Light' "—and sent it to the next magazine on his submission hierarchy, *Amazing Stories*.

And still the stories continued to bounce back, rejected: *Collier's* bounced " 'My Object All Sublime' " early in July, so he started that one on the rounds also, sending it first to Campbell. *Thrilling Wonder Stories* returned "Patterns of Possibility," but at least this time it came with an explanatory note: the plot was "too trite—no complications." A few days later, Campbell returned " 'My Object All Sublime,' " saying essentially the same thing: too familiar. Campbell seemed to be going out of his way to treat him as a fellow professional; even though these letters were not so long and chatty, they gave him potentially useful feedback.

Around the beginning of July that summer, Heinlein was in Shep's Shop, a secondhand bookstore on Hollywood Boulevard, close to Western Avenue. He was trying to find the issues of *Amazing Stories* in which Doc Smith's "Skylark of Space" serial had appeared. Shep's specialized in used pulps and had a lending library and motion picture stills—a miscellany of clutter that made it a likely place to look for such bits of science-fiction history. Those issues were not in stock, but as he was leaving the shop, a tall, gangling young man stopped him and introduced himself as Forrest J. Ackerman—"4SJ," as he signed himself, or, just as often, "4e." Ackerman recognized Heinlein from the campaign posters that had been up around town the previous summer and told Heinlein he had duplicates of those issues and would be glad to sell them.

Heinlein had joined the local science-fiction fan group, the Los Angeles Science Fiction League (which became the Los Angeles Science Fantasy Society—LASFS—in March 1940) in the spring of 1939, shortly after he began writing, but had somehow not met Ackerman, whose energetic promotion of all things science fiction was to see him voted the "World's #1 Science Fiction fan" by his peers. They found they had many interests in common—Ackerman, for instance, spoke Esperanto, which Heinlein had learned as a teenager, because it was going to be the language of the future. Ackerman's girlfriend, Myrtle R. Douglas, promoted Esperanto, too, using the Esperanto name "Morojo" for herself. Heinlein invited Ackerman home to continue the discussion, and that led to dinner invitations. Ackerman was surprised when the August issue of *Astounding* came out a few weeks later, with Heinlein's first short story, "Life-Line."[5]

Heinlein was writing again—but slowly. There was always a cluster of family obligations in July and August. His own—thirty-second—birthday was on July 7; exactly a week later was his mother's sixtieth birthday. Family affairs were becoming sizable productions in Los Angeles, even though his father was in the V.A. hospital. His brother Rex would be moving again shortly, and he arranged to have someone come to collect the trunk Robert and Leslyn were storing for him.

Heinlein's story "Life-Line" appeared on the newsstands one day toward the end of July. By that time, he was starting to germinate a couple of new stories, and he wanted to work on them. Back in May he had stalled on a story that was coming clearer to him now: he had figured out how to tell the story of the Second American Revolution in his connected history-of-the-future, starting out with the notion of a high-tech underground operating in a regressive and medievalized theocratic United States.

Heinlein was a deeply spiritual person, but he had never had any attraction to the creeds and dogmas of any church, Christian, Buddhist, Shinto, or Pagan—none of them. Churches did not stir him to religious awe; the monkey antics they—*some* of them—allowed themselves were revolting to him.[6] This is a much more common attitude than is generally realized; for a goodly segment of the spiritually aware, churchgoing is what you do *instead of* religion. There can be an aesthetic appreciation of the theater of ritual and ceremony and the feel of historical "depth" one gets from attending a Latin mass and sharing an experience that goes back for nearly two thousand years, to a time when the Roman conquerors let the Sanhedrin cruelly execute a Jewish dissident and reformer—highly moving, but it is the aesthetics of theater and not religion.

Robert Heinlein's religion was America and what it meant to the world and to human history—and could mean again.[7] A people governing themselves without fear or favor of princes or prelates was a thing wonderful and precious—perhaps doomed to pass again into the dust of history, but inextinguishable as a human ideal. That was the divine light that shone on humanity's struggle—and it would rise again and again, inextinguishable.

Heinlein had just started to write "The Captains and the Priests" when President Roosevelt made a national speech on the petroleum reserves issue, on July 20, 1939. A cloud on the horizon, "no bigger than a man's hand," was beginning to loom, and the possibility he might be called back into politics was firming up: Heinlein was the California Democratic Party's local expert in matters naval, and the state's oil industry was fighting legislation that affected the Navy's operational fuel oil reserves.

The California oil industry, it was feared, was in imminent danger of collapse because insane levels of overproduction were destroying the domestic market. Each oil producer was pulling every barrel of oil out of the ground that it could. At the same time, a naval preparedness report said that oil reserves were dangerously low: the oil glut was being shipped overseas, particularly to Japan, where it was used for that country's military adventures—a state of affairs Heinlein found appalling. "There are practices which are vicious in themselves, regardless of law or government, and selling iron and oil to Japan in the 1930s is one of them."[8] And, of course, even if the Navy never used the operating reserves, it was unbelievably foolish not to have them ready if needed.

A voluntary program for limiting oil production had all but collapsed by 1938. Several states had already passed oil and gas conservation programs. The California State Legislature passed an oil conservation program in July, which the big oil producers threatened to derail by sending it to a popular vote on the November ballot. There could be little doubt, Heinlein knew, that he would be called upon to put in time working on this: the Navy's interests were too tied up with California oil to let this pass.

When they called, he would answer—but he would wait for the call and continue to write while Leslyn, who was still involved with state politics on a day-to-day basis, kept a watchful eye on the qualifying process.

"The Captains and the Priests" did not flow as easily as it should. It felt like hackwork, and what he was saying violated so many of the taboos of pulp magazine fiction, it was possible he would not even be able to sell it. He worked hard to make it entertaining.[9]

He finished his first draft early in August and then took time out for three chores: first, a regular monthly follow-up letter to Gorham Munson at the L.A. Social Credit chapter, to inquire about the status of *For Us, the Living*,[10] and then a quick letter to thank M. Isip, the artist who had illustrated his story in the August issue of *Astounding*, for enhancing the drama of the scene he pictured.[11]

The third chore was to find a way to keep himself from dropping details in the outline of the world-future-history he was working on. The notes he had been keeping about his revised outline of his future were getting too complicated as he added more detail; it was becoming too time-consuming to shuffle through that mass of handwritten notes every time he wanted to use a reference. Sinclair Lewis had a similar problem in the novels and stories set in his fictional city of Zenith in the fictional midwestern state of Winnemac, with passing references in one story to characters and issues featured in others. He had recommended a wall chart to keep the data organized.[12] Heinlein tore one of his old navigation charts in half[13] and made a wall chart he could take in at a glance.

Returning to work, Heinlein retyped the long manuscript, with a new title. Perhaps the theocratic background and the Freemasonic underground had reminded him of something George Washington had quoted from the Bible in his farewell address: princes and prelates had been put down on these shores for good, and the ordinary man "shall sit down under his own fig and vine, and none shall make him afraid." Heinlein mailed "—Vine and Fig Tree—" to Campbell in the middle of August 1939 and started to organize his outstanding projects.

Gorham Munson finally responded to his inquiry about the status of *For Us, the Living*, a postcard saying it was going to be difficult to place, promising a more detailed critique later. And Heinlein had busywork to take care of, too, keeping manuscripts in circulation. He had only two story sales, which was still uncomfortably in the one-swallow-does-not-make-a-summer range. He had to establish markets, and that just wasn't happening yet.

Earlier in the year, Heinlein had been encouraging Elma Wentz to follow her ambitions into commercial writing. She had been doubtful about the mechanics of generating a story, but he told her there was nothing to it. You could plot a story in as little as half an hour. Challenged, he had done just that, outlining a shaggy-dog story that made fun of self-important anthropologists who went about making up explanations for things like the Easter Island statues—"beyond any possibility of doubt"—without any evidence at all. He made up an alternative story, an extended joke about an election in ancient Mu—material he knew she was familiar with from the EPIC campaigns, with Sinclair lampooned as the candidate, and Cleve Cartmill and Roby Wentz parodied as operators—and gave the three-page outline to Elma to flesh out. She came back with a 7,500-word draft titled "Beyond Doubt," which he could work on—mostly cutting—when he had time.[14]

The other project he had in mind was the long anthropology story he had put aside in May, "Lost Legacy." He had outlined and sketched some of it out as a political campaign electing a vigorous young man like Jerry Voorhis to the presidency, but he intended to write it soon, probably before "Beyond Doubt," another "politics" story, was cut and ready to market, so he moved the focus of "Lost Legacy" from politics to education—and used the same pen name he was using for "Beyond Doubt," Caleb Saunders, since it was not part of his future history, either.

In the meantime, he was developing a good idea for a short—a really good one, the kind that doesn't come around too often—and began to write this one before he tackled the "Lost Legacy" novel he had started back in May and put aside. This one was all mood, best written down while the inspiration was fresh. He poured into "A Business Transaction" (so titled because it wasn't) local color from his childhood in Missouri, but most of all he captured in one sequence of poignant flashbacks a life of yearning to follow the call into outer space, the next frontier where the wild geese went. The tone was bittersweet and perfect, the storytelling simple and straightforward.

Campbell's letter accepting "—Vine and Fig Tree—" on August 25 had been the most backhandedly complimentary thing Heinlein had ever received. It was full of complaints, mostly about how the religious theme would offend his readership—but the tone of the letter was pure delighted-frustration, like a dog growling over a fresh bone he kept turning over and over, gnawing at the good stuff.

The story, by practically all that's good and holy, deserves our usual unusually-good-story 25% bonus. It's a corking good yarn; may you send us many more as capably handled.

But—for the love of Heaven—*don't* send us any more on the theme of this one. The bonus misfires because this yarn is going to be a headache and a shaker-in-the-boots; it's going to take a lot of careful reworking and shifting of emphasis.

Ye gods man, read your own dicta at the end of the yarn as it now stands (incidentally, you don't think, on the basis of the material's own logic, we could print that safely, do you?) And consider the sort of reaction that yarn, as it stands, would draw down on us! Even after considerable altering of emphasis, it's going to be a definitely warmish subject to handle.

You say, in your concluding part, that religion is dogma, incapable of logistic alteration or argument. Evidently you believe that. Then, on that basis, what reaction would you expect this yarn to evoke in the more religious-minded readers? Your logic, throughout, is magnificent and beautifully consistent. That's swell. *I* love it. Lots wouldn't, you know.

I'm reworking it, I'll be forced to eliminate some beautiful points possessed of an incendiary heat, so far as controversy goes. Consider, man, the reaction if we let that bit about the confessional pass! As a useful adjunct to a dictator's secret police, it undoubtedly is surpassingly lovely; as an item to print in a modern American magazine, it's dynamite. That's out like a light. . . .

I genuinely got a great kick out of the consistency and logic of the piece. You can, and will, I'm sure, earn that 25% bonus for unusually-good stuff frequently.[15]

Heinlein could not help but be pleased—amused and complimented.

And Campbell's specific comments showed that he was most impressed by things Heinlein had put into the story as throwaways—details that added believability to the backstory. If he could tease out some coherent, specific discussion of what Campbell liked about what he was doing, he could write specifically to Campbell's needs and stop all this out-and-back-again with stories that weren't selling. The $300 and then some that "—Vine and Fig Tree—" brought in would pay down the mortgage for six months!

Dear Mr. Campbell:
Your letter accepting VINE AND FIG TREE arrived today, and you have no idea what a lift it gave this household. We have been undergoing a long, dry spell—I was beginning to think I was definitely poison ivy to editors. No other editor has even been friendly. I had developed a case of the mulligrubs. Then—your letter arrived on my wife's birthday, constituting the perfect birthday present.

Incidentally, the major portion of the check is going to go a long way toward lifting the mortgage on Castle Stoneybroke.

I agree with you absolutely in your criticisms of the story. I knew the story violated a lot of taboos and didn't think it could be sold and published under any conditions. I was very sick of it by the time it was finished, but Mrs. Heinlein and I decided to waste postage too and send it off once, in the belief that you might enjoy reading it, even though it couldn't be printed.

I shall avoid the more ingrained taboos in the future—at least for market.

He discussed other story possibilities, then showed a little leg:

If Cosmic Construction Corps stands up, I have outlined a long series of shorts, using the implied culture of that story as a backdrop. Some of them use Libbey [*sic*] of C.C.C. as central character, others have different central characters. The central characters in one story appear as minor characters in other stories, à la Forsyte saga and Cabell's Biography of Manuel. They are not sequels. Each story will be independent and the action of one story does *not* lead up to the next.

Enclosed is a short ["Requiem"]. I hope you like it. In a way it's my pet.[16]

So far all of the stories he had sold Campbell were in that outline of the history of the future. That was a vein he could continue to mine—and *For Us, the Living* would earn its keep even if it never got published!

Campbell bought "Requiem" almost immediately, on the last day of the month of August, even though, he said, he didn't care for it himself: he wanted to float it as an experiment with his readership, to see how they reacted to these more sentimental stories.[17] In the meantime, he urged Heinlein to work at the longer lengths, where his strength seemed to lie.[18]

The next day, the international news was shattering: Germany had rejected Great Britain's ultimatum to return to its borders after the invasion of Poland, and the suddenly revealed Hitler-Stalin pact had American communists spluttering. England declared war on Germany, and the French were mobilizing. On September 3, 1939, Heinlein composed a memorandum/prediction for his own files, "A note from Robert A. Heinlein of this date to R.A.H. of some later date, just to keep the record straight":

Great Britain has just declared war against Germany. France joins them.

Germany has not attacked Britain nor France. Germany has attacked Poland, after demanding Danzig (a German city) and the corridor (German territory) and being emphatically turned down. I do *not* justify Germany's attack, but let's keep the record straight. Britain is *not* entering this war to save democracy (Poland is a dictatorship), nor because of the "holiness" of her treaty obligations (remember both Ethiopia and Csechoslovakia [*sic*]—a democracy, incidentally, and loyalist Spain.)

So far as I can see, Britain is entering this war because Germany is getting stronger than she likes. She has decided to fight Germany because she thinks she can lick her now, and isn't sure she can later—let's not be sanctimonious about it.

This war isn't being fought for Thomas Mann, nor Albert Einstein, nor for other persecuted Jews. Nor is it being fought for "democracy." It's being fought to preserve the worst and most unjust features of the Versailles Treaty. Let's get that straight. And stop Hitlerism makes as much sense as Hang the Kaiser.

Hitler is a symptom of Versailles—we caused him. The insanity he typifies we caused.

This is where we came in—want to sit through another show?

He added a handwritten postscript:

I'll bet two bits that from here on anyone who is not pro-British will be called un-American![19]

Anything he was going to get written needed to be done as fast as possible. Not only was it possible he would be recalled to active duty if the United States entered the war, the local oil conservation campaign was heating up. He queried Campbell on the long anthropology story while Campbell was "editing at" "—Vine and Fig Tree—."[20]

On top of all the other stress in his life, he had a blowup with his brother Rex, who was dropping the name "Ivar" inside the family. Rex had told him he would have someone call for the trunk Robert and Leslyn were storing for him, but had not made a definite date for it. Early one Sunday morning, after a late Saturday night at *chez* Heinlein, two of Rex's Army buddies showed up with a truck to collect Rex's trunk. Leslyn was never a morning person in the best of circumstances, and she particularly resented being wakened this way. Perhaps she went a little over the top with the strangers (something that had been happening more and more frequently for the last few years), for by the time Robert came down it had degenerated into a screaming argument. Robert separated them by physically taking the men down to street level and unlocking the garage. He got them out of there with Rex's trunk and calmed Leslyn down.[21]

Rex called, angry, and Robert had had more than he could take. All the suppressed rage of thirty years came boiling out, and he let Rex have it with both barrels for not having the simple courtesy to let them know about the pickup and thereby causing such an uproar. That was it, as far as Robert was concerned: Rex was out of his life—and good riddance.[22] A few years later he said, "The *first* time he was rude to Leslyn, I closed the book on him, permanently."[23]

Before tackling "Lost Legacy," Heinlein pulled out the list of story notes he had made back in the spring, and separated them into two columns— one, science fiction, for *Astounding*; the other, fantasy, for *Unknown*:

Stories for Unknown	*Stories for Astounding*
Potemkin Village [ultimately published as "They"]	Tourist Trouble (or "—the Natives Are Friendly—")
"I am the cat" 3rd person	Warm Ice
Danger—One Way Traffic	Safety Precaution 75 [science-fiction version of "Danger—One Way Traffic"]
Reversed Memory	General Services, Inc. [ultimately published as " 'We Also Walk Dogs' "]
Maybe "Morpheus, Inc."?	General Housing, Inc.
The other "Life-Line"	Labor, Inc. (interplanetary slavery) [the germ of "Logic of Empire"]
Regeneration (M is *not* T) working title is Resurrection, Inc.	Production, Inc. (entropy pantograph)
	Sauve qui peut!
The Soul Detector (a telepathic heterodyner)	Mining on Venus
The Shadow of Death: *novel* [this was one of the two ideas conflated together for "Methuselah's Children"]	Youngster cruise (target practice)
	General Foods, Inc. (not now ready)
Story treating black magic as *good* (not yet worked out and possibly too	Lynch's Death Dodgers as racket man

Stories for Unknown	*Stories for Astounding*
hot. It would deal with the whole ethical problem)	
	Space Navy, the regeneration of the "bad boy"—a Little Tailor type.
Patterns of Possibility: a free will-destiny problem in time (Later) [Published as "Elsewhere" and collected as "Elsewhen."]	"Fire Down Below!" 2 part serial of the revolution in Little America, source of U-238 used in atomic power. Principal interests; underground culture, and fatigue as a tactical factor. Also the logistic problem in strategy.
Da Capo, or "This is Where We Came In": story starts with a man's death and ends when the obstetrician spanks him—metempsychosis.	
Dream inversion story, cf. Dunn (If I can do it.)	Week End Watch; slipstick Libbey's [*sic*] roommate at the Academy gets a court martial *and* a commendation.

Astounding had a reader's popularity poll that would show how "Life-Line" had fared with the readers in its October issue. Campbell had started the practice of tallying all the reader comments as votes and publishing the results as a small department, the "Analytical Laboratory." "Life-Line" was listed second in the issue, after Lester del Rey's "The Luck of Ignatz," which had been the cover story that month.

Even better, there was a letter of comment praising the story as one of the best published in 1939, from Isaac Asimov. Asimov's name was familiar, because he wrote to the science-fiction magazines frequently, but also because he had had a few stories published in *Amazing* earlier in the year—about the time Heinlein had started writing, in fact. Asimov was a colleague as well as a fan. A few weeks later Heinlein received a personal letter from Asimov. He was only nineteen years old, a chemistry student, and fiercely bright—and amusing, as well. He told Heinlein he thought Jehovah got all the good press and Satan needed to hire a good press agent.[24] That was an idea that could be developed into a story—one day.

Heinlein started to work on "Lost Legacy" and was almost immediately interrupted.

The expected California oil conservation initiative qualified and was designated Proposition 5.[25] Governor Olson, a former EPIC, sent Heinlein a personal appeal to help coordinate the Navy's support for the Yes on 5 Committee. The Governor wanted him to take charge of the southern counties—from Fresno south through Imperial and Riverside counties,[26] where he had worked so intensively between 1935 and 1937. The oil cartel must *not* be allowed to torpedo the regular legislative process on this issue.

It was not something Heinlein was eager to take on—it would mean more than a month away from home, traveling from local office to local office in the high desert and living out of a suitcase.[27] The cause was just, but the personal effort it would take was something he could just not afford any longer. He was beginning to realize the limitations of the life of a freelance writer: once you stop punching the keys, there is nothing between you and starvation except a sixty-mile commute each day to an engineering workshop. . . .

But Governor Olson arranged to make the sacrifice more bearable: the Yes on 5 Committee would hire him for a month as a professional consultant—at a substantial salary. Heinlein could not even raise an objection to the people he would be working for: his immediate boss on this campaign would be Ed Pauley, a man whose integrity he respected.[28] The combination of his detailed knowledge of these Southern California counties, his naval background and interest, and the salary made it impossible for him to refuse. He applied for one of the new Social Security account numbers, so he could be paid by the Yes on 5 Committee.[29]

Heinlein let Campbell know he would have to interrupt work on "Lost Legacy" for the duration of the campaign[30] and organized his working files so that Leslyn could keep the writing business going while he was out of town. He typed up a list of his research into the existing markets with all the relevant information he could think of. With that information, Leslyn ought to be able to handle everything that was in circulation at the moment.

Proposition 5 failed—1,755,626 (61.3 percent) to 1,110,316 (38.7 percent).[31] Heinlein must have been aware this was probably the last political campaign he would run; it would have been a pleasant thing to lay down his laurels with a clear victory, but you have to take what the voters give you. He supervised the shutdown of the southern-counties operation and went back to writing "Lost Legacy."

The writing went very smoothly. This was a story he could be enthusiastic about, unlike the agony of piecing "—Vine and Fig Tree—" together, bit by bit. He had originally planned "Lost Legacy" to conclude (except for a brief, pastoral postlude) with the election of a new president of the United States, a young and vigorous progressive patterned after Jerry Voorhis, and that ending, at least, was written.[32] But over the summer he rethought that plan: a long period of public reeducation was probably necessary before this could be accomplished—starting as young as possible, with children as little corrupted by the prejudices of their elders as possible. This time in his story plan the Boy Scouts of America was the entering wedge for a new progressive tradition.

But he had a little business to take care of first. Forrest Ackerman told him about two new science-fiction magazines that were in preparation, *Astonishing* and *Incredible,* edited by New York fan Frederik Pohl. They were offering only a half-cent-per-word rate, but Heinlein was not getting any better offers for " 'My Object All Sublime' " or " 'Let There Be Light' "); they had by now been rejected by all the higher-paying markets, though he couldn't definitely see why.[33] He sent them both to Pohl under the Lyle Monroe byline. He also sent another status inquiry to Gorham Munson about his other problem child, *For Us, the Living.*

The November issue of *Astounding* came out with "Misfit," his second story. While he was writing, the cash register rang again: Fred Pohl wanted " 'Let There Be Light,' " but he also wanted to use Heinlein's name instead of the Lyle Monroe pseudonym.[34] It was not an unreasonable request, but Heinlein was not willing to go along with it. It is easy to guess his reasoning: that story had been rejected by every other market, and even if he hadn't gotten any useful comments from the editors about *why* it wasn't up to snuff, it was pretty clear that it wasn't: publication of a dog under his own name might dilute whatever commercial reputation he was starting to make in *Astounding.* At the same time, he did not want to alienate a potential buyer.

The tactic he decided to use was to nudge Pohl, to see if he would come up to market rates: if he would pay the one-cent-a-word rates *Astounding* was giving him, then there would, *ipso facto,* be no "dilution" of the commercial value of his name: "I am sorry to have to say that I am not free to publish under my own name for a lower rate than one cent per word," he told Pohl. "If you still wish to use my own name on those terms, please let me know."[35]

But the offer for the lower-grade story put Heinlein on a cusp: up to a week before, he had been able to sell *only* to Campbell—which meant science fiction, of course, or fantasies that could be disguised as science fiction. And of all the miscellany of humor and fantasy and philosophical speculation and utopia he had out circulating, the only work that had sold to anyone was stories from that history-of-the-future scheme he had adapted from *For Us, the Living*. If his current story, "Lost Legacy," did not sell—his favorite of everything he had written to date[36]—he would have to put aside the story ideas that did not fit into the future history scheme. He could not afford to spend the time and effort writing material he could not sell.

He sent "Lost Legacy" to John Campbell—and decided to work up one of the future-history stories from his "road city" idea that had been inspired by H. G. Wells's moving roadways. He made engineering sketches and load calculations, trying to get a picture of the scale of these road-cities and the kind of industrial infrastructure they would require. These behemoths dominated a short period in that history-of-the-future.

Science-fiction writers rarely paid any attention to the actual engineering of their marvels of the future, the building and maintaining of them. These cities required *massive* infrastructure—on the scale of the national highway system and the major engineering projects that had been completed in the last five years: the Hoover Dam, the Grand Coulee Dam, the bridges at San Francisco, and the Tennessee Valley Authority project that was just ramping up.

Heinlein was writing "Road-Town" on December 6, 1939, when Campbell responded to "Lost Legacy"—the same day Ray Palmer returned "Patterns of Possibility" without a line of comment. Campbell was rejecting "Lost Legacy" "because it's good. It should be great."[37] As his comments went on, it became frustratingly clear that Campbell had misunderstood the entire point of the story: he thought it was about supermen—"Here, you have the story of a whole colony of supermen"—whereas Heinlein thought he had made it clear this was about stuff that was latent in *every*man. He had failed to write it clearly enough.

Campbell liked the story Heinlein had carpentered together with sweat and agony, and thought the one that rolled easily was missing a "motivating principle." Again, that backhanded compliment: "I don't think you've got the makings of a good hack, but I'm ardently hoping for a dozen more top-notch yarns that are real writing."

The combination of the *Amazing* rejection and the *Unknown* rejection on the same day took the wind out of his sails. He just couldn't work up enthusiasm for the story in his typewriter.[38] He sat staring at the page in the machine, unable to come up with the next sentence. He gave up in disgust with himself and started to organize some chores around the house to keep himself busy.

But the information about what Campbell did like about his writing was piling up, and Heinlein felt he was zeroing in on his editor's particular tastes for the history-of-the-future stuff. He thought he could target them exactly with future stories. The ideas started flowing again for the "Road-Town" story, and within a week he put away the housepaint and brushes and ladders. Instead, he would get back to work and send Campbell science-fiction stories from his history of the future. He had another H. G. Wells–inspired story he could write easily—a switch on something he had put into *For Us, the Living,* about the island prisons-without-walls for malcontents Wells had mentioned in *A Modern Utopia.*

"Requiem" came out in the January issue of *Astounding,* hitting newsstands just before Christmas 1939, and Heinlein was very irritated to discover that Campbell had written a four-line concluding paragraph that spoiled the tone as well as the drift of the story. Could the man not recognize the theme at all? Did he have a completely tin ear for rhythm and flow? Heinlein did not say anything about it at the time, but the following year, when their personal relationship had grown stronger, Leslyn mentioned to Campbell Robert's reaction: "Bob feels . . . it spoils the end . . . by nudging the reader and saying, 'See, do you get the point?' and repeating the snapper."[39] Still later, Heinlein expressed himself in very direct terms: "I still simmer when I think of the four lines you added to 'Requiem'; they killed the punch"[40] and "And you damned near ruined 'Requiem' by adding four lines to the end which led the reader up a blind alley, clear away from the real point of the story."[41]

Heinlein was beginning to realize, as he got Campbell's range, that what could be sold to him—and therefore to *Astounding* and *Unknown*—was sharply limited by Campbell's own range and prejudices. He might, for example, not be able even to recognize a good story if it fell outside the boundaries of his prejudices.[42] Jack Woodford's advice in *Trial and Error* was exactly on target: to succeed in this game, you have to find out what your audience wants to hear and beat the drum for it, loudly and enthusiastically.[43] Only, it wasn't as simple as Woodford made it sound. In this case, at least, his "audience" was the editor, not the reader.

Heinlein finished writing "Road-Town" during a visit from Robert Cornog, a friend who had taken his doctorate at the University of California–Berkeley and was now working at Lawrence's radiation laboratory in Berkeley (he was codiscoverer, with his mentor and adviser, Luis Alvarez, of

deuterium and tritium). Cornog dazzled Heinlein with talk about the forefront of atomic physics, a discipline that was about to break wide open. German (and Jewish) mathematical physicist Dr. Lise Meitner had published the
calculations she had started on the train fleeing from Nazi Germany, calculations that would permit a vast, uncontrolled release of energy from a very
compact source, nearly instantaneously. Atomic bombs had just become
possible.

OUT AND ABOUT:
THE LONG, STRANGE TRIP

The casual Saturday "at homes" Robert and Leslyn had started for political purposes gradually changed over the course of 1939 into a writers' group for the local science-fiction professionals. If anything, the changeover of personalities could only have sharpened the sense of being involved in something purposive and progressive: socializing with writers instead of politicians required less concentration on creating unity out of divisiveness—fun they did not have to work at so hard.

When Henry Kuttner and "Cat" (C. L. Moore)[1] moved to Laguna, they started coming up at least weekly. Cleve Cartmill introduced William Anthony Parker White, called "A.P.," who was working for *United Progressive News* as a theater and music critic while trying to get work as a screenwriter. He was also an established mystery writer—"H. H. Holmes" was his pen name—with four published books under his belt. A.P. was witty and lively, and he elevated the tone of the group. It became the "Mañana" (Spanish for "tomorrow") Literary Society—or MLS—since its purpose, White said (though Heinlein appropriated the remark),[2] was to save civilization by letting writers talk out stories instead of writing them. "[Heinlein] did tell a story about someone talking a plot during one of those meetings, and everyone present went home and wrote the story, and the tale goes, they all sold the stories to the same editor!"[3] Heinlein and Cartmill hoped to tempt White into writing science fiction.[4]

Annette McComas, wife of J. Francis McComas, called the MLS "one of the most delightful features of those years . . . The club provided some very merry times, in spite of the threats of war hanging over our heads":

> The club parties were a lot of fun. They became a haven for every visiting
> published (and frequently unpublished) science-fiction writer. Visitors and

parties went together. Some of the locals and visitors included Henry Kuttner, C. L. Moore, L. Sprague de Camp, L. Ron Hubbard, Cleve Cartmill, Arthur K. Barnes, Leigh Brackett, and Willy Ley, Jack Williamson, and various and sundry wives and girl friends.[5]

A few of the fans from the local science-fiction club would be invited from time to time. Nineteen-year-old Ray Bradbury was rambunctious and so energetic that it made Leslyn tired to be in the same room with him; it was too much like having to manage a large and unruly puppy[6]—but Robert sensed in him a certain quality he wanted to encourage: Bradbury wrote one thousand words a day, every day, after hawking *The Los Angeles Daily News* on street corners. That impressed Heinlein, who confided to one interviewer: " 'I read some of his stuff.' He leaned toward me for emphasis. 'It was awful. I said to myself, 'Here is a great writer.' ' "[7] Bradbury's discipline and perseverance would force him to learn his craft.

Heinlein patiently critiqued anything Bradbury brought him. When Bradbury brought him a manuscript that wasn't bad at all, Heinlein walked it over to Rob Wagner at *Script* magazine. Bradbury later related[8] that Heinlein agented his first sale.[9]

Gorham Munson finally wrote back on January 7, 1940, that *For Us, the Living* was, in his opinion, unsalvageable without a complete rewrite, reconceiving it from the ground up and working from story to philosophy, not the other way around. Heinlein had become (somewhat) inured to rejection, but he did not want to invest the necessary effort into rehabilitating this manuscript when he had more immediate projects. He put the manuscript away in his files.

He had started a long novelette for *Unknown* about industrial magic, but it needed more time to ferment, so he put it aside. Campbell bought the moving roadway story, retitling it "The Roads Must Roll"—an improvement, Heinlein thought, over his original rather flat title: "His reasons: 'Roadtown' doesn't say anything; it just lies there. But 'The Roads Must Roll' suggests action, an urgent necessity, and an unexplained mystery . . . for *roads* do not *roll!* What is this? Let's take a look and find out."[10]

In quick succession Heinlein wrote and sold Campbell another story he had mined out of *For Us, the Living,* "Coventry,"[11] and an atomic power story, "Blowups Happen," which had been suggested to him almost simultaneously by conversations with Bob Cornog and a letter from Campbell.[12] Things were going so well, in fact, that Leslyn sent a poem, "Lilith," to

Campbell for *Unknown*—it was "philosophical" enough, but not in quite the same direction Campbell was trying to take the magazine.[13]

The "Blowups Happen" sale on February 24, 1940, was a red-letter day for the Heinleins. They had been dedicating most of the proceeds from the writing to pay down the mortgage on the Lookout Mountain house, on the theory that if they could get out from under the debt, they would be able to live more comfortably on the resources they had. Heinlein had used one of the traditional political fund-raising visual aids to keep his mind on the job: a giant cardboard thermometer to show the amount remaining on the mortgage as he paid it down. When he used the check for "Blowups Happen" to pay off the last of the mortgage, he threw a mortgage-burning party to celebrate.[14]

The writing was generating other correspondence: Isaac Asimov had started corresponding months earlier, but Willy Ley had also written, enthusiastic about "Misfit" and "If This Goes On—" when the first installment appeared in February, with a gorgeous cover by Hubert Rogers. One reader commented enthusiastically: "A striking cover like that, without a trace of the luridness commonly associated with the pulp mags, really attracts favorable attention."[15] Heinlein wrote Rogers a fan letter of his own—more positive and enthusiastic than the thank-you notes he had written to Isip and Wesso.[16] In addition to Willy Ley's friendly and collegial letters, some of the letters from fans and readers developed into a correspondence interesting in its own right.

The Heinleins were also becoming immersed in the social life of Los Angeles's science-fiction fandom at the time, attending at the regular Wednesday-night meetings at Clifton's Cafeteria in downtown Los Angeles. Science-fiction clubs can be a "gateway drug": socializing leads to reading the amateur magazines issued by fans—"fanzines," as they came to be known—and then to writing letters of comment to the fanzines[17] . . . and then the hard stuff: Ray Bradbury asked Heinlein for a piece of short fiction for his fanzine, *Futuria Fantasia*. Heinlein wanted to oblige, but the only thing he had on hand that might do was a sketch called "Successful Operation," about a pineal gland transplant for a totalitarian dictator. Heinlein had been awakened to the state of German prison camps as early as 1936, when *EPIC News* had run a personal-experience exposé by Isobel Steele.[18] He let Bradbury have it, retitled "Heil!," to publish under his Lyle Monroe byline in the issue dated "Summer 1940."

Since Campbell perpetually complained about his need for stories for *Astounding* and longer material for *Unknown*, Heinlein started passing along

Campbell's ideas to the other writers in the MLS,[19] and he pushed Roby Wentz and Bill Corson to think about writing up some of their own ideas. Now that he felt he was definitely over the hump in getting started with the writing, he could foresee the next stage of his evolution as a writer. Pulp writers often faded out after a while and stopped selling, for one reason or another. "If my stuff starts slipping," he told Campbell, "and is no longer worth top rates,"

> I prefer to quit rather than start the downgrade. Same thing I had to say once before with respect to rejections—I don't like 'em and will quit the racket when they start coming in. I know this can't go on for ever but, so help me, having reached top, in one sense, I'll retire gracefully rather than slide down hill.[20]

He told his Authors Guild representative, Arthur Leo Zagat, the same thing, expressing it as a definite "intention to quit pulp."[21] But Heinlein felt personally grateful to Campbell for giving him a chance and knew Campbell was in a Red Queen's race to keep *Astounding* on track with the new program for science fiction, in which he had assumed an important role. It was not entirely logical, he knew, but he felt obligated to raise up an army of writers to take his place.[22]

If the "Magic, Incorporated" novelette sold to *Unknown*—and he thought it should, as he had pitched it directly to Campbell's prejudices—they would be flush for a while, and Heinlein knew just what he wanted to do with the "extra" cash: he called in all his outstanding political favors and got a pass as an observer to the 1940 Democratic National Convention in Chicago that July. It was by that time an open secret that President Roosevelt was going to declare for an unprecedented third term. That convention was going to be an historic occasion, and he wanted to be there. And, by coincidence, Korzybski was giving a seminar in Chicago just a week after the convention ended. Heinlein's kid brother, Clare (who had entirely stopped using his first name, Jesse), was studying at the University of Chicago. He asked Clare to find them an apartment they could rent for a month.

And if they were going to Chicago in July, they could go first to New York—take in the World's Fair, visit with the local writers. And editors. Robert's U.S. Naval Academy classmate John S. Arwine lived in New York and made a good living as an unwed mother—that is, writing "true confession" stories (among other things).[23] He would put them up.

The April and May issues of *Astounding* decided the issue (*Super Science*

Stories came out in May with "Let There Be Light" under the Lyle Monroe byline). Both installments of "If This Goes On—" were rated best in their issues, and the reader reaction to the novel was overwhelmingly positive. But the most satisfying result of the novel's appearance came from outside science fiction—from the Navy. Apparently one of his Academy classmates picked up an idea he had tossed off in the novel and jury-rigged an implementation before the next issue hit the stands. It was soon in use throughout the fleet, though it was classified so that he could talk about it only obliquely and in generalities, if at all.[24]

Heinlein first investigated passage to New York for himself and Leslyn via a Navy vessel, but none would be available until July. Instead, he and Leslyn left Hollywood early in May for a long overland trip by car. They were in Kansas City on May 10, visiting Robert's friends and family, when Germany sidestepped the "invincible fortifications" of France's Maginot Line and invaded the Low Countries for the second time in the century. Robert and Leslyn left Kansas City on the fourteenth of May, to arrive in New York four days later and take in the 1939 World's Fair as the crisis deepened. On May 29, the British sent every vessel they could float to converge on the Flanders fishing village of Dunkirk to evacuate their troops from Nazi-occupied France. Winston Churchill made his stirring "Never have so few done so much for so many" radio speech. The lights had gone out in Europe, but he promised that the gallant Britons would fight on, even through an invasion of the home isles.

Heinlein and John Campbell found they complemented each other in odd and not entirely predictable ways, both interested in out-of-the-way and underappreciated data. Campbell introduced him around to all the other New York *Astounding* writers.[25] Willy Ley was even more interesting and entertaining in person than in his letters. When Doña Campbell, John Campbell's wife, had to leave the room during a conversation, she instructed him, "Willy! Be dull!"[26] Heinlein was also taken to one of Fletcher Pratt and John Clark's Friday-night *Kriegspiel* sessions—a naval battle simulation played out on a grid marked on Pratt's living room floor with wooden models of ships—and there he met L. Sprague de Camp, science fiction's reigning master humorist.[27]

They met L. Ron Hubbard when they gave a dinner party; they thought he might be the catch of the trip—explorer, raconteur, and liberal. Heinlein had been *very* impressed with Hubbard's realistic treatment of the professional commissioned military officer in the installments of "Final Blackout" that had appeared before they left for the trip.[28] "He is our kind of people in every possible way."[29]

The Heinleins were also introduced to the various local fan communities. Robert was invited to the Queens Science Fiction League on June 2, 1940, to talk about "If This Goes On—" and met a number of the prominent local fans, including Sam Moskowitz.[30] Not wanting to become a prize or a football for one feuding faction of New York fans against another[31]—the feuds were ongoing and vicious at the time—he invited the major opposition faction, the Futurians, *en bloc* for a Sunday "at home," through Robert A. W. Lowndes.

It was common knowledge within the science-fiction community that the Futurians were conventionally "red," and he wanted to head off a wrangle, so he laid down some ground rules in the invitation:

> Re communism—I have read Das Kapital. I know and have been "worked on" by many of the leading party members on the coast. . . .
>
> Re technocracy—I have taken the study course and spent a lot of time with prominent west coast members, including many hours of close discussion with Johnson, the west coast organizer.[32]
>
> Re socialism—I first started reading the Appeal to Reason in 1919. I am an old friend of Upton Sinclair's. I am thoroughly familiar with most collectivist literature of every sort.
>
> Re anarchism—same sort of thing. I know many of the west coast libertarians. I could make a similar list of right wing movements.[33]

He later, and privately to Lowndes, refined his position:

> My . . . opposition to communism, et al. (including Technocracy), was based almost entirely on matters of civil liberty; it was not based on opposition to socialism, per se. Socialism can be good or bad, depending on how it is run . . . I never could stomach the indifference of our native commies and fellow travelers to matters of physical freedom, intellectual freedom, and democratic consent. In my own personal evaluations there is no possible economic benefit of sufficient importance that I would choose it in preference to the freedoms specified in our Bill of Rights and elsewhere in the Constitution and customs—they aren't perfect but they are enormously better than the set to be found anywhere else in the world—and I include England, all of Scandinavia, Switzerland, New Zealand, and Australia.[34]

He was on vacation, he said, and interested in discussing the radical ideas he had been studying for the last twenty years—but not in being a verbal punching bag. By reputation, what these kids regarded as "good clean fun" could be more like a shark attack.[35]

One morning two weeks into their New York stay, early in June, Heinlein woke in Arwine's apartment with an odd sense of disorientation. Something in a dream had brought up that childhood sensation that the adults were in a conspiracy to deceive him, that they didn't do the same things when he wasn't around. He scribbled notes to himself about the story, to be called "Potemkin Village" (since someone was setting up and dismantling reality around his protagonist)—enough to turn it into a horror story—and let it germinate.[36]

The next day, June 5, 1940, they went on the road to Washington, D.C., where Jerry Voorhis welcomed them enthusiastically and issued them a souvenir member's pass to the House of Representatives.[37]

When they returned to New York, Heinlein was able to finish his short story, which turned out a creepy, paranoid fantasy he retitled "They." On June 11, he took it down to Campbell's office by subway, and Campbell bought it on the spot, for *Unknown*. They still had a lot to talk about. "Coventry" was coming up in the July issue, and reader reaction to "The Roads Must Roll" was already starting to trickle in—another hit. Campbell definitely wanted more in that same vein. Heinlein mentioned his history-of-the-future wall chart, and Campbell seemed fascinated by it: he even wanted to publish it (and the cash register rang again). Heinlein had brought along *For Us, the Living,* to leave with Campbell when he moved on to Chicago. But Campbell had something else on his mind.

Street & Smith had recently told Campbell that he couldn't sell any more of his own fiction to competing publishers—it didn't look good. Nor could he sell to himself for *Astounding*. That would look even worse. Campbell's career as a science-fiction writer was effectively over. But he had a good solid novella, titled "All," and he suggested that Heinlein could write it up as a serial and he would buy it.[38]

Heinlein was cautiously enthusiastic. He could use the proceeds from a serial to buy a used car in better condition than the one he was driving—and he could probably get a better deal in the Midwest than he could in California, so the timing was right for him. He had met Doc Smith briefly in New York (and they found each other "muy simpatico"[39]). Smith was one of the science-fiction writers Heinlein had admired for more than ten years, and Smith had invited him to visit at his home near Detroit.[40] Heinlein could ask

Smith for help with the purchase of the car, and that would justify a side trip to Michigan for a visit.

Campbell described the plot of "All" to him in detail and even came up with a new pseudonym, a fake Scottish one, combining Robert's middle name with Leslyn's maiden name: Anson MacDonald.

Heinlein was not entirely happy with "All,"[41] but it was a guaranteed sale, and he would have a few weeks free in Chicago before and after the convention and the General Semantics seminar to write it.

They were booked (as "Robert Monroe and wife") for two weeks (June 14 to 28) at Camp Goodland—a nudist, "mixed sunbathing" resort in New Jersey—and he needed the time to relax as the war crisis jitters continued to ramp up: on the day they left New York, the German Wehrmacht invaded and occupied Paris.

At the end of June, the Heinleins pulled up stakes again and moved on to Chicago, where they camped out for a few days with Clare and his wife, Dorothy, until they could pick up the keys to the summer rental Clare had found them in his own apartment house near the University of Chicago campus. They registered for the General Semantics seminar, which they hadn't had a chance to do before, and found that A.K. (as Korzybski was called by the inner circle of General Semantics, to which the Heinleins had been admitted) had arranged VIP status for them—a very pleasant surprise. This year, when asked for his occupation in the seminar application Heinlein stated that he was a "retired Naval officer, Free lance fiction writer, Politician." Leslyn had shown her occupation as "Housewife; secretary to husband's writings; General hand[y]man in political campaigns." She had still not made it all the way through *Science and Sanity*.[42]

Heinlein used the time before the convention to organize his writing projects. He tried first to work up a story based on an unfolded tesseract. Campbell had liked the idea, but Heinlein found it hard to build a comprehensible story around it: he found it frustratingly hard to explain the basic ideas to nonmathematicians in any understandable way. He tried out various demonstrations on Leslyn and on Clare's wife, Dorothy, using toothpicks and bits of modeling clay, and found they had trouble visualizing the relationships, even with the three-dimensional model to play with.[43]

Heinlein put aside the tesseract story and typed up his notes for the "All" story.

"All" was about a United States invaded and conquered by an Asiatic military clearly referencing the new military Japan (but just as clearly was based in the old, racist Yellow Peril pulps). In the great tradition of 1930s super-science stories, Campbell had a small group of (white) American soldiers who had escaped the invasion and destruction of American forces rallying with a new invention—predictably, a "ray"—that had come just in the nick of time. They were led by a wise old stuffed shirt and sneaked their advanced technology into the conquered country under the guise of a new religious cult.

Making a novel that would be acceptable in the new (and, frankly, more literate) field of modern science fiction took a great deal of work. Heinlein livened up the stiff, boys'-club atmosphere of the super-science story, making the Americans more contemporary in their personal styles. And he also wanted to reduce the pulpish Yellow Peril angle. "It was a hard story to write, as I tried to make this notion plausible to the reader—and also to remove the racism which was almost inherent to his [Campbell's] story line."[44]

The fix he ultimately came up with was to recast the story in sociological terms, instead of racial terms—spin the conflict specifically as a conflict of *cultures* rather than of races. To make the matter explicit, he incorporated a Nisei (Japanese-American) character who would have a tragic and heroic role. Dealing this way, one issue at a time, Heinlein was acting out a larger agenda Campbell had brought to science fiction; gradually Campbell and Heinlein and the rest of the new generation of science-fiction writers left pulp standards behind. Such writing became recognized as a Golden Age of science fiction.

It was uncomfortable trying to work in the heat, and the apartments didn't cool off much even in the evenings. Most nights, about 9:00 P.M., he and Leslyn made a pitcher of wine coolers (sometimes lemonade) and invited Clare and Dorothy for an hour and a half of lively conversation in the open, if not precisely fresh, air of the apartment house's roof, ten stories up.[45]

Campbell wrote to him in Chicago with his reaction to *For Us, the Living*. It was just about what could be expected: he suggested it be rewritten by throwing out all the nudism and free love and reworking the backstory from a political evolution to a technical revolution, based on atomic transmutation.[46] Heinlein knew there was no point in arguing. He replied mildly:

> To me there is a close and causal relationship, or rather a functional and structural relationship between economic customs, sexual customs, dress, taboos, language, political institutions, etc. I think that the dress customs, sex conventions, language habits, etc., of the mid-Victorians were a direct

expression of the economic practices of the time, and *vice versa,* oh, most certainly vice versa! This is not economic determinism, but a loose expression of a theory of function in culture.

There are other things in that book which would offend much more deeply than nudity and different sexual mores. I believe that you didn't mention them because you yourself are an odd and unorthodox man. To you they were an "of course." But they would not be to most people. Puritanism is not simply, nor even primarily, a matter of sex and modesty. We are living in a period of Puritanism (or moral authoritarianism) but most people are totally unaware of it because we have dropped some of the superficial trappings of traditional puritanism. *It is impossible to overemphasize the influence of moral dogmatism in this culture.* Most people are so thoroughly brought up to it that they can not be made aware of it, even when it is pointed out to them. (Is a fish aware of water?) Nor is it possible to overemphasize the influence of moral dogmatism in economics.

Nor is it possible to break with superstitious nonsense and lead one's own life. One either conforms to a culture, or fights it. There is no middle ground. Organisms exist only in environment. One can decide to ignore a culture, but the culture will never ignore one in turn. No can do. It's like deciding to ignore the law of gravitation—it won't let you!

So—finding myself in a culture which is distasteful to my inner needs, I adapt to it as comfortably as possible, and try mildly from time to time to change it here and there.[47]

About much of this, Campbell was dubious. He particularly objected to the close relationship Heinlein saw between social customs and economic conventions[48]—a progressivist, social-engineering notion that traces back through Herbert Spencer to the founding socialist, Henri de Saint-Simon: "The institutions of a people are nothing but the application of its [ethical] ideas."[49]

Since the book was dead in the water, it was a moot issue, but a datum to keep in mind as he tailored future material to Campbell's tastes—"odd and unorthodox," though very much worth cultivating. Campbell's conversational style has been compared to having a manhole cover dropped on you,[50] verbal sledgehammers incapable of nuance. But that kind of shock effect has a chance of dislodging your thinking out of ruts and away from the level of slogans—clearing away mental cobwebs. "I just like to shake them up," Campbell decades later told Barry Malzberg.[51]

The Democratic National Convention opened on July 15, the day the

Battle of Britain began, with the first of repeated German air attacks against British airfields on the home islands. In Chicago, it was exceptionally hot and humid and uncomfortable. Heinlein had been in and through Chicago many times, but his recent political experience, particularly with the migrant camps in the Imperial Valley, gave him new eyes. Between the Loop downtown and the green and pleasant lands of the University of Chicago campus there lay—and still lies—mile after grim mile of ghetto-slums, poverty and despair rolling out of the dilapidated, turn-of-the-century detached carpenter's gothic houses like sweat off a field hand's back. "One night there, I saw five people burned up in one of those death traps," he recalled.[52]

As a party insider, Heinlein had obtained press credentials that allowed him on the mezzanine and a Special Appointee pass "good at any gate and anywhere in the Stadium," both signed by James A. Farley, the president's chief political fixer. Heinlein got into the spirit of things, wearing a red, white, and blue straw skimmer.[53] Almost immediately the Heinleins ran into Jerry Voorhis again.

They found the convention much more staid than expected, with not much of the spittoon-and-cigar-smoke backroom atmosphere that traditionally went along with the national party conventions. Everybody seemed self-conscious that the convention was being broadcast on the radio. Things were so quiet, in fact, that he took his sister-in-law Dorothy one evening.

The draft for Roosevelt, he thought, was genuine rather than staged—or possibly genuine as well as staged, but genuine in any event, and he was satisfied with the result, though disturbed about Roosevelt's acceptance speech, in which he floated the idea of a reintroducing conscription.[54] Heinlein was dead set against conscription, under any circumstances, and saw no long-term benefit in becoming embroiled in the European war. It might even be reason enough to cross the aisle and vote for Wendell Willkie:

> If I become convinced that Wilkie will save us from a semi-totalitarian condition, i.e., the draft, and bids fair to understand what is needed for modern national defense, I will vote for him. *If*—I am not yet convinced and don't like him for other reasons.[55]

Even when affirming the principle of party loyalty, Heinlein nuanced it. Perhaps the difficult division in California politics over the past four years—between mainstream Democrats and the party's radical-progressive EPIC leadership—had made him acutely conscious of where, precisely, his loyalties lay. A less supple mind might fall to one side or the other of the razor's edge. But you had to achieve whatever you could at the moment, given the materials you had available to work with, and like-minded people could work together no matter what their party affiliation. This was certainly true of his relationship with John Campbell, whom he characterized to his friends as a "rock-ribbed Republican."[56] But, he told Campbell,

> I don't think of you and myself as a republican and a democrat, but rather as two different men with different backgrounds and different *data* but who are both intelligent and socially minded and who are working toward much the same social objectives as best they may, each in his own environment.[57]

That is, they had (roughly) the same social goals, even though they disagreed about strategies for achieving them.

The General Semantics seminar was held about a week after the convention,[58] in a suburb some distance from the downtown and the lake, and near the University of Chicago, but just as hot and humid. Immediately, they all picked up where they had left off the previous year in L.A., kicking around ideas for a General Semantics demonstration-movie that was supposed to be fully entertaining and instructive at the same time—a tough proposition.

The Heinleins also met new people, including Japanese professor of English at the University of Wisconsin, S. I. Hayakawa. Hayakawa, like Heinlein, had been directed to Korzybski by Stuart Chase's 1938 *Tyranny of Words*.[59]

After the seminar, Heinlein wrote "Six Against the Empire" through three grinding weeks of Chicago August heat and humidity. He was not completely happy with the results, but shifting the Yellow Peril story from racial to cultural differences was the best he could do and stay within the framework of Campbell's outline. If he strayed too far, it would no longer be "presold." He sent the completed manuscript off to Campbell, retitled "Sixth Column," taking the Fifth Column of the Spanish Civil War one further.

Robert and Leslyn briefly considered staying in Chicago for the Labor Day weekend, when the second "world science fiction convention," called Chicon, would take place. But he and Leslyn had been away from home for nearly three months by that time, living out of suitcases, and there was a limit to how much they could prolong the trip. Campbell expedited the payment for them, and when the check arrived—$584.62, including an extra quarter-cent bonus for exceptional quality that was becoming routine for him—they got ready to make that trip to Michigan to visit with Doc Smith and buy a used car.

It was time to start letting Campbell down gently about churning out pay copy at the same rate he had been doing. Heinlein later said that he would probably want to get out of pulp writing within a couple of years,[60] and this thought might already have been percolating in the back of his mind in the fall of 1940. Since Campbell had said he was coming to depend on Heinlein's production, Heinlein wanted to bring in enough new material for *Astounding* and *Unknown* to be able to "retire" when the time came. He wrote that he would probably not do so much fiction writing when he got back to Hollywood[61]: his eyes were starting to bother him. He might not be able to keep up steady work at writing.

He asked Campbell for his preference among the stories he had in development: the tesseract story was on hold; he had a reincarnation novelette he was calling "Da Capo"; "Fire Down Below" as a two-part serial for *Astounding*; and another two-part serial, "The Shadow of Death," which was just a germ at this point: "Conflict between ordinary men who live to be 60–70 and men who live to be over 200. A strong tragic story with plenty of necessary detail."[62]

He also offered Campbell an oddity story that may have been inspired by Forrest J. Ackerman's "Assorted Services" project. Ackerman had given up a regular paid job and for nine months in 1940 collaborated with a friend, Ted Emsheimer, offering to do "anything for anyone, from borrowing a book to reminding about birthdays."[63] Heinlein's General Services company also offered miscellaneous personal services for a fee—to compensate for the personal servants who had disappeared from middle-class American life in the last thirty years—but took on much larger projects as well. He warned Campbell:

> The basic notion is not a science-fiction notion—at least I don't think the readers will think that the art of business organization and the development of a new field of enterprise (one which is *not* based on some scientific advance) is a science-fiction story. Of course I can stick in a lot of pseudo-science window dressing, as I did in "Coventry," but there is no *basic* science development involved. Judging by the reader response, that method was successful in "Coventry" (which was *not* a science-fiction story, except by misdirection!) but the method does not seem to be as readily applicable to General Services, as I write it.
>
> There is a story there, but it seems to be a Sinclair Lewis story rather than an *Astounding* story.
>
> I have been thinking about having the General Services company outfit

the colonizing expedition that founds Luna City. That might make it a story, by sheer tour de force.[64]

Campbell was a little alarmed at the prospect of a slowdown in his best, most dependable producer.

You may have to slow down because of the eyes, but *please* don't desert the ship. Damn it, I like your stuff, and so—which is vastly more important—do the readers. . . . It takes three to four years at least to find a top-rank author's replacement, so hang around for a while.[65]

He wanted the tesseract story soonest, but the long-lifer story sparked many comments.

Robert and Leslyn drove over to Jackson, Michigan, on August 17 and were met by Doc and Jeanne Smith, and their sixteen-year-old daughter, Verna, all warm and welcoming, energetic and intelligent people—"muy simpatico," as he later wrote about the meeting.[66] They talked about doing a collaborative novel—a mainstream novel, perhaps, for *The Saturday Evening Post* or *Collier's*. Heinlein had a good character in mind and suggested they set it in the food-service industry, to take advantage of Smith's background in cereal chemistry.

Smith had been thinking about what he wanted to get them in the way of a car, and had investigated the used-car market while waiting for them to arrive. He thought he had found one that might do for them. His test-driving terrified and amazed Heinlein: Doc gunned the engine (sound enough) on a back road, his head bent so far over, ear resting on the frame (to listen for squeaks by bone conduction) that he couldn't see the road ahead. Heinlein was in the passenger seat, terrified, but "trying hard to appear cool, calm, fearless—a credit to the Patrol."[67] He bought the Chevy sedan for $585—the Street & Smith check plus thirty-eight cents out of pocket. They christened the car *Skylark IV*.

On August 23 they were done with traveling: they posted Robert's routine notice of his whereabouts to the Navy Department and left for Los Angeles, arriving on the twenty-eighth—Leslyn's birthday. "Blowups Happen" had just appeared in the September *Astounding*. "Coventry" had placed first in that magazine's Analytical Laboratory (as the readers' poll was called), and Campbell's lead editorial was about Heinlein's story in this issue. And there was one letter commenting on "Coventry," with another backhanded compliment. "The Devil Makes the Law" came out that month, too, in *Unknown,* under the Anson MacDonald byline. Heinlein had definitely and finally "arrived."

And with story orders in hand for another year's worth of income, Heinlein picked up his writing routine again, and agonized through the tesseract story, now titled " '—And He Built a Crooked House—.' " The day he sent it off (September 12, 1940), Doc and Jeanne Smith arrived in Los Angeles for an overnight visit, and the Heinleins took the Smiths to dinner with Jack Williamson, Ed Hamilton, and Leigh Brackett, stopping in at the LASFS meeting in downtown Los Angeles. Williamson and Hamilton had shown up that summer, traveling cross-country from east to west while the Heinleins were traveling cross-country from west to east, and were already well acquainted with the Mañana Literary Society crowd. Jack Williamson, in particular, delighted Heinlein. He was a very quiet, shy man, unassuming—a little too unassuming, in Heinlein's opinion:

> Two writers have influenced my writing most: H. G. Wells and Jack Williamson. But you influenced me more than Mr. Wells did. (I hope not too many readers noticed how much I've leaned on you. *You* spotted it, of course. But you never talk . . . [68]

In between stories and social events, scheduled and unscheduled, the Heinleins were painting the house and sprucing things up in the garden. They wanted to be ready to jump if war boiled over.[69] In the meantime, Heinlein would keep punching the money machine to build up their reserves before taking a little much-needed personal time: "I've acquired, without assimilating, too many impressions lately, and it's time I took stock. My mind is as cluttered as a neglected desk drawer."[70]

They had arrived back in Los Angeles on the day John and Doña Campbell's first child, Philinda Duane Campbell, was born, so P.D. and Leslyn shared the same birthday. Discreetly they offered to be godparents to P.D.[71]— an offer that delighted Doña. But John Campbell had family close by, and he wound up asking his father and stepmother. John and Doña Campbell let the Heinleins know they would prefer to have them as foster parents, if it ever became necessary. This was a responsibility Robert and Leslyn took very seriously:

> Leslyn and I intended to have children when we got married, but a combination of circumstances made it difficult. I came down with T.B.; I was re-

tired which brought half-pay; the years piled up and now Leslyn is thirty-six and the world is in a hell of a mess. If she should become pregnant inadvertently, we would acquiesce cheerfully. In the mean time we have no plans for children of our own.[72]

Heinlein was having trouble with the General Services story. He was thinking about having his General Services contract the building of Luna City, just to connect it into his history of the future,[73] but the story wasn't coming together. Campbell offered him another idea, about a spaceship that missed its mark—interesting, but it would be a while before he could get to it. He put General Services aside and wrote "Logic of Empire."

He did take time out for one thing: H. G. Wells was coming to a bookshop in Pasadena in late October for an autograph party. It was Heinlein's first chance to meet Wells, and he would not miss it. Heinlein took his treasured copy of the 1910 revision of *When the Sleeper Wakes*. Wells was surprised—and pleased—to see the antique. He inscribed it to "Lieutenant Heinlein."[74] This meeting—the only time Heinlein and Wells met—has some of the historical resonance for science fiction that Mozart hearing the young Beethoven has for music.

When Harry Warner, Jr., a fan, wrote asking for something of Heinlein's he could publish in the second anniversary issue of his fanzine, *Spaceways*,[75] Heinlein cautiously agreed, though he didn't want to become embroiled in the feuding that was endemic on the East Coast. He was in any case spending too much time at the typewriter for the good of his health. But he had an odd, humorous, stream-of-consciousness piece about all the things a writer does to avoid actual writing he called ironically "How to Write a Story."[76] It had failed to place while they were gone—they had found it in the mail when they got back—and was so odd that he would otherwise have trouble finding a place for it. He subscribed to *Spaceways* as he was already subscribing to Will Sykora's *Fantasy News*.

Fred Pohl wrote and expressed regret he had missed meeting them in New York. He wanted more story submissions.[77] Heinlein didn't have any new material not already committed to Campbell—and particularly none he could afford to divert to lower-paying markets. But he did have the five early stories that had not sold. He was particularly interested in getting "Lost Legacy" into print, and offered all five (three of which he had already submitted to Pohl) on the sole condition that Pohl didn't do any editorial monkeying about with the idea-content. Pohl's editorial comments about "Beyond

Doubt" and "Lost Legacy" struck Heinlein as perceptive and workable,[78] but the prospect of selling off the last of his ugly stepchildren at fire-sale rates caused Heinlein to reevaluate his overall strategy.

If it should ever happen that he couldn't keep hitting the high-pay markets like *Astounding,* he did not intend to be forced to live on the low-pay/slow-pay markets. There were easier and less personally humiliating ways of making a living: he would get out of the business at once, rather than take the chance of having some lowlife like Ray Palmer make cracks in print about him "slipping" because his stuff was rejected.[79] And the notion that he might put a friend—Campbell—through the unpleasantness of having to reject him was very unpalatable, and he told Campbell ("John" now; their letters began addressing each other by first names during the summer) so, in so many words.

> Right now I know I am a profit-making commercial property, because the cash customers keep saying so in the Analytical Laboratory, but I don't intend to hang on while slipping down into fourth or fifth place. No, when I quit, I'll quit at the top, in order to insure that our business relations will never become unpleasant or disappointing to either of us. Which is a long and verbose way of saying that I value your friendship very highly indeed and intend to keep it if I can.[80]

In the meantime, the lost-starship idea was germinating into a story. He wrote "Universe" to fit into his history of the future, set about a quarter century after "Misfit," and mailed the story to Street & Smith on December 1. "It was a dilly of an idea, John, and I appreciate you letting me work on it. I hope that it satisfied you."[81] It did, and Campbell shoved at him another pregnant technical idea—one that again dovetailed with a political story he was germinating from a conversation he and Bob Cornog had had: radioactive dust used as a weapon—really nasty atomics.

"Such nice ideas he has," Heinlein told Campbell.[82] In the same letters, he began outlining a proposal for a serial about the conflict of long-lived and short-lived that made Campbell frantic with delight, if the lively discussion that stretched over a period of weeks is any indication.

Heinlein's professional life went well that fall. But as the year drew to a close, a local fan, Bruce Yerke, decided to write a flippant and satirical fanzine article about the Heinleins' political activities. Heinlein knew Yerke's underlying purpose was to get him involved in a public argument with the L.A. fans about Technocracy, and he was not going to succumb. He had avoided making any kind of public comment about Technocracy so far—privately, he considered Technocracy a particularly vicious kind of industrial fascism:

> It is a state run without democratic consent, an absolute authority, no checks and balances—like it or lump it. I am inclined to believe that in due time American versions of Hitler and Mussolini would maneuver their way to the driver's seat, and that we would have a hell of a time getting them out. In any case the social set-up as described in the study course provides no way of getting them out. In our present set-up no matter how bad an administration is, we get a chance every couple of years or so to "turn the rascals out."[83]

In any case, he hated that kind of pointless public argument that went around and around and never went anywhere. It got him upset without producing any beneficial stimulation. "I most bodaciously will *not* get into a fan mag debate."[84] Heinlein asked Yerke not to publish the article:

> Every person has things about them which they do not like to have dragged out into public. I've led a very active life and made a powerful number of mistakes. If you go digging into my record, much of which is public and easily available, you will find a lot of things which I would much rather forget, but which are facts.
> But my friends don't go out of their way to remind me of them.[85]

Yerke published the article anyway.[86]

So far as Robert and Leslyn were concerned, that was that: they had let him know they would not consider it friendly, and Yerke had decided to not be a friend. They quietly let it be known they would not go anywhere Yerke was—which alarmed several of the local fans, since that meant they would not appear at the LASFS Christmas party. Yerke was pressured into writing an awkward, not-quite-apologetic letter. "I take it that you don't intend any harm," Heinlein replied, "but, for me, you play too rough." People naturally react badly when they are satirized, he explained; what else could he have expected?[87] Robert and Leslyn would attend the LASFS Christmas party, but any continuing and closer relationship with those fans was no longer in the Heinleins' plans.

The radioactive dust story was ready on Christmas Eve and mailed off with the working title of "Foreign Policy"—and that was the year's work for

Heinlein. His subscription copy of *Unknown* (the January 1941 issue) had arrived, with Cleve Cartmill's first published story, "Oscar." Cartmill had not received his copy yet, so they took the magazine over and gave it to him as a Christmas present. "Greater love hath no man than that he giveth his new copy of *Unknown* to a friend before he had a chance to read it himself. Looks like an exceptionally good number, too."[88]

That evening, Robert made time alone to prepare a Christmas surprise for Leslyn. When they were in bed reading with the radio on, he slipped out to the dining room where he had set up the Zenith automatic record player he had bought for her. It "broadcast" to a radio frequency, and when he got back to the bedroom, he discreetly tuned the radio, then got back in bed. One of the ten disks on the changer was a platter he had recorded himself, with a Christmas message for her. When the radio called her by name, Leslyn started: "She did a double-take that money could not buy. And the longer it played the more excited she got."[89]

So his gift was a success. The new record player was also accompanied by a sizable check to buy more records. One of Leslyn's gifts to him that year delighted him just as much—a bedside memo pad with a tiny built-in light that came on automatically when you removed the pencil from its holder: "Just the thing," he said, "for an insomniac writer."[90]

21

EXPANDING HORIZONS

First news of 1941 was Campbell's reaction to "Foreign Policy": there was no *good* solution to the dilemma it posed. Atomic weapons create a stalemate in power politics. Campbell had mixed reactions but decided the story's weaknesses—its very unsatisfactoriness—could be its greatest strength if he spun it as a challenge to the reader. He retitled it "Solution Unsatisfactory," calling attention to the story's challenges.[1]

Another potential sale was on the horizon: that Monday, Campbell sent a night letter saying he had forwarded the manuscript for "Sixth Column" to a book publisher, Henry Holt & Company, and, at the same time, to a Chicago radio producer, Ralph Rose, who was looking for science-fiction properties. Heinlein arranged for Clare to act as his local agent and keep any fees the properties earned. He and Leslyn had wanted to figure out some way to help underwrite Clare's doctoral program, and that might do it painlessly. At the same time, Clare suggested Robert get a Hollywood agent, and he did, making arrangements with H. N. Swanson for film and media representation.

In January, they became a two-writer family again. As the first installment of "Sixth Column" came out in the January issue of *Astounding,* Leslyn's poem "The Ballad of Lalune" came out in the January issue of *Weird Tales*—Leslyn's first published writing since 1939.

Heinlein revised "Lost Legacy" to Fred Pohl's editorial comments. Gradually the half dozen stories Campbell rejected were selling, one by one, to lesser magazines.

With the money coming in and the immediate pressure of writing commitments in abeyance, Heinlein probably felt he could afford to take a little time off and do some household renovation projects. Making a studio for himself was at the top of the list. He had been writing in a corner of the living room, which could be very distracting, sharing space with guests and Leslyn's continuing political activities. He had been putting off making a new space for his own use because he expected to be called up for active duty at any time, but the crisis had gone on for a long time now.[2]

The garage was over twenty feet tall, with a lot of floor space. He and Bill Corson installed a loft, starting in January, before the worst of the rains came on (February is Los Angeles's month for gullywashers and hailstorms). They didn't bother getting a permit for the work, but sneaked materials in under cover of night and even cut the windows and outside door at night so that the neighbors would not catch on and complain. When the structure was completed, including a stairway to the street, he posted a sign Bill Corson created for him on the outside door, to discourage random visitors and door-to-door salesmen:

ENDOSTROPHIC THERAPY ROOM. KEEP OUT!
DO NOT KNOCK!!!
Use upper door—it works quite well

The "upper door" was the main house—down the stairs, across the driveway, and up a curved flight of brick steps, where Leslyn had posted her own sign:

Anyone knocking on this door before eleven A.M.
will be buried free of charge.[3]

Toward the end of 1940, Campbell had recommended Heinlein take up photography as a hobby,[4] and Heinlein was able to write back that he already had a bad case of the camera bug: he used a Contax 1.5 he had bought from a German refugee—that was why he was building a darkroom and sculpting studio in his renovation. "I am completely nuts now on the subject of cameras," he told Campbell. This produces a vicious cycle: "I have to write stories to support my camera, darkroom, buy gear, etc., but I really haven't time to write stories because photography is a full time occupation."[5] Nude photography was what he spent much of his free time and spare cash on. Heinlein never had any difficulty getting women to pose nude for him— which astonished his friends and acquaintances. To him, it was simply a numbers game: "If you approach a woman right, one out of two will pose nude for you," he told Forrest Ackerman.[6] "Leslyn's chaperonage is the main reason why I can get anyone to pose for me I want for the purpose," Heinlein told a fan he had met at Denvention.[7] The Heinleins also had belonged for several years to a camera co-op that hired live models at group rates. In 1941, the co-op brought him the perfect model, Sunrise Lee. She could not fall into an ungraceful pose. A nude study of her hung in his house for the rest of his life.

The studio was finished enough to move into by the beginning of February. He got a writing study, a sculpture and photography studio—and a darkroom, because he liked to develop his own photos (many of which were nudes, for which privacy was required in any case)—and a wood-working shop in the back of the shortened garage, plus much-needed extra bookshelves, and a second bath and spare bed for his insomniac "white nights." The writing studio he put to immediate use. His brother Larry had asked for a $100 loan until April, so to underwrite the loan he wrote up his General Services story for Campbell and titled it "'We Also Walk Dogs.'"

But he also had his eye on bigger things. The radio adaptation of "Sixth Column" wasn't going anywhere. Ralph Rose had disappeared, and the book deal Campbell was trying to broker collapsed as well. Campbell wanted the long-lifer serial Heinlein had outlined, though the story seemed a little "skimpy" for a serial. Heinlein decided to combine it with another story idea in his files, a super-science epic he had outlined, by having his long-lifers forced off Earth. He would use Doc Smith as the pattern for his lead character, Woodrow Wilson "Lazarus Long" Smith. Doc Smith's ancestors for five generations back had lived to be more than a hundred years old.[8] But he made him a very pragmatic rogue by mixing him with a literary character. He later told Jack Williamson:

I took your immortal Giles Habibula, mixed him with your hero in Crucible of Power . . . and made another, after carefully filing off the serial numbers and giving it a new paint job. You invented the hero in spite of himself, the one with feet of clay, human and believable—and I knew a good thing when I saw it. The result? Lazarus Long. Lazarus, who never wanted trouble, always tried to duck out, never hesitated to stack the deck or tell a shameless lie if those tactics were safest for his hide.[9]

Heinlein mailed the first serial installment on March 5, asking for comments he could incorporate in the last two-thirds of the serial.

"While the Evil Days Come Not" was written in a very unusual way for him, through letter after letter of discussion of the serial's various tropes and turns. This exchange was a much-expanded version of the way "Sixth Column" had been written, with discussion and feedback as he went along. Campbell's comments were not all encouraging; but it was often the disagreements that made the most impact on the shape the story took on.

The comments that caused Heinlein the most trouble had to do with Campbell's skepticism about Heinlein's planned *non*-secret of long life: his people lived longer because they *believed* they would live longer. Campbell wanted a scientific explanation, and Robert wanted to avoid the super-science cliché, since nobody could really say for sure that it *had* to be physical factors that determined everything. The issue was still open as he turned in the second installment of what was beginning to look like a four-parter. Campbell persisted: the psychosomatic long life bit just didn't work in the story. Heinlein capitulated and found a "physical" explanation he could live with; the buyer presumably knew his market better than the mere writer. But perhaps this caused him to go stale on the project for a while. He went back to work finishing up the renovation, struggling with plumbing, perhaps to get his mind off the "Evil Days" serial. In any case, he finished the last installment on March 26—a "fairly radical departure"[10] from the usual run of science fiction serials since there were no battles of any kind.

During the planning and the writing, Campbell and Heinlein had, in letter after letter, chewed over aspects of Heinlein's Fortean idea of encountering a race of intelligent beings owned by their gods, the Jockaira, which he shorthanded as "dog people." "The yarn's good," Campbell told him after receiving the draft of the final installment.

But the last chunk here tends to sag every time they hit one of the new planets. Reason: You don't have any real conversation with—or meeting with—the Jabberwocky or whatever you called 'em [Jockaira], or the Little People. Jawohl; I know. You can't talk to 'em sensibly. I still want to "hear them talk." I don't. Therefore you're a liar and it didn't happen at all, and I don't believe you—at least not emotionally. Wherefore I think we've got to do some heavy faking. . . .

In other words, I'd like you to take your carbon, go over it, and rewrite most of the dog-people part in dialog. Haul out all the "we can't establish contacts, really" until the explanation of what really happened when the gods finally threw them off the planet. Your experts can warn, but most of your pragmatists—and isn't Long pretty much one?—will feel that, even if they can't get *all* the words right, and they are missing something here and there, they can straighten that out better when they're finally settled.

They've got a job to do; settling. The precisionists can fuss and stew, but their precision can wait till the proper time.

Then the mask comes off, and they see what was behind that veil of language, and it really will scare them silly. The nice, kind, pleasant friend turns into something unholy, revolting to the very nature of men. The peaceful world is suddenly under the shadow of awful, lurking *things,* hiding unseen in their temples. *Yeeow!* Get me out of here![11]

The writing of "Evil Days" (which Campbell retitled "Methuselah's Children") marked an unnoticed watershed in the Heinleins' life together. Gradually, Robert's intense involvement with Leslyn as sounding board and story doctor had begun to taper off. His own "story sense" was becoming surer, but the feedback he was getting from Campbell—his editor—was more directly useful.

The April issue of *Unknown* hit the stands, with "They," and his mail from both fans and fellow writers continued to pick up, filled with compliments on how successfully he had pulled that one off. Ironically, his "offbeat" story "They" was his most successful so far. His ninth wedding anniversary, on March 28, made him reflective: "We think very highly of the institution of matrimony and believe it is here to stay. Since we have spent twenty-four hours a day, literally, in each other's company during the major portion of that time, you may take it as laboratory tested and approved."[12] "[Leslyn] convinces me that there is something outside the ego besides otherness, enmity, and enigma."[13]

"Beyond Doubt" appeared in the April *Astonishing,* so his obligation to Elma Wentz was finally discharged. The early polls in *Astounding* showed "Sixth Column" in first place. He joined the Authors Guild on Jack Williamson's recommendation.

Revisions on the "Methuselah's Children" serial slowed to a stop as he got the story refined to Campbell's satisfaction, but Campbell shoveled a new idea at him, addressing his letter to "Dear Anson" [MacDonald]:

While Bob's on his vacation—and has a long novel coming up—maybe "you" can be mulling this one over for a novelette—which we most desperately need. We need half a dozen novelettes, as a matter of fact.

Setup: the CT ships. The CT ships are employed in a form of meteor and asteroid mining—the deadliest, most dangerous going. And its rewards are, naturally, proportionate.

CT stands for *contraterrene*—contraterrene matter.[14]

Heinlein was not sure enough of his background in physics—contraterrene, or "anti," matter had been possible in theory since Paul Dirac predicted the positive electron in 1929 but Heinlein wanted to think about it before agreeing on the series of stories. "I don't have a story yet on contraterrene," he told Campbell, "but I will get one I know."

> . . . I've got to work out some major human problem to center the story around, some problem created by, or solved by, the peculiarities of contraterrene. If necessary, I suppose I could use some fairly stock plot against a background of contraterrene mining, but the gag is too good for that; unless you are immediately pressed for copy, I'll turn it over in my mind for a few days before starting to write.[15]

He asked Robert Cornog for another briefing, and they spent two days working through the fundamentals before Cornog was called to Washington, D.C., to consult on something or other hush-hush.[16] Heinlein set the story idea aside. When it was ready, a story idea would drop out of the preparation—and it wouldn't drop until it was ready.

In May 1941, "Universe" and the Future History chart were published, as well as "Solution Unsatisfactory," bylined Anson MacDonald. Since *Astounding* was going to a larger format, Campbell was in desperate need of material. Heinlein promised to start writing the sequel to "Universe" on June 1, whether or not he actually had anything to say—a safe promise, since he had chopped off the second half of a planned serial to make up "Universe."[17] He could start writing anytime he could work up interest in pounding the typewriter again. In the meantime, Heinlein sent Campbell the two stories he had revised for Pohl. Campbell actually bought the shortened (ten-thousand-word) version of "Patterns of Possibility," which Heinlein had retitled "It's Impossible!"—but Campbell apparently didn't like even the retitle, as it appeared in the September 1941 issue under the somewhat misleading title "Elsewhere"[18]—and it was different enough from the "Anson MacDonald" or "Robert Heinlein" material to justify using the "new" pseudonym Heinlein had placed on the revision for Pohl's use: Caleb Saunders.

Heinlein immediately wrote up a gimmick story he had been working out in his head: all the characters in the story are the same person at different times of his life, made possible by using multiple overlapping loops-back of time travel.

I have had a dirty suspicion since I was about six that all consciousness is one and that all the actors I see around me (including my enemies) are myself, at different points in the record's grooves. I once partly explored this in a story called "By His Bootstraps."[19]

It was light entertainment. A puzzle story.

That yarn has been received in a fashion that has amused me. I regarded it as a piece of pure hack-work myself, but it stood higher than a really serious story in the same issue. Some people have been quite upset by it, judging from the letters I received. It was based on two ideas: a wish to do a time story which faced, rather than avoided, the intellectual paradoxes inherent in an orthodox Euclid-Newton time theory, and secondly, a wish to embroider the theme that the Possible is not necessarily the Emotionally-Conceivable. You will see that the question of how in the hell Bob Wilson managed to furnish his own First Cause is structurally the same as the old dilemma: if God made the world, who made God?—which is a legitimate question (although usually dressed up in other language) and quite unanswerable in any emotionally convincing fashion.[20]

But once that effort was concluded, on May 11, 1941, everything stopped for him:

I am not writing at present. I went stale after finishing "By His Bootstraps." (There is a small but noisy minority who contend that I went stale *before* finishing it.) I have returned to manual labor for a week or two, after having, for the first time in my life, spent a week staring at a typewriter and moaning. However, I expect to get to work on the "Universe" sequel around the 1st of June—unless I do a novelet first. That means one less story than I had previously indicated; sorry—the old hack refused to budge.[21]

Although he never recorded what his manual labor amounted to, the timing is right for him to have designed and installed a sprinkler system that would "rain" on the house and lower the temperature.

Heinlein had been invited to be the guest of honor for the third World Science Fiction Convention, or "WorldCon," held in Denver over the Fourth of July weekend, for which he was expected to given an important speech, and he didn't have *any* idea for it. The timing was awkward this year: Korzybski was going to give a seminar in Denver the following month. He and Leslyn would have to stick around for about six weeks to take in both events. It was time to get moving on the speech.

There is only one thing to do in these circumstances: steal from the best. H. G. Wells had given a speech in 1902 titled "The Discovery of the Future," about the social effects of technological change. Heinlein combined that idea with some propaganda about Korzybski, on the theory that he might be able to do the same thing for the 1940s: lay out the groundwork of the knowledge it would take to live in the future, picking up where Wells had left off with his three sociological fact books.

In June, Heinlein started writing the "Universe" sequel, knowing it was as good as presold, and he could use the proceeds to underwrite the trip to Denver. His and Leslyn's expenses were already covered, but he wanted to make a special loan to one of the local fans, Walter Daugherty. Daugherty was to be married at the end of June and go to the Denvention—that's what the fans were calling this Denver WorldCon—for their honeymoon.[22] "It's the first time we have ever chaperoned a honeymoon," he told Campbell.[23]

Then came a burst of good news—the first good news about the European war in four years: Hitler had turned on his erstwhile ally, Stalin, and invaded Russia on June 21, along an 1,800-mile front. "Isn't the news of the German-Russian war wonderful?" Leslyn wrote. "No matter which of them wins, it's good for us."[24] That sent them off to Denver on June 27 in a burst of good cheer. They filled *Skylark IV* with luggage and Daugherty's movie and phonograph recording equipment—he intended to record the convention for posterity.

This was a good trip. They stopped at Boulder Dam and at the Grand Canyon to stretch their legs, and at Pikes Peak and the Garden of the Gods, Daugherty functioning as relief driver and general source of entertainment. At the Colorado Springs rest stop there were horses nearby, so Daugherty demonstrated his horsemanship for their approval and amusement.

The Heinleins had taken a suite on the fourth floor of the convention hotel, the Shirley-Savoy. When they checked in on July 2, two days before the convention was scheduled to start, they found a number of fans already there. The Heinleins opened their suite as an informal hospitality center for the preconvention activities, and worked hard at making the mostly teenaged fans feel comfortable. Shortly they had thirty young fans (boys, mostly) sprawled on the floor and spilling out into the hall (and consuming two cases of Coca-Cola).[25]

The early WorldCons were not like today's gigantic affairs: with only two hundred or so people, Robert and Leslyn were highly visible. He was probably the most sophisticated and cosmopolitan person the fans had ever come into contact with, and he seemed to them like something out of a movie.[26] Forrest Ackerman was impressed by their easy hospitality—and particularly by the fact that Heinlein treated the black bellman who brought up their room-service order "like a normal human being." That just wasn't *done* then, crossing that social color line. Even his mannerisms and affectations—the bit of stagecraft business he did, lighting a cigarette to cover an incipient stammer—struck Ackerman as suave and sophisticated.[27]

Heinlein's personal stock with the convention members soared on the first day when he saved the sponsoring committee from embarrassment by offering to cover a $25 award that had been promised by a new science fiction magazine, *Comet,* but that had failed to materialize.[28] And he had followed that up by a just-one-of-the-guys routine: there was a masquerade program for which he was caught unprepared. He got into the spirit of the thing, without a costume of any kind, entering the competition as "Adam Stink, the world's most lifelike robot"—a parody of the robotic hero of *Adam Link,* a popular series by brothers Earl and Otto Binder, writing as Eando Binder. Leslyn's costume was a subtle but definite psychological statement for anyone who could read it: she came in Oriental drag as Queen Niafer of Cabell's *Figures of Earth*[29]— the "small dark thing" companion of Count Manuel of Poictesme, the very ordinary and small-minded wife of an artist-conqueror-redeemer.

The masquerade smoothed the way into Heinlein's speech. Ackerman introduced him, calling Heinlein the "Olaf Stapledon of American Science-fiction."[30] Dr. Daugherty's recording equipment started spinning, and Heinlein got up to give his own "Discovery of the Future."[31]

Heinlein had taken as his theme "time binding"—Korzybski's 1922 insight about what distinguishes humans from animals: the ability to plan across time and to pass knowledge and other forms of wealth from generation to generation. He wove this into Doc Smith's theme from the previous year at the Chicago convention: science fiction was socially useful, he said, because it trained its readers to know, on a very deep level, that *tomorrow is going to be different*. And with this knowledge, humankind at last possessed the tools to shape its own future. Science-fiction readers were thus at the leading edge of a great wave in human evolution—an important part of Wells's Open Conspiracy.

Science-fiction readers in 1941 were social outcasts. To be told— seriously—that they were personally an important element in human progress was apparently just as intoxicating for them as the same realization had been for Heinlein in 1930.[32]

There is a certain type of personality, however, unfortunately common in science-fiction fandom, for which adoration is a red flag. A dozen or so of these boys—mostly Technocrats, Heinlein thought (though in another place he refers to New York fans, Futurians)[33]—followed him around and made a "steady and malicious effort" to whittle him to size. This irritation loomed large in his mind. "They were so rude that I did not enjoy [the guest-of-honor experience]."[34] He wondered—for years—why the more socially adept fans didn't rein them in.[35]

On Sunday evening, the convention hosted a banquet for their guest of honor, and Heinlein made an impromptu thank-you speech, a soufflé he felt fell flat and wasn't very funny, because he was "tired enough for twins by then."[36] He sat down, feeling defeated and hardly paying attention to the next speaker, Franklyn Brady, who surprised him with a present—seven of them, actually—for his birthday. Brady and Bill Deutsch had quietly passed the hat and took up a collection to honor him. Leslyn was in on the gag: she had told them what books he might appreciate.

Up to that moment, Heinlein had thought that his time and effort had been wasted, that the science fiction fans despised and resented him. He was visibly shocked—and deeply touched—by this gesture of affection. "He was so filled with emotion that he came very close to tears. He was really thrilled."[37] Frank Brady "asked me to read the titles aloud," Heinlein told Campbell later.

> I got all choked up and couldn't do it.
>   Here is what they gave me:
>   *The People, Yes*—Carl Sandburg
>   *The Prairie Years*—Carl Sandburg
>   *Young Adventure*—Benét
>   *John Brown's Body*—Benét
>   *Stargazer: The Biography of Galileo*[38]
>   *Experiment in Autobiography*—H. G. Wells
>   *The Oracles of Nostradamus*.[39]

An eighth book—Stephen Vincent Benét's collection *Thirteen O'Clock*—had to follow him home, as Bill Deutsch could not find a copy for sale in Denver.

Once the convention was over, the Heinleins had to make a decision: could they stay in Denver for the General Semantics seminar Korzybski was giving in five weeks or should they go back to Los Angeles and make a second trip to Denver? Ultimately, Robert and Leslyn decided against attending the seminar at all—possibly because they didn't have progress to report on the projects Robert was theoretically working on.[40]

> We hoped to be able to attend both conventions (as Guest of honor we couldn't very well cut the first one but we couldn't afford to stay in Denver a whole month. We also didn't want to stay any longer than we could help as we lived there once!)[41]

They returned to Hollywood by way of Wyoming, Utah, and Nevada, the Great Salt Desert, Reno, the Donner Pass, and the Sacramento Valley.

On the day they arrived back in Hollywood,[42] Heinlein was interviewed for a local writers' magazine. "Doc" Lowndes (whom they had met in Denver and who was now editing the pulp magazines *Future* and *Science Fiction*) returned " 'My Object All Sublime,' " saying it was too long—but he could use a story at four thousand words. That was the last of Heinlein's unsold stories from spring 1939. He could cut this story to make the sale, but the prospect did not inspire any immediate interest. He was having trouble settling on any idea good enough to write.[43]

Willard G. Hawkins, who had been at Denvention, worked for the World Press and thought the transcript of his speech could be placed with *Author & Journalist* magazine, for which he did the printing and publishing. Doc Smith wrote saying he was ready to come to California and work on the collaborative novel they had talked about last year. Smith sketched out his ideas for a 100,000-word book with a naval—or perhaps merchant marine—background, which would make use of Heinlein's experience base. They could include a subplot dealing with the hidden international spies and saboteurs, so-called "fifth columnists," and flesh out the story with

> Some open struggles, a few fist-fights and gun-fights. Possibly a trainwreck and/or near the climax, a torpedoing or some such disaster. These things, and whatever incidental mayhem seems to be indicated, would be my dish.[44]

Heinlein countered with a suggestion for a food-service background, as Doc Smith was a cereal chemist, but there was a lot of work to do before the rough ideas they were kicking around could be turned into a story.

Photos of the convention began to arrive, sent by the other camera bugs he had met at the Denvention, and that was entertaining.[45]

In his doldrums, Heinlein drifted into an extended "political" correspondence with Doc Lowndes, who had represented himself as a Technocrat/pacifist. It was probably this discussion of the Technate and its potential for brutal, insect totalitarianism that tickled something in Heinlein's mind, something that started with the Selenites in H. G. Wells's very ambiguous *First Men in the Moon* but went . . . somewhere else. He felt a story coming on—"a strong *new* idea (oh, fairly new, anyhow)," he told Campbell[46]—and with the weird, atmospheric quality that had caught so much attention with "They."

No matter whether writers portrayed aliens as conquerors or victims or as wise "elder brothers," they always used the underlying assumption that there would be a rough parity between humans and aliens. Some of Charles Fort's ideas suggested an entirely new direction to take such a story, picturing aliens so far above us intellectually that they might not even interact with human beings—any more than we interact with goldfish in a bowl.[47] Sir Arthur Conan Doyle had touched on some of this atmosphere in his *Post* story, "The Horror of the Heights."

He finished the story in a week and a half, retitling it "Creation Took Eight Days" (since his original title, "Goldfish Bowl," might reveal too much about the story to the readers), to suggest higher orders of creation than the human. This, he thought, was the one of the strongest things he had ever written—groundbreaking and "daring,"[48] just the kind of thing Campbell wanted for *Astounding*. It went off to him on August 11, 1941.[49]

Ten days later (the letter is dated August 21, 1941), Heinlein received a very odd letter from Campbell, headed "Dear Mr. Heinlein." That was strange to begin with: they had been on first-name basis since last June.

> I am afraid that "Creation Took Eight Days" will have to come back. I don't know whether this was intended for *Astounding* or *Unknown*. It might possibly fit either.
>
> The basic trouble is that it lacks point; nothing of particularly convincing importance occurs in the story. I am afraid it simply has no punch.
>
> I suggest you lay this one aside for a while and look it over in three or four months and see if you don't agree with me.[50]

It was signed with his full name, not simply "John."

That was disturbing on many levels.[51] The chatty, voluble, friendly John had completely disappeared and was replaced by this coldly formal stranger. That kind of unexplained sudden reversal might have triggered depressing, mildly paranoiac doubts about the impossibility of achieving any real understanding of another human being. (A. P. White [Anthony Boucher] received a similar rejection letter from Campbell within a day or so.) Campbell seemed to have missed everything that made the story important to Heinlein: what he had taken as a slow buildup of horror, Campbell had dismissed as "lacks point."

Heinlein dealt with his feelings of personal rejection as he had learned to, by chopping off the immediate experience of the emotions to process later. As for the professional rejection . . . if he could miss his target that badly, this was the early warning signal that triggered the up-or-out policy he had set for himself a year ago. And that, surprisingly, gave him a sense of relief, of being finally unchained.

> So—at long last came the envelope I had been looking for, a rejection instead of a check. I had a quick pang of regret over the money I didn't get which was washed away by the pleasant knowledge that school was out at last. I spent the whole day taking pictures. I spent the next day starting the excavation for a swimming pool, a project which I have had in mind for five years, which I have been ready to commence for some months, but which takes time, lots of it. I could hire it done by staying at the typewriter, but that was not the idea—I wanted the heavy physical exercise which a pick, shove, and wheelbarrow provides.[52]

He still had a few stories that would appear in the pulps—"Lost Legacy" appeared in the November issue of Pohl's *Super Science Stories* (Pohl had left the magazines—or been fired; it wasn't clear), chopped up and atrociously edited and under the inapt title "Lost Legion." The magazine was on the stands in August, and he began receiving mail about it almost immediately. Together with "They," "Lost Legion" was already becoming one of his most successful stories, and the "Lyle Monroe" pseudonym seemed no obstacle at all to the colleagues who wrote him about the story.

And he had nonpulp writing projects on his back burner: in addition to the projects he had agreed to take on for Korzybski, he wanted to write up the money game he had invented for *For Us, the Living* as a tract in monetary theory. He had a publisher ready to take it, if and when it got written.[53]

> The above plans, although numerous and involved, are leisurely in their nature—which is what I have been wanting. I want to be able to stop, sit

down, and "invite my soul" for an hour, a day, or a week, if I feel the need for it. I don't know yet what my principal task in this world is, if I have one, but I do know that I won't find it through too much hurry and striving. Nor by accepting other people's standards.[54]

Campbell's next letter was friendly again—and contained no mention of the rejection Campbell must have known would trigger Heinlein's retirement. Heinlein replied in the same vein until an opportunity should present itself to say what he might find to say about the subject.

In the meantime, life went on. Robert knew Campbell was counting on product from his Mañana Literary Society protégés and suggested he write a regular weekly "marketing letter" for this West Coast writers' colony, so they would be able to compete on even terms with the New York writers who could just drop by Campbell's office for the latest scoop on what he was buying.

Cleve Cartmill and his fiancée, Jeanne Irvine, were becoming jittery at the relatives' plans for their wedding at the end of September and decided to move up the date to August 18. Robert and Leslyn drove them to Las Vegas—then, in the days before Bugsy Siegel invented the casino strip, barely a wide place in the road. "I drove the Mojave Desert twice in twenty hours, and it made an old man out of me. That makes two honeymoons we have chaperoned in six weeks; I am quitting the business."[55] Nor had the writing business shut down just because he was no longer spending all day at the typewriter: now that he wasn't writing full-time for pulps, he could consider writing a mainstream novel or marketing something to the slick magazines. A friend,[56] Virginia Perdue, offered to introduce him to her agent (who had gotten her mysteries in serialization in *The Saturday Evening Post*).

Just then, Fred Pohl wrote saying that he had left Popular/Fictioneers suddenly to form an agency and he wanted Heinlein as a client. That was awkward: just the day before, Heinlein had told Doc Lowndes *he* could agent the two stories that were still outstanding (" 'My Object All Sublime' " and "Pied Piper"). That was all the stock Heinlein had on hand at the moment. He told Lowndes he could offer them to Alden Norton, which would give him a "back channel" to find out about Pohl's situation, particularly with reference to the atrocious editing "Lost Legacy" had received. Some of the edits were dumb but at least comprehensible (that business that Ambrose Bierce, who was (positively) portrayed as a character in the story, might come back from his long absence and sue was typical); but a lot of the edits seemed like random monkeying around that made no sense.[57] The title under which it was published, "Lost Legion," didn't make any sense at all.[58] Lowndes discovered that Alden Norton, the owner at Popular who had taken over Pohl's editorial duties, claimed he had published the manuscript as it came to him.[59] Pohl said Norton chopped it up, and Heinlein thought Pohl had a lighter editorial hand than that.[60]

Heinlein had nothing for Pohl to agent, but he could refuse to sell to Popular. He put the matter in Doc Lowndes's hands: "If he [Pohl] got a dirty deal from them and wishes his friends to boycott them, I don't care to do business with them. Will you please consult with Freddie on this point and see how he feels about it?"[61]

And then, the rejection of "Creation Took Eight Days" began to be resolved. Campbell wrote sheepishly, as close to an apology as he could get (without actually apologizing):

A boomerang's pretty good at coming back and smacking down the thrower, but an evil disposition practically never misses. I evidently succeeded in biting myself on the back of the neck with thoroughness and dispatch. Those rejection notes. Trouble with being an editor is that you're not able to afford being human—which is a statement, and not to be interpreted as a gripe. You and Boucher are perfectly right, I'm wrong—but I'll tell you how I got that way.[62]

Those curt, cold rejection letters had been written and signed while under the influence of a bad case of influenza and not entirely *compos mentis*. Later, when he had more leisure to figure out what had struck him so wrong about "Creation," Campbell was able to develop more coherent comments: the story didn't cue the reader as to the *kind* of story it was. It could probably be salvaged by reslanting it.[63] Heinlein thought the same true of A. P. White's story, rejected at the same time and in the same way.[64]

Heinlein was relieved that the friendship had not crashed. He wrote back immediately:

I hope this letter finds you fully recovered from flu. I don't see how you managed to write as kind and decent a letter as you wrote to me, feeling as rocky as flu makes one feel. I was afraid that my letter to you would make you sore, although I did my best to explain myself. It seemed to me that you might be expected to feel that I was being ungrateful and childish in my attitude. I'm glad you did not take it that way, I don't ever want to have a misunderstanding with you, John, I don't think we ever would have, face to face, but letters are feeble methods of communication at best.[65]

Trying to do business with friends was emotionally draining.[66]

In the meantime, he softened his retirement news by telling Campbell that if he got an idea for a story that would suit Campbell's needs, he would feel free to write it, and, until either the Heinlein name or the Anson Mac-Donald byline cracked the slicks, they were both available for pulp—or Lyle Monroe or Caleb Saunders at lower rates. He offered to do a serial under these terms, since Campbell was so short of material, recapitulating the way they had worked out "Methuselah's Children" by draft-comment-revision during the writing process, but at a more leisurely pace.

This big project would generate a cash surplus in the Heinlein family exchequer (even after buying Leslyn a scandalously expensive fur coat), which they could dedicate to another visit with the Campbells in New Jersey, probably around the holidays.

Willy Ley wrote saying that he was going to visit his old friend Fritz Lang and wanted to spent time with the Heinleins. Cheered, Heinlein settled down to clear his desk before Ley got into town, cutting " 'My Object All Sublime' " to the size Doc Lowndes had said he could probably sell. He thought that the hack editing "Lost Legacy" had received might have lessened the commercial value of the Lyle Monroe pseudonym, so he came up with Leslie Keith,[67] combining the names of Leslyn and her sister, Keith. He offered the story to Campbell under either pseudonym, at fire-sale rates, since he didn't have an actual *commitment* from Lowndes.

Robert and Leslyn were having dinner one night in September with his old friend Elwood "Woodie" Teague when an unpleasant incident occurred. Teague had been at the Naval Academy with Heinlein, though he left before graduation to go into banking and had done quite well for himself. A "black reactionary," he would argue politics with Heinlein for hours on end, but he had done everything he could to promote Heinlein's political career.

We were very close—when their baby girl was killed in an accident, it was us they sent for. We spent a week with them then, going home only to sleep. I arranged the funeral, and fed him liquor, and held his head. And so forth. More of the same, over seventeen years.[68]

Somehow, over the years, the subject of race had never come up before. Teague suddenly went off about "the Jews," making anti-Semitic remarks that would have been at home in the mouth of a Nazi.

At first, Heinlein thought Woody was just kidding, in extremely bad taste, but Teague assured him he was not kidding.

> I sat there for another fifteen seconds, thinking about my lawyer, who is a Jew and one of the finest men I know, and about my campaign treasurer, another Jew, and about their kids. Anyhow, I decided that I couldn't let it go on and ever look them in the face again.
>
> So I stood up and said, "Woodie, apparently there has been a mistake made. It appears you didn't know that I am half Jewish." Then I turned to Leslyn and said, "Come on—we are going home," and went out to get our coats.[69]

This was a complete surprise to Leslyn: she knew as well as Robert that his background was Protestant at least six generations back, and Bavarian Catholic before that. Moreover, Robert *never* lied. ("I don't tell a lie once in five years; when I do, it's arc-welded and water tight."[70]) But she caught her cue and followed his lead.

> Is it any wonder I love the gal? She looks little and soft and feminine, which she is, but she's got mind as hard and tough and logical as a micrometer gage.[71]
>
> Anyhow we left, leaving a social shambles behind us—went home to nurse a stomach attack and a migraine, respectively.

If nothing else, Woody would keep his mouth shut—"one less loud mouth to fan the fire of racial intolerance."[72] But fuming about bigotry and racism apparently got him thinking about race and genetics—and utopias.

Nine days after the dinner with Woody Teague, Heinlein wrote Campbell that he had an idea for a serial: once the problems of economics and politics are solved, "what is left—genetics, what are we going to make of the human race?"[73] Aldous Huxley's *Brave New World* barely scratched the surface of the possibilities—and Olaf Stapledon's *Last and First Men* had simply glossed over the difficulties.

The problem was, the story had to be set in a utopia, and he had no idea how to tell a story with the kind of conflict the readers wanted to see in a utopia. That was a technical problem he would have to thrash out to his own satisfaction before he could write the story.[74] He laid out the problem, serial numbers suitably filed off, in a letter to Robert A. W. Lowndes:

> . . . the basis of drama is tragedy and Utopia aint tragic. In this field you can do *short* stories about minor incidents in an otherwise-Utopian culture, but I defy you to do a story 50,000 words or longer about the *future* and have that future be a Utopia—and sell it! To a pulp book in this field I mean. No, the cash customers want their meat red and dripping; if you don't give them actual gore, you must give them strong socio-economic conflict, and that means no Utopias. If you postulate that the earth is a Utopia, then you must find some other scene in the universe which is *not* Utopia, and lay your conflict there.[75]

By that time, "By His Bootstraps" and "Common Sense" had been out on the stands for ten days, and Campbell was able to cite reader comment about "By His Bootstraps." Heinlein had thought the story a hackwork soufflé, tossed off. Campbell assured him it was not—it was a major story. Jack Williamson wrote, too, calling it "an astounding technical feat."[76]

The interview he had given a journalist for *Writer's Markets & Methods* came out in the magazine's October issue, and Heinlein was the cover and lead story of the magazine. "The write-up made me sound so omniscient that I was tempted to call myself up and ask for some advice and a little coaching," he told Campbell.[77] But even this came with a price: Willard Hawkins wrote that *Author & Journalist* would not use the Denvention speech—or the gag article Heinlein had sent them, "How to Write a Story." Because of the interview in *Writers' Markets & Methods*, an editor had decided "not to use anything concerning [Heinlein] for a while." Hawkins was embarrassed, since the *Author & Journalist* submission was his idea in the first place—but nobody likes to be seen as trolling another magazine's leavings.[78]

Then Forrest Ackerman showed up one day with a copy of the speech printed in Technocracy-green ink. He had transcribed it from Walt Daugherty's photograph records and mimeographed it as his own "Novacious" publication.[79] Heinlein was not pleased—and was particularly displeased that Ackerman had traced Heinlein's signature onto his mimeo stencils without asking permission.[80] When Campbell received a copy from Ackerman, he told Heinlein he should have submitted it as an article for *Astounding*. "As it is, I'll probably steal hunks for editorials."[81] Campbell rejected " 'My Object All Sublime,' " and Heinlein sent it on to Doc Lowndes, who bought it and scheduled it for the February 1942 issue of *Future*.

At the end of September, Robert and Leslyn found themselves saddled with a new responsibility that was going to be eating up more cash: Leslyn's brother-in-law Mark Hubbard, a petroleum engineer in the Philippines, had been financially supporting Leslyn's mother, Florence Gleason "Skipper" MacDonald, since 1934. Now he had taken a new job with a salary cut and could no longer afford the $50 per month he was giving Skipper for her support. It's your turn to take over now, he told Heinlein.

Unpleasant as the prospect was, Heinlein wrote back assuring Hubbard he would take up the slack and thanking him for his past generosity, which "postponed for me a nasty problem."[82] At the very worst, she could stay with Leslyn and him and share bread and board.

The genetics story was not coming together at all—and Heinlein was developing a nice case of insomnia.

I am getting into a state of nerves about this damned serial. I've thought about it longer and harder than any story I've ever done, and the result of said thought is damned unsatisfactory. I am about convinced that the story is unsuitable for magazine market; Leslyn and Willy are both stubbornly insistent that I do it, and that I do it straight, with no corning up for the trade. The trouble is neither lack of material nor lack of interesting ideas (interesting to me), but that the subject seems to me to develop in terms of very heavy philosophical ideas, essentially tragic and almost devoid of action possibilities. The more I work on it the more it seems like a goddam Russian novel, or one of Eugene O'Neil's less successful efforts.[83]

Ley, in fact, was extremely forceful in his opinion: "Willy said, 'You write it. I vill go back to New York and jam it down his [Campbell's] throat!' "[84]

Because of Campbell's publishing schedule, Heinlein had to get *something* written in order to fill the gap. He promised to start writing by the first of November, even churning out transparent hackwork to fill Campbell's pages, if it came to that. "Do you have any idea," he asked Campbell, "any idea which is strong enough to be the central conflict of a book-length serial? . . . If it were not for the steady march past of the days, I would not holler for help—but comes next week and I must *write*."[85]

Campbell suggested Heinlein take a break—aim for a novelette, which would give him more time—but at all cost stay within his area of strength:

What you contributed to science fiction was a direct expression of what I'd been vaguely groping for—personalized, emotionalized science fiction

instead of intellectualized stuff. Your prime strengths are two—reality of
personalities who have reasonable emotional reactions, and a reality of
technical-political-social culture against which they can react. . . .

Your cultures have all been expressed through the people of those cultures. . . . If you want to present philosophy, you have the choice of textbook methods, or dramatization, wherein your puppets act out the points
to be illustrated. I have the feeling that the thing that's stopping you is that
you can dramatize only the failure of a philosophy with respect to the genetics story—a successful philosophy with which it could be contrasted, to
give the story the necessary pull between two sides, is unavailable.

Your story might jell for you if you developed in some detail two reasonable, opposing philosophies, both ultimately failures since men are human, not superhuman, but such that each has points of strong appeal.[86]

That gave Heinlein enough of a clue to get started. His solution to the economic problem was through Social Credit—or something very much like
it—and that led him back to *For Us, the Living*. His thinking had evolved
somewhat since 1938:

I did not stay sold on C. H. Douglas' economic theories as expounded in
Social Credit, but I did stay sold on the notion that our economic troubles
lay principally in our fiscal system and that they could be remedied without doing away with private ownership. I remain so convinced . . . I believe that civil liberty and human dignity is most easily achieved in a
system based on private capitalism and private ownership. I'm not fanatic
about it either way; I like public libraries, and I like public roads; I'm
afraid of all-out socialism even when it isn't the Marxian variety.[87]

He had developed one "conflict" story out of *For Us, the Living* already—
"Coventry." He turned the story assumptions of "Coventry" upside down
and shook until something interesting fell out—a society that was overvio-
lent, instead of overcivilized.[88] He started the story, titling it "False Dawn,"
then crossed that out as he got a little further into the story, retitling it
"Problem Child," and then re-retitling it " 'Utopia' Means 'Nowhere' " as the
story evolved. Finally, he put on the manuscript the title that had occurred to
him at the end of September, "Beyond This Horizon."[89]

He sent the first ten thousand words to Campbell and sketched out what
comes next, asking for comments he could work into the next segment—just
the way they had worked "Methuselah's Children." He was making good

progress, at the rate of two thousand words a day, but he queried Campbell to do a review of Willy Ley's *The Days of Creation*. He would do it for free, for the chance to plug Ley's book.[90]

Heinlein continued developing his what-comes-next-after-utopia story between letters to and from Campbell, adding in a caricature of his hero from *For Us, the Living*, making him a Republican stockbroker type. The story gradually came together for him much the way "Methuselah's Children" had. He worked especially hard to keep it from bogging down in philosophy, since he was illustrating

the basic problems of epistemology, the relations between map and territory.

Symbol	Referent
Map	Territory
Gene chart	Man
Finance structure	Physical economic process
Eidouranian	Physical universe

. . . And a gene chart, even an ideally perfect one, is not *all* there is to a man.[91]

By Thanksgiving Heinlein was in the full flood of production, but when he wrote Campbell saying he wanted to toss personal survival after death into the mix—and by the way he wanted to do someday a "long story about Rhysling, the Blind Singer of the Spaceways"—Campbell realized Heinlein probably wouldn't ever be able to get to the antimatter machine shop idea that had been hanging fire for months. He offered it instead to Jack Williamson, who had bogged down on a serial of his own.[92] Williamson wrote to Heinlein that he didn't want to trespass on another writer's territory.[93] Heinlein gave his blessing through Leslyn, as he didn't want to take a break from writing. His output had soared up to four thousand words a day.[94]

In one of his now-regular weekly business letters, Campbell asked Heinlein to get the Mañana Literary Society working on a "really good lie" for a new department of science-fictional "tall tales" he was bringing to *Astounding*—"Probability Zero." Heinlein passed the suggestion along but couldn't spare the time to work on anything like that himself—the director of the Port of San Pedro had sent him a circular asking all retired officers to volunteer to route merchant traffic in the port.[95] Heinlein knew how to read between the lines, and what this circular probably told him was that the

Navy was trying to free up all active duty personnel, as fast as possible. War was imminent.

Campbell suggested Heinlein come to New York to finish "Beyond This Horizon" there—but that was not a practical solution, Heinlein told him.[96] It was too late to move now:

> If the Japanese start a war with us, as it looks as if they intend to, then they will do so this coming weekend and probably on Sunday, as they have a record of surprise attacks and they certainly know our Navy's habits on weekends.[97]

He would be called back into service in New York and be unable to finish the book, even if he came there. And in any case he would need the proceeds from the serial to finance his recall to active duty in that case—uniforms and kit—so he was committed to finishing the book in Los Angeles. Then, if the Japanese did not attack, he could leave by train for New York on Monday, December 8.[98] He would need the vacation—he was overstressed.[99]

Heinlein put on a burst of speed and worked twenty-four hours straight on the serial, finishing the last ten thousand words of "Beyond This Horizon" in rough draft early in the morning of December 1, 1941. Leslyn proofread it as it came out of the machine, and he mailed off the rough copy before having breakfast at 7:00 A.M.[100] and going to bed.[101] He wrote up his review of Willy Ley's book from notes and sent it off to Campbell the following day.[102] Campbell had the payment expedited—a thousand dollars that arrived on Saturday, December 6, 1941, too late in the day to deposit.

22

"And put aside childish things . . ."

It was just after noon on Sunday, December 7, 1941, when a news bulletin broke into the regular radio broadcast: the Japanese had attacked Pearl Harbor. As details started coming in, Heinlein realized that the Japanese had taken exactly the same tactical approach he had participated in, in war games nine years earlier.[1] The sense of personal loss was overwhelming:

> The thing hit me with such utter sickening grief as I have not experienced before in my life and has left me with a feeling of loss of personal honor such as I never expected to experience. For one reason and one only—because I found myself sitting on a hilltop, in civilian clothes, with no battle station and unable to fight, when it happened.[2]

Admiral Kimmel had made no preparations *at all*: he should, at the very least, have had his forces at sea during an international crisis; but, instead, the entire fleet was in harbor, and flight squadrons neatly lined up on Hickam Field.[3] *Oklahoma,* the ship of Heinlein's 1927 practice cruise, had taken three torpedo hits early in the attack and sank in her berth, turning over until her masts touched bottom and stabilized her. More than four hundred men were killed, many trapped beneath the hull. More—Cal Laning was at Oahu. There was no news of him or of his ship, *Conyngham,* in dry dock at the time of the attack.[4]

Even worse, the Japanese had simultaneously attacked U.S. Naval outposts on Guam and Wake Island and mounted a major offensive on the Philippine island of Luzon, where Leslyn's sister and brother-in-law and two nephews were.

Heinlein reported in by telephone to the Personnel Office, Eleventh Naval District (San Diego). He asked to be assigned to active duty immediately.

They acknowledged his request as of "1255 7 December 1941." That act took a great weight off his shoulders.

> For myself, the situation, tragic as it is, comes to me as an actual relief and a solution of my own emotional problems. For the past year and a half I have been torn between two opposing points of view—the desire to retain as long as possible my own little creature comforts and my own snug little home with the consistent company of my wife and the companionship of my friends and, opposed to that, the desire to volunteer. Now all that is over, I have volunteered and have thereby surrendered my conscience (like a good Catholic) to the keeping of others.
>
> The matter has been quite acute to me. For the last eighteen months I have often been gay and frequently much interested in what I was doing, but I have not been happy. There has been with me, night and day, a gnawing doubt as to the course I was following. I felt that there was some-thing that I ought to be doing. I rationalized it, not too successfully, by re-minding myself that the Navy knew where I was, knew my abilities, and had the legal power to call on me if they wanted me. But I felt like a heel. This country has been very good to me, and the taxpayers have supported me for many years. I knew when I was sworn in, sixteen years ago, that my services and if necessary my life were at the disposal of the country; no amount of rationalization, no amount of reassurance from my friends, could still my private belief that I ought to be up and doing at this time.[5]

Now that the crisis had come, all his priorities were instantly reordered. Heinlein put in a long-distance call to John Campbell, to tell him the trip to New York was off, and found that he had to break the news of the attack. Campbell took it very calmly; Heinlein thought at first he didn't believe it. "I'm not kidding; you know," he insisted. But Campbell was in the middle of his own version of the "semantic pause."[6] Heinlein was past that now:

> My feelings toward the Japs could be described as a cold fury. I not only want them to be defeated, I want them to be smashed. I want them to be punished at least a hundredfold, their cities burned, their industries smashed, their fleet destroyed, and finally, their sovereignty taken away from them . . . Disarm them and *don't turn them loose*. We can treat the in-dividual persons decently in an economic sense, but take away their sover-eignty.[7]

The declaration of war on the Empire of Japan was a foregone conclusion and came immediately. As soon as the banks opened on Monday, Heinlein deposited the check for the serial. Leslyn started mending his old uniforms, to do for the moment, while he reported in person at San Pedro to start the process with a frontal attack on the weakest side of his case to be reassigned to active duty: he demanded a physical exam. They turned him down when the scarring on his lungs showed up in an X-ray, but the medical officer was sympathetic and cooperative: he agreed to send a copy of the report to D.C. by mail, so that Heinlein might start the appeal process for a waiver.

In the meantime, Heinlein used the delay to get his affairs in order. He bought a new uniform immediately with some of the cash he had just gotten for "Beyond This Horizon" and planned the work that would get the house fixed up to rent during the war—a new water heater and a fireproof roof, at the least. Bill Corson could house-sit, if necessary: he had just taken the examination for consular service and was waiting for his civil service papers to come through. That would free up Robert and Leslyn to jump fast, if they needed to, and in any direction. "In the course of a long life, one should be prepared to abandon one's baggage several times. The trick is to do it without too much shock."[8]

The dominoes were not done falling. Hitler declared war on the United States, and on December 9, Congress declared war on Germany—Japan's ally. The era of isolationism was finally at an end. The U.S. garrison on the island of Guam surrendered. The Wake Island garrison surrendered less than two weeks later, on December 22. Hong Kong fell, and Singapore; only the Philippines, where former Chief of Staff General Douglas MacArthur had been caught in the middle of fortifying Manila, held out. No word came from the Hubbards, Mark and Keith. No word from Cal Laning.

Heinlein set in motion the paperwork for a Navy Reserve commission, once the local board had waived him for any duty afloat or ashore. He conceded he would not be medically qualified for duty at sea, between his chronic seasickness and tuberculosis, but argued they could use him for shore duty, PR, or math instruction at the Academy, or "any administrative job in which fresh knowledge of Naval technology is not of paramount importance."[9] BuNav acknowledged his request for duty but pointed out it was overwhelmed with such requests at the moment.

Having failed to slip by the naval bureaucracy in the crisis, he was going to have to talk his way in—and that gave him plenty of time to fret. Leslyn decided to make herself useful as a fire spotter in the canyon hills, which she could do even though she didn't drive. Heinlein kept himself occupied by following the news as it came in by radio, writing agonized letters to friends and family, and calling around to all the local installations, trying to find someone—anyone!—who wanted his services enough to request him and give him an entering wedge. "I should have volunteered six months ago," he concluded sadly.[10]

> I have known since the fall of France, that there was work to be done and that I was morally obligated to assist in it. But I was making money and enjoying life, at least superficially—tomorrow seemed soon enough. Now, when I have been jarred awake, I am having to sit here, fidgeting, waiting for orders which will let me go to work. What that work will be I have not the slightest idea. . . . I would like awfully well to live through it and come out healthy, but if I don't—well, it's what I believe in. I don't feel a damn bit courageous; in fact, I feel scared, but I imagine some of the three thousand at Pearl Harbor were scared too. The job has to be done.[11]

His own family had immediately scattered to the winds. Larry had been stationed in Arkansas, commanding two battalions of engineers. He was already gone—destination unknown. Ivar had been approved for limited duty, by the Army, where he had gone after his hospitalization for tuberculosis, and would probably wind up teaching at West Point. Clare's wife, Dorothy, worked; Clare would undoubtedly be moved up to 1-A status (physically fit for active military duty) and be drafted just months before getting his doctorate.[12] Leslyn was quietly making herself nuts because she couldn't get any word from her sister in the Philippines.[13]

When a Canyon neighbor, Curt Siodmak, asked him to critique a manuscript and suggest where it might be marketed for magazine publication, Heinlein directed him to Campbell, since *Astounding* and *Unknown* were the only possibilities he could see. *Donovan's Brain* was damned good—good enough to help replace him and the other writers Campbell was going to lose from his *Astounding* "stable."[14]

And that brought up another thought: Leslyn could write science fiction while he was in the service. "My stories have always been collaborations between Leslyn and myself, in which I did the writing. I think it quite possible that she could and would turn out quite a bit of printable copy, continuing the same collaboration."[15] And by the same token,

Doña could take over editing *Astounding* and *Unknown* if and when John went into active service. Campbell doubted Doña could be hired as editor.

They were exchanging letters on the average of every forty-eight hours, and some of Campbell's side comments were alarming. Campbell and his New York friends were mouthing off, apparently, with opinions either ignorant or incautious, about the Navy's poor "preparedness," and Fletcher Pratt was actually talking about troop movements and battle stations. They should both know better: that kind of loose talk could get fighting men killed. Some of Campbell's griping was just twaddle. Exasperated, Heinlein tried to inject some common sense into the mix:

> You may gather the idea that I am suggesting that you lack adequate information in politics. You are jolly well right. John, you are so ignorant of political matters that your opinions on politics, sociology, and (usually) economics aren't worth a tinker's dam, except as brilliant flights of fancy. You are a hell of a nice guy, good-hearted, liberal, and quite intelligent, but you haven't information enough to be intelligently critical of the party you support.[16]

And as to Pratt and his coterie of *Kriegspielers* . . .

> If [Pratt] knows no more than the rest of us, he does not yet have sufficient data on which to pass judgment. If he has a pipeline to Washington, then he is in possession of state secrets and should keep his mouth shut. . . . I earnestly advise you and commend to cool heads everywhere (you might pass this on to Sprague) the course of saying nothing in the way of an opinion *as yet* and of quieting down as much of the Sunday-morning quarterbacking as they can.[17]

Leslyn wrote separately to John, on the same subject:

> The gathering at which Pratt shot off his face you spoke of as madder than "the public at large"—as if they don't consider themselves really part of the public at large. Don't you realize what that bunch are, John. *They're an "organized fan" club.*[18]

The thought that this friendship that had meant so unreasonably much to Robert—and Leslyn—might be breaking up was one emotional burden too many for him; after writing about his friends and classmates on *Oklahoma*, he lost his self-control:

> I broke down on that last paragraph and started to blubber, something I have been needing to do for three and a half weeks, no, four weeks, something I have not done in years. I thought Leslyn was safe upstairs, but she heard me. It resulted in a little plain talk between us in which we had both been holding back.[19]

Leslyn herself had been under great emotional strain since the fall of Manila had been announced on January 2. She had just had a cry, which she had tried to hide from Robert, of tortured self-recrimination because she had not talked Keith into at least sending her nephews back to the States. Now all of them were in occupied territory—and her brother-in-law had been away from home, prospecting in Davao, when Luzon fell. Their shared grief gave them a moment of catharsis and led to them getting their priorities straightened out.[20]

Campbell was equally disturbed about the conflict and wrote acknowledging that their reactions were understandable, given the way he had framed the issues.

> The greatest disturbance caused by your two letters last time was a very genuine fear that I might have busted up a friendship that meant a great deal more to us than any single friendship should, perhaps, for our own emotional safety. Those who can like us and whom we can like in an equally wholehearted manner are few—and the more important for that. . . . Your statements were accurate and called for; the degree of bitterness in their manner of expression was understandable and, under the circumstances, equally called for.[21]

Campbell came as close as he ever would to explaining himself in a self-aware way:

> Not all my flat-footed opinions are intended as such. That I sometimes pull some bad ones that I do intend as serious judgments is undoubtedly true; everybody does or we'd be prophets. I try not to act on opinions I'm unsure of; I'll willing to be corrected. And—I have a tendency to pull flat-footed opinions when someone throws one at me that I feel is too flat-footed. . . .
>
> I think my explanation . . . will make it clear what I've been doing. I'm

writing the guff to you primarily because I want adequate answers to arguments I've met and tried to answer. Telling a guy with an ugly rumor not to spread it is like telling the water to wait here a while till you get back and build a dam. Make the rumor look silly and he won't take the trouble to pass it on. . . .

I am not fighting you or the Navy; I'm doing my damndest to kill some of the utterly screwy ideas I do meet. And I'm sending along some of them for more ammunition.[22]

Robert wrote back, expressing his relief.

Anyhow, let me begin by saying that I read your letter with a feeling of profound relief—relief that you weren't sore at me, or, if you had been, you had inhibited it by the time you wrote your last letter. . . . This whole interchange of letters has been of great benefit to me. Specifically, notwithstanding the fact that the stages of the sequence were painful, the sum total effect has been to buck up my morale immeasurably, and to achieve in me a relaxed, comparatively calm, attitude, which might have taken months to achieve if it had not been for your letters.[23]

In the middle of this exchange, Heinlein got the break he had been looking for: his old friend from his Navy days Buddy Scoles, now a lieutenant commander and in charge of the Aeronautical Materials Laboratory at the Naval Aircraft Factory in Philadelphia, wrote, asking if he would do an article for *Astounding* to lay out the range of the practical problems his laboratories at the Naval Aircraft Factory were facing. At the end of his letter, almost casually, he added:

Incidentally, how would you like to go back to active duty and go to work here in the Factory? I could assure you a most interesting job with not too much to do, if you think your health could stand the God-Awful climate here in Philadelphia.[24]

That fit perfectly with Heinlein's plan: he needed someone to request his services, and this was very nearly ideal. He dashed off a postcard agreeing enthusiastically and scheduled a long telephone call to make arrangements. Scoles flew to D.C., and Heinlein wrote to Campbell, telling him about it—and giving credit where due: this job was directly attributable to the stories of his John had published.

It might be only a matter of days before his orders came through. He opened up further to Campbell:

> I haven't anything which could properly be termed a religion. My thoughts on religious subjects are matters of intellectual rather than emotional conviction. The nearest thing to a religious feeling I have, and, I believe, strong enough to justify calling it religious feeling, has to do with the United States of America. It is not a reasoned evaluation but an overpowering emotion. The land itself as well as the people, its culture in the broadest most vulgar sense, its history and its customs . . . I have no God. The only thing which always inspires in me a feeling of something much bigger and more important than myself, which calls up in me a yearning for self-sacrifice, is this country of ours. I know it is not logical—I presume that a mature man's attachments should be for a set of principles rather than for a particular group or a certain stretch of soil. But I don't feel that way . . . Every rolling word of the Constitution, and the bright, sharp, brave phrases of the bill of rights—they get me where I live. Our own music, whether it's Yankee Doodle, or the Missouri Waltz, or our own bugle calls—it gets me.[25]

Now that they knew where they might be going, Leslyn settled on the kind of defense work she wanted to get into. She wanted a factory job—

> possibly even one of these jobs they use twelve-year-old boys and midgets for . . . I'm stronger and in better health than a 12-year old (thank God I don't have to go through the agonies of adolescence again) or a midget, and I've a quicker ability to learn than most. And I'm no bigger than most.[26]

At the Naval Aircraft Factory, she decided, she would apply for constricted-space riveting in the cramped places that can only be reached from *inside* an airframe.[27] She then came down with what looked like an attack of food poisoning that lingered on worrisomely for days. But it was not food poisoning: it was gallstones. Her doctor said she might travel, but there was risk of another attack at any time. Leslyn preferred to take the risk. "Knowing her temperament and evaluations, I concur," Robert wrote the Campbells.[28]

Scoles assured them that the way was cleared at the Naval Aircraft Factory, even including housing. Their lives were swept and garnished, ready to leave Los Angeles for Philadelphia, when Scoles reported a catch: no orders could be issued until Heinlein was cleared with the Discipline Section. Scoles suggested Heinlein call a Captain Stewart in D.C. to find out what was going on.

Captain Stewart had never heard of Lt. Robert Heinlein—had never heard of Lt. Cdr. Scoles—but would look up his records. A few days later, he called back: Heinlein's records had an admonition regarding lack of good judgment dating from *1934*—which made no sense at all. He was sick with tuberculosis for most of 1934. But in any case, Stewart could not possibly recommend him for duty.[29]

This could take months to resolve by mail and phone. He would have to present himself in person to various personnel offices in Washington, D.C., and make an intolerable nuisance of himself until they gave him what he wanted, just to be rid of him. He arranged with Hank and Kat Kuttner to rent the house (since Bill Corson, it turned out, was going into the Army). He and Leslyn packed up the car and left for D.C. the next day, planning to stay with Robert's childhood pal Don Johnstone in Arlington. He dropped Scoles an explanatory note from Yuma, Arizona.

They powered through, making the trip from Hollywood to Washington, D.C., in three rainy days. They paid a quick, overnight visit to Buddy Scoles in Philadelphia, where Scoles told him part of his job would be recruitment in many departments; Heinlein suggested, off the top of his head, that L. Sprague de Camp had a background in mechanical engineering and might be a good candidate for the kind of materials testing and design work Scoles had in mind. Then they continued traveling north to take up semipermanent residence with the Campbells at their new home in Westfield, New Jersey, around the middle of February. This kept them within striking distance of Philadelphia or D.C. to the south. They had been on the road for more than two weeks, and Leslyn's gallbladder trouble had come back. She needed an operation to have the gallbladder removed.[30]

The trip had been unusually expensive, and their cash reserves were exhausted. Suddenly, their financial crisis had become acute. Heinlein tried to clear his mind and settle down to write a novella for *Astounding*. Campbell had been after him to do something with uncertainty in the subatomic field driving scientists insane, so presumably that story would be salable. For his protagonist, he remembered a *Popular Mechanics* article he had read more than twenty years ago, about an engineer afflicted with the degenerative muscular disease myasthenia gravis. He had set up a system of power-multiplying gadgets to manipulate things he was too weak to handle with his own muscles. The image of a fat man floating in the air might have come from H. G. Wells's short story "The Truth About Pyecraft," since Pyecraft goes on to become a ballroom dancer; Heinlein's character Waldo (named after a suburb in Kansas City[31]) goes on to become a "ballet-tap" dancer.

But Heinlein was also already at work for Scoles. His first recommendation, L. Sprague de Camp, had applied for a commission in the Naval Reserve (but was sick with a case of adult whooping cough that kept him weak and underweight).[32] Heinlein set up a meeting in John Arwine's New York apartment with de Camp, Scoles, Campbell, and himself.[33] De Camp was willing; Scoles would issue a letter requesting his services as soon as his commission came through. Campbell would stay with *Astounding* and do what he could on the side to whip up interest in Scoles's recruitment program.

Heinlein also wanted Isaac Asimov for defense work. Even before he and Leslyn had left California in January he told Campbell: "By the way, talk to that young idiot Asimov—he wants to go fight. M.S.'s in physical chemistry aren't cannon fodder."[34] On March 2, Heinlein met Asimov for the first time, accidentally, in John Campbell's office, when Asimov came over to pick up the painting Hubert Rogers had done for his story "Nightfall."[35] Asimov's skills as a laboratory chemist would surely be of some use to the Materials Laboratory.

A week later, Campbell invited Asimov to his home in Westfield, New Jersey, where Heinlein got him drunk for the first time in his life with a Cuba Libre and showed some slides of his nude photography—in this case, a recent session with Catherine Crook de Camp. Asimov tried to act like a man of the world under this assault of alien values—and apparently "passed inspection."[36] At the end of March, Scoles sent Asimov a job offer at the Philadelphia Navy Yard.

Heinlein's first recruitment efforts for Scoles were a success—fortunate, since neither pushing nor pulling seemed likely to get him recalled to active duty. The holdup with the Naval Discipline Section turned out to be something that almost could not be coped with: an officer in the Discipline Section had a personal "down" on him (never explained in the correspondence where it was mentioned) and would not be budged. Heinlein's application, and all his papers, came to the Discipline Section and stalled—the paperwork was even "lost." Heinlein and Buddy Scoles started the process over again, but they knew it was probably futile. In the back channels they tried to find out why the way was blocked. It wasn't completely hopeless: worst coming to worst, Scoles had authority to hire him as a civilian engineer—and Heinlein had a line on a job for the State Department, as well.

In any event, at the moment Heinlein was chained to the typewriter by other circumstances, and he could use the time to write his way out of debt. The writing on the "Waldo" novella had gone haltingly, but he had to come up with a second novella, or a serial. "It seems I *can* write, war or no war," he told Cal Laning (who had survived the attack on Pearl Harbor and reestablished contact in February 1942),

> but my writing is not as good and it is a tremendous chore—it seems so damned futile and silly to be punching a typewriter while the rest of you are taking the brunt. God knows I'm no hero, but it is distressing to sit around in this emasculated condition when there is work to be done.[37]

Leslyn's operation yielded "eight perfectly matched gall stones"[38]—and a fit of depression that put her at least momentarily into the black and alien frame of mind that was so disturbing to Robert. "She told me afterwards," Heinlein told Doña Campbell a decade later, "that she had decided that I was trying to poison her. She admitted this to me during one of her mellow moments."[39]

As his serial "Beyond This Horizon" began appearing in *Astounding* in April 1942, Heinlein put together an offbeat story with paranoiac elements, taking the sense of the illusion of the world's appearance he had exploited in "They" to another level, combined with the brotherhood of evil he had whipped up for "Lost Legacy" and the haunting image that concludes Cabell's *Figures of Earth,* of the real world being only a reflection in a window that, opened, revealed only nothingness. He called it "The Unpleasant Profession of Jonathan Hoag." Hoag's "unpleasant profession" was art critic. Creepy and shuddery—but in its oppressive sense of a frail human couple caught up in the workings of vast and unseen figures perfectly capturing the mood in the early days of World War II. Campbell bought it and scheduled it for the October issue of *Unknown Worlds,* to be published under the byline John Riverside, following "Waldo" by Anson MacDonald in the August issue. "Unpleasant Profession" would be, with the exception of two reviews of Willy Ley books as they came out, the last of Heinlein's writing to appear until after the war ended. But Heinlein's name had already disappeared from *Astounding* and *Unknown Worlds* after the October 1941 issue: all of his last prewar work was published under pseudonyms (both "Goldfish Bowl" in March 1942 and "Beyond This Horizon" in April and May 1942 appeared as by Anson MacDonald).

The Heinleins had been very comfortable with the Campbells. The Campbells' daughter, P.D., (whom they referred to as their godchild, even if it was not a formal arrangement) was a delight.

> She started making eyes at Bob the first day he arrived, and has been working on him ever since. She's been flirting with Leslyn very effectively, too,

and has 'em both fetching and carrying for her. She won't talk—so far has seen no need for it, as far as I can make out. She can point and roll her eyes with marvelous efficiency.

But the result of the attention has been wonderful to behold. She likes the boys. Bob is hers, her exclusive slave and attendant. The other night he and Leslyn curled up in the same chair, and hey, presto! there was Peeds tugging at Leslyn's hand and making annoyed sounds. Leslyn let her lead her away, and Peeds deposited her on the couch, and went over and climbed in Bob's lap herself. So Doña came over and sat in my lap. Peeds was over in about 15 seconds, pulling at Doña's hand, and presently having deposited Doña safely, came back to me herself.[40]

John Arwine had been turned down for active duty and had applied and been accepted in the Coast Guard. His apartment was vacant, so the Heinleins moved into Manhattan in April, though they continued to receive mail in New Jersey. They could entertain in New York, and received visits by the Leys and Hubert Rogers, among others. Sprague de Camp took them to an Authors' Club dinner where they "met Fletcher Pratt, Pendray, Octavus Roy Cohen, Will Cuppy . . . half of Ellery Queen, and several others."[41] They also entertained the local fans at dinner on at least one occasion.

Heinlein extended his recruitment efforts to idea-work from his colleagues, and had some success with both Campbell and Will F. Jenkins, who wrote under the pseudonym of Murray Leinster. He asked them to write up their thoughts and forwarded the written memoranda to Buddy Scoles.

Life did, annoyingly, go on. The Heinleins received word from Henry Kuttner that he and Catherine had had to move out of the house on Lookout Mountain—Catherine was pregnant and had fallen, requiring an operation that left her with stitches in her neck and the prospect of being immobilized for the entirety of her pregnancy. Although it is not mentioned in the letter, the Kuttners must have told the Heinleins their house had acquired a ghost or two.[42] Henry Kuttner had to take an apartment downtown, closer to the hospital. There was almost nothing the Heinleins could do from three thousand miles away, except wish them well. They put their house in the hands of a real-estate agent, to find a tenant.

Heinlein's series of appeals wasn't going anywhere—and might not, ever. He applied again for an active duty assignment[43]—on the very day that his old CO, Captain E. J. King, was appointed by President Roosevelt to assume the combined offices of Commander in Chief, U.S. Fleet, and Chief of Naval Operations (March 20, 1942).

As I heard it, the Selection Board offered the new President, in office one month, a list of five names. Roosevelt is reputed to have torn up the list and reached down 32 numbers and named the "boy captain" (40 yrs old) that he had known and liked years earlier (1918) when FDR was AsstSec-Nav in WWI.[44]

By the end of April 1942, Heinlein and Scoles's back-channel inquiries finally yielded some information about the Discipline Section block: it was actually related to the admonition Heinlein had received from the Secretary of the Navy in 1935, when he and Leslyn had written a sarcastic letter to the editor of their local progressive paper, the *Hollywood Citizen-News.* Someone in the chain of command had decided this meant Heinlein was a communist sympathizer who ought to be kept out of contact with servicemen. He might gnash his teeth forever; the Navy would not recall him to active duty. Robert and Leslyn had to start thinking about more permanent living arrangements.

Scoles put their backup plan into motion: if Heinlein was taken on as a civilian engineer for the Naval Aircraft Factory, he could apply again after receiving fitness reports that would strengthen any new application. On May 2, 1942, Heinlein received an appointment to the Navy Yard as "Assistant Mechanical Engineer, P-2, in the Engineering Division, Naval Aircraft Factory, Navy Yard, Philadelphia, Pa" with a six-month trial period and indefinite extension thereafter.[45] Within two days they had found a small apartment in Lansdowne[46]—far enough away from the overchlorinated, unfiltered Philadelphia municipal water supply to have good drinking water; close enough to have a bearable commute.

And his other efforts were bearing fruit, too: L. Sprague de Camp was over his case of whooping cough; he came back from a three-week vacation in Florida and passed his physical on May 3. Scoles put in a request for his services. There would be a two-month wait until the next session of the Naval Training School started at Dartmouth College. In the meantime, Scoles asked de Camp to take a civilian job as Assistant Mechanical Engineer. He would work at the same grade as Heinlein until he graduated the Training School and was commissioned a full lieutenant—a grade higher than Heinlein had been retired at eight years earlier. De Camp was an officer in the Navy, and Heinlein was a mere civilian engineer. Never mind: it was war work.

I have today [May 11, 1942] accepted a civil service appointment as a mechanical engineer at the Naval Aircraft Factory, Navy Yard, Philadelphia, Pennsylvania. Have notified 11th Naval Dist. to stop retired pay.[47]

"DO WITH THY HEART WHAT THY HANDS FIND TO DO . . ."

The physical plant of the Aeronautical Materials Lab (AML) was not prepossessing: several hangarlike buildings separated by unpaved stretches that became innavigable mudflats during the rainy season. The distances between the buildings were so great that they kept racks of bicycles outside the buildings, and everyone used them for basic transportation around the Yard. Heinlein commented wryly:

> A naval officer of rank, years, and poundage on a bicycle is a touching sight. And . . . visualize me in business suit, necktie, and hat pedaling with dignity up to the Commandant's office. Also riding without using the handle bars. Oh, I'm a gallus snapper all right![1]

People did not drive, even between widely separated buildings: by 1942, gasoline rationing was already in effect. Five gallons per week was the ordinary ration, and Heinlein would not indulge in the various rationalizations that could have allowed him a bigger allowance. Nor would he countenance others doing so: gasoline was rationed because it was needed for the war effort, and nothing, he felt, must get in the way of that. This was one subject about which he had no sense of humor at all.

One of his coworkers, Joel Charles, cut off the paper tags from tea bags one day as a gag and offered to sell "T" stamps—gasoline ration—to Heinlein in a public hallway, a black market transaction. Years later, Charles recalled the incident to Heinlein: "You unwrapped them, took one look, then handed them back very disdainfully with the remark, 'you're lucky they weren't real.' My 'joke' had all the impact of a collapsed dirigible."[2]

Sugar and whiskey were also rationed, but Cuba Libres were Heinlein's favorite drink (made with rum and Coca-Cola),[3] so he was not seriously compromised in that (so long as the Coca-Cola Company could finagle enough cane syrup to get by).

Nor was public transportation an option. There was subway service in Philadelphia, but it did not go all the way to the Navy Yard. You had to take a shuttle bus from the subway. "Robert told me," Virginia Heinlein recalled, "that [the Philadelphia City Fathers] had stolen the money for the subway continuation down to the Navy Yard."[4] Philadelphia's municipal politics had never seriously been challenged by reformers, operating instead by good, old-fashioned graft.[5] In the meantime, commuters carpooled to the Navy Yard from the suburbs.

Within the buildings, there was an awe-inspiring bustle of activity. The ground floor was a huge, open shop, with gantry cranes rumbling overhead, conducting engine tests (very loud) and structural stress tests.[6] A wing test was especially exciting and always drew a crowd of sidewalk superintendents as they crushed the wing or broke it literally in two.[7]

The floor above was a large room with dozens of desks, each one inhabited by a person who was supposedly an expert in his or her subject. Heinlein was going to have one of those desks—if he could get the intradepartmental squabbling over him under control. Once his availability was announced, there was a tug-of-war over his assignment—flattering but also annoying because he couldn't get down to work until the various department and section and subsection heads got their priorities straight.[8]

Heinlein's immediate assignment was to supervise the new cold-and-pressure chamber for the AML's high-altitude projects, which included the creation of a "high-altitude pressure suit"—the prototype of a space suit. The new altitude chamber was a white-painted steel cylinder about the size of a large steam locomotive boiler. He also supervised installation and operational tests for the Cold Room—a large, cubical, Freon-cooled chamber. Everyone then had to undergo medically supervised tests for resistance to anoxia (oxygen deprivation). L. Sprague de Camp described the experience:

We sat on a bench in this insulated steel cylinder with oxygen masks in our hands. As the pressure fell, corresponding to altitudes of ten thousand feet, twenty thousand feet, and so on, I noticed that the white paint on the walls of the chamber seemed to turn yellow, while the hiss of air in the pipes seemed to sound like church bells. Before anyone passed out, the medical officer had us don our masks, whereupon the wall turned white again and the church bells ceased.[9]

But Heinlein was not even allowed to take the test: the flight surgeon eliminated him just on the basis of his medical records. Sprague de Camp took
over the high-altitude projects when he returned from Officer Training
School.

Heinlein was reassigned where he could give some more attention to his
secondary duties: hiring engineers. He continued his recruiting efforts among
the science-fiction writers. John Campbell wrote him in mid-May that L.
Ron Hubbard was in New York, wounded, and he might be available, since
he was a civil engineer.[10] But Hubbard quickly obtained an assignment
captaining a subchaser, and that took him to the West Coast and to San
Francisco—though the Kuttners reported a Hubbard sighting on the streets
of Los Angeles one day in July:

> He mentioned meeting you [Heinleins] and in flattering terms I shan't re-
> peat for fear of turning your heads. Isn't he wonderful and astonishing?
> We have the strange faculty of meeting him in the middle of the sidewalk
> when neither of us knows the other is in town. It's happened twice now.[11]

The AML was expanding so rapidly that Heinlein had to recruit engineers
everywhere he could—a very scarce commodity when all the young men
were in the services. But he knew there would be an untapped source: he
spent the last months of the academic year scouting technical schools all over
the East, looking for female engineers. Female engineers would be draft-
exempt. He amused himself between interviews checking—and refuting (to
his satisfaction)—Doc Smith's idea that a woman could have either brains or
beauty, but when he saw at first hand the unfair treatment women were accorded by universities, he became incensed.[12] At the University of Delaware,
he found that female engineering candidates were not even *permitted* into the
School of Engineering.

> I almost went through the roof . . . then took nasty pleasure in chewing
> out the President of the University in the presence of a large group of
> people, by telling him that his University's medieval policies had deprived
> the country of trained engineers at a time when the very life of his coun-
> try depended on such people.[13]

Between trips, the work piled on. Scoles kept him on administrative and
personnel work because everyone could see that "his technical competence,
managerial ability, and ability to relate to others placed him in a class by

himself."[14] By July, when the high-altitude chamber gushed clouds of chill fog into the humid Philadelphia air, Heinlein was buried in paperwork, suffering from a constant backache and kidney problems, sleep deprivation, and incipient exhaustion—and frankly depressed about the whole situation:

> I hate Philadelphia, I hate this blasted, hot, humid, mosquito infested climate, and—Lord help me—I hate my job. There is plenty of important work being done here but I am not doing it. Instead I do the unimportant work in order that others with truly important things to do may not be bothered with it. Necessary and useful, but I dislike it. I happen to be cursed with the sort of ability that makes the perfect private secretary, the ability to attend to multitudinous details for other people, picayune but necessary details, none of which interest me and none of which use up any important part of my brain. I see that reports get out, I see that letters are written on time, I soothe the feelings of senile, half-witted, permanent-appointment civil service clerks when the boss wants to do something not included in their sacred bureaucratic procedures. I write memos requesting copies from General Files of directives written months or even years before in order to prove to timorous functionaries that we really are permitted to do something we intend to do anyhow. I count gas masks, or order them to be counted, and report that someone has stolen one pair of rubber boots from one of the air raid lockers. (*That* presents a really nice problem in the inanities of administration, Air raid equipment can *not* be locked up, else its purpose is defeated, yet it is government property and must be accounted for.)
>
> Over it all and greatly contributing to my malaise hangs the gloom of a war which isn't going any too well, which at the moment we seem to be losing. I have no doubt that we will win in the end but after how long and at what cost? I don't expect the high command to confide in me but I am beginning to wonder when we are to read of something better than strategic retreats, something better than careful explanations of why a second front cannot be opened.
>
> No, my morale isn't so hot—but I have and will retain a grim determination to hang on and do this job the best I can. But I don't have to like it and don't. I know that it is a privilege to serve and I know that I am damned lucky not to be in a fox hole somewhere, or clinging to a life raft—but I still think Philadelphia stinks and I wish to Christ they would retire everybody over fifty![15]

They needed a vacation. Leslyn had not been able to get the kind of factory work she wanted and so had been taking business courses downtown to sharpen her administrative skills. But they got a three-day weekend break from the overtime at the end of July, and visited with the Campbells.

Sprague de Camp was at Officer Training School in the summer, but he had asked his wife, Catherine, to find them a place to live in Philadelphia. Burdened with a toddler (Lyman), she appealed to the Heinleins for help in the nearly impossible task of finding a living space for the three of them plus her uncle, Frank Badeau.[16] In July and August, the Heinleins put Catherine up in their tiny apartment in Lansdowne.[17] Eventually, a local real-estate agent told her of an attic apartment in a big house a block away from the Heinleins' apartment. It was the Pennock mansion, the "family seat" of a wealthy florist, now deceased. The widow Pennock wanted social references from Catherine, which was somewhat startling. Catherine's references must have been satisfactory: by the time Sprague returned from OTS in September, she had moved Lyman and Uncle Frank into the garret and started homemaking.[18]

The Heinleins and the de Camps spent many of their off-hours together (not that there were many—wartime work schedules called for six days a week), picnicking on the lawn of the mansion or walking the two miles into Philadelphia to visit with Isaac Asimov and his new wife, Gertrude.

Leslyn completed her business courses—and promptly got a job as Junior Radio Inspector at the Navy Yard. She was not in the same building as Robert, but they could commute to and from, and eat lunch together. The Plastics & Adhesives section, where Heinlein wound up, made a point of taking lunch together as a group at the cafeteria, which they called "Ulcer Gulch." Leslyn joined them.

The table was entertaining for the talk, if not for the fare—most often a stew made from tripe and other mystery meats better left uninquired-after, or scrapple, a local specialty that is, to put it delicately, not to everyone's taste. Isaac Asimov, who joined the Ulcer Gulch crowd a year later, in the summer of 1943 (after his wife left for a visit with family in Canada),[19] immortalized Ulcer Gulch.

Deprived of his sandwiches and his lunchtime reading, Asimov complained continuously, in a deliberately comic way—though not without justification, in fact—about the food. Heinlein would not countenance morale-destroying grumbling.

> When . . . I spoke eloquently of cardboard potatoes and wilted lettuce and
> middle-aged roast beef, Heinlein passed a ukase to the effect that from

then on anyone who complained about the food would have to put a nickel into the kitty. (When enough had accumulated, I think he was going to buy a war bond.)

I objected bitterly, for I knew it was aimed at me. I said, "Well, then, suppose I figure out a way of complaining about the food that isn't complaining? Will you call it off?"

"Yes," he said.

After that, I had a mission in luncheon life that took my mind off the food, at least. I was going to find a way of complaining that couldn't be objected to. My best solo attempt, I think, was one time when I pretended to be sawing away ineffectually at a dead slab of haddock and asked with an innocent air of curiosity, "Is there such a thing as tough fish?"

"That will be five cents, Isaac," said Heinlein.

"It's only a point of information, Bob."

"That will be five cents, Isaac. The implication is clear."

Since Bob was judge, jury, and executioner, that was that.

But then someone new joined the table who did not know the game that was going on. He took one mouthful of some ham that had been pickled in formaldehyde and said, "Boy, this food is awful."

Whereupon I rose to my feet, lifted one arm dramatically, and said, "Gentlemen, I disagree with every word my friend here has said, but I will defend with my life his right to say it."

And the game of fine came to an end.[20]

Even after his transfer to engineering, Heinlein continued to work as a kind of unofficial personnel director for the whole installation, according to J. Hartley Bowen, a section chief in "another part of the [Air Materials] Laboratory."[21] The personnel mix was a potentially explosive combination of new-minted engineers fresh out of college, a grab bag of naval officers from ensign to commander, on temporary rotation, and well-pickled civilian engineers. The mix needed a lot of stabilization. Civilian and Navy officers—particularly those trained in the old, aristocratic traditions of the naval officer class—did not mix well. Heinlein was constantly watching out for those instantaneous tips of emotional balance that could erupt into open conflict.

Sprague de Camp was very much aware of this problem. When he came back a commissioned lieutenant, he noted the friction he seemed to be at the center of and asked Heinlein for advice. Thoughtfully, Heinlein told him to "clip those beetling brows."[22] He could speak more freely with a colleague from *Astounding* than he might with one of the other engineers. De Camp had bushy eyebrows, but that's not what he meant: Heinlein's advice was to be more pleasant, not to glower so much, and perhaps insist less on the perquisites of his rank. Naval-officer aristocracy came too naturally to de Camp. (The advice seems to have fallen on deaf ears, as he was still observed to be overly punctilious two years later.[23])

As with many ministerial virtues, Heinlein's hands-on personnel micro-management had its own set of defects, and the more stable individuals sometimes bore the brunt of the arrangements: Heinlein once browbeat Isaac Asimov into volunteering to work on Yom Kippur, taking advantage of Asimov's amiable desire to help his Jewish coworkers arrange to have Yom Kippur off instead of Christmas. In a way, it was a compliment to young Isaac—not that he could be manipulated this way, but that Heinlein thought he was emotionally strong enough to bear some of the burden of compromises.

In September, they finally got some word about Leslyn's family in the Philippines. Bill Corson, who had contacts in the consular service, sent them a postcard: "Whole Hubbard gang interned (as of Feb.) Santo Tomas University. Nothing since, but will check anon."[24] The "whole Hubbard gang" meant Keith and her two boys. Her husband, Mark Hubbard, had been on another island. He had simply vanished.

By October, winter was coming on, and Heinlein's schedule was no more settled than it had been in the summer. He decided it was not practical for him to try to commute by carpool from Lansdowne, so he found a small apartment on South Hicks—a one-block street south and west of Rittenhouse Square, close to the railyard. This was a minor miracle in overcrowded Philadelphia (but his work recruiting out-of-state engineers had undoubtedly given him some expertise in handling housing problems).

"The Unpleasant Profession of Jonathan Hoag" appeared in *Unknown Worlds,* under a new pseudonym, John Riverside.

That fall, Buddy Scoles's tour of duty was up, and just before Thanksgiving he was transferred somewhere on the West Coast. Nobody knew exactly where anyone went in those days: everyone tried to be conscientious about unnecessary talking. Heinlein himself was so tight-lipped that many of the people he associated with on a daily basis never knew exactly what projects he was working on.[25]

His new boss was "a nice guy whom I knew slightly in the *Lexington* a good many years back."[26] But the change introduced another element of uncertainty into Heinlein's work—less administrative work and more engineering. He was very rusty as an engineer.

Leslyn, on the other hand, was happy with her factory job, though she worked every other Sunday and went at it, perhaps, too intensely for the good of her health. "The work is quite hard on her," he told John Arwine. "But I think she can stand it."[27] The strain on Leslyn was obvious, too, to Forrest Ackerman, with whom they were both corresponding:

> [T]his was so serious to her, that she just knocked herself out twenty-four hours a day in the war industry, I believe, just doing everything she could to shorten the misery of her sister. The Heinleins during WWII had no use for anybody who wasn't engaged in the war effort, particularly as a soldier or marine or airman.[28]

Ackerman had volunteered for the Marines, but at 130 pounds, he was not taken. Eventually he was drafted into the Army, where his personal oddities made him a target:

> Well, when I went into the Army, the first day of that I felt like I had died. I was gonna go to hell. I was 29 years old, I didn't drink, I didn't smoke, and I was a virgin. And I went, God help me, you know, when the soldiers find out about this, every bully's gonna pick on me. I'm gonna be the target, you know, this sissy Ackerman.[29]

He asked for one of Heinlein's nude photos to put up in his locker and around his office. Without having to talk about his prowess as a ladies' man, he could let everyone assume he was a regular guy, and no one ever questioned him. He credited Heinlein with literally saving his life.[30]

Heinlein certainly approved of the use they were put to: anything that screened off personal privacy from Mrs. Grundy, with or without stripes, was always okay by him.

Heinlein's name had not quite disappeared from the pulp magazines, however: an enthusiastic review promoting Willy Ley's *Shells and Shooting* came out in the November 1942 issue of *Astounding*. It may have been commissioned verbally by John Campbell to fill a last-minute one-page hole, since the review does not appear on the table of contents for that issue, and Campbell would certainly have gotten Heinlein's name on cover or contents if he could possibly have managed it—but in any case, Heinlein wanted to take any opportunity to promote Ley's science writing.

And that was all the writing he had done for pulp—perhaps all he would ever do.

Even if his entire pulp production were forgotten, however, he had been immortalized: In the fall of 1942 William A. P. White finished a *roman à clef* mystery novel, *Rocket to the Morgue,* using the characters and situations from the Mañana Literary Society. The characters were blends, taking a bit from this person, a bit from another, but recognizable if you knew the players. John Campbell, who most certainly did know the players, read proof on the typeset galleys: "I dunno whether it's a good murder mystery novel or not," he told Heinlein. "I had too much fun reading the story and recognizing people."[31]

Heinlein was most of the chief suspect, Austin Carter. Campbell was in it, under his pseudonym Don A. Stuart, and White even put himself in as the detective, but also as his science fiction pseudonym, Anthony Boucher.[32]

> It's more fun than anything I've seen anywhere anywhen. He made Leslyn into a mystery writer, and made "Joe Henderson" out of 25% Ed Hamilton and 75% Jack Williamson, and "D. Vance Wimpole" out of L. Ron Hubbard with amazing clarity. Also, half the gags in the book, if not more than half, are simple reporting . . . He used incident after incident that I knew; probably there are dozens of others you'll recognize.[33]

The book was in print by December, dedicated to Heinlein. He was flattered. He and Leslyn read it straight through in one sitting, he told White, looking over each other's shoulder. "You handled me charitably," he wrote to White. It gave him the experience of being an outsider looking in, which was rare and exciting. He could not pretend to evaluate it objectively: "For me it was simply the most fascinating book I have ever read."[34]

Not even overwork to the point of exhaustion put a serious crimp in the Heinleins' omnivorous reading—or Robert's, at any rate: Leslyn devoted her spare time to the neglected art of sleep. Robert particularly enjoyed C. S. Lewis's *Screwtape Letters* when they came out in an American edition by Macmillan in 1942.[35] These letters had appeared in *The Guardian* in 1941, from the viewpoint of a senior demon giving infernal advice to his nephew, a tyro imp, on how best to corrupt human souls. The conceit tickled Heinlein's fancy.

Vincent McHugh, whose 1936 *Caleb Catlum's America* Heinlein was still using as a touchstone to measure the compatibility of potential friends, pub-lished his fourth book, *I Am Thinking of My Darling*—a response to H. G. Wells's *In the Days of the Comet*—making good use of McHugh's experience as a city planner for New York. Now McHugh was writing and directing film documentaries for the Office of War Information.

But Philip Wylie's *Generation of Vipers* so exactly said things Heinlein be-lieved desperately *needed* to be said that Heinlein's enthusiasm ran away with him, and he gushed for an hour about the book to a very *un*interested fan, Rusty Hevelin, who came to visit for a couple of hours one day in 1943.[36] That book was almost an essayistic parallel to what Heinlein had tried to get across in "Beyond This Horizon" (both were published in the same year, 1942): "Our Civilization has not yet," Wylie said early in the book, "even dreamed of applying science to *itself*."[37] At one point in the introduction, Wylie had even quoted Ouspensky in an injunction dear to Heinlein's heart: "Think in other categories."

Nor would Heinlein's own writing career lie down and decently die so he could stop minding the store: a book editor named Bronner contacted Hein-lein to use "Life-Line" and " '—And He Built a Crooked House—' " in an anthology, and Heinlein wrote to Campbell for releases of the rights. When the stories were sold to Street & Smith, he had originally tried to vend only "first American serial rights"—rights to publish in the magazine—but Street & Smith bought "all rights," without exception—and Campbell as-sured him the company's policy was to revert the rights to the author, freely and without charge, whenever he had any actual use for them. Even if Street & Smith made the contract, the author would be entitled to 25 percent of the proceeds. Many of the other pulp chains would buy all rights and simply pocket the proceeds of secondary sales.

Street & Smith was very concerned at that time about exploitative reprint magazines masquerading as paperback books. Campbell thought that might be the case here, since Bronner was extremely vague as to important details, such as who his publisher might be. Street & Smith refused to release the rights and killed the sale, saying if anyone was going to do an anthology of Street & Smith properties, they would prefer to do it themselves.[38] One week later, however, they sold anthology rights to Donald Wollheim for " '—And He Built a Crooked House—.' "

Heinlein had arranged a sale that would total $146 net to him; Street & Smith had blocked that sale and turned around and sold one of the stories for $19 net to him. Even though Heinlein was not writing currently—and he might never go back to pulp—this practice struck him as unreasonably predatory. But he said nothing to Campbell about it at the time: "I took it and shut up, as I was up to my ears in war research and had neither the time nor the money to fight the arrangement."[39] This was the first mass-market paperback science-fiction anthology, *The Pocket Book of Science Fiction,* edited by Donald A. Wollheim and published in 1943.

Without any real plans for going back to writing, Heinlein was nevertheless making notes for stories whenever something provocative came up. The stories that were appearing in the newspapers of the men at war—of suffering and of heroism and dedication—were inspiring. And he saw heroism and dedication even at the aircraft factory, of a quieter kind. When he did switch over from personnel to engineering early in 1943, he was thrown into contact with Tony Damico, a blind machinist. Damico was an absolutely fascinating man—and a perfect "fit" with the idea of Rhysling that had been kicking around in Heinlein's mind for a few years now. He hadn't felt up to writing it because he had trouble putting himself in the shoes of a blind man. "Being sighted myself, I had trouble characterizing a sightless man; he would not come into focus."[40] Talking with Damico—a nightclub entertainer before the war who had retrained himself into a machinist—gave Heinlein an abundance of details, but also an inspiring idea of what was possible.

Heinlein felt he was idling where he was and mentioned the urge to write in a letter to Campbell. Campbell's reply was shrewd.

> Your urge to work on stories may be prophetic, or a symptom of one of two things. Either that the plant there is beginning to run reasonably smoothly, or that it's—well, shapfu. The "hap" standing for "hopelessly and permanently," and that your mind, whether you have or not, has decided that there is, none the less, a way to get along in chaos.[41]

Some progress was possible, even in "Snafu Manor," as Heinlein's group of friends and colleagues there had begun to call the Naval Air Experimental Station (their little corner of the AML). "Snafu" is a military slang acronym, standing for "Situation Normal: All Fucked Up."

Heinlein's first evaluations as civilian engineer came in early March 1943— first-rate—and he was promoted from "Assistant M.E., P-2" to "Associate M-E, P-3," with a nice bump in pay (from $2,600 to $3,200 per annum). He was made second in charge of the Plastics & Adhesives section of the Materials Laboratory, under Henry Sang.

Sang was a young civil service engineer who had become part of the Heinleins' social set. They found him very compatible, and he lived close by in downtown Philadelphia, too, so they saw each other frequently after work.

In June, Heinlein was detached again, this time to Pittsburgh, to recruit junior engineers for the AML.[42]

The war was not good to Robert and Leslyn Heinlein: the frustrations of a constantly increasing workload, searching for technical solutions that didn't exist in the technology of 1943, flogging himself for not being at the front, and the bitterness over what he was not allowed to do, Robert was becoming humorless and superior. "Holiness is a bad habit, and one that frequently catches mutual admiration societies," Bill Corson admonished him in August 1943. Leslyn's workload, too, was constantly increasing, and she fretted over her sister and nephews in a concentration camp in the Philippines.

Both Robert and Leslyn were taking out their frustrations on at least one of their friends. Robert did notice the liquor disappearing at a greater rate than usual, but he thought Bill Corson was responsible. Corson came from his Army camp in New Jersey to spend the weekends with them frequently—perhaps too frequently, since in his letters of this period Heinlein often mentions having houseguests nearly every weekend, Corson mostly, and no alone time at all. But neither Robert nor Leslyn would say anything to discourage a man on active duty in the Army. Although Corson had "a wonderful-to-see effect on Heinlein père,"[43] he could, he admitted, be socially oblivious.[44] But he protested they were using on him the same tactics they used to keep Asimov's puppyish energy under control (Asimov was charming and funny and enthusiastic and oblivious: if you didn't tramp on him—hard!—he'd run you over innocently and cheerfully), and Corson felt they portrayed him as consistently and invariably wrong about anything and everything.

Leslyn complained that she felt taken for granted by Corson and relegated to household drudge while he was there. Any perceived threat to Leslyn brought out a swift and vehement response from Robert—by letter, since they had been dropping hints that Robert escalated into a firm instruction that they wouldn't be having weeknight guests for a while.[45] Corson admitted some culpability, but protested:

I've never yet been able to sort out the times when I'm to take an esoteric hint or wait for a pointed bluntness, of which latter you are abundantly capable. . . . I'm neither utterly dense nor psychic. . . .

> I don't think I could get you to see that you had ever made any mistakes, Wobert. For a long time I've seen that . . . it was taken for granted no matter what came up that I was always wrong. I guess maybe you believe that pretty thoroughly by practice, now . . . I don't think I'm very likely to be able to convince you that I'm *ever* not in the wrong . . .[46]

Heinlein and Corson worked out a mutual understanding: Heinlein replied immediately that he hated to take a holier-than-thou attitude with anyone, but especially Corson—but the process took months by exchange of letters. Perhaps there was another factor at work, as well. Years later, L. Sprague de Camp observed:

> Seems to me that Johnny Arwine suffers from the same disease that you do, which is a tendency to idealize your friends and then to be terribly hurt when they don't come up to your expectations. I seriously hope you have a proper appreciation of the vices, faults, and shortcomings of the de Camps, as I should hate for you to be thus drastically disillusioned about us some day.[47]

Catherine de Camp added by handwritten insert: "Or have you been already?"

Perhaps the tension was being focused on Corson, since nothing could be done about their personal and professional situation. If so, Corson may have let the people in Heinlein's immediate circle escape a blowup.

By October 1943, it was clear that the Navy was not going to reactivate Heinlein's retired status under any circumstances. But he had another bow to his string: John Arwine had got active duty in the Coast Guard—and the merchant marines were always a possibility. Now that supply ships had to have a military escort, the merchant marines had assumed critical importance to the war effort: it took ten tons of supplies, most of them shipped overseas, to maintain a man in the field for a year. No shipping, no warfare. Heinlein began doing research for either of those options. "I'm *alarmed*!" Bill Corson wrote Leslyn:

> For gossake, don't let our Wobert go Merchant marining, because they shoot bombs and torpedoes at you when you do that. He's uh . . . too close to maturity to swim all over the north Atlantic on winter nights. . . . It's just that damned erratic conscience of his, and it's high time he came to an understanding with it and ceased to allow it to bulldoze him.[48]

Heinlein began clearing the decks, cleaning up his affairs so he could make a rapid move once he was approved for the merchant marines. He also had some medical problems to take care of.

Lifestyle stress is often "somatized," put into the body; many people get ulcers; Heinlein got an annoying case of hemorrhoids. He went to a doctor who specialized in reducing the inflamed tissue by injections, without the usual operation, and started the regimen as his application for the merchant marines came up. But nobody would take him for active duty.

> It looked for a few minutes as if I were going to make it—no legal impediments, no need to resign my navy commission, fully qualified for bridge or engine room. Then the medical board got a look at my retirement papers and refused to examine me. According to the board here, no waiver for a history of pulmonary TB had ever been granted. Sorry. Thanks for coming in.
>
> They did offer me a job teaching navigation ashore. The hell with that. Might just as well stick where I am. There still remains a possibility of a waiver through Washington but it is a very remote chance. I expect to pursue it but I regard the matter as settled.[49]

Nevertheless, he continued the treatment for hemorrhoids. The regimen was only partly successful at first, and he developed an infection that made his life increasingly miserable. What with overwork and poor diet (the result of wartime rationing), his immune system couldn't combat the infection. He caught an early case of the flu that was making the rounds that year and, in his debilitated state, developed an abscess "in a location where I could not see but was acutely aware of it."[50] It progressed to a state for which he had to be hospitalized in November 1943, for three months, at Jefferson Medical School. He went on medical leave without pay and reactivated his Naval retirement pay.

The first operation in late November dealt with the abscess and started the process of dealing with the hemorrhoids surgically. "Having the flu and simultaneously having your asshole cut out with an apple corer (Leslyn says she thinks that is what they used) is an annoying and debilitating experience."[51] He had a second surgery in early December, under spinal block instead of general anesthesia. He lost a great deal of blood and was very weak for some time after. There was no replacement blood available, as all blood collection was for combat, not for civilian hospitals. They were short on nursing staff, too.

One student nurse had the 8-bed ward I was in plus three more like it—so any patient who could possibly get out of bed had to use the W.C.—no bed pans or bed urinals for them. I could get out of bed, but I could not get as far as the W.C. without fainting. After falling twice I learned an expedient: push a straight chair ahead of me. When my vision would start to black out, I would collapse across the chair and that would break my fall. It worked. A usual trip to the W.C. would average three faints, but I never got hurt again. A good thing as the flu epidemic hit the hospital and these little nursing students worked until they keeled over, and there was no one to replace them.

I remember one morning when the student nurse in charge of us came in, stuck thermometers in our mouths, went out—did not come back. For about three hours nothing happened—no drinking water, no breakfast, nothing. About 11 A.M. a visitor to a patient showed up with a rack tray of glasses of water, then in a couple of hours some food arrived. I never saw our little student nurse again but I found out later what had happened. She had walked into the corridor . . . and collapsed. She was found there, out cold, and was carted somewhere else and put to bed. The hospital staff, already stripped down to minimum by the War, was hit by flu, and perhaps a third of the usual number were holding things together as best they could.[52]

Heinlein's temperature fluctuated erratically, and he thought he might be coming down with TB again, though the blood and sputum cultures were negative.[53]

Heinlein was still in the hospital in January of 1944, when Leslyn was contacted by the Red Cross: the Swedish "mercy ship" *Gripsholm* had managed a repatriation of some fifteen hundred prisoners of the Japanese in the Philippines, and specifically from Santo Tomas, where Keith and the boys were being held. The ship traded Japanese refugees they had picked up in Goa for the expats. Keith and her two sons were on that ship!

Leslyn had been working with her brother-in-law's boss to get them out, sending money (she later estimated it at about $5,000 altogether). A survivor, Peter Wygle, later said:

The *Gripsholm* incident was infamous among the prisoners, for access to the rescue ship was controlled by a small group of rich Americans; many women and children were left behind, as apparently bribes controlled who got on the boat to escape.[54]

The Lyle-Heinlein family about 1905. BACK ROW, LEFT TO RIGHT: Aunt Anna; Rex Ivar Heinlein (senior) with Rex Ivar Heinlein (junior) in arms; Bam Lyle Heinlein. FRONT ROW: Thelma; Rose Adelia Woods Lyle (seated); Lawrence Lyle Heinlein; Grandfather Alva Evans Lyle; Park Lyle. *Courtesy of Robert A. and Virginia Heinlein Prize Trust*

The first known photograph of Robert Heinlein, probably taken in front of Grandfather Lyle's house in Butler, Missouri, 1907. *Courtesy of Robert A. and Virginia Heinlein Prize Trust*

The Heinlein children, 1910 or 1911: Larry (tallest), Rex Ivar (middle), Louise, and Robert (seated). *Courtesy of Robert A. and Virginia Heinlein Prize Trust*

Bobby Heinlein's graduation portrait, 1924—"one of the nicest, sweetest boys in his graduation class" according to classmate Alice Marie.
Courtesy of Robert A. and Virginia Heinlein Prize Trust

A girl who is prominent in dramatic, scholastic, journalistic and debate circles is Elanor Curry. She has attained perhaps what is the greatest scholastic accomplishment of which any girl is capable when she was elected captain of the entire girl's debate squad. Her dramatic ability is assured, in that she is an ex-vice president of the Speech Arts club, and the fact that she was a member of the Crier and Herald staffs in '23 assures her journalistic ability. The **Cornish-Baker Photo.** supreme tribute to **Elanor Curry.** her popularity was paid her when in her junior year she was elected president of the renowned Pundit club. Her unusually heavy list of activities and the scholastic standing which she maintains indicate that she has plenty of energy.

Elinor Curry, Heinlein's first wife, in high school. Her name is misspelled in the caption and text.

Alice McBee about the time she and Heinlein became engaged, 1927.
Courtesy of Robert A. and Virginia Heinlein Prize Trust

Heinlein in midshipman whites with his parents at Rex's graduation, 1927. *Permission to reproduce this photo (provided from Bam Heinlein's effects) by Andrew Lermer, on behalf of the entire Heinlein family.*.

Ensign Bob, about 1930. *Courtesy of Robert A. and Virginia Heinlein Prize Trust*

Leslyn as Wood Sprite, a professional actress résumé photo about 1928–1930. *Courtesy of Colin Hubbard, M.D., and Robert A. and Virginia Heinlein Prize Trust*

Robert and Leslyn's wedding portrait. *Courtesy of Colin Hubbard, M.D., and Robert A. and Virginia Heinlein Prize Trust*

Robert and Leslyn's formal wedding group portrait, March 28, 1932. *Courtesy of Colin Hubbard, M.D., and Robert A. and Virginia Heinlein Prize Trust*

The newly married ensign and wife in Ensenada, California, 1932. *Courtesy of Colin Hubbard, M.D., and Robert A. and Virginia Heinlein Prize Trust*

Sally Rand publicity photo inscribed to Bob and Leslyn. *Courtesy of Robert A. and Virginia Heinlein Prize Trust*

Playing fashionable croquet in the summer of 1934. *Courtesy of Robert A. and Virginia Heinlein Prize Trust*

Heinlein playing chess, 1936 or 1937.
Courtesy of Robert A. and Virginia Heinlein Prize Trust

Cleve Cartmill, about 1947. Heinlein may have taken the photo himself.
Courtesy of Robert A. and Virginia Heinlein Prize Trust

Robert Heinlein and Jack Williamson discussing a writerly
problem in the Mañana Literary Society, about 1940.
Courtesy of Robert A. and Virginia Heinlein Prize Trust

Glamour Bob—a studio photo
taken by Bill Corson in 1940.
This photo was used on book
jackets through the 1950s.
*Courtesy of Robert A. and
Virginia Heinlein Prize Trust*

Heinlein in his new writing study, 1940.
Courtesy of Robert A. and Virginia Heinlein Prize Trust

Heinlein captured in a hall conference with another engineer in the Plastics and
Adhesives section of the Naval Air Experimental Station, about 1943.

Courtesy of Robert A. and Virginia Heinlein Prize Trust

Virginia Doris Gerstenfeld in Washington, D.C., 1943, age twenty-seven, when she was working for BuAer. This may be one of the photographs taken by skating buddy Fred Fleischman while he was working for Edward Steichen doing war photography, but the photographer is not identified. *Courtesy of Robert A. and Virginia Heinlein Prize Trust*

Virginia Gerstenfeld at NAES, 1944. *Courtesy of Robert A. and Virginia Heinlein Prize Trust*

"Killer Cal" Laning showing the results of his unexpectedly aggressive and unexpectedly successful command of his ship *Hutchins* at the Battle of Leyte Gulf in 1944.

Courtesy of Jillian Giornelli and Judith Laning for the Estate of Cal Laning

L. Sprague de Camp, Isaac Asimov, and Robert Heinlein interviewed for the
Naval Air Experimental Station magazine, *Wind Scoops,* in 1945.
Courtesy of Robert A. and Virginia Heinlein Prize Trust

John Arwine in the Merchant
Marines, about 1945.
*Courtesy of Robert A. and
Virginia Heinlein Prize Trust*

Robert Heinlein in 1945 immediately after leaving the Naval Air Experimental Station.
He has been sick and overworked, and his condition shows in this picture.
Courtesy of Robert A. and Virginia Heinlein Prize Trust

Ginny Gerstenfeld in Los Angeles, 1946. "Ice fairy Virginia, First in the Dance!" The photo may have been by Heinlein; the caption certainly was.

Courtesy of Robert A. and Virginia Heinlein Prize Trust

Heinlein in Ojai while waiting for his divorce to be heard in 1947. The photographer was not identified, but Virginia Gerstenfeld may have taken this picture.

Courtesy of Robert A. and Virginia Heinlein Prize Trust

Robert and Virginia Gerstenfeld probably on one of Ginny's weekend visits to Ojai in July or August 1947. *Courtesy of Robert A. and Virginia Heinlein Prize Trust*

Robert Heinlein and Virginia Gerstenfeld, probably in the San Fernando Valley in September 1947. Heinlein lives in a trailer park while refurbishing his "piano box in a former life" house trailer in order to leave Los Angeles.
Courtesy of Robert A. and Virginia Heinlein Prize Trust

Willy Ley and Doofus, 1945 or 1946.
Courtesy of Robert A. and Virginia Heinlein Prize Trust

Heinlein in front of his and Ginny's first house in Colorado Springs (rented 1948), where they lived while he wrote *Red Planet*. They kept the house until he went to Hollywood to make *Destination Moon*. *Courtesy of Robert A. and Virginia Heinlein Prize Trust*

The money Leslyn and Mark Hubbard's boss raised apparently bought Keith and the boys onto *Gripsholm.*

The entire trip, from Goa to the Philippines to Port Elizabeth and Rio to New York, took seventy days. Leslyn went to New York City that January of 1944 to take charge of them, only to find out that the Red Cross had lost track of them entirely. They had come thousands of miles only to be lost in New York City. Leslyn was frantic.

But Keith and the boys had been put up in a cheap hotel room—and in a few days were relocated to a better hotel by Mark Hubbard's employer.[55] Leslyn gathered them in and took them back to Philadelphia while Robert was recuperating.

Robert was not doing well: the surgery had left him "with no rectum to speak of,"[56] and he had a third operation coming up in the new year. In the meantime, he could not sit up at all, though, paradoxically, he could stand or lie down. Keith's boys were entertaining but exhausting—a little too much for the sickroom, so they were shipped off to stay with the Campbells in New Jersey for a while. "I am a bloody mess," Heinlein said of himself, "and disgusted with myself."[57]

Even in his weakened condition, he was able to keep up with a few aspects of his war work—morale-building letters to a British soldier, his friend and colleague Ted Carnell. He had begun submitting stories to Carnell's project for a British science-fiction magazine in 1940, and their casual correspondence developed into a friendship (even though Carnell's project collapsed and he had to return his purchases). Carnell had gone into the British army, and Robert and Leslyn helped out by keeping his subscriptions to *Astounding* and *Unknown* current. On the last day of 1943, Heinlein began his recovery by writing to Carnell:

> You are being especially honored, sir. I am sitting up and typing in your honor—the first time I have sat up in two months. No, nothing very serious. I have been reasonably comfortable; I have been able to stand up and walk; I have been able to lie down; I have been able to dine regally, reclining Roman banquet style. But I have not been able to sit.[58]

Keith and Leslyn were night and day opposites. She took an instant dislike to Bill Corson, for example, and this made entertaining him on his every-other-weekend trips awkward.[59] When Keith expressed approval of their friend John Arwine, Robert wrote to Arwine: "I think that for the first time in history the two MacDonald sisters have decided that they both like the same man. There may be some hairpulling."[60] Keith was weak from the long imprisonment, and she was ill for months. The winter weather in "Filthydelphia" bothered her. Sometime in the fall—the date is nowhere recorded—she collected the boys and went back to the milder weather of Laguna Beach, California—really too close to her mother for anyone's comfort, but . . .

> Skipper is just as much of an old harridan as ever, but I crack the whip over her pretty drastically. If she gets out of hand or bothers Keith too much, she gets a sharp note from my lawyer with a reminder of the source of her support.[61]

From the evidence of later events, traced back to this time of the war, Leslyn must have been in multiple spiritual crises, with no help in sight. She had always been thin, but her weight dropped to eighty-five pounds, and she continued to push herself into overwork.[62] Normally, she would have turned to Robert, and he would have done whatever it took to jolly her out of it—if she would let him. But overwork and illness had taken its toll on him, too: Robert had no extra strength to lend her this time. The relatively minor problems began to tip over her psychological balance, like a stack of dominoes. She began to sleep ten to twelve hours a day. Robert's own psychological balance was none too good; Bill Corson's frequent teasing of Leslyn about her sleeping habits provoked another explosion:

> You've nagged her about her need for sleep for a good many years now. I should have shut you up about it before this. Don't ever mention it again. . . .
>
> We are very fond of you *but, God damn it—quit treating us as if we were your parents!*[63]

When she and Robert were true partners—in politics and in the writing—Leslyn appeared satisfied, more or less, with the power-behind-the-throne role she built for herself, as a political operator (she had continued with political work of her own even after Robert "retired" from politics) and as a story doctor for Robert and for the other working writers in the Mañana Literary Society. She had a congenial social role: the brilliant, knowledgeable authority on story structure.

But once Robert turned to Campbell to work out the stories he was selling to *Astounding,* her role in the process began to wane. Effectively, she became an outsider—just in time for her family to fall into danger.

Her father had known the solution: there was warmth in the bottle with the dimples.

KEEPING ON—

Robert's third and final operation of this series took place on January 24, 1944—"expensive, damnably painful, and the whole business an embarrassing indignity."[1] The operation left him weak, and he had to wear an enormous dressing Bill Corson said looked like a diaper.[2] But he was able to sit up for twenty minutes at a time, using a rubber ring. "I've lost twenty pounds," he wrote to John Arwine, "and am just beginning to be able to scratch my head without resting between strokes."[3]

The doctors told him he could look forward to gradual improvement—*if* he kept to his bed. This, he would not do: he was ready, he said, to go back to work by the end of the first week in February.

This episode convinced him, finally, to give up the idea of trying to get into combat:

I have no desire to be shot at nor to be killed; even more I do not wish to sleep in foxholes, contract malaria, be wounded painfully and lie in the mud, stand midwatches, freeze to death on the forecastle, go eighty hours without sleep, or do any of the other horridly uncomfortable things that constitute the romantic pageant of war. I'm simply going to be bored to distraction and worked to a rag doing things I don't want to do in a town I hate. I know I am damned lucky and I shall try to remember every hour that guys who don't like it any better than I would are doing all those things and dying at the end of it. But I think you will understand that I had to try in every possible way to join up with the rest in order to be able to live with myself. And that my motivation was composed in equal parts of patriotism, compassion, and sinful pride, and that I never could get the elements sorted out in my own mind.

I think it was getting flu even more than the surgery that convinced me that I was a dead letter for combat purposes. I had just completed a series of cold shots. They did not protect me. I now realize that I would almost certainly fold up physically if any real strain were put on me . . . simply be a handicap to any combat outfit, a man who would have to be hospitalized, without being wounded, at the earliest opportunity, probably with another attack of TB.[4]

Leslyn, too, was distracted and overworked; she also had been down with the flu that winter and had lost ten pounds she could ill afford to lose. But interest in her new work helped sustain her: in September 1943, she had been promoted from the factory- and quality-inspection work she had been doing for two years into personnel management for the six-hundred-man machine shop and was doing effective work:

They like her and trust her on first contact and her reputation spread ahead of her. She was a fine inspector but she [is] ideally suited to this work both by training and experience—and by temperament. In the first place she has a highly developed feeling for simple justice and a fine subtle mind which can deal with the complications of social relationships, get them sorted out, and make people happy. She has the union shop stewards pitching on her side. She loves her work but it is harder than inspecting. . . . Her deep earnestness about her job and her determination to give her full strength and ability to winning the war makes me very proud.[5]

Heinlein resumed working early in February,[6] conserving his health most carefully:

I go to bed right after supper, come hell or high water, *every* night but Saturday. I am watching my diet and have gained six pounds since leaving the hospital. My temperature stays normal and I feel better each week. I am determined not to fold up again while the war is on and I plan to do so, not through sheer nerve (That didn't work!) but through caution. My life is pretty dull but pretty healthy.[7]

The combination of boredom and overwork was debilitating, and he had been contemplating doing some writing again. He was of two minds about it[8]: Isaac Asimov had continued to write for *Astounding,* producing stories in his Foundation series and contributing occasionally to the local Naval Air Experimental Station (NAES) bulletin, *Air Scoop*. Heinlein's dilemma was that if he had enough energy left over to write stories, some poor naval aviator downed in the South Pacific could probably use the extra effort he could put in, to help keep him out of the drink.

But, on the other hand, if Heinlein went nuts, that poor aviator wouldn't get the benefit of *any* of his efforts, stringing beads in a loony bin. He had queried Campbell about doing a review of Willy Ley's new book, *Rockets: A Prelude to Space Travel.*[9] Campbell gave him the go-ahead. "I sure would like to do that 60,000 word novel," Heinlein wrote Campbell,

> but I see little prospect of it at the present time. It would have been nice to have done it while laid up—if I had been sick in any other way! But one must sit down to type for any length of time and sitting down is still somewhat of a chore. But I certainly would like to get back to writing. . . . This long sickness has completely bollixed up our plans—and bank account![10]

The war news was both encouraging and frustrating. U.S. forces invaded Europe at Normandy on June 6, 1944, and opened the European front that had been needed for a very long time. The day after the invasion of Normandy, Isaac Asimov, Sprague de Camp, and Heinlein were interviewed for an article in *Air Scoop* that stressed the creative thinking that science-fiction writers brought to the war effort. The article appeared in August. By the time Heinlein's enthusiastic review of Willy Ley's *Rockets: A Prelude to Space Travel* appeared in the July 1944 issue of *Astounding*, the German army began putting rockets to practical, immediate use, launching their new V-1 buzz-bomb rockets (the *Vergeltungswaffe*, or "vengeance" weapon) across the channel at Britain. The reportage in newspapers and radio went around the world, and everyone was suddenly aware that science was at war. The Norden bombsight, radar, and, above all, the Manhattan Engineer District were still out of the public eye.

On July 20, 1944, a "Conspiracy of the Generals" was launched in an attempt to assassinate Hitler. He escaped with only minor injuries, more convinced than ever he was protected by a lucky star. He set in motion purges that killed twenty thousand people in the German army, including Erwin Rommel, Hitler's best hope of reversing the war in Germany's favor. Hitler was determined to carry the war to victory or the destruction of Germany itself.

In the South Pacific, the "Navy's War" was running into trouble: the intense Japanese resistance to the taking of Saipan on July 6, 1944, signaled a change of strategy on Japan's part: there would be no fall-back-and-regroup strategy as the Allied forces moved from island to island in the South Pacific. They were now intent on making the home islands too expensive for the Allies to consider taking them—buying time to rebuild.

In the United States, the parties' nominating conventions came around in the summer of 1944, and Franklin Roosevelt was renominated for an unprecedented fourth term. Roosevelt's fragile health was no secret in the high levels of the Democratic National Committee; Roosevelt would probably not live to see the end of his fourth term. The short list for the "replacement" President, who would be running as Vice President, had several candidates, but Roosevelt went outside the list and browbeat Harry Truman into accepting the nomination. Truman was considered a lightweight by the party regulars, though Roosevelt knew he was a very loyal New Dealer.

Somehow Heinlein had never connected with Truman in Kansas City politics (though they were at some of the same functions at the same time when Heinlein was a boy), but he looked up the Senator's record and was generally pleased.[11] Despite coming to Congress as the "Senator from Pendergast," he had done solid work investigating corruption in war industries; he had made speeches trying to alert people to the genocide of the Jews going on in Germany. And he had personal qualities Heinlein liked—particularly his personal loyalty: He had stood by Tom Pendergast during his tax evasion scandal and imprisonment in 1939, not ducking out on the public association: "As for his K.C. origin, I, too, got my start in the Pendergast machine; it didn't ruin me, I don't think it has ruined Truman."[12]

But the vice presidency would probably saddle Truman with the problem of the peace—an unsolvable morass, if Woodrow Wilson's experience meant anything. Looking to the long term, he suggested to John Arwine in April 1944 that the party might be better off to "trap pass" the Republicans and throw the 1944 election:

> Then *we*'ll be the critics and *they* will be the ones who have got to satisfy the public . . . If *they* have the responsibility they may find themselves forced to indulge in a little constructive statesmanship, because we will be sitting on the sidelines, jumping up and down and screaming our heads off about the sell out. I really suspect that the results might be better than those which would result from a vengeful Senate working over Roosevelt's efforts.[13]

This was a kind of long-range strategic thinking on Heinlein's part that was much too far outside the automatic grab-it-and-keep-it party mentality. When he later suggested the idea to Susie Clifton, to be passed on to Helen Gahagan Douglas,[14] Mrs. Douglas praised the idea as "objective, far-sighted, and sensitive to public thinking"[15]—but not within "the art of the possible."

In August, Heinlein was transferred from the Naval Aircraft Factory Engineering Division to the NAES Materials Laboratory, Plastics & Adhesives section, to work on the mechanical problems of Plexiglas aircraft canopies. He might (there are no records on the point) have instituted this lateral transfer himself, to break a political impasse where he was. He had incurred the wrath of a superior because he refused direct orders to hide from the Navy the falsification of test results from the Naval Air Materials Center (under pressure to get war matériel into the field)—facts embarrassing to the head of the AML. "He considered me a disloyal sonuvabitch and never forgave me for . . . such narrow loyalty-of-organization was a prime reason why NAMC was so scandalously inefficient in helping to win the war."[16]

Other departments, and even other facilities, wanted his services: John Campbell was maneuvering to get him assigned to the National Defense Research Committee's new technologies section in New York, where Campbell was working on a hush-hush project set up by the University of California and occupying an entire floor of the Empire State Building.[17]

There had been a request for him to switch over to technical writing for electronics, for which he wrote a carefully noncommittal letter saying that he was ready to go where assigned but that he thought he could best serve his country where he was, concluding, "I have no special training, other than the usual Naval Academy engineering courses, for the work I am now doing, but I have spent fifteen months learning its details." The head of NAES would not release him.[18]

> By the time BuShips [Bureau of Ships] got around to requesting my services from BuAero [Bureau of Aeronautics] I was doing urgent engineering work which would have suffered if I had left and which appeared to be a good deal more important than the work BuShips had for me.[19]

Heinlein was—finally—able to derive satisfaction from his job:

> This dear old place is just as offensive as ever but I find it a little more bearable because I am now so busy and have the warm and comforting feeling that my work is effective in the combat areas within a very few weeks after I finish it.[20]

The lateral transfer into the Materials Section at NAES appears to have been a "book" transfer that did not affect Heinlein's actual day-to-day working arrangements. He stayed second in charge of the section, Henry Sang his immediate superior.

Sang was single, and there are subtle indications, in a casual comment made by another close friend, that Leslyn might have been interested in him.[21] Robert and Leslyn's marriage commitment was still strong, but Leslyn, too, was free to pursue her own sexual liaisons.[22] Robert was still *hors de combat,* living too quietly to get himself into many interesting situations.

The Heinleins' open marriage was a direct reflection of their liberal political philosophy, an extreme liberalism of a type that nevertheless cannot be exactly characterized as "left wing"—and that cannot so much be called a "political" philosophy as a philosophy of life, extending to all aspects of their life. Most of their friends and acquaintances saw them as "ultra-liberal,"[23] without, apparently, having any exact or nuanced comprehension of their liberalism. In their days of political activism, they had learned to avoid engendering or participating in controversies by getting the other person to talk about himself, finding areas of agreement or commonality, nodding and appearing to agree with whatever was said (within reason). They learned to speak the proper shibboleths, and work out their opinions and strategies only when talking with people they could trust to understand the nuances of their social evaluations. Outsiders saw them only as "like me, one of us"—or "not one of us."

In Heinlein's case, it is possible to see that he did fit into a "labeled" political philosophy. His lifelong preoccupations with marriage reform, combined with sound-money matters, mark him as a Freethinker, the radical wing of the Democratic Party at the turn of the twentieth century. By 1940 this political platform had all but disappeared from American political life, and Freethinkers wound up going into either Republican or Democratic parties, depending on how they felt about what was to become conventional left-wing liberalism.

But in 1944 and 1945, it was possible to remain a Freethinker and regard the left-wing tolerance of totalitarians—particularly the United States' Soviet ally—as an *aberration,* to be corrected after the war, after the more immediate problems were resolved.

On the whole, Heinlein considered himself a very lucky man to have found Leslyn, and his sense of personal loyalty to her was very strong, coloring even the way he looked at her.

She is a damn smart looking wench when she gets her war paint on and her Sunday clothes. But I also see her in dungarees, after a night sleepless, heading for the factory, maybe no make up yet. She still looks good then, because it's not her clothes or her makeup I am looking at.[24]

The occasional bouts of instability, which had been growing more frequent, were simply something to be coped with for the duration—an *aberration*.

When the Paris uprising started on August 22, 1944, the war in Europe could clearly be seen to be winding down. Leslyn received another promotion—which meant more responsibility—and began managing a number of shops instead of just the one. Her hands-on work with personnel was being noticed.

In September, they got a new chemist for the Adhesives projects, fresh out of BuAer in D.C.—Lieutenant Virginia Gerstenfeld. On her first day, she was taken to her new billet in the Plastics & Adhesive section during a general staff meeting. Only Heinlein was on the floor. When her supervisor left,

> he looked me up and down and said "Lieutenant, your slip is showing." That was my introduction to Robert. He had a laugh in his voice as he said that. I ducked into a ladies' room and pinned up the offending strap which had broken.[25]

She had the desk just behind his. Heinlein showed her around the laboratories and took her down to the coffee mess in the Adhesives lab, then over to Ulcer Gulch for lunch and introduced her around the section. That evening, he and Leslyn took her to dinner, and afterward he walked her over to the YWCA, where she was staying, a few blocks from the Heinleins' apartment. The Y was in a bad district. Heinlein offered to find her a place downtown— a minor miracle, considering the housing shortage (the Navy couldn't even provide housing for its staff), but a routine act (for him, she found) of helpfulness.[26]

Lieutenant Gerstenfeld was somewhat distracted at the time: she had put in for transfer to San Francisco to be able to see her fiancé, George,[27] when he periodically rotated stateside from the South Pacific. But the Navy's "Practical Joke" department was handling her career,[28] and she had wound up in Philadelphia by mischance.[29] She threw herself into the job, learning the plastics and adhesives field. "The Navy has its own way of doing things," Lieutenant Gerstenfeld later remarked:

> They put you into a job, and it is either sink or swim—you do it, or you are moved elsewhere. So I learned something about plastics (I already knew a bit about them) and adhesives. But now and then I would need some help with something, and Robert was always handy—and helpful.[30]

Lieutenant Gerstenfeld—"Ginny," as she preferred to be called, having been put off her given names, Virginia and Doris, by her mother[31]—was thrown together with Heinlein as they worked on the Plexiglas canopies for the B-29 bomber, trying to find a way to prevent them from spontaneously exploding outward.

It rapidly became evident that Ginny Gerstenfeld was something unusual as government engineers went: she was not "going through the motions" on the civil service plan; she was actually paying attention to her work. She found an anomaly in the standard "drop test" used to measure the tensile strength of the batches of Plexiglas—dropping a ball bearing of known weight from a known height onto the plastic to see whether it would shatter. They had been using incorrect measurements: every tensile strength test the laboratory had done for the last two years was off and needed to be done over.

Heinlein was almost—but not quite—inured to that kind of thing by now: that was why NAES was "Snafu Manor." There had been hundreds of engineers working with those tests: only Gerstenfeld had caught the discrepancy.

Always on the lookout for competent help, Heinlein had his eye on her thereafter, and turned to her when he needed something done right. He was also approvingly impressed that she paid no attention to the Navy officer's ethos. Navy officers did not get their hands dirty, but Lieutenant Gerstenfeld would routinely change into dungarees and perform whatever tests she could do herself, on "C" and "D" priority work—things that would never get done at all if she didn't do them.

That was also the start of what came to be a close friendship between the two of them. Heinlein found her "gung-ho but non-reg"[32]—independent in a way that was highly entertaining, even (or perhaps especially) when it involved differences of opinion he could not quite go along with. She wore a navy blue ribbon in her hair one day, because there was nothing in the regulations that forbade it, and she stuck to her guns, even though it scandalized Heinlein and the regular Navy types.[33]

Gerstenfeld had lost her brother in submarine warfare the year before, and for a very long time Heinlein thought she had joined up to "replace him,"[34] though she straightened him out one day: she had simply joined up the first moment the Navy would take her after the enabling act set up WAVES (Women Accepted for Volunteer Emergency Service) in 1943. She was disappointed that the statute specifically forbade women in combat and restricted them to shore duty, but if that was what she could do for the war effort, that was what she would do.[35]

She was also a thoroughgoing Republican—an example of liberal freethought attitudes that took the less customary route into the Republican Party. She agreed with him—and H. G. Wells—for example, that a world sovereignty with its own international police force was a necessary part of postwar peacekeeping.

> Hang it all, why don't the powers that be realize that the only way we'll at-
> tain a lasting peace is to have every nation give up some of its sovereign
> power and have a world federation of countries with an international
> police force to back it up? Not another League . . . [36]

Heinlein had recently learned to live with a close friend who was a Republican (though he was somewhat jaundiced about Campbell's "slightly open-mouthed adoration for 'big businessmen' ").[37] But the bottom line was, Campbell was there when it counted, and so was Gerstenfeld. She was a more liberal conservative than Campbell.

Heinlein really began paying attention to her as a person, she later said, when she mentioned she had walked the precincts in New York.[38] Anyone who had his—or her—hands on the levers of democracy was a comrade, so far as he was concerned, and that by itself made Ginny Gerstenfeld an order of magnitude more important, in the greater scheme of things, than John Campbell.[39]

Heinlein always sought out and valued acquaintances who had their own minds, who were their own persons. Ginny Gerstenfeld was not an ordinary or conventional person. She was both intelligent and also stimulatingly different. They were very compatible, Heinlein found, but she was an "exception that proves the rule," since she didn't much care for General Semantics or James Branch Cabell—or one of his important touchstones, *Caleb Catlum's America*—but did love Kipling. She was a law unto herself—an individual.

Most important, she was capable of surprising him with a refreshingly direct and sensible approach to obstacles she encountered. That made her an exceptionally valuable coworker and friend.

Gerstenfeld was interested when Heinlein told her about his own political background, and the writing, even though she had never been particularly interested in science fiction. She asked to read something he had written, and he gave her what he had on hand—which was fortuitously the issues of *Astounding* in which his "Beyond This Horizon" serial appeared since he had been in

Philadelphia. She found it thought-provoking, though she didn't warm to the Social Credit ideas in the book (Heinlein himself had begun to drift from the strict SoCred line by that time).[40] Most important: it didn't convert her into a *fan*—and particularly not a fan of his writing.[41] That made her even more valuable as a friend, since he could get from her what every writer needs and few can get, honest criticism.[42]

Gerstenfeld's living arrangements precluded much socializing after work: she moved out of the downtown apartment Heinlein had found her—she couldn't keep her uniform clean because of the soot and cinders from the nearby 30th Street Railyard—and found a place in the Main Line suburb of Merion. She commuted to the Navy Yard by carpool, which took her out of the Heinleins' NAES social circle, except for lunches in Ulcer Gulch. As winter came on, her own social circle revolved around the local skating club. She had been a fanatic ice-skater and ice-dancer since she saw Sonja Henie's review in 1938. Her fiancé, George Harris, was her dancing partner. She was invited to join the Philadelphia Skating Club and Humane Society (so called because the members carried rescue equipment for people in danger on the iced-up Schuylkill River).[42]

When President Roosevelt visited the Philadelphia Navy Yard just before the elections—one of the few appearances Roosevelt made during that campaign—NAES emptied out, except for Gerstenfeld, who did not think much of his domestic policies or the New Deal. "But he's your commander-in-chief," Heinlein admonished her. She continued stubborn and refused to go.[43] Heinlein did go.

He had last seen Roosevelt in 1940, at the third-term nominating convention. Heinlein was aware of Roosevelt's faults as a politician and as a man; even John Campbell's complaint that he chose people badly had some merit. But Heinlein thought if anyone else had taken the presidency in 1933, there might have been a bloody revolution in this country.[44] Roosevelt's willingness to experiment socially and economically had let some of the head of steam out of the boiler that was America in the Depression years, and so he was owed a debt of gratitude by all patriots.[45] Heinlein was shocked, therefore, by the President's appearance and came back to NAES pale and worried: President Roosevelt looked sick—dying, in fact.[46]

The war was again brought home to him personally in October when Cal Laning was involved in the Battle for Leyte Gulf—the largest naval engagement in history and the opening engagement of the Allied invasion of the Philippines. Laning was then commanding the destroyer USS *Hutchins*.

Laning ordered *Hutchins* in closer against kamikaze attack. As the Navy and Marines retook the Japanese islands, against desperate resistance, the Japanese high command had devised a strategy that struck many people inside the Japanese government as a corruption and perversion of Bushido: the kamikazes, suicide pilots, living torpedoes—some as young as fourteen and some bolted into their airplanes so they could not escape their fate. *Hutchins*'s courageous behavior on this occasion earned Laning the nickname "Killer Laning" in press photos—as well as a commendation from the Navy.

But Laning's "extraordinary heroism"—"in keeping with the highest traditions of the Navy of the United States"[47]—was not his main contribution to this battle: *Hutchins* had been refitted with the newest Combat Information Center (CIC) equipment in its last overhaul at Pearl Harbor in 1943. The CIC collects and evaluates and redistributes information about the engagement ("field intelligence") while it is going on, to organize the battle plans in real time. Laning called on his electronics knowledge, years of reading science fiction, and his long, speculative bull sessions with Heinlein back in their Academy days to reorganize and integrate *Hutchins*'s CIC. "And it works and sinks and shoots down Japs," he told Heinlein.[48] Although histories of World War II naval engagements pay scant attention to the improvements in CIC during the war, integrating field intelligence from the new technologies of sonar and radar with visual data, they do remark often on the surprisingly aggressive—and successful—behavior of destroyers in the Battle of Surigao Strait (one of the four major battles in the Battle of Leyte Gulf). Laning's innovative work with CIC put him in the forefront of CIC development, and he repeatedly acknowledged the role Heinlein's fiction had played in the accomplishment and urged his friend, "Save yourself for some super-stories."[49]

Even if Scoles's experiment at NAES never produced anything particularly useful, science fiction had justified its existence in World War II.

Heinlein continued to work in a state of quiet exhaustion. Ginny Gerstenfeld remarked once that they seemed to have cut the day in half since the start of the war, and he quipped it must be a shortage of materials[50]—and the work doubled and then tripled, taking up all his time, even on Sundays. He did not stint on entertaining friends in the service who passed through Philadelphia. Jack Williamson had been accepted for the Army and was training in weather reporting. He was passing through Philadelphia early in December 1944 and took the Heinleins, the de Camps, the Asimovs, and L. Ron Hubbard to a steak dinner—a welcome relief, as meat was still rationed. By that time, also, the financial strain was becoming acute: Heinlein and Leslyn were supporting six people in three households—he and Leslyn in Philadelphia, Keith and the two boys in Laguna Beach, with Skipper in her own setup nearby. They also had a new source of anxiety: a rumor reached them from the Philippines that Mark Hubbard, Leslyn's brother-in-law, might still be alive, caught by the Japanese at last, after twenty-nine months of guerrilla resistance in the bush.

The work was exhausting and overwhelming, and it continued to increase. In addition to his regular work, Heinlein took on a special "crash priority" project for Captain—now Fleet Admiral and Chief of Naval Operations (CNO)—King.[51] Nearly simultaneously, he got a request through back channels for some high-priority input from his science-fiction colleagues on a strategic problem intractable by conventional means. The Japanese kamikaze program was a serious annoyance to Naval operations.

In theory, the demonstration of Japanese fighting spirit would break the Americans' will to fight. It didn't happen that way. For the most part, the Americans were simply horrified—and it only confirmed the general opinion that the Japanese were moral monsters who had to be crushed out of existence.

The Navy was taking more combat casualties due to kamikazes than were the Army and the Marines ashore. The conventional response—improved detection and defense—wasn't working well enough. Heinlein was asked by OpNav-23 to come up with some unconventional responses.[52]

Even though the kamikaze program was not, by itself, a great impediment to the war in the Pacific, it was one more symptom of a problem that was becoming central, so far as Heinlein was concerned: Germany and Japan now had to be obliterated *as cultures:* "This is not revenge," he explained, "this is pragmatic necessity. This murderous damn foolishness has got to stop."[53]

Early in the fall of 1944, Heinlein started a science-fiction think tank among his colleagues scattered around the Atlantic northeast—Campbell and his assistant, L. Jerome Stanton, from New York, and Stanton's roommate, Theodore Sturgeon; George O. Smith and L. Ron Hubbard came with that group, too, by train every weekend, to the Heinleins' apartment.

Heinlein threw himself into the kamikaze project.[54] This, at least, gave him the satisfaction of something concrete that could be accomplished and not blocked by senseless bureaucracy.

OpNav-23 used to come to my apartment on Sundays to get the latest work ahead of channels and discuss it—and if he liked it, he could start the breadboarding that same night and have it flown out and tested at sea

by Ingram's special force off Hampton Roads that same week long before
the paperwork could pass through several hands.[55]

There were, however, certain inconveniences associated with the project:
there were no hotel accommodations available in wartime Philadelphia, and
nearly everyone needed to stay overnight. Some slept on the floor in the
Heinleins' hallway; others slept overnight with Henry Sang.

This gave the Heinleins a chance to become better acquainted with L. Ron
Hubbard, and they found him a fascinating person. He was in Princeton in
September 1944,[56] and Campbell roped him in for the think tank. Both the
Heinleins found him very compatible, though Sprague de Camp and Jack
Williamson were both suspicious of him. Heinlein was fascinated by Hubbard's larger-than-life quality—and by the number of wounds he had already
taken in his country's service.[57] He was a prime talker, the kind of conversa-
tionalist who could draw people out. He was also good story material. One
evening at the Heinleins' apartment, Robert remarked on a persistent dust
devil hanging around the odd cornices of the building, and Hubbard glanced
over and said, "Oh, that's just Kitten," and went back to his conversation with
someone else. Robert excused himself and immediately made a note of the remark.[58] Three years later it would become a short story, "Our Fair City."[59]

Soon after starting up the kamikaze think tank, Heinlein was then handed
yet another "crash priority" project to discover how to build nonmetallic
"radomes"—aerodynamic blister on the underside of an aircraft—to house
newly invented, ultrasecret radar equipment.

Radar—*Ra*dio *D*etection *a*nd *R*anging—was the great secret of World
War II, after the Norden bombsight (a mechanical analog computer that fa-
cilitated precision, high-altitude bombing); multiple groups were working
on radar in the United States and in Britain (Arthur C. Clarke among them).
E. J. King, Heinlein's old captain on the *Lexington,* had been advanced by
President Roosevelt to Chief of Naval Operations, and he personally supervised this project and another crash project dealing with radar proximity
fuses. Admiral King wanted reports on his desk by 8 A.M. each Monday, and
Heinlein made sure to get the latest results by Saturday night, plus special reports for breakthroughs. Heinlein tagged his most dependable engineer to
help out with this project—Ginny Gerstenfeld.

I made Hobson's choice, as dependable engineers were scarce, most of
them being either old civil servants with no other speeds but ahead slow
and stop, new wartime civil servants lacking either adequate professional

training or experience or both, male reserve officers who weren't really engineers at all but were devoted to the Navy's endless paperwork, and female reserve officers some few of whom were graduate engineers but most of them were not. That left me, a mechanical engineer with considerable experience in Navy planes and their problems, and a female reserve lieutenant [Virginia Gerstenfeld], chemist with seven years professional industrial experience before she enlisted and whose service had been BuAer and Mustin field . . . [*sic*] and was the only WAVE in her shop who changed from blues to dungarees each morning and got her hands dirty.[60]

By late 1944, it was clear that the war in Europe was winding down. The Allied forces had overwhelming numerical superiority and were pushing the Germans back on all fronts. The Italian peninsula had been completely retaken, and the Russians were moving on Germany. Hitler had one last move to make: on December 22, 1944, Germany began a massive push—its last—that came to be known as the "Battle of the Bulge," because on the hundreds of thousands of pushpin maps people used to follow the European Theater of Operations (ETO) war news as it was reported, Germany's positions suddenly bulged out in the Ardennes forest. On New Year's Day, 1945, Hitler threw the entire Luftwaffe into his "Great Blow" operation, bombing Allied airfields in Belgium, Holland, and northern France. But the damage the Luftwaffe took from defenders was devastating. A week later, Hitler ordered a general German withdrawal, and by January 16, all the positions previously held by the Allies had been retaken. The war in Europe was almost at an end. Now came the Navy's War.

25

STABILIZING, SOMEWHAT

Robert and Leslyn had decided before Thanksgiving 1944 to postpone Christmas for the duration. They were barely scraping by, their two wartime salaries supporting six people in three households. That December, Leslyn's mother, Skipper, died suddenly—Leslyn cryptically said later of "food fads."[1] That caused their financial crisis to ease a little. They started buying war bonds again for the savings account.

And on Christmas Day, although they would not find out about it for five months, Mark Hubbard, Leslyn's brother-in-law, was shot at Bilibid Prison in the Philippines and then set afire while still alive. That December, Leslyn lost most of her immediate family, and she was never the same again.

Leslyn also had to bear up under the unbearable pressure of her war work, and did it surpassingly well: "Whenever she moves into a shop," Heinlein wrote friends in England, "she cuts down absenteeism enormously."

We have statistics on it; it will be possible, when it is all over, to calculate just how many journeyman mechanics she has been equivalent to, in terms of shop hours saved for military productions. Then I shall recalculate it in terms of bombers. She was very anxious when the war started to make something with her own hands, something that would be directly destructive to the Jerries and the Nips. But this is better; had she stayed on the assembly line, she would have been just one productive worker. By using her really exceptional talents as a personnel troubleshooter, she is equal to at least a dozen highly skilled old hands.[2]

Heinlein never talked about their relationship during that time in specifics, except to note that she was sleeping even more than usual for her. But between the lines of what little was said, it can be guessed that her uncontrollable rages became frequent and alarming. She retreated into herself, unreachable—by him. She was reaching out to every individual in her shop even as she withdrew from him. And there seemed to be nothing at all he could do about it but endure.

There was so *much* for both of them to endure.

When L. Ron Hubbard got orders in January 1945 to go to San Francisco, he celebrated by bringing Heinlein a whole box of his favorite candy bars. In sugar-rationed wartime, this was an incredible act of generosity.[3] Hubbard would be in and out of Southern California, and Heinlein suggested that he look up another friend of his, Jack Parsons, a brilliant, self-taught rocket engineer and another personality as fascinating in his own way as Hubbard.[4]

Heinlein had come to despise his job—the waste, the inefficiency, the absolute rigidity of the bureaucratic red tape that tied everything up in knots and made it nearly impossible to get anything useful done. If he stopped and thought about it, his work environment filled him with disgust and moral revulsion—so he thought about it as little as possible.

> I found here my conception of the navy had been incorrect or at least incomplete . . . and I began to be ashamed of being a naval officer (yes, *ashamed*). Presently the heroic exploits of the fleet compensated in part and gradually I began to understand the mechanism which produced, automatically, Snafu Manor. It does not produce bastards but it gives them scope. . . .
>
> —and I *hate* such bastards. Not impersonally, and intellectually, but emotionally—I hate 'em—and it is damn well time more naval officers hated 'em and determined to change the situation which gives them power.[5]

Perhaps one reason Philip Wylie's *Generation of Vipers* resonated so much with Robert was that it explained how much of the bureaucratic situation was a natural consequence of the prewar organization, and of the conditions of American life in general. Both government hiring policies and the Navy's internal working methods encouraged safe, conservative thinking, "never taking your finger off your number," in Navy jargon. But understanding, contrary to the saw, does not beget forgiveness.

In self-protection, he *didn't* think about it, if he could get away with it. He dealt with the problems at hand, one problem at a time. He turned his numerous personal and professional contacts into a support network he could sometimes use to work around the bureaucratic snafu at NAES.

They needed a special speed-camera for certain tests, for instance, but it would take a bale of paperwork and probably two years of waiting to get it through channels. Because Heinlein talked photography constantly with John Campbell and his group, however, he knew that George O. Smith already had the equipment he needed. One tiny problem at a time could be solved—if you didn't mind bending the regs.

But Robert's and Leslyn's health—physical, mental, spiritual—continued to deteriorate. It did not pass without notice. When Henry Kuttner was mustered out of the Army in Red Bank, New Jersey, in January 1945, as too invalid even to be used as a typist, he went back to writing there in New Jersey, to raise enough money eventually to get his wife, Catherine, out of the "filthy climate"[6] and back to California. The Kuttners visited the Heinleins on February 3, 1945, and were taken to "another science-fiction dinner," memorialized by Isaac Asimov:

> As was not true of the first dinner party [for L. Ron Hubbard, the previous year], the food and service were horrible. It embarrassed Bob (who was hosting it) extremely.
>
> The peak moment of embarrassment came when someone tried vainly to get a waiter to bring a fork, and Heinlein, finally, by main force, stopped one in midflight and demanded a fork. The waiter nodded, walked over to another table piled high with dirty plates and assorted garbage, and looked over the scraps for a possible fork. We yelled out, "Never mind," and the diner who was short a fork made do with his fingers.[7]

It was not the dinner that disturbed the Kuttners, though:

> We are rather troubled to realize that both of you seem to be strung on taut wires these days, compared to three years ago . . . After the tensile strength is exceeded, it's a damn sight harder to get the resilience back in a hurry. The hypertension's sneaked up on you both so gradually you're probably not conscious of it, but it's certain there, submerged under the surface, and we are worried about it and expect you to blow up presently and suddenly.[8]

Others were becoming concerned, as well. Heinlein had to assure John Arwine (with some embarrassment, since Arwine was in service in the South Pacific and actually in physical danger):

> By strict refusal to indulge in late hours and to take on things we couldn't do, we are now in as good health as we have been at any time since the war

started and quite prepared to out last and out work any god damn Jap or German civilian.[9]

Early in 1945, Ginny Gerstenfeld came to him with a problem. She had been working on the inflatable life rafts all naval aircraft carried as emergency equipment. Her test sample for a batch of life-raft adhesive had jelled and so, of course, could not be used as an adhesive at all. She put in an order for a replacement test sample when her immediate superior, John Huddick, stopped her. BuAer wanted *this* batch and wanted it *now*. Huddick told her to pass it *as if it had been tested*. Gerstenfeld was astonished—and dismayed: life rafts assembled with this stuff could come apart as they inflated. Her immediate reaction was to refuse the order, but she asked for time to think over the matter and went to Heinlein for advice.[10]

She was perfectly correct—and these were orders she could not possibly obey with a clear conscience. But rationality can destroy you in an unsane situation: if she simply refused the order she might be brought up on charges of insubordination and handed a General Court Martial (GCM)—a very serious matter.[11] The order to falsify test results was clearly illegal, but in wartime, a GCM might not want to hear mitigating circumstances to insubordination. Heinlein told her to sit on the matter for a while—do nothing yet—while he had a talk with her supervisors, probably thinking he might be able to straighten it out with a politician's diplomacy.

But the Adhesives section supervisors didn't see anything out of the ordinary about the situation, anything mitigating at all. BuAer had made its request and that was that. Their job was to accommodate BuAer. Heinlein tried to explain it patiently but found himself getting angry. Somehow, the "discussion" got out of control and degenerated into a shouting argument—with no practical results at all. He found himself shaking and dizzy—and alarmed at the intensity of the emotions he was experiencing.[12]

Heinlein's stress had mounted to the point where he was losing control, and he couldn't afford to lose control—not for himself, not for Leslyn, not for the war effort. He went immediately to his local internist and asked for an evaluation.[13]

The doctor examined him and decided the problem was less mental in this case than physical. He prescribed a mild sedative, "a pleasant mixture of vitamins and barbiturate called (as I recollect) 'Elixir E,' or some such. Either his reassurances or the joy juice or both quieted me down."[14] Heinlein also made further restrictions in his lifestyle to reduce the demands on his time, and with additional rest and the help of the mildly narcotic sedative, he found he could maintain an even strain.

But he had to deal with the immediate problem. Heinlein knew how to handle this—the Navy way: when you can't avoid illegal or irrational orders, he told Gerstenfeld, the thing to do is *not* to refuse them, but to ask for them *in writing*. That way, your own ass is covered, and any repercussions would go to the person who put his orders in writing. In the constipated bureaucratic environment of Snafu Manor, that took care of the problem.

Heinlein might not be enraged any more, but Huddick and his superior had wakened in him a determination to fix this one thing that was within his power to fix here and now; he "taught [Gerstenfeld] how she could trip our chief engineer even more effectively by a two-stage action that was strictly regulation."[15] Leslyn, when she heard about it, told him that she had run into similar incidents, and they bothered her, too, because it meant soldiers would be killed by the stuff coming out of the Naval Aircraft Factory. It was a systemic problem, and the whole of the Navy, Robert came to see, was rotten with it:

> It took a war and the unusual experience of serving in the Navy as a civilian to open my eyes to just how abysmal our shortcomings, as an officer class, are. The class as a whole is so self-satisfied, so shot through with complacent belief in their own natural superiority, that I doubt if the Young Turks in the outfit can have any real effect on it, toward reform. . . . They are a dying breed, like the dinosaurs. The epitaph should read, "Dead through arrogance, ignorance, stupidity, and inability to adapt to a changing world.[16]

The taking of Iwo Jima on March 26, 1945—650 miles south of Tokyo— brought Allied positions within striking range of the Japanese home islands, and the war in the Pacific entered its concluding phase. The Japanese garrison had been told that they would not be reinforced and that they were the last defense of the divine emperor. They were to resist to the last man, and they did—fiercely, desperately, insanely. Much of the island's civilian population they herded onto the heights of Mount Suribachi, where they were encircled. The Japanese forced civilians to—and over—the precipice as they defended the mountain to the last cartridge.

The raising of the American flag on the heights of Iwo Jima's Mount Suribachi on the morning of February 23 was memorialized by sculptor Felix W. de Weldon, and remains an iconic image of World War II.

It was also a moment of critical cusp for the entire remaining history of the twentieth century: on the basis of the battle statistics from Iwo Jima and Okinawa, the General Staff estimated that a conventional island-to-island campaign to invade and conquer the Japanese home islands could result in a range of 250,000 to an inconceivable *one million* Allied casualties.[17] It was a horrifying prospect, from which there was no possibility of escape unless the Japanese could be brought to surrender.

Cal Laning was out of harm's way for the moment—and possibly for the duration. *Hutchins* had dropped him in San Francisco, and he wrote cheerfully of his continuing psychic experiments, with his wife, Mickey, acting as a medium for an appropriately military "spirit-guide."

> During my absence a Navy wife introduced Micky to automatic writing and the principal "spirit" talking to Micky was one "Charles Hammond," formerly a U.S. sailor. H[ammond] predicted the date of my return to the states 5 months ahead of time, to 2 days inaccuracy. He has missed many other predictions. He is valued by Micky and myself mostly for his humorous conversation. We communicate by using two people on a pencil. I enclose part of his scribblings of the night I phoned you, with our translation.[18]

Perhaps this struck Heinlein as a frivolous occupation for a soldier in time of war, but this is not a criticism he would make of a genuine hero like Killer Cal Laning. Heinlein replied that he had given up those experiments,

> for much the same reasons I gave up fooling with hypnosis—did not understand how it worked and had reason to feel that there were unknown dangers with no compensating results.[19]

And he no longer had time for anything but results.

That was only on his end, though: Leslyn practiced "white witchcraft" to ward and protect all their distant friends. Ted Carnell wrote—half (but only half) teasing—to thank her for his and his wife Irene's numerous narrow escapes on duty and during the bombing of London.[20] Leslyn was perfectly serious about her warding and other magical practices: "Swanson, by the way, is one of the victims of my getting cross. He annoyed me once—and a couple of years later he was dead-as-dead."[21]

Laning was called to Washington, D.C., to work on implementing the radar project for Search and Detection. On the way to Washington, he made a side trip to Philadelphia to visit with Robert and Leslyn. It was not the renewing experience Robert had hoped it would be: "Cal was quite definitely surprised and disappointed in me that, after 3 years I was not running the place—lack of stripes and civil service [illegible] he brushed aside—I should at least be mayor of the palace."[22]

Even worse, he brushed aside their concerns about the quite literally deadly bureaucratic snarl at Snafu Manor. "What I'm cross about," Leslyn wrote Laning,

> is that we tried to tell you that there is near sabotage going on up here on the part of the brass hats . . . And, Cal, your remark to Bob about being "disappointed" in him for not "coping with the situation" and "ultimately dominating the problem" was as silly as criticizing a cripple for not being able to make a championship broad-jump . . . What you were doing— whether you knew it or not—was cruelly rubbing Bob's nose in the face that he is just a p.f.c—"a poor f— civilian."[23]

Some "poor f— civilian"s were better off than others: the intense fighting on Iwo Jima and Okinawa sent the first wave of wounded and disabled back to stateside hospitals, and Leslyn found herself with a novel problem in personnel administration: retraining the disabled—particularly the blind—for jobs in war industry. Working through their depression was the hardest part. She set up a special program for disabled veterans using a secret weapon, a personnel blockbuster in the person of Robert's blind machinist friend, Tony Damico. Robert had met Damico in 1943 and tried out on him a story idea he had been kicking around for a couple of years by then—about "Rhysling, the blind singer of the spaceways." He had an idea that a blind man "sees" more beauty than a sighted man. "Tony agreed emphatically and gave me details to back it up."[24] As Heinlein talked with Damico, he found himself forgetting that Damico was blind, and having to remind himself to speak loudly and clearly before he got too close to the power tools in operation. He did not need to identify himself: Heinlein's voice was as fixed in Damico's mind as his face was to his sighted colleagues.[25]

Damico's production was up to shop average, and his safety record was perfect—unusual, even for a sighted machinist. Leslyn brought Damico to the reorientation classes, and the disabled veterans responded to him almost instantly. He got through to them in a way nobody else could. "It was amazing, miraculous—and enough to tear your heart out."[26]

April 1945 was a very eventful month for Heinlein and his circle, as well as for the war. Early in April, John and Doña Campbell's second child was born. They named her Leslyn, and there was no shilly-shallying about god-parenting this time: the Heinleins were her godparents. Also in April, L. Ron Hubbard—across the continent in Los Angeles—took up Heinlein's sugges-tion to meet Jack Parsons.

Parsons was a rocket engineer working at Cal Tech—one of the most bril-liant and creative of the scientists and engineers there, in fact. Heinlein and Parsons might have met in many ways, as they had science fiction and eso-teric philosophy, among other things, as common interests—both fields in-volving relatively small circles of acquaintance in Los Angeles. But as it happens, they met through rocketry, as members of the American Rocket Society. The Sunday *Los Angeles Times* had run an article about Parsons and his coworkers Frank Malina and Edward Forman at GALCIT (the Guggen-heim Aeronautical Laboratory at Cal Tech) in November 1939, shortly after Parsons's paper on powder rocket fuels had been published in *Astronautics*.

Parsons was preoccupied with Aleister Crowley's newly founded religion of Thelema and an adept of Crowley's Golden Dawn variety of sex magic.[27]

Parsons knew Hubbard's science-fiction writing and found him a com-patibly offbeat personality. (When Parsons inherited a mansion in Pasadena in 1942, he had advertised in a local newspaper for boarders to share the house, specifying he was looking for "atheists and those of a Bohemian dis-position.")[28] "Mundane souls," science-fiction fan and resident in the man-sion Alva Rogers recalled in a memoir, "were unceremoniously rejected as tenants."[29]

On April 12, 1945, President Roosevelt died at Warm Springs, Georgia, of a cerebral hemorrhage.

That immense presence, guiding the war, was suddenly gone. The news flashed around the country, and hundreds of thousands of Americans knew grief greater than any war news had brought them. The "backup Presi-dent" the Democrats had nominated less than a year earlier was summoned to the White House to take the oath. Finding Eleanor Roosevelt there, Harry S. Truman civilly asked if there were anything he could do for her. Mrs. Roosevelt blinked owlishly at him: "Is there anything *we* can do for *you*? For you are the one in trouble now." Prophetic words: the Russian army was approaching Berlin; Harry Truman was left to make the unmakeable peace.

The news hit NAES in the last hour of the day shift. Even those who hated Roosevelt were stunned by it. The others grieved. The next day, Robert and Leslyn wore black armbands to mark their mourning. Mourning was nearly universal, and intense. The death of a sitting President is always psychically traumatic for Americans, but this was special, even so:

> Isaac Asimov came to my desk, and in telling me how he felt, said "You see, I've never lost a member of my family before." He made it as a perfectly straight remark, quite unaware that his statement, emotionally true, was not literally correct. Our presidents do not usually inspire such personal feeling, but Mr. Roosevelt did—most loved him, some hated him, none were indifferent to him.[30]

And all the work of the war accelerated as President Truman took office. As the American and Russian armies advanced on Berlin, the Buchenwald concentration camp was liberated (April 11, 1945—the day before President Roosevelt's death), and all the rumors too horrible to be believed were confirmed:

> The bodies of human beings were stacked like cord wood. . . . All of them stripped. . . . The bottom layer of the bodies had a north/south orientation, the next layer went east/west, and they continued alternating. The stack was about five feet high and extended down the hill . . . for fifty to seventy-five feet. Human bodies neatly stacked . . . [a]n occasional limb dangled oddly. . . . There was an aisle, . . . and more stacks. The Lord only knows how many there were.[31]

On April 20, 1945, the day Hitler celebrated his fifty-sixth birthday in his Berlin bunker, President Truman met with Rabbi Stephen Wise, chairman of the American Zionist Emergency Council, to discuss resettlement of Europe's surviving Jews in Palestine. President Roosevelt had tried to set the postwar shape of Europe in February, at the Yalta Conference, naïvely confident of Stalin's good will, but that agreement was already coming apart: Ambassador Harriman warned that Stalin would not honor the Yalta agreements. The peace had just become much more difficult—yet its momentum was unstoppable. There was no question, even, of buying time: on the day that the United Nations Conference on International Organization met for the first time in San Francisco, April 25, 1945, to begin the process of creating the Charter of the United Nations (one of the terms of the Yalta agreement), Secretary of War Stimson was joined in the Oval Office by General Leslie Groves, to brief President Truman on the existence of the greatest, most closely held secret of World

War II, the Manhattan Engineer District and its work on the atomic bomb. This weapon could make an invasion of the Japanese Home Islands—with its anticipated one million Allied casualties—unnecessary. Three days later, Mussolini was torn to pieces by a mob in Rome and his broken body hung from a lamppost. The Russian army entered Berlin on April 30; Hitler—or his body—had disappeared. The Nazi "Thousand-Year Reich" was gone, and the German war machine took only a week to make unconditional surrender. V-E Day—Victory in Europe!

Heinlein had always been apprehensive about winning the war in Europe—up to the very day of the capitulation. "I think we made a Garrison finish and that we were damned lucky to win."[32] Indeed, as the cleanup of the German government proceeded, reports appeared in American newspapers of the superweapons still in preparation, among them a "stratosphere rocket bomb"—an intercontinental ballistic missile that could bomb New York or D.C. from launch sites in Nazi Europe. That one was to have been ready by November 1945.[33]

It would take a real world government to keep this from being just another interlude between wars.

But the war was not over; they had only hit a—welcomed!—cadence: "On V-E day . . . There was very little excitement. In my section I took down the war map of Europe which Isaac Asimov had been keeping, and replaced it with one of the Pacific. For us this is the end of the first act."[34]

As the war shifted to the Pacific—the Navy's War—the Heinleins finally received word about the death of Mark Hubbard, Leslyn's brother-in-law. The full story was deeply moving: he had been on a geological research expedition on the southern tip of Luzon island when the Philippines were overrun on December 10, 1941, and he could not get back to his family in Manila. He dynamited the gold mines he owned, to keep them out of Japanese hands. He made sure that his rolling stock went to the Resistance, then "faded into the bush" and moved from island to island, "using his practical engineering knowledge to set up bush radios and power them with alcohol-driven generators, having also set up the stills to make the alcohol."[35]

Late in 1944, he contracted malaria and, down to less than a hundred pounds, was betrayed into Japanese hands. He endured torture for months, and then, on Christmas Day in 1944, he was shot and burned alive at Bilibid prison, during the Japanese retreat from Manila. Though he was physically disqualified from the draft—"so cross-eyed he stared into his own ears"[36]—he was retroactively enlisted as a "First Lieutenant Infantry (Irregular)" and awarded a posthumous Purple Heart. Keith and the boys received the award and forty-two months' back pay.

Heinlein tallied the war's attrition on his own class at the Naval Academy: the class had mustered in, in June 1925, with 626 members. By July 1, 1945, Heinlein counted 118 left alive and in the Navy.[37] He had lost many friends in the Pacific already.[38]

Nevertheless, the end of the war was clearly in sight, and even the war industries were starting to readjust for a peacetime economy. NAES went back to a five-day workweek and began releasing staff. Heinlein had to take up the slack, taking on the duties of a second engineer. "I expect to drown in a sea of laboratory instructions between now and V-J Day," he wrote to the Campbells.[39]

Even so, Heinlein began to think seriously about going back to writing for a living[40]—not complaining this time, not the result of discouragement. He had developed a permanent case of sinusitis, for which he needed to spend time in a desert climate, away from "Filthydelphia" (as he called the city),[41] baking out the infection. Health issues aside, there were prospects that made a resumption of writing a practical possibility—taking up an actual career, not just a temporary expedient to pay bills. That spring, he had been approached by Westminster Press to write a book for boys. Westminster's Juvenile editor, William Heyliger, had a rough idea of the kind of book he wanted to see—a Jules Verne–esque exploration of what small-town American boys' lives might be like in the future, twenty years or so.[42] The idea was tempting, and Heinlein thought seriously about it. Just before Pearl Harbor he had intended to raise his sights from pulps to the slick magazines and book publication,[43] which pretty much implied then that he would leave science fiction behind. But science-fiction publishing had begun to branch out during the war. Although boys' books did not have any literary prestige, this would be a book publication, and in a field in which he was well read.

But he did not move on it then: there was a war on, and the practical results were daily experiences for Robert and Leslyn Heinlein, reinforced by the art and the music of the war era.

Since late in 1944, Nelson Eddy's recording of "The Ballad of Rodger Young" had been playing on the radio, and that song became intensely meaningful to Heinlein.

Young, an infantry private, had been killed on July 31, 1943, in the campaign for the Solomon Islands. He had been a runt—five feet two inches—and so nearly deaf that he had given up leadership of his squad and asked to be demoted to private because he feared missing an order in battle that would get his squad killed. He was wounded when his squad was pinned down by a hidden Japanese machine gun nest protecting the Munda airstrip on the island of New Georgia, and a second time when his return fire pinpointed his position. He had crept forward and begun to throw hand grenades, covering his squad's withdrawal. He was shot a third time and killed. This was the "finest traditions" of the infantry. When Private First Class Frank Loesser heard about the posthumous Congressional Medal of Honor awarded Rodger Young in January 1944, he had written the song. It was released later that year. For Heinlein, "The Ballad of Rodger Young" was symbolic of the war and of what even he, sheltered and sequestered in the Philadelphia Navy Yard, experienced on a daily basis.

"We had a very nervous-making day last week," Heinlein wrote Campbell,

> but one of the most remarkable and significant of my life. First, it was Leslyn's day to work with her blind marines in the shop—work she loves and has worked up herself, but hard on her emotionally—then, as we came out of the lunchroom that noon, we found ourselves listening to a speaker outside—it was . . . just a guy in uniform talking about action he had seen. But I could not walk on past. The man brought it to you and laid it in your lap, with the blood still flowing. . . .
>
> I couldn't leave until he had stopped talking. I skipped my one and only chance to buy my weeks' cigarette ration in order to hear him, but I could not leave. It was while he was talking that I decided that I could not with clear conscience take a day off until I had my work in better shape.
>
> Well—that night we went across the street to dinner. Miles' and Rod's was crowded. There was a marine with one leg sitting on the couch. He said, no, he wasn't waiting for a table; he had had to move because the hard chair hurt him—his leg wasn't healed. Presently a party started coming out, another one-legged marine with a corpsman, then a bluejacket with a crutch under the stump of his arm, then a man with no legs, carried. The marine said with respect to the bluejacket, "There's the bravest guy in the ward. One arm, one leg, one eye, and one ear—and he *jokes* about it."
>
> We went in as the marine left, feeling pretty shaky, but thinking that the party was gone. But there was still one marine in there, apparently all right. As the last one on crutches left, this one said, "*There's* the way I'm going to walk." Just then a corpsman returned, said brightly, "bet you thought I'd forgotten you," and turned around, presenting his back to the

kid. The kid put his arms around the corpsman's neck and the corpsman carried him out, like a sack of flour. There was just enough of him left to sit down.

I got up and went out and locked myself in the head and bawled my eyes out for about fifteen minutes. Then we took a walk around the block and came back. I was all right by then but I couldn't get Leslyn to eat.

I wish more people could have seen them.[44]

This last year and a half, Heinlein had finally been able to see practical— and satisfying—results to some of the excruciatingly frustrating work he and Leslyn had been doing. On his side, he had been able to find an interim solution to the radome problem, and when Cal Laning was able to facilitate an order for 150 of them, he even moved it from research to production.

The Plexiglas canopy problem was not solved—he had been conducting mostly fruitless discussions with all the local producers of optical plastics and had come to the conclusion that the problem probably couldn't be solved until there was a breakthrough in technology. He did not know until years later that the breakthrough already existed: one of the companies he had contacted, Rohn & Haas, "had a Plexiglas product in their German plant that would have met our specs and the Philadelphia plant knew about it."[45] By that time, he might have been able simply to shrug it off: that kind of self-sabotage was routine by the end of the war, and he had become—somewhat— inured. He wrote up his research in the single engineering report (of about two hundred) that survived from his wartime work in Philadelphia; *Report on Cockpit Canopies—Free-blown Type—Thermal Stability—Evaluation of, by Aeronautical Materials Laboratory Naval Air Experimental Station, Naval Air Material Center Philadelphia.*[46] His successors could build on his research.

The kamikaze problem might not have any solution at all. Various suggestions were made from time to time, and tried out in combat,[47] but nothing they could come up with made any appreciable difference.

On Leslyn's side, the feedback was more immediate. The war matériel produced by the shops she supervised was often in use in the Pacific Theater of Operations (PTO) within weeks—so the reduced absenteeism when she was on the shops' floors translated directly into additional production of war matériel. This must have braced her up emotionally: the psychotic episodes went away, and for a time they had their old, affectionate relationship back.[48]

Heinlein had finally begun to feel that what they were doing was a useful— even important—contribution to the war effort, and he was not inclined to give over any of his carefully husbanded energies to mere entertainment. The Westminster proposal that he should write a boys' book would stay on the back burner *for the duration*.

In the meantime, new markets for his writing continued to open up. Sometime late in 1944, Heinlein's friends and fellow writers Roby Wentz and Cleve Cartmill had become involved in a new pulp magazine chain being fronted by Leslie Charteris, writer of the popular "Saint" mysteries. Bond-Charteris Enterprises were headquartered in Beverly Hills and planned to start some new Western and mystery magazines on the West Coast. They had approached Heinlein to write for a new mystery magazine. Henry Kuttner was already negotiating with Charteris and his group to ghostwrite Charteris stories.[49] Mystery writing was not something that interested Heinlein much, but he passed word along to his friends.[50]

Hardcover publishers were only slowly beginning to integrate science fiction into their lines, but editors of a new medium—small-format "pocket books" (possibly encouraged by the wartime paper shortages)—were eager for science fiction, particularly reprints of the best prewar stories. Several paperback anthologies were in process by 1945, and all of them wanted some of Heinlein's stories. Reprints he could manage; it just required correspondence, not the time and energy of original writing. And the secondary-sales checks, though smaller than the original sale, were a welcomed addition to the severely wounded Heinlein exchequer, still supporting two households.

He got a request to reprint "Life-Line" and again asked Street & Smith for a release. Heinlein generally agreed with Street & Smith's management that the new pseudo-magazine paperbacks were detrimental to the industry and was prepared to use discretion, but what he thought didn't matter. Street & Smith unilaterally changed the terms of the deal: it would release anything for which the writer had an immediate sale use unless the stories were for reprint paperbacks, which would be handled on a case-by-case basis.

Heinlein had been warned of the possibility this might happen: Henry Kuttner had written to him in September 1944 saying Street & Smith was refusing to release paperback rights to him.[51] Heinlein was angry, but he couldn't manage the time to pursue a protracted case through the Pulp Section of the Authors Guild; he would just have to live with whatever crumbs of "found money" Street & Smith would let him have, *for the duration*—which might mean another year or two.

On the morning of August 6, 1945, everything changed.

26

DANGEROUS NEW WORLD

Early in July 1945 the imperial Japanese government had approached the Soviet government to open diplomatic discussions for a negotiated peace. By this time, however, it was clear that what the Japanese wanted was a "breather," to rebuild their shattered war machine, and that was not acceptable: there could be no prospect for an actual peace so long as the military was in control of the Japanese government. From Japan, the Allies would accept nothing less than unconditional surrender. They would not give any guarantees, though on July 27, 1945, in the Potsdam Declaration the United States, jointly with Britain and China, assured the Japanese of humane treatment.

President Truman knew what the Japanese did not: the day before the Potsdam Declaration, the USS *Indianapolis* had delivered the U-235 core of the "Little Boy" atomic bomb to Tinian Island. The plutonium bomb, code-named "Fat Man," to be used after Little Boy, had been tested in the New Mexico desert on July 16, 1945, code-named "Trinity." The results at the Trinity site at 5:30 A.M. were awe-inspiring, terrifyingly far beyond anyone's expectations (the yield was calculated at twenty thousand tons of TNT—the equivalent of two thousand bomber loads, delivered in a single instant at one point on Earth). The detonation flash of light was seen over the entire state of New Mexico and in parts of Arizona, Texas, and Mexico.

Some of the Manhattan Project scientists had argued for a demonstration of the fearsome, awe-inspiring, terrifying new weapon for Japanese and other international observers, but President Truman ultimately decided to use the bomb as its own demonstration. The Japanese high command was known to deal with unfavorable war news by ignoring it—a policy known as *mokusatsu*, meaning "kill with silence." It was hard enough to credit their own reports of the bomb's impact. If the Allies lost the shock value of the weapon, and the Japanese high command minimized the reports of their observers, then the dreaded invasion of the Japanese Home Islands would have to go forward. President Truman could not convince himself to risk a million new Allied casualties—to say nothing of the casualties the Japanese would take. The invasion of the home islands, code-named Operation Downfall, was scheduled for early November 1945. Devastating air strikes on Japanese military and industrial targets would precede Downfall, each bomber now dropping ten thousand pounds of high explosive, in waves of hundreds of bombers per sortie. Heinlein hoped that would be enough—not merely for its *Schrecklichkeit* ("dreadfulness"), but to destroy the Japanese cottage industry in war matériel and bring the imperial war machine to a state of collapse. The lesson of the German bombing of London was not lost on him:

> Modern war is like an iceberg, with the part that sticks up representing the combat forces, the concealed part the industry and train behind him. . . . No. I have a dirty feeling that this is our last chance; we had better make it good.[1]

Early in the morning of August 6, 1945, the specially modified bomber *Enola Gay* approached the industrial city of Hiroshima, flanked by two observation planes carrying cameras and scientific instruments to record the event. They had left Tinian Island at 2 A.M.; now the city's workday was starting. At 8:16 A.M., in clear weather, *Enola Gay* dropped its payload, the U-235 bomb code-named Little Boy. A quarter mile in the air, it exploded, with a blinding flash and an inconceivable rumbling. In the blast and backdraft, buildings simply fell out of the sky, and a cloud of dust and smoke rose into the sky.

The Japanese General Staff sent observers to find out about the mysterious explosion in Hiroshima—thirty thousand deaths, tens of thousands of casualties, hundreds of thousands of survivors digging themselves out of rubble. They learned its cause with the rest of the world, sixteen hours after the explosion—early evening on the East Coast of the United States—when President Truman went on the air and publicly announced it.

Heinlein had known about a secret War Department project involving uranium and did his best to keep talk about the subject in his presence to an absolute minimum, preferably none at all.[2] Now, atomics were a reality—and the future rushed in.

Even while he struggled to grasp the enormity, his mind flashed ahead to the *meaning* of the event. "That's the end," he said flatly.[3] The end of the war, almost certainly—but also, Good-bye to All That, the end of the whole world as it was before August 6, 1945—and also the opening up of an unprecedented opportunity to change things for the better.

American newspapers frantically assembled their reports from every source they could find. Although many people had no way to grasp the scale of the event or its importance, some intuited immediately that things had changed. An editorial in the next day's *Kansas City Star* said: "We are dealing with an invention that could overwhelm civilization."

Two days later, on August 9, 1945, the second bomb, a plutonium bomb code-named Fat Man, was dropped on the port of Nagasaki, with results no less devastating. The same day the Soviet Union invaded Manchuria with one million troops. If Japan did not surrender unconditionally, the juggernaut of "swift and utter destruction" promised by the Potsdam ultimatum was upon them. Japan surrendered unconditionally on August 14, 1945. The war was over.

The news came at 7 P.M. on the East Coast, and civilians and soldiers crowded into public places to share this glorious moment. Heinlein was already at work on the postwar. That day he had written his letter of resignation from the civilian engineer job at NAES, to be effective August 18, citing "Reason for Resignation: (a) End of war. (b) Health—I've been holding together, trying to last to the end. (c) My permanent home is on the west coast; my permanent profession is *not* engineering."[4] He had accumulated vacation time that would carry him through September if he wished, but he had conceived a huge and exciting project that would involve the Navy and American industries, and push America into the future headfirst.

That morning, before the surrender came through, he had sent a five-page memorandum to his boss, John Kean, titled "Tentative Proposal for Projects to be carried on at NAMC,"[5] outlining a program to invest the Naval Aircraft Factory's research and development resources in the next stage of aviation—rockets and missiles. Atomic weaponry was the single fact that overwhelmed, true—but the key to atomic weaponry was deployment. Combine the atomic bomb with the V-2, and—

> 1. I believe it is evident to any sober-minded technical man that the events of 6 Aug. 45, et seq., should cause us carefully to re-examine all plans, proposals, and projects which obtained before that time. . . . In the broad sense, we are out of business, just as thoroughly out of business as were

wooden ships after the battle of the Monitor and the Merrimac. On the other hand we need not be out of business if we reorient, see what may be done with our exceptional resources in the way of trained personnel and mechanical equipment, and then determine what we *should* do in the interest of the United States of America in particular and humanity in general.

A week after hearing the news, he had grasped the essential elements that would shape the postwar world.

It is a simple fact that (1) we can not afford a war ever again, (2) the atomic bomb cannot be abolished, nor can it be indefinitely kept from other peoples. We must ride the lightning and ride it well. I conceive the atomic bomb as being the force behind the police power for a planetary peace . . . such a force there must be if we are not to be ourselves destroyed.

The Naval Air Materials Center, which was the research wing of the Naval Aircraft Factory, should organize "a major project" with all the usual apparatus of its wartime R & D projects, to develop a man-carrying rocket out of V-2 technology. The first step could be an unmanned "messenger rocket" to the Moon, guided by the new radar target-seeking technology, but (eyes on the Navy's target):

It must be noted that it is really much easier to build a successful Moon rocket than to build a proper war rocket. Nevertheless either problem can be used to solve the other—the choice between the two is a choice in diplomacy and politics, not in engineering.

The public, he said, is now ready for such a project, and Robert Goddard had suggested a good test in his 1920 technical paper: the Moon rocket could carry a fifty-pound payload of carbon black. An explosion just before touchdown could disperse it far enough for the mark to be seen on Earth, even by quite low-power amateur telescopes. That was politics. "The unique prestige which would accrue to the United States of America, to the U.S. Navy, and to NAMC in particular cannot be expressed." And that was diplomacy. At the very end, he dropped a little personal diplomacy, concluding with a final, delicate hint that he, Robert Heinlein, was uniquely qualified to guard and guide such a project.

The memo went up channels, from John Kean's office to the head of the

Naval Aircraft Factory, where it quietly died; another copy went through Navy Department channels. Cal Laning, on his way to Washington, could monitor its progress from inside the Navy bureaucracy while working up his own proposals for an artificial satellite program. He appealed to Heinlein for help with writing up his proposal, but in the third week of August, when Laning visited them in Philadelphia, Heinlein was frantic with his own full program, mobilizing support outside the Naval bureaucracy for a government-and-industry "five companies and Guggenheim"[6] rocketry project that would be a necessary complement to the Navy's rocket program. He suggested instead that L. Sprague de Camp might be able to help with the writing. He also gave Laning an introduction to Willy Ley, who had just been hired to work on commercial weather rockets.

A project of the magnitude Heinlein envisioned needed massive support. By excruciating years of exhausting and mostly unrewarding effort, he had positioned himself at the center of a huge web of contacts, and some of them could be turned to account. He began working his network to stir up support for his own government-and-industry rocket project.[7] Before he was ready to leave Philadelphia, he mapped out a route of side trips on the way back to California:

- to a steel plant that could be moved from war production to manu-facturing the specialized alloys needed for rocket research;
- to a high-explosives engineer with the kind of mental flexibility and project-coordinating experience to do the kind of thing Heinlein had done for Buddy Scoles in 1942;
- to the core group of atomic scientists who were fretting over the po-litical and diplomatic implications of atomics in the postwar world.

Heinlein could organize and bring these elements together, but he could not afford to get directly involved in any of these subprojects: when he got back to Los Angeles, there would be important political and propaganda work to do—the political end of this technical project, persuading the taxpayers to pay for it!—and for that, shaking his atomics stories loose from Street & Smith got moved several notches up on his list of priorities. He could no longer afford to be stymied by the kind of arbitrariness and indecisiveness Street & Smith had shown in the summer concerning the release of his story rights.

Heinlein's last day at NAES was on Friday, August 17; on Monday the twentieth he was in New York, at the Street & Smith offices, prepared to

pound desks and make a general nuisance of himself until he got general releases on those stories.

He had asked for those two releases in a telephone call to John Campbell
shortly after the Hiroshima bomb had dropped.[8] Street & Smith had simply
ignored him for two weeks, apparently unwilling to let go of the rights it had
acquired, in Heinlein's opinion, by fraud[9]—and even with his personal guarantee that he would not sell to cut-rate competitors. (The last reprint deal he
had set up, for "Life-Line," just before the bomb was dropped, paid him as
much for the story as Street & Smith had paid for the initial sale—hardly
"cut-rate.")

Heinlein had to be very, very firm with Campbell: either he got those
releases—now—or he would go over Campbell's head, to Ralston, the managing Vice President of Street & Smith, and take up the whole sordid business, point by point. He got the releases—the only ones Street & Smith would
give him then.

This kind of personal confrontation was emotionally difficult for him, and
only the fact that it was utterly necessary could have forced it on him now.
Campbell, he knew, was caught in a bind, trying to accommodate him, both as
a friend and as one of his most popular authors. Campbell wanted him writing
for *Astounding*. But Campbell was also too ready an apologist for Street &
Smith, too loyal an employee, making absurd "defenses" of the policies.[10]

Heinlein had been putting off his difficulty with the John Campbell/Street
& Smith relationship since 1941[11]: he simply could no longer do business
with Campbell and still maintain their friendship.[12] Finding a good agent
moved up on his list of priorities.

The next day Heinlein was back in Philadelphia to finish packing up for
the move. John and Doña Campbell would take the few household furnish-
ings that were worth shipping, so he and Leslyn could fit almost everything
they needed to take into *Skylark IV*. But he had one more good-bye to make
before he took off.

Ginny Gerstenfeld had been out of town for the last couple of—
crowded—weeks. Her fiancé, George Harris, who was also her ice-skating
partner, had come back from the South Pacific in the summer, and they had
competed in the ice-skating championships in Lake Placid, New York. They
placed second in ice-dancing, concentrating so intensely on the competition
that they missed the news of the dropping of the bomb. When the Japanese
surrender came, on August 14, George and she were the only Navy personnel
in Lake Placid, so Gerstenfeld put on her uniform and went out marching
with the Army.

She was back in Philadelphia late in August and met Heinlein, to say good-bye. They talked a little about the bomb, about what atomics might mean in the future. "He left me on a street corner in Philadelphia with a kiss. Our first."[13]

Robert and Leslyn left Philadelphia in *Skylark IV* on August 23, 1945, stopping near Lewistown, Pennsylvania, where Robert wanted to rope in Charles Edwards, the chief accountant of the Baldwin Locomotive group of companies. Baldwin's Standard Steel Division had extensive in-house experience in building the new jet and rocket engines, and the company had a history of advanced research in aeronautical materials.

Edwards was receptive; to give him help convincing the Baldwin board of directors, Heinlein's old boss at NAES, John Kean, would be approaching Frank Tatnall, the Baldwin-Southwark Research Director, about the project. Baldwin could put effective outside pressure on the Navy for a rocket program.

Next stop: La Porte, Indiana, to see Doc Smith. Doc was enthusiastic about any sort of rocket research, and, so far as Heinlein was concerned, a perfect candidate for project manager:

> Although he is fifty-five years old, he is a better man than I am, more energetic and with a faster mind . . . experienced and successful in the direction of research teams.[14]

By the time the Heinleins got to Indiana, however, Smith's useful industrial contact was no more: he had gotten into an argument over Kingsbury Ordnance's poor quality control and quit. Now he was working for Allis-Chalmers, as Assistant Chief Metallurgist—and Allis-Chalmers had no interest in rockets or in research of any kind. Farm machinery was their bailiwick.[15]

But it was still a fruitful visit: Smith gave him a completely different strategic approach to atomics he hadn't heard before. Heinlein set out his understanding of the current situation in a letter that month to John Arwine:

> As I see it, we finally finished off the war by plunging the globe and ourselves in particular into the greatest crisis, the most acute danger, in all history. I am not deploring it. I know that the discovery of atomic power was inevitable and I know that you can't turn the clock back, nor turn sausage back into hog. It is here. We've got to face it and deal with it. I am overwhelmingly thankful that we got it first and that it was brought out into the open by the war. Now we have a fighting chance to save civilization as

we know it and the very globe we stand on. If the Axis had gotten it first, we would have had no chance. It might have been a thousand years before freedom and human dignity would ever again have been known.

But I am bitterly afraid of the way we may handle it. There are two crazy approaches to the matter which are beginning to be heard. The first says, "We got it. We'll hang onto it. From now on they got to do what we tell them to" . . . The second crazy viewpoint regards the atomic bomb as just another weapon, powerful but bound to be subjected in time to an effective counter weapon, and that as a matter of fact things haven't changed and let's get back to normalcy and forget all about war.

There is a third reaction, one of deploring the whole thing, of passing resolutions expressing regret that we ever used so barbarous a weapon, apologizing to the poor mistreated Japs, and calling on Congress to do away with the whole thing, tear up the records, make it a lost art, forever proscribed as forbidden knowledge.

You might call these three types of dunderheads the bloody minded, the common or garden unimaginative stupid, and the custard head. God deliver us from all of them.[16]

All right-minded people—of course Heinlein's position—wanted to place atomic weaponry under international control.

Smith distrusted the idea of international control and suggested instead that the United States should maintain a big military presence and "go it alone," perhaps enforcing a *pax americana*.

Heinlein did not agree, but Smith made cogent practical arguments, which Heinlein nevertheless thought might not be politically achievable: the arguments sounded too much like the prewar debates about arming Guam and were likely to be scotched by squeamishness about high taxes and the rush to "normalcy" and washing machines.[17]

From La Porte, Robert and Leslyn went to Kansas City for a family visit with Louise and the three little Bacchi, and then on to Santa Fe, New Mexico, to see Robert Cornog.

They had not heard from Cornog since the start of the war. Heinlein's work on getting the rights back from Street & Smith for "Blowups Happen" and "Solution Unsatisfactory" must have brought him back to mind: Cornog had given him the physics background for those stories. It was suspicious—the kind of suspicions Heinlein would not have voiced to anyone—that so many of the atomics men he had known by name or by reputation before the war quietly dropped out of sight. Cornog had popped up again at just that time: he had been working for the Manhattan Project,[18] designing instrumentation for the bomb. He and Heinlein had arranged a quiet visit now that the lid of absolute secrecy was off. Cornog's plans for the postwar world fit well with Heinlein's: he was looking around for work in rockets and was quietly discussing such a project with an engineering firm in Pasadena.

The rocket men in those days were sheerly brilliant, innovative. Progress could be expected to be meteoric. Cornog had known Jack Parsons for years, of course, but during the war, he had had a chance to work with Dr. Tsien Hsue-shen, the Chinese rocket scientist who had founded the Guggenheim Aeronautical Laboratory at Cal Tech (GALCIT) before the war, with Parsons, Frank Malina, and Theodore von Kármán. In 1944 GALCIT became the Jet Propulsion Laboratory, and Dr. Tsien would go on to work with the V-2 project in this country after the war. Dr. Tsien was one of the few people Heinlein had ever met whom he recognized immediately as smarter than he.[19] Cornog introduced Robert and Leslyn as political operators to the group of Manhattan Project scientists who were worrying over the postwar implications of atomics. The scientists had already faced up to the hard facts of dealing with the genie they had let out of the bottle. "Well, they fell on our necks. They practically kissed us—at finding a layman of their own view point. We . . . found ourselves drafted into the position of unofficial political advisor for the nonce."[20]

Two years earlier, H. G. Wells had published a pamphlet, *Phoenix,* talking about the cutting edge of the massive coming revolution, as a fruition of his Open Conspiracy, articulated as early as 1926 in *The World of William Clissold.* These young men were the ones he was talking about, with their "clear, cold, hard realization of the essential rightness, and therefore the essential community, of their ideas."[21] Here was the fruit of Wells's foresight, coming together before Heinlein's eyes—humbling and inspiring at the same time: "The men who built the atom bomb asking us quite seriously what they should do next to achieve their social aims," he wrote wonderingly. And then, "I was floored." It was something worth giving your life to—and just the inspiration the Heinleins needed at this moment.

> Leslyn and I felt our hearts lifted up to discover how real, sincere, and conscientious was the feeling of responsibility these boys have for the power they have let loose in the world. There will never be an atomic war if they can help it.[22]

The scientists' particular problem at the moment was that they were gagged by the security restrictions—and they knew that anything they sent up "through channels" would get to Leslie Groves's desk and be killed there. Heinlein's recent experience with Navy bureaucracy suggested a way around the blockage: address any statements through channels directly to the Commander-in-Chief.

None of them had thought of that approach. They had been organizing themselves for some time already and had worked out a consensus among the thousand or so scientists:

We found, when we arrived, that they had formed an association, comprising an overwhelming majority of the professional men there, for the specific purpose of convincing congress and the country that such should be done. They propose that the so-called secret be made public, but that all atomics work throughout the globe be under the surveillance of international police, acting for a planetary super-government which would be armed with the atomic bomb. They say that atomics work is of such a nature that it cannot be concealed and therefore could be policed. They believe that the alternative is an armaments race between nations, each developing its own atomic weapons, each in fear of the other. If war came (as it would!) under such circumstances, we would be subjected to surprise attack which would destroy us in a matter of minutes.

So far as I can see, I am forced to agree with them.[23]

If the United States tried to hold on to bomb technology, it would be hated and feared as no other nation in history. "We will automatically be marked for destruction in a hundred secret conclaves," Heinlein wrote.[24]

The greatest danger, he thought, came from the smaller nations now that the basic research had been done and it was potentially a cheap weapon.

Shucks . . . we could be wiped out by Switzerland, or Sweden—or Argentina. . . . I would judge that, using the Smyth report as a laboratory manual, ten million dollars and three years should enable any competent research team to build a workable bomb. Bolivia could afford it. Portugal could afford it.[25]

The one state he did not at this time suspect was Soviet Russia. Uncle Joe had too much at stake to risk: "Forget Russia—she has the same overpowering reasons for wanting to keep the peace that we have. She is a 'have' nation. She can't afford this new sort of war. She has too much to lose."[26] Dealing with Russia was a tactical necessity in making this whole scheme—as impractical as it sounded—work at all: once an arms race started, it could not be stopped; the one chance at survival was to stop the arms race before it got started:

> We have *got* to get along with Russia. . . . The help of Russia is indispensable to the setting up of a world police force. Right now, while *we* have the bomb, we might be able to talk business with her. Later on, when Russia has the bomb too, there is much less chance of getting them to give up their secretive, nationalistic ways and to surrender their own military might to a superstate.[27]

But he was not sanguine about the realistic possibilities:

> Russia has reason to be suspicious of us. Twice since World War I the United States has invaded her for the open purpose of overthrowing the present government. For years we refused her diplomatic recognition and we still continue to subject her, throughout our newspapers, to an unbroken stream of abuse, lies, and suspicion. (That Russia has treated us badly in many ways is beside the point—I'm talking about why she mistrusts us. Why it will be so difficult to get her to go along no matter how generous and altruistic a scheme we may propose.) When you combine the suspicion Russia has of us with the suspicion that we have of Russia you get a combination which looks hopeless—unless both sides are utterly convinced that survival depends on it.[28]

The dynamics of the Cold War, that had dawned on Robert so chillingly in 1940, with the writing of "Solution Unsatisfactory," were a cold and present reality. Robert and Leslyn decided that their first priority was to help these dedicated young scientists ride the tiger. Robert immediately began to factor them into his plans.

They were not able to visit the Trinity site itself, more than fifty miles southeast of Albuquerque—the entire area was still cordoned off—but Cornog gave them a small chunk of the bubbly, translucent green glass they were calling "Trinitite"—the sand fused into glass beneath the first atom bomb blast. Leslyn, Robert sensed, was afraid of it, and he handled it gingerly himself, since it was mildly radioactive. He kept it shielded in metal, in a brick fire-safe in their basement.[29] The Trinity site was opened up by General Groves a few days after they left, on September 9, 1945. Already the ranchers forty to sixty miles from the Trinity site were reporting that their cattle had lost patches of hair on the sides exposed to the bomb blast or to the radioactive dust from it—the first victims of fallout. What they might find next April, when this generation started dropping calves, was a chilling thought.

They stopped at Meteor Crater in Arizona—"an eerie, frightening place. I still want to go to the Moon, but, if it's like this sample, I want a good bar handy."[30] The desolation might have served as local color for an article that was coming together in his mind—"Men in the Moon," about placing atomic weapons research on the far side of the Moon.

Then on to the coast by way of Boulder Dam, through Los Angeles, and down to Laguna Beach arriving September 9, for a visit with Leslyn's sister and nephews.[31] Keith had remarried, but her new husband, John Adams, had been sent to the Philippines, too, to her horror. Now she was recuperating from an operation she had had in August—for uterine cancer. After a two-day visit, the Heinleins returned to Los Angeles on September 11, 1945—not quite home at last.

They found Hollywood somewhat changed—and not for the better:

Item: Instead of the clear, golden, overpowering sunshine Los Angeles county now has Smog, occasioned apparently by the synthetic rubber plants and sich. Not a thick Pittsburgh smog, not even the Philadelphia variety. Nevertheless there is a high haze of which the natives (and I) complain bitterly. The City Council threatens to take Steps, involving precipitrons and such. I hope they do. I want a sun that will knock you down dead if you fool with it, the kind of sun we saw coming across the desert. This sunshine takes half an hour to give a sunburn instead of the former fifteen minutes. I wish I had a vacuum thermocouple at hand.

Besides that prices are considerably inflated, particularly real estate and restaurant prices. Food in the markets is considerably cheaper and better in quality and variety than in Philadelphia, but a meal in a restaurant costs about what it does in Philly. Housing is almost unobtainable. However I think both of those items will improve rapidly as the Boomers head home, looking for jobs, and as the Army concentrations hereabouts thin out. The

Japs and the Nisei [interned by President Roosevelt during the war] are coming back which will help.[32]

Hollywood, he concluded, isn't what it used to be, and possibly never was.[33]

They also found that their tenant at the Laurel Canyon house had not moved out yet, and apparently had made no preparations to do so. After the Kuttners moved out in 1942, a local realtor had found a tenant for them, Johnny Paxton, a screenwriter for RKO Pictures. The termination-of-tenancy notice their real-estate agent had served on him turned out defective in its language, so they started the process all over again. The new notice gave the tenant a month's notice and another month to vacate. They could not expect to take back possession until sometime in October.[34] The house looked more run-down than simple lack of maintenance could account for. "Our poor house has been mistreated and it will take me three months to get it into proper shape again."[35]

The trip to Laguna had postponed their housing problem, but now they had to face it. The small town of the prewar years could not accommodate the wartime population boom: *all* housing was gone. *All* hotel rooms were filled. Overcrowding had become so critical that there was now a city ordinance limiting hotel stays to a maximum of five days, *for the duration,* until the wartime jobs went away and the city's industrial Okies went back where they came from. The Heinleins circulated the word that they were back and reconciled themselves to moving every few days.

Heinlein set up his typewriter wherever there was a table. Once he made arrangements with his sister Mary Jean to receive their mail, he dashed off update letters to the three people most closely involved in his rocket project: John Arwine, who was functioning as a kind of senior adviser; John Kean, who was working up industrial contractors from the other side of the country; and Cal Laning, his mole inside the Navy bureaucracy. Cal gave him the welcomed negative assurance that the project Heinlein had proposed in his August 14 memo had at least not yet been killed.[36]

As people got the word they were back, their combined business-and-social life picked up again. The business part took priority: Heinlein had decided that working as a political operator again was more important than writing for market—not partisan politics *per se,* but as a way to get some actual facts about atomics injected into the national political process. They had dinner with Robert and Susie Clifton on September 17, to get a sense of the new political landscape in Southern California. Susie Clifton—the model for the Sacramento lobbyist and political operator he had put into "Magic, Inc."[37]—had continued plugging away at Democratic politics during the war and was now a major party operator in the state. There would be strings attached to getting back into California politics, but Heinlein had worked his way up to the county and state committees by 1938, positions of some influence; the potential power might well be worth the effort and expense. Heinlein expressed cautious enthusiasm for the prospect, and the Cliftons put him to work right away: they gave him the job of convincing Bette Davis to stop obstructing a local resolution for internationalization of the bomb, in the Hollywood Independent Citizens Committee of Arts, Sciences, and Professions. "Here in town," he said dryly, "my cursory knowledge of such things is enough to make me a local expert. One thing leads to another."[38]

When Cornog came out to Pasadena, he and the Heinleins met for dinner at the home of Jack Parsons. Parsons's GALCIT projects had gone over to the newly formed (1944) Jet Propulsion Laboratory, and he had formed Aerojet to work on rocket-assisted takeoff for the new jets that the Army Air Force was developing. But Aerojet had just been acquired by General Tire, and Parsons was at loose ends. The timing was perfect to rope him into the Moon rocket project.

Parsons's personal life was a little messy: during the war, he had gotten involved with Aleister Crowley's new religion, Thelema, and his occult magick-working group, the Ordo Templi Orientis (OTO). His first wife, Helen, had run off with the head of the local chapter of the OTO, but Parsons didn't seem much disturbed by that fact: he had taken up with Helen's eighteen-year-old sister, Sara Northrup, a vivacious blonde he would introduce casually as "Betty."[39] Nevertheless, Parsons, almost completely self-taught, was an original creative thinker—one of the founding geniuses of American rocketry in the generation after Robert Goddard's pioneering work.

The Navy's plan to set up a guided missile research center at Point Mugu brought Buddy Scoles to Southern California, too, and he wanted to help.[40] Heinlein put Cal Laning in touch with Scoles.

Laning was arranging to have a Navy edition printed of the Army's Smyth Report on the technology of atomics—issued just two weeks after the Hiroshima bomb was dropped—but he had sent copies of the historic first edition to Heinlein in Philadelphia. What with the move, they had gone astray. Laning had already resent one to the Laurel Canyon address, and he sent another, care of Heinlein's sister Mary Jean, who was providing them an accommodation address. This copy was inscribed to Heinlein:

> Received from Manhattan Publicity about 15 August First Edition! For Lt. R. A. Heinlein in appreciation of assistance to this office on radar development and general "anti-Kamikaze" technical advice.
>
> /s/ C. B. Laning[41]

Even with the stress of overcommitment and having to move every few days, Heinlein found things about Hollywood that were still right. He wrote encouragingly to Henry Sang, who intended to follow them to Southern California. After warning Sang of the changes he would find from the glowing descriptions quoted above, Heinlein went on:

> Now for the pleasant aspects of Hollywood: The place really hasn't changed much. People stroll and loaf on the Boulevard. Breakfast is served from nine till noon. The whole joint has a small town honkytonk air, a little more crowded but not much. No one seems to be in a hurry. Sports clothes are normal dress and a housewife shopping in a sun suit is a common sight. But I have almost wrecked the car once or twice over the prevalence of midriffs. Midriffs on sunsuits we are used to but have you ever seen a formal afternoon dress which was a midriff style? The woods are full of them. The women here are clean, bare, and usually pretty, frequently beautiful, just as I remembered it. Special selection has definitely resulted in a much higher level of pulchritude and they let one take a good look at it, bless their well scrubbed little hearts.
>
> I just took time out to stare out the window at royal palms, fig trees, pepper trees, deodars, and eucalypti. The sun is brighter, despite the smog, than I ever saw it in Filthydelphia. It is good and the war boom did not ruin it.[42]

As the end of September approached, it became obvious that Paxton (their unwanted tenant) was not going to vacate their house in Laurel Canyon. He would have to be evicted—forcibly if necessary. They had Sam Kamens, their lawyer, institute eviction proceedings. Within a few days, the lawyers worked out an agreement for him to vacate on November 10—too late, unless the winter rains held off, to do any serious exterior repairs this year.

In the meantime, the stress was taking its toll on Leslyn: she was obviously worn out, her heath deteriorating. Since they were having to live in hotels anyway, they decided to make it count. "On Sunday we move to Murrieta Hot Springs Hotel, Murrieta, California," Heinlein notified his former boss at NAES, John Kean, who was also working on the rocketry project,

> where we expect to remain a month to six weeks (depending on our ten-ant) and where we expect to soak up some sunshine and rest. It is a resort hotel, with mineral spring, swimming massage, and desert sunshine. Leslyn needs it badly and I can use some myself. Leslyn has been quite sick this week, nervous indigestion, throwing up steadily, and down to 78 lbs. in weight. Our bastardly tenant was simply the last straw which keeled her over.[43]

They had come across the resort in 1941, looking for a weekend getaway. Leslyn had called it "an old haunt of my childhood, which is *just* the sort of health resort we are looking for."[44] Now the season was over, the rates were reasonable, and the half desert there still had good weather this late in the year.

Packing up for the trip to Riverside County, Heinlein pulled out the piece of Trinitite Cornog had given him and tried to find out if it would fog a photographic plate. It was *very* radioactive: the rubber band that held it to the plate fluoresced bright green. He stored it away in its metal box, very carefully.[45]

The spa was just exactly what they needed. They both studied the new material they had to master and tried to reclaim their equanimity:

> We sun bathe, we take the baths, we walk, and we sleep. Leslyn has ac-quired a fine all-over mahogany tan and has gained six pounds. I am tan-ning somewhat more slowly but feel more nearly well than I have for four years. Sinusitis, acquired in Filthydelphia, still plagues me, but I hope to bake it out.[46]

His typewriter was his constant companion, and the R & R allowed him time to think and catch up with friends and family, still very widely dispersed. John Arwine made Lieutenant Commander. Robert's oldest brother, Larry, had been one of the four Army people who had constituted the entire U.S. occupying force in Japan for about three weeks[47] (he had, in fact, been the first American ashore on the island of Honshu); their younger brother, Clare, had been sent to Japan to be part of the military government there, until the original plans were called off, and his ship was sent to Korea instead.

Heinlein's Moon rocket proposal was winding its way up the Navy's bureaucratic hierarchy, Cal Laning tracking its slow progress. Heinlein's part in the initial contact-making was done, and now the circle of people available to work on that and related projects continued to grow. Laning had gotten in touch with Jerry Voorhis, who was about to introduce an internationalization bill into the House, and Willy Ley.

On his trips to Southern California, when he wasn't staying with the Heinleins, Ley had always stayed with his friend Fritz Lang, who now was talking about doing a Moon rocket picture. Ley put him in touch with the Heinleins. But Robert Heinlein's goals had shifted somewhat from the big rocket project he had discussed with Cal and Willy and others in Philadelphia, and he needed to articulate it for them.

> The change of intention is this: Leslyn and I feel that the present crisis, in re atomics, is so critical that nothing else is of comparable importance. It is my carefully considered opinion that the United States will probably be destroyed as a nation, with a loss of life in excess of fifty million, within the next ten years, unless present trends are drastically changed. Since we believe this, we intend to spend as long as necessary in political action primarily. I will probably do little if any writing not directed toward politics, one way or another.[48]

Changing present trends, even with all the resources he could muster, was a tall order, and the odds, he knew, were against being able to do it—rapidly enough to matter, anyway.

The political situation did not occupy his mind completely; lately he had been corresponding with Armand Coign, a reader—not an organized fan hooked in with Forrest Ackerman's crowd—who had written him a couple of searching, philosophical letters about "The Unpleasant Profession of Jonathan Hoag." Heinlein found the correspondence helped keep him oriented to what was important, building his life strategy from the ground up.

> I don't know the explanations of this world, but, to my mind, blind chance and materialism are nonsense. As for myself, I think that I have lived a very long time and I do not think that any catastrophe, not even the destruction of my body, can destroy me. I expect to go on. For what, I do not know, but I have a great zest for living and a feeling of kinship for everything that grows or moves.
>
> My inner, basic evaluations, quite beyond logic and not subject to ver-

bal defense, classify some things as good and some as bad. I want to fight and strive for what I feel is good. This is translated into overt action, for which I am never certain; nevertheless, I do not stay my hand. I do what seems best and hope that my moral judgment proves to be correct. . . . This globe is not big enough both for me and for creatures who will not grant to others equal rights. In the long run (a few thousand years, perhaps,) one or the other of us has got to go. . . . The people of good sense and good will have got to be awakened to the nature and urgency of the crisis or the custard heads and the bloody-minded will most certainly lead us to our doom.[49]

A year later, he told Coign his task at hand lay with the immediate and practical necessities:

Although a "mystic" by nature, I conceive my immediate task to be with much more mundane matters. I have certain small bricks to lay in a great wall which I did not design and will not now see completed.[50]

And each persuasive article he churned out for popular consumption was a brick in the overall design.

Murrieta Hot Springs proved conducive to work: Heinlein made good progress on his atomics articles. By the end of September, he had finished the first of a series, "Man in the Moon," and he started another article about how to prepare for atomic war.[51] As he got back into the swing of writing, and the demobilization commenced, his friends were beginning to move around. Jack Williamson and the Kuttners were expected for long visits soon. As soon as the Heinleins got back into the house, it would fill up—with Henry Sang and his fiancée, among others. They were finally able to pay forward the Campbells' hospitality to them in 1942.

They particularly looked forward to seeing L. Ron Hubbard and his wife, Polly. They had always met Hubbard on the East Coast (he had a permanent address at the Explorers Club); Polly apparently preferred to stay behind in Seattle. Now Hubbard was about to be medically retired in December and told Heinlein he and Polly wanted to move to Hollywood.[52] Hubbard had recently been hospitalized on the East Coast with an ulcer and other war-related complaints, but now he was in Southern California on temporary duty—and was coming to spend a few days at the spa with Robert and Leslyn.

Leslyn, Robert said, had an affair with Hubbard;[53] this is the most likely time for it to have taken place. Robert's regard for Hubbard—and Hubbard's for him—was not affected in the least.

This was a very profitable visit; when Hubbard heard that Heinlein was looking around for an agent, not one of the homegrown science-fiction boys, he was able to recommend Lurton Blassingame, a prestigious New York agent. Blassingame, a former (Hollywood) writer himself, who had started his agency in 1929,[54] agreed to take Heinlein on as a client, based on the commercial viability of his prewar science fiction. He agreed with Hubbard's assessment that Heinlein was "wasted on pulp."[55]

The first project Blassingame was given to handle was the article Heinlein had just completed, the first of his "world-saver" articles, "Man in the Moon."

Hubbard was with them at Murrieta Hot Springs on October 21 when they got word that Paxton had vacated the house early and they could take possession.

SETTLING IN

The house was an absolute mess, and in the necessary cleaning up and clearing out, they found more damage than they had known about. Paxton had left his dog in the house rather than taking it outside to do its business. There were corners soaked with urine and other stains. The floor had to be sanded back to the wood and refinished. Some of their personal items were missing, and some of the packing cases they had left in the garage had developed dry rot.

Repairs would make quite a dent in their nest egg of war bonds—the small amount they had managed to accumulate since Skipper died. Heinlein heard that Buckminster Fuller was going into the housing business; he had designed a "Dymaxion" House, to be built using aircraft manufacturing methods. It was supposed to cost just about what a Cadillac would cost. Heinlein placed an order for a Dymaxion; they could raze Quintus Teal's old place at 8777 Lookout Mountain and live like human beings in a modern house—the Model-T version of a modern house, at any rate.[1]

Even before unpacking the household goods, they set up Heinlein's work area and made a second desk in the studio for Hubbard, using packing boxes and an old door. They both had to get to work churning out pay copy. Although Leslyn's health had begun to improve, she was still suffering from exhaustion. Her doctor ordered her confined to bed. First she had placed wards around the house to protect against the ghosts the Kuttners had noticed in 1942—"especially one against a thing that keeps trying to come up the basement steps."[2] To keep her occupied once her magical work was done, Heinlein asked her to take over the correspondence. She could answer most of the letters longhand, from her bed.

Henry Sang and his intended/significant other, Grace Dugan (called "Cats"), showed up, as promised. Heinlein encouraged Sang to try commercial writing: "The guy can write and should be a fine addition to us typewriter bums. I always feel a glow of wellbeing when I entice a working man into giving up and becoming a consumer."[3]

They cobbled together another makeshift desk for the studio. The five of them figured out arrangements to keep out of each other's way—a rule of silence in the working studio, for example, with a 25¢ fine to enforce it. They ran the food arrangements on the Navy's wardroom plan, with Henry Sang acting as mess treasurer. It worked, after a fashion—and Heinlein was glad he was able to offer hospitality in this housing crisis, to pay forward the kindness John Campbell had shown, taking him and Leslyn in when they came east in 1942.

> We will probably have more house guests from time to time for several months; five more of our friends face immediate eviction—they may land on us. Fortunately the somewhat anarchistic arrangements of Squalid Manor is suited to accommodating an indefinite number of civilized people.[4]

However, some of the people he had invited from the East Coast could not be accommodated even under these circumstances. Heinlein asked Campbell to tell Ted Sturgeon, who was going through a rough time, that they had no space at all at the moment. Sturgeon was offended—not because the invitation had been withdrawn, but because Heinlein had not had the *cojones* to write to Sturgeon personally and do his own social dirty work.[5] Heinlein apologized: "You are perfectly correct," he told Sturgeon.

> I was wrong, and I most humbly ask your forgiveness. . . . I mention these things not as a true defense but in hopes that you will be tolerant of my failure and believe that I was rude through negligence rather than intention.[6]

Sturgeon was forgiving, telling Heinlein it's best to get these things into the open air rather than allow them to fester.[7]

Hubbard was not doing too well, either; he was jumpy, nervous, and unstable—everyone had noticed it. He had a tendency to fly off on obsessions that were not always very firmly grounded. He had become a "high-maintenance" friend, and it took hours of working with him to keep on an even keel—a situational problem, Heinlein was sure, and one he would recover from in time.[8] The war had been hard on a lot of people—though comparisons with blinded and disabled veterans of the fighting always made him feel small. Hubbard was in the "wounded veteran" category and deserved all the patience Heinlein could muster.[9] When John Arwine came through Los Angeles, demobilized, in November, Heinlein was glad to see him put heads together with Hubbard and come up with a project that would provide satisfying and important work for themselves:

> John Arwine and Ron Hubbard have whipped up a plan to organize *all* the scientists for the purpose of channelizing some of the rational thought for this [atomic weapons] crisis. I think they can accomplish it. They have organized CalTech already.[10]

Heinlein's writing business was already picking up. Just as he had expected, the first reprint request for one of his atomics stories came through in October 1945, less than two months after the bomb. Crown Publishers was bringing out an anthology with "Universe" and "Goldfish Bowl." Edmund Fuller, the publisher, also wanted "Solution Unsatisfactory" and offered a half-cent a word—a very good price for a reprint. He was going to shoehorn it into the anthology over the objections of the editor—Groff Conklin— who was supersensitive, he said, on the subject of "anti-Soviet" propaganda (though he admired Heinlein's other work).[11] Well, for that matter, so was Heinlein. This choice for the anthology particularly pleased Heinlein because "Solution Unsatisfactory" had put a female physicist on display, and he lost no opportunity to remind people that this whole discipline had been kicked off by Dr. Lise Meitner—a woman who had been virtually written out of the histories of atomics and who was, really, the only completely indispensable mover and shaker in it.[12]

To his new agent Heinlein proposed three books, two of them postapocalyptic novels: *Hour of the Knife,* "a novel of how America cudgeled the rest of the world into accepting a world state," and *After Doomsday,* a novel about the twenty-minute World War III. The third proposal was *How to Be a Politician,* and with 1946 being an election year, it ought to appeal to civic-minded voters. For this, he reverted to a sentiment expressed early in the war to John W. Campbell:

> It requires no special aptitude nor talent to be active in politics. Patience is the only requisite. Second, the things which may be learned by direct political activity are worth knowing, difficult to acquire secondhand, and almost a *sine qua non* in understanding the world around us.[13]

In December 1945, Heinlein also struck a deal with Hubbard about *For Us, the Living,* which had been packed away all during the war years. Hubbard would rewrite it, to turn it into a salable novel, and take top billing. He would have a free hand, so long as he didn't denature the political and social evaluations in the book—and they would split the proceeds fifty-fifty.[14] Almost immediately after they signed the contract, however, Hubbard gave up his space at *chez* Heinlein and moved in with Jack Parsons. Nothing was ever done on *For Us, the Living.*

Jack Parsons rented out rooms in the large house in Pasadena he had inherited, seeking odd and eccentric characters of all kinds. This suited Hubbard's needs, and he moved in. Parsons had assumed leadership of the Los Angeles chapter of Aleister Crowley's Ordo Templi Orientis (OTO), and he gave weekly presentations of the "Gnostic Mass" in the attic of his house.

The Gnostic Mass was a theatrical piece, rather than a true religious rite, suitable for introducing newcomers to the basic concepts of Crowley's religion of Thelema.[15] Heinlein himself had attended a performance, saving the program and a paperbound copy of Crowley's *Book of the Law* for future reference.

Parsons found Hubbard "the most Thelemic person I have ever met."[16] Hubbard immediately became comfortable in Parsons's eccentric ménage— and soon started an affair with Parsons's live-in lover and magickal assistant, Sara "Betty" Northrup. Although testimony on the subject is divided,[17] it appears that Parsons had little objection to make when Hubbard took over Betty's affections; Betty's affections were habitually strewn around pretty indiscriminately, and not just as a matter of adolescent friendliness—a fact Robert did not pick up on immediately, but Leslyn did:

> . . . she even had Bob convinced that I was being catty until about seven other women whom he admires for their friendliness to other women told him the same things about the lovely Sarah (then known as Betty) . . . that I had been trying to get him to listen to.[18]

Instead, Parsons immediately threw himself into a magickal project to call down an elemental to take her place.

Heinlein did manage to write at least one piece of fiction in December 1945. In keeping with his resolve to explore new fields, it was a mystery story, of the hard-boiled variety—"rough stuff," as he called it.[19] Henry Kuttner had already struck a deal with Leslie Charteris to ghostwrite for *The Saint's Choice*: Charteris would resell Kuttner's stories as his own work, since his name commanded several times the rate Kuttner's did. Cleve Cartmill and Roby Wentz were already working on Charteris's editorial board, as was A. P. White,[20] which made it virtually a West Coast operation. White suggested Heinlein try his hand at mystery,[21] and Cleve Cartmill talked him into it.[22]

Charteris needed a great deal of new material, and the repairs to the house were eating a big hole in the Heinlein exchequer. Heinlein said he would come up with an outline for a mystery book and began casting around for a short story subject. He came up with a sexy "magic mirror" show he had seen at a Hollywood bar on Sunset and Gower before the war. Taking his cue undoubtedly from Jack Woodford's advice, he started "They Do It with Mirrors" with a sex-angle hook: "I was there to see beautiful naked woman," he started. "So was everybody else. It's a common failing."[23]

His typewriter was malfunctioning intermittently so Heinlein drafted much of the six-thousand-word story working longhand for the first time in years. He created a brand-new pseudonym for mystery writing—Simon York. Charteris bought the story for *The Saint's Choice*.

In January 1946, he wrote another of his atomics articles, "America's Maginot Line"—this time pointing out how inadequate conventional weapons were to address the strategic demands of atomic weaponry. Cal Laning said he had an "in" at the War Department, and Heinlein sent him "Men in the Moon" so he could walk it through the security-clearance process. Initially, Heinlein hadn't wanted to get security clearance, distrusting the narrow self-interest of the Navy's bureaucracy. "America's Maginot Line," he knew, was certain to anger people in the military hierarchy: Heinlein was arguing that America's arsenal of very expensive conventional weapons was no more effective against atomic weaponry delivered by missiles than France's Maginot Line had been against Germany. Offense had so far outrun defense that trying to rely on conventional weaponry was virtually an invitation to a preemptive strike with atomic weapons.

I believe that present plans for national "defense" are not only useless and a waste of money but tend to lull the public into thinking that "older and wiser" heads have the situation under control. . . . Unless we abolish war (*war*, not the atom bomb!) by forming a world sovereign power, armed with the A-bomb and the latest gadgets and charged with enforcing disarmament with especial reference to atomics, I think a new war, resulting in the destruction and conquest of the United States, is inevitable.[24]

Moreover, the market was changing so rapidly that the normal delay could make these articles obsolete. But Laning argued that his contact might be able to shorten the delay from months to a matter of days.

Heinlein then finished "Pie from the Sky." He had one or two more articles in him, but it was already becoming clear that events were changing so fast around him that the role he had originally conceived for himself, getting the Moon rocket project going, was not going to materialize. Internationalization was their last, best hope. That was not likely, either:

> I have strong and terrible forebodings. I see around me a nation hell-bent on new washing machines, Congress diddling around with mighty trifles, and the military engaged in a bureaucratic cat fight over consolidation while brasshats talk quite seriously of aircraft carriers, super-block-busters and such like obsolete junk. . . . [25]

In a similar vein, he confessed to Campbell: "Frankly, I'm scared—no longer on the thalamic level, but a cold apprehension of disaster on the cortical level."[26] But he had about reached the limit of what he could do with his existing resources. He decided to submit the articles for clearance—just to test the waters and see what the official attitude would be. He finished "Why Buy a Stone Ax?" on January 10 and sent it to Lurton Blassingame: "The most expensive thing in the world is a second-best military establishment."[27] Three days later he sent off "The Last Days of the United States." And that would be the last of the atomics articles for a while.

Laning's confidence in his inside man was well placed: even though the clearances for "Men in the Moon" (written in September 1945) did not come through until June, the January 1946 articles, with the help of Laning's contact, were cleared in January 1946. "Your services in re clearance invaluable," he wrote Laning:

> I am no nearer publication than I was; it appears almost impossible for a person without an established reputation to get such things published. Nevertheless, they remain on the market and my conscience is easy for having tried.[28]

Writing these articles had been a chore—and probably a useless chore. Heinlein never felt as comfortable doing persuasive articles as he did writing fiction. "It has not been easy," he told John Campbell, "roughly ten times as time consuming as writing fiction."[29] But some of the pressure to get things moving was starting to come off since Jerry Voorhis had introduced an internationalization bill into the House; Heinlein and his friends would no longer have to beat the bushes themselves to drum up support. Heinlein thought he might be able to let up on the world-saving writing for a while.

In addition to the writing, his political work was ramping up. He helped found Americans for Democratic Action, for the explicit purpose of getting communists out of the Democratic Party. It was a futile gesture: the very first meeting was targeted for CP takeover. He later concluded that he could have figured it out even sooner if he had not been away from the players and the game for such a long time.[30]

This was very frustrating to him. "I dislike to see communism being made a political issue in the United States," he told Fritz Lang,

> because it is a false issue which plays directly into the hands of the most reactionary elements in the country. . . . Communists never manage to elect communists . . . but they have great luck in electing guys like Bilbo. The activities of the American communists are the greatest single asset of the black reactionaries in this country.[31]

Heinlein's self-education was continuing, too. Bob Cornog had settled in Hawthorne to work for Northrup Aircraft, and the advanced ideas Cornog was tossing off were dazzling—orbital rockets, robotic navigation by the stars, jamming guided-missile controls, which Cornog called "the Heinlein effect" and incorporated into Northrup reports on guided-missile research. Cornog suggested the need for a space station above the Heaviside layer, since radar had a hard time "seeing" missiles coming in vertically. Heinlein had suggested a geostationary orbit that would always stay over one spot on the planet, but Cornog was holding out for a lower orbit.[32]

Early in February 1946, the Navy bounced a radar signal off the Moon, and Laning reported that the Navy bureaucracy was actually apportioning real money for rocket research.[33] Gleefully, Heinlein suggested propaganda bits that could be turned to the Navy's use for lining up even the most conservative Admirals behind the space navy concept. He recycled Dr. Robert Goddard's carbon-black idea one more time and gave it a twist to prang the conservative generals:

> Imagine waking up some morning to find that Stalin has announced that a party has landed on the Moon and has claimed the Moon—and that the autonomous socialist soviet republic of Luna (six men, two women, all

Russian scientists or technicians) has petitioned the USSR for membership and the Grand Soviet Council has been graciously pleased to act favorably! Then suggest that the Russians, with their great fondness for gargantuan poster display, might decide to put a hammer-and-sickle on the face of the Moon—an easy job to do with a jeep rocket and a few tons of lampblack, crop-dusting style, on that airless planet where even finely dispersed pigment settles straight to the ground and stays put. I should think that while an admiral is thinking about that horrid prospect—a hammer-and-sickle he can stare at from his front porch; a USSR base which *looks* at him— would be just the time to get a favorable endorsement out of him for rocket money.[34]

Their early effort was beginning to pay off; things were in good hands and progressing. That would clear his desk somewhat. "I am probably one of the most confused men in the United States," he told Willy Ley: "By nature I am a man with a one tack [*sic*] mind. I can handle a large number of details if directed toward one objective—but plural objectives throw me into a neurosis of frustration."[35] With the reduction of his objectives to something more manageable, his new agent, Lurton Blassingame, wanted him to get back to writing fiction.

Blassingame reminded Heinlein of the old request for a juvenile from Westminster. Heinlein was still dubious: the publisher wanted a short-term future set in a small town, which seemed unrealistically claustrophobic to him. Also, Heinlein had disliked having to work within the conventional taboos of writing for the pulps: writing for children would have even more, and more restrictive, taboos.

He had other possibilities if he wanted to take them: John Campbell wrote asking for more stories from the Mañana Literary Society.[36] Heinlein wrote back, telling him about the book proposals he had on the fire, and other projects he was fiddling with in the back of his mind.[37] The "Risling story"[38] was starting to take shape for him, to wind up the Future History. He might fill in the gaps one day, but there was a catch to working with (or for) Campbell: Street & Smith was still buying only "all rights," and Heinlein would no longer sell anything but first American serial rights. In fact, he wanted a general release of everything of his that Street & Smith held and let Campbell have it with both barrels, calling him on Street & Smith's inconsistency.[39]

Campbell's boss, Henry Ralston, accidentally saw the letter and objected to some of Heinlein's intemperate language, which forced Heinlein to assemble all the exchanges he and Campbell had had on the subject over the last six years. Ralston's impression of Street & Smith's policies with regard to rights didn't match up to the actual behavior of the company executives—though Heinlein did apologize for the intemperate tone of the letter. He had to draft the letter three times because just recounting the history factually made Campbell look inconsistent and careless, and he wanted to avoid putting Campbell under the hammer.[40]

Ralston replied after three weeks, with a blanket no—no bulk transfers of groups of stories, and no release of rights "for publication in the so-called pocket-book style of publication."[41] Since Heinlein was unable to guarantee that Street & Smith would release the properties, that letter virtually killed his chances of negotiating deals for radio or motion pictures. "I can't do business with no authority to negotiate and no knowledge of exactly what S&S will approve."

> In Hollywood stories are submitted simultaneously and you conduct a Dutch auction. I suppose Ralston knows that—he should—in any case I called his attention to the special circumstances and asked for a specific answer, but he ignored the matter. I'd be a fathead to go to all that expense [of special prep] on a story, only to find that S&S would not release. Ralston's fine, paternalistic policy simply means that I can't possibly sell to the movies the stories I've written for [*Astounding*].[42]

He hadn't mentioned the boys' book to Campbell, perhaps because any book pitched to fifteen-year-olds would probably be too young for *Astounding*'s audience, which seemed to be made up of established professionals, if Campbell's reader polls could be trusted.

That February, Heinlein's old boss at the Philadelphia Navy Yard, John Kean, sent him an inflammatory newspaper clipping: an article bylined Alfred M. Klein had appeared in *The Philadelphia Record* on January 20 portraying Heinlein's work at the Naval Aircraft Factory, along with that of Isaac Asimov and L. Sprague de Camp, as a silly and expensive blue-sky wartime boondoggle by the Navy Department, who had set them up in a laboratory. Campbell was quoted as supporting the idea of such a blue-sky project—and then he went on to puff his own (*Astounding*'s) role in technological prediction, citing his efforts to get Cleve Cartmill's story "Deadline" published against the opposition of the FBI. Campbell had been the self-aggrandizing subject of *New Yorker* articles in August 1945—so John Campbell and his silver tongue saved the Allied war effort all by himself.

Heinlein found Campbell's statements highly inappropriate. "It tended to produce in me an explosion—which I restrained as I have had too many personal beefs lately, anent getting the house back, etc., and other grief."[43] Sprague de Camp was ready to sue the *Record*—and Heinlein took the question to his local lawyer, who thought they might have a grounds for an action in libel. If de Camp brought suit locally, Heinlein would support it.[44] As to Campbell: "I am honestly fond of John; he has many virtues as well as faults and I will make every effort to avoid parting brass rags with him, even though I hardly expect to sell to him again."[45]

With their wartime savings dwindling, Heinlein started thinking seriously about that boys' book for Westminster. The main sticking point was writing for *juveniles*. He talked it out, over dinner, with Fritz Lang. Lang had become something of a "friend of the family"—one of those wise, older, and more experienced men whose advice Heinlein valued and sought out. Periodically Lang would call up the Heinleins and invite them out for dinner.

This time, Lang listened seriously to Heinlein's objections and thoughtfully told him he wasn't getting the big picture. Writing for children could actually be more important than writing for adults: it was a chance to shape the attitudes of the next generation[46]—and what could he possibly do that was more important?[47] That was a very persuasive argument, and Cleve Cartmill said essentially the same thing.[48]

> One added: 'Hell, don't write "boys books," write a book that you know a boy would like to read.' Nevertheless, such was my lack of confidence, that my first step was to go to a book store and buy more than a dozen books which the shopkeeper assured me were ones that were popular with the present-day kids. Most of them concerned aviation and were heavily filled with cops & robbers sort of adventure.[49]

He started taking notes, keeping in mind the injunction *not* to write a "boys' book," but instead to write "a book that you know a boy would like to read."

The other major option he had been considering was getting back into Democratic Party politics. Since returning to California, he had been approached twice to run again for the state legislature. He couldn't work up any enthusiasm for that prospect. On February 16, 1946, he wrote the Honorable Jerry Voorhis that another offer had materialized—one more tempting:

> Judge Bob Clifton called up the other day and suggested that I try for Congress this time, since Pat is going for Senate and no major liberal

democrat has announced. Off hand I was opposed to the idea—I spent every cent I had and wore myself out with very little help save from you and a handful of others when I tried to displace Charlie Lyon [in 1938]. Public office *per se* has no lure for me. But I admit it would be wonderful to participate actively in the present crisis.[50]

Heinlein's main objection was the prospect of having to go through the same meat grinder he had been through in 1938. Neither his health nor Leslyn's could take the strain at this point. Leslyn had gained back some of the weight she had lost but, even confined to bed and with no social life at all, she collapsed unpredictably, with alarming tachycardia and other disturbing symptoms:

She was very sick again this morning, recurrent vomiting, heart pounding, etc. She just has no reserve; she wore herself out on the war, completely. I realize now that she did the final year on nerve. Not that I could have stopped her—she has courage, that one.[51]

He couldn't turn Clifton and the local Democratic organization down flat . . . but he couldn't see doing it at all without Leslyn's indispensable help.

I finally answered that I would run *provided* a committee called on me to inform that the funds were already in the bank, including salary for a suitable manager approved by me, and provided that the campaign *per se* would not be my worry. I doubt very much if that will happen. I could make it happen by a little maneuvering but I won't walk across the street to seek office until someone else evinces very serious interest. I don't want anymore campaigns funds "pledged" and then almost impossible to collect—I've been through that mill![52]

That should be the end of the matter, Heinlein thought: "It has not been my experience that candidates are often drafted for candidacy quite that emphatically."[53]

In the meantime, he started on the boys' book for Westminster. After his current round of research, Heinlein had come to the conclusion that he could do this. He told his agent:

Off hand, I think of a juvenile in S-F as being a book of the Tom Swift and the Motor Boys type, aimed at the early 'teens and having heroes three or four years older than the reader, so that he may imagine that he himself might take part in such adventures in the near future. The style should be fast, simple, and not written down. It should hook as fast as a pulp story and have continuous adventure, with authentic science, not too much elaborated. No sex or love interest, naturally. I have no doubt of my ability to do such stories, well enough to meet the competition.[54]

He came up with a melodramatic action plot like the Tom Swift stories, about boys building a rocket. Blassingame forwarded the outline to Heyliger, the editor at Westminster, and suggested that Heinlein hold off doing anything about the book until March 7, when they would have Heyliger's reaction.[55]

That didn't suit Heinlein: once he was charged up to write, he usually just threw himself into the project until it was done. He occupied himself fretting over an offer from Crown for an abridged collection of the Future History stories, but the publisher, Edmund Fuller, was talking about some very extensive editing that might gut the series.[56]

When the phone company finally activated their telephone service toward the end of February, Heinlein wrote a few letters notifying friends and business contacts. The one to L. Ron Hubbard and Jack Parsons would do double duty: neither of them had been seen in weeks, and the Great Silence was puzzling; he had forwarded Hubbard's Navy pension check to Parsons's address in Pasadena, but Hubbard needed at least to tell him what he wanted done about his mail.[57]

Heinlein started to write, concentratedly, *The Young Atomic Engineers and the Conquest of the Moon,* with some deliberate fudging on the science and particularly on the engineering, to bring all the action within the framework of the story.[58] He kept in mind his conversations with Fritz Lang, since the same considerations would apply to any film.

And in fact, as he wrote, he started making notes for a book on interplanetary travel that would parallel *Young Atomic Engineers* so he would have a proposal to take to Lang as the basis for the collaborative film project Lang had been talking about. Heinlein was in touch with current politics and current engineering on the problem, and it could work very well as a pseudo-documentary of the immediate future.[59]

But the important thing was the tone of *Young Atomic Engineers.* Above all, he did not want this to be what H. G. Wells had once called the "artificial and meretricious frivolity . . . forced upon the young."[60]

Before starting this story I established what has continued to be my rule for writing for youngsters: *Never* write down to them. Do not simplify the vocabulary nor the intellectual concepts. To this I added subordinate rules: No real love interest and female characters should be only walk-ons. The story should have lots of action and adventure . . . [and] plot use of difficult intellectual or scientific concepts; the kids *enjoy* getting their teeth into such—much more so than their parents.[61]

The life lessons he had learned from the Horatio Alger books were still relevant here and now. Later, he explained his intentions:

I have been writing the Horatio Alger books of this generation, always with the same strongly moral purpose that runs through every line of the Alger books (which strongly influenced me; I read them all). "Honesty is the best policy."—"Hard work is rewarded."—"There is no easy road to success."—"Courage above all."—"Studying hard pays off, in happiness as well as in money"—"Stand on your own feet"—"Don't ever be bullied"—"Take your medicine"—"The world always has a place for a man who works, but none for a loafer." These are the things that the Alger books said to me, in the idiom suited to my generation; I believed them when I read them, I believe them now, and I have constantly tried to say them to a younger generation which I believe has been shamefully neglected by many of the elders responsible for its moral training.[62]

The conventions and taboos of children's writing were restrictive, but he decided he could work within the taboos and still show different racial and cultural types working together. He firmly instructed his agent to withdraw the book from any publisher who objected to this feature of the book:

I have deliberately selected a boy of Scotch-English pioneer ancestry, a boy whose father is a German immigrant, and a boy who is American Jewish. Having selected this diverse background they are then developed as American boys without reference to their backgrounds. You may run into an editor who does not want one of the young heroes to be Jewish. I will not do business with such a firm. The ancestry of the three boys is a "must" and the book is offered under those conditions. My interest was aroused in this book by the opportunity to show to kids what I conceive to be Americanism. The use of a diverse group . . . is part of my intent; it must not be changed. . . . I am as disinterested as a referee but I want to get over an object lesson in practical democracy.[63]

The writing went rapidly: he sent off the first several chapters to Blassingame early in March and finished it by the middle of the month, dedicating the book to his nephews through Leslyn's sister, Keith—Matt and Colin Hubbard. Blassingame said it looked like a very salable manuscript, calling it a "good job"[64]—though Heyliger did reject the book: rogue Nazis on the Moon were a little far out of his line. Blassingame took the book to Winston, which was establishing a line of science-fiction juveniles. He could offer it as the first of a series, for Heinlein had several series titles already outlined in his head: "the YAE [Young Atomic Engineers] on Mars, or the Secret of the Moon Corridors, the YAE in the Asteroids or the Mystery of the Broken Planet, the YAE in Business or the Solar System Mining Corporation."[65]

Heinlein was brimming over with more book ideas. He wanted to do a book about power politics in the atomic age, developing the ideas in "Solution Unsatisfactory." He also wanted to do a World War III novel, sparked off by an action of the rogue Nazis he had put into *Young Atomic Engineers*—a novel that would graphically show the probable results of an atomic war. Then a contemporary-scene book about the engineering and political and organizational effort that was going into making space travel a reality. This one he planned to show Fritz Lang, as they had talked about this kind of thing for the space movie Lang wanted to do next.[66]

But what he went to work on immediately was his handbook for practical politics. He would have to work very fast and finish in one month in order to catch the election-year trade.

As he started *How to Be a Politician* in March 1946, peace descended suddenly on *chez* Heinlein: the Sangs found a cottage in Fallbrook, California, a hundred miles southeast of Los Angeles, and left the Heinleins by themselves in their own home for the first time since Pearl Harbor, as Bill Corson had stayed with them until they left for the East Coast in January 1942.

In the course of the past year the house has sheltered a total of nine writers; we have been running a sort of separation center, hostel and rest camp for the members of [the] Mañana [Literary Society] leaving the service. Most of them are scattered by now.[67]

That spring, Leslie Charteris's *The Saint's Choice* failed, and the editors returned the manuscript of "They Do It with Mirrors." Mystery writing didn't really appeal to Heinlein—and in any case, Kuttner's experience with Charteris turned out not an unalloyed success,[68] so Heinlein never went back to mysteries. When the manuscript was returned to him in May 1946, he sent it on to Blassingame, who eventually sold the story to *Popular Detective,* a minor tec pulp.[69]

Nevertheless, things were finally beginning to look up for the Heinleins. Leslyn's health continued to improve, and she had regained enough weight that she popped a brassiere leaning over one day.[70] In February Robert had found an effective treatment for his chronic sinusitis—half a million units of penicillin taken as a fog in oxygen, supplemented with penicillin-saline nose drops between treatments. He could breathe normally again for the first time in years.[71] Breathing normally was turning out to be a mixed blessing, though. He could smell the alcohol on Leslyn's breath when she fell down, and it was unpleasantly likely that some of her nervous prostration had been, at least in part, "falling-down drunk" these past several months. At Robert's insistence she "went on the wagon" for a time, until Robert was satisfied he had been mistaken.[72]

It was not for him to criticize anyone's ways of coping with ill health and fatigue, but as a practical matter, he got rid of all the liquor in the house— and became irritated with L. Ron Hubbard when he found him sneaking in liquor.[73] He stopped drinking himself, to minimize temptation. The temporary abstention was lifted—and Leslyn collapsed again, alarmingly. "She is off the wagon now," Heinlein wrote to John Arwine in May, "with my advice and consent."

> Her capacity for liquor is just as large as it ever was, not large but adequate. She can drink as much or more than I do and not show it—or she can suddenly collapse and have to go to bed when she has not been drinking at all and has had adequate rest.

Heinlein had no experience at all in dealing with alcoholics—and as great a capacity as any man for seeing what he wanted to see:

> Partly by elimination and partly by analysis, I am now of the opinion that her trouble derives almost entirely from too great a sensitivity to the woes of the world—she can't really get interested in her own garden when there is famine abroad and while the shadow of the Atomic War hangs over us.
>
> Truth of the matter is she needs serenity to recoup, but she is not vegetable enough to accomplish it easily in a world in which there is now no

serenity. She knows too much about what is going on and her imagination integrates too well.[74]

But such self-deception works well only when it puts the issue out of mind. They had a halcyon period for a few months of relative good health in the spring and early summer of 1946 and were able to resume a social life.

They were both excited by the V-2 tests that started that April in the New Mexico desert, at White Sands. Cal Laning wrote to them about the first one,[75] and the newsreel footage they saw in a Hollywood movie theater sparked a desire to see one up close.[76] Laning didn't have any pull himself but thought they might be able to get press credentials. If they could all get there at the same time, they could have a private "rocket convention." And Laning had some real progress to report: the Bureau of Aeronautics had set up a "Space Ships" subsection with its own personnel.[77] Space was on the Navy's formal agenda now, and once a project is in the budget, with its own bureaucracy, it can become self-sustaining. The Navy had put in its claim for priority in American rocketry.

With that news, Heinlein could—finally—retire from the struggle in good conscience and become an applauder-on-the-sidelines. His own rocket project disappears from his correspondence.

They set about the finicky task of finding hotel accommodations in the New Mexico desert that June, and were able to get reservations at a whimsical hotel they had run across in Las Cruces, "complete with The Dog with Eyes As Big as Saucers" who functioned as night watchman.[78]

These V-2s let the American rocketry program take over all the German rocket research—a fitting turnabout, as the Germans had pirated Goddard's original patents to get their start. The Army of Occupation had captured one hundred partially assembled V-2s in the Harz mountain manufactures—and the core of the cadre of German rocket scientists who had fled Peenemünde to avoid being captured by Russians. Nazi scientists were at the heart of the American rocket program. For Congressional background on the developments, Heinlein recommended that Jerry Voorhis get in touch with Willy Ley, who was also in Washington, D.C., at the time:

Willy is former science editor of PM, an anti-Nazi refugee, a New Dealer, and a rocket engineer. He is working with Laning. Willy's decision not to take Hitler's shilling may have won the war for us, in sober truth, for it was one of his former assistants [von Braun] who built V-2—after Willy left.[79]

Leslyn had encouraged Laning to bring Willy Ley into the loop about their planned "rocket convention" in New Mexico, with some confidential advice: "Consult with Willy about this—but don't let Willy have a veto vote. He's one of the prima donnas, himself. We love Willy better than some of the other boys—but he has to be gentled along like the rest of 'em."[80]

Something odd was going on with L. Ron Hubbard and Jack Parsons. Late in February Parsons had acquired another sex-magick assistant, a gorgeous, exotic green-eyed redhead named Marjorie Cameron, whom he referred to as an "elemental." She was going by the name of "Candy," short for "Candida" (the yeast that makes candidiasis yeast infections).[81] Heinlein was one of the first people he introduced her to. She later remarked that she didn't take much to Heinlein: he was "too slick, too Hollywood," with his ascot and pipe.[82]

Parsons had put up most of the capital to form a business buying and selling yachts. Hubbard and Betty Northrup were heading off to Florida to buy the first vessel, which they would sail back to California. It seemed a dubious venture to Heinlein:

I don't understand Ron's current activities. I am considerably disturbed by them—not angry but disturbed on his own account. I don't think he is doing himself any good. As near as I can tell at a distance he seems to be off on some sort of a Big Operator tear, instead of straightening out and getting re-established in his profession.[83]

Lurton Blassingame wrote expressing doubt about the commercial viability of Heinlein's proposed political book. Leslyn answered for him, so he wouldn't have to break his concentration:

It is too late to stop now. It's like trying to catch up with Man o' War on foot, to withdraw him from the race after he's reached the quarter-post! Joking aside, Bob's method of writing is to start very promptly once the decision to do a certain job is made, and he writes seven days a week until finished—a full-length book in about three weeks. It is disastrous for him to stop in the middle of a piece of work—the writing time already consumed and the waiting to start a new job after stopping are a total loss financially—and it subjects him to considerable nervous shock. He has a one-track mind—once he's on a given track. . . . Consequently, you've got to stop him before he starts. He'll gentle down and take the next lane over—and go *whoosh* down *that* track.[84]

The book was done within the month—even before Winston, too, rejected *Young Atomic Engineers* (on April 19). But the "Why Buy a Stone Ax?" article was picked up for the July 1946 issue of *Facts* magazine.[85]

The other articles were not faring so well. Blassingame returned the manuscript for "America's Maginot Line" after it was rejected by *Salute* magazine, *The American Mercury, Infantry Journal,* the United States Naval Institute *Proceedings,* and *The Christian Science Monitor.* "Men in the Moon" received clearance from the Navy, and *Collier's* was interested in it—or at least *part* of it.

Heinlein thought he might improve the chances of *How to Be a Politician* with a foreword by some highly respectable political figure, and he wrote to two men whose prestige put them above partisan politics, Henry Stimson (1867–1950), President Roosevelt's Secretary of War, and Justice Owen J. Roberts (1875–1955), a Philadelphia lawyer and the elder statesman who had conducted the court of inquiry in 1942 that sent Admiral Kimmel to a General Court Martial over the Pearl Harbor attack. Neither of them was interested in doing an introduction for his book. "I found it amusing," Justice Roberts wrote to Heinlein's agent, "but cannot say much for its literary quality."[86] Heinlein's third choice was Bernard Baruch, who was busy at the time fronting the "Baruch proposals" for internationalizing atomic weapons and research to the United Nations. The book began circulating, though with disappointing results. An unnamed editor at William Morrow wrote Blassingame that it was "a book that would be good for people to read but, from past experience, I don't think many will."[87]

Since the idea of his running for Congress had quietly been dropped, it was unlikely that Heinlein would do anything more political this year than "campaign for candidates for Congress who seem to understand the meaning of atomics and One World."[88] There were no Democratic candidates for president who fell into that classification. He granted President Truman's essential goodness but found the lack of practical options frustrating: "Poor Mr. Truman," he said, "is a very good man and tries hard but he is not up to it."[89] The matter of international cooperation on control of atomic weaponry was such an overridingly important issue that Heinlein forced himself to wrap his mind around an impossibility: his own liberalism might force him to change parties.

If things shape up the way I expect them to, next year I will reregister Republican and start plugging for Stassen. I think that Roby [Wentz] and

Cleve [Cartmill] will probably join me in the endeavor. Forty-four in-structed convention votes, won early in the campaign, might start a landslide.

Yours for a planetary government![90]

Some of the attraction wore off, though, as the presidential campaign ramped up: Harold Stassen came to California to stump for a reactionary senator who had just voted against a loan to Britain "and every other pro-gressive measure."[91]

Heinlein was keeping a close watch on the world political situation. The British loan was critical, he thought, if only because it would allow them to import more food. Food was a problem everywhere in the world—and one that could easily become a flash point. Whenever possible, he sent packages of sugar and chocolate and canned hams and this and that to Ted Carnell, since American rationing was winding down. Rationing of some items had been discontinued months before. In the United States, items like butter and sugar—and tires—were hard to find, but they were no longer officially con-trolled substances. The rest of the world, Britain included, was much worse off: "We have wired our representatives that we want drastic rationing re-sumed," Heinlein wrote Ted Carnell in June 1946:

and any other measures necessary to squeeze every possible calorie out of this country and into China, German, Italy, India, etc.—not on Britain's account; if I read the news correctly you folks are not hungry even though your diet is perhaps not very interesting. I fear the aftermath of the pres-ent world food crisis. We can throw our victory away in the next twelve months, if we have not done so already.[92]

(Carnell's toddler, the Heinleins' godson, Michael, got most of the candy, but Carnell wrote back his personal thanks—it had been seven years, from 1939, since he had tasted chocolate![93])

In the meantime, Heinlein kept plugging away. "My agent is getting a little vexed with me," Heinlein wrote to John Arwine, "as he has been opening up a market for me for science-fiction slick":

He is demanding copy of that sort and I am about to satisfy the demand, a few shorts first, and then a serial or two. It is a fair speculation; the market is there, created by the war—and the stuff that does not sell can be peddled to my established market in pulp.

I can't get interested in writing which is not, to my mind, socially useful. By continuing to do the sort of speculative (or "Science") fiction I
used to do, but slanted for slick, I can satisfy my itch to preach and prop-
agandize, reach a bigger audience and make some dinero.

(I should have been a preacher. Had I been able to retain the puritani-
cal, Bible-Belt faith in which I was reared, I would have been. As it is, I am
that uncomfortable and ill-adjusted animal, the preacher with no church,
a windmill tilter—a *persona* you can recognize!)[94]

He recycled some of his back file of notes for a Future History story and
wrote "Free Men" as a fiction complement for his "How to Be a Survivor" article. Blassingame commented that the scale of the story dwarfed the characters; it read like a French Resistance story and would be very hard to sell in
this market.[95]

Jack Parsons's April business deal with Hubbard had fallen through in an
embarrassing way: by May 10, Parsons was suing Hubbard and Betty
Northrup to recover some of the boats they had bought, and Heinlein heard
that Ron and Betty were heading for New York. In the meantime, the Heinleins
had taken in another of Hubbard's discarded ex-girlfriends—Vida Jameson.[96]

Vida was the daughter of Malcolm Jameson, a naval officer and science-
fiction writer who had died of cancer in 1944. She told Robert and Leslyn
Heinlein she had taken up with L. Ron Hubbard in 1945, during the time
he was shuttling between D.C. and New York and Philadelphia, and had
been Hubbard's date for a dinner party Heinlein had thrown for him and
other visiting science fiction firemen.

She received her discharge from the WACC in California and Ron wrote
to her and suggested that she come down and be bookkeeper and business
manager for [Parsons's business venture] Madcap Enterprises. After a couple of months in a welter of unpaid bills, unanswered letters, and confused
finances which characterized the four or five companies which Jack, Sarah,
and Ron had floated she was pretty thoroughly browned off, but, amaz-
ingly enough, had been able to restore a semblance of order to some of the
enterprises and had, at the same time, gained some weight, got over the
worst of the discharge jitters, and improved her health. Sunshine, fresh
air, and good cooking (her own!).[97]

Vida Jameson's life had fallen apart when her father died, and again when
Ron and Sara/Betty ran away together in April 1946. Robert and Leslyn liked

her—a practical-minded liberal whom Leslyn called "practically a twin sister."[98] They rescued her from "Madcap Enterprises," to live with them in Hollywood. She was one of the civilized people who fit into their domestic arrangements without a hitch.

After a week or so, Vida decided to return to New York to visit her mother. Robert and Leslyn had hopes of persuading her to come back in the fall and stay with them for a longer period. The re-formed Mañana Literary Society unanimously agreed. "She leaves a large hole in our pleasantly wacky lodge."[99] Robert and Leslyn put her on an airplane and took Henry Sang and Grace Dugan to Arizona for an impromptu wedding (the Heinleins were best man and matron of honor) and working vacation, combining pleasure with pleasure.

> I got spiffed on champagne and attended a local Sabbat at the boiling mud pits below sea level in Imperial Valley. . . . The Sabbat was a great success and I made a speech, but it is the last time I ever try to dance every dance at one of those affairs. We lolled in the sun at Palm Springs thereafter and admired the snow on the top of San Jac and the undressed sunburned women and gradually oozed back home.[100]

This vacation really felt like a vacation. "I do believe," Heinlein told John Campbell, "that at last I have found out that the war is over."[101] He was ready to dive back into a pile of manuscripts—short stories—before Willy and Olga Ley arrived in July or August. But there would be a spot of journalism first, when they went to the V-2 firing in June—if they could get tires, which were no longer rationed, but not readily available (unless you were willing, as Heinlein was not, to go to the black market). Henry Sang offered them his car, which had four new tires—or they might take a bus, if they could get authorization or press credentials.

They had worked hard for months, and their life together was straightening out. Leslyn wrote an acrostic poem for him signed with an acrostic, her initials, L.M.H., making "Little Miss Hitter-Skitter":

Rarely seen is such a soul,
Only every now and then,
Beautiful and sweet to know.
Everyone has such a goal,
Reached by only favored men—
Thus it is I love you so.

Heart so big and full of care,
Everything's within your scope.
I, and others, find our hope,
Not afraid, if you are there.
Large of purpose, oh my Bear,
Ever toward the light you grope,
If it fails, you *can still cope,*
Never leave me, is my prayer.

L.M.H.[102]

28

WRITING FACTORY

One day early in June 1946, Leslyn answered the doorbell and was startled to see Heinlein's old NAES coworker Virginia—Ginny—Gerstenfeld on their stoop, suitcase in hand. She had come directly from the train station.

The Heinleins had known she was on her way, but Ginny had talked in her letters about making her way slowly across the country, seeing the sights. They hadn't expected to see her until the fall, when perhaps she would enroll in UCLA. Leslyn invited her in: "[W]hen someone just came 3,000 miles to pay you a surprise call you can't just say 'Go 'way. I'm busy.'"[1]

Gerstenfeld had been demobilized in March and found herself at loose ends. She had broken off her engagement the previous winter,[2] and her mother was determinedly throwing her at family friends, trying to get her married off. Her own friends, she said, had all become bridge-playing house-wives with no conversation. There just was nothing left for her in New York.[3] She wanted to travel overseas, since she had never seen anything but the East Coast of the United States, but could not get a booking.[4]

Then she heard about the GI Bill. It would pay for books and tuition if she went back to school. Gerstenfeld decided she would work toward a graduate degree in her specialization, chemistry, someplace on the other side of the country, since that would get her out of New York and away from the East Coast. "I had planned to go to Berkeley when a letter from Robert changed my mind, and I matriculated at U.C.L.A."[5]

UCLA, she found, had an accelerated program for veterans, straight to doctorate, bypassing the master's degree. If she took the maximum course load, plus summer sessions, she could get the degree before the GI benefits ran out—but she would have to jump to get into this year's summer session. She booked a train straight through to Los Angeles.

Gerstenfeld had not planned to *stay* with the Heinleins, though she was invited in, at least overnight: they were mercifully free of houseguests at the moment, though all the work spaces were occupied, and they had a full calendar.

Leslyn had been coaching another budding writer[6] while Robert churned out pay copy. He was working up story notes for "The Horse That Could Not Fly" (later published as "Jerry Was a Man") and for "The Green Hills of Earth." Even turning down most invitations left them frantically busy, but Robert's mother and sister had recently returned from a family visit in the Midwest. Robert and Leslyn had trekked out with the family that very day to visit his father in the veterans' hospital (never a very satisfying prospect: sometimes he didn't even recognize them). And the arrangements for the trip to White Sands were surprisingly complicated.

Gerstenfeld got herself registered for the summer session that would be starting in two weeks and found a boardinghouse close to the campus. She did not have much opportunity to see the Heinleins socially, but she invited them to a dance session at the local ice-skating rink in Westwood. They had never had a chance to see her skate in Philadelphia, since her rink was only open in the winter, and in the winter of 1944–1945 all the Heinleins' spare time was taken up with the kamikaze think tank and the extra work for Admiral King. Now they were enthralled by it.[7] Robert, in particular, was englamored. It put an entirely new light on Ginny: she was no longer a pretty, athletic, girl—woman—with a slight adult-acne problem;[8] on skates she became something from the half-world. When he got home he wrote his impressions in a poem:

"Dance Session"

The squeegeed ice in the great dim hall
Was clean and blue and fit for the ball;
So the music sounded and the lights glared out
And the cruel steel blades went swirling about
In flight fantastic and fancy free,
In crisp, clean spins, with gusty glee—
Etching the ice with outré art,
While the cruel bright blades sliced sharp in my heart.

Out of the leaping, rushing spate
A voice sang out for three-lobed eight:
The ice fauns paired with their elfin sprites
To start their intricate woven rites

In complex, structured demonstration
They captured Art in one equation;
In sweet incredible enthymeme
She proved the logic of cold Moon beam.

Out from the pattern of Killian and Blues
Emerged the sprite whom the Ice Gods choose
To show us weary earth-bound creatures
The cool, sweet lines of Beauty's features.
Rosy her long limbs, snow white were her gants,
Timeblue was her jerkin, and merry her glance—
Hoyden her hair bow, among the gallants.
Ice fairy Virginia, First in the Dance!

(Oh, great was the shock of the sudden stop
When the music ceased and the pattern broke
And fairyland melted in cigarette smoke
In the warm dull light of a coffee shop!)

RAH—June 46[9]

A couple of elderly professors had been there at the same time, learning to dance. If they could learn, Robert and Leslyn thought they certainly could.[10] Gerstenfeld set them up with beginner's lessons.

They wouldn't buy good equipment—quality skates were very expensive—and that worked against rapid progress, but their biggest limitation was that they were both afraid of falling on the ice. Robert had lingering problems from his wartime surgeries, which he would not talk about. Leslyn was so terrified that she could not force herself to pick up the speed necessary for some of the figures.

After their lessons and her own workout, Gerstenfeld would come home with them, usually on Saturday afternoons, and coach them privately. She spread a lot of pillows around on the floor and showed them how to take a fall.[11]

That didn't much appeal to either of them, but they both continued with the lessons. Robert found the mechanics of skating fascinating: they forced him out of certain mental ruts he wasn't aware he was in.

Most of the turns, spins, etc., depend on conservation of *angular* momentum. I found it almost impossible, at first, to understand the descriptions of the turns and had no luck doing them, until I did analyze them in terms of physics. Then it became fairly simple—only "fairly," as the precision juggling required still calls for muscular co-ordination which I am still acquiring. Calculating the path of a projectile is not the same thing as *being* the projectile—and some of the dances, the Fourteen-Step for example, are done at forty miles an hour.[12]

The lessons were interrupted in late June for Robert and Leslyn's first trip to White Sands, to see V-2 shot number 6. Cal Laning was coming to White Sands with some admirals to evaluate this shot, and hoped to be able to find time to get together with them. They drove across the great Southwest desert, from California through Arizona, through half of New Mexico to Las Cruces in the south. This time they planned to see the Trinity site—and visit Jack Williamson at his ranch near Pep, New Mexico, not far from Portales. They would go to Santa Fe over the holidays, then home by way of Monument Valley and the Grand Canyon.

Heinlein wrote to Ginny Gerstenfeld while they were gone, a handwritten letter full of local color about White Sands, addressed "Dear Ice Sprite" and signed off "Our love."[13] Her reply the next day is equally chatty, and she refers to having a date with Cleve Cartmill,[14] who had divorced his first wife, Jeanne, before the end of the war.[15]

The big rocket launch on June 28 was impressive—awe-inspiring. Heinlein took Stereo Realist pictures of everything that wasn't absolutely classified—though, unfortunately, the pictures did not come out in processing.

The nervous tension in the control blockhouse, just two hundred yards from the rocket, was thick enough to cut. "If anything goes wrong," the observers were cautioned, "fall flat on your faces."[16] The V-2 has a very distinctive silhouette, a squat cylinder, like a pencil stub fifty feet tall with fins at its base. A crane steadied it, at a long angle, a ring around the point. Twenty minutes before the launch, the control blockhouse let off a smoke bomb. Eighteen minutes later, two red star shells alerted all the men in the launch area to take cover. They ran for the blockhouse. Then flame flashed out of the base and smoke billowed up. Heinlein caught his breath and held it.

She rose slowly and gracefully, straight as an Indian's back, till she hung some fifty feet in the air suspended on a column of orange-red flame. The roar hit us—the quality of a blow torch but with the massive violence of all the subway trains in Manhattan. It pushed against the chest.[17]

When the rocket was high in the sky, the "sun-bright flame" disappeared, and the blockhouse radio operator announced, "Twenty-five miles up!"

Heinlein looked around, dazed. The towers were still trembling from the blast of the liftoff: it was *unbelievably fast.* "This ship had climbed more than twenty-five miles from a standing start in the length of time a man can hold his breath through shock."[18] It disappeared from naked-eye sight at forty miles' altitude and went on to break the current record at one hundred miles (the report the next day in *The El Paso Times* said only that it was "over 75 miles"[19]), followed by radar as the vapor trail twisted weirdly in the clear desert sky above them.

Lieutenant Colonel Turner, the CO at the White Sands base, voiced an observation that has been made many times since:

> "You know," he said, "I've fired everything from the smallest to the biggest; this is the only sort of shoot that gives you just as much of a kick the last time as the first."[20]

A week later, two days after his thirty-ninth birthday, Heinlein wrote a 1,500-word article, "Journey of Death," "to justify my status as a member of the press."[21] He found this very difficult to write:

> The trouble is, I know too much that is confidential about rocket progress in this country, which greatly hampers me in writing about it. Where another writer may speculate in an interesting fashion, I don't dare open my kisser because I know the speculation is perfectly true.[22]

This article never sold, even though the clearance officer told him it was "very suitable for publication."[23] Perhaps he had waxed too poetical:

> *Jornada del Muerto* the Spanish called this remote and menacing stretch of New Mexican desert, in honor of the many who did not quite make it, who died and left their dessicated bodies to the buzzards. It is still the Journey of Death.
>
> At the White Sands Proving Grounds near Las Cruces Army Ordnance engineers are taking the first steps in another deathly journey in this

desert; there they are testing and investigating the great German V-2 rockets that were used to shell London.

Perhaps parts of it were a little too lugubrious for commercial markets:

> In sight, though still unrealized, is the round-the-world rocket, capable of free flight of unlimited duration, hanging in the sky for weeks, months, or years, ever ready to drop atomic death on any city selected by its masters.
>
> Do not console yourself that these rockets can protect us. The United States has no monopoly on rocket research. . . . Other brilliant engineers, speaking other tongues than ours, can place such angels of death in outer space, ready to carry *us* on that last journey. And no brass hat or scientist anywhere has been willing to state that there is any defensive measure at all against rocket attack. We can search and we can hope—but no defense is in sight.[24]

He wrote more directly to John Campbell about the experience: "I will state that it is the most thrilling thing I have ever seen in my life—the Grand Canyon did not give me the boot that this thing does."[25]

Ironically, Leslyn's more journalistic report on the firings did sell, first on the front page of a local, neighborhood sheet, *The Canyon Crier,* of July 19, under the headline "Canyonite Only Lady to Witness V-2 Test" and subtitled "Rocket's Red Glare." Later in the year, Forrest Ackerman sold it to a French publisher, Gallet, representing himself as Leslyn's agent—and *then* told her he was offering it around. That $7.00 sale engendered a certain amount of anxiety: Lurton Blassingame was her agent as well as Robert's, and he specialized in international sales. Leslyn insisted that Ackerman regularize the relationship by working through Blassingame, to minimize the damage to her business relationship—and Robert's. Ackerman couldn't understand what the fuss was about. He sent Blassingame a letter asking for his cut of the agency fee.

Blassingame was bemused rather than angry. Leslyn apologized:

> You have run into one of the occupational diseases of science-fiction writers—fandom. Forry Ackerman is the best of the lot, but he can be a damned brat at times. . . . I imagine that his letter to you was impertinent, to say the least. It was necessary for me to refer this very trivial matter to you in order to get it through his head that Bob now has an agent, and that all of our literary business must go through you. Fans have a gay way of expecting professional writers to whip off a little 2000 word story or

article, just for the sheer pleasure of seeing their names in print in some fan magazine. . . .

Fans are no positive factor at all in the career of a science-fiction writer, but they can have a certain negative or nuisance co-efficient, which has to be watched.[26]

They found Ackerman virtually unchanged by the war—perhaps a little more self-involved. Heinlein had reached the conclusion that if he wanted to keep Ackerman's friendship, he would have to treat Ackerman like a very young person without much life experience.

I have decided to take him as he is and regard him as a young friend of limited viewpoint, sweet and charming, but not to be considered as one of the adults. By such, I hope to avoid being irritated at his unwavering juvenile attitude and his refusal to take an adult part in this busy and troublesome world. I really am fond of him.[27]

In mid-1946, Ackerman was also promoting a fannish charity, the Big Pond Fund, to bring a science-fiction personality, fan or professional, over from England for the World Science Fiction Convention when it started up again in 1947 (the WorldCons had been suspended during the war). Ted Carnell was selected as the first recipient of the Big Pond Fund.

Carnell had just gotten his new science fiction magazine, *New Worlds,* in circulation, and this trip would give American fans a chance to look him over. Heinlein and Carnell had already been in correspondence over this proposed trip. Carnell had American royalties he could pick up and so had the ancillary expenses of the trip covered—and Heinlein had been doing as much as he could for the Carnells, sending packages of foods that were still rationed in England. But his own sales from the writing business were down, and he and Leslyn were living on reprint offers. The packages of foodstuffs they could handle—and they would continue to send packages periodically for years. Forced to choose between food packages that would directly help Ted and Irene and Micheal[28] and an impersonal donation to a charity, he chose the food packages.[29]

Naturally, Heinlein did not want to be forced to explain this to Ackerman—and have it get out in local fandom that he was too poor or too tightfisted to make a charitable contribution. Ackerman's frequent and increasingly insistent appeals for a donation became more and more irritating, so Robert and Leslyn began to avoid him.

They had resumed ice-skating lessons when they got back to Los Angeles from Los Alamos. The lessons were probably coincident with a change in Ginny Gerstenfeld's personal status with them. She was moving from interesting friend to "family member"—a pattern that was somewhat familiar to Leslyn already. Ginny was interested in Robert, even if she wasn't herself entirely aware that her friendly affection was becoming a crush. Leslyn welcomed Ginny into the family as a matter of course, though she would probably never have the same easygoing, affectionate relationship with Ginny that she had with Vida Jameson.

Jameson came back to Hollywood in August and moved in again with the Heinleins and became part of the ice-skating crew.[30] Between them, Robert and Leslyn had offered to teach her how to write for market—but not "creative writing." Robert's position, articulated many times over the years, was that either you had the basic creative stuff, or you didn't—though "Robert had a notion that anyone could write and sell a story, if they tried."[31] But you could teach the nuts and bolts of mechanics: how to slant a story to a market. In his few comments on this "coaching," Robert stressed only Leslyn's role as "story doctor." Leslyn apparently worked with Jameson about story mechanics. What Robert may have taught her he never mentioned, but the subjects that appear casually in his correspondence suggest he may have coached her on basic prosodic technique—how to achieve your effects; how to "hear the characters talk."[32]

Though normally Heinlein refused all social invitations while writing—and in any case, he had been sick for several weeks—this kind of social life, seamless with the ordinary mechanics of living, he could handle. It was, in fact, a pleasure. Vida Jameson was far and away the best novice they had ever taken under their collective wing—and very easy to have around the house, as well. "We are having a wonderful time together. If it hadn't been for Ron [Hubbard] going off the deep end we'd never have become so well acquainted with her—and swapping Hubbard's friendship for hers is clear gain."[33]

Heinlein was ill in July and August, with some sort of kidney ailment—then with a bad reaction to the sulfa drugs used to treat the kidneys—before he was ready to go to work again.

I'm better now, but I still don't know just what was the matter with me. Sinusitis, pyelitis, sulfa poisoning, wrenched back, high fever, and dandruff that I know of. I'm not pregnant, but we've been supporting five doctors, one GP and four specialists, in luxury.[34]

And the work piled up. The Navy wasn't quite done with him yet: his August 14, 1945, memo continued to work its way up the naval bureaucracy. It was a perfect short abstract to head all the minor projects that involved rocketry and electronics and guided missiles. One year after the memo, Cal Laning wrote to him, warning that the newly created Air Force might preempt the Navy's priority in space. He suggested Heinlein ghostwrite an article for the slicks, to go out under Laning's name: "Why Navy Crews Should Man Our Space Ships." The subject was interesting and important, but Heinlein was uneasy about ghostwriting; it was not a legitimate practice for a professional writer, he felt. He countered with a proposal for an "as told to" byline, "the standard arrangement of *reputable* ghosts."[35]

But Laning feared that his own name—which was what the Navy people would be looking at—would be ignored with a double byline; he would look like a "front" rather than a credible advocate.

Naval Operations took the prospect seriously enough to bring up Heinlein's memo and the Moon rocket proposal at a cabinet meeting. President Truman asked whether such a rocket could be launched from the deck of a ship. The current plans based on scaling up the V-2 required land-based launching facilities. The Navy's project was killed, and space became the Air Force's baby.[36]

Two weeks later, the newly formed U.S. Air Force announced it would put a guided missile on the Moon in eighteen months. "Just who is writing science fiction these days?" Willy Ley complained. "The placing of a rocket on the moon is, of course, the science part of it, the 18 months is Fiction."[37]

Heinlein picked up his Rhysling story notes again in August. Perhaps the work with Vida Jameson and Leslyn on story mechanics helped him reframe the story into a contrast between a formal eulogy that cleaned up the man's life story and the actual, unsavory details of his life. He drafted the story in one sitting, skipping over the places he planned to put in samples of Rhysling's verse. It turned out a powerful and moving story.

Over the next ten days he wrote and rewrote and polished the verse. Some of it was intentionally doggerel, but some of it had very memorable and affecting language. Rhysling's songs of the spaceways were supposed to be international, so he translated some of the verses into French and German—and even Esperanto.[38] There was something about the title, though, that nagged at him:

I had a vague feeling in the back of my mind that it was not original with me; I thought that I might have seen it in a story of Hank [Kuttner]'s,

"Hollywood on the Moon"—but I did not know that it had ever been used as a song title.[39]

The story needed only a couple hundred words cut to tighten it up to just the right length. He sent it to his agent on September 27 with instructions to market it to the slicks before trying any of the pulps (even though his outline notecards noted it was originally to have been his "Swan Song for *Astounding*"[40]). Just then, Blassingame was able to report that Alice Dalgliesh, the juvenile editor at Scribner's ("A quiet, pleasant person in her fifties"[41]), had liked *Young Atomic Engineers*—their first solid nibble for the book. He had given her a copy of the discussion of possible sequels. She was coming soon to Los Angeles, and the Heinleins might meet her in person.

"Green Hills of Earth" sold to *The Saturday Evening Post* on September 30, 1946. Heinlein's long dry spell had broken.

> And it means a lot to me; it marks, I hope, the point of inflexion in a long, hard struggle to reconvert to peacetime activity. It has not been easy. One or both of us have been sick all the time; when I was free to write, I wrote frantically, under disturbed conditions and not very well. I've kept my nose to the grindstone with damn few rewards for the effort. This sale to the Saturday Evening Post really gives me a lift. (First thing I ever submitted to them, by the way—I feel good about it.)[42]

At about the same time, his "Back of the Moon" was picked up by *Elks Magazine* for the January 1947 issue—half of the article anyway; the editors didn't want the Moon colony stuff, since it was already old hat even to their readership.[43]

Heinlein tried at first to keep the "Green Hills" sale under wraps, not wanting to tempt fate until he had the check in hand—or the bank had it, at any rate—and the *Post* was committed to the story. He had a hard time believing it even after he had cashed the check and the story was scheduled.[44] A sale to the *Post* of all the slick magazines, was most ironic: it was a bastion of the bourgeois, and he took some gentle ribbing about that from his friends once he let the word out.

On the whole, his colleagues were pleased with his good fortune. Isaac Asimov was personally depressed because he was having trouble recapturing his own markets, but he saw that it was a net gain for the field as a whole.[45] Even the respected astronomer Robert S. Richardson (also a writer of science articles and fiction for *Astounding*), who turned out to have been a classmate of Leslyn's, heard about the sale and congratulated him, delicately suggesting they might get together to talk about projects.[46]

Two weeks after the sale was made, Vida Jameson was in bed with a cold, and Heinlein dug out some of his old *Weird Tales* pulps so she could read his favorite Northwest Smith stories by C. L. Moore. In the middle of reading, she sat up in bed, startled: she had discovered the title of Heinlein's *Post* story in a passage in "Shambleau" where Northwest Smith is humming "The Green Hills of Earth" to himself.[47]

Heinlein immediately apologized to Catherine Kuttner for unconsciously appropriating her intellectual property and asked for a formal release to use the song title.

The Kuttners, too, were delighted to learn about the sale to the *Post* and happy to make the release. They wrote him gloating congratulations.

> Perhaps the best thing about the sale, from our viewpoint, is that you haven't been standing still during the war years; you didn't go right back to where you were in 1941, but went on to something where you could use more of your potentialities. We are very pleased indeed, and can't wait to boast to John [Campbell—*Astounding*], Leo [Marguiles—the Standard pulp chain], Mort [Weisinger—*Thrilling Wonder Stories*], et al.[48]

By that time he had written and sold a second story for the *Post*.[49] "Space Jockey" was a story about a space pilot whose job took him away from home, to his wife's distress. It was the kind of perennial human story that might have featured a long-distance trucker or a railway engineer—the kind of story most familiar to readers of the *Post*—and this allowed Heinlein to portray the inexpressibly exotic professions of the new frontier in space in very comfortable human terms. This exactly fit into the propaganda purposes he had started writing with more than a year ago. With "Space Jockey," he had found the *Post*'s range and might be able to make sale after sale there.

The "Green Hills" sale to the *Post*, though, had personal fallout: John Campbell had put a blurb about the story in *Astounding* when Heinlein started talking about writing it, back in the summer. Campbell should not have done that, just on the don't-count-your-chickens-before-they-hatch theory, and he especially ought not to have done that because Heinlein had told him very explicitly that he wouldn't sell to Street & Smith until they changed their rights-purchase policy. Apparently Campbell didn't think Heinlein was serious about that:

> It is a sad business and I deeply regret that it should have worked out with hurt feelings, for John nursed me along a lot at the beginning. I owe him a debt which cannot be cleared up with money—it stays on the books. . . . I should have gotten an agent long ago, and avoided direct business dealings with friends.[50]

But John Campbell *was* a friend, and a writer, after all. It was impossible to argue with the rate per word that the *Post* could offer and *Astounding* could not. In addition, this sale implied that Campbell's decade-long editorial struggle for the acceptance of science fiction was coming to fruition.

In the middle of all this, Ginny Gerstenfeld mysteriously dropped out of their lives. Leslyn had quit skating entirely after a bad fall, and Robert had to cut back on his own lessons when he was working, though he was continuing to make progress skating.

Heinlein worried about Gerstenfeld and told her so. She had not wanted to bother him with her personal crisis, she told him in a letter, but her father was ill and her mother was worried about making ends meet, so Gerstenfeld had given her mother all her savings and pulled back all her expenses, even dropping out of skating. If anything should happen to her father, she told Heinlein early in November, she would have to return to New York to take care of him.

> Leslyn has asked me not to worry you with my troubles and I've tried, but you have a knack for getting at what's worrying me, and the only way I can comply with her wishes in this matter is apparently to stay away from you and to avoid talking to you.
>
> I love you very dearly, and would do anything to make you happy, but I don't see how I can keep you from worrying about my troubles when you find them out and from trying to do things for me. I really don't blame Leslyn for being annoyed about that, because I would be too, if I were in her place. So, it seems to me that the only solution is to stay away.[51]

Heinlein's response is not recorded. In any case, he had a lot of condolences to write that November: the 1946 elections were a Republican landslide. Jerry Voorhis was caught in the avalanche and turned out of his seat by Richard Nixon.

A deadlocked struggle between a Democratic President and a Republican Congress could be absolutely fatal to the prospects for world peace. Heinlein began floating the idea that President Truman could gain the strategic long-term control of the situation for the party by a gambit—resigning now in favor of Senator Vandenberg (after appointing him Secretary of State, to make him eligible for the succession) and gearing up to take back the presidency in 1948. Two years of deadlock, followed by four years of new isolationism, would just about finish the country.

Susie Clifton had just run one of the few successful Democrat campaigns in the country, getting Helen Gahagan Douglas elected to the House. Heinlein congratulated her on her victory and outlined his idea in more detail on the day after the election:

1. Moral Reason—to achieve democracy in fact.[52]

Truman had not been elected—and the Republican landslide showed that the voters would have gone Republican if they could. The Constitution didn't have any mechanism comparable to the "vote of confidence" in British practice that could force a general election to avoid the deadlocks the United States had experienced in 1918–20 and 1930–32, "and are now about to have again."

2. Practical Reason on the Level of Statesmanship—to achieve a functioning government in a period of crisis. . . .

There were enough angry Republicans to block any proposal that came from the State Department of a Democratic administration.

3. Practical Reason on the level of Partisan Politics—to permit the possibility of the election of a Democratic Administration in 1948.

If Truman remained in office, the Democrats would be blamed for everything that went wrong until the next election. They would have handed the Republicans a perfect campaign argument.

The Democrats had nothing to lose, Heinlein argued, and much to gain.

There is one more factor, hard to classify—Mr. Truman has the unique opportunity of being in a position to pick the Republican candidate for president in 1948. If we are to have a Republican president, would it not

be much better for it to be Mr. Vandenberg (in the Atomic Age!) than
Taft, Dewey, Bricker, or Warren![53]

Susie Clifton forwarded his letter to Representative Douglas, who wrote him
a polite thank-you—but it was a strategy too bold and too risky for the practical politicians: "I can only say that, if the people we should have to appeal
to were objective, far-sighted, and sensitive to public thinking, your plan
might be taken seriously!"[54]

He began circulating a bit of doggerel in letters:

"Brave New World"

Consider, when you're blown to bits
By robot plane and atom bomb,
Opinions of those demi-wits
From Willie Hearst to Good old Mom:
"We're safe behind our oceans here,
From Panama to icy Baffin;
We're safe and sovereign, never fear."
Cute? Why, Pal, we'll both die laughin![55]

Of the half dozen world-saver articles Heinlein had written, only half of
one was picked up: "Man in the Moon" appeared in the January 1947 issue
of *Elks Magazine*. However, the current run of luck at *chez* Heinlein in the
fall of 1946 continued excellent: the *Post* also bought Vida Jameson's first
submitted story—and scheduled it for the same issue as Heinlein's.

Three months of effort—and Mother Heinlein's Double-Whammy
Coaching Course is vindicated again!
     (Honest to goodness, I think Leslyn is probably the best story doctor
on either coast. Her instinct is almost unerring.)[56]

Heinlein started on a third story for the *Post* in November. Willy Ley was
visiting until November 18, and he and Lang were over at all times of day or
night. Ley always stimulated Heinlein, whose writing was fresher and easier
after a visit from Ley[57]—but he couldn't get any work done until a day or so
after Ley left town. The story he wanted to write was based on a couple he

knew who were never satisfied with where they were, so always moved around. " 'It's Great to Be Back!' " sold to the *Post* like clockwork. He had written it at what seemed its natural length, then had to cut it drastically to fit into the *Post*'s six-thousand-word limit for fiction. "It was a little like getting one of Billy Rose's show girls into one of my dresses to get it down to 6000 words," Leslyn wrote Lurton Blassingame about the revision.[58]

Alice Dalgliesh, his editor at Scribner's, wrote telling him that the Junior Literary Guild had picked up *Rocket Ship Galileo* as a 1947 selection, on a split-royalty deal. That would add another ten thousand copies to the edition when it came out, at a net to him of ten cents a copy. He revised the book slightly in January 1947, after Scribner's readers gave him notes on the book's pacing.

The *Post* knew it had something special on its hands in "Green Hills of Earth" and planned to do some unusual promotion: the story was advertised with half-page ads in major daily newspapers around the country on the eve of publication—"TONIGHT YOU VISIT MARS!" with a halftone cut of Fred Ludekens's spectacular illustration of the story.[59] The *Post* was also going to feature the story—and its artwork!—in its weekly four-sheet *Keeping Posted,* and for that biographical material was needed. William Holt, the editor at the *Post,* noticed that Jameson and Heinlein had the same address and queried as to who was the pseudonym and who the real person. Heinlein put on his best company manner, to amuse them, when he replied:

> When I received your letter of January 7th I felt an overwhelming impulse to throw myself on your mercy and report as follow: "Gentlemen, you have me. I confess that Vida Jameson is simply one of my pen names, as are Rex Stout, Erle Stanley Gardiner, and Clarence Buddington Kelland."
>
> Yes, it is a surprising coincidence. My wife's favorite theory is that 8777 is the address of a girl's school and that little Robert and little Vida were winners of honorable mention in the annual literary contest, which caused my wife, as headmistress, to submit their efforts to Dr. Franklin's distinguished journal. Bill Corson, another member of the Mañana Literary Society (more about the society later), points out that there is no such person as Heinlein in the first place, it being merely the name the members of the society give to the "Plotto" machine they own jointly. My own favorite theory is that 8777 is the mail-drop of a Communist cabal engaged in a conspiracy to gain a monopoly over *The Saturday Evening Post* and then destroy it, by suddenly withdrawing its support.

Their home, he explained, was the West Coast headquarters of the Mañana Literary Society, and the editors should not be surprised to find more manuscripts bearing that address:

> In truth, Miss Jameson and I are not even collaborators. I have always had an ambition to help young lady authors by assisting them in gaining experience which would permit them to write true confession stories, but I have encountered an amazing amount of awfully stuffy resistance. The fact behind the coincidence is that two of the several writers whom my wife coaches, to wit, myself and Vida, happened to hit the *Post* at about the same time and at a time when Vida is living with us because of the well-known housing shortage.
>
> It's a darn good thing, incidentally, that my first sale to the Post antedated Vida's by a couple of weeks, or I would have gone into a permanent decline. I've been a professional writer for a good many years; Vida has been one for a matter of weeks—and made her very first sale to the top magazine market. I am delighted that the kid sold to the *Post,* but, if, after plugging away for years, I had been beaten out in attaining this market, even by a matter of days, by a youngster and a beginner, I would have blown my top. I might even have taken a job.[60]

He went on, making an effort to charm them at the *Post*:

> We both wish to thank you for letting us know that our stories are to appear in the February 8th issue. We plan to have a small, tasteful neon sign constructed, demountable so that it may be mounted fore and aft atop the family automobile when out driving and then shifted to the front porch when we are home, and reading: SEE FEB 8TH SAT EVE POST. I like to get fat checks but I just love to see my name in print. Would a psychiatrist make anything nasty out of that fact?

Jameson's story, "The Thirteenth Trunk," was picked up by ABC for radio broadcast just before the February 8 issue of the *Post* came out. Leslyn, who had been acting as agent for Heinlein's world-saver articles as they came back from Lurton Blassingame, expected interest to pick up, and that would give her greater entrée for the material she was now handling for Bill Corson, Henry Sang—even a short story by Jack Parsons. She was sending the most likely of these directly to Blassingame, keeping the others in circulation to lower-paying markets.

Ron Hubbard wrote a letter that December from New York, on Hotel Belvedere stationery, "heartily and affectionately" congratulating Heinlein for "finally [going] conservative" and cracking "that citadel of reactionism," *The Saturday Evening Post*. His brief note, simultaneously self-deprecating and roguish, closes with the wry observation that he knows he's in "the Heinlein doghouse" and therefore he expects no reply.[61] The reference to being in the Heinlein doghouse was serious. Before leaving Southern California with Sara/Betty, L. Ron Hubbard had burned—or at least severely damaged—his bridges with the Heinleins, and Robert felt morally compelled to drop him—not for the psychological instability and irresponsibility that seemed to have seized him, or for "broken dishes, plaster, etc. I can go on forgiving and excusing a wounded veteran indefinitely,"[62] Heinlein wrote in a series of notes attached to Hubbard's letter in Heinlein's files—or even the divorce he was trying to obtain from his wife, Polly. But Hubbard had caused trouble with Leslyn's sister by getting their nephews all worked up about a mysterious "China venture," with frills that left them all aghast:

> No, it was enticing a boy, a son of another veteran, to whom I had been left in locis parentis. When my sister-in-law [Keith] called me—China—knives—guns—etc—your goose was cooked with me.
>
> As a wounded veteran I am still obligated toward you and will help you if I find you down and out, but I no longer trust you. You may show this letter to anyone you wish.
>
> I think a lot of those ribbons on your chest, even if Polly doesn't. You're an authentic hero, even though a phony gentleman. I'll give you money to get you out of a jam but I don't want you in my house.[63]

That was a bad situation, no doubt about it—messy and getting messier, Leslyn said:

> Ron is a very sad case of post-war breakdown. The details are too complex and too personal to be bruited about by letter. Suffice it to say that although Bob and I feel as if the Hubbard we knew had been possessed by some entity out of one of the more horrid Unk[nown Worlds] stories, we do not feel that Polly has helped the situation one bit. Ron is a very volatile personality—when he was around us he was a very different person from what he has become under the influence of his latest Man-Eating Tigress.[64]

Sprague and Catherine de Camp disagreed about Hubbard's personality deficiencies being a recent acquisition. "I don't think he's a case of post-war
breakdown at all," Sprague de Camp wrote in reply:

> I think he always was that way, but when he wanted to make a good im-
> pression or get something out of somebody he put on a first-class charm
> act. What the war did was to wear him down to the point where he no
> longer bothers to put on the act.
>
> I saw the other side of his character before the war and decided then
> that he was not to be trusted. You told me that you'd heard of his fascist
> leanings and were agreeably surprised to learn that he wasn't that way at
> all, but was a fine upstanding liberal. But I'd heard him give quasi-fascist
> harangues on the slimy iniquity of all politicians, and remembered the
> similar sentiments in *Final Blackout*. How do you know he was putting on
> an act for me, and revealing his true nature for you, and not the other way
> round? Because he wanted to conciliate the Heinleins whom he knew to
> have strong political convictions? Personally, however, I doubt if such an
> opportunist can have firm political convictions, fascist or otherwise.[65]

The news concerning the Hubbards' divorce was somewhat confused by
Laning's creative social information passed among their set. "Cal is an excellent Naval Officer and a brilliant scientist," Leslyn wrote the de Camps after
a particularly incorrect version of the Ron-and-Polly-Hubbard divorce situation, "but as a reporter, he'd make a fine fiction writer. His nearest and dearest have long ago learned to discount Cal's friendly exaggerations in social
and personal reports.[66]

29

SEPARATION. ANXIETY.

That January of 1947, Vida Jameson was finally able to find a place that suited her, and the Heinleins were again without houseguests. It was a pleasure for them to have the house back, to be sure, but perhaps not the best thing for Leslyn to be too much by herself after Vida left. Cal Laning finally stopped his months-long dithering and in January proposed a collaborative article about a naval space fleet—"A Spaceship Navy" or "A Spaceship Corps."

As "The Green Hills of Earth" hit the newsstands just before February 7, telegrams and letters began pouring in, congratulations and also awe and delight. His fan mail abruptly increased to new levels, and Ben Hibbs, the editor at the *Post,* wrote saying that this story attracted more reader mail than any other story they had ever published.[1] The praise made an ironic counterpoint to Leslyn's renewed irritability and depression. She was also drinking again.

Heinlein arranged a long vacation trip for the two of them in February, to the desert. From Twentynine Palms, where they could sunbathe on the hotel's patio in the nude, Heinlein wrote once to Ginny Gerstenfeld, a note on the hotel's stationery. Leslyn added a postscript: "This is practically the first place we've ever found which is *not* on a railroad, truck route or airline. It's so quiet I'm almost asleep. More later. Love—Leslyn."[2] They wandered around without itinerary for most of two weeks. Robert wrote to Ginny again from Blythe, telling her about the local rodeo they had attended—not a tourist affair, but a benefit for an injured local boy. Leslyn enclosed another handwritten postscript, also signed "Love," but Robert tucked into the envelope something Leslyn might not have seen—a three-by-five-inch index card on which was typed one line: "I think about you all the time."[3]

But work called, and they had to return to Los Angeles eventually. Scribner's and the Literary Guild didn't like the second title Heinlein had given *Young Atomic Engineers*; the next set of revisions on the article with Cal needed to be done; and he had to correct a misprint in the *Post*'s biography of him (he had been described as a naval aviator, which wasn't true). Heinlein really needed the release of exercise. He had been ordered by his doctor to take up horseback riding—no excuses!—but that was almost impossible to arrange in Laurel Canyon. He compromised with the doctor by throwing himself back into skating.[4]

The writing on the collaborative article with Cal Laning went along somewhat bumpily in March and into April because there wasn't as much technical data as Heinlein thought was needed to support the claims they wanted to make. Laning now was chivying him along, playing on Heinlein's sense of duty to the cause:

> Inasmuch as you can't be here, either trust me as to determination of the undercurrent of this article, or cut free from our teamwork in distrust. Heinlein Hollywood is not Heinlein Washington, but he can have an observer there if he will. . . .
>
> I can cease to be a powerful factor in the National Defense scheme if the article is not acceptable scientifically, and I don't mean by science the extrapolation of curves. . . . If you can't build me up to a position of real influence from the level I've reached, and the radical but sound attitude you have educated into me, you will lose the only tool you have in the Armed Services. Be goddamned clever.[5]

Almost as soon as they got home, it became impossible to keep Leslyn's drinking a secret. Robert emptied her caches of liquor into the sink as he found them[6]—and thought she was getting back to battery. But one evening when Ginny Gerstenfeld was up at the house for dinner, she went into the kitchen after groceries had been delivered to see if she could help put things away. She found Leslyn "swigging liquor directly from the bottle"[7]—she hadn't even taken the time to put the whiskey in a glass.

After struggling with her basic impulse to ignore—not her business!—Ginny took Robert aside and told him about it. He was embarrassed that she had seen it, but he must also have been at least a little relieved, not to have to cover up the problem—and not to have to bear the burden of the secret by himself. The strain of trying to cope, he later said, was making him a little crazy, and his friendships suffered because of it.[8] Heinlein searched the house and found stashes of liquor hidden in unlikely places.[9] He dumped them down the drain again, just as he had done in 1946, but more would appear magically: since she didn't drive, Leslyn had an account at the local grocery store in Laurel Canyon and could have more delivered at any time. He couldn't cut her off without virtually imprisoning her in the house (and letting the grocer know they were having a family fight over it), neither of which he was willing to do).[10]

Robert became convinced Leslyn was just one of those persons who could take adversity just fine but were overwhelmed by success.[11] What Robert knew at the time was that Leslyn had been in psychological crisis for some time already, her family mostly lost to her, and the props of her personality removed one by one over the years. She had been happiest as the acknowledged *éminence grise* of Heinlein-the-political-operator; she had been comfortably functional as the mentor of a budding writer and then a society of writers—a role that diminished as Heinlein turned more to his editor for such feedback, but returned with the advent of the postwar writing factory. Once both Robert and Vida could no longer be seen as in some sense her "protégés," Leslyn was just out of the picture—had, in fact, no "picture" to be in. Without family or any satisfying personal role, she was cut adrift, with nothing to lose. She followed her father down the neck of a bottle.

With Ginny Gerstenfeld providing backbone and helping him keep the house in order, Heinlein insisted Leslyn get help from someone if she wouldn't take help from him. He got her to a psychiatrist Grace ("Cats") Dugan Sang had recommended, Dr. David Harold Fink. Fink had gained a national reputation when he published a series of self-help books starting with *Release from Nervous Tension* in 1943 and *Be Your Real Self* in 1950. In 1947, however, he was in private practice; Cats Sang ran into him when she moved to Fallbrook with Henry Sang.

The treatment was not successful.

There is a joke in the psychological profession: how many therapists (psychologists, psychiatrists) does it take to change a lightbulb? Answer: Only one—but the lightbulb has to *want* to change.

Leslyn did not want to change. She broke up the united home front that April by ordering Ginny out of her house, setting that particular bridge on fire. Predictably, this drove Robert and Ginny together. Ginny wrote to him their first unequivocal love letter:

My beloved.

 Oh, my darling, how much I miss you already—not waking with you today and not seeing you and hearing your sweet voice—

 I said "goodnight" yesterday because I felt as if I were going into a dark tunnel—the end, where? Who knows? And I'm not sure how long I'll be able to take it either. When I returned to you, I told you that it was because I couldn't live without you and that is truer now than it was then, if that's possible.

I love you so very much, and I want to see you happy. If anything would accomplish that, I'd do it, but I do want to be near you. I need you in a way I've never needed anyone or anything in my life before. I'm just beating my head against the brick wall of forces that hold us apart. Oh, Lord, if only we lived in the Stone Age when only the things that were vital mattered to anyone.

My heart is crying for you—I want most desperately to be with you tonight, my love—

Your Ginny[12]

Over the last year, Ginny's thoughts had been turning more and more to Robert. Her own engagement had evaporated after the war, and none of the boys she met at UCLA had sparked any lasting interest. Most of them, of course, were much younger than she—by ten years or more—and uninterestingly callow. There were a certain number of older students, getting their degree, as she was, on the GI Bill, but there were no sparks.[13]

Robert, on the other hand, was almost ten years *older* than she—handsome, compatible, and (most important) *funny* when he had the time and energy for it. But the reality overwhelmed her practical side. She was especially vulnerable, too, at that time, because the fits of lassitude she had been struggling with since Washington, D.C., were becoming alarmingly more frequent. She went to a doctor and was diagnosed with thyroid deficiency, for which she had to take daily medication.[14] Physically and emotionally she was at a low point, and the loss of the family solidarity knocked the props out from under her. The intensity of Ginny's abrupt fall into love was startling to her.

Heinlein allowed none of this emotional disturbance to show to the outside world. In a contemporary letter to the Kuttners, he chats about his ongoing DIY, getting the house back in shape, with no intimation of trouble:

We've been redecorating throughout and now the house is so goddam clean that we are thinking of moving out. Kitchen in royal blue and butter yellow—whee! bedroom in white and royal blue; studio in ivory; enormous green rug in L.R., with rust colored drapes. You wouldn't recognize the joint. I think we've chased the ghosts out and hope you will be happier in the place next time you stay with us, than you were in '42. Leslyn has made and planted hands and charms of other sorts through the house, especially one against a thing that keeps trying to come up the basement steps. I've put a mirror on that door, which is good in itself; if the hand and the mirror don't work, I shall try garlic flowers, knife-drawn lines, and dripping water.[15]

By May, Leslyn was more or less confined to bed at the doctor's orders and in a state of mind that could only be called psychotic, much of the time. Robert tried to keep things going, doing the housework himself and turning down all invitations for them. He kept up a front to friends:

I am beginning to be afraid that Leslyn used up her reserve during the war. Her health may be permanently impaired—no endurance and no resistance to infection. Me—I'm a little older and a little slower, but I am in much better health than at the end of the war. Even my sinuses don't bother me much now. There's a dance in the old gal yet, Archie.[16]

Nevertheless, he was miserable and irritated, so worked up he often couldn't sleep, and on a merry-go-round he could not get off: the writing business was bustling, and he had a hard deadline of the end of May to have the final version of the article for Cal Laning.[17] A letter written two months earlier to his close friend John Arwine illustrates Heinlein's state of mind during this entire period:

During the past eighteen months there have been more times when I wanted to be dead than there were times when I wanted to go on living. . . . I think I have discovered that I can manage somehow to endure anything that happens to me. I may be mistaken—there may come a morning when I will slit my wrists, or I may turn my face to the wall and quit answering anything that is addressed to me. But I don't think so; I think I can stick it out somehow. . . .

Leslyn's troubles have paralleled mine and in some ways have been worse. I shan't discuss them, except to say that we heterodyne each other, my troubles make her troubles worse and vice versa. Each of us would do almost anything to make the other happy; the results have been quite the opposite. Both of us have been in such a stew that we have not been able to give the other support and calmness in time of trouble. Each of us knows it and regrets it; our intentions are good but our performance falls short of our intentions.[18]

But the work, too, was often frustrating: when the editors at *Collier's* expressed interest in the article he and Laning had cowritten, Heinlein was not in charge of the negotiations, even though he *had* to work at the writing to get it done by their deadline of May 29. Laning showed no sympathy or understanding of the mind of the public—but Laning was the man on the spot, and the negotiations were in his hands.

Heinlein had another spate of stories appearing: "Columbus Was a Dope" had gone to the pulps at fire-sale rates and appeared in the May issue of *Startling Stories*. That one had missed on every slick market. The mystery story he had written for Charteris in 1946 appeared in the May *Popular Detective*, slightly cleaned up. Rogers Terrill, the editor at *Argosy*, wanted to buy a story based on a dream Heinlein had one night about California flooding after an earthquake, "Water Is for Washing"—but wanted some minor revisions.[19]

And Heinlein sold a fourth story to the *Post*, "Little Boy Lost." In a letter acknowledging the sale to the *Post*'s fiction editor, Stuart Rose, he tested the water for a broader range of fiction:

> I'm a bit afraid of being typed for "space opera" only. Would you care to see a business romance with an engineering-firm background—or a whodunit—or boy-meets-girl in a political campaign—or a domestic comedy on ice skates—or even sea, air, or western. I have background experience for any of these.
>
> I can do fantasy—but Wilbur Schramm is tough competition. That guy is good!
>
> I can do speculative science-fiction of any sort, as well as space stories—for example, an industrial atomic-power story.
>
> There is an unlimited supply of 4- to 5,000 word shorts with a space-travel background, for example a disaster incident in a military spaceship of the U.N. peace patrol. How long will the market hold up?
>
> Can you stand a tragic novel about World War III? Or a short story about a man who tries to out-guess a rocket bomb attack on the United States?

And he probed also for receptivity to longer fiction:

> I would like to do a serial about the opening of space travel. Title: "The Man Who Sold the Moon." The background story would be the same, at an earlier period, as my Luna-City stories; the story would be of D. D. Harriman, the first great entrepreneur of space travel. It would be concerned mainly with the financial and promotional aspects of the first Moon trip,

rather than with the physical adventure. This is, I believe, a fairly novel ap-proach to the space-travel story, and concerns what is, in fact, the real hitch in opening up the solar system—money, the huge initial investment and the wildcat nature of the risk. Does it sound like a serial—or, possibly, a novella?[20]

The *Post* editors did not express enthusiasm. Heinlein puzzled over this and asked his agent what he could do to keep his slicks audience. Blassingame forwarded a comment he had received[21] recommending Heinlein get personal coaching from Thomas Uzzell. Uzzell had been the fiction editor at *Collier's* and dealt with technique, plot, and "literary psychology" in his 1923 book *Narrative Technique,* the standard textbook for story technique. Blassingame thought he might get something by a quick look through *Narrative Technique,* but he didn't see any particular need for personal coaching.

Heinlein was doubtful about this kind of coaching in any case. He was getting the kind of coaching he needed from Blassingame and from Leslyn's story sense.

Each of you have a sympathetic understanding of what I'm trying to ac-complish and try to help me do it, instead of trying to get me to do some-thing entirely different.[22]

And he doubted he could use any tricks Uzzell could teach him about conventional plotting—he just didn't use conventional plots:

My notion of a story is an interesting situation in which a human being has to cope with a problem, does so, and thereby changes his personality, character, or evaluations in some measure because the coping has forced him to revise his thinking. How he copes with it, I can't plot in advance because that depends on his character, and I don't know what his charac-ter is until I get acquainted with him.[23]

But he got a copy of the book anyway, since he had gotten good use of Jack Woodford's *Trial and Error* book when he first thought of commercial writ-ing. But he put it aside until he got off deadline with the Laning collabora-tion, which *Collier's* had definitely bought.

The *Collier's* editor had been vague about what he wanted, which made revision a maddening process. The strain was starting to get to him.

Leslyn, I am sorry to say, is sick again. I am chief cook and bottle washer and am rushed to death. I wonder when this rat race will let up. There have been times since V-J day when I thought I was losing my mind.[24]

He was able to handle it at all only because Ginny came over periodically and pitched in to help. The rift in April apparently was resolved somehow.[25] He even managed time to write a chatty letter to the de Camps:

I have been neglecting you kids or palming off postcards on you in exchange for nice chatty letters. This time I will do quite a bit better through the courtesy of Ginny Gerstenfeld. I have got a boiler shop running this weekend. Some vet[eran] students from UCLA are working around the house repairing, doing odd jobs, and gardening, and Ginny is enabling me to turn out an enormous stack of mail by means of her shorthand, a talent I didn't know she had. When I finish dictating, she will get to work at my machine, and I will go outside where I am engaged in the most enormous and improbable venture in engineering—to wit, putting in an irrigation system to cover completely two city lots. The whole house has been in a turmoil for weeks as we have been repairing and redecorating the entire joint and rebuilding the entire garden. While I carried on simultaneously four separate literary ventures. I tell you this that you may understand why my personal correspondence has been so damned sloppy.[26]

Heinlein finished the revision of the article for *Collier's* with four days to spare. On Lurton Blassingame's recommendation, he had arranged for a Hollywood agent, Lou Schor, to handle two potential projects for radio. Schor wanted to capitalize on his new association with a *Post* writer and had his publicist run a puff story in the May 27 issue of *The Hollywood Reporter*—a common ploy in the entertainment industry to make self-promoting announcements and create buzz.

Hollywood was a tiny and inbred community, even more so then than it is now. Heinlein's motion picture agent in Hollywood was H. N. "Swanny" (or sometimes "Swanie") Swanson—an affiliate of Lurton Blassingame's literary agency. Swanson became very angry when he saw the story. He had been representing Heinlein on a handshake basis. Now he sent over a boilerplate seven-year contract that seemed to assume Heinlein was going to be a staff writer of some kind for a studio, either movie or television. This conflict Heinlein absolutely did not need. Between his own health crises and

Leslyn's he was constantly on edge. The work he could do was the only thing holding him together, letting him push through it.

His deadine for *Collier's* completed, Heinlein picked up Uzzell's book and read through it carefully. *Narrative Technique* was very different from Woodford's practical guide to writing to market. Uzzell's directions for developing a commercial story followed commercial formula patterns, and Heinlein's mind simply did not work that way. He found himself locking up when he tried to follow Uzzell's advice.[27] "That book durn near ruined me! It brought on the only really dry period I have ever had. I could plot—but I could *not* write a story."[28] After a month of dithering, he vented his frustrations on Ginny as he helped her move to downtown Hollywood.[29]

Ginny had become disgusted with the couple she was keeping house for, and in any case her expenses were outrunning her income. She had decided that she couldn't afford to stay in school for the summer session this year; she would have to get a real job. She found a residential hotel for women—actresses—in downtown Hollywood. Robert had a car; she asked him to help her move her books and clothes and typewriter.[30]

One of the things Robert most valued about Ginny was the utterly serious, deadpan way she treated any problem—but particularly one of his problems. This time, she cut right to the heart of the matter: " 'Plot,' " she said, "is something dreamed up by professors of English to explain what born storytellers do without thinking about it."[31] He was a born storyteller, she told him. Throw the book away: it had nothing to teach him.

And he did toss the book in the trash can (something he almost never did: books were sacred) and tried to put it out of his mind.

Late in May, Leslyn's state of mind changed again; now she seemed almost placid and contented. But there was a cold and impenetrable cruelty to her. She told him she had tried to commit suicide—she later said, by rubbing herself with radioactive glass, though the piece of Trinitite that Cornog had given him was stored in a safe and buried under the woodpile.[32] Confined to her bed all month, she could not have gotten to it at all.

This was profoundly shocking to Heinlein. He knew instantly that there was only one chance for both of them—only one way to break the spiral: he told her she needed to call their lawyer, Sam Kamens, and get a divorce, on any terms she cared to name.[33] She could cash in the war bonds to live on, and he would take the cash in their savings account. That would give them each about $600—that should be enough to hold them both until they could work out something. He agreed to pay $40 a month in an informal "alimony" until she got settled.[34] He would need the car, but since she didn't drive, that shouldn't matter much to her.

Heinlein forced himself to get on with it. He packed a bag, took his typewriter and some papers from his studio, and left.[35] On June 16, he closed down their joint checking account and paid the outstanding bills. A few days later, he made it official: the date of separation they listed in Leslyn's Complaint for Divorce was June 20, 1947.

His month of Uzzell-induced inactivity meant that he had no fiction out in circulation and therefore no immediate prospects of a sale (with the exception of the *Collier's* payment, due sometime within the month—which would have to be split with Laning). He would have to crank out something as soon as he could get settled, but his mind kept going round and around his own failure to be what Leslyn needed. The grief and guilt took him and stayed. More than a year later, he was still mourning:

> [T]his is my beloved Piglet who has nursed me, and whom I have nursed, my partner and staunch right hand in many a difficult venture, my confidant, the wife of my bosom, the creature that I cared for more than anything else in the world, of whom I was proud, whose goodness I admired, an honest gentleman among Philip Wylie's Moms.[36]

Sam Kamens worked out the provisions for a settlement agreement that was ready for execution on June 24. Because there were no children, and it was not a complex estate, they could agree on a clean division, almost to walk away with what they each had in their hands at the moment: they had already divided the cash assets evenly and agreed to make no claim on what the other had in his or her possession or might earn in future. Leslyn got the house and all its contents, except Robert's working papers. That was a very considerable "bump" to her: the house had appreciated in value since they had bought it for $3,000 in 1935; she had already moved out and put it on the market for $10,000. In return, she agreed to give up any further claim on the literary estate—practical, in the short term, since the slicks sales had stopped and the royalties from reprints were so minor then that the bookkeeping involved in splitting them fifty-fifty would be more than the income would justify (and in any case, Street & Smith's stranglehold on the reprint rights meant Heinlein couldn't exploit them properly anyway). They informally agreed for Robert to continue the "alimony" Leslyn was receiving, even though the settlement document specified that they released each other from alimony—among other possible claims.[37]

The day he signed the papers, Heinlein found a secretarial service on the corner of Fairfax and Santa Monica Boulevards, in what is now West Hollywood, that would receive and forward mail for him, and notified his agent of the change of address. He told Blassingame Leslyn could be reached through Kamens.

There were endless details to take care of, and the necessary work helped keep him busy. They hadn't told anybody yet, and they didn't know what people's reactions would be. Heinlein found a hotel and worked out what to do next. One day he called Ginny at the Studio Club and cashed in the favor she owed him: he asked her to help him move things out of the house before it was sold.

They went together up to the Lookout Mountain house. Leslyn was not there. Robert took his business files and working reference books, and his desk and some other small furniture, and boxes and boxes of personal items, most of which went immediately into storage at the local Bekins. Then Ginny accompanied him to Arcadia, where his mother was living with Andy and Mary Jean Lermer, and stayed in the car while he went in to tell his family. That was very hard for him.[38]

He spent several days sorting through the personal papers he had accumulated. Sack after sack of letters—almost his entire personal history in California politics, and correspondence with family and friends that did not bear on his business—he had Ginny burn in the hotel's incinerator, patiently feeding them a piece at a time to avoid choking the fire.[39]

Leslyn had started talking about the separation and divorce—she had, he later discovered, been bad-mouthing him to friends for months before the separation, portraying him as evil and psychotic, abusive to her.[40] He began receiving letters from people back east: apparently Sprague de Camp had gotten all up and down the eastern seaboard spreading the word.

Ginny suggested that he had nothing to gain by talking about it; it would only lead to situations in which he felt called upon to explain himself—and that could only lead to recriminations and self-justification. Better to say nothing than to be drawn into that.[41]

Heinlein realized at once that what was wise was also the most practical thing for him to do.

Robert and Ginny were out driving in the Valley on one occasion when he had to duck into a drugstore. Ginny spied a largish bottle of cologne— King's Men—and bought it for him. Robert scolded her for spending money on something like that, but he used it, and he kept the bottle quietly hidden away when the cologne was all but gone.[42]

Ginny put her practical problem solving to work on his other big problem. He couldn't get up enough concentration to get anything done, between having to move every few days (city ordinances limited hotel stays to about five days at a time) and having sympathetic friends drop in unexpectedly.[43] The situation would be the same anywhere he went in the city. Ginny found a ranch outside Ojai, seventy-five miles north of Los Angeles in Ventura County, that rented rooms—Rancho Amelia. After dumping more boxes in storage, they went up to Ojai and got him installed there in a private room, where he could set up his typewriter and work in peace. He left Los Angeles quietly, on Sunday, July 6, the day before his fortieth birthday, not mentioning the departure to his friends.

Installed in his room, he put Ginny on a bus back to Los Angeles Sunday night. He had missed his childhood bet that humanity would be on the Moon before his fortieth birthday—but July 7, 1947, was nevertheless an important transition for him. "And the evening and the morning were the first day," he wrote to Ginny that night. "Also, Life Begins at Forty."

> The first hitch of my life gone, the second starting auspiciously. With Ginny's help I intend to make it a better job than the first. Thank you for loving me, my dear. Thank you for worrying about me and helping me and most especially for putting new life into me and making me young again. Thanks for the birthday cards and your cheery smile and for the watch . . . and most of all for your sweet, indominatable spirit. It's a new borning on a bright new morning and you have made it.[44]

It was quiet in Ojai. As soon as he met his fellow residents and the staff, he knew he would enjoy the place.

> The social atmosphere of this blessed valley is so fraternal, so Arcadian, that Ventura seems by contrast one of the seven ports of sin.
> Nevertheless I would take Port Saïd *with* Ginny, rather than Carcassonne without.[45]

The only defect was that he couldn't get a post office box there and had to take his mail c/o General Delivery, Ojai. If he stayed there any length of time, he would have to make better arrangements. He found a decentish restaurant for lunches and dinners, in a bowling alley, which suited him just fine.[46] He could sit back and watch the undemanding spectacle of life on the hoof, knowing that he had to get back to work. He had to generate stories, and he also had a big rewrite job to do on "Beyond This Horizon," before that serial could be published in book form. He was not looking forward to that task.

The major publishers were understandably timid about taking on science-fiction lines—they had no experience at all marketing science fiction and were reluctant to invest in developing the expertise for what might, after all, turn out to be the fad of a season.[47] But there were some small presses devoted to science fiction and fantasy, run mostly by science-fiction fans. Lloyd Eshbach had founded Fantasy Press in 1946 to reprint in hardcover the best of the magazine science fiction, and he wanted *Beyond This Horizon* for his line. They had signed the contract early in April,[48] and the small advance had been spent. It was time to make the revisions.

The serial had been written under the wire in the last days of the prewar peace, and there were a lot of changes Heinlein wanted to make, reworking inelegancies, removing or changing some of the elements that were in there for John Campbell's amusement, and adding enough material to smooth out some of the transitions. It would be a complete rewrite, with the torture of re-typing the whole manuscript. He had developed some speed at touch-typing, but his accuracy—or lack thereof—made it a slow and tedious process.

Ginny volunteered to put her professional clerical experience to work for him again and smooth-type the revisions on *Beyond This Horizon*.[49] At a high school rummage sale she had picked up an old Underwood portable typewriter for her classwork at UCLA,[50] and her evenings were free. He was delighted—it would save many days' agony and let him get back to producing fresh copy. He gave her his marked-up manuscript, and she took it back to Hollywood with her.

The months-long drought in his professional life came to an end then: the day after his fortieth birthday, *Collier's* finally bought "A Spaceship Navy" for $1,250[51]: ten times his Navy retired pay for one month. That was just about twice the word rate paid by the *Post*. "But, so help me, it aint worth it!" he told Ginny.

I've made as much money in less *time* writing pulp—this thing was a chronic headache.

Nevertheless, I gotta make dough.[52]

Laning was depressed over the editing: they had taken out a lot of the fac-tual material and left in all the sensational and dramatic stuff Heinlein had introduced to try to liven it up. Laning was afraid that his reputation would be damaged rather than enhanced,[53] though he was already talking about another collaborative article, on aviation applications of radar.

The $562.50 that was Heinlein's half of the fee (after Blassingame's 10 percent commission and 50 percent to Laning) went into his operating fund. Now he could consider something he and Ginny had talked about in the weeks he had been living in motels: he could buy a low-end house trailer and be able to move freely about the country—with Ginny;[54] they could live together without the restrictions hotels and boardinghouses imposed on them. His initial calculations were not encouraging:

> This situation won't improve any by the middle of next month, except by squeezing money out of this typewriter, for it costs me a minimum of $4 a day to live, $2 rent, $2 meals, which is almost exactly my income after alimony, leaving nothing for weekends, cleaning, haircuts, etc. But it *is* enough to get me a trailer, even if I hit a dry stretch—which I have no intention of doing. And now I'll close, resisting the temptation to start another page, for I have three hours more work ahead of me.
>
> My deepest love, my sweet!
>
> Bob[55]

Ginny had more faith in him than he did: she was already buying dishes and small appliances for the trailer.[56]

Whither he went, she made it clear to him, she would go—like Ruth. This was a major decision on Ginny's part: it meant giving up her plans to obtain a doctorate at UCLA; but more than that, it meant becoming a Bad Girl. Good Girls—and Ginny Gerstenfeld's mother had trained her into a very good girl—did not shack up with married men, and that was what the trailer meant. Moving in with a man-not-your-husband was an irrevocable watershed: sex was one thing; living together quite another.[57] Nevertheless, this was what she wanted. She was in love with Heinlein and wanted to marry him as soon as it was possible to do so. She had cleared all her personal emotional hurdles; she was committed.

Heinlein might have been somewhat less committed at this stage. The risks were considerable, and they weighed on his mind. When the divorce was granted, the court would issue an "interlocutory decree," but until the final decree of divorce (the "decree *nisi*") came through, a year after the hearing, he was still legally married to Leslyn. "Cohabitation"—living together out of wedlock—was illegal everywhere in the United States, and being discovered cohabiting could land both of them in jail.

It could also mean that the divorce might be invalidated—or some ridiculous penalties thrown at him. It could also mean the end of his new career writing books for boys, since Scribner's would not want to be associated with someone who wound up in the papers labeled a "notorious adulterer." Sophisticated people might let it pass, but there was enough prudery in the children's book business that Scribner's could invoke a morals clause in his contract—a clause nullifying the contract if Heinlein were found engaged in any of several activities considered unsavory—and that would be that. And that would be just the first of the dominoes to fall: his name would no longer be an asset to the *Post* and *Collier's* and the other high-paying slick magazines. He would be forced back into pulp writing—and he might have to take on a new set of pseudonyms there, too. Katie Tarrant, John Campbell's very Catholic editorial assistant, already thought he was "bad clear through."[58] Campbell might not stand up to pressure from Ralston or the business office.

There were serious risks involved if worst came to worst—but the worst-case scenario hardly ever came to pass if the parties used normal discretion. In the meantime, friends relayed to him some of Leslyn's loose talk about having him followed by detectives, and that was nerve-racking enough to keep him cautious about making his relations with Ginny conspicuous, even in Ojai. When Ginny came up from Hollywood on the weekends, Robert paid for a room for her—in another building, since his own building was fully occupied (Armelda, the owner-manager, wouldn't tolerate any hanky-panky, no matter how much she liked Robert!)—and Robert joked that Ginny came up to see the new litter of kittens more than to see him.

But one thing he could do: he began signing himself "Robert," the name by which Ginny called him. "Bob" was for his previous life, his life with Leslyn. Some of his friends continued to address him as Bob, and he did not insist they make the change, using the "Bob" sign-off to them well into the 1980s.

Robert's relationship with Ginny progressed into the "pet name" stage—he told her about his mother calling him her "little stove" when he was a baby. He called her Ticky and developed a stick-figure caricature of her with triangular dress and cats formed out of backwards *S*'s, resulting in hundreds of "Ticky pictures" over the years. Himself he called "Wuzzums"—a little different from the "Pig" and "Bear" routine he and Leslyn had used.

Heinlein forced himself to sit down at the typewriter every day, but often as not, he would get himself into an emotional tailspin over Leslyn and get nothing productive done. Ginny spent her evenings at the Studio Club for the next month, retyping *Beyond This Horizon* on one of the deal tables that came with her room. The table was a little too high, so she piled a couple of telephone books on her wooden chair and sat on them, high enough to reach the keys comfortably. The typing was not as much a chore as trying to read Heinlein's handwritten corrections.[59] Looking at his chicken scratches gave her a headache—and the phone books wrecked her back, but she persevered, taking another batch home with her each weekend.[60]

Ginny lucked into a stenographer's job at a brassiere factory—five days a week, without the usual half-day on Saturday, so it would allow them to spend more time together. She complained that it was dull. To amuse her, Heinlein wrote her a story that enchanted her:

Once upon a time there was, in a specially favored city, a little girl named Ticky. This she was called because she was busy like a ticking clock, all day long. Tick, tick, tick went her heels; tick tick tick went her knitting needles; and, most especially, tick tick tick went her mind. Her hair was the color of flame in the bon fires, her eyes were the changing green of the sea when sunshine plays down through it to the sands and the sea flowers. Her nose had not yet made up its mind what it would be and her mouth was shaped like a question mark. She greeted the world as a child greets a laden Christmas tree and there was no badness in her anywhere.

"Mother," asked Ticky one morning when the sun was bright and time was slow and sleepy and the pigeons were discussing new spring outfits, "can I eat my lunch in the cutter? Can I, please? Can I?"

"'May I,' Ticky," her mother said automatically. "Yes, I suppose you may, but do be careful and so forth and so forth—" So Ticky took four potatoes, fat Idahoes that would roast well, and some celery left over from dinner, and a tomato, and two cupcakes, and a bit of cold broiled ham, and some butter. Then she thought about it and took some more butter.

She met her special chum in the vacant lot across the street and down the block and they got busy. Now this vacant lot backed onto another street where the children were not so favored. There was a little boy who lived on the fourth floor there. First he leaned on his back porch railing and watched. Then he came down and hung on the fence and watched. Then he came near them and stood on one foot and watched. "Whatcha doin?" he asked. As if anyone couldn't see! For Ticky was buttering a

potato—first you push it from the ends, to break it, burning your fingers.
Then you lick your fingers. Then you drop the butter in. Then you—
    "Try it," said Ticky, "and—"
    (catch this same space tomorrow for more adventures of Ticky)
    Ticky
    Ticky at Camp, or Why a *Blue* Ribbon is not like a *Red* Ribbon
    Ticky in School, or Growing Pains make Big Girls
    Midshipman Ticky, or the Pie-Bed Mystery at Holyoke
    Ticky in Washington, or peril among the Bureaucrats
    Ticky at Snafu Manor, or Love has a low priority.
    Ticky in Hollywood, or You can't stay on ice forever.
    (In preparation) Ticky in a Trailer Coach; Ticky at Pike's Peak; Ticky
in Mexico City; Ticky on the Moon.

                                            love, love, love,
                                            Bob[61]

Heinlein also had accumulated a number of other writing chores during
the time of his crisis with Leslyn, and they were becoming urgent: a "resident
expert" job on science-fiction writing, for one. Since The Bomb, there was
suddenly a lot of interest in science fiction, and a kind of minor industry had
already grown up, advising teachers and especially librarians how to recognize good science fiction and sort the wheat from the pulp chaff. Heinlein
was supposed to write a short introduction to the theory and practice of science fiction for beginners. He was still collecting notes for "On the Themes
of Speculative Fiction."
    The editor at Scribner's had approved his space cadet idea for a second boys'
book, so he put that on the back burner to germinate ideas. " 'It's Great to Be
Back!' " appeared in the *Post* on July 26, 1947, the third of the four stories he
had sold to them. Heinlein also tried to develop straightforward stories of contemporary life for the slicks market—that was their bread and butter. Next he
wrote a "veteran's" story, working up his notes about the man who had frightened himself to death in the TB ward at Fitzsimmons. If it was carefully told,
so that nothing pegged it to 1932, he could let the reader assume it dealt with
World War II veterans. That story had haunted him for fifteen years, with its
encapsulation of fortitude versus extraordinary courage—good enough reason
to suspect it would work well in the slicks. He put a carbon set in the typewriter
and stared at it for a day. Nothing came. And then, suddenly, it began to come,
in dribbles. "It sort of smells," he wrote to Ginny,[62] but it did progress, and at
least the logjam was broken. He got through "Three Brave Men" and sent it off

to Blassingame to market—but two deaths in a routine medical procedure and no upbeat ending caused it to run into problems. "This story has been rejected more times than a wet dog at a garden party," he later told another editor.[63]

> *American Legion* magazine sent it back with the comment that they liked the story but as a matter of policy did not print fiction which implied that medical services in our veterans hospitals were defective. Another editor claimed that it was a known fact of psychology that it was impossible to frighten a man to death, so the story rested on a false premise. (That's the trouble with truth; it lacks the plausibility of fiction.)[64]

Between bouts of correcting manuscript and generating story, Heinlein was able to power through his "speculative fiction" article, two thousand words with a working title "How To, in Four Tricky Lessons." In 1941, he had repackaged Jack Woodford's advice to writers presumptive, cautioning that they could not afford to take themselves too seriously: writing is a commercial product. Now Heinlein expanded those thoughts into five rules for commercial writing:

1. You must write.
2. You must *finish* what you start.
3. You must refrain from rewriting except to editorial order.
4. You must put it on the market.
5. You must keep it on the market until sold.[65]

Making these rules into professional habits, he said, had more to do with writing and selling speculative fiction to its commercial markets than any amount of theoretical background. Failing at any one of these points was the main reason there were so few professional science-fiction writers—and so many failed wannabes.[66]

By the time he got the article to Blassingame, the original editor who had asked for it had changed his mind. The piece went on the open market[67]— and was almost immediately snapped up by Lloyd Eshbach, Heinlein's publisher for *Beyond This Horizon*; it was just exactly what Eshbach needed to round out a slim book of critical essays he was putting out, *Of Worlds Beyond*. One of Heinlein's personal heroes, Eric Temple Bell ("John Taine"), later told him, "That book should be made available in writing classes."[68]

And his personal life was beginning to settle. He hadn't lost as many friends as he had feared. Allan Gray, his buddy from the Naval Academy, wrote him sympathetic and understanding condolences acknowledging the sadness of such a breakup. "Somehow I had it all figured out that you and Leslyn came about as near to knowing what you wanted and having accepted the necessary deficiencies, as anyone I knew."[69] Bill Corson, the Wentzes, and the Sangs had already assured him of their continuing friendship. And as Sprague de Camp brought the gossip to their social set on the East Coast, reassurances came from them, too. Isaac Asimov expressed sympathy, as did Willy Ley: "Olga and I are very sorry about it all, but we also realize that you must have had good and sufficient reason."[70] With most of them, he was glad to be able to drop it—to not have to talk about it. Most of them tried not to take sides, though Vida Jameson was definitely Leslyn's friend, and her fiancé, Cleve Cartmill (who seemed to be diving into a bottle himself),[71] sided with Vida.

When the Corsons or the Sangs invited him for dinner—frequently— they even made a point of not talking about his domestic situation, offering the by-now-misplaced consolations of liquor[72] (for a time following the separation, Heinlein feared he might also be an alcoholic[73]) but also congenial companionship and conversation instead about "the War-Prophets, the 'flying saucers' or who rubbed out Bugsy Siegel."[74] Cal Laning, though, was another matter. Heinlein had been unsure how Cal Laning would react: Leslyn had been his find, and his own girl before Heinlein took her away in 1932. Now Laning assured him of continuing regard and respect. "Of course I am No. 1 with you in regard to your divorce," Laning wrote:

> That is, you are my friend of extraordinary bonds, beyond comparison to my attachment to Leslyn. I am terribly sorry to see the break up and sympathetic with each of you. I do believe you are probably clear sighted, whatever the reasons are.[75]

That assurance apparently eased his mind somewhat. Heinlein wrote back:

> I greatly appreciate your comment about my domestic bust-up. One of the things I had to consider was just how many friends I would have left and it is very heartening to discover how small the attrition was.
>
> I knew this bust-up would distress you especially. I am very sad about it myself but it had become necessary if I was to retain my sanity and regain my health—as it is I tried to hold things together about three years too long. I don't want to indulge in recriminations, nor to justify my actions,

but I know you will believe me when I say that I did not want it to happen and did not go ahead while I saw any hope of getting back to peaceful understanding—you may hear quite a different story from Leslyn.[76]

And in fact, Leslyn had been spreading "quite a different story"—several of them, in fact. "Thanks for the tip about not talking about my affairs," he wrote Laning.

> Leslyn has been shooting off her face all over town and I have run across her tracks many times. . . . I have been most careful to keep my affairs to myself. Leslyn has done just the opposite—which gives me a black eye at first, I suppose, but in the long run my policy of privacy and silence will justify itself, I believe.[77]

Indeed, as time went on, Robert found that Leslyn's poisoning of the well had been going on for months:

> I find that my friends have been keeping their mouths shut for a long time and that Leslyn had been spilling her guts to anyone who would listen for many months before I left her, and she overdid it. She had been describing me as psychotic and building up an involved case to prove it. Bill and Lucy [Corson] told me that they used to listen to these long harangues and find me the same as I always had been and had concluded thereby quite a while back that Leslyn was loony as could be. Bill says that he had worried for months for fear I could not leave Leslyn and then felt obligated after I did leave her to pass on to me a lot of grisly stuff to insure that I would not come back to her. The latter decision cost him some worry. Bill is not disposed to stick his nose in other peoples' business.[78]

Remarkably, not one person who left any recorded commentary about this time in published memoirs or public archives had anything to say in support or defense of Leslyn.

Leslyn had sold the house and its contents, receiving, after fees and taxes, $8,500. Abandoning their painfully collected books hurt.[79] He had intended to go through the books after she took her pick of them[80]—but that was what "abandoning your baggage" meant.

Once the divorce hearing was over—in August, presumably (though, as July wore on, Leslyn had still not filed the divorce papers)—he planned to travel, get entirely out of the Los Angeles area and all its social complications.

His world-saving days were over—and the international situation had clarified chillingly.

> Incidentally, I'm making use of this bust-up to decentralize. . . . Time has run out; Russia has made it clear that, in time, she expects to fight. I assume that she now has the Bomb and will have sufficient stockpiles by the time she has an efficient long-distance carrier. I suppose we will be smashed. You have more data than I have, but, from the outside, I see no hope, other than possible good luck and good political breaks. My writings continue to talk "One World," but I'm whistling in the dark.[81]

In the same letter he requested that the "orange-slice" pole-to-pole orbit he worked out for the article with Laning be registered with *Proceedings* of the United States Naval Institute as the "Heinlein grid."

Robert did not speak of Ginny in his letters to his friends, but she had quietly become a fixture in his life. Her father had a heart scare that July, and she worried that she might have to go back to New York to take care of him. She did not want to leave Robert at this fragile time—and feared that the relationship would break apart if she left now. Nonsense, Robert told her.

> You have already restored me to the point where I can get by without going to pieces in your absence. . . .
>
> Do not fear separation. We are tenacious ones, each of us. I won't change my mind; I am sure that you won't. . . . Do what you need to do and feel sure that Robert will be behind you, backing you up, approving your decision and helping you to accomplish it—and loving you.
>
> I love you, Ginny, and want you to be happy.[82]

Fortunately, it turned out to be a false alarm. And Heinlein *was* back in production. Ginny was on his mind, and story ideas started to come out of their conversations. She must at some point have lamented the fact that she still had to share a bathroom at the Studio Club, just as she had to share the bathroom at the house where she was working before, because the next story he started turned on that gimmick. "A Bathroom of Her Own" imagines Heinlein being in a political campaign against Ginny. He would have been in trouble! "Female candidates are poison to run against at best," he wrote in the story:

> [Y]ou don't dare use the ordinary rough and tumble, while she is free to use anything from a blacksnake whip to mickeys in your coffee.

Add to that ladylike good looks, obvious intelligence, platform poise—and a veteran. I couldn't have lived that wrong.[83]

Blassingame thought it was well written, but it might have trouble finding a market: "Since the hero isn't very interested in getting elected, the drama's slight. Hope it goes."[84]

Heinlein's boys' book for Scribner's, *Rocket Ship Galileo,* was about to come out, and the publisher wanted some promotional work—a knowledgeable historical overview of trip-to-the-Moon stories from the past—at five hundred words for its house organ, *McClurg's Book News.* He gave them about 750 words titled "Tomorrow, the Moon," reaching back to Lucian's *True History* and *Icaromenippus* (about 160 C.E.) and going up to *Rocket Ship Galileo.* They could edit it to fit what space they had. He gave his new Hollywood agent, Lou Schor, a power of attorney to market *Rocket Ship Galileo.*

On August 14, Leslyn filed her petition for divorce, citing "[a] course of cruel conduct . . . against her will and consent and without cause or provocation, causing the plaintiff to suffer grievous mental anguish and humiliation."[85] Apparently, she had delayed filing, hoping for a reconciliation. Four days later, she wrote to Jack Williamson, in a tone very different from what Heinlein was hearing about from their mutual friends:

> I have put off this letter for some two months, hoping that I might have better news for you. But it appears that my hopes were quite futile. What I thought was going to be a summer trip for the two of us, turned out to be a request on Bob's part for a separation and divorce. Bob feels that I am entirely to blame, and perhaps he is right. But it has taken me some time to get used to the idea that fifteen years of habits and associations must be broken.[86]

The summons was issued two weeks later, on August 28, together with a Request to Enter Default (meaning that the petition was not being opposed). That meant the hearing was imminent. Heinlein packed up his things and came back to the Los Angeles area.

30

ALSO ON THE ROAD . . .

Heinlein wanted to get moving, get out of Los Angeles, away from the mess the divorce had generated.

> However the trial was delayed beyond the estimated date—it is now set for the 22nd [of September]—and I did not dare leave California until my affairs were straightened up.
>
> I have to hang around town because of her [Leslyn's] unpredictability. I don't want to find myself in the East, with my get-away money gone, when my next stop should be Nevada—I've got to wait until she actually goes through with it. This stalling around has put the damndest pinch on me financially that I have experienced in years. And the waiting makes it hard to write decent copy.[1]

He waited, moving from hotel to hotel, seeing no one except Ginny. He had invitations—and he appreciated them, more than he could properly express—but he found that kind of socializing just too hard on him emotionally:

> I am able to stay on an even keel only by dissociating myself as completely as possible from my former life.
>
> I plan to stay away from former associates and haunts until my emotional experiences have had time to age a bit, until I have become more or less indifferent to my Piglet. Even writing this letter brings up such emotions of sorrow that I can hardly control my tears. I have no doubt as to my course of action—my life with her had become intolerable—but I am by no means indifferent to her. No need to go on about it.[2]

Heinlein made a temporary solution to his housing problem: he invested his dwindling cash in a tiny "house" trailer he nicknamed his "Gopher

Hole": "I think the G.H. had formerly been a piano box," he told Doc Smith much later. "It was all we could afford at the time and was really a fishing-trip trailer rather than a true mobile home; what I wanted was the Airstream Line, but I could not afford it."[3] He set up housekeeping in a trailer court in the far northern end of the San Fernando Valley, about thirty miles from Hollywood.[4] His new trailer was so small that he had to keep his condensed reference library in the car's trunk, but he kept himself busy while waiting, installing light and electrical fixtures.[5]

Collier's published his much-cut article cowritten with Cal Laning as "Flight into the Future" on August 30, 1947. The reaction was not what they expected at all: it was almost as if people had been collectively holding their breath, waiting for someone to say something. And now that someone had, the dam broke: editorials appeared in newspapers about the Spaceship Navy concept, and the article was referenced in radio broadcasts.

> There was an inquiring reporter broadcast out here featuring the question "would you like to be a passenger in the first Moon rocket?" I listened to it and found that it was based on "Flight Into the Future." I don't know who set it up. I could inquire but it doesn't really matter—we got the publicity no matter who wrote the show.[6]

Heinlein sent Laning a clipping of a front-page article *The Los Angeles Examiner* had published. *The New York Post* gave it six inches with a picture of a rocket. Instead of being called on the carpet, Laning received congratulatory notes from his superiors—and from the head of Army Ordnance. Laning's sister-in-law had overheard two naval officers waiting in an airport, hoping that he would put out a series of those articles. He immediately proposed another collaboration (with the same back-and-forth about ghostwriting).[7]

Laning took the opportunity in the same letter to caution Heinlein not to talk about his domestic problems—unless he felt he absolutely had to get it off his chest. Heinlein was frank about his feelings in the situation:

> I have seen very few of my acquaintances since I left home and have consistently refused to stir the dirt with them. . . .
>
> My health is fair, my morale just so-so. Breaking this up after so many years is very depressing—I find myself overtaken every now and then by a catharsis of sorrow. However, Leslyn's behavior since I left has offered me no hope at all that I could expect any improvement if I went back. I'll let

the details age for a year or two until I see you, but there is no rational doubt in my mind about the step. As it is I hung on three years too long.[8]

Though, as a practical matter, he would not—could not—have left Leslyn when exhaustion from constant overwork and the loss of most of her family apparently kicked off this crisis back in 1944. Nor could he have known at that time that it was not one more instance of the passing instabilities that had blown over for the last eight years. Bill Corson had seen Leslyn a few days earlier at dinner and confirmed Heinlein's judgment: "If it will be of any help to you . . . and to help you past any last-minute doubts, hear this now: the Piglet is not improving. At all. The ailment is in full spate."[9]

That assurance did help. As the hearing came closer and the opportunities to back out dwindled away, he was in a state of increasing anxiety: "[When I got your letter] I was in a terrific state of emotion and I had to know, I just had to know, whether or not there was any reasonable prospect that Leslyn had pulled up her socks. Your statement . . . settled my mind."[10]

At 9 A.M. on September 22, 1947, the hearing went forward before Judge Alfred Pannessa in Department Sixteen of the Los Angeles Superior Court, and fifteen minutes later the "Interlocutory Judgment of Divorce" was issued, uncontested.[11]

That must have relieved enormous tension.

And now that the moment was upon them, both Robert and Ginny had second thoughts about going off together. Ginny said, "I believe we were in truth shocked at ourselves."[12] But the worst danger was now over, and discretion—and absence—would get them through the next year. Not even the $8,500 Leslyn had realized from the sale of the house would pay for detectives to trail him around the country. Whether planned or not—Ginny later remarked, "We got the trailer for anonymity"[13]—the course he took was cautious and discreet: living in a trailer, they would leave no trail of documents behind them—no registering at hotels as "Mr. and Mrs. Heinlein"— and the risk of exposure would be reasonably small.

Ginny's life was packed up and in Bekins storage; she had not registered for the fall semester at UCLA, and classes had started without her. But as to casting her lot with Robert, she had no real doubt. This was not "like" her, she knew—but if she was going to be with Robert, she had to *be* with him. If she just let him wander away, there was no point to any of the mess.[14] She was ready to go.

They left within a day or two of the hearing,[15] driving across the desert and over into Arizona's central mountain country in one day's drive. In late September, the summer weather among Arizona's Ponderosa pine-covered mountains was just beginning to go crisp, but Heinlein was there not so much for the weather as for Mars Hill, Percival Lowell's personal observatory in Flagstaff. He picked up copies of one of Lowell's original sketches of Mars, both hemispheres, showing plains and deserts and canals.[16]

He felt so invigorated that he set up his typewriter. He had not been able to work at all for the last month, and it had been even longer since he had written any science fiction. He had a gimmick story in mind, about a construction worker on the Moon—a union guy like many he had known, who complained about the job but could be counted on when the chips were down. The gimmick he had in mind was a little too rough for the slicks: sealing a pressure leak by sitting on it—which might kill a skinny guy but leave a fat man alive. "Easy Job" he wrote over a five-day stretch, finishing on October 1. A letter from Lurton Blassingame reached him a few days later:

> What in the world has happened to you? You were going like a gasoline-soaked fire for a time, but since your separation, there has been almost no copy from you. I do hope you have not become discouraged, nor that you are ill.[17]

Heinlein had more story ideas to work up, but he had to do something about the backlog of correspondence that was stacking up. Ginny took shorthand dictation and then typed drafts he could correct by hand.[18] This continued for a while, and it was a help—though perhaps it was a little too much help. Heinlein tended to get carried away when he was dictating (and come to his senses five thousand words later). They fiddled around with their routine and settled on his roughing out a reply on the typewriter, which he could correct by hand. Ginny would then copy in "smooth" final.[19] It must have been helpful for Ginny to have something to do: once the observatory was exhausted as entertainment, there was very little for her to do in Flagstaff.

The weather was cooling down, so they picked up one day and moved a few hours' drive south to Tombstone, Arizona, where there was more sightseeing. Heinlein had been in Yuma before, but Tombstone was something else: the city fathers had set aside the old part of the town as an Old West exhibit, built around the legendary O.K. Corral.[20]

Ginny kept herself occupied: She knew he was in pain and also that he had to work through it on his own. When he wasn't staring off into space, nursing his private pain—or, better, generating another story—or working, he could be very affectionate and astonishingly whimsical for such a serious and substantial person. Each day she got breakfast for him, and he always came back to the trailer with a "Ticky hum," a little rhyme with perfect scansion he sang to her, always to the same tune, but different words each day, sometimes holding his pajama top up and acting the part of a little boy performing for his elders, or a little girl curtsying. He teased her about not taking these Ticky hums down in musical notation and preserving them for posterity.[21] It was a habit he kept up for the rest of his life.[22]

While Ginny climbed Tombstone's Boot Hill and took in the other local attractions, Robert set up his typewriter again. He wrote outdoors whenever he could, since the interior space of the trailer was only four feet wide and seven feet long. Using the pull-down table he had installed blocked the kitchen sink and butane stove, and there wasn't anyplace else to sit.

One of Heinlein's perennial topics of discussion with Bill Corson was finding someplace out of the fallout patterns for first strikes on the coastal cities. The subject had come up again in their most recent exchange of letters, and Corson had reminded him to keep an eye out for suitable locations.[23] It might have been that correspondence that gave Heinlein an idea for a short-short written in Tombstone, "On the Slopes of Vesuvius."

Rocket Ship Galileo came out on October 13, and Alice Dalgliesh at Scribner's had approved his rough outline for a second book. He planned to write his space cadet story over the winter,[24] once they got settled, but something she had said when she visited with Robert and Leslyn in Los Angeles the year before had evidently stuck with him, for what he wrote next was a complete change of direction for him.

Alice Dalgliesh had written children's books herself, since 1924, and an autobiographical story, *The Silver Pencil* (1944), had been a runner-up for the Newbery Medal. She remarked that there were many more writers for boys than for girls. Heinlein's agenda in doing these juvenile books was for girls as well as boys. He saw no reason he couldn't write a girls' book[25]—writers always have to put on a persona and write through that persona. He would just put on the persona of a teenaged girl. "Miss D[algliesh] told R[obert] once that she wished she had an author who could turn out a girls' juvenile each year just as regularly as R[obert] did; he told her that he would try one—and she just laughed at him."[26]

At the time Heinlein had just filed the idea away, but it was a challenge he could not resist—"difficult but fun," he said of it.[27] "Poor Daddy," written in October 1947, turned out an ice-skating story: perhaps the "Mother"

character was a portrait of Ginny as she was now—startlingly, straightfor-
wardly multicompetent—and Puddin' an imaginative portrait of Ginny as
she might have been as a teenager. Heinlein himself would be "Poor Daddy,"
euchred into taking up ice-dancing to keep up with his wife as a preventative
for jealousy. His agent thought the story lightweight but charming.[28] Ideas
for several others had popped into Heinlein's head while he was doing it, and
he thought one day he might have enough stories to make a collection, possibly using a female pen name.[29]

As soon as he finished that story, Heinlein moved on to the next item on his
agenda. At one of the kamikaze think tank meetings in 1944, L. Ron Hubbard
had casually named a dust devil that hung around the Heinleins' apartment in
downtown Philadelphia, and Robert had dashed off an idea note at the time.
Over four days in October 1947 he worked up a story he called "Our Fair
City," about a progressive journalist making friends with a sentient (and very
cooperative) dust devil named Kitten, and using her to ridicule Philadelphia's
(thinly disguised) corrupt political machine out of office.[30]

" 'Our Fair City' amused me," Blassingame wrote back when Heinlein
mailed it off, "but reactions to this type of fantasy vary widely so I'm not absolutely sure a check will result. Here's hoping."[31]

Rocket Ship Galileo was already making waves, only a couple of weeks after its publication date: Heinlein's mother reported that she had got the last
copy in the local Bullock's; his sister-in-law Dorothy (Clare's wife) wrote
that the books were flying off the shelves in Cincinnati—and the bookseller
urged her to tell him to write another one immediately "for it's exactly the
kind of book all the boys want to read."[32] Irving Crump, the fiction editor at
the Scouting magazine *Boys' Life,* wrote asking for stories with the same kind
of scientific or technical background as in *Rocket Ship Galileo.*[33] That was
confirmation that he was in the right groove to get his "propaganda message"
across to young people.

Heinlein didn't really have "plans"—the only thing on his agenda was a
trip to New Orleans for Mardi Gras in February, if feasible, and possibly
after that, on to New York to see the Campbells and Arwine and his other
East Coast friends. Willy Ley was not among the friends he would be seeing:
over the last year Ley had found himself on the horns of a very unpleasant
dilemma and had made, by Heinlein's lights, the wrong choice. Shortly after
the V-2 firing in June 1946, he had mentioned to Heinlein that Wernher von
Braun, his former underling in the German Rocket Society, had been captured along with the V-2s and German rocket engineers and was now, as Cal

Laning reported in October 1947, was going to be working on the American rocket program. "I only hope that the U.S. Army will not suddenly find him [von Braun] 'charming' in addition to being useful," Ley told Heinlein.[34] But that is just what happened. Ley had rapidly discovered that if he wanted to stay in the loop with rocket development, he had to find some way to work with von Braun, which dismayed him—but turned Heinlein's stomach: von Braun was not merely a member of the Nazi Party, he was an SS officer. This friction caused Heinlein's friendship with Ley to cool; Ley stopped answering Heinlein's letters and spoke angrily of him to John Campbell as "self-righteous." On Heinlein's part: "I'm sad about the whole thing—but I really can't stomach Nazis—and I can't sponsor a man who condones them. I'm not sore at Willy, I am just out of touch, don't know what goes on there, and no longer feel sure of him."[35]

Heinlein was ready now to write his next boys' book for Scribner's, the space cadet story, which he was thinking of calling *Hayworth Hall*. He needed to settle in one place for a while—which meant they should move now rather than put it off. Winters get icy in the high deserts. His cash reserves were dwindling, and that put limits on what he could do until some of the stories he had written over the past summer sold.

Leslyn had been telling people that he was getting out of science fiction entirely, which was not quite true. Bill Corson viewed the prospect with alarm: "No one writes such good stf and it sells swell. Why do you do this thing? Desist."[36]

Heinlein might be able to squeeze by through the winter even without a sale. He must have run a complex minimax calculation, balancing his cash reserves against the destinations he could reach in the Sun Belt. He came up with Dallas–Fort Worth as his solution.

Late in October, they drove across half of Arizona and all of New Mexico and into Texas. They pulled into Fort Worth two days after leaving Tombstone and found a trailer park for four dollars a week with a shared bath. Heinlein set up his typewriter and began writing again. He had another idea for the *Post*—an entirely earthbound science-fiction story with a nicely ironic twist: a claustrophobe—a rocket pilot traumatized by an accident in space—had to overcome his fear of open spaces in order to rescue a kitten on the window ledge of an apartment building.

Heinlein could feel himself loosening up. He didn't mention Ginny even to his closest friends, but she was very, *very* good for him. He summarized his improvements in a letter to Bill Corson:

I've gained 20 lbs, my sinuses are okay, and I sleep like a top without sleepy pills. I've had one drink in six months—and that with Scoles, to keep from hurting his feelings. I get up early and eat three meals at civilized hours. On the basis of the above alone, I know that the Great Change is what I needed. As to my morale, it is certainly as good as it has been for the past four years—what I have left now is heartache, loneliness, and sorrow that it turned out the way it did, instead of frustration, anger, exasperation, and hopelessness, combined with an agony of indecision. Since all the authorities maintain that what is biting me now passes with time, I have no reason to feel down-hearted no matter how sad I may be now.[37]

His agent agreed that "Broken Wings" was good enough for the slicks— "This is the best one you've done in some time. Congrats!"[38] But the *Post* turned it down. Blassingame started offering it around to the other slick magazines. Heinlein hadn't sold anything new since leaving Leslyn, except a couple of essays. Nobody seemed to want his fiction anymore. "My stuff lately seems to be too corny for slick and quite unsuited to pulp. I keep turning it out; some of it ought to sell someday."[39]

He started working on *Hayworth Hall*, fiddling around with it for days, searching for that moment when it would just click and flow out of the fingers. But that wasn't happening. He was not blocked. He always had a hard time getting started on a long job. Henry Sang wrote an understandingly sympathetic letter about his "difficulties" in taking his writing in new directions: "I know how catastrophic and hopeless such phases can seem to a creative mind." Sang was confident that Robert's success was inevitable, but cautioned that "changes in the pattern of one's life can be harrowing and can exert curious and temporarily incurable retarding influences on one's ability to express oneself."[40]

The one thing he had sold post-Leslyn was articles, and Cal Laning was still trying to come up with another technical article for the slicks. He had given up on having Heinlein ghostwrite it and agreed to a joint byline. Heinlein offered him a deal: he would agree to another fifty-fifty split if Cal would advance him $75 a week during the actual writing—and if he actually needed to travel to D.C. for it, an advance for expenses. He just couldn't afford to write pure speculative material at the moment.[41]

He also heard from Leslyn indirectly, through Sam Kamens. They had exchanged letters off and on over the summer, in some of which he opened up to her about his misery at the separation and divorce,[42] but this was different—a business matter. She had left the Los Angeles area, too, and was now working at the Point Mugu Missile Range north of Los Angeles, which Buddy Scoles had helped set up after leaving the Naval Air Experimental Station in Philadelphia. The Heinleins seemed to have a knack for catching Scoles just before he moved on to something else: he was retiring from the Navy on November 1, 1947, with a tombstone promotion to Rear Admiral. Leslyn had used her personal friendship with Scoles to get an administrative job at Point Mugu and had moved to nearby Port Hueneme. She wrote offering to waive the support Robert was paying her—they both called it "alimony," though it was not a court-ordered payment. She sounded much calmer now. Her letter to him was oriented, reasonable, and loving:

> Dear Bob:
>
> I am pleased that you and Sam [Kamens] agree with me that I should waive the payment of the $30 per month allowance, so long as I am employed, and am making more money than you are. If at any time you start making big money again and wish to send me the allowance, I shall bank it, so long as I am making a living wage.
>
> Enclosed is a carbon copy of this letter, in case you wish to send one to Sam Kamens to keep with our other papers in regard to financial settlement.
>
> I also wish you and Sam to know that I have opened a saving account in the Oxnard branch of the Security First-National Bank, and starting next payday I will be putting one Saving Bond every other payday in a safe deposit box in the Oxnard bank. Under my holographic will in the Hollywood bank and the way in which the bonds are made out, these savings you are also heir to.
>
> Fondly, as ever,
>
> Leslyn[43]

That was a definite improvement. He was cheered when Corson wrote that Leslyn seemed happy in Port Hueneme. It could not be anything more than a start toward normalizing their relationship: reconciliation was completely out of the question.

> We remain as far apart in understanding as formerly, however—she sees nothing in the complaints I made but puritanical spite, masked as concern for her welfare, and overbearing bossyness. Well, perhaps she is right, but we will never agree. But I do miss her company like hell. It's a funny thing,

but even when we were most at odds, we enjoyed each others company more than almost anything on earth.[44]

This sentiment could not have appealed to Corson, who wrote implying that even this apparent stability when Leslyn first moved to Port Hueneme might have been a blip, rather than a long-term trend. He warned that Leslyn was sharing his letters with others, along with her own asides, "acid and witty."

> Dear Wobert,
>   Extensive survey of the Mugu area reveals considerable deterioration from even what you remember. Worse, by considerable, and sordid withal. Do not tease, torment and tantalize yourself over that which exists only in your mind—the person we remember fondly does not seem to be extant any more. Forgive my mentioning it?[45]

The situation was even worse than Corson implied: Henry and Cats Sang visited Leslyn after she moved to Hueneme and were alarmed by what they saw. They did not tell Heinlein at that time—not wanting to distress him any more—but they did talk it over with Bill Corson, who ultimately, when Heinlein was stronger, decided to pass the information along. Heinlein summed it up this way:

> Liquor at all hours. Leslyn apparently ate no food at all the entire . . . weekend . . . nightclubs with Leslyn insisting on paying all checks. Strange little characters who would wander in, have a couple of drinks, and wander out, an apartment filthy and unfinished (plenty of furniture in storage and plenty of money with which to get it out, but no rugs on the floor), no food in the house, and a refrigerator used only for drinks. Sink filled with dirty dishes. Wash basin filled with dirty clothes soaking in cold water. . . .
>   There was just one bed and Henry and Cathy finally went to bed in it. Leslyn was to sleep on a chaise longue; however, Henry says that he heard her wandering around all night long mixing drinks, puttering, and that once he got up and found her sitting in a window seat with a drink in her hand, staring out doors. The next morning she greeted them merry and bright and chipper, drink in hand. Breakfast was powdered coffee made with lukewarm tap water. She either did not bother or was not equipped to boil water. The normal reaction would be to recoil in disgust.[46]

Telling Ginny about this, Robert added, "Well, I feel that, too, but mostly I am overwhelmed with sorrow."[47]

Naturally, when Heinlein fretted, he could not concentrate on the novel for Scribner's. He gave up even trying and cast around for something else to occupy him. He thought about working up the Moon rocket serial the *Post* had turned down, but there was bad news on that front, as well: "Little Boy Lost" (which the *Post* retitled "The Black Pits of Luna" for its January 10, 1948, appearance) would be the last of the science fiction the editors there wanted at the moment. Ben Hibbs, his editor at the *Post,* told him "politely but bluntly" that his stories "had not stood up in their doorbell reader surveys."[48]

The recent string of rejections by the slicks for stories like "Broken Wings" he found disturbing; those were specifically slanted to the slick markets.[49] Heinlein took a short break: the Shrine Circus was in town at the beginning of December, and he and Ginny went to take in the event. The baby elephants took him right outside himself and made him smile.[50]

That trip to the circus must have been just the tonic Heinlein needed. He sat down again with *Hayworth Hall* and commenced the struggle again. He and Ginny spent three solid days calculating on big sheets of butcher paper some of the Hohmann transfer orbits he was writing about. They did the calculations independently and compared the results. Her calculations were more accurate, he found, than his own—no surprise: women had always made better "computers" than men.[51]

The writing went much more smoothly this time—for a while. He usually started to write these long projects with just the bare outline of the major events in mind, and the thematic relationships; the actual details were filled in as the characters developed and interacted. Once the characters were mentally fleshed out enough that he could hear them talking, he could begin to write[52]—and very often his notes "degenerated" from an idea to a plan to dialogue and by that time he would abandon the "outline" and just begin to write.

His characters this time were more lively than the trio of boys in *Rocket Ship Galileo* and correspondingly had a stronger "pull" on the story line. And they were simply not going to go where he had planned for them to go. He had initially intended to dramatize the space patrol concept—a kind of souped-up version of H. G. Wells's "Wings Over the World" (from the prewar movie *Things to Come*) for the atomic age—by having his central character, Matt Dodson, be called on to bomb his own hometown.[53] But as he got into it, that ending rang more and more false: as a practical matter, the Patrol would not ever put a cadet in that position, ever. It just wouldn't work.

Nothing he tried seemed to work. Without that kicker, the story fell apart on him. That realization hit him and took him down, flat on his back. Ginny was alarmed:

> . . . for about two weeks in the middle of that book [December 1947], Robert just lay on the sofa and moaned. I did not know what to do—or think. . . . It was the first time I had actually seen him at work on writing, and I did not make any very helpful suggestions—I just did not realize what he needed at that time.[54]

Heinlein remembered the event somewhat differently:

> [A]fter I had written half of *Space Cadet* I lay on a couch for thirteen days and groaned, and snarled at Ginny for every suggestion she offered for the plot. At the end of that time I got up, put all of her suggestions together, stirred them and finished the book.[55]

Reconceiving a plot is not normally so traumatic a process for most writers—but Robert Heinlein was not "most writers." His "just storytelling" was wound up in multiple dimensions, and all the elements were crafted to reinforce each other and have multiple facets that the reader might not consciously perceive but would sense nevertheless. Heinlein was trying to do something that looked superficially like formula but was much more complex and tightly woven, based on his idea of what boys wanted to read and how that fit into his propaganda purposes. It was not a simple matter of setting up a scene according to the formula and letting things proceed from there: the entire structure had to be taken apart, strand by strand, and fitted into a new pattern that had just as much complexity and thematic density as the original.

Winter had come on by that time, and Robert and Ginny were living more and more in the trailer, trying to economize as the money ran out. Ginny wanted to get a job as a secretary in downtown Fort Worth, but Robert put his foot down: married women did not take jobs that might take the bread from someone worse off than they were.[56]

But he should have let her get out of the trailer more: as it got colder and ice formed on the ground, Ginny bore up under the confinement, but small hardships became major annoyances. Cabin fever was setting in. One day, a sweetish, rotting odor spread through the trailer—a smell Heinlein recognized at once from his Midshipman's days on *Utah* in 1926: there were potatoes rotting away in the tiny icebox; probably one had slipped into the drip pan that collected the melting ice. If they had been in a better mood, they might have laughed at it. But they were on their way to living on potato soup—unpleasant echoes of Heinlein's infancy.

He went back to work on the book. He *had* to make this work.

One day she [Ginny] wanted to spend thirty cents—thirty lousy cents— and I wanted to know *why*?

She beat around the bush about it—Ginny becomes very inarticulate when she is upset, whereas I get still more verbose. This puts her at a great disadvantage in a family quarrel. Well, we had a hell of a row about it, one of the worst we have ever had. I could not see why she simply wanted to blow in—waste—the price of a supper for both of us when we were so low on money that we couldn't even buy gasoline, hitch up and head south to warmer weather—and no prospects of any money coming in any time soon and no one in the whole wide world that we could turn to. I am afraid I was pretty brutal with her. For thirty cents.

I finally squeezed it out of her. She wanted it for bus fare . . . to go down town . . . to go window shopping . . . to mingle with the Christmas shoppers and look at the pretty things she couldn't possibly buy . . . just to get away for a few hours from that 4×7-foot space, be by herself in a crowd of people, not to have to keep quiet so that I could work, or (worse still) listen to my nagging and bitching when I was stuck.

Thirty cents. I told her to go ahead, of course, once I knew what was troubling her, and Ginny had her day of "shopping." It seemed to do her a lot of good and she never complained nor asked for anything again.[57]

Heinlein made it his business to see that she never had to ask again.

Christmas that year was very memorable. Their trailer lot had a pine sapling on it, about four feet high. Ginny made strings of popcorn and cranberries and decorated the tree with bits of bread and bacon fat, to attract birds. It also attracted the neighborhood's local mutt. He ate the bread bits off the tree, so Ginny give him larger bits of bread. Robert laughed and called him their "Broad-gauged Texas Bread-Wolfer."[58] They had acquired a family.

It got very cold. There was snow on the ground and no heat at all. Robert bundled up with every article of clothing he could get on, in layers, but his fingers would go numb, making it almost impossible to type. One morning, Ginny slipped on a patch of ice on the stair, coming out of the trailer with a glass pitcher in each hand. She landed on her tail in the ice and burst into tears, not because of the pain, but out of fear she had broken the pitchers, which they could not afford to replace. They were intact—not even nicked—and the pitchers didn't matter in any case, but that kind of devotion was touching and irreplaceable.[59]

Presents were one of the few things for which Robert would let Ginny touch the savings she had put away from her work in Los Angeles. A wildly extravagant gift might well show how full and overflowing her heart was—but, of course, it could also be an implied criticism. Ginny found a way around the dilemma by making a gift herself. Robert liked long, loose dressing gowns that reached all the way down to the ankles—a Japanese style it was impossible to find in stores. She ordered Springmaid cotton fabric and a pattern, and sewed the robe herself, in yellow, with Springmaid girls all over it—and another in red cotton trimmed with the Springmaid fabric. She also made a little doll—a caricature of herself—out of a pair of the silk gloves she had worn as a little girl, with cardboard body in the shape of a Ticky picture, with cotton puffs for fuzzy slippers and a red, white, and blue ribbon. After he went to sleep on Christmas Eve, she arranged it in his Christmas stocking, peeking out over the top.

Heinlein had done a little sneaking around himself. On Christmas Eve, he found an excuse to go out and found a bottle of perfume for her that he could afford—$2.00 in a drugstore.

In the morning, Heinlein was overwhelmed by the robes—and by the Ticky doll, even more than the robes. After breakfast, he propped up the Ticky doll by his working setup (and kept it on his desk for the rest of his life). It inspired him that day; he wrote most of a chapter.[60] Ginny was sentimental over her perfume, too, knowing that it was a widow's mite. She kept the bottle for the rest of her life.[61]

In January—January 2, 1948—the dam broke: Heinlein received a telegram asking to buy one of his pulp novels to be made into a book. Erle Korshak had set up a partnership with Mark Reinsberg in Chicago, to found Shasta Press, and they wanted to publish an expanded version of "Methuselah's Children" as one of their first projects. The advance was small—$200—but he was hungry, and it was a good deal for him, to get into boards. It would be his third hardcover book.[62]

The very next day, "Gentlemen, Be Seated" sold to *Argosy*. His post-Leslyn sales slump was broken.

31

ONCE MORE, DEAR FRIENDS . . .

The sale to *Argosy* was more than moral encouragement: as Robert's savings had dwindled, they had been "eating my piano," as Ginny later said.[1] She had asked her mother to sell it for her, and they lived on the proceeds of that sale, and Heinlein's Navy pension, until the *Argosy* sale and the advance for *Methuselah's Children* came through, at about the same time.

With money in hand, they could get out of the ice and snow. Heinlein felt free to go downtown and stand in line on January 5, 1948, to purchase a necessary luxury—one of the first copies of Alfred Kinsey's pioneering scientific study of sex, *Sexual Behavior in the Human Male*.[2]

Erle Korshak had already raised the possibility of publishing the entire Future History in boards. Early in 1946 Edmund Fuller at Crown Publishers had talked about doing such a project, but the editing Fuller contemplated to make it fit into a single, "frighteningly long" volume would have gutted the series.[3] Heinlein told his agent to secure the rights from Ralston at Street & Smith before they even tried to work a deal: he did not want to get caught between Korshak and Ralston and have another book deal go down the drain.[4]

Now that they could afford it, Ginny wanted him to do something about his neglected hair. He had not had a haircut in months.

When I am writing a story, I *won't* stop to go and get my hair cut. However, I am willing to pause between breakfast and the days work and let her move my ears down. She got disgusted the first time I wrote a novel after we were married and bought the tools—I was pretty shaggy. Her first haircut was not a real success, but she soon picked up some skill and now no-one ever suspects that I get my hair cut at home—until I boast about it, which I do whenever possible.[5]

The book, now retitled simply *Space Cadet*, was nearly finished.

The professional logjam continued to break up: on February 1, 1948, the *Post* purchased book rights to "The Green Hills of Earth" for an anthology of stories it planned to issue, and Heinlein's Hollywood agent, Lou Schor (then working for Mercury Artists Agency), told him that Howard Hughes was interested in making a Moon picture out of *Rocket Ship Galileo*. In 1948, Howard Hughes's name was magic: Hughes had succeeded to Thomas Edison's reputation as a wizard inventor. He also held at one time every major aviation record. He had begun making films in the 1920s and now, in his forties (he was two years older than Heinlein), was still one of the most dashing figures in Hollywood. Schor speculated wryly that Hughes might ". . . become so excited about the project that he'll forget about the picture, build a spaceship, and hie himself off to Lunar City-to-be. And with his luck, he'll make it!"[6]

Heinlein had been in touch with the astronomical artist Chesley Bonestell since May 1947,[7] and Schor had informally "packaged" Bonestell into the picture project as early as December 1947.[8] Bonestell's astronomical paintings were astonishingly realistic, and, though originally trained as an architect (he designed the façade and distinctive gargoyles of the Chrysler Building in New York), he was an experienced matte painter for film work as well, having worked (sometimes without screen credit) on *The Hunchback of Notre Dame* (1939), *Citizen Kane* (1941), and *The Magnificent Ambersons* (1942). In 1944 he had published a series of Saturn paintings in *Life* magazine that created a public stir. The prospect of combining his almost *trompe l'oeil* astronomical paintings with matte work for a film was enticing. No one else could have done it at all. "I would not have attempted the picture," Heinlein later told an old Kansas City friend, "had I not had him lined up first."[9] A film began to look more and more like a real possibility, rather than a pipe dream.

Heinlein had intended to go to New Orleans for Mardi Gras if the finances would permit. On February 8,[10] between snowstorms, they packed up and left Fort Worth, dropping down to the Gulf Coast and then to New Orleans. The wide-open nature of New Orleans during Mardi Gras amused and bemused. He marveled at the crowds and the costumes, some extravagant, and the street theater, and tried to savor it all.

I tried a couple of the gourmet restaurants around New Orleans and in particular one named Broussards. The food was wonderful, and the prices no higher than Hollywood Boulevard, but the thing that tickled me the most about the place was one of the stunts that they do to amuse the tourists, meaning me. I ordered Crêpes Suzette for dessert. When it was served, the lights all over the room were turned out in order to permit the flaming brandy to show up. During this time the waiter sang "Madelon." This was their regular routine for Crêpes Suzette. When serving Napoleon brandy, they ring a ship's bell. They had a number of little stunts of that sort. The cooking all over New Orleans is usually remarkable, even in quite ordinary and unfamous restaurants.[11]

Heinlein had originally intended to put up in New Orleans for a while, but he found, unexpectedly, that the "dirty mud and smell of oyster shells"[12] depressed him, so they continued past New Orleans fifty-seven miles farther, into Mississippi and to the Gulf resort town of Pass Christian.

This is the stretch of country described in *Collier's* under the heading of Salt Water, Sin, and Salubrity. It is a famous resort stretch of coast. Mississippi has prohibition but there are liquor stores and bars everywhere and there are slot machines in every drug store and restaurant. The slot machines around here are very nice. I think they send a man around to put in more nickels every little while, for they appear to pay off about 120%.[13]

Robert handed Ginny several nickels and put his hat under a slot machine. "There were several men around and they laughed when he did that; but [Ginny] hit a jackpot, and we walked out."[14] They went to take in a picture with the profits—a revival of *Gone with the Wind*.

Now that they were more flush, they could live in a real house for the rest of the winter. They found The Oleanders, a huge, rambling house on stilts. It was seventy years old, with thirteen-foot ceilings, a fireplace in every room, and nine-foot doors, with a front yard running down to the Gulf. The house itself was only one hundred yards from the high-tide mark, and the estate was surrounded on three sides by what looked very much like jungle. The house was infested with termites and ghosts and rented for $40 a month: they made arrangements to take possession by St. Valentine's Day and went back to New Orleans, an hour's drive away, to enjoy themselves.

There are a million people in New Orleans on Fat Tuesday—in a space that could not possibly, Heinlein told Bill Corson, accommodate more than 100,000.[15] The town was wide open. They enjoyed themselves immensely this time through, though the most lingering memory of Mardi Gras was of aching feet, since there was no place to sit down in that crowd. They wore masks, and Heinlein wore a feathered cap to complete his costume.[16]

In New Orleans, Heinlein sold the trailer to a young couple just getting married. After Mardi Gras he and Ginny returned to Pass Christian and to work on his books. He had to expand the serial "Methuselah's Children" into a book, and he had to cut *Space Cadet*—and he had to be canny about it.

Alice Dalgliesh wasn't entirely happy with *Space Cadet*—it was a little different from the formula in *Rocket Ship Galileo*; the characters, she thought, were not so sharply defined, and her eyes glazed over in the technical material—despite which she and her assistant, Virginia Fowler, found the book "fascinating."[17] Their sense of his readership was better than their conscious philosophy about writing for children.

Heinlein cut the book from 73,000 to 70,000 words and had it to her by the end of the first week in March. He needed the $450 advance to pay his taxes.

While Heinlein was revising *Space Cadet,* Cal Laning wrote saying he had decided definitely that he wanted Heinlein to come to Washington, D.C., and help him finalize the new article on how radar could be applied to air traffic control. By the end of February, Laning had finished his draft of "System in the Sky" and sent it to Lurton Blassingame for preliminary comments. It was time to make the travel arrangements to D.C.—not a simple matter.

Laning had offered Heinlein his basement, but, he cautioned, there were complications:

> You can certainly shack up with us. Mick [Cal's wife and Leslyn's friend], is still antagonistic—I believe mostly as a result of Leslyn's handling though partly because she feels you represent too strong a claim on my affections. I am sure that the visit would work out in improved relations.[18]

But Robert could not bring Ginny with him, effectively saying to Mickey Laning, "Oh, by the way, here's my current shack-up I left your friend for, and won't you invite her into your home, too?" If he was going to go to Washington, they would have to separate for at least a couple of weeks. Ginny could go on to New York without him, and he could join her there when he was finished in D.C.

Meanwhile, Ginny acquired a kitten from a neighborhood boy, a rust-colored tom she called Pixie. "I started out as a dog man—and still *am*," Heinlein wrote years later, "but the relationship with cats is not the relationship with dogs. Dogs are human; cats are e.t.s—Martians probably. Very odd people and all different and quite unhuman."[19] Ginny, however, was as cat-mad as Mark Twain.

Pixie was entertaining: he would launch himself at the trailing skirt of Ginny's ankle-length housecoat and climb up to her shoulder, where he would perch, cleaning her hair. But Robert grouched because the cat tied them down to Pass Christian just when he was making arrangements to move.[20]

Then the situation became even more complicated: he heard from Bill Corson that Leslyn was carping about some personal items he had kept—a briefcase she had given him in 1934; a Tchaikovsky phonograph record. He sent the briefcase back by way of Corson and asked him to buy the album for her as a replacement. That kind of thing still gave him twinges of grief. "This whole matter is still a source of great pain to me," he told Corson.

> I was so upset as to be useless and unfit to live with the entire day follow-
> ing the receipt of your last letter but I do want you to know that I greatly
> appreciate the news about her that you relay to me and comments thereon.
> Please continue. It is a great help to me and has done more than anything
> else to confirm me in my resolution to stay away from her.[21]

She was receiving $50-a-month payments from Corson on a $1000 loan they had jointly given him earlier, so he had to stay in touch with her. Heinlein didn't, and that's the way he wanted to keep it.

Town and Country magazine bought "Broken Wings" on March 1. They retitled it "Ordeal in Space," to point up both the science-fiction elements and the ironic twist.

Heinlein was starting to get ready for the move to Washington, D.C., when Fritz Lang wrote him. They had corresponded in December, once Heinlein had a more or less permanent address.[22] Now Lang wrote saying he was wrapping up a film project and it was time for them to collaborate on the trip-to-the-Moon film they had been talking about periodically since Heinlein had come back to Hollywood after the war. Lang had been approached by the astronomer Robert S. Richardson, but Richardson's story idea was "hopeless."[23] Lang wanted Heinlein to come back to Hollywood to work on this project; he knew Heinlein had the right attitude about it: no mad scientists, nothing fantastic—let the inherent drama speak for itself. "An interesting human story," Lang framed the project, "against the background of the first rocket to the moon."[24]

"Your suggestion of Moon story collaboration tantalizes," Heinlein wrote back, but he was already committed to D.C.[25] He proposed to cut short the stay in New York he had planned after completing the article with Laning and come to Hollywood in April. Lang thought this would work.[26]

This put Heinlein square up against a big problem: Ginny had reconciled herself to a brief separation, planning to meet up again in New York after he finalized "System in the Sky" with Cal Laning. The trip to California would mean a much longer separation—months longer at the very least. Ginny could no more accompany him back to Hollywood than she could camp out with him in Cal Laning's basement, and for much the same reason: they would be much, much too visible there to slip under Leslyn's radar, or the law's, or his family's, for that matter.

But he *could not* turn Lang down. There are no letters or other documents telling how the arrangements were made—Heinlein was still not referring to Ginny at all in his correspondence—but if their later relationship is at all typical, he must have sat Ginny down one evening and laid out the situation for her as dispassionately as he could manage. She could only have been sad about it: if they separated now, there was a real possibility they might not be able to get back together later. But Ginny faced up to the necessity; she could not have disagreed with his logic. This was an opportunity he *had* to take.

On March 25 they loaded up *Skylark IV* for the trip to Washington, D.C. They must have been sadly conscious this could be their last trip together. Perhaps he later wrote a poem to himself about this painful and ambiguous moment and stuck it in his files—very different from the thumping, Kipling-esque verse he had written for "The Green Hills of Earth":

"Wise Choice"

Of course it's the sensible thing to do;
Our love was founded on shifting sand.
You owe me nothing, nor I to you.
We're both agreed, and here's my hand.
So go your way and I wish you well
I know that you wish the same to me.
No need for candle, nor book, nor bell—
I'm sure we'll often meet for tea.
If we can't be lovers at least we're friends.
There's no denying the fun we've had.
The waltz is over, the music ends.
It could not last but it wasn't so bad.

You never quite lose what you've already had
So I'm not bitter and you're not mad.
If you're content I'll even be glad.
Rational actions need never be sad.
So finish your cup; I'll fetch your hat.
A friendly kiss and then we part.
You're startled—that noise? No, it wasn't the cat;
But only the sound of a breaking heart.

In Washington, D.C., Heinlein settled into Laning's basement and bent his efforts to finishing up the "System in the Sky" article Laning had drafted. Laning just was not a commercial writer.[27]

Ginny discreetly visited for a few days with a friend from her Bureau of Aeronautics days, then went on to New York by train. She went about getting reestablished—finding another residence hotel, another secretarial job—but the luster had gone out of her life. She didn't even have family there anymore: both of her parents had remarried and had no place for a thirty-year-old daughter in their lives.

She looked up John Arwine and went out on a couple of dates with him. He was already separated from his wife and about to get a divorce—a nice enough guy, but no sparks.[28]

Heinlein joined her in New York a couple of weeks later and camped out with Arwine. The two men arranged to drive west together, leaving just before Ginny's thirty-first birthday. Heinlein would drop Arwine off in Las Vegas and then go on to Los Angeles.

Heinlein arrived in Hollywood around May 4, 1948 (a postcard from Victorville, northeast of Los Angeles, was postmarked on May 3). This time, he had to stay close to Lang's home and office. He could not bunk with friends; none of his friends were in the Hollywood area anymore, so he would have to put up with the inconvenience (and expense) of moving from hotel to hotel every few days, since the postwar ordinances coping with the population explosion were still in place. He wrote to Ginny almost daily.

Lang was ready to go to work, too. He had already started pitching a project around Hollywood, to be titled *Rocket Story*,[29] based on his earlier talks with Heinlein about a realistic treatment of the early days of space flight. Heinlein found the early stages of building a film project mystifying and frustrating. He put the best possible face on it for Ginny's benefit: "I'm not used to the Hollywood method of writing a story yet. It just seems like sitting around and chatting, but it's fun."[30] Their partnership was supposed to share the writing jointly, with Heinlein supplying all the technical expertise for the story and Lang the technical expertise for film. But the complicated deal maneuvers Lang floated seemed pointless and confusing to him.[31]

He did keep busy on other matters: it helped his reputation locally that he had two stories out—"Gentlemen, Be Seated" in *Argosy* in April 1948 and "Ordeal in Space" in the May issue of *Town and Country*. Nearly as soon as he arrived in Hollywood, he was invited to give a talk to a group of children's librarians at a "Book Breakfast" of the County Librarians' Association meeting in Los Angeles on May 5, 1948, sharing the "stage" with eight writers, including soon-to-be Newbery Medal–winning children's librarian-turned-writer Mabel Leigh Hunt[32] and Theodor Seuss Geisel, who was to become much better known as Dr. Seuss. Although Geisel had been writing children's books since 1936, in 1948 he was still best known for his Flit ads, Oscar-winning documentary films, and the cartoon *Gerald McBoing-Boing*—and for the series of "Private Snafu" newspaper cartoons he had done with Chuck Jones during World War II. Heinlein's boys' books were written for an older readership than most of this particular group aimed at; he talked about how the "gravity gauge"—the difference between the Moon's gravitational field and the Earth's—might change the strategic situation so completely that anyone who got to the Moon first didn't need atomic weaponry; he could throw rocks from the Moon and be a serious threat. The speech was picked up as the theme of *The Los Angeles Times*'s report of the breakfast the next day.[33]

Heinlein got reacquainted with his friends and found it possible to have a social life of a sort—but it was opening up old scars. "This return to Hollywood is having an odd emotional effect on me," he wrote Ginny.

> I can't define it because I can't analyze it, but I think I will be free of most of the bad associational effects of the place after this one trip. However, just at present seeing old friends and old places is squeezing out emotional feelings that have been dammed up. For one thing, after a year of avoiding my friends and keeping my mouth shut I find myself talking about my bustup with Ed, with Roby [Wentz], with Bill, with Lucy [the Corsons] particularly. And probably I shall talk with others. At the time it is both painful and relief-inducing, like removing a bandage or tearing off adhesive tape. I don't know how I shall feel about it in the long run.[34]

The daily sessions with Fritz Lang were starting to take on a surreal quality. Heinlein practically forced the story issue by offering the basic situation of *Rocket Ship Galileo* and evolving a more adult-oriented story line out of it. Lang seemed preoccupied spinning deals, and Heinlein didn't understand more than a third of the maneuvering he wanted to do.[35]

This semi-stalled state was beginning to have a serious downside for Heinlein as his cash reserves drained away: it was *very* expensive to live in Los Angeles. He had been lucky enough to find a room to rent, on Highland north of Franklin,[36] so he no longer had to move every few days—but he would have to do some commercial writing, quickly, in order to stave off total collapse of his finances. Fortunately, several markets had asked for stories: Irving Crump, the editor of *Boys' Life* magazine, had written before Heinlein got to Hollywood,[37] asking for a twenty-thousand-word serial; *Town and Country* and *This Week* magazines were both looking for short stories.[38]

And Lang kept spinning deals. He wanted his production company— Diana Productions—to take over the copyright of the story they were generating, without fee. Heinlein thought it was time for him to consult his agent: maybe Lou Schor could explain the whys and wherefores of this deal to him.

> As to Fritz, at first everything was lovely, then I told him that I must go see my agent and talk things over with him. He wanted to know why Lou must know anything about our venture, an attitude that I did not like. I told him that Lou was displaying other properties of mine, interplanetary, as he knew. I pointed out that it was better to bring Lou in, pay his commission, and have him on our side. He agreed but it seemed to surprise him very much that Lou was offering *Rocket Ship Galileo* for sale.
>
> Why it should surprise him I don't know, since he had seen the book and actually owned a copy, but it did. He then took the stand that I must make up my mind between *Rocket Ship Galileo* and the venture with him before we could talk about anything. I wanted him to talk with me and Lou to see what the situation was and figure out what was mutually advantageous—i.e., Fritz has no financing as yet. Lou thinks he can float a moon rocket story; maybe we can use Lou. No, no, a thousand times no! I was subject to five hours of temperament, nine P.M. to two A.M. at Fritz's house. All of which added up to the notion that Fritz would not see Lou because "he had nothing to say to him." There's no need to go into all the involvements. Lou thinks that Fritz is trying to pull a fast one in which I would speculate on a possibility while giving up the right to peddle the moon story elsewhere and taking my chances that a picture might eventually bring me some money while Fritz draws fifty thousand or so as director's salary *in advance profits*.[39]

Heinlein didn't think Lang was being that dishonest: Lang was a personal friend of several years' standing—but certainly there was an uncomfortable level of paranoia. And there were other matters that made him uncomfortable: "A couple of phrases used in my presence," he told Cal Laning, "plus a remark about Paul Robeson made by his closest friend and collaborator . . . convinced me that Fritz was either a commie or a fellow traveler."[40]

Well, I was prepared to trust him completely when I came out here, but his displays of temper at the very idea of talking things over with my agent have left me quite jaundiced. Actually, I think Fritz is quite honest by his lights and sincerely hurt that I should have let an agent come between us. He feels that he is honoring me with the association and that I should be grateful. Well, I am, but when it comes to the money side of it, it seems to me that I should be paid just as soon as he is. And I don't see why that we remove from the market a story which he's not interested in. Oh, well, I doubt if we shall reach any agreement, in which case Lou will go ahead and see what he can do without Fritz. Perhaps it's just as well. I still have qualms about Fritz's leftist leanings, and I would hate to be associated with a story which might turn out to fit the party line. But mostly I don't give a damn.[41]

He just didn't go back to Lang's house. "The deal with Fritz Lang is probably falling through," he wrote Lurton Blassingame on May 18, 1948,

but I am not unhappy about it. Lou Schor does not like the proposed contract, and especially does not like the fact that Lang wants me to agree to withdraw *Rocket Ship Galileo* from the market before he will go ahead. Schor is expecting to sell *Galileo*.[42]

Two weeks later, Lang wrote, saying this obviously was not working out. "Let's call it quits and part friends"[43]—which Heinlein thought was about all that could be salvaged from that. Schor quietly went about trying to salvage the film deal—if not with Lang, perhaps with someone else.[44]

FRESH STARTS

When the project with Lang collapsed at the end of May 1948, Heinlein's trip to Los Angeles became open-ended, and the possibility of money problems and family problems had to be dealt with. Lou Schor, his Hollywood agent, confidently expected to sell *Rocket Ship Galileo* for film, and the adult-oriented story Heinlein wanted to develop for film (only loosely related to *Rocket Ship Galileo*) might be salvaged in one way or another, so leaving Hollywood again was not an option.

But the social problems Heinlein had anticipated from his return to Hollywood did start to come about: Leslyn had started hinting that she wanted to meet with him, probably to talk about a reconciliation. He was stalling her, but he could not keep that up indefinitely[1]—and what he heard of her current condition from friends who had visited her recently made him heartsick. "Because you never saw her before she got sick," he wrote Ginny in New York, "you cannot compare her with the person I knew and loved."

And now she is sicker than ever, in a dire and desperate condition, and there is nothing at all I can do to help her. It tears my heart out and makes me want to weep. Of course, I can't help her. She's gone too far into her dream world. All I could get is her lashing-out resentment at my attempt to force her to give up her sodden ways. I know that she isn't lovely and that she did it to herself. For one thing, I can't stop the march of years and apparently she can't stand growing old and must convince herself by her own means that she is young and desirable. I can't help it, but it leaves me with a sickness that I cannot readily get over. Forgive me, dearest, I can't shut Leslyn like a book and lay her aside forgotten. She was part of my life. She *was* my life. It will take time for me to build up a new life. I still love her and grieve to my roots for what she has become.[2]

That letter, sent on May 14, 1948, was not reassuring to Ginny in New York. She was not, in fact taking the separation as well as she seemed to be. She kept up a cheerful and encouraging stream of letters to him, but the gnawing doubt that they would ever reconnect was growing, and that letter may have tipped the balance for her. New York simply had nothing for her anymore. The unsatisfactory conditions she had left two years before had not changed: with no family life and a limited social life—her old friends, she said, were all just doing the same old things, and she couldn't interest herself in the minutiae anymore.[3] Nor could she have even a satisfying professional life: she got a job as a typist.[4] Four days after Robert sent his letter confessing he still loved Leslyn, Ginny wrote him from her women's residence hotel in New York:

My dearest one,

In my last letter I told you something of what is going on around this place—how down-grade it is. The girls are leaving it like rats a sinking ship.

But tonight something happened that made me particularly heartsick and sore. A new girl came in, a poor deformed creature. The house is half empty now, and I suppose Mrs. Koepp only let her in for that reason. She isn't crippled, but she's terribly deformed. For some reason, she reminded me of Cleve [Cartmill], though.[5]

At dinner, she sat down, and they left a little oasis around her. I heard the girls discussing her, that she made them feel ill, that they didn't see how Mrs. K could expect any person to share a room with her, etc. It made me feel ashamed and sorry to be a part of the human race, to see the way they recoiled from the unfortunate woman. I had to leave the room.

Why do I have to go on living? I've wondered so many times since Sonny died [her brother was killed in submarine combat during the war] why it couldn't have been me instead.

I'm paying the price of my sin. I must go on living and accept my punishment without complaining. I don't see why I do live, though. I've no wish or will to, just simply a business of going through tiresome day after tiresome day. Life is simply a burden to me. How sweet it would be to know that I'd attained peace, at last. . . .

I know now that I've lost my battle for you. It's all over, and I've given up. I had hoped, though, that something very sweet might come of it, but now it's all over. A good life to you, and a happy one. I've given up the struggle because I'm too tired to go on with it.

Goodbye now,
Ticky[6]

Her irrepressible spirits reasserted themselves within hours, though, and she posted an all-better-now apology the same night, hoping the retraction would reach him before—or at least *with*—the "first cousin to a suicide note."[7] Heinlein found her depression alarming. He was not afraid of Ticky, he assured her—though possibly of in-laws and bills.[8] Ginny wrote him a bracing, no-nonsense, no-self-pity letter a few days later:

Darlingest one,

Do you realize that it is a month today since you left New York. One half, I hope, of the time gone. You haven't said anything about returning to the city. When do you expect to be back here?

Your letter dated "May 23rd, I think" arrived today. My sweet, evidently you've missed one point, which I've tried and tried to put across to you. You've been good about writing, and I appreciate it. I've tried to be good about writing too.

But the fact is, I feel much the same way you did early last summer. I don't want to see my old friends, any more than you did. I've been divorced too, and I'm hating it too. And I'm every bit as heartsick about the thing as you were. I've been pushed out and made to feel all alone, and I'm sick and sore. Much worse than you think.

You've said to me that it isn't as bad as I think. Well, it's a lot worse than you think. I'm not just making this up—it's a fact. And the fact that I haven't anyone to whom I can turn has made it quite dreadful. I'm suffering over a busted-up marriage too. . . .

What bothers me is that you don't seem to want to do anything so that you can get over your fears, and try again. After all, you *will,* someday, and you'll have to overcome the same things the same fears. It seems to me that the sooner you *do* something concrete, the sooner you'll be well again. I'm not trying to push you into something you don't want, because I believe that deep down inside of you you really want it. But what I am saying is that the longer you let those things go, the greater will be your fear of them.

I will try to be patient with you, but remember that I've been through the same thing. And more recently. I need something to tie to, and I think that you do too. You can't spend all of your life reliving the past.

Believe me, I do love you, otherwise I'd have quit trying to help you long before this. Truly, I'm trying to help you.[9]

The subject of their relationship—and of marriage—continued to be prominent in their correspondence.

Heinlein's family was also a matter of concern. His father was still in the hospital, and his mother and sister were living unhealthily in each other's pockets.

When he realized that his parents' golden wedding anniversary was coming up in 1949, and he might still be in Hollywood by that time, Robert wrote to his brother Rex, with whom he had not communicated for ten years, and suggested that they pretend to have reconciled, for their parents' benefit.[10] Rex wrote back that, so far as he was concerned, there was no breach between them and therefore no need for reconciliation.

In addition to his increased living expenses in Los Angeles, *Skylark IV* was in the shop, and no sooner did the mechanics fix one thing than another broke down. The car was ten years old and had been worked hard: he was having to replace the whole thing, piece by piece. It was becoming the biggest drain on his finances.

Still, sometime in the last half of May 1948 Heinlein settled in to write some salable fiction. Casting around for a subject, he must have thought back to the Shrine Circus he and Ginny had taken in last December, when they met the baby elephants. Separated now from her, with only her Christmas Ticky doll for company, he wrote one of his most sentimental stories, "The Man Who Traveled in Elephants." It was very meaningful to him, and it remained one of his favorite stories,[11] but he was not certain of its prospects. He worked on the story, off and on, for more than a month. "I think it's a good story," he told his agent, "as good as some of Benét's. But fantasy is very tricky stuff and may make 'em laugh where it should make 'em cry. We'll see."[12] He asked Blassingame to try it on the slicks first—the *Post, Collier's,* possibly even *Cosmopolitan.*[13]

The story must also have been on Heinlein's mind when he wrote his update for the twentieth anniversary *Muster Notes,* the book compiled periodically for reunions of the Annapolis Class of '29: "For my money, the United States—the country itself—is the finest possible hobby and the greatest show on Earth!"[14]

Lurton Blassingame had been shopping *Space Cadet* around for serial publication now that Scribner's had purchased the book rights. Irving Crump, the editor at *Boys' Life,* wrote saying he had read the galleys for *Space Cadet* and couldn't use it because of the comic drinking scene—Boy Scouts do not drink alcohol under any circumstances—but he was still open to a twenty-thousand-word serial.[15] Heinlein didn't have a suitable story in mind at the moment, so he put it in the back of his mind, to grow an idea.

While Heinlein was writing, his Hollywood agent, Lou Schor, was working, as well. Possibly Schor had become interested in developing the business of what is now called "packaging" in film. Without Lang, he could not make a package deal, but he could keep juggling the elements until something likely came up.

Schor's friend George Pal had mentioned that he was looking for something unusual—off the beaten path. The kind of fiction-documentary Heinlein and Lang had been talking about might be just the thing. Schor introduced Heinlein to an established screenwriter who was just coming off a long project, Alford van Ronkel, nicknamed "Rip." They began the talk-talk process of story development, starting off again from *Rocket Ship Galileo* and developing a more adult story line while van Ronkel's current project wound down.

It might take a month or more to write the screenplay, van Ronkel told him, which gave Heinlein some free time. He got his ice skates out of storage and began skating again at the Westwood and Hollywood rinks. One time, his skating instructor took him to coffee with another student—Harriet Nelson, of the *Ozzie & Harriet* radio show.

Van Ronkel wrapped his picture, and Lou Schor prepared a collaboration contract giving both Heinlein and van Ronkel equal rights in the project they were developing. They executed the contract on June 21, 1948, and began working on development five days a week at van Ronkel's house—a much more stable working environment than the residence hotel Heinlein had found in Hollywood.

During the weeks between Lang and van Ronkel, Heinlein had decided his next book for Scribner's would be about a family of undersea farmers in the next century—to be titled *Ocean Rancher*.

> I contemplate using as a postulate of the story the notion that continued abuse of the soil and continued increase in population pressure have forced the human race to turn back to the ocean for the major portion of their food supply. Using such a postulate, I can show an ocean-farming family, all the members of which are as casual about going under water as western ranch families are about climbing on horses.[16]

As the month of June wore on, and while he was finishing up the last revisions on his second collaboration with Cal Laning, Heinlein was looking around for suit-diving instructors in San Diego—suit diving was more appropriate for living underwater than skin diving—and Buddy Scoles recommended a real expert, Edward "Jake" Jacobs. Jacobs's wife, Sylvia, it turned out, was family—another writer represented by Lurton Blassingame. She set him up with a local L.A.-area diving school, and by the end of June he began taking practice dives in the cumbersome suits in use then.

Another sale, the day before his birthday—"Our Fair City" sold to *Weird Tales*—put a little walking-around money in his pockets, and he had a big royalty statement for *Rocket Ship Galileo* coming in August, so all he had to do was hold out and keep up production. Lou Schor told them that he could begin setting up a financing deal as soon as the script was ready to be copied.

Sometime early in July, van Ronkel must have asked Heinlein to help move the script along by writing a formal treatment, which was a major project all by itself.

In Hollywood, screenwriters work on projects in stages. A "treatment" is a narrative version of the script, going scene by scene through the story, but written out in paragraph form. An experienced screenwriter like van Ronkel could pick up a treatment and recast the story into screenplay format almost effortlessly.

Heinlein's conception of the film project was much broader than usual for a writer: he was coming up with ways to create novel screen effects and solving technical problems of film making as he went along. As a screenwriter, van Ronkel must have been aware that that is both good and bad. Producers and directors don't want a mere writer to tell them how to go about their business, and putting too much "direction" into a script is an amateur mistake. On the other hand, some of the stuff Heinlein was coming up with was new and useful. Van Ronkel must have foreseen that part of his role in their partnership would be to function as a filter between Heinlein and the producer when the marketing process began.

Heinlein's treatment for *Operation: Moon* (as the project was called at that stage) was highly detailed—ninety-seven pages, completed on July 21, 1948. That speeded up the writing process: the first draft of the script was nearly done by the end of July, and Lou Schor went into action. At a Hollywood party given by cinematographer Lee Garmes,[17] Schor introduced van Ronkel to his producer friend George Pal. Pal had already had some modest success under his belt producing the Puppetoons series, but he had been looking for something new and different to take on as a feature film project. Pal was intrigued enough by van Ronkel's pitch to ask for a more formal pitch meeting with him and Heinlein. The three of them clicked and quickly struck a deal: Pal would take on *Operation: Moon* as producer: he would start looking for financing for the project.

The main function of a film producer is to provide the financing for the film and control all the spending on the project. After that, he may or may not take on the function of a "line producer," seeing to the various details of the production. Pal went to New York to pitch the project to Paramount in the first week in August.[18] He had a tough sell in front of him: there was no long tradition of lucrative science-fiction films behind him in 1948, and "everybody knew" that trips to the Moon were "crazy Buck Rogers stuff," suitable only for low comedy.

Nevertheless, Pal was enthusiastic about the documentary style Heinlein and van Ronkel had worked out for the project and thought he could sell it. If Pal struck out with Paramount, Schor still thought he might be able to sell it to Hughes.[19] The Hollywood buzz had it that another producer was mounting a Moon trip picture and might steal a march on them—which must have been alarming, but might actually work to their advantage, since producers tended to follow a herd mentality and wander where they thought everybody else was wandering.

Heinlein had a windfall at the end of July: royalties from advance sales of *Beyond This Horizon*. He autographed a sheaf of inserts for the edition and, when his own advance copies came in the mail, he inscribed one for Ginny, with a Ticky picture of her typing away perched on two telephone books and captioned: "Amanuensis Extraordinary and Copyist Plenipotentiary." He also, without telling her in advance, bought a new portable Smith-Corona typewriter for her, to replace the used Underwood she had banged to death retyping *Beyond This Horizon,* and shipped it to her in New York, his first "unbirthday" present. She was delighted with it, showing it off to the other women in her residence hotel.[20]

Perhaps this was the occasion for the only piece of Virginia Gerstenfeld's verse extant:

> *To the sweetest Wuzzum in the whole country*
> *From whom I've had letters recently*
> *But seldom. It surely would be awful nice,*
> *And Ticky'd answer in a trice,*
> *If he'd write more often. But very busy is he*
> *Writing stories and a movie,*
> *And he hasn't time for letters.*
> *(Oh, when will he burst those fetters?)*
> *Today after hunting long and lean,*
> *I've acquired some dichloroethylene,*

With which to mend my Plexi box,
Which I broke with awful knocks.
Then some knitting he will see,
At which to rejoice mightily,
For out of that very box will come,
A sweater to replace his Navy one.

It would be nice to know a date,
How long for Wuzzum must I wait?

This thing makes sense, in little ways,
But I've been planning it for days—
It's fun to write you these quatrains,
Like forgetting heat in chiliblains.
Speaking of heat, the weather's been awful,
And of New York I've had a crawful.
The subways are like a Turkish bath,
And I've lost weight til I'm like a lath.
Sleeping, too, is an awful chore,
And I'll be glad when it's cool once more,

Ticky's appointments to fix her teeth,
Start on Saturday. Please bequeath
A posy to her if she dies before [21]

The project was in good hands. Heinlein could contemplate leaving Los
Angeles while Pal was pitching the script in New York—as soon as his royalties for the last six months' sales of *Rocket Ship Galileo* came through in mid-
August. He had three "back orders" for stories, plus the undersea farming
book for Scribner's.

Heinlein was a little shaken up because of a recent accident while suit
diving: the diving suits in use then consisted of a shaped bag with an enormous spherical helmet, the whole set of diver and gear weighing about four
hundred pounds. The version Heinlein's instructor was using had peepholes
through the helmet, rather than a circle of glass in front; both versions were
essentially nineteenth-century technology that Jules Verne might have recognized. [22] On one of his three practice dives, when he was on the bottom
of a cove off Santa Catalina Island, he found he had not been strapped in

properly, and he was pulled out of the helmet and into the mass of the heavy, shapeless suit, banging the back of his head and crushing his nose. He struggled to get a grip on something—anything—but was blind and helpless.

Sensing his struggles, his instructor hauled him up by main force, but Heinlein was too heavy to lift out of the water. He struggled ineffectually to get back up into the helmet.

Finally, they got him into the boat, with just a skinned nose and a lump on his head—but so exhausted by the struggle that he had no strength left in his arms and had to have help just to stand. Heinlein found out something about himself that day: he was one of those people who do not panic in an emergency—but he was scared, without entirely being aware of it. Half an hour after the accident, when he had been skinned out of the suit and changed from the red flannel "aviator" long johns he wore as undergarments for the diving suit, and back into Skivvies, he suddenly lurched to his feet and made for the rail and threw up.[23]

He put on a brave front for Ginny and Lurton and John Campbell: "I was in no real danger—but I now have an acute, emotional appreciation of the old standard s-f situation of the man in a spacesuit whose air is giving out!"[24]

Heinlein hadn't felt any nausea while the emergency was on, but he was grateful he hadn't had to throw up in the helmet: "It is *not* a good idea to get sick inside your helmet; it not only trickles down your armpits, it clogs your valves and ruins your visibility."[25] He planned to get back into that suit, but it would have to wait until he could get settled. "Much as it scared me," he told Ginny later, "I would not have missed this mishap for anything; it is a thousand dollars worth of authentic material."[26]

With the screenplay nearing completion and marketing actually getting under way, it was time for him to leave Los Angeles. His family was in an uproar that summer. Mary Jean was sick and worried about both Bam and Rex. By August, Heinlein's father was starting to be interested in things again, and that had everybody in a tizzy: you just don't recover from involutional melancholia. That was the orthodox medical opinion—which, apparently, wasn't worth anything at all. But it meant that Heinlein now had family obligations he could not escape.

He had taken care not to let his mother know that there was a possibility he might be back in Hollywood for an extended period, but when he contacted his brother Rex, back in May, about his parents' golden wedding anniversary, Rex had told others in the family, and shortly Robert's mother phoned, hinting he could take some of the burden off Mary Jean if he settled here permanently. "The answer to that is, *no!* . . . Oh, nuts, I try to think about it as little as possible."[27]

Also, his sister Louise had been diagnosed with breast cancer and was scheduled for an emergency mastectomy. Bam was traveling out to Albuquerque to take care of the little Bacchi,[28] and the family was back-and-forthing about visiting and care arrangements that threatened to suck him in.

> I don't know just what my duty is. Men have to keep their jobs. My job is writing. I can't just drop a job without writing off the financial return expected. In this case I have several other people to whom I am committed. I don't know. I feel as if I were failing to carry my weight. I'm rather in a tizzy. . . . I am weeks overdue on this screenplay and very impatient. It is possible, even probable, that we have been beaten to the punch by another producer. I've run out of cash except for the royalties due in three days on *Rocket Ship Galileo,* and I don't want to drive cross-country alone, and I'm a big crybaby.[29]

He added: "If the money gets low, Wuzzum's morale goes down into his boots. This is a Natural Law."

In addition to the family problems and the financial strain, Heinlein had been struggling with himself. At the age of forty-one, he knew himself, his habits and inclinations—and had no inclination to lie to himself about them. Ginny's fears they might never reconnect were not entirely groundless. It was a serious question, whether he could reasonably promise to curb his wandering eye, to "cleave only unto her." "Honey," he wrote seriously to Ginny, "I've reached the dangerous age."

> Like Kipling says, "There are times that you think that you mightn't and times that you know that you might." I expect to keep it pretty well under control—but I hope you won't kick me out if I slip. Don't judge this frank statement too harshly. There is literally no way for me to tell you just what goes on inside me in the way of erratic judgment when I begin to spin around my gonads. Anyhow, you lecherous little wench, if I were not subject to such spasms of cockeyed rut-controlled, lack of judgment . . . I wouldn't now be proposing to make a fairly honest woman out of you.
>
> I'll try to behave but I am not giving any iron-clad promises. I *think* I will behave.[30]

The period of separation from Ginny—and the obvious emotional strain the separation placed on her—had forced him to resolve his own self-doubts.

I'm tired and have had several disappointments, frustrations, and dilemmas lately and I'm feeling poor. A sale would help a lot, especially the sale of this movie. I don't *have* to have it, but it would mean freedom to do things comfortably and pleasantly. I could pay the Jacobs for what they have done for me free—and they need the money. I could give mother a lump sum and thereby buy myself a limited freedom from family responsibility.

And I could marry Ticky without a nagging worry as to whether or not I could feed her.

Yes, wench, I want to marry you! Little as I care for the institution of marriage as it is set up at present, I want your company and your help and your love and the lift I get from having your small and rather screwball presence around me. I had hoped to sell this screenplay before coming out flatfooted with plans—coming, as it were, to lay a bag of gold at your feet. I know that you have never held out for a thin dime, but the subject of money matters to me when I haven't got it. The presence of poverty and the fear of poverty goes way back into my childhood; I wanted us to start out right, with a good bank balance and a healthy chunk of paid-up life insurance as an estate. Well, maybe I'll get it yet. But I do want to marry you. . . .

I think you'll be taking a hell of a risk in marrying me, but it may be better than living in a rooming house and going to an office or lab. Anyhow, I love you, wench—I love you to pieces and I plan to beat you up every Saturday night.

How about it?

W.[31]

Ginny seriously considered the proposal:

Other women: How about crossing that bridge when we come to it? I darned well wont kick you out if you slip. Hey! Rut-controlled lack of judgment! Connected with Ticky too! I'm not sure I like that! Objection.

(Objection will be overruled, I'll bet.) Seriously, though, if you don't feel like being monogamous, that's up to you. I promise not to try to hinder you. You'll have to judge for yourself what's best for you. I shall be as nice to the ladies as I know how, but I don't think you'd kick over the traces too hard. Anyway, it might just be that you'll settle down after a little

fling, and what's the sense of trying to guess the future? Let's just take those
things in our stride, shall we?

. . . About families, well, the less said, the better.

Sure, I'll take the hell of a risk, because I love you too. It's not just go
get out of the rooming house and job. Anyway, I kinda like the job. And
I'm looking forward to the Saturday night beatings. Masochist, that's me.

I love you, darling, and I want to see you happy, and no matter what it
takes to make you happy, that's what I'll do.

All my love,
Ticky[32]

Robert wanted to settle down into a stable relationship—with Ginny and
not in Los Angeles. Ginny didn't want to live in New York. Robert proposed
Colorado Springs, one of his favorite places in the entire country.[33] He
would put off writing stories until he got there. "That is, it would be nice to
write them there if Ticky were there. . . ." after fifteen grueling weeks of separation.[34]

Heinlein prepared to leave Hollywood bogged down by a cold. He wrote
a "drop dead" file of notes (that is, in case he were killed or incapacitated),
recommending Jack Parsons for technical advice on the rocketry if anything
happened to him. He also left in van Ronkel's hands a letter firing Lou Schor
as the agent for the writing partnership as of September 1 and removing his
power of attorney to agent *Rocket Ship Galileo*. In the month since he had
made the introduction to Pal, van Ronkel had become dissatisfied with his
performance as an agent—more dissatisfied than Heinlein—but Heinlein realized Schor couldn't function without the full confidence of both partners.
Van Ronkel could use the termination of agency at his discretion.

Heinlein left Hollywood on the last day of August. As he made one last
check at his mailing service, he found waiting for him his six author copies of
Space Cadet.

For company on the long drive, he pinned the Ticky doll Ginny had made
for his Christmas stocking to the front seat, and took off across the great
Southwest desert. A gas station attendant told him the Ticky doll had been
flirting with an Indian.[35] On his way to Colorado, he stopped in New Mexico to
see his childhood friend Don Johnstone. Johnstone remembered the occasion:

I was living in Los Alamos, and one evening got a phone call from Bob,
who said he was at a motel in Española. I invited him up to the hill—told
him I'd have a pass at the gate for him—but he said no, he wanted me to

come down to Española, and he'd tell me why when I got there. I did and he did, and it turned out that, as he put it, he had made a "lucky guess" some time before, had been grilled at length by Security people, and the last place in the world he wanted his name to show up was on the admission list of any atomic energy facility.[36]

Heinlein arrived in Colorado Springs on the second or third of September 1948. His year of waiting for the divorce to be final would be up in three weeks—on September 22. That would be time enough to get settled in, and then he and Ginny would get married.

Life would be very different. Not only was she a very different person from Leslyn, but he was a different person with Ginny than he was with Leslyn—and that was, finally, fine with him. Ginny could not come out until sometime after he arrived in Colorado Springs—her boss would not release her before a proper two weeks' notice—but the delay would actually work in their favor, as, now the proposal was definite, there was no point any longer to the risk and the emotional discomfort of living together illegally. Ginny had brought up the subject explicitly before he left Los Angeles, before he was committed:

> I'll tell you, honey, I've wavered back and forth about living in sin again, but have decided that it really isn't for me. Sometimes, when I've been desperately lonely, I've thought I would kick my hat over the Moon, but since you've been talking of marriage, I don't really see the sense of jumping the gun for a mere two weeks or so. Honestly, darling, that just doesn't make sense to me. There's an old Chinese proverb, about not raping the girl when you're going to marry her the next day, and that's the way I feel about it. Not to mention the fact that I really would like to get a few nice things to wear for Wuzzum and say goodbye to family, etc.[37]

Nevertheless, Ginny would fly out to Denver (though she hated flying) as soon as she could get away from her job in New York, and he would meet her there. Jumping the gun for a mere two weeks or so was better, all said and done, than those same two weeks alone in New York.

She initially had trouble getting a reservation and finally found a flight on a "nonscheduled" airline. Heinlein did not care for that, so he pulled in favors and found her a controlled seat on a major airline. She would arrive on September 11, 1948, so he would have several days in Colorado Springs to prepare before she got there.

As soon as he got into town, Heinlein started scouting for a rental and two other items he wanted Ginny to find when she got into town. For housing, he found an old, furnished, Spanish-style house at 1313 Cheyenne Boulevard. He was even able to purchase a used piano—a Wurlitzer spinet—to replace the piano she had had to sell last year, when they were so broke in Fort Worth. The other item—

> [I] finally tracked down a kitten in a litter belonging to a mama cat who is a free citizen; she belongs to no one but is the official mouser for an entire block. I catnapped him, a beautiful little orange-flavored tom, with fluffy hair.[38]

This kitten would have to be Pixie II, commemorating the kitten she'd had to give up in Mississippi, so he came up with a formal name of the bombastic sort suggested by *Old Possum's Book of Practical Cats*: Ethelrude Pixilated Colorado.[39]

On Saturday, September 11, 1948, Robert took a commuter flight up to Denver to meet Ginny's flight from New York.

For the next ten days, Robert and Ginny had to keep a very low profile. They acquired a companion kitten for Pixie II—a tan-colored kitten they named Café au lait au sucre—"Caffy." Pixie and Caffy took to each other immediately, noisily mock-battling all morning and sleeping together in the afternoon, then more rounds of sparring in the evening. The decree *nisi* would be issued in a little less than two weeks. They quietly went about their business, not calling much attention to themselves until they could be married and take up their new life. The kittens provided most of their social life.

Heinlein began planning his workload for the rest of the year: he wrote to Alice Dalgliesh asking for her latest deadline for the ocean ranching book so that he could schedule more suit diving—possibly in Florida.[40] She found the idea "thrilling" but cautioned him not to get too technical—and if possible put in a girl this time.[41] That was not a problem, since he was planning to build the story around a family.

September 22 came and went, and no word from Los Angeles about the divorce. Both Robert and Ginny were holding their breaths: if this situation went on too long, everything would be spoiled. On September 23, Lurton Blassingame told him that both Ginny's parents had contacted him simultaneously, wondering what had become of Ginny.[42] Both Robert and Ginny jumped to fix that one—but the social white lies needed to keep things smooth could very easily become too big to handle. Robert had not mentioned Ginny in any of his correspondence for the last year. Now it was time to take the wraps off, since in a matter of days the masquerade would be over anyway. "I'll try to clear up the mystery," he told Blassingame:

> I've acquired the habit of keeping silent about my private life because of how I have been forced to live these past five years—I'm afraid I have come to carry it to extremes. . . .
>
> Yes, I'm married again. I would have gotten around shortly to telling you so, by the usual formal announcement. The mix-up with Ginny's parents came about this way: She wired both of them as soon as she got here but did not give an address as we had not yet obtained a house. When we located a house, she wrote to each of them and put the letters in her purse, intending to stamp and mail them downtown.
>
> We found them about a week later, the next time she wore that purse.[43]

They couldn't keep things quiet much longer, and while people might wink at a couple living together a few weeks before marriage, if it went on too long . . .

Bill Corson had written suggesting Heinlein find someone local to follow up on the decree *nisi*, as these things didn't just happen automatically.[44] Heinlein asked Sam Kamens—his Los Angeles lawyer and Leslyn's lawyer for the divorce—to look into it and do whatever was necessary, since Leslyn apparently wasn't up to finalizing the divorce. Leslyn, in fact, had disappeared from her job at Point Mugu—"compulsory resignation because of refusal to do work the way her boss wanted her to do it," Bill Corson told him, adding, "Complicated to unknown extent by liquor."[45] She turned up "in a sanatorium at Long Beach, taking the cure."[46] She had joined AA.[47]

Kamens sent Heinlein a form "Affidavit for Final Decree of Divorce," and Heinlein found a notary in Colorado Springs on Columbus Day, October 12. The affidavit was filed with the court on October 15, three weeks and two days after the year was up—five weeks minus one day since they had set up housekeeping in Colorado Springs without benefit of clergy.

Even living as quietly as possible, they had neighbors, and they had started to make friends in Colorado Springs. Ginny had even agreed to do an ice-skating exhibition for the Broadmoor Hotel and Resort in the winter. They had started to put down roots.

But they had a clock problem: when they got married, the announcement would appear in the local newspaper, and everyone would know they had been "living in sin" for the last six weeks. At the very least, they would be snubbed. It was common knowledge that in this kind of situation, some of the local merchants might make trouble. It was not out of the range of the possible that the local constabulary might suggest the community didn't want to be associated with "their type."

If they could not handle the transition discreetly, they would have to pull up stakes and move again.

The Final Judgment of Divorce was issued, pending recording, on October 19. On October 20, 1948, Sam Kamens telegraphed Heinlein and followed it up with a letter: "All conditions complied with contract terminated."[48]

Heinlein was impatient to make it legal. New Mexico did not have the three-day waiting period to issue a marriage license—and if they were married out of state, it wouldn't appear in the Colorado Springs papers. That would solve their social problem perfectly.[49] The next day, October 21, 1948, they drove to Raton, New Mexico, just across the state border, and were married before a Justice of the Peace in a Methodist church.

Here is a poem I wrote for our wedding:
The bride was old/the license was new/the money was borrowed/the groom was blue. (Ginny didn't like it.)[50]

ACKNOWLEDGMENTS

When Virginia Heinlein called on January 1, 2000, to ask me to write a formal biography of her husband, neither of us had quite the vision of the gargantuan thing it was to become.

What I did not know was that Mrs. Heinlein had been searching for a biographer for more than a decade. She had even tried her own hand at writing it but did not feel equal to the task. Brad Linaweaver, the mutual friend who introduced us, later told me that he knew before anyone—before Ginny, even—that I was the biographer she had been searching for. Brad has supported this biography above-and-beyond for all the years it has taken to get it into print: Brad Linaweaver is truly the grandfather of this biography.

It is more than a conventional grace note to say that this biography would literally not have been possible without the full support and cooperation of Virginia Heinlein. She opened doors, made rough places plain, introduced me to friends and family—to Eleanor Wood, literary agent extraordinaire, and to Rita Bottoms, Head of Special Collections and Archives of the University Library at the University of California, Santa Cruz. Mrs. Bottoms's help with the Robert A. Heinlein Archive, then mostly sealed, in the months before she retired was generous—and as nothing to the help she has given in the years since.

Some of Ginny's introductions came too late: *all* of Heinlein's contemporaries would have been in their eighties and nineties; almost all were already gone. An interview Ginny arranged with Admiral Ignatius "Pete" Gallantin, Retired (U.S. Naval Academy, Class of 1933), provided information and insight about the Naval Academy during Heinlein's tenure there. Admiral Gallantin did not live to see the end results of his help.

Other introductions were fruitful and multiplied from generation to generation: an e-mail exchange with Kathy Petty, one of Heinlein's grandnieces, was the first of many discussions with other surviving family members, and particularly the genealogists and family historians of that generation, Andrew Lermer, Jr., and William Ivar Bacchus. It was through Bill Bacchus's good offices that I was privileged to interview Dorothy Martin Heinlein (Robert Heinlein's sister-in-law), then aged ninety-two. Sitting around the table with many of the generation of Heinlein's nieces and nephews in 2007 at the Centennial celebration of Heinlein's birth was a wonderful experience— and this roomful of bright, quick, wry, and witty Heinleins gave me a faint taste of what young Robert Heinlein's family dinners must have been like.

But the biography benefited, as well, from the myriad inputs of an interested Heinlein community. Individuals shared anecdotes, tape recordings, and historical research to illuminate the subject. As well as sound advice on the writing, Philippe Paine provided special expertise as an historical researcher, digging through crumbling, seventy-five-year-old rental records in Kansas City to uncover the traces left by Elinor Curry Heinlein. Thanks are owed, as well, to Deborah Houdek and Geo Rule, Missouri and Civil War historians, who independently researched Robert Heinlein's first wife but chose not to exercise their right to publish first so that the biography could have the privilege instead. Such forbearance is not humanly credible. I suspect angelic intervention.

Dr. Robert James, friend and invaluable critic, reviewed the manuscript at various stages. Special thanks are due, also, to James D. Gifford, who is in a sense the founder of the new generation of the Heinlein community. Jim Gifford was characteristically generous to this newcomer, sharing research materials he had developed over decades. His groundbreaking *Robert A. Heinlein: A Reader's Companion* laid the foundation and plan of a broad city, of which this book is but one ornament. He also, along with Peter Scott and Tim Kyger, took on most of the burden of the 2007 Heinlein Centennial celebration, which allowed the editorial revision of this book to proceed apace. Tim Kyger, longtime friend and space and aerospace professional lobbyist, also monitored the narrative of the aerospace history in which Heinlein was involved.

The late Dr. Phillip Homer Owenby shared his extensive 1994 taped interviews with Mrs. Heinlein to supplement those I made in 2000–2002. The late Leon Stover, Ph.D., Litt.D, allowed me to read and take extensive notes of his unpublished biography of Robert Heinlein, *Before the Writing Began,* as well as to assist slightly in readying it for submission—an act of particular generosity. For recovery and access to records, thanks are due to L. N. Collier, Esq.; Bill Higgins and Bill Mullins; Charles W. Miller, Ph.D.; and Beth Simmons as well as four generations of the Mosch family of professional miners in Colorado, whose records exceed those of the state.

The assistance of literally hundreds of individuals is gratefully appreciated, even though I cannot name all of them here. Any errors or infelicities, however, are my own and no reflection on their generosity.

Thanks also are due to my editor, David Hartwell. No better-prepared editor could have been found anywhere in the field.

And, last if not in any way least, to the Trustees of the Heinlein Prize Trust, Arthur M. Dula, J. Buckner Hightower, and James Miller Vaughn, Jr., whose continuing support of this project has been outstanding and indispensable.

WILLIAM H. PATTERSON, JR.

APPENDIX A

FAMILY BACKGROUND

Robert Heinlein was, like a great many of his relatives, interested in his family history both in America and in Europe before his great-great-great-grandfather immigrated here before the Revolutionary War. He was, furthermore, proud of the family tradition that Heinleins had fought in every American war. Kept out of combat in World War II himself, he supported his many friends in the armed forces—"Killer Cal" Laning, John Arwine, Isaac Asimov, Jack Williamson, and L. Ron Hubbard—and he was awed and inspired by his brothers' parts in the conflict: Lawrence Lyle Heinlein, who rose through the ranks from private to major general, was one of the handful of Americans who made up the Japanese occupation forces for a few weeks in August and September 1945. Jay Clare was in the first small force occupying Korea. It was their proud tradition as well as his own.

When he was able to travel in Europe, Heinlein made a point of finding out about the Heinlein and Lyle ancestors in Germany and in Ireland, and of sharing his findings with the other members of the Heinlein Family Association. Interest in Heinlein and Lyle family genealogy continues unabated in the next generation, and the special assistance of two of Heinlein's nephews knowledgeable in family lore, William Ivar Bacchus and Andrew Lermer, Jr., in putting together this appendix is acknowledged with gratitude.

The name "Heinlein" was originally—meaning before the family came to America—a moderately common Bavarian Catholic name. Even though the Heinleins have a lively interest in their family genealogy, the ground is confused because of multiple immigrations to the United States, at different times, deriving from different branches of the same family and from entirely different families. There were apparently two Heinlein families that came to the United States at about the same time in the mid-eighteenth century, both coming through Philadelphia and settling first in Bucks County, Pennsylvania. While this is a curious coincidence, it is not particularly startling: William Penn had traveled extensively in the Low Countries and the Rhineland to promote his proprietorship in the New World, and any converts deriving from Penn's proselytizing would naturally come through Philadelphia and make their way to the area being settled at the time.

The Heinleins of southern Germany were not necessarily all part of the same large family; the surname was adopted by unrelated families of peasants in Bavaria, the Rhineland, and Alsace when surnames began to be used in the fourteenth and fifteenth centuries—although Robert Heinlein once indicated that he had found reference to the name existing prior to the eleventh century. In another place he said that the earliest use of the name he had been able to discover dates from A.D. 1290 and refers to "Isaak Heinlein," a farmer in the Trier region of the Palatinate. An achievement at arms was awarded to one Josef Heinlein of Stuttgard in A.D. 1652. In the middle of the eighteenth century, the family from which Robert Heinlein descended is presumed to have been based in the southern German city of Nuremberg. Heinlein himself traced a Nuremberg goldsmith in his distant ancestry and on that basis suspected that the name might once have been Jewish.

> I encountered a number of Heinleins in south Germany and the city records of Nuremberg show that a "Peter Henlein" whose statue is there actually spelled his name as you and I do—I conjecture that the name was originally "Heimlein."[1]

"Heimlein" might mean "little secret." "Heinlein" might mean "little moor." At any rate, "Uncle Peter" (as Robert Heinlein's brother Lawrence jokingly referred to him[2]) had a statue—and a postage stamp!—because he invented the watch escapement.

Lutheranism predominates in northern Germany and indeed all the Baltic countries, but there are significant numbers of Roman Catholics in southern Germany. The family lost its association with Catholicism in America.

The founder of the American branch of the Heinlein family from which Robert Heinlein descended was Matheis (Matthias) Heinlein (1710?–1765?), who arrived in Philadelphia on October 31, 1754, in the *Bannister,* out of Holland, with his wife, Margaret (born Anna Margrethe Heisler), his oldest son, twelve-year-old George (in some early records "Jerich"), and two daughters, Eva and Sarah. In the mid-eighteenth century, Philadelphia was the principal port of entry to America, because of the city's reputation for religious tolerance and the presence of an abundance of good land west of the city (which then ended around Eighth Street).[3] The family moved to Durham Township, Bucks County, and settled on a tract of partly farmed land on the southern slope of Bucher Hill—then frontier territory. One of the daughters, Sarah, married James Morgan, Daniel Boone's uncle. The records of Berks County have Matthias Heinlein, a master hatter, living and working in Reading, Pennsylvania, then a center of hat manufacturing. He lived on one of the lots laid out by the Penns when they came up the river out of Philadelphia to establish a town. They must have been well thought of as neighbors in this frontier area: in 1797 Margaret Heinlein sponsored the baptism of a neighbor's (Ludwig Gobel's) daughter, her namesake: Anna Margrethe Gobel. She would have been quite aged at the time.

George Heinlein (1742–1805) appears in the Durham Township records of Bucks County in 1772, where he was listed as renting land from the Durham Furnace Company, from whom he purchased land in 1776. He worked as a potter and farmer—and he served as captain of the Durham Township militia throughout the Revolutionary War, thereby starting the military tradition of the Heinlein family in America. After the war, George moved into what is now Monroe County, and when his father died, he moved again, into Washington County, Pennsylvania. At his death in 1805, he was buried on the family plantation. The burial ground, which may also have contained the graves of other members of his immediate family, has since been ploughed under.

The name Lawrence enters the family in the third American generation: George's son Lorenz (1770?–1867), probably born in Reading (Bucks County). He must have been the War of 1812 Heinlein—though he also lived through the Civil War in his remarkable ninety-seven-year lifespan.[4] He married a woman named Anna, but nothing further is known of her. Of Lorenz, Robert related a family anecdote:

> My great-great-great grandfather Lawrence Heinlein died prematurely at the age of ninety-seven through having carelessly left his cabin one winter morning without his gun—and found a buck deer on the ice of his pond. Lack of his gun did not stop my triple-great grandfather; this skinful of meat must *not* be allowed to escape. He went out on the ice and bulldogged the buck, quite successfully.
>
> But in throwing the deer my ancestor slipped on the ice, went down, and a point of the deer's rack stabbed between his ribs and pierced his heart.
>
> No doubt it taught him a lesson—it certainly taught me one.[5]

Lorenz's name also appears in some public documents in the anglicized form, "Lawrence." A land grant is recorded for this Lawrence Heinlein in Northampton County, Pennsylvania, in 1800, and Lawrence, his father, George, and a James Heinlein are shown on the tax rolls of Northampton in 1799. For reasons unknown, James Heinlein changed the spelling of his name to "Hineline."

Lawrence's will, written in May of 1832, in Washington County, Pennsylvania, mentions Acy, Edward, Thomas, Rebeccah, Harriet, and Peggy Maria. Another daughter, Eleanora (b. 07/09/1766), had died in 1806. She had been baptized in the Trinity Lutheran Church in Reading, Pennsylvania, though Lawrence's birth is not noted in the parish records anywhere in Bucks County. Another daughter, Sarah, was also not mentioned in the will. She had married Charrick Vandermark and died in 1815.

Lorenz Heinlein's son Asa (1795–1869) was born in Pennsylvania. The 1860 census lists his year of birth as 1794, and another source says "about 1802." He married Hannah (or "Susannah") Culver (born in New Jersey, where there is another clutch of unrelated Heinleins) in either 1797 or 1805 and moved his large family (seven children) westward into Guernsey County, Ohio, near the Pennsylvania border, with three of his brothers and their children. There is some inconsistency among the records as to when this move took place, but Asa's oldest son, Lawrence (1828–1901), was born in Guernsey County, Ohio, in April 1828. Both Asa and son Lawrence may have fought in the Mexican-American War of 1846–1849, though there is no surviving documentation to support this speculation. Lawrence would have been eighteen years old when the war started in California; his father, Asa, would have been in his early to mid-forties. A second marriage is recorded for Asa, to Susannah Maria Culver Rose, a much younger woman.

The family thrived in eastern Ohio, "plenishing the land," as Robert Heinlein once wrote,[6] and slowly spreading out into the surrounding areas. By the end of the nineteenth century, this branch of the family had reached and settled in Blue Mound, Illinois, where a family Bible on the farm of F. M. Heinlein, one of Lawrence's sons (and great-uncle of Robert), listed the birth and death dates for many members of the family.

In 1852 Lawrence married Elizabeth Johnson (1830–1909), and a prominent strain of Irish blood entered the family. Elizabeth was born October 14, 1830, in Lancaster County, Pennsylvania (1831 in some sources), a member of the Ulster-Irish Johnson family (originally "Johnston," though the family dropped the "t" somewhere in the eighteenth century, or at any rate did not use it consistently). Heinlein's great-great-grandfather (through his grandmother Elizabeth), Thomas V. Johnson (1786?–1850), had immigrated to the United States in 1822.

At the time of the Civil War, Asa Heinlein was still living, though at the age of sixty-six it is unlikely that he enlisted. Lawrence Heinlein would have been thirty-three years old when war broke out, and he is, therefore, the Civil War Heinlein.[7] Lawrence's oldest son, Samuel Edward (Heinlein's paternal grandfather), would have been about seven years old in 1860.

After the Civil War, Lawrence moved his family by covered wagon to Bates County, Missouri, settling in the town of Butler in 1883, where he farmed until his retirement in 1896.

The genealogy of the Heinleins in Missouri is somewhat confused. There are several Heinleins in Missouri before the Civil War, but the data from the 1850 federal census and the 1864 Missouri State census show only one (rather large) family—that of John M. Heneline (later spelled as Heinlein), of Gasconade County, in central Missouri. John Heneline was born in Germany, circa 1805. Although this is a common variant spelling of the Heinlein name, this was an independent immigration, probably by a completely unrelated family. This John Heneline had come to Missouri during the early days of settlement with his German-born wife (1815)—coincidentally also by way of Ohio. But the Henelines had immigrated to *northwestern* Ohio, while the Matthias Heinlein line was in eastern Ohio, near the Pennsylvania border. There are no Heinleins (of any variant spelling) in Ohio in the 1830 census, only two in 1840, and eleven by the 1850 Ohio census. The bulk of the 1850 names are in Crawford County, also in northwestern Ohio. By 1880, there are plenty of Heinleins, Heneleines, Heinlens, and Henlines in the northwest of the state.

To make matters even more confusing, after the Civil War there was also a series of migrations of unrelated Heinleins from Germany directly to St. Louis, 260 miles across the state from the Kansas City area. The coincidental involvement of Ohio in both sets of family trees continues to create confusion in Heinlein family genealogy.

Lawrence's family is recorded in various census records:

Samuel Edward Heinlein (6/12/1853–3/1/1919), born in Illinois.
Mary Alice Heinlein (2/07/1860–3/22/1861), died in infancy.
Francis Marion Heinlein (5/1/1857–1/20/1927).

"Frank" apparently stayed in Illinois to farm instead of moving with the family to Missouri. He lived in Blue Mound, Illinois, and died in Decatur,

Illinois, keeping the family Bible on which much information in the Heinlein family's genealogy is based. F. M. Heinlein apparently had three marriages, though the full name is known only of his first wife: Althea May Brodes. The others were Rhetta and Mary.

> *Alma Ann Heinlein* (4/23/1862–3/30/1925) married J. A. Wear and lived in Butler, Missouri.
> *Oscar Allen Heinlein* (12/16/1864–10/31/1931), born in Christian County, Illinois, near Springfield and died in Butler, Missouri.

"Uncle Oscar" married Kate Canterbury (03/11/1881–5/24/1926), a native of Butler.

> *Leonard Smith Heinlein* (12/14/1869–1/18/1872)—another childhood death; nothing further is known; and
> *Harvey Wallace Heinlein* (9/9/1873–4/2/1931). He also had two marriages—to Ruth Dare and to Aura Neptune. It is recorded that he died in Long Beach, California.

Lawrence's oldest son, Samuel Edward, was Robert Anson Heinlein's paternal grandfather. He had married Elizabeth Kitchin (or "Kitchen," 1853–1881) on February 24, 1876, in Christian County, Illinois. Their firstborn, Rex Ivar Heinlein (08/08/1878–11/13/1959), born in Christian County, was Robert Anson's father. Samuel Edward and Elizabeth had one other child, a girl: Jessie Clare (01/17/1881–1961?). Elizabeth died just two weeks after Jessie was born. Jessie married William Ira Ayers (b. 2/23/1856).

After Elizabeth's death, Samuel Edward remarried, to Maria Woods Baldwin (1857–1932). For reasons unknown, Maria is not mentioned at all in contemporaneous family correspondence, though their children, Lawrence Ray Heinlein (b. 11/11/1886), Mina Ladine Heinlein-Hurst (b. 12/24/1888), and Alice Irene Heinlein-Pemberton (b. 3/7/1895), were lively correspondents of Rex's family, and Aunt Alice made a particular impression on young Robert. An oral history dictated by Maria Woods Heinlein to Alice Pemberton is an important resource of Heinlein family history.

Robert's maternal grandparent, Alva Lyle, M.D., first came to Missouri before the Heinleins, but he moved around a great deal and was much longer in settling down.

The Lyle name is Irish in origin, a variant of "L'Isle," meaning "from the (or an) island." The surname appears in Irish records as early as 1170, which suggests an aristocratic or quasi-aristocratic origin for the family, as this is centuries before surnames came into popular use among commoners. In combination with Heinlein's Irish paternal grandparents (Johnson), the Lyle Irish half of his heritage caused Irish to predominate over German, despite the German name. And there was "some Cherokee Indian in the family, too, and a trace of African."[8]

Oral tradition in the Lyle family (who do not seem to have had the same lively interest in family genealogy as did the Heinleins) indicates the family had been in America about the same length of time as the Heinleins—that is, predating the great wave of emigration out of Ireland following the Great Irish Potato Famine of 1848—and early-nineteenth-century census information seems to support this tradition. One Robert Lyle is known to have been born in 1808 in Muskingum County, Ohio. In 1829, he married Anna Evans, born also in Muskingum County, in 1811, and their son, Alva Evans Lyle, was born in March 1843 in Perry County, Ohio. The family moved, again westward, to Minnesota in 1856, where Alva grew up, receiving a primary education of which he later spoke approvingly. He, too, though very young, appears to have served for a brief time in the Civil War (after a fashion): there was a family story passed down to Robert that young Alva, at the age of twelve, ran off to join the Union Army as a drummer boy. His father went after him and took him back to Minnesota.[9]

The Lyles seem to have been unusually restless, even in a time of migrations, westward movement, and Manifest Destiny. Alva Lyle came to Bates County, Missouri, in 1868, as part of the first wave of resettlement following the Civil War. He arrived in a region that was completely devastated, burned fields and rubble. These new settlers had to rebuild new towns and farms practically from the ground up. In one letter, Robert Heinlein mentioned that his grandmother lived in a log cabin. Perhaps it is his grandmother Lyle he is referring to, since both Heinlein grandmothers married into well-established families.

The northwestern part of Missouri had been devastated by the Civil War and the border war between Kansas and Missouri, which had been going on since the 1850s. Missouri was remembered as a "dark and bloody ground" by veterans and their descendants. But the devastation of the area surrounding Kansas City was special even so.

The western border area of Missouri had essentially been at war since the early 1850s, with Missouri pro-slavery gangs crossing over into Kansas to raid the Abolitionist strongholds, and Kansas gangs ("Jayhawkers" and "Liberators") crossing over the Missouri line to exact revenge. The Missouri Compromise of 1820 had set up this situation, admitting Missouri as a slave state at the same time Maine had been admitted as a nonslave state—"Free Soil." Thereafter, one state would be admitted Free Soil for every state admitted as a slave state. The proportions of representation in Congress could thus be kept stable for a time.

The U.S. Congress in 1854 passed the Kansas-Nebraska Act, permitting (requiring) the voting residents of the territories to determine how they would be admitted to the Union under the Missouri Compromise. Therefore, the question of whether Kansas would be admitted as Free Soil was overwhelmingly important.

There were fifty thousand slaves—half the slave population of Missouri—ranged along the western border with the Kansas Territory, an immense concentration of wealth, constantly increasing in value as the slave trade was shut down. Thousands of pro-slavery Missourians immediately rushed into Kansas, hoping to capture the legislature. In response, Abolitionists, particularly from New York State, immigrated to Kansas for exactly the same reason. Missouri "Bushwhackers" tried to close Missouri River traffic by terrorist attacks on riverboats. Free Soilers countered by coming in through Iowa State (which had been admitted Free in 1846).

The levels of violence escalated into what has been called the Kansas Border War, but which were really the opening movements of the Civil War: two days after a Missouri gang shot up the Abolitionist town of Lawrence, Kansas, in 1856, John Brown, a new Kansas settler, took a sword and hacked up five pro-slavery men and boys in Kansas on the banks of the Pottawatomie River—apparently random targets of opportunity, as none had anything to do with the raid. The Abolitionists won control of the Kansas legislature after that, and Kansas Liberators began to raid in Missouri.

The Kansas Border War was incorporated into the Civil War, the raiders from each side (Quantrill's Raiders, the Cole Younger gang, etc.) co-opted into the national armies but loosely: they had their own agendas, which they pursued in their own way.

When the Union Army moved into the area, it found the border counties of western Missouri an impossible problem. Two-thirds of the population surrounding the Marais des Cygnes (pronounced "Mardezines" by the locals) marshlands, it was estimated, were either relatives of the pro-slavery guerrillas or actively supporting them by provisioning and sheltering them. After a particularly destructive raid by Quantrill and his Raiders on the town of Lawrence, Kansas, Brigadier General Thomas Ewing, the Union commander at Kansas City, decided on a drastic solution: depopulate the entire area.

General Order No. 11, issued August 25, 1863, ordered every human being out of Jackson, Bates, and Cass counties within fifteen days—except those who had satisfactorily proved their loyalty to the Union cause. Twenty thousand people were driven from their homes, their farms put to the torch (after being looted by the Union cavalry), a heart-wrenching flood of refugees in misery. The phrasing of the order, "Leave not a stone standing on a stone, and raze the ground," was remembered by survivors for decades and repeated to their children and their children's children.

Those who could pass interrogation and took a Union loyalty oath were dispersed to refugee camps in Kansas. After the deadline, the grain and hay found in the district was to be burned, to keep it out of the hands of the guerrillas. Almost all antebellum records were destroyed by fire. The painter George Caleb Bingham witnessed the atrocity at first hand and later memorialized it after the war in his picture *Order No. 11*. He portrays General Ewing personally driving a family from their home.[10]

After the Civil War the area was repopulated, but not by the original displaced families, many of whom stayed in Kansas, where they had been resettled. Others moved farther westward, perhaps to Nevada or Arizona, or even California. Still others went to Arkansas. The new population for the three counties devastated by General Order No. 11 came mostly from Ohio, and they brought with them an upper midwestern cultural tradition. Even today, Kansas City is a midwestern city, distinct from the Southern and Ozark subcultures in the rest of Missouri. Both the Heinleins and the Lyles were thus the distilled product of an evolutionary filter, in the same sense as Darwin was to talk about the migration to the New World as an evolutionary filter in *The Descent of Man* (1871).

The Lyles and then the Heinleins came to an area that was rebuilding from the ground up. The first railroad bridge over the Missouri River—the Hannibal Bridge at Kansas City—was completed in 1869, the same year the transcontinental railroad opened. Kansas City was thus set up to become a major entrepôt for the nation's westward expansion. Generations later, all of the Heinleins' homes in Kansas City, by coincidence, were on the old Santa Fe Trail—and before World War I many of the local landmark buildings of the neighborhoods were oriented to the Trail, rather than to the streets they sat on. As a boy, Robert was fascinated by Westport Landing,[11] the place where pioneers gathered to leap off on their journey across the plains and over the Rockies to the West Coast. Three years after the opening of the transcontinental railroad, there were seven rail lines going into and through Kansas City. The frontier had moved west, and Missouri was now the middle of the country.

By the time the Heinleins arrived in 1883, the surrounding area was booming. Some of the family settled southeast of Kansas City, in the town of Butler (county seat of Bates County), but Samuel Edward Heinlein removed to Kansas City, working for the Emerson-Brantingham Co. and Midland Manufacturing Company, a producer of agricultural implements.

Alva Lyle stayed in Bates County. In 1871, he found himself in Papinville, the first settlement in Bates County (named for a Canadian trader), and decided to become a medical doctor. At that time, the accustomed way to become a doctor was to learn from an established practitioner, so Alva apprenticed himself to August Rhoads, M.D. (b. 1838?), and attended a series of medical lectures at Washington University in St. Louis. Missouri history books emphasize that medical teaching in St. Louis was unusually advanced at that time. But most of his training was *practicum,* spent "walking with" Dr. Rhoads.

In March 1873 he was "graduated," but it is not clear whether this consisted of a certificate of proficiency issued by Dr. Rhoads (the more usual custom) or by the new medical school in St. Louis. Dr. Lyle set up a practice in the town of Metz, in Vernon County, Missouri, and the following year (1874) married Miss Rose Althea Adelia Wood (born 1850 in Morrow County, Ohio), daughter of Anson S. Wood and K. (Sophia) Monroe. It is thought that Adelia Wood's mother's family was a collateral branch of President James Monroe's family, which would give Robert Heinlein an "Old American" descent through all four of his grandparents.[12]

Though Dr. Lyle's parents had both immigrated to Bates County by this time (as cemetery records show them both buried in the same cemetery in Bates County), the Lyles must have spent some additional years moving from place to place as the young doctor sought a stable and lucrative practice and his family continued to grow. Daughter Anna was born in 1876 or 1877 and followed by another daughter, Bam, on July 14, 1879. Her birthplace is given as Grinnell, Iowa. Her name is not short for "Alabama," as has been conjectured; she was named for an Aunt Bam—"an old heller who . . . was forever traveling," visiting relatives.[13] When Aunt Bam was ninety-nine years old—this would be in the 1940s—she broke her hip and could no longer travel, so she "turned her face to the wall" and died.[14] (Heinlein later combined qualities of his aunt Bam and his mother's sister, Anna, as the basis for

Hazel Stone in *The Rolling Stones*.) Apparently, Bam was not given a middle name.

In 1881 Dr. Lyle moved his practice back to Missouri, to the village of Sprague, in Bates County. His mother, Anna Evans Lyle, died December 1, 1888, and was buried in Green Lawn Cemetery in Bates County.

Some years after Bam's birth, while the family was still living in Sprague, Missouri, there was another addition to Dr. Lyle's family, under curious circumstances. Dr. Lyle had an extramarital affair with a schoolteacher, which resulted in an illegitimate boy, Park Lyle, born in 1893. Remarkably, Dr. Lyle told his wife about it, and she took Park into the family, raising him as her own child. The actual circumstances surrounding Park's birth and informal adoption have never been documented. Apparently, Park Lyle never learned about his illegitimacy.

Rose Adelia Lyle can only have been a remarkable woman—the first of many in Robert Heinlein's life.

Dr. Lyle shortly had an opportunity that he may have used to assist the cover-up by relocating his practice again, away from the gossipy Mrs. Grundys of Sprague.

In 1893 Dr. Lyle, then fifty years old, took the unusual step of moving his family with him to Chicago for a year while he took a continuing-education course in the medical school at Northwestern University, to learn about Pasteur's new germ theory.

Although Bam Lyle was never inclined to talk much about herself (Robert said of his mother that she didn't let her fingers know what she was doing),[15] the experience was deeply formative for her. Bam was not a particularly intellectual person, though she had a rather intellectual father who may have been something of a natural teacher: she recalled stopping with him in about 1889 or 1890 in Kansas City to figure out an underground foundation. In 1893 she was fourteen years old, and her world was repeatedly expanding and re-forming itself around her.

For one thing, she saw her first black man on the train going to Chicago, a dining car attendant going about his business, serving diners—a traditional "George" of railroad travel before the turn of the century. She was startled and not a little frightened.[16]

During the year the Lyles were in Chicago, Bam did not go to school but instead spent her time at the Columbian Exposition, the World's Fair of 1893—which was probably as educational as school might have been for her. Certainly she was impressed by the wonders and new experiences that came to her. A "glahz vahz" she saw at the Exposition ("glass vaze" being the usual pronunciation in the Midwest when she was growing up) became something of a family joke. What she mainly took away from Chicago was the memory of talks with her father about germ theory: nothing was ever quite clean enough for her after Chicago. She spent the rest of her long life scrubbing everything.

But she was at a pivotal place in a pivotal moment in American history. The 1890s were a period of particular turmoil for the United States. Following the Chicago Haymarket Riots of 1886, the public was terrified of strikes, terrified of the Labor movement (these dangerous anarchists were striking for an eight-hour day), and terrified by the Panic and Depression of 1893—the worst in the country's history. Businesses collapsed by the thousands. Banks closed in record numbers.

This period of social and moral ferment has been glossed over in history books, reduced to a quick mention of William Jennings Bryan's "Cross of Gold" speech (though it confusingly had something to do with silver coinage) and the Populists, who are given a sentimental portrait as prairie peasants earnestly playing with the co-op movement. They are related, somehow, but it is not quite clear how or why.

On May 3, 1893, a wave of selling took place on the stock market. The Panic of 1893 began—and Chicago was in the middle of it all. It was time for the Lyles to move back to Missouri.

Dr. Lyle wound up in Butler, Missouri, where he established a general practice making rounds in a horse-drawn buggy. When she was old enough, Bam enrolled in the Butler Academy, in the same class as Rex Ivar Heinlein, despite having taken a year off from school. The Academy gave a difficult and comprehensive general education, somewhat comparable to a junior college. They graduated together in 1896. Doubtless they were courting when, two years later, the Spanish-American War was declared.

Cuba had been in open revolt against Spain since 1895 (with the Philippines, another Spanish possession, following in 1896). Americans—and particularly Missourians—followed the news from Cuba with great interest; St. Louis was a hub for distribution of Cuban sugar and tobacco to the Midwest and West. Missouri agricultural and manufactured products were finding a market in Havana, and there were significant Missourian business interests in Cuba.

In January 1898, Cuban insurrectionists attacked newspapers that supported Spain's proposals for "limited autonomy," and the U.S. Consul-General in Havana interpreted the attacks as a threat against Americans. He asked for a warship to be sent to Havana. President McKinley responded by sending the USS *Maine*. On February 15, 1898, the *Maine* exploded in Havana Harbor, killing 266 American sailors. Two months later, on April 16, the U.S. Army began to mobilize. Spain declared war on the United States on April 22, 1898. The United States declared war on Spain on April 25, 1898, retroactive to the twenty-second. The Spanish-American War was under way.

Rex Ivar Heinlein, following his family's conscious military tradition, signed up with the first wave of volunteers and enrolled as a private in the Second Missouri Volunteer Infantry, Company B, on May 4, 1898. The next day, Bam Lyle presented him with a small (three-by-four-inch) pocket *New Testament and Psalms,* inscribed with sentiments doubtless conventional but also doubtless heartfelt:

> Rex Ivar Heinlein
> Co. B 2nd Reg.
> Butler, Mo.
> Be true to self
> and country
> BAM
> *May 5, 1898*

He left Butler for muster at Jefferson Barracks the next day, after a farewell banquet.

The Second Missouri left Jefferson Barracks for Camp Chickamauga, Georgia, on May 18, arriving on May 21. They were assigned to the First Brigade of the Third Division of the First Army Corps, commanded by General John R. Brooke.

This was the Rough Riders' war—the war of the charge up San Juan Hill, the Buffalo Soldiers, William Randolph Hearst's frenzied "Remember the *Maine*!," and the Marines taking Guantánamo Bay. It was also the war of the Philippines, of General Aguinaldo, of the capture of Guam. But that is the war of romance, of Yellow Kid journalism and fictional history and popular myth. It was not the war Rex Ivar experienced.

Missouri had made no adequate preparations to equip, transport, or feed the volunteers. The Army was just as badly disorganized in Georgia. There were food shortages and no sensible plan for organizing and equipping the volunteers. A dispute within the Army resulted in failure to issue uniforms. Many soldiers lived through the month wearing only blankets. Haste and inefficiency resulted in poor handling of foodstuffs and unsanitary camp conditions. The

canned beef was barely edible—the scandal over the "embalmed beef" provided to the military in the Spanish-American War prepared the ground for the
public furor that in 1906 led to passage of the Pure Food and Drug Act.

After a month at Chickamauga, Rex Ivar's regiment was sent to Lexington, Kentucky, then to Albany, Georgia. They were mustered out of service
in March 1899, without seeing Cuba. Rex Ivar had been detached even earlier, desperately ill. He was "brought home on a shutter," as his relatives recalled, and spent months recovering. Nevertheless, he was included in the
public celebrations: the civic boosters of Butler threw a grand banquet for
the returning war heroes. A flyer on glazed newsprint announced in multiple
typefaces:

> Welcome, Gallant Soldiers! The citizens of Butler, desiring to express in
> a substantial manner their appreciation of the gallant soldiers who so
> promptly responded to their Country's call "to Arms," less than one year
> ago, and are again at home, having been honorably mustered out of the
> service of "Uncle Sam," will hold a GRAND RECEPTION and Ban-
> quet, in Butler on Evening of Friday, March 10th, 1899, to which every
> soldier from Bates County in the late Spanish-American war is invited to
> be present, as a guest.

The Cuban portion of the war ended with the Treaty of Paris on December 10, 1898, though fighting continued in the Philippines until 1902.

Rex Ivar always remembered his service in the Spanish-America War with
pride; Robert remembered his uniform hanging, pressed, in his parents' closet
decades later,[17] and drew at least some of the inspiration that led to *Starship
Troopers* from Rex Ivar's thoughts about the Spanish-American War—the
conviction, expressed in 1912, when Heinlein was only five, that "only those
who fought for their country were worthy to rule it."[18]

Rex Ivar Heinlein and Bam Lyle were married in Butler on November 20,
1899.

The story of Robert Heinlein's immediate family picks up in the main
text.

CAMPAIGN BIOGRAPHY

Leon Stover's unpublished biographical sketch of Heinlein, *Before the Writing Began*, quotes Heinlein's autobiography written for his campaign staff in 1938.

Political record:

1934   Precinct group organizer in Sinclair's campaign. Board of Directors of West Hollywood Democratic Club.

1935   Precinct group organizer for James M. Carter's campaign for council (3rd district in Imperial Valley). Managing Editor "End Poverty News" in city election. Assistant to state organizer and business manager in End Poverty League. Member of convention arrangement committee for first EPIC convention. Drafted End Poverty League constitution with Saul Klein and Luther Bailey.[1]

1936   Campaigned for Ordean Rockey [UCLA poly-sci—successful] primarily in finance committee. Mrs. H. managed Rockey-for-Congress Ball. Elected Democratic County Central committee in the primaries and thereafter 59th District chairman. Appointed to Democratic State Central Committee.[2] Appointed to Veterans Division of the National Committee. Precinct work for Democratic ticket in 59th District. Both Leslyn and he worked in Harlan Palmer [ed. HOLLYWOOD NEWS] campaign for 59th District. Appointed by John Anson Ford (sitting on LA County Board of Supervisors) to investigate relief and WPA.

1937   Precinct organization for Ford's mayoral campaign. Member of County Central Committee to investigate Metropolitan Water District Strike at the San Jacinto tunnel. "Resigned chairmanship of 59th District in August 1937 in anticipation of running for Assembly. Was drafted by the Democratic County Central Committee to be chairman of Organization . . ." Announced candidacy on 3/15/38.

Notes

Introduction

1. RAH, *Time Enough for Love* (1973) volume 2 of the Virginia Edition: the Definitive Collection of Robert A. Heinlein, 253.

2. Eleven minutes of the featurette is included as a Special Feaure on the DVD collection *The Fantasy Film Works of George Pal* (1985).

3. Transcribed from Virginia Heinlein's personal videotape of Robert A. Heinlein's appearance on CBS television, July 20, 1969. CBS destroyed the original videotape, and a copy was provided them from a digitization made by the author in 2001 (with Mrs. Heinlein's permission).

1. The Heinleins of Butler, Missouri

1. Virginia Heinlein, letter to author, 11/16/00. For an extended examination of the Heinlein and Lyle family history, see Appendix A.

2. The "understanding" was framed, in the reminiscences Virginia Heinlein received from Robert Heinlein, as an explicit promise, which was voided when Oscar married and had a son. Virginia Heinlein, IM (instant message—a real-time Internet communication) with author, 06/21/2000; Virginia Heinlein, letter to author, 11/16/2000. However, Oscar Allen Heinlein's marriage to Kate Canterbury did not take place until 1910—three years after Rex Ivar Heinlein left Butler for Kansas City—and Oscar Allen, Jr., was not born until 1911.

3. In a birthday letter to RAH, dated 07/11/71, Maj. Gen. Lawrence Heinlein recalled: "I remember I had to ride herd on Ivar the day you were born to keep him out of the way."

4. RAH, letter to Tom Eaton, 12/12/73.

5. Material about the Heinlein family in Kansas City from H. Bruce Franklin, *Robert A. Heinlein: America as Science Fiction* (New York: Oxford University Press, 1980), 6–9.

6.   At different times, Robert Heinlein gave different dates for the family's move
     from Butler to Kansas City, 1907, 1909, and 1912, possibly because Bam made
     a practice of taking the children for extended visits back to Butler. An undated
     letter (sometime in the 1970s) from Kansas City Public Library archivist David
     Boutros, responding to a reference request by Heinlein, suggests using the 1910
     Census and the city directories from the period 1907–1912 to determine when
     the entire family officially reported residence in Kansas City. No follow-up to
     this suggestion was found in Heinlein's files.

7.   Bam Heinlein, letter to RAH, 07/07/51.

8.   Virginia Heinlein, taped interview by author, Second Series, Tape C, Side A.

9.   Stammering, also called stuttering, typically begins in early childhood, with a mean
     onset age of thirty months, according to E. Yairi and N. Ambrose, "Onset of Stut-
     tering in Preschool Children: Selected Factors," *Journal of Speech and Hearing Re-
     search* XXXV: 4 (1992). This is the primary language acquisition phase for children.

         Heinlein specifically attributed his difficulty to his family and particularly his
     two-year-older brother, Rex. Psychologists at Leeds University and Goldsmith
     College also report a high correlation of stammering with bullying and abuse
     (reported in *The London Times Educational Supplement* [06/11/99]).

         It is certainly possible that Heinlein's brothers were too rough on him,
     though his different attitudes toward his older brothers in adolescence do not
     suggest any intentional cruelty or abuse.

10. Franklin, *Robert A. Heinlein: America as Science Fiction,* 8.

11. RAH, letter to John W. Campbell, Jr., and Doña Campbell, 01/20/42.

12. RAH, letter to Dr. Chris Moskowitz, 09/06/61.

13. Virginia Heinlein, taped interview with author, Second Series Tape B, Side A.

14. Franklin, 8.

15. RAH, telephone interview by Ben Bova, 06/29/79. This interview was never pub-
     lished commercially, but the corrected transcription has been included in the non-
     fiction volumes of the Virginia Edition collected works of Robert A. Heinlein, 2010.

16. Heinlein fictionalized this incident in his last book, *To Sail Beyond the Sunset*
     (1987).

17. Virginia Heinlein, conversation with author, March 2 or 3, 2001.

18. RAH, letter to Tom Eaton, 11/06/73.

19. RAH, *I Will Fear No Evil* (New York: G. P. Putnam's Sons, 1970), 250–51.

20. RAH, letter to Harlan Ellison, 09/06/61.

21. RAH, letter to Judith Merril, 05/16/57.

22. Pendergast did have a rival: Joseph B. Shannon led a minority splinter faction of
     the local Democratic Party, known as the Rabbits (the Pendergast faction was

known as the Goats), but the Pendergast faction was clearly in the ascendency: the Rabbits had to make patronage deals with the Goats. Shannon was eventually kicked upstairs, into state politics.

23. An undated three-by-five-inch index card in Heinlein's hand found in a miscellaneous box of papers contains Heinlein's salient recollections of his life in 1912. The card may have been made during his preparations in 1972 to write *Time Enough for Love.*

24. Virginia Heinlein, summarizing remarks made by Heinlein to her, relates this incident in her preface to *Requiem: New Collected Works of Robert A. Heinlein and Tributes to the Grand Master,* ed. Yoji Kondo (New York: Tor Books, 1992), 236.

25. RAH, letter to Ruth Clement Hoyer, 05/22/46.

26. RAH, interview by Alfred Bester, *Publishers Weekly* (July 2, 1973), 44.

27. RAH, interview by Alfred Bester, *Publishers Weekly* (July 2, 1973), 44.

28. The incident is recounted in his 1973 Forrestal Lecture, partly published as "Channel Markers" in RAH, *The New Worlds of Robert A. Heinlein: Expanded Universe* (New York: Grosset & Dunlap, 1980) and again in his 1976 Guest-of-Honor Speech for MidAmeriCon, published in *Requiem,* ed. Yoji Kondo.

2. Growing Up, Kansas City

1. RAH, letter to Tom Eaton, 12/12/73.

2. RAH, letter to Lewis Patterson, 07/26/73.

3. RAH, letter to Marion Zimmer Bradley, 04/06/63.

4. RAH, letter to Leon Stover, 06/08/86.

5. Ian Stevenson, M.D., *Twenty Cases Suggestive of Reincarnation*, 2nd ed., revised and enlarged (Charlottesville: University Press of Virginia, 1960, 1980).

6. Solipsism, strictly speaking, denies the validity of other; treating self and other as parts of the same overarching reality is a different philosophical concept, but one that had, apparently, by the time Heinlein's fiction began to appear, become less familiar than solipsism, since the mistaken label is so widely applied.

7. RAH, letter to Theodore Sturgeon, 02/11/55.

8. RAH, letter to Robert Bloch, 03/18/49.

9. Heinlein's short story "They" (1941) embodies this feeling. His outline notes for this story begin: "Idea is based on the feeling I had as a kid that everything as I saw it was a deliberate plot to deceive me, that people didn't do the things I saw them do when I wasn't watching them." Heinlein's friend Cal Laning told biographer presumptive Leon Stover that these same feelings were still important motivating factors for Heinlein twenty years later, at the end of the 1920s. Leon Stover, conversations with author, 1999.

10. RAH, letter to Bam Heinlein, 07/11/62.

11. RAH, letter to Alice Dalgliesh, 02/17/59.

12. RAH, unpublished interview by Ben Bova, conducted 06/29/79.

13. RAH, letter to Robert D. Kephart, 11/08/73.

14. Virginia Heinlein, taped interview by author, First Series, Tape 12, Side A.

15. Dorothy Martin Heinlein, wife of Jesse Clare Heinlein, conversation with author at the Heinlein Centennial, 07/06/2007.

16. Virginia Heinlein, letter to author, 07/14/2001.

17. Howard Thurston (1869–1936) mounted his own show in 1902; in 1907 he took over Harry Kellar's show and increased the size and effects to a three-hour production, which toured the world several times, beginning in 1908, and toured the United States frequently until his death in 1936. His stage show required ten railway cars to transport the props, scenery, and effects. His most famous illusion was the "floating lady."

18. Virginia Heinlein, taped interview by author, First Series, Tape 12, Side A.

19. During World War I, in addition to clothing drives and metal salvage drives, people were encouraged to collect and salvage other resources to aid the war effort. One of the stranger resource drives was to collect peach pits to be burned into charcoal, which could then be used in filter masks for the new poison-gas warfare being tried out in France.

20. RAH, letter to Tom Eaton, 12/12/73.

21. Virginia Heinlein, taped interview by Phillip Homer Owenby (1994).

22. H. G. Wells, *The World of William Clissold* (New York: George H. Doran, 1926), vol. 1, 61.

23. RAH, letter to Leon Stover, 06/08/86.

24. RAH, letter to Marion Zimmer Bradley, 04/06/63.

25. Virginia Heinlein, letter to Lynnie Ayer, 04/09/75.

26. Jay Clare Heinlein, biographical recollections of RAH, undated but probably 1989, in preparation for the biography to be written by Leon Stover. (Jesse Clare, later in life, formally changed his name to Jay Clare.)

27. Interview with Frank Robinson (unpublished), submission draft, p. 4.

28. RAH, letter to Leon Stover, 06/08/86.

29. RAH, letter to Alfred Bester, 04/03/59; in a letter to Joanna Russ, 04/10/79, he implies the books were borrowed from the Kansas City Public Library.

30. RAH, letter to Judy Lynn Benjamin, 12/12/73.

31. RAH, draft (unsent) letter to George "McC" (the only identification), 02/13/58.

32. RAH, letter to Marion Zimmer Bradley, 03/04/63.

33. RAH's official biography for More Junior Classics, 04/10/57.

34. RAH, letter to Ruth Clement Hoyer, 05/22/46.

35. Wells was already having disagreements with the Marxist, class-warfare strains of socialism in England, grown popular since the takeover by the Bolshevik communists of the moderate, Menshevik revolution in Russia. Marxism was the Zionism of socialism, and Russia was its homeland. Wells thought Marxist socialism—communism—intellectually and morally defective.

36. RAH, letter to Leon Stover, 06/08/86.

3. A Jazz Age Teenager

1. RAH, letter to Alice Dalgliesh, 02/17/59.
2. RAH, letter to Ted Carnell, 02/22/65.
3. Feruling: striking (a student), usually on the hand, with a rod usually of wood or iron.
4. Bam Heinlein, quoted in a letter from RAH to Rick Lawler, 11/21/73.
5. Bam Heinlein, quoted in a letter from RAH to Rick Lawler, 11/21/73.
6. RAH, letter to Alice Dalgliesh, 02/17/59.
7. See *The Centralian* for the years 1920–1924, but particularly a list of his activities in his 1924 (graduating) yearbook, p. 76.
8. RAH, letter to Richard Pope, 09/25/74; no copies of the ads or pictures have been preserved.
9. RAH, telephone interview by Ben Bova, 06/29/79.
10. Heinlein's Guest-of-Honor Speech for MidAmeriCon, 1976, published in *Requiem*, ed. Yoji Kondo, 209.
11. RAH, letter to Harlan Ellison, 09/09/61.
12. RAH, letter to Leon Stover, 06/08/86.
13. Virginia Heinlein's recollections, recounted in correspondence with Ron Harrison, memorialized in Harrison's letter to Virginia Heinlein, 09/02/92.
14. RAH, letter to Harlan Ellison, 09/09/61; see also RAH, letter to Poul Anderson, 10/02/61.
15. Wells recounted his sense of inspiration (and then disappointment) with Wilson in *The World of William Clissold* at pages 294–325, but his sense of America as the country of the future had been a continuing trope in Wells's journalistic works since his first trip to the United States in 1906.
16. RAH, letter to Poul Anderson, 10/02/61.
17. RAH, unpublished telephone interview by Ben Bova, 06/29/79.
18. RAH, letter to Tom Eaton, 12/12/73.
19. RAH, letter to Marion Zimmer Bradley, 04/06/63.
20. RAH, letter to Marian Zimmer Bradley, 04/06/63.
21. Several scrapbooks are preserved in "The Robert A. Heinlein Archive" of Special Collections and Archives of the University Library, University of California,

Santa Cruz. The oldest, its binding now disintegrated, covers Heinlein's youth through his Naval career.

22. Don Johnstone, quoted in Dorothy Martin Heinlein, "Relatively Speaking" (unpublished paper written ca. March 2006).

23. RAH, letter to Chris Moskowitz, 09/06/61. The timing of the loan of his brother to the FBI's predecessor is not fixed in the correspondence, except that Lawrence Heinlein was a major at the time, which places it in the 1920s and most probably during Heinlein's high school days.

24. RAH, letter to Alice Dalgliesh, 02/17/59.

25. RAH, letter to Alice Dalgliesh, 02/17/59; see also Virginia Heinlein, taped interview by author, Second Series, Tape B, Side B (September 12–14, 2000).

26. John Fiske was an American evolutionist, very popular in the last decades of the nineteenth century, who defended Darwin, Herbert Spencer, and Huxley. His own contribution to Darwinian thinking was to point out the evolutionary significance of humans' prolonged gestation and infancy.

27. RAH, letter to Alice Dalgliesh, 02/17/59.

28. J. Neil Schulman, *The Robert Heinlein Interview and Other Heinleiniana* (Culver City, Calif.: Pulpless.com, 1990), 146–47. The interview was conducted in 1973.

29. Self-help and self-improvement movements flourished in the United States during the late nineteenth century, nourished by circuits of lecturers and entertainers. The Chautauqua circuit was the best known of these "lyceum bureaus"—"the most American thing in America," as Theodore Roosevelt called it—and lasted well into the 1930s. Lecturers were the backbone of the Chautauqua, but also musical revues and classical and contemporary Broadway plays.

30. Schulman, *The Robert Heinlein Interview and Other Heinleiniana,* 146–47.

31. RAH, letter to Mr. Josselyn, 08/28/53.

32. RAH, letter to Robert Bloch, 10/11/71.

33. RAH, letter to Sheri Harris, 03/19/83.

34. R. S. Leigh, Bureau of Navigation (BuNav), letter to RAH, 09/19/23.

35. The Pendergast machine evolved and deteriorated over the years as control passed from brother to brother to son. Until the 1930s, it was rather more benign, based in Jim Pendergast's saloon: city graft to a concrete-and-paving business owned by Tom Pendergast, illegal gambling, and wholesale liquor sales during Prohibition. The line between political machine and crime organization blurred further in 1926, when a Chicago-style mobster was ceded control of part of the machine and expanded illegal activities to prostitution and protection.

By 1933, the scandal over the Union Station Massacre (which also affected Heinlein—see chapter 14) focused attention on Tom Pendergast, who was losing enormous amounts of money on horse racing and consequently demanding more and more money from his machine/crime organization. Eventually (1939) Pendergast was jailed for income tax evasion—by the same prosecution that sent Chicago's Al Capone to jail. An attempt to revive the Pendergast machine in the 1940s had only limited and temporary success. The age of the machine was over.

36.   President Warren G. Harding's Secretary of the Interior, Albert B. Fall, granted oil leases in Wyoming (the "Teapot Dome" oil field) and California in exchange for personal loans at low and no interest—a bribery scandal that erupted in 1922, two years into the Harding administration.

President Harding's slogan for his Republican administration had been "less government in business; more business in government." But the business turned out to be the machine politics of Tammany Hall and Kansas City, on a national scale.

President Harding died of a heart attack in 1923, but the Teapot Dome scandal tainted his administration's historical reputation. It was not completely resolved until 1929, in an anomalous decision Heinlein noted elsewhere: Secretary Fall was convicted of receiving a bribe that Doheny (of California) was acquitted of giving.

By coincidence, that same Doheny was the founder of the family fortune that established the trust fund that supported Larry Niven while he was learning to write science fiction.

37.   RAH, "The Happy Days Ahead," *Expanded Universe*, 537.

38.   RAH, letter to John Campbell, 11/05/46.

39.   Undated clipping from *The Kansas City Star* preserved in Heinlein's scrapbook.

40.   The clipping, the anonymous letter of complaint, and the petition are all preserved in Heinlein's scrapbook.

41.   *The Centralian* (1924), 76.

42.   *The Centralian* (1924), 78.

43.   Alice Marie Evans, Christmas card to Robert and Virginia Heinlein, 1973.

44.   RAH, letter to Poul Anderson, 12/13/61.

45.   The relevant clippings in Heinlein's personal scrapbook were pasted in without dates but must have been before graduation in June 1924.

46.   Deleted text from "The Happy Days Ahead," Ms. in 181b of *Expanded Universe*, RAH Archive, UCSC, page 595 of ms.

47.   RAH, letter to John Campbell, 01/20/42.

48.   RAH, letter to Forrest J. Ackerman, 02/25/49.

49.   RAH, letter to Christopher B. Timmers, 01/31/72.

50.   Capt. C. Marchant, Company C, 110th Engineers, letter to RAH, 08/28/24. The letter is part of RAH's "Naval Jacket," that is, the dossier of the Navy's records. RAH's Naval Jacket is in the RAH Archive, UCSC.

51. RAH, letter to Poul Anderson, 09/06/61.

52. The formation of this junior college is mentioned briefly in the Will and Ariel Durant joint autobiography; Robert's sister-in-law Dorothy Martin Heinlein remembers that the Kansas City Superintendent of Schools had renovated the downtown facility of the first high school in Kansas City, which had since been abandoned, and offered two years of college for a tuition of $8 per semester, with classes provided from 8 A.M. to 4 P.M. five days per week. The tuition was apparently first-rate, as when she transferred to another college she was told to sit out her French classes for the first semester. "Relatively Speaking" (unpublished paper written ca. March 2006).

53. RAH, letter to Poul Anderson, 07/21/61. In another letter (to Lt. Sandra Fulton, of the U.S. Navy, dated 08/07/65) Heinlein says the teacher of calculus was a Negro.

4. Plebe Summer

1. "The Class of Nineteen Twenty-nine," *The Lucky Bag* (1928), 228. *The Lucky Bag* is the name of the United States Naval Academy's annual yearbook.

2. Telegram preserved in RAH's scrapbooks at RAH Archive, UCSC.

3. RAH, letter to Robert Louis Stevenson, 12/12/73.

4. RAH, letter to F. M. Busby, 07/22/61.

5. RAH, letter to Jerry Pournelle, 02/16/68.

6. RAH, Plebe Summer letter addressed to "Folks" on Carvel Hall stationery, dated only "Monday" (June 15, 1925).

7. Edward F. Hutchins, commenting on Novak's portrait in the 1929 *The Lucky Bag*.

8. Class history for Plebe Summer, *The Lucky Bag* (1929), p 68. Heinlein captured a little of this excited confusion in the early chapters of his 1948 juvenile novel, *Space Cadet*.

9. RAH, Plebe Summer letter addressed "Dear Dad," dated "Saturday" (probably June 20, 1925).

10. RAH, letter to Ayako Hasegawa, 06/11/81.

11. "Rank" denotes a particular position in a particular table of organization; "rating" is the grade attained within the Navy as a whole.

12. "The pap sheet" is a conduct report. *The Lighthouse: The Plebe's Bible* (1929), 23.

13. Most of the detailed information about discipline and circumstances at the U.S. Naval Academy at Heinlein's time in these chapters is derived from an afternoon's interview with Admiral Ignatius "Pete" Gallantin, Class of '32, given the author on March 31, 2001, in the Admiral's home in Atlantic Beach, Florida. Admiral Gallantin was sworn in in 1928.

14. RAH, letter to Robert D. Kephart, 11/08/73.

15. RAH, letter to Bam Lyle Heinlein, undated but sometime in July 1925 "I went out for track today in high jumps. The head coach thinks he is going to make a jumper out of me."

16. RAH, letter to Alfred Bester, 04/03/59: "As for personal combat or even body-contact sports (other than those involving bedsprings), well, I never climbed into a boxing ring in my life without wishing to Christ that I were somewhere else! I disliked boxing and wrestling so much that, as soon as I had passed my first-class tests in each, I quit them permanently."

17. RAH, Plebe Summer letter addressed "Dear Sis" (probably Louise Heinlein), dated "Friday" (possibly July 31, 1925).

18. Virginia Heinlein, taped interview by author, Second Series, Tape C, Side B (September 10–12, 2000).

19. RAH, letter to Alfred Bester, 04/03/59.

20. The pragmatic and utilitarian rationale Heinlein advanced in "The Tale of the Man Who Was Too Lazy to Fail" (part of *Time Enough for Love* [1973])—namely, to avoid being tagged for the more dangerous sports—did not apply in his own case (for one thing, weighing in under 110 pounds, he was in little danger of being tagged for the football squad or, indeed, any of the body-contact sports). The basic story of "David Lamb" belongs to another Plebe, Delos Wait, whom Heinlein knew, filled out with some general autobiographical information about hazing and life at the Academy—plus, of course, his customary writerly distancing and "making strange," a device for convincingly portraying a tale told by a 2,600-year-old man to people with no cultural context to understand the details.

21. See, for example, RAH's letter to Jerry Pournelle, 03/14/63.

22. RAH, *Expanded Universe,* 452.

23. RAH, letter to his mother, 07/07/25.

24. Virginia Heinlein, taped interview by Phillip Homer Owenby (1994), Tape 11, Side A.

25. "Youngster Year" section of the class history in *The Lucky Bag* (1929), 86–89.

26. RAH, Plebe Summer letter to his mother, dated "Thursday" (probably June 25, 1925).

27. RAH, Plebe Summer letter to his mother, dated "Friday" (probably July 3, 1925).

28. RAH, Plebe Summer letter to his mother, dated "Tuesday" (probably June 23, 1925).

29. The listing immediately follows "Worldly Wisdom" and consists of the names Tedder, Latimore (settled!), Jacobs, Anderson, Finnegan. Only Finnegan's name recurs in Heinlein's personal history.

30. RAH, Plebe Summer letter to his mother, Tuesday 07/07/25.

31.   RAH, Plebe Summer birthday letter to his mother dated "Sunday" (probably July 12, 1925).

32.   "Plebe Summer" section of the class history in *The Lucky Bag* (1929), 68.

33.   RAH, Plebe Summer letter to his brother Larry, dated "Thursday" (probably August 20, 1925).

34.   RAH, letter to Ayako Hasegawa, 06/11/81.

35.   I have been unable to discover who "Bljdf" might be.

36.   RAH, Plebe Summer letter to his father, dated "Saturday" (probably June 27, 1925).

37.   RAH, Plebe Summer letter to his mother, dated "Wednesday" (August 26, 1925).

38.   RAH, Plebe Summer letter to his father, dated "Monday" (probably July 6, 1925).

39.   "Extra duty" is defined in the 1929 *Lighthouse: The Plebe's Bible* as "a form of hazing practiced by the Executive Department."

40.   There is a photograph of the fire engine in the 1928 *Lucky Bag*; a photo captioned "Fire in Isherwood Hall" appears on page 70 of the 1929 *Lucky Bag*.

41.   RAH, Plebe Summer letter addressed "Dear Folks," dated "Sunday" (August 23, 1925).

42.   RAH, letter to his parents, 08/25/25.

43.   RAH, Plebe Summer letter addressed "Dear Folks," dated "Sunday" (August 23, 1925).

5. Plebe Year

1.   Jack Thornton, "J. Fish," *The Heinlein Journal*, No. 10 (January 2002), 10.

2.   RAH, letter to Dr. R. P. Boas, 06/21/79.

3.   RAH, telephone interview by Ben Bova, 06/29/79. The old seawall along which Albert Abraham Michelson's measurements were made was removed for the construction of new buildings; a brass line set into the concrete in the plaza east of the Nimitz Library preserves the location of the seawall, and therefore of Michelson's experimental measurements of the speed of light when he taught at the Academy.

4.   Admiral Ignatius "Pete" Gallantin, interview; 03/31/2001.

5.   Admiral Gallantin interview.

6.   Admiral Gallantin interview.

7.   Although in use for a very long time, the term *middie* for *midshipman* is considered insulting at the Naval Academy today; *mid* and *mids* is considered acceptable.

8.   Admiral Gallantin interview.

9. Heinlein and Teague met up again and resumed their friendship when Heinlein settled in Los Angeles in 1934.

10. Admiral Gallantin (Class of 1932) confirmed the overall accuracy of the picture of hazing at the Naval Academy in *Time Enough for Love* in his taped oral interview with the author, 03/31/2001.

11. RAH, *Time Enough for Love,* 78–79.

12. Cal Laning, letter to Virginia Heinlein, 05/21/87.

13. RAH, *Time Enough for Love,* 79.

14. Heinlein left no direct description of the hazing he received at Gurney's hands, except for some of the details he memorialized in *Time Enough for Love*; all the other details here are recounted by Virginia Heinlein as recollections passed on to her by Robert Heinlein.

15. RAH, *Time Enough for Love,* 76–80.

16. Heinlein carried a personal notebook through his years at the Academy; it was given by Virginia Heinlein to the author.

17. The episode of the ketchup bottle and Heinlein's reaction is recounted in Virginia Heinlein's e-mail to the author, 01/05/2002.

18. The Black N is the flip side of the Navy's Gold N given for athletic achievement. Since 1912 it has been given out for serious offenses against military discipline, meriting a week in the Academy's brig, then the captured Spanish-American War ship *Reina Mercedes* (the *Reina* has since been removed). For each additional Black N offense, an asterisk would accompany the N. Gurney's five asterisks meant a total of six weeks spent "in hack" (naval slang for "under arrest").

19. Virginia Heinlein, e-mail to author, 05/27/2002.

20. RAH's inscription to Marsh Gurney on the 1960 list of inscribed copies of *Starship Troopers* to be sent out. See n. 22, *infra.*

21. Virginia Heinlein, letter to author, 06/14/1999; see also Virginia Heinlein, e-mail to author, 05/27/2002.

22. RAH's 1960 list of inscribed copies of *Starship Troopers* to be sent out: "To Marsh Gurney, '26 who made me memorize log tables, the Mary Gloster & beat my tail—and thereby shaped my character for the rest of my life."

23. RAH, *Time Enough for Love,* 78.

24. Admiral Gallantin interview.

25. Virginia Heinlein, taped interview by author, Second Series, Tape C, Side B (September 10–12, 2000).

26. RAH, letter to Marion Zimmer Bradley, 12/25/63.

27. Lawrence Lyle Heinlein to RAH, 01/01/26, in Heinlein's scrapbook, RAH Archive, UCSC.

28. RAH, letter to Bam Heinlein, dated "Tuesday" (probably dating from about April 1926, as it is before the Gymkhana that year).

29. RAH, letter to his mother, dated "Tuesday" (possibly February or March 1926).

30. "Dark Days" is U.S. Naval Academy slang usually applied to the months of February and March, when the winter has been unrelieved too long.

31. Academy slang for dating.

32. Draft undated but probably about May 1926.

33. Dorothy Martin Heinlein, "Relatively Speaking" (unpublished paper written ca. March 2006).

34. RAH, letter to Jerry Pournelle, 03/31/63.

6. Youngster Year

1. RAH, letter to Alice Dalgliesh, 02/17/59.

2. Admiral Gallantin interview.

3. "Youngster Cruise" entry, *The Lucky Bag* (1929), 79.

4. Memorialized in the 1927 *Lucky Bag*, 92.

5. *The Lucky Bag* (1927), 96.

6. RAH, letter to Stephen King, 08/08/84.

7. "Youngster Cruise" entry, *The Lucky Bag* (1929), 82.

8. Virginia Heinlein, taped interview by author, Tape 7, Side A (February [27?,] 2000).

9. Virginia Heinlein, taped interview by author, Tape 7, Side A (February [27?,] 2000).

10. Although this recounting is taken from Virginia Heinlein's recollections of the incident told her directly by her husband, Heinlein also recalled this incident in *I Will Fear No Evil* (1970), slightly adapting it to the fictional recollections of the much older protagonist, Johann Sebastian Bach Smith.

11. Mrs. Heinlein's various e-mail recollections of Heinlein's factual recounting of this incident vary in small details; in one recounting, they purchased the car for $75 and sold it in Kansas City for $50 (06/14/2002); in another, they purchased the car for $50 and sold it for $75 (06/10/2001). In the first taped interview— the first series (which runs from late February to the first few days of March 2000)—she says, "When they got to Kansas City, they sold it for $45, which was more than they paid for it."

12. There are in Heinlein's letters several approving references to the "adult" entertainments offered by Kansas City under the Pendergasts, which must include this period as well as his later (1934) trip home. See, for example, RAH's letter to Earl Kemp, 01/20/57.

13. There are many informal recountings of this part of the Pendergast machine's

history. See, for example, David McCullough, *Truman* (New York: Simon & Schuster, 1992), 207.

14. RAH, letter to Lois Lavendar, 02/17/68.

15. RAH, letter to Larry Niven and Jerry Pournelle, 06/20/73.

16. Admiral Gallantin interview; Virginia Heinlein, in an e-mail to the author dated 01/05/2002, says this was the case with the first-ranked scholar in Heinlein's class.

17. Bill Mullins, "Biographical Notes on Robert Heinlein and His Family and Associates," *The Heinlein Journal,* No. 20 (January 2007), 8.

18. Dr. Eric Picholle, the foremost French authority on Heinlein, suggests Heinlein probably meant *avec des points d'arête.*

19. RAH, letter to Jerry Pournelle, 03/14/63.

20. The 1929 *Lucky Bag* has a very extensive discussion of this trip, and the details of this telling are drawn substantially from the *Lucky Bag* class history.

21. Preserved in Heinlein's personal scrapbook at the RAH Archive, UCSC.

22. RAH, handwritten letter; no addressee, in scrapbook.

23. Virginia Heinlein, letter to author, 12/12/2000.

24. James R. Harrison's reports had been running near the middle of the daily paper from the arrival of the midshipmen on Thursday through Saturday; the full report on the game was the lead article in the Sunday *New York Times:* "110,000 See Army and Navy Battle to a 21 to 21 Tie in First Game in the West." The quotation is on the page 28 continuation of the story.

25. "Youngster Year" entry, *The Lucky Bag* (1929), 87–88.

26. Virginia Heinlein, IM with author, 12/16/01.

27. RAH, letter to T. B. Buell, 10/03/74, p. 62.

28. RAH, letter to Ruth Clement Hoyer, 05/22/46.

29. James M. Merrill, *A Sailor's Admiral: A Biography of William F. Halsey* (New York: Thomas Y. Crowell Company, 1976), 70. The staff officer is not further identified.

30. RAH, letter to T. B. Buell, 10/03/74.

31. RAH, letter to Fred Smith, 05/28/57.

32. RAH, letter to Fred Smith, 05/28/57.

33. Virginia Heinlein, taped interview by author, Misc. Notes First Series, Tape A, Side A (September 4–8, 2001).

34. RAH, *Starman Jones* (New York: Charles Scribner's Sons, 1953; Pocket Books, 2005).

35. RAH, letter to Chris Moskowitz, 09/06/61.

36. RAH, letter to Luis E. Bejarano, 11/08/54.

37. Remarks of a classmate named Faigle, quoted in RAH's letter to his mother, 07/11/61.

38. Admiral Gallantin interview.

39. The *Navy Register* itinerary of the 1927 practice cruise squadron, courtesy Special Collections of the Nimitz Library, U.S. Naval Academy.

7. Second Class Year

1. "Second Class Cruise" section of the class history in the 1929 *Lucky Bag,* 91.

2. Class history, *The Lucky Bag* (1929).

3. RAH, letter to John Campbell, 01/04/42.

4. RAH, *Tramp Royale* (New York: Ace Books, 1992), 41.

5. RAH, Foreword to "Cliff and the Calories," *Expanded Universe,* 355:

> When I was a freshman in college, the nearest connection for marijuana was a drug store a hundred yards off campus, for H or C it was necessary to walk another block. But bootleg liquor (tax free) would be delivered on or off campus at any hour.
>
> Did I avail myself of any of these amenities? None of your business, Buster!

6. Virginia Heinlein, letter to Denis Paradis, 12/13/82.

7. RAH, letter to Alfred Bester, 04/03/59.

8. If, indeed, they had not already become engaged; there is no documentation for the timing of the engagement; years later, in a letter dated February 17, 1968, to Lois Lavendar, Heinlein says simply that he and Alice McBee were "engaged to be married," without mentioning the timing of the engagement. His September leave in 1927 was simply the most likely time for such a proposal to have been made and accepted.

9. Heinlein's graduating portrait in the 1929 *Lucky Bag* shows a Black N with *two* asterisks.

10. Virginia Heinlein, letter to author, 06/23/99.

11. William F. Halsey and Lt. Comm J. Bryan III, *Admiral Halsey's Story* (New York: McGraw-Hill, 1947).

12. Virginia Heinlein, letter to author, 06/23/99.

13. In a letter dated February 2, 1949, to Forrest J. Ackerman, Heinlein stated he "never indulged in [hazing] as an upperclassman," which could be exactly, if only technically, true, as the Second Class year, his first year as an upperclassman, was not regarded as commencing until the October academic term started.

14. Oscar Allen Heinlein, Jr., letter to RAH, 10/02/72.

15. Frank E. Wigelius, letter to RAH, 09/24/84.

16. RAH, letter to Forrest J. Ackerman, 02/25/49.

17. *Stranger in a Strange Land,* where Mike is watching the monkeys in a zoo and has his "anthropophany."

18. Preserved in RAH's personal scrapbook of his Annapolis years, transcribed in Virginia Heinlein, taped interview by author, Second Series, Tape D, Side A.

19. "Second Class Year" section of the class history, *The Lucky Bag* (1929), 98.

20. RAH, letter to Larry Heinlein, 08/25/53.

21. Preserved in RAH's first scrapbook; described in Virginia Heinlein, taped interview by author, Second Series, Tape D, Side A.

22. Information preserved in RAH's first scrapbook.

23. Virginia Heinlein, taped interview by author, Tape 1, Side B (February [28?,] 2000).

24. The telegram was not preserved and thus cannot be dated precisely. Heinlein says only that he received word and could not get emergency leave: with a three-day trip home he would have missed even the funeral.

    The seemingly contradictory assertions that Alice McBee was in a car accident but that she died of "appendicitis" initially gave rise to suspicions that Alice McBee was pregnant and died in childbirth, or, possibly, of a botched abortion since appendicitis was a very common cover story given for pregnancy among unmarried women. However, the timing cannot be made to work for Heinlein to have impregnated her; he and she would have had to be in proximity sometime between March and May of 1927, and Heinlein was at Annapolis at that time. The best way of resolving the contradiction is to suppose that Alice was in a serious car accident and during her long recovery developed acute appendicitis and died from it.

25. RAH, letter to Lois Lavendar, 02/17/68. This is the only mention of this incident in all his correspondence.

26. "Second Class Year" entry, *The Lucky Bag* (1929), 99.

27. "Fencing," *The Lucky Bag* (1928), 342.

28. Another event memorialized in Heinlein's scrapbook is less odd than it appears: on May 4, 1928, Robert received a telegram from his oldest brother, Larry: "You are father to a fine boy born 11:00 last night weigh 8 lbs. 12 oz. Everything fine." It is unlikely this was a practical joke, since Robert would have known Larry and Alice were expecting a child. It was probably a slip of the pen, and Lawrence meant to say Robert was now an "uncle" for the first time. There was now a "next generation" in his family: Lawrence Lewis ("Bud") Heinlein.

29. In addition to the increased load of academic work, the Second Year men were expected to help with the preparation for the year's graduation ceremonies. They took charge of organizing the Ring Dance, a social highlight of the June Week ceremonies—pictured in the 1928 *Lucky Bag* with couples of midshipmen and their drag entering through a giant, gilded representation of a class ring, where

the dance instruction they had received year by year would pay off. But the Class of '29 also had their own Ring work to do. Their Ring Committee had been formed in their Youngster year, and they had spent almost two years comparing designs and costs. They would put their rings on after the Class of '28 graduated and they became First Class men.

30. Allan "Gus" Gray is mentioned only infrequently in Heinlein's correspondence, and little is known of him. Cal Laning, however, became one of Heinlein's closest and longest friends. They had not met in Kansas City, since Laning went to a different high school, and their social circles did not intersect.

8. First Classman

1. "First Class Cruise" section of *The Lucky Bag* (1929), 105.
2. As Heinlein later abandoned this wish to be self-made and also destroyed his correspondence from this period (for other reasons), there is only one surviving piece of evidence of his attitude at this time, a 1930 letter to "Barrett" Laning quoted later.
3. RAH, letter to Marion Zimmer Bradley, 03/04/63.
4. RAH, letter to William Rotsler, 08/23/74.
5. In the unpublished manuscript of *Before the Writing Began*, Leon Stover maintains that Heinlein and Rand had an ongoing sexual relationship, resumed each time they were in the same part of the country—not impossible; not even improbable. There is, however, no surviving documentary evidence to this effect, and I have elected not to include the assertion in this biography.

    It is possible Stover received the information from Cal Laning or from Heinlein's childhood friend Don Johnstone, but neither they nor Stover's records were available, and it is therefore not possible to confirm or deny the assertion.
6. Curiously, the Land Trips listing in Heinlein's scrapbook does not show a final leg of travel back to Annapolis. It's not impossible that he boarded some vessel in New York Harbor for the last leg of his journey back to the Academy.
7. Admiral Gallantin interview.
8. Cal Laning, letter to Virginia Heinlein, 08/29/78.
9. L. H. Dentel (Robert's high school principal), letter to RAH, 07/09/52.
10. Virginia Heinlein, letter to author, 06/23/99.
11. Virginia Heinlein, letter to author, 06/23/99.
12. RAH, letter to Laura Haywood, undated but in 1973.
13. Virginia Heinlein, e-mail to author, 01/05/2002.
14. Frank Wigelius, letter to RAH, 09/24/84.
15. In a letter to Robert A. W. Lowndes, dated 08/15/41, Heinlein's second wife, Leslyn, describes (rather than gives the names of) four close friends at the Academy, but while the list includes descriptions of Perreault, Laning, and Wait, it does not

include John Arwine or Gus Gray, both of whom maintained friendship with Heinlein for the entirety of their remaining lives, or Elwood "Woody" Teague, another close friend from Academy days; another classmate, Robert N. S. Clark, he knew of but did not meet and befriend until they were both stationed on their first billet, USS *Lexington*.

16. *The Lucky Bag* (1929), 345.

17. After telling Wait's story as a dinner-party anecdote for decades, Heinlein wrote it as "The Tale of the Man Who Was Too Lazy to Fail" in *Time Enough for Love* (1973). In a taped interview with Leon Stover, Virginia Heinlein recalled that Wait wrote a letter to her after Robert Heinlein's death in which he recognized and approved his fictional portrayal as David Lamb. Tape 3, Side 3, p. 23 of the transcript.

18. RAH, letter to Dr. Samuel Herrick, 07/16/52.

19. The Quest is mentioned but rarely in Heinlein's correspondence, but Cal Laning talked freely about it with Leon Stover, and it is discussed in some detail in Stover's unpublished manuscript, *Before the Writing Began*, especially on page 127. Stover thinks the name may have come from H. Rider Haggard.

     The best short description of The Quest was provided in a letter by Cal Laning to Virginia Heinlein after Heinlein's death: "Possibly the most interesting event in our relationship was the 'Quest.' When the three of us [Gus Gray being the third, though Laning does not mention the name here] decided to divide the fields of knowledge and find out what was the significance of the universe, the one which we thought the old folks were keeping from us."

     Laning goes on to suggest that they found the solution to their Quest in *Universe: A Verifiable Solution to the "Riddle of the Universe,"* a book published privately in 1921 (publication information is given only as "Westchester, NY") by a retired naval officer, Scudder Klyce (a graduate of Annapolis, Class of 1902). However, except for the coincidence of the names—"Scudder" is a background figure in some of Heinlein's Future History stories—and the title "Universe," there are no references to this book in Heinlein's *oeuvre* (whereas there are hundreds of primary and secondary references to books that dealt with related subjects: P. D. Ouspensky's *Tertium Organum* and *A New Model of the Universe*— books probably recommended by Leslyn Heinlein).

     Klyce's *Universe* was for a very long time a rare and obscure book, despite an introduction by John Dewey, then very nearly at the peak of his reputation as "America's Philosopher." However, Klyce and *Universe* attained a minor notoriety when the book was depicted in Alan Grant's Anarky graphic-novel series in *Detective Comics* (the first incarnation of Anarky as a Batman antagonist ran from 1989 to 1999). In 2006, a facsimile reprint of the 1921 publication of *Universe* was issued by Sacred Science Institute.

20. Laning's testimony as memorialized by Stover in *Before the Writing Began*, 138.

21. Laning's testimony, memorialized by Stover in *Before the Writing Began*, was that
     Laning would hypnotize dates, and then he and Heinlein would bed them, singly
     or—Stover's words—"double dating in bed." See page 127 of the manuscript.

22. See, for example, RAH's letter to Barrett Laning, 08/21/30, quoted and in fac-
     simile in Leon Stover's unpublished manuscript, *Before the Writing Began*; the
     parts Stover quoted in text are given in full in chapter 12 herein.

23. RAH, letter to William Rotsler, 08/23/74. The name of the artist-friend was
     not given.

24. RAH, letter to Richard Pope, 09/25/74.

25. Graduating portrait of Seraphin Bach Perreault written by Robert Heinlein, *The
     Lucky Bag* (1929), 318.

26. The Norfolk–New York leg is recorded in his scrapbook-preserved list under the
     heading "Land Trips," which implies that the Annapolis–Norfolk and New York–
     Annapolis legs were taken on board a naval vessel.

27. RAH, letter to Richard Pope, 09/25/74.

28. RAH's midshipman's jacket (dossier) obtained from Special Collections of the
     Nimitz Library, U.S. Naval Academy.

29. "June Week" section of *The Lucky Bag* (1929), 119–20.

30. Virginia Heinlein, letter to Leon Stover, 04/07/89. Stover says in several places,
     but most directly on page 127 of *Before the Writing Began*, that The Quest actu-
     ally had two purposes—the investigation into what the adults were hiding, com-
     bined with lechery. This is probably Cal Laning's interpretation, sixty years
     later.

9. Frying Pan and Fire

1. Nearly all the details of this chance encounter, including Heinlein's own aston-
    ishingly open comments on the impact it had on him and on his subsequent
    character development, come from a single letter written by Heinlein to the
    woman in question, Mary (Briggs) Collin, 08/06/62.

2. RAH, letter to Mary Collin, 08/06/62.

3. RAH, letter to Mary Collin, 08/06/62.

4. RAH, letter to Mary Collin, 08/06/62.

5. RAH, letter to Mary Collin, 08/06/62.

6. RAH, letter to Earl Kemp, 01/20/57. Actually, Count Basie recalled, they *were*
    dressed, after a fashion: "One high-priced place called the Chesterfield Club of-
    fered a businessman's lunch served by waitresses clad only in high heels and cel-
    lophane aprons." Cited by McCullough in *Truman*, 198.

7. Virginia Heinlein, letter to author, 02/07/2000.

8. RAH, letter to Mickey and Cal Laning, 10/16/73.

9. Cal Laning, letter to Virginia Heinlein, 08/29/78.

10. In an IM with the author on 06/13/2002, Virginia Heinlein speculated that Sammy Roberts had a car and took them on road trips.

11. Research report commissioned for this biography from Philippe Paine, 11/16/2000.

12. Elinor and Robert's ticket to the 1925 ROTC ball is preserved in Heinlein's earliest scrapbook.

13. This marriage certificate was kept in the Heinleins' safe-deposit box and provided for the biography by Virginia Heinlein in 2000.

14. In a personal conversation with the author, Jerry Pournelle commented that he had worked with R. N. S. Clark in the 1970s, and Clark told him that he was best man at Heinlein's first wedding. However, this is difficult to reconcile with Heinlein's statement (RAH, letter to Mickey and Cal Laning, 10/16/73) that he did not become acquainted with Clark until they served together on the *Lexington*—that is, a few weeks after the marriage to Elinor Curry. Perhaps Clark did not know about the marriage to Elinor Curry, or else he had forgotten it and was referring to the 1932 marriage to Leslyn MacDonald in San Diego, since Heinlein rarely mentioned the 1929 marriage.

15. Dorothy Martin Heinlein, wife of Robert's brother Clare, in an unpublished interview with the author at the Heinlein Centennial in Kansas City (July 5–8, 2007), provided the information that RAH did not tell his family about the marriage. They certainly became aware of it at some time, as Mary Jean Lermer (Robert's younger sister) introduced Elinor as her "ex-sister-in-law" in 1939.

16. Virginia Heinlein, letter to author, 02/07/2000.

17. Virginia Heinlein, IM with author, 05/13/2000.

18. Philippe Paine, research report 11/20/2000.

19. Virginia Heinlein, taped interview by author, Tape 2, Side A (February [27?], 2000).

20. Probably Cal Laning, as Laning later (03/25/89) told Virginia Heinlein in a letter discussing the presumptive biography that he was "co-respondent" in the divorce that followed. (But see note 14 of chapter 11 discussing what a "co-respondent" would have meant.)

21. Virginia Heinlein, letter to Leon Stover, 04/08/89.

22. He remained on very good terms with Cal Laning, even in the short term, as is evidenced by his one surviving letter to "Barrett" dated 08/21/30.

This letter was acquired from Cal Laning by Leon Stover and is now, together with the rest of Laning's complete file of his correspondence with Robert Heinlein, in the possession of David Aronovitz, a collector and dealer in rare books and manuscripts. Mr. Aronovitz has declined to make any of the Laning-Heinlein correspondence available for use in this biography; only material quoted in *Before the Writing Began* was available for use here.

23. The more usual Navy way was for the husband to get a free pass for liaisons away from home while the wife remained, at least on the surface, a faithful homemaker. Heinlein never discussed this first marriage, but the open nature of his second is well (if discreetly) documented, and Heinlein later called his own "unjealous" nature a lifetime feature of his character. RAH, letter to Mary Collin, 08/06/62.

24. RAH, letter to Cal Laning, 08/01/30.

25. Cal Laning, conversation with Leon Stover, recorded in Stover's unpublished manuscript, *Before the Writing Began*, at page 127.

26. Although the letter and its reply have not been preserved, the transmittal cover sheets from the Academy to *Lexington,* with a complex series of endorsements, have been preserved. The contents of the letter are inferred from the fact that the draft application exists in Heinlein's midshipman jacket but there is no carbon of a finalized application; nor does the American Secretary of the Rhodes Trust have any record of the application or the award of a Rhodes Scholarship to him.

27. Heinlein never discussed the Rhodes Scholarship at all. That he regretted the loss of the opportunity and attributed it to the marriage is inferred from his later letter to Cal Laning, 08/21/30, by which time he had come to regard Elinor as "poisonous, like mistletoe."

28. Report dated 07/31/29, C. E. Riggs, Chief of the Bureau of Medicine and Surgery to Chief of the Bureau of Navigation. "Re RAH: Physical Examination for flight training in the case of Heinlein, Robert Anson."

   There is a certain irony in this, for Admiral Halsey failed his own entrance examination for the flight school at Pensacola in 1932 due to eyesight. Two years later, the Bureau of Aeronautics (BuAer), headed by Admiral Ernest King, gave Halsey a waiver to get him into Pensacola. James M. Merrill, *A Sailor's Admiral: A Biography of William F. Halsey,* 11.

29. RAH, letter to T. B. Buell, 10/03/74.

30. RAH, letter to T. B. Buell, 10/03/74.

31. RAH, letter to T. B. Buell, 10/03/74. Heinlein's extremely voluminous and extremely detailed letter about his time on *Lexington* provides most of the detail on which this portion of the biography is based.

32. RAH, letter to T. B. Buell, 10/03/74, p. 2.

33. This seems to imply that the scale of 1930s currency compared to that of the naughty aughties was about 1 to 80 or so; that is, a piece of pie now sells in national chain restaurants (the Automat having disappeared) for between $3.50 and $5.50.

   Thirty billion dollars in 1929 dollars would therefore be the equivalent of more than $2.4 *trillion* in 2010 money. The stock market crash of 2008 was frequently compared to that of 1929, but the scale was not even close.

34.   RAH, letter to Laurie A. MacDonald, 03/01/72.

35.   RAH, letter to Laura Haywood, undated except "ca. Dec. 73."

36.   Robert's grandfather Samuel Edward Heinlein remarried after the death of his first wife and moved to Long Beach, where he and his second wife, Maria, had three other children, Robert's uncle (Ray) Lawrence Ray and two aunts, Mina Ladine and Alice Irene.

37.   Ron Steward, letter to RAH, 02/06/47.

38.   RAH, letter to Ray and Kitty Heinlein, 11/18/59. Heinlein continues, telling them how their example helped him in the grim time when he had to plan his own father's funeral:

> What I learned that week stood me in good stead this week . . . and I had help, too, because I had Edward Ray walking beside me, steadying me, keeping me going, with a big grin on his face, reminding me of details, helping me out when I needed it. Ed always did say that he and I were partners and that anything he had was mine—and meant it and did share with me. This week, when I needed some of his courage and his strength, he was on hand and shared it.
>
> No, I'm not seeing ghosts nor hearing voices—I simply mean that Ed has been very close to me this week and that fact helped enormously to get me through the rough part.
>
> I don't know why Dad had to suffer through so many years . . . and I don't know why Ed had to be taken from us when he was so young and strong and buoyant. But what I cannot understand it is necessary to have the courage to accept—and I think I have acquired some of that courage both from Ed and from Dad.
>
> May the Lord make His face to shine upon thee and give thee peace.
>
> All my love
> Bob

39.   *The Tacoma News Tribune,* 06/21/61.

40.   RAH, letter to Joanna Russ, 04/10/79.

41.   RAH, letter to T. B. Buell, 10/03/74, p. 11.

42.   RAH, letter to T. B. Buell, 10/03/74, p. 11.

10. New York State of Mind

1.   Heinlein kept a penciled record of "Land Trips" in his personal scrapbooks from 1923 to 1934.

2. Virginia Heinlein, taped interview by author, First Series, Tape 3, Side B (February 1, 2000).

3. RAH, letter to Poul Anderson, 09/06/61.

4. More than once, Heinlein mentions cruising in bars with his lesbian model, but see particularly RAH's letter to Marion Zimmer Bradley, 04/06/63.

5. A black-and-white rotogravure photo of one of Gertrude Vanderbilt's Rodinesque sculpture groups was preserved in Heinlein's first personal scrapbook.

6. RAH, letter to Marion Zimmer Bradley, 04/06/63.

7. Heinlein never gave any extended reminiscences about his time in Greenwich Village, but the various mentions in correspondence of specific incidents show that he was immersed in the several "arts" crowds ranging from those at the hangouts of artists' models to Dorothy Parker and the *New Yorker* crowd, while he included some photos of the new sculpture in his scrapbooks.

8. RAH, letter to Dr. Chris Moskowitz, 09/06/61.

9. Or here already: in 1895 the future Edward VII had said "we are all socialists nowadays," repeating an earlier aphorism of Sir William Harcourt. Dewey's essays were published later that year (1930) as *Individualism: Old and New.* Heinlein never mentioned that book—or Dewey—specifically, but the late Phillip H. Owenby, in his 1996 unpublished doctoral dissertation, *Robert A. Heinlein: Popular Adult Educator and Philosopher of Education,* identifies the Pragmatism of C. S. Peirce and Dewey as a major influence in Heinlein's philosophy. In any case, it was a subject of interest by a prominent current intellectual, and Heinlein might well have read Dewey's book or the essays as they came out. In any case, the book is illuminating for some of Heinlein's later writings, such as *Beyond This Horizon,* as showing the state of thinking about individualism and socialism that was "in the air" when Heinlein was a young man.

10. Wells, *The World of William Clissold,* 536. Although Heinlein several times endorsed Wells's books of social philosophy (see, for example, "The Discovery of the Future," his 1941 Guest-of-Honor Speech for the Third World Science Fiction Convention), it was always in very general terms, without mentioning specific books (except for the trilogy of sociological books, *The Outline of History* [1920], *The Science of Life* [1930], and *The Work, Wealth and Happiness of Mankind* [1937]). There are no direct and specific references to, say, *Ann Veronica* (1909) or *Christina Alberta's Father* (1925) or *Meanwhile* (1927), even though it is highly probable that he read them. Similarly, there are no direct references to Wells's clearest explanation of his Open Conspiracy concept, *The World of William Clissold* (1926), so it is impossible to tell whether Heinlein read this book specifically. Nevertheless, *Clissold* is the clearest and most convenient state-

ment of Wells's social philosophy, and it, together with *The Open Conspiracy (What Are We to Do with Our Lives?)* of 1928, kicked off a political movement very active especially in England well into the 1940s. By looking at *The World of William Clissold* we are able to get an outline of Heinlein's dialogue with Wells's thought—his "wellsianism," rather than specific references to specific books.

11.   RAH, letter to Robert Lowndes, 03/15/56.

12.   RAH, letter to Dr. Chris Moskowitz, 09/06/61: "I considered the elephant to be the perfect subject for sculpture then. I admit that my tastes widened somewhat later—I began to feel that h. sapiens, female model, was probably the epitome of 3-dimensional curves for sculpture or anything—but my interest in elephants did not lessen thereby."

13.   RAH, letter to Marion Zimmer Bradley, 04/06/63. Wine recurs often in these reminiscences, few though they are. Prohibition was still in effect in 1930, and wine, beer—indeed, liquor of all kinds—was obtainable only with a certain amount of effort and expense: the 75¢ bottle of muscatel mentioned above as standard inducement for a date would have cost the equivalent of about $60 in 2010 dollars—not a minor consideration at the time.

Although economic conditions were to worsen steadily over the next several years, Heinlein came to a New York already on a depression footing. Nineteen thirty was the year that men selling apples on street corners became a common Depression-era sight (a little after Heinlein rejoined *Lexington*). Washington State apple producers had a bumper crop in 1930, and distributors sold crates of apples to the unemployed on credit:

> A man could buy a crate for $1.74, stand on a street corner, and sell apples for five cents each. With luck he could sell a crate full of sixty apples within a day, take in $3.00, pay the distributor, and have $1.25 . . . and those who could afford to do so bought the fruit out of sense of responsibility. Apple selling became a common big-city activity, indeed a symbol of coping with the depression. (David E. Kyvig, *Daily Life in the United States, 1920–1940: How America Lived Through the "Roaring Twenties" and the Great Depression,* rev. ed. [2002; repr., Chicago: Ivan R. Dee, 2004]), 225.

14.   There is only one surviving letter-record of these experiments (which Laning continued long after Heinlein had moved on to other things), dated 07/13/41. It is possible the file of Laning's correspondence with Heinlein now in the collection of David Aronovitz may contain more—and more illuminating—material.

15.   In a letter to Robert A. W. Lowndes, 06/07/40, Heinlein said he began reading *Appeal to Reason* in 1919—that is, at the age of twelve.

16.   J. B. Rhine had just begun conducting experimental trials at Duke University, but the first results would not be published until 1934, under the title *Extra-Sensory Perception*.

17.   Upton Sinclair, *Mental Radio* (New York: A. & C. Boni, 1930), 5.

18.   See, for example, his workup notes for "Lost Legacy," in the RAH Archive, UCSC.

19.   Leon Stover, letter to author, 05/25/97.

20.   In 1974 Heinlein was contacted by a biographer, T. B. Buell, who was assigned to write an updated biography of King. King had become Fleet Admiral King during World War II and was therefore one of the most important naval figures of the century. Buell routinely contacted all surviving men who had served with King.

       Heinlein wrote a long letter in reply, sixty-three pages, single-spaced, in which he poured out observations of King and discussed his personal history with King on board *Lexington*. It would be cumbersome to cite every fact that comes out of this irreplaceable resource; suffice it to say that most of the information in the following chapter comes from that long letter.

11. Robert and Uncle Ernie

1.   RAH, letter to T. B. Buell, 10/03/74, p. 61.

2.   RAH, letter to T. B. Buell, 10/03/74, p. 30.

3.   RAH, letter to T. B. Buell, 10/03/74, p. 31.

4.   RAH, interview in *Xignals* (the newsletter of the Otherworlds Club), 1986.

5.   RAH, letter to Harlan Ellison, 07/27/67.

6.   RAH, letter to T. B. Buell, 10/03/74, p. 38.

7.   Martha King married Freddie Smith (West Point Class of 1929), and Heinlein stayed in touch with them for the next several decades—they were neighbors in Colorado Springs in the early 1950s, when Smith was at the Air Force Academy, and Smith entertained Heinlein several times when he was traveling overseas. Most notably, Smith was the officer who debriefed him and Ginny after the trip in 1960 to the U.S.S.R.

8.   RAH, letter to T. B. Buell, 10/03/74, p. 35.

9.   RAH, letter to T. B. Buell, 10/03/74, p. 34.

10.   See, for example, RAH's letter to T. B. Buell, 10/03/74, p. 16 and *passim*.

11.   RAH, letter to Cal ("Barrett") Laning, 08/01/30, quoted in part in Leon Stover's unpublished manuscript of *Before the Writing Began*. The letter was part of the complete file of Laning-Heinlein correspondence which Cal Laning gave Leon Stover and now is in the possession of David Aronovitz.

12.   RAH, letter to Poul Anderson, 12/13/61. Heinlein uses this incident to illustrate his point about moral standards determining moral choices.

13. RAH, *Time Enough for Love*, 90.

14. In a letter to Virginia Heinlein after Robert Heinlein's death (03/02/89), Cal Laning told her that Elinor named Laning as "co-respondent" (a technical term that has now disappeared from divorce proceedings, meaning the second party in an adulterous affair). But the actual court papers do not list him at all, and the grounds for the divorce were not adultery; no co-respondent was needed in this type of action—and in any case, Laning could only have been a co-respondent in an action brought by Robert against Elinor; Elinor would have been accusing *herself* of adultery.

15. Property Settlement in Cause No. 337,884, *Elinor Heinlein* vs. *Robert A. Heinlein,* Circuit Court of Jackson County, Missouri, at Kansas City.

16. Minute Order of Jackson County Circuit Court dated "33rd day of the September Term, 1930. Wednesday, October 15th, 1930." Document obtained from Jackson County Circuit Court and forwarded courtesy of L. N. Collier, Esq.

17. Microfilm print of divorce decree of Mr. Heinlein and Ms. Curry, dated 10/15/30, received from the Clerk of the Jackson County (Missouri) Circuit Court and entered in official records November 5, 1930. Document kindly provided by L. N. Collier, Esq.

18. RAH, letter to T. B. Buell, 10/03/74, p. 20.

19. "The Weekly Retrospect" (unsigned and uncredited) in *The Observer of the U.S.S. Aircraft Carrier* Lexington IV: 21 (08/08/31), 1.

20. "Events of the Week," *The Observer of the U.S.S. Aircraft Carrier* Lexington III: 44 (02/28/31), datelined Balboa, Panama, C.Z.

21. RAH, letter to T. B. Buell, 10/03/74, p. 3.

22. RAH, letter to T. B. Buell, 10/03/74, p. 4.

23. RAH, letter to Poul Anderson, 09/06/61.

24. RAH, letter to Poul Anderson, 09/06/61.

25. RAH, afterword to "Searchlight," *Expanded Universe*, 452–55.

26. RAH, letter to Christopher B. Timmers, 01/31/72.

27. RAH, letter to Christopher B. Timmers, 01/31/72.

28. The incident is related in the Afterword to "Searchlight" in *Expanded Universe*, 517.

29. "Case History—Urethritis R. A. Heinlein" (handwritten in 1933); this document is part of RAH's Naval Jacket in the RAH Archive, UCSC.

30. RAH, letter to T. B. Buell, 10/03/74, p. 22.

31. RAH, letter to T. B. Buell, 10/03/74, p. 23; see also RAH, letter to John P. Conlan, undated but after May 25, 1973.

32. RAH, letter to T. B. Buell, 10/03/74, p. 33.

33. RAH, letter to T. B. Buell, 10/03/74, p. 17.

34. RAH, interview by Frank Robinson, *Oui* (December 1972), 76.

35. RAH, letter to Alfred Bester, 04/03/59.

36. RAH, letter to T. B. Buell, 10/03/74, p. 31.

37. RAH, letter to T. B. Buell, 10/03/74, p. 31.

38. "Case History—Urethritis" (hand dated January 1933) in RAH's naval jacket, RAH Archive, UCSC.

39. Dorothy Martin Heinlein, "Relatively Speaking" (unpublished paper written ca. March 2006).

40. On July 6, 2007, at the Heinlein Centennial in Kansas City, Dorothy Martin Heinlein told of running into "Bob's ex" at a play she attended in Kansas City with her sister-in-law Mary Jean in 1939, but the intervening years have turned up no documentation.

 Virginia Heinlein recalled in a letter to Leon Stover dated 04/08/89 that Robert's sister Mary Jean also met Elinor "with her new husband" on the same occasion. However, the phrasing is ambiguous and might mean that Mary Jean (rather than Elinor) was with her new husband—she had married Andrew Lermer in January 1939.

41. Virginia Heinlein, taped interview by author, Miscellaneous Notes, Tape A Side A (September 4–8, 2001).

12. Leslyn MacDonald

1. Much of the available biographical information about Leslyn MacDonald was developed by Robert James, Ph.D., and published in "Regarding Leslyn," *The Heinlein Journal*, No. 9 (July 2001), 17–36, and his supplemental follow-up "More Regarding Leslyn," *The Heinlein Journal*, No. 11 (July 2002), 11–14. As more newspaper and other archives are placed online, new details continue to become available.

2. See Bill Mullins, "Biographical Notes on Robert Heinlein and His Family and Associates," *The Heinlein Journal*, No. 20 (January 2007), 11. The article also contains information about Leslyn's experience at the Pasadena Playhouse.

3. Leslyn MacDonald's father, Colin MacDonald, a Canadian bookkeeper and hotelier, had died in Santa Barbara in 1929, of cirrhosis of the liver brought on by acute alcoholism. In RAH's letter to William A. P. White, dated March 22, 1957, Colin MacDonald is described as a "bottle-a-day man."

4. *World Theosophy Magazine* (April 1931) quoted in Robert James, Ph.D., "Regarding Leslyn," *The Heinlein Journal*, No. 9 (July 2001), 19.

5. RAH, letter to Ted Carnell, 02/13/46.

6. Robert James, Ph.D., "Regarding Leslyn," *The Heinlein Journal,* No. 9 (July 2001), 19.

7. Although it is unlikely Leslyn discussed her practice of "white witchcraft" at their initial meetings (her involvement is casually mentioned by others in later correspondence and will be documented as it arises in this narrative), Leslyn was clearly already versed to some degree in some mystical and occult matters (such as Theosophy) that bore on Laning and Heinlein's Quest.

8. This summary is synthesized from a number of letters Heinlein wrote to others over the period of his marriage to Leslyn MacDonald (a few are preserved in public archives), rather than deriving from a single or even a small number of sources.

9. Leslyn (Heinlein) Mocabee, letter to Phyllis and William Anthony Parker White [Anthony Boucher, pseud.], 09/15/53, and Virginia Heinlein, e-mail inverview with Robert James, Ph.D., 05/31/2001.

10. This sentiment imputed to Laning is drawn from Leon Stover's unpublished biography, *Before the Writing Began.* There is no documentation to this effect in the fragments of correspondence in Heinlein's archive (and Laning's file of letters is not available for research); however, much of Stover's work was based on extensive personal interviews with Laning, and much of the discussion there of Heinlein's sexual life is not documented anywhere else.

11. In his unpublished manuscript, *Before the Writing Began,* Leon Stover claimed that this aspect of The Quest had been brought to a close by the group's discovery of a book titled *Universe,* self-published in 1921 by the retired naval officer Scudder Klyce. Klyce claimed the book "unifies or qualitatively solves science, religion and philosophy." I have been able to find no documentation for Stover's claim (it is entirely possible that the facts were outlined orally to him by Cal Laning and never committed to print—or else that they were in the file of letters Stover later sold).

It is something of a mystery how even inveterate bookstore and library surfers like Laning and Heinlein might have come across such an obscure publication, but it is possible that Dewey's *Individualism: Old and New* might have led them to *Universe,* as Dewey wrote an introduction for Klyce's book, which is listed in his collected papers.

12. RAH, letter to Poul and Karen Anderson, 07/19/62.

13. Los Angeles Voter Registration records for 1932.

14. RAH, letter to Laura Haywood, undated except "ca. Dec. 73" penciled on his file copy in RAH's hand.

15. RAH, letter to Laura Haywood, undated except "ca. Dec. 73" penciled on his file copy in RAH's hand.

16. In his 10/03/74 letter to T. B. Buell, Heinlein misremembers the date as March 15, 1932, and the groups as Red and Blue.

17. Thomas Fleming, "February 7, 1932—A Date That Would Live in . . . Amnesia," *American Heritage* (July/August 2002).

18. RAH, letter to T. B. Buell, 10/03/74, p. 46.

19. In Heinlein's long letter about King to Commander T. B. Buell (10/03/74, pp. 57–58), he indicates King was in fact passed over in the next round of promotions and that gossip at the time attributed it to this incident; however, due to the reshuffling of assignments following Admiral Moffett's death and to President Roosevelt's personal intervention in the selection process, King did become an admiral only two years after leaving *Lexington.*

20. RAH, letter to T. B. Buell, 10/03/74, p. 57.

21. Quoted in Fleming.

22. Fleming, "A Date That Would Live in . . ."

23. RAH, letter to T. B. Buell, 10/03/74, p. 50.

24. Leslyn (Heinlein) Mocabee, letter to Fred Pohl, 09/06/53 and quoted in Robert James, Ph.D., "Regarding Leslyn," *The Heinlein Journal,* No. 9 (July 2001), 20.

25. Leslyn (Heinlein) Mocabee, letter to Fred Pohl, 05/08/53.

26. Leslyn (Heinlein) Mocabee, letter to Fred Pohl, 06/09/53.

27. Dr. J. E. Pournelle, e-mail to author, 05/20/2009. Dr. Pournelle notes that Clark told him directly that he had been best man at Heinlein's wedding, but did not mention *which* wedding it was. The 1932 wedding to Leslyn MacDonald seems the most likely, as they were not well acquainted at the time of the 1929 wedding to Elinor Curry.

28. This refrain can be found at various points in the documentation, both by Laning himself and by other people who quoted him. But see especially Laning's offer to help with the biography, in a letter to Virginia Heinlein dated 09/13/88. It is also quoted in an e-mail from Virginia Heinlein to Robert James, 05/31/2001.

29. RAH, letter to T. B. Buell, 10/03/74, p. 8.

30. Quoted words and incident from RAH, letter to T. B. Buell, 10/03/74, p. 14.

31. RAH, letter to T. B. Buell, 10/03/74, p. 14.

32. RAH, letter to T. B. Buell, 10/03/74, p. 14.

33. RAH, letter to T. B. Buell, 10/03/74, p. 15; the ellipses were in Heinlein's original language.

34. This and the next quoted words come from RAH, letter to T. B. Buell, 10/03/74, p. 15.

35. RAH, letter to T. B. Buell, 10/03/74, p. 15.

36. Both Virginia and Robert Heinlein mentioned this, but no such document was found with his naval jacket; it is possible that the request was submitted to BuNav as part of ship's papers, rather than with Heinlein's papers.

37. RAH, letter to T. B. Buell, 10/03/74, p. 46.

38. Virginia Heinlein, taped interview by author, Tape 2, Side A (February 27, 2000).

39. The nature of the order was not specified in Heinlein's recounting. The incident of written orders is related in RAH's letter to T. B. Buell, 10/03/74, pp. 41–42.

40. RAH, letter to Robert Bloch, 10/11/71.

41. RAH, letter to T. B. Buell, 10/03/74, p. 21.

13. Swallowing the Anchor

1. Virginia Heinlein, IM with author, 12/06/2001.

2. RAH, letter to Doña and George Smith, 02/03/51.

3. Virginia Heinlein, e-mail to Robert James, 06/03/2001. Leslyn might not have been the culinary technician that Virginia Heinlein was, but in September 2004, as this book was being prepared for press, Bill Mullins found a reference in an online search to a recipe Leslyn submitted for publication in *Sunset Magazine*, for a Watercress Spread she had served "[a]t a housewarming party for 60 guests," along with the last half of a poem bylined Leslyn M. Heinlein:

> I think I'll make a little sign
> To hang each day at four:
> Tea Served Within. Admission Free
> And Room for Just One More

The search organization has not permitted locating the specific issue in which this material appeared—though a mention of St. Patrick's Day suggests March 1935 (or possibly 1936). A further fragment of text concludes:

> Last year her husband retired from the Navy and they bought a house in Hollywood, and this year she's going to pick some flowers. For 3 years, every time she planted sweet peas the Navy heard about it, and sent the Heinleins somewhere else.

As new archival material is put online, new facts become available.

4. RAH's Request for Assignment to Duty addressed to BuNav on 12/13/41.

5. RAH's Request for Assignment to Duty addressed to the BuNav on 12/13/41.

6. Lawrence Lyle Heinlein must have been divorced from Alice Lewis Heinlein sometime between 1926 and 1932, but the event does not show up in Heinlein's

surviving correspondence from the period. Family members queried about it through the good offices of Heinlein's nephew Bill Bacchus in 2006 and 2007 could not develop any definite information. It was not talked about within the family.

7.   Francis Pottenger, M.D., letter to RAH, 08/15/33.

8.   Heinlein discusses his treatment in a letter to Rex Ivar on 03/10/33; his thoughts were interrupted by the Long Beach earthquake, which he describes from his home in Arcadia, about sixty miles east-northeast of the epicenter of the quake, in Huntington Beach.

9.   The daily schedule, written out in Leslyn's hand, is in Heinlein's naval jacket in the RAH Archive UCSC.

10.   The letter is dated March 10, but the earthquake that interrupted the writing is reported as taking place at 5:54 P.M. on March 11, 1933. The discrepancy can be attributed to the official designation in Greenwich Mean Time (U.T.C.), across the International Date Line (and therefore on the following date). March 10 at 1:54 P.M. was the correct local date.

11.   RAH, letter to Lurton Blassingame, 07/30/47.

12.   Order of Commandant, 11th Naval District, 04/15/33. In RAH's naval jacket, RAH Archive, UCSC.

13.   RAH, letter to Rex Ivar Heinlein, 03/10/33.

14.   RAH, letter to Colonel Fehrenbach, 10/07/78.

15.   RAH, letter to Colonel Fehrenbach, 10/07/78.

16.   Leslyn (Heinlein) Mocabee, letter to Fred Pohl, 05/08/53. We know of a few of Leslyn's extramarital affairs in the 1940s, and she recorded her quirky sexual behavior following her divorce from Robert Heinlein, so it is quite likely that she had her own adventures. But Leslyn was more reticent about her own adventures at this period, and Robert never spoke of them at all, so no information has survived.

17.   RAH, letter to Rex Ivar Heinlein, 09/29/64.

18.   Kyvig, *Daily Life in the United States, 1920–1940: How Americans Lived Through the "Roaring Twenties" and the Great Depression,* rev. ed., 236.

19.   RAH, letter to Rex Ivar Heinlein, 09/29/64.

20.   In one form or another, this joke has had a very long life and is widely quoted on the Internet to illustrate the difference between socialism and communism. In its original context, the joke is cited in "The Extent of Recovery and Success of the New Deal to 1941," in *The Home Front, 1914–1918* by Malcolm Chandler (Oxford: Heinemann, 2002).

21.   RAH, letter to Tom Eaton, 11/06/73.

22.   F. M. Pottenger, M.D., letter to RAH, 08/15/33. RAH's naval jacket, RAH Archive, UCSC.

23. Heinlein told this anecdote, including its provenance, many times over the years, and wrote it as a story eventually included in *Expanded Universe* under the title "No Bands Playing, No Flags Flying," but see, for example, RAH's letter to Judith and Dan Merril, 08/28/61.

24. RAH, letter to Harlan Ellison, 07/27/66.

25. RAH, letter to Mary Collin, 03/04/63.

26. RAH, prefatory material in *Expanded Universe*, 452.

27. Primitive versions of the water bed had been in existence since at least 1844, and a water bed is mentioned in H. G. Wells's *When the Sleeper Wakes*. The matter is explored in Kate Gladstone: "Water Beds, Pre-Heinlein: An Investigation," *The Heinlein Journal*, No. 15 (July 2004), 3–4.

28. RAH, letter to John Zube, 10/08/71.

29. "Notes on Case of R. A. Heinlein" [by same], Lieutenant (JG) U.S.N., 01/11/34, preserved in Heinlein's naval jacket, RAH Archive, UCSC.

30. Leslyn Heinlein, letter to John W. Campbell, 11/27/41.

31. First name not given in Heinlein's notes.

32. In all of Heinlein's many mentions of Dr. Howard in correspondence, and even on Dr. Howard's formal statement of Heinlein's case to the naval board, no first name is given.

33. "Report from Doctor Howard, January 20th 1934" in Robert Heinlein's naval jacket, RAH Archive, UCSC.

34. Letter to RAH from U.S. Naval Unit, Fitzsimmons General Hospital re: Change of status to sick in hospital, dated 03/05/34; RAH's endorsement is dated the same date. RAH Naval Jacket, RAH Archive, UCSC.

35. Heinlein never recorded how he met Cornog. A recent biography of John Whiteside (or "Jack") Parsons, *Strange Angel*, by George Pendle, suggests Cornog and Heinlein may have met at a nudist colony in Denver; however, Cornog's oral history at UC Berkeley's Bancroft Library states firmly that he met Heinlein at the downtown Athletic Club in Denver while Heinlein, in uniform, was judging a chess match.

36. Order in RAH's naval jacket, RAH Archive, UCSC.

37. R. N. S. Clark, letter to Leslyn and Robert Heinlein, 06/17/46.

38. There is no documentation as to how Heinlein learned of the lodes' availability or how he came to enter into the arrangement. However, given that Pendergast men had been arrested in Denver on at least two occasions since 1931, the inference that someone in the Pendergast organization might have been looking for someone with a clean reputation to front for him is at least colorable; otherwise, it is hard to imagine how Heinlein might have run across this opportunity on his own.

39. See, for example, RAH's interview by Alfred Bester in *Publishers Weekly* (July 2, 1973), 44.

40.   The lawyer's name is not given in Heinlein's surviving correspondence, though there was no particular mystery about him; possibly the name was given in correspondence that was destroyed in Heinlein's first great housecleaning in 1947.

41.   McCullough, *Truman.*

42.   The Colorado State records have no holdings for the Sophie and Shively Lodes, though they are shown on claim mines: the records are organized by mining company rather than by name of the lode.

43.   RAH, letter to Rip van Ronkel, 05/04/49.

44.   The fact that Heinlein held the exploitation rights only temporarily (the bond) and through a lease, a private arrangement with the then owner of the claims, makes it more difficult to locate any records. The arrangement is simply not reflected in the state's record-keeping.

45.   Rex Ivar Heinlein, letter to RAH, 08/03/53.

46.   RAH, draft letter to Tom Eaton, 12/12/73.

47.   RAH, letter to Rip van Ronkel, 05/04/49.

48.   McCullough, *Truman,* 200–201.

49.   Heinlein's naval jacket, RAH Archive, UCSC; see also RAH, letter to Larry Niven, Jerry Pournelle, 06/20/73.

50.   RAH, letter to Jack Parkman, 03/16/57.

51.   The 1934 California Voter Registration records show them at 905 *La Salle,* which would be in Inglewood, near the present site of the Los Angeles Airport, but this seems to be an error, as they were receiving mail in West Hollywood by August 30, 1934.

52.   Virginia Heinlein, letter to George Warren, 03/09/79.

53.   For Cal Tech being Heinlein's first choice and UCLA his second, see Leon Stover's letter to Virginia Heinlein, 05/25/89.

54.   Research in UCLA records by Robert James, Ph.D., communicated to the author in personal conversation, 2000.

55.   RAH, letter to Bill Corson, 02/20/48.

56.   RAH, letter to Damon Knight, 01/19/57.

57.   RAH, letter to Dr. Zimmerman, 08/01/73; see also RAH, letter to Damon Knight, 01/19/57.

58.   Heinlein's letter to Mandelkorn has not been preserved, though Mandelkorn mentions this passage in his undated reply letter written sometime in 1934 or 1935.

59.   Virginia Heinlein, taped interview by Phillip Homer Owenby (1994), Tape 11, Side A. Here Mrs. Heinlein says, "He got a recurrence of TB," and at various points in correspondence Heinlein said flatly that he had a tubercular relapse then (see, for example, RAH's letter to Jack Parkman, 03/15/57). But there are no medical records for treatment then, and no ancillary evidence of, say, a trip to

the Naval hospital at San Diego at that time. Furthermore, within a very short time, Heinlein was putting a great deal of energy into his political project, which suggests that he did not believe he was having a relapse of TB. Perhaps his "symptoms" were more related to situational stress and insomnia and passed without consequence.

14. Baptism of Fire

1. The great majority of the background information in this chapter about the 1934 California gubernatorial election, the EPIC (End Poverty in California) movement, and Upton Sinclair comes from Greg Mitchell's magisterial *Campaign of the Century* (New York: Random House, 1992), which details California and national newspaper and magazine coverage of the campaign on a daily basis. Constant direct citation of facts would be tedious, so citations to this work have been restricted, for the most part, to quotations taken from the book. The chapters on EPIC and related movements in Arthur M. Schlesinger, Jr.'s *The Politics of Upheaval, 1935–1936*, vol. 3 of *The Age of Roosevelt* (New York: Houghton Mifflin Co., 1960, 2003) were also helpful. There are some slight differences between Schlesinger's treatment and Mitchell's, and in the case of conflicts, I tended to rely on Mitchell's fuller treatment. References to the Schlesinger book are given as they occur in the text.

    All of Heinlein's correspondence and personal papers relating to this period of his life and the 1934 California gubernatorial campaign are lost—presumably destroyed in 1947. A small amount of direct information about Heinlein's participation in this campaign can be gleaned from his handbook for politicians: *How to Be a Politician,* published in 1992 as *Take Back Your Government!* These few references allow some reasonable inferences about events Heinlein must have witnessed, even where direct documentation is not available.

2. Schlesinger, *The Politics of Upheaval,* 112.
3. Wells, *The World of William Clissold,* 180.
4. Schlesinger, *The Politics of Upheaval,* 112.
5. "California Climax," *Time* (October 22, 1934), 2.
6. Upton Sinclair, *I, Governor of California, and How I Ended Poverty: A True Story of the Future* (1933), quoted in Schlesinger, *The Politics of Upheaval,* 112.
7. Schlesinger, *The Politics of Upheaval,* 100.
8. *Los Angeles Times* (August 29, 1934), quoted in Mitchell's Introduction to *The Campaign of the Century,* x.
9. *Los Angeles Times,* quoted in Mitchell, *The Campaign of the Century,* 321.
10. RAH, *Take Back Your Government!,* 19. The dating to late September is tentative, as Heinlein did not specify the date; but he does note that he was directing

the local (West Hollywood and Beverly Hills) Democratic club six weeks later, and if this took place before the election, then his volunteering cannot have taken place *later* than the last week in September.

11. Wells, *The World of William Clissold*, 253.

12. All documentation of Heinlein's actual thought processes about this decision has been lost (it was probably burned, along with many other bags of personal correspondence, in 1947), but, a dedicated Wellsian and an American socialist-liberal, Heinlein could not have failed to note the irony of Wells's praise for these antiliberal realtors. His own decision to go into real estate would thus be a blow to reclaim the professional organization for Wellsian managerial socialism.

     Such a supposition has the minor virtue of suggesting an explanation for such an odd move into a field so far from his normal interests.

13. RAH, letter to Judith Merril, 11/07/62.

14. "California Climax," *Time* (October 22, 1934), 2, quoted in Mitchell, *The Campaign of the Century*, 356.

15. Kyle Palmer, quoted in Mitchell, *The Campaign of the Century*, 428.

16. Alderman Jim Pendergast is quoted on page 152 of McCullough's *Truman*: " 'I've got friends,' he would say cheerfully. 'And by the way, that's all there is to this boss business—friends.' " Jim Pendergast died in 1911, but his personal style in both ward-work and in electioneering persisted through Heinlein's contact with T. J. Pendergast's machine, and the grassroots style of Sinclair's campaign was very compatible. Both the theory and the experience are preserved in *How to Be a Politician*, written by Heinlein in 1946. See, in particular, chapter 7, on precinct work.

     The book was published in 1992 under the title *Take Back Your Government!* but is presented under its original title in the Virginia Edition (the first hardcover publication of the book, as well).

17. "Father Coughlin" was Charles Edward Coughlin (1891–1979), a radio priest with an estimated at forty million Catholic followers for his weekly broadcasts. More political than religious, Coughlin initially endorsed and promoted the New Deal—but also after 1936 promoted Hitler and Mussolini and issued anti-Semitic propaganda. Some radio stations began refusing to carry the program, and he was forced off the air by the National Association of Broadcasters in 1940.

18. Quoted in Mitchell, *The Campaign of the Century*, 476.

19. Quoted without attribution in Mitchell, *The Campaign of the Century*, 498.

20. Quoted in Mitchell, *The Campaign of the Century*, 494.

21. A more detailed description of the rally can be found in Mitchell, *The Campaign of the Century*, 504.

22. RAH, *Take Back Your Government!*, 240.

23. Heinlein's experience in this election is noted without corroborating detail in *Take Back Your Government!/How to Be a Politician,* where Heinlein omitted all identifying detail as a matter of policy.

24. Jerry Voorhis, quoted in Mitchell, *The Campaign of the Century,* 546.

25. Schlessinger, *The Politics of Upheaval,* 123.

26. This was a good prediction for Olson to make; four years later (albeit after repudiating his EPIC membership), Olson was elected Governor of California by EPIC Democrats.

27. Upton Sinclair, quoted in Mitchell, *The Campaign of the Century,* 541.

15. Party and Shadow Party

1. RAH, letter to Lieutenant Sandra Fulton, 08/07/65.

2. RAH's 1938 campaign biography, quoted in Leon Stover's unpublished manuscript, *Before the Writing Began.*

3. Unbylined front-page article by Max Knepper, in *Upton Sinclair's EPIC News* I: 41 (March 4, 1935).

4. The observation was made in the same month in 1939 that *The Grapes of Wrath* was published. Donald Worster, *Dust Bowl: The Southern Plains in the 1930s* (New York: Oxford University Press, 2004), 53. Interestingly, this observation was quoted in the CliffsNotes for *The Grapes of Wrath.*

5. The text of Robert Heinlein's report of his individual findings was not preserved, but much of his work duplicated the research of other individuals and agencies at about the same time (for which reason he never pursued it further). This particular example, attributed to a finding of "relief officials," was quoted in Worster's *Dust Bowl.*

6. RAH, letter to John W. Campbell Jr., 01/05/42.

7. RAH, *Take Back Your Government!*, 19.

8. *EPIC News* (April 8, 1935), 16.

9. "Girl Knocked Unconscious by Police, Blood Flows in J.C. Anti-War Strike Riot. Second Co-Ed Hurt on Being Driven from Speakers' Stand. Policemen Jeered. Demonstrations Prove Quiet at UCLA, Other Campuses," *Hollywood Citizen-News* (March 12, 1935), 1.

10. RAH, letter to Cal Laning, 11/26/50.

11. *The New York Times* famously ran a masthead slogan "All the news that's fit to print."

12. RAH, letter to Cal Laning, 11/26/50.

13. This refers to an incident on March 15, 1935 (after the "Red Squad" riot), in which the local school board refused to allow an airing of protests against the

clubbing incident by "students, parents and sympathizers." "Battle over Co-Ed Attack Grows Tense. Board Refusal to Grant Hearing on Clubbing Fails to Daunt," *Hollywood Citizen-News,* March 16, 1935.

14. "Town Meeting" section, *Hollywood Citizen-News,* March 17, 1935, 21.

15. The suspicion that Leslyn may have added Robert's military rank rises because Heinlein never before or after failed to include the exact rank at which he had retired, "Lt., J.G." with the mandatory "Ret."

16. "Speaker Hits 'Vigilantes' in Imperial Area," *Hollywood Citizen-News,* March 18, 1935, 7.

17. *EPIC News* carried an Open Forum on the subject of whether EPIC should join in the United Front in its May 13, 1935, issue.

18. RAH, letter to Cal Laning, 11/26/50.

19. The *Times* was quoted in the *EPIC News* report of the convention published on May 27, 1935.

20. RAH, letter to Hon. Jerry Voorhis, 11/06/46.

21. RAH naval jacket, RAH Archive, UCSC.

22. RAH, letter to Cal Laning, 11/26/50.

23. The City Directory for 1935 gives a Grand Avenue address for them, which may have been the old Sinclair for Governor campaign headquarters.

24. *Muster Notes,* 1935. *Muster Notes* is the book produced for each class reunion.

25. Per RAH's Naval Personal History Questionnaire, prepared by RAH in 1951; their voter registration was changed to the Lookout Mountain address as of 1936.

26. Ford's investigation of graft and corruption in the administration of Los Angeles mayor Frank Shaw, and in particular the car bombing of private investigator and former policeman Raymond Frank in 1937, is widely detailed in histories of the period, but see the L.A. Almanac, http://www.laalmanac.com/history/hi06f.htm.

27. Nor was I able to find any reference to Heinlein—or indeed, to any of the other less well-known investigations Ford commenced in 1936 and 1937—in Ford's personal papers lodged with the Huntington Library. Only a single box deals with Ford's first four years as a Los Angeles County Supervisor.

28. RAH, letter to E. O. Voight, 05/13/58.

29. This information is from the 1936 entry from Heinlein's 1938 campaign biography written for his volunteer staff. The only known surviving copy of this campaign biography was in the possession of Judge Robert Clifton, who gave it to Leon Stover for use in preparing his stub biography *Before the Writing Began.* The present whereabouts of Dr. Stover's papers is not known.

30. *EPIC News* III: 14 (August 13, 1936), 1.

31. RAH, letter to Alfred Bester, 04/03/59.

32. RAH, *Take Back Your Government!* But also see RAH's letter to John W. Campbell Jr., 01/17/42. This is a sentiment also echoed in one of Heinlein's "political" novels, *Double Star*.

33. See, for example, RAH's letter to Judge Robert Clifton, 03/15/82.

34. RAH, letter to Phil Farmer, 11/21/73.

35. RAH, *Take Back Your Government!*, 185.

36. Leslyn Heinlein, side comment in RAH's letter to Robert Lowndes, 08/23/41.

37. RAH, letter to Cal Laning, 11/26/50; see also RAH, 1938 campaign biography, distributed to his campaign workers.

38. RAH, *Take Back Your Government!*, 182.

39. This pattern of completing each other's sentences was remarked on often a few years later when Robert and Leslyn Heinlein entered the world of science fiction and was even noted in a Robert Lowndes editorial in 1941, concerning "the Lyle Monroes." ("Lyle Monroe" was a pen name Heinlein used for lower-paying markets.)

40. This working as a team though the public attention was focused on Robert was noted in Heinlein's Guest-of-Honor Speech for the Third World Science Fiction Convention in Denver, July 7, 1941 (transcribed and published by Forrest J. Ackerman as "The Discovery of the Future," and republished in *Requiem,* ed. Yoji Kondo). This was three years after their intense joint involvement with political activities ceased, but the habit was well fixed by that time.

41. Implied by remarks of Leslyn (Heinlein) Mocabee in a letter to Fred Pohl, 05/08/53.

42. RAH, letter to William A. P. White, 03/27/57. The specifics of the problem were not recorded contemporaneously, either by Heinlein or by Leslyn—just general mentions decades later. In this letter, Heinlein tells White that the crisis of the divorce in 1947 had been building up since 1936.

43. RAH, letter to "Capt. Jack" (A. Bertram Chandler), 08/27/78.

44. Virginia Heinlein, editorial comment in *Grumbles from the Grave* (New York: Ballantine/Del Rey, 1989), 114.

45. Leslyn (Heinlein) Mocabee, letter to Fred Pohl, 06/09/53; the "How to Spot a Commie" title cited by Robert James, Ph.D., in "Regarding Leslyn," *The Heinlein Journal*, No. 9 (July 2001), on page 21, was crossed out in Leslyn's holographic letter and replaced with "Communists are Religious Fanatics."

A page-by-page search through the unindexed *Rob Wagner's Script* at the Beverly Hills Public Library's periodicals holding room from the January 1935 issue through March 1937 (the magazine also did not have a table of contents for each issue) did not turn up the article under either title or any possible non-pseudonymous byline.

46. RAH, letter to Poul Anderson, 09/25/61.

47. RAH, letter to Robert Bloch, 03/18/49. In this passage, Heinlein is speaking about the period of his EPIC political activities; but these sentiments he maintained and expressed in very similar language for many decades. The consistency of Heinlein's political positions over a very long period creates a problem in interpreting the man, as many of his 1930s-liberal positions came to be regarded by contemporaries of later decades as reactionary (even though he maintained the same philosophical and political matrix characterized by Isaac Asimov viewing Heinlein in the years of World War II—only five years after our period in this passage—as "ultra-liberal"). Heinlein was never "a conservative" in the simple sense, and an attempt to view him, even in his later years, as a "rightist" is seriously mistaken.

48. RAH, letter to Robert Bloch, 03/18/49.

49. Heinlein wrote a white paper on the communism-fascism problem in 1938 for his Assembly District campaign. In it he first articulated his position that communism was simple "red fascism," as evil as black and brown fascism; he repeated this view in 1949 to Robert Bloch and again in 1983 to Dr. B. M. Treibman. However, that white paper was in the Judge Clifton papers given to Leon Stover and since lost.

   This quotation is taken from research notes made of Leon Stover's unpublished manuscript, *Before the Writing Began*. Dr. Stover's kind permission to read and make notes of his manuscript is gratefully acknowledged.

   No copies of that white paper have been found. No other contemporaneous documentation is known to exist; all the testimony we have from Heinlein writing in the 1940s and 1950s, mostly about his attitudes during the 1930s. (In fact, in a discussion about an attempt to get a security clearance, Heinlein wrote a long letter dated November 26, 1950, to Cal Laning, in which he goes over his entire political career and anticommunist attitudes throughout. That letter was written to be given directly by Cal Laning to an investigating security officer and so attempts to deal in detail with any evidence he suspects will be in the record.)

50. Leon Stover, in *Before the Writing Began*, states directly that Heinlein and Sally Rand had an ongoing sexual relationship, pinpointing the dates of specific assignations. Possibly some or all of this material is documented in the file of the Laning-Heinlein correspondence which has not yet been made available for re-

search. There is no documentation from other sources that contributes to this point, so the evidence cannot be weighed.

51. There are no good print biographies of Sally Rand, but several online biographies of Sally Rand as well as a day-by-day history of the California Pacific International Exposition recount this incident. See, for example, http://www .yodaslair.com/dumboozle/sally/sallydex.html.

52. *Caleb Catlum's America* stayed with Robert Heinlein for the rest of his life. In 1972 he paraphrased the introduction of *Caleb Catlum* for his reintroduction of Lazarus Long in *Time Enough for Love* (1973).

53. The Heinleins' candidates went 50–50; Ordean Rockey was elected to the state assembly, but Harlan Palmer lost the race for Los Angeles District Attorney, amid accusations of ballot stuffing by the incumbent, Burton Fitts.

54. "Sir" Arthur Bliss, after 1950.

55. RAH, letter to Leon Stover, 06/08/86.

56. RAH, letter to Ted and Irene Carnell, 04/02/52.

16. Party Animal

1. This phrase is used dozens of times throughout Mitchell's *Campaign of the Century*.

2. Mitchell, *The Campaign of the Century*, 560.

3. *EPIC News* IV: 40 (February 28, 1938), 5.

4. Wells, *The World of William Clissold*, p. 189.

5. Katherine Petty, e-mail to the author, 12/12/2000.

6. Virginia Heinlein, taped interview by author, Tape 12, Side A (March [4?], 2000). Since there is no documentation about the move, it is probable, rather than certain, that Robert and Leslyn took Rex's trunk at this time, since no other occasion in which they might have acquired it appears in the record.

7. In a letter dated 02/03/67 to Lurton Blassingame—that is, thirty years later— Heinlein remarked, "This is the only thing I have ever been afraid of—that I would go the way my father did."

8. Since the 1990s, involutional melancholia has been replaced as a diagnostic category by late-onset depression, which is not the same thing. The older literature is now available in microform or online. The professional reevaluation started in the 1980s; for a representative article summarizing the medical thinking at the time, see R. P. Brown, et al., "Involutional Melancholia Revisited," *American Journal of Psychiatry* CXLI: 1 (January 1984).

9. RAH, letter to Jerry Pournelle, 03/31/63.

10. Michael S. Bahrke, Charles E. Yesalis III, and James E. Wright, "Psychological and Behavioural Effects of Endogenous Testosterone Levels and Anabolic-Androgenic

Steroids Among Males: A Review," published online at http://www.mesomorphosis .com/articles/bahrke/bahrke09.htm.

11. Presumed from the timing of the announcement, as chicken pox epidemics typically spread in early spring. Leslyn mentioned this episode of chicken pox in a letter to Jack Williamson, 05/20/42; both facts are cited in Robert James, Ph.D., "Regarding Leslyn," *The Heinlein Journal*, No. 9 (July 2001), 21.

12. Clipping from unidentified Los Angeles paper—possibly *EPIC News*—in Robert Heinlein's personal scrapbook, 04/09/38.

13. RAH, letter to John Payne, 08/22/59.

14. Corson, in fact, not only invented new types of guns, he professionally published several articles on guns over the years. See, for example, "Vented Pistol Barrels" in *Rifle Magazine* XIV: 2 (March–April 1982), 32–24.

15. In the last two "Straw Ballots" run by the *EPIC News* in May, Heinlein is joined in the listing by Morey S. Mosk (without affiliation)—though Heinlein is shown as "leading."

16. McCullough, *Truman*, 234.

17. RAH, letter to Fritz Lang, 05/02/46.

18. RAH, *Take Back Your Government!*, 148.

19. RAH, letter to Tim Zell, 02/28/72.

20. Virginia Heinlein, letter to author, 01/30/2000 and 02/27/2000; see also Virginia Heinlein, IM with the author, 06/17/2002.

21. RAH, *Take Back Your Government!*, 92.

22. And ten years after *Take Back Your Government!* was written, Heinlein used some of this material again, in *Double Star*.

23. RAH, *Take Back Your Government!*, 126.

24. RAH, letter to John W. Campbell, Jr., 09/21/40.

25. RAH, *Take Back Your Government!*, 37.

26. Program preserved in RAH's personal scrapbook, now at the RAH Archive, UCSC.

27. A sample of the postcard is preserved in the RAH Archive, UCSC.

28. Reportage on the primary campaign is extremely sparse, and none of it indicates any direct exchange or debate between Heinlein and Lyon in any of the local papers.

29. RAH, *Take Back Your Government!*, 126.

30. The postmortem was mentioned by Heinlein in *Take Back Your Government!*, 126.

31. RAH, *Take Back Your Government!*, 222.

32. A characterization in RAH's letter to Robert Lowndes, 07/18/41, 5.

33. Robert Clifton became a judge of the California Superior Court in 1943 and was known thereafter as "Judge Clifton."

34. RAH, *Take Back Your Government!*, 224.

35. RAH, letter to Clare and Dorothy Heinlein, 07/07/73.

17. The Next Thing

1. Robert Heinlein's 1938 campaign biography in the papers of Leon Stover, quoted in *Before the Writing Began*.

2. RAH, letter to Fritz Lang, 05/02/46.

3. Heinlein never memorialized the precise steps in his move out of political management, but, in any case, this is the way he actually did it—simply stop taking on new jobs and ease out by a process of attrition after the 1938 election.

4. RAH, letter to Poul Anderson, 10/30/59.

5. RAH, *Expanded Universe*, 4.

6. *Thrilling Wonder Stories* (October 1938), 112–13.

7. *Astounding Science-Fiction* (July 1938), 73.

8. RAH's membership application for the 1939 General Semantics Seminar in Los Angeles, published in *The Heinlein Journal*, No. 11 (July 2002), 7.

9. RAH's Guest-of-Honor Speech at the 1941 World Science Fiction Convention ("Denvention"), reprinted as "The Discovery of the Future," in *Requiem*, ed. Yoji Kondo.

   And speaking of human nature, Orson Welles's Halloween-night broadcast of his adaptation of H. G. Wells's *War of the Worlds* may have frightened the country, but Heinlein left no recollection of hearing the broadcast.

10. The precise dates on which Robert Heinlein started writing were never recorded, but a letter written to John Campbell on December 18, 1939, says he wrote his book-length manuscript "a year ago." Since it was mailed out, after retyping, in January 1939, the writing must have been started around Thanksgiving 1938, in order to give him, a beginning (and very slow) typist, time to retype the 300-plus pages of his manuscript.

    In an interview given in 1941, Heinlein said that after the campaign concluded (in early November), Leslyn went into the hospital for an appendectomy (not mentioned anywhere else), leaving him at loose ends, and this is when he wrote the book "and finished it in three weeks." Bernice Cornell, "The Sky's No Limit," *Writers' Markets & Methods* (October 1941), 7.

11. RAH, letter to John Campbell, 07/29/40.

12. RAH, letter to Leon Stover, 06/08/86.

13. Bellamy's survivors endorsed EPIC, his daughter calling it "a continuation of the principles advocated by my father" when she and her mother, Edward Bellamy's wife, toured the United States in 1936, visiting the headquarters of

various progressive and liberal movements. *EPIC News* III: 26 (November 23, 1936), 1.

The text of Marion Bellamy's 1936 lecture on her father was printed in a fifteen-page pamphlet, *Edward Bellamy Today*. James J. Kopp's discussion in "Looking Backward at Edward Bellamy's Influence in Oregon, 1888–1936," *Oregon Historical Quarterly* CIV: 1 (Spring 2003) is representative of the spread of Bellamy's Nationalist Clubs throughout the United States and references in particularly corresponding events and activities in California.

14.   See RAH's letter to Robert A. W. Lowndes, 10/01/41. At the time this letter was written, Heinlein was generating his post-utopian novel, *Beyond This Horizon*.

15.   Charles Fourier was an early French socialist, of the generation after the French Revolution, who worked out a plan for communities—called "phalansteries"— large enough to be self-sustaining based on the kind of work different temperaments like to do. Fourier's thought was never very prominent in the development of European socialism (though still prominent enough to be attacked by Marx and by Engels in the *Anti-Dühring*), but his ideas dominated the waves of utopian socialist experimentation that emerged in the United States in the middle third of the nineteenth century, after about 1840.

16.   Compare Erich Fromm's foreword to the 1960 paperback edition of *Looking Backward,* which shows how Americans' radical socialism fits into the American frame of reference:

> The aim of socialism was that man should . . . transform himself into a being who can make creative use of his powers of feeling and of thinking . . . In the nineteenth century and until the beginning of the First World War, socialism . . . was the most significant humanistic and spiritual movement in Europe and America.
>
> What happened to socialism?
>
> It succumbed to the spirit of capitalism which it had wanted to replace . . . Thus socialism became the vehicle by which the workers could attain their place *within* the capitalistic structure, rather than transcending it; instead of changing capitalism, socialism was absorbed by its spirit.

17.   See, for example, Virginia Heinlein's letter to author, 03/04/2000: "Robert did favor Social Credit as a possible answer to economic problems." Heinlein went on to write about Social Credit, or fiscal theories quite similar in some respects to Social Credit, in three major works, most explicitly in *For Us, the Living*

(1938) and *Beyond This Horizon* (1941, 1942), and he discussed some of the economic principles also in *Time Enough for Love* (1973).

18. RAH, letter to Cal Laning, 11/26/50.

19. Heinlein's complete manscript file for *For Us, the Living* was destroyed presumably in 1987, and the manuscript used for its 2004 publication was reconstructed from a photocopy of a photocopy of the retyped manuscript. All other manuscript materials have been lost, and so this picture is a speculation based on practices known to have been in use a few months later.

20. Heinlein later said he taught himself to touch-type by retyping the manuscript of *For Us, the Living*; at the start of the writing, then, he was not a touch typist. Virginia Heinlein, taped interview by author, Tape 7, Side A (March [1?,] 2000).

21. See, for example, RAH's letter to John W. Campbell, Jr., 07/29/40.

22. Leslyn (Heinlein) Mocabee, letter to Frederik Pohl, 05/08/53.

23. RAH, letter to William A. P. White, 03/27/57.

24. There is almost no detailed discussion of Leslyn's episodes in the correspondence, most of the material in the relevant time frame having been burned in 1947, but in any case, Robert was extremely protective of their private life and might not have discussed it with anyone. There are remarks from both Robert and Leslyn in correspondence about the behavior of Leslyn's mother, and Robert told both William A. P. White and Doña Smith that he saw certain resemblances in Leslyn's behaviors; in addition, there is one eyewitness report of behaviors much later, in 1947 (Virginia Heinlein, taped interview by the author). That Leslyn would not discuss the flashes of temper and withdrawal is inferred from her rather extreme resistance to psychological help when offered at a crisis time years after these events.

The most detailed glimpse of these events comes from reading between the lines of poison-pen letters Leslyn herself wrote, the best examples of which are found in the Frederik Pohl archives, and the explanatory responses Heinlein wrote to people who had received the letters. The letters themselves were kept in a separate file that was not found in Heinlein's papers after his death (presumably they were burned in 1987); a significant letter from William A. P. White (Anthony Boucher, pseud.) in 1957, written on receipt of such a poison-pen letter and inquiring delicately of Heinlein whether the intervention of St. Dymphna should be sought (the patron saint of the mentally afflicted), has not been found in either White's or Heinlein's papers, though Heinlein's responsive letter, dated 03/27/57, is extant. Another significant (Heinlein) letter, which goes over some specific accusations in another lost poison-pen letter, is addressed to Doña and George Smith and dated 02/18/52.

25. Leslyn herself referred to her mother as "a combination of Lucrezia Borgia and Catherine of Russia." Leslyn (Heinlein) Mocabee, letter to Fred Pohl, 05/08/53.

26. Obituary of Colin MacDonald in the *Los Angeles Times* (June 2, 1929), 26. The obituary, which says he died on May 31, 1929, calls him a "San Francisco hotel man" who had been assistant manager at the Fairmont for ten years. At the time of his death, he was managing a hotel in Santa Barbara, California.

27. This is the conclusion reached by Robert James, Ph.D., in his biographical profile of Leslyn Heinlein, "Regarding Leslyn," *The Heinlein Journal*, No. 9 (July 2001), 17–36.

28. Both Robert and Leslyn Heinlein were extraordinarily discreet about their extramarital affairs. Robert himself only admitted that they existed, without ever giving details, even to his wife and close companion of forty years, Virginia Heinlein.

   Presumably on the basis of undocumented personal discussions with Cal Laning, Leon Stover maintained in conversations with the author and in his unpublished biographical sketch, *Before the Writing Began*, that Heinlein had an ongoing affair with Sally Rand, for instance, which would be renewed whenever they were in the same place at the same time. Virginia Heinlein suspected on the basis of "the way he talked about her" that Heinlein had an affair with the writer Virginia Perdue. Virginia Heinlein, taped interview by author, Third Series, Tape A, Side A (March 27, 2001).

   In none of the scant surviving correspondence of Leslyn (Heinlein) Mocabee does she refer to her own affairs, though in some rather unbalanced poison-pen letters written after a series of strokes in 1952 (the correspondence with Frederik Pohl is in his papers in the Red Bank, New Jersey, archive), she accuses Robert of sexual infidelities frequent and ongoing. In another context, Robert told Virginia Heinlein of just one affair of Leslyn's—with L. Ron Hubbard (Virginia Heinlein, taped interview by author, First Series, Tape 2 [September 2000]). Forrest J. Ackerman recalls his shock at Leslyn's accusation that *Robert* had a sexual affair with Hubbard—not completely impossible (as Heinlein implied in an essay in *Expanded Universe* that he had experimented widely with both drugs and unorthodox sexual practices) but improbable. As Ackerman went on to say, "Both of them were such womanizers that they wouldn't have any time for the same sex! I don't know if she was hallucinating, or what." Forrest J. Ackerman, interview by Robert James, June 9, 2000.

   Dr. Stover also maintained that Leslyn was so unhappy with enforced "wife swapping" and nudism that she took to drink. This is not an altogether credible conclusion, given that her alcoholism emerged during the war years, thirteen or fourteen years later, but since such a conclusion, if factually grounded at all, could only have been based on input from Cal Laning, together with the complete volte-face of Leslyn's attitude toward Robert after their divorce (suggesting that she may have been accommodating herself to expected behaviors rather than engaging in behaviors she desired for herself), it is not unreasonable to conclude that Leslyn may have been less happy with the pattern of the marriage than Robert was (an unfortunately not-uncommon pattern).

There is no evidence one way or another, so it is impossible to say whether Leslyn simply never intended to have what we now call an "open" marriage or whether she did but found it less to her taste once in the lifestyle and either did try to communicate this to Robert, without success, or did not make the attempt but kept it bottled up—a pattern she did manifest (among others) during the crisis period immediately before the divorce in 1947.

The psychological stresses of the war years, the falling off of her central role in achieving and maintaining Robert's prominence as a writer, and a possible dissatisfaction with the lifestyle of their marriage may all have contributed to the unhappy person Leslyn (Heinlein) Mocabee was to become.

29. Virginia Heinlein, IM with author, 05/28/2000.

30. Heinlein struggled with this insight for many years, until he reached a satisfactory articulation with *Stranger in a Strange Land* in 1961. His explanatory letters to his agent, Lurton Blassingame (10/21/60), and his editor, Howard Cady (04/09/61), suggest these themes had been in his mind for a very long time—and in fact, the first attempt to articulate them may well have been in *For Us, the Living*.

31. RAH, letter to Ralph Gould, 11/17/73.

32. RAH, letter to L. Sprague de Camp, 10/26/52.

33. RAH, letter to George Warren, 07/25/83.

34. Jack Woodford, *Trial and Error: A Dithyramb on the Subject of Writing and Selling*, rev. ed. (1933; repr., New York: Carlyle House, 1938), 327–28.

18. And the Next

1. The Works Progress Administration, or WPA (in 1939 renamed Works Projects Administration), was a New Deal program that provided employment in the middle of the Great Depression by underwriting socially useful work. In addition to construction projects, the WPA had a program that employed writers and artists to create comprehensive guides to each state. California's was edited by noted science-fiction writer Mildred Clingerman. In the case of the art classes Heinlein refers to, the WPA probably employed artists to teach beginners' classes.

Leon Stover, on what evidence is not known, claimed that Heinlein's first novel, *For Us, the Living*, was written in 1937 as part of a WPA writer's project;

however, the timing and circumstances of the writing of the book do not support this claim.

2. RAH, letter addressed to "Red [Rex], Kathleen, Tish, Karen, Lynnie, Charcoal, et Cie," 10/09/54.

3. RAH, letter to Bjo Trimble, 11/21/61.

4. RAH, letter to Poul Anderson, 10/02/61.

5. Pronounced Kah-SHIB-skee.

6. For this and the following remarks, see Heinlein's 1941 speech "The Discovery of the Future," printed in *Requiem,* ed. Yoji Kondo.

7. Curiously, Heinlein never made specific reference to *Manhood of Humanity,* though he *must* have read it in order to be knowledgeable about time binding.

8. Again, see "The Discovery of the Future." In this speech, Heinlein attempted to convey what he found important and exciting about Korzybski's General Semantics.

9. Robert Heinlein's Application for the Los Angeles General Semantics Seminar held on June 2–4, 1939.

10. Leslyn Heinlein's Application for the Los Angeles General Semantics Seminar held on June 2–4, 1939.

11. On Leslyn's Application for the 1939 Los Angeles General Semantics Seminar, she had started the book and was reading it "slowly." A year later, on her application for the 1940 seminar in Chicago, she had "partially" read *Science and Sanity.*

12. See, for example, RAH's letter to Daniel F. Galouye, 02/05/69.

13. Leon Stover, on what evidence is not known, insisted in *Before the Writing Began* that Leslyn had acted unofficially as a story doctor at Columbia Pictures before her marriage, though how that might have worked in practice is not clear. The information may have come from Cal Laning; Columbia's business records from that period give no hint that might help to interpret this claim; nor is she credited or acknowledged in any of the surviving industry directories of the period consulted at the Beverly Hills Public Library.

14. RAH, letter to John W. Campbell, Jr., 12/21/41.

15. Leslyn (Heinlein) Mocabee, letter to Frederik Pohl, 05/08/53.

16. All these story ideas are taken from the "Story Notes" file in the RAH Archive, UCSC.

17. Heinlein did write a tongue-in-cheek stream-of-consciousness sample of his creative process, published in a condensed form in Harry Warner, Jr.'s fanzine, *Spaceways,* in 1941, as "How to Write a Story." The article was reprinted in its longer manuscript form in the *Robert A. Heinlein Centennial Souvenir Book,* July 7, 2007, and is included in the nonfiction volumes of the Virginia Edition.

18. There is no direct evidence on Leslyn's reaction to "Life-Line." From passing remarks later it is clear that Leslyn saw and approved the story; there is no suggestion of an unusual procedure for this first short effort, so I have assumed that the working relationship he talked about later held for this one, too.

It is very likely that direct remarks were made in Heinlein's contemporaneous correspondence—but virtually all of his papers relating to this period of his life were burned in 1947, when he was clearing out his possessions at the time of the divorce from Leslyn.

19. Heinlein later told both Sam Moskowitz and Leon Stover that he had submitted "Life-Line" to *Collier's,* but the documentary evidence contains no confirmation of this, and the timing makes it unlikely in any case; the cover letter submitting the story to Campbell was dated April 10, less than a week after it was finalized, and the story was accepted by *Astounding* on April 19, 1939. The most likely conclusion is that Heinlein was confusing this story with other early stories he *did,* on the evidence of the documentation, submit to *Collier's,* possibly " 'My Object All Sublime.' "

20. Virginia Heinlein, letter to author, 05/31/99.

21. RAH, letter to John W. Campbell, Jr. 01/17/42.

22. There are two versions of this story. The basic version, given as "how long has this wonderful racket been going on," is given by James Gifford in *Robert A. Heinlein: A Reader's Companion,* (Citrus Heights, Calif.: Nitrosyncretic Press, 2000), 111, possibly referring to one of Heinlein's recountings in the *Xignals* interview (in the December 1985–January 1986 issue). Virginia Heinlein, in conversation with the author in 2001, added the second part.

23. "If This Goes On—" file, RAH Archive, UCSC. The drafts are dated May 12, 1939.

24. RAH, letter to Gorham Munson, 05/24/39.

25. There are no surviving drafts for this story, offered as "Prometheus 'Carries the Torch' " and then as " 'Let There Be Light,' " in Heinlein's archived files. The story development sketched here is implied by the published story figures and their relationship to story devices common in science-fiction magazines of the 1930s.

26. RAH's Accession Notes dated 04/02/67 for Opus 4, " 'Let There Be Light' " ("Prometheus 'Carries the Torch' ").

27. John W. Campbell, Jr., letter to RAH, 05/16/39, in the Opus 5 manuscript file for "Misfit" in the RAH Archive, UCSC. In his Accession Notes, Heinlein misremembers the date as May 20, 1939.

28. RAH, letter to John W. Campbell, Jr., 05/21/39.

29. RAH, letter to Gorham Munson, 05/24/39.

30.   See the marked-up first submission draft in the Opus 5 manuscript file for "Misfit" in the RAH Archive, UCSC.

31.   See RAH's letter to Frederik Pohl, 10/23/40.

32.   RAH, letter to Frederik Pohl, 11/01/40.

33.   Miles J. Breuer, *Astounding* (May 1930).

34.   John W. Campbell, Jr., to RAH, 05/31/39. *Marvel* was a new science-fiction pulp with a reputation for sexual titillation that classed it (perhaps not entirely fairly) as one of the sex-and-sadism "shudder pulps."

35.   And indeed the character of Mary Lou Martin is extraordinary in the context of its times. In this very early story, Heinlein built up a portrait of a couple with one character trying to enforce codependency while the other tries to move the relationship to a level of greater intimacy. Codependency would not become a feminist issue for another thirty-five years, but Heinlein has, without the guidance of theory, performed the task we rely on art fiction for: turning raw, personal observation into illuminating fictional characters.

19. Not Quite Done with Politics

1.   This description is taken from Heinlein's Guest-of-Honor Speech at the 1941 World Science Fiction Convention ("Denvention"), published as "Discovery of the Future" in *Requiem,* ed. Yoji Kondo, 166.

2.   James Gifford points to the resemblance of the names of Cleve Cartmill and Cleve Carter in *Robert A. Heinlein: A Reader's Companion,* 132. He also speculates that "Carter" might also refer to Austin Carter, Heinlein's ringer in Anthony Boucher's mystery *Rocket to the Morgue*—but that mystery was not written until two years later (and not published until three years later).

3.   William Sloane, letter to RAH, 06/20/39.

4.   Heinlein said this and expressed related sentiments often in his early letters to Campbell, but see, for example, Heinlein's letter to Campbell dated 08/29/39.

5.   Ackerman's recollections of his first meeting with Heinlein were recorded in a taped interview of Forrest J. Ackerman by Robert James, Ph.D., on June 7, 2000. Dr. James kindly provided a transcription of his interview.

6.   In response to some random gossip that Heinlein had wanted to become a Jesuit, Virginia Heinlein remarked: "One of his [Robert's] favorite expressions, which I don't believe you heard, was 'Become a monkey in a monstrosity [monastery?].'" Virginia Heinlein, letter to Leon Stover, 05/01/89. Speaking of Rosicrucianism, The Watchtower Society, and "the more ordinary religions," Heinlein told John Campbell, "They all look wacky to me and I avoid them." RAH, letter to John W. Campbell, Jr., 09/27/40; consider also the emotional tone of Heinlein's dis-

cussion of religious faith in his letter to Howard Cady, his editor for *Stranger in a Strange Land,* dated 04/09/61. Jubal Harshaw's almost visceral disgust for formal religions may well be an exaggeration for fictional purposes of Heinlein's own private attitudes.

7. RAH, letter to John W. Campbell, Jr., 01/20/42.

8. RAH, letter to John W. Campbell, Jr., 01/20/42.

9. RAH, letter to John W. Campbell, Jr., undated but between 12/06/39 and 12/14/39.

10. RAH, letter to Gorham Munson, 08/02/39.

11. RAH, letter to M. Isip (by way of John Campbell), 08/03/39.

12. In a letter dated 07/23/60 to Willy Ley, Heinlein says only that he got the idea from Sinclair Lewis. No discussion of writing methods was found in Lewis's books of the period, but very few of his articles for periodicals have been collected. A major radio interview in 1935 is mentioned in Mark Shorer's magisterial biography of Lewis, in which Lewis is said to have discussed his working methods, and this radio interview may be the source. Research has not yet turned up a copy or transcription of the interview.

13. In the navigation-chart version of the Future History, all the entries are handwritten; another (slightly later) version of the chart in the RAH Archive, UCSC, is on the back of a cardboard campaign poster; the version sent to John Campbell for publication in 1941 was adapted from the later version.

14. The manuscript was not submitted until December 1939, when it was sent first to John Campbell.

15. John W. Campbell, Jr., letter to RAH, 08/25/39.

16. RAH, letter to John W. Campbell, Jr., 08/29/39.

17. John W. Campbell, Jr., wrote a letter to RAH, dated 08/31/39; the letter does not specifically mention the sale of "Requiem" but does encourage him to work in longer lengths; nevertheless, Heinlein's contemporaneous records on the archived envelope in which the manuscript materials for the story are stored show that as the date on which "Requiem" was purchased by Street & Smith; the letter formally accepting the story as an experiment for *Astounding*'s readers is dated 09/11/39.

18. John W. Campbell, Jr., letter to RAH, 08/31/39.

19. Memorandum in "Wartime" file, RAH personal papers, RAH Archive, UCSC. It should be noted that the current Archivist has undertaken a project of reorganizing the papers, and it is not possible to predict where the document will be finally placed.

20. RAH, letter to John W. Campbell, Jr., 09/07/39.

21. This anecdote is fleshed out from a brief recounting of the incident in a letter

from Virginia Heinlein to Leon Stover, dated 04/19/89, concluding: "Leslyn was furious about it, and managed to make Robert furious, too." Since this is an event that happened before Virginia Gerstenfeld knew the Heinleins directly, the description can only have come from with Heinlein himself (or another family member—Virginia Heinlein may have been told the incident in 1949 when she helped negotiate a reconciliation of the brothers—a story that will be told in its context); there are a few, scant additional details in casual mentions of the incident by Heinlein in other correspondence.

22. This incident is told by Virginia Heinlein, taped interviews by the author, Second Series, Tape B, Side A; see also Virginia Heinlein, letter to Leon Stover, 04/19/89.

23. RAH, letter to John and Doña Campbell, 01/17/42.

24. This letter was not preserved in Heinlein's correspondence; we know of it only because Heinlein mentioned it in a letter to Asimov in 1984, telling him he was essentially a godfather to *Job: A Comedy of Justice* because of that letter.

25. The full text of the Initiative may be found at http://holmes.uchastings.edu/cgi-bin/starfinder/9212/calprop.txt. No print version of the text was located.

26. Mentioned in RAH's letter to John W. Campbell, Jr., 12/21/41; the letter from Governor Olson has not been preserved in Heinlein's files and may have been destroyed in 1947.

27. RAH, letter to John W. Campbell, Jr., 10/16/39.

28. RAH, letter to John W. Campbell, Jr., 12/21/41.

29. Application for Social Security Card dated 10/24/39 in RAH Archive, UCSC.

30. RAH, letter to John W. Campbell, Jr., 10/16/39.

31. The information is archived online at http://holmes.uchastings.edu/cgi-bin/starfinder/9212/calprop.txt, "Abbreviated Listing, Record 344."

32. Pages of "Lost Legacy" at its "Fire Over Shasta" stage with the election of the young progressive President are preserved in the RAH Archive, UCSC, "Lost Legacy" manuscript file; it is impossible to say whether the entire story was written, or just this ending, as Heinlein occasionally did write (as well as plan) the beginning and end of a story.

33. RAH, letter to Frederik Pohl, 10/23/40; these stories stayed in circulation for quite some time and were even offered a second time to John W. Campbell, Jr.; the October 1940 submission to Pohl, however, carries the strongest summaries of the marketing history of these still-unsold stories.

34. Frederik Pohl, letter to RAH, 11/15/39.

35. RAH, letter to Frederik Pohl, 11/28/39.

36. RAH, letter to John W. Campbell, Jr., undated but between 12/07/39 and 12/14/39.

37. John W. Campbell, Jr., letter to RAH, 12/06/39.

38. RAH, letter to John W. Campbell, Jr., 12/18/39.

39. Leslyn Heinlein, letter to John W. Campbell, Jr., 01/27/41. They are discussing Heinlein's reactions to a proposed edit of "Solution Unsatisfactory," which he likened to Campbell's end-edit of "Requiem." When Heinlein was writing, Leslyn often wrote business letters for him.

40. RAH, letter to John W. Campbell, Jr., 02/07/41.

41. RAH, letter to John W. Campbell, Jr., 09/06/41.

42. Heinlein made these observations in several places, but see RAH's letter to Lloyd Biggle, 09/30/76.

43. Woodford, *Trial and Error,* 1938, 328.

20. Out and About: The Long, Strange Trip

1. C. L. Moore is confusingly referred to as "Catherine," "Cat," and "Kat" in Heinlein's correspondence, apparently because Henry Kuttner also used different forms of the name. It appears that C. L. Moore did not often write letters to the Heinleins, more often than not passing comments and so forth through Kuttner. There are only a few letters written by her in Heinlein's archived correspondence.

   To make matters even more confusing, Grace (Dugan) Sang, whom the Heinleins met in Philadelphia, was known as "Cats."

2. Virginia Heinlein, taped interview by Leon Stover (1988), Tape 1, Side B.

3. Virginia Heinlein, letter to author, 05/12/2000.

4. RAH, letter to John W. Campbell, Jr., 05/10/41.

5. Annette McComas, ed., *The Eureka Years: Boucher and McComas's Magazine of Fantasy & Science Fiction 1949–1954* (New York: Bantam Books, 1982), xiv.

6. Jack Williamson, *Wonder's Child: My Life in Science Fiction* (New York: Blue Jay Books, 1985), 127.

7. RAH, quoted in Michael J. Patritch, "One Hundred and Fifty Minutes into Forever: A Meeting with Robert A. Heinlein," *Thrust* XXXIII (Spring 1989), 10. Bradbury is not named directly, but the inference is clear.

8. Ray Bradbury, "Ray Bradbury Takes the Stage," *The Heinlein Journal,* No. 8 (January 2001), 6.

9. Ray Bradbury, "It's Not the Heat, It's the Hu—," *Rob Wagner's Script* (November 2, 1940), 6.

10. RAH, letter to Larry Niven and Jerry Pournelle, 06/20/73.

11. I have elected not to write much in the way of critical commentary here, but it seems inappropriate to allow "Coventry" to pass without remark. "Coventry" is surely one of the most unusual stories ever published in science fiction—so unusual, in fact, that the existing commentary on it is somewhat incoherent. The

story is unusually stuffed with literary references, explicit, oblique, and incorporated into story structure. For example, in addition to explicit references to Emerson Hough, Jack London, and Zane Gray (among many others), the story is structurally intertextual with *A Tale of Two Cities* and *The Tempest*—as well as H. G. Wells's *A Modern Utopia*, both directly and by way of a reference to an Edmond Hamilton story drawn from *A Modern Utopia*.

The story is structurally unusual, as well: It superficially presents as a romance, with MacKinnon the romance protagonist. But Heinlein has doubled the romance story structure, giving the descent into the nightmare world (and subsequent recognition and restoration) to another character, Fader Magee, so that Magee is actually the romance protagonist; the point of view character has what looks like a romance descent—but it is instead him being granted his heart's desire, only to discover (as Cabell insisted before Heinlein) that contentment is somewhere else, if anywhere.

Instead of a romance recognition scene, MacKinnon's recognition is a Dark Night of the Soul. The story is built around MacKinnon's self-healing—the "other road" that the protagonist of *For Us, the Living* might have taken but did not. The relationship of MacKinnon to Magee is intersubjective—in 1940!—MacKinnon's restoration outlining the nature of what is not so much a restoration for Magee as the birth of a new man—as the baptism symbolism of the traverse of the river separating Coventry from Covenant suggests.

Most remarkable of all, the end of the story incorporates what is clearly a Brechtian *Verfremdungseffekt,* throwing the commercial romance completely off its tracks so that comic catharsis cannot proceed.

From the very beginning of his writing career, Heinlein has experimented and wrestled with form and structure in a way quite foreign and antagonistic to pulp formula, a way never paralleled by any of his science-fiction colleagues—in a way, in fact, which has been completely and mystifyingly invisible to them.

12. RAH, letter to John W. Campbell, Jr., 01/20/40.

13. John W. Campbell, Jr., letter to RAH, 02/16/40. No copy of the poem is known to have survived.

14. The mortgage-burning thermometer still exists in the Opus 0 file of the RAH Archive, UCSC.

15. Joseph Gilbert, letter in the "Brass Tacks" letter column of *Astounding Science-Fiction* (April 1940), 160.

16. RAH, letter to Hubert Rogers, 02/03/40.

17. See, for example, a letter of comment Heinlein wrote at about this time for *Sweetness and Light,* Spring 1940 issue.

18. The installment series began in *EPIC News* III: 20 (October 10, 1936), but the archive consulted did not have many subsequent issues, and I was not able to discover how many installments ran.

19. Phyllis White (widow of William A. P. White), letter to author, 03/13/1997.

20. RAH, letter to John W. Campbell, Jr., 02/17/41; the earlier discussion is not preserved with the correspondence, and Heinlein may have been referring to in-person discussions about Heinlein's up-or-out personal policy.

21. RAH, letter to Arthur Leo Zagat, 07/16/41.

22. RAH, letter to John W. Campbell, Jr., 09/06/41.

23. Virginia Heinlein, letter to Leon Stover, 03/29/89.

24. In fact, the few discussions of this "gadget" that appeared in correspondence with Campbell and in a brief, passing mention in a later essay are so vague that Dr. Ed Wysocki has spent more than a decade trying to identify it. His work has been based on a study of the naval technology of the time and the naval careers of Heinlein's Academy classmates, as well as an analysis of the stories themselves. Dr. Wysocki set out the problem in an article for *Shipmate,* the Naval Academy Alumni Association magazine, in 1995. The results of his research are to be presented in a forthcoming book.

25. It is very unfortunate that Heinlein and Campbell were not exchanging letters during the time they were visiting together, as these meetings with interesting individuals were not documented or memorialized at the time, except for several short pen portraits of Heinlein and his circle written by John Campbell to his friend Robert Swisher and published in the first two volumes of *The John W. Campbell Letters,* published by Perry Chapdelaine. The second volume contains correspondence with A. E. van Vogt, as well. The third volume, to be issued in conjunction with the Virginia Edition, will contain both sides of the Heinlein and Campbell correspondence.

26. RAH, letter to John W. Campbell, Jr., 11/09/46.

27. See, for example, Heinlein's Introduction to de Camp's *The Glory That Was and Other Stories,* written in 1952.

28. RAH, letter to John W. Campbell, Jr., 05/04/40.

29. RAH, letter to John S. Arwine, 01/28/45.

30. Moskowitz memorialized the occasion in a late essay, "Heinlein and Me," published in Ed Meskys's fanzine, *Niekas* XXXIII (1985).

31. Heinlein's motivation is set forth in the invitation, quoted below.

32. I have not been able to identify this Johnson; histories of the Technocracy movement rarely identify anyone not on the very top levels of the hierarchy and tend in any case to be more interested in goings-on in New York. Moreover, although

it has a chapter devoted to Technocracy in Los Angeles in 1935, *Glory Roads,* by Luther Whiteman and a friend of Heinlein's, Samuel L. Lewis (New York: Thomas Y. Crowell, 1936), mentions no Johnson. Perhaps, being a "west coast organizer," Johnson was not sufficiently oriented to Southern California to fall within their subject matter.

33. RAH, letter to Robert A. W. Lowndes, 06/07/40.

34. RAH, letter to Robert A. W. Lowndes, 03/15/56.

35. No actual memoir of the occasion was written down or survives; the only fact known about it, from a mention of the occasion in a letter Leslyn (Heinlein) Mocabee wrote to Frederik Pohl in 1953, is that Leslyn made and served her very Californian culinary specialty: tamale pie with green salad and red-wine-vinegar dressing.

36. Heinlein's memo of the circumstances is contained in his story notes, in the "They" manuscript file at the RAH Archive, UCSC, and available for online download through the Heinlein Prize Trust's Web site.

37. Pass dated 06/05/40 in the RAH Archive, UCSC; these members' passes have no significance as "influence."

38. Heinlein related this anecdote in *Expanded Universe,* at page 93, and again in his Accession Notes for the "Sixth Column" working papers for the RAH Archive, UCSC.

39. RAH, letter to Ralph Gould, 11/19/73.

40. RAH, letter to Ralph Gould, 11/19/73.

41. RAH's Accession Notes for "Sixth Column" in the RAH Archive, UCSC.

42. The quoted information is taken from the Heinleins' applications for this seminar, preserved in the records of the Institute of General Semantics. Copies of Heinlein's applications were reproduced in Kate Gladstone's article "Words, Words, Words: Robert Heinlein and General Semantics," and Leslyn's were reproduced in "More Regarding Leslyn," both in *The Heinlein Journal,* No. 11 (July 2002), 4–8 and 11–13, respectively.

43. RAH, letter to John W. Campbell, Jr., 07/29/40.

44. RAH, letter addressed to "Mr. McLean," 11/06/73.

45. Dorothy Martin Heinlein, "Relatively Speaking" (unpublished paper written ca. March 2006).

46. John W. Campbell, Jr., letter to RAH, 07/25/40.

47. RAH, letter to John W. Campbell, Jr., 07/19/40.

48. John W. Campbell, Jr., letter to RAH, 07/25/40.

49. *Oeuvres Complètes de Saint-Simon et Enfantin* (Paris, 1865–76), Vol. 19, 30.

50. Poul Anderson made this remark at a memorial panel held at the World Science Fiction Convention in 1972, shortly after Campbell's death.

51. Barry Malzberg, *Breakfast in the Ruins: Science Fiction in the Last Millennium* (Riverdale, NY: Baen Pub., 2007).

52. RAH, letter to Alice Dalgliesh, 02/17/59.

53. Dorothy Martin Heinlein, "Relatively Speaking" (unpublished paper written ca. March 2006), 9.

54. RAH, letter to John W. Campbell, Jr., 07/19/40.

55. RAH, letter to John W. Campbell, Jr., 07/25/40.

56. RAH, letter to Cal Laning, 10/25/40.

57. RAH, letter to John W. Campbell, Jr., 07/29/40. The passage that is cited was added as a postscript on August 1.

58. The Heinleins' application for the 1940 seminar indicates the seminar was to start on July 8, but there is no mention of attending the seminar in the correspondence written before July 15, while there is a mention in a letter Heinlein wrote to John Campbell on July 29 that the seminar is "almost over." Perhaps there was a preliminary or registration session on July 8, which was the date of the applications.

59. Videotape of a 1985 interview of Hayakawa in the possession of Steve Stockdale, IGS Dallas/Ft. Worth office.

60. RAH, letter to John W. Campbell, Jr., 09/06/41; see also RAH, letter to Robert A. W. Lowndes, 07/18/41, in which he speaks of his desire to get out of fiction writing immediately, and also RAH, letter to Arthur Leo Zagat of the Authors Guild Pulp Writers' Section, 07/16/41, in which he says he intends to get out of pulp writing if and when his remuneration drops to the base rate the PWS is advocating.

61. RAH, letter to John W. Campbell, Jr., 08/11/40.

62. RAH, letter to John W. Campbell, Jr., 08/11/40.

63. Harry Warner, Jr., *All Our Yesterdays* (Chicago: Advent Publishers, 1969), 113.

64. RAH, letter to John W. Campbell, Jr., 09/27/40.

65. John W. Campbell, Jr., letter to RAH, 08/14/40.

66. RAH, letter to Ralph Gould, 11/19/73.

67. RAH, "Larger than Life: A Memoir in Tribute to Dr. Edward E. Smith," *Expanded Universe*, 494.

68. RAH, letter to Jack Williamson, 03/20/76.

69. RAH, letter to John W. Campbell, Jr., 09/14/40.

70. RAH, letter to John W. Campbell, Jr., 09/14/40.

71. RAH, letter to John W. Campbell, Jr., 09/14/40.

72. RAH, letter to John W. Campbell, Jr., 11/02/40.

73. RAH, letter to John W. Campbell, Jr., 09/27/40.

74. Leon Stover, who received the book as a personal bequest from Heinlein, is

under the impression this incident took place in 1937, but Heinlein's letter to Doc Smith dated 10/24/40 says that they were planning to go see Wells "next week" and that he had never seen him in person before.

75. Harry Warner, Jr., letter to RAH, 09/10/40.

76. RAH, letter to Harry Warner, Jr., 10/22/40.

77. Frederik Pohl, letter to RAH, 10/07/40.

78. RAH, letter to Frederik Pohl, 11/25/40.

79. Raymond A. Palmer was then editor of *Amazing Stories* and was well known for making such caustic remarks about writers in his editorials. He went on to become a professional embarrassment when he published Richard Shaver's Dero stories after World War II and argued people should take the Shaver Mystery seriously. Heinlein's opinion of Palmer was actually more emphatic than has been rendered here, as this shoptalk with E. E. Smith dated October 24, 1940, indicates:

> I don't like Palmer. I don't like the way he does business. I don't like his habit of discussing in print the fact that he has rejected stories of writers named by name. I don't like the moronic level to which he has lowered the once-dignified and serious business of speculative fiction. I don't like the arrogant contempt with which he treats anyone who does not share his own cheap tastes.

80. RAH, letter to John W. Campbell, Jr., 11/02/40. Portions of this letter are reprinted in *Grumbles from the Grave*.

81. RAH, letter to John W. Campbell, Jr., 12/01/40.

82. RAH, letter to John W. Campbell, Jr., 12/01/40.

83. RAH, letter to Robert A. W. Lowndes, 07/18/41.

84. RAH, letter to Robert A. W. Lowndes, 07/18/41.

85. RAH, letter to Bruce Yerke, 12/09/40.

86. *The Damn Thing*, no. 2, is carried in the Eaton Collection of Science Fiction at the University of California, Riverside. It must have been published some days at least before Heinlein's letter to Yerke dated 12/09/40, as Heinlein mentions a remark about it made the previous Wednesday at an LASFS meeting.

87. RAH, letter to Bruce Yerke, 12/09/40.

88. RAH, letter to John W. Campbell, Jr., 12/27/40.

89. RAH, letter to John W. Campbell, Jr., 12/27/40.

90. RAH, letter to John W. Campbell, Jr., 01/15/41.

21. Expanding Horizons

1. John W. Campbell, Jr., letter to RAH, 12/30/40.

2. Heinlein began receiving circulars from the Navy in September 13, 1940, offering active duty postings in desk jobs (that first one sought instructors at Great Lakes), but preferred, as he told John W. Campbell, Jr., (09/18/41), to wait until called—or until offered something closer to his training and interests (say, in propaganda, which he requested as his preferred assignment in his 12/13/41 Request to BuNav to be returned to active duty).

3. Both signs are described in RAH's letter to Henry Kuttner and C. L. Moore, 09/11/41.

4. John W. Campbell, Jr., letter to RAH, 12/27/40.

5. RAH, letter to John W. Campbell, Jr., 06/21/41.

6. Forrest J. Ackerman, interview by Robert James, Ph. D., 06/09/2000.

7. RAH, letter to A. D. Doc Kleyhauer, Jr., 08/15/41.

8. RAH, letter to John Kean, 09/20/45.

9. RAH, letter to Jack Williamson, 03/20/76.

10. RAH, letter to John W. Campbell, Jr., 03/26/41.

11. John W. Campbell, Jr., letter to RAH, 03/28/41.

12. RAH, letter to Henry Kuttner, 03/29/41.

13. RAH, letter to Robert Moore Williams, 03/31/41.

14. John W. Campbell, Jr., letter to RAH, 04/08/41.

15. RAH, letter to John W. Campbell, Jr., 04/17/41.

16. RAH, letter to John W. Campbell, Jr., 05/29/41.

17. RAH, letter to John W. Campbell, Jr., 12/01/40.

18. The title was changed again by Heinlein to the more aptly suggestive "Elsewhen" for collection into *Assignment in Eternity* in 1953.

19. RAH, letter to Theodore Sturgeon, 02/11/55.

20. RAH, letter to A. D. (Doc) Kleyhauer, 12/03/41.

21. RAH, letter to John W. Campbell, Jr., 05/21/41.

22. RAH, letter to John W. Campbell, Jr., 06/21/40.

23. RAH, letter to John W. Campbell, Jr., 07/14/41.

24. Leslyn Heinlein, letter to Jack Williamson, 06/22/41.

25. RAH, letter to John W. Campbell, Jr., 07/14/41.

26. This is the way Forrest J. Ackerman remembered the occasion in a 2000 interview with Dr. Robert James; Earl Kemp spoke of Heinlein twenty-one years after the convention, comparing him to Franchot Tone, an actor noted for his portrayals of Café Society sophisticates in the 1930s and into the 1940s (the comparison is in Kemp's "Heinlein Happens" essay, written in about 2003 for Alexei Panshin's Abyss of Wonder Web site, and may, naturally, be a later

development of Kemp's opinion, though he speaks of it as being a contemporaneous reaction).

27. Forrest J. Ackerman, interview by Robert James, Ph.D., 06/09/2000; punctuation slightly modified; similar material is in Ackerman's memoirs, "Through Time and Space with Forry Ackerman," originally published in the Rich and Nicki Lynch fanzine *Mimosa* XVII (October 1995) and available online in multiple places.

28. Warner, *All Our Yesterdays,* 107.

29. Warner, *All Our Yesterdays,* 103, where the name is spelled "Queen Nipher."

30. Forrest J. Ackerman, interview by Robert James, Ph.D., 06/09/2000.

31. A CD-R of this speech has been made from an audio tape, transcription in 2001 made directly from Dr. Daugherty's 78 rpm disks by the Heinlein Society.

32. Apparently on the basis of this speech, Heinlein's name was associated in some fannish histories—perpetuated in the literature of the National Fantasy Fan Federation (N3F) well into the 1970s—with the "Fans are Slans" movement of the early 1940s, claiming that science-fiction fans are superior to "mundanes."

33. RAH, letter to Forrest J. Ackerman, 08/04/52.

34. RAH, letter to Lurton Blassingame, 10/03/58.

35. See, for example, RAH's letter to Samuel J. Moskowitz, 01/25/61, and RAH's letter to Marion Zimmer Bradley, 07/15/64, from which:

> The unique problem of organized fandom is one that I have wondered about for many years. Here is a group made up largely of well-intentioned and mentally-interesting people—how is it and why is it that they tolerate among themselves a percentage of utter jerks?—people with no respect for privacy, no hesitation at all about libel and slander, and a sadistic drive to inflict pain. Marion, I do not understand it.

36. RAH, letter to John W. Campbell, Jr., 07/14/41.

37. Forrest J. Ackerman, interview by Robert James, Ph.D., 06/09/2000.

38. Probably Heinlein is referring to *The Star Gazer: A Novel of the Life of Galileo* by Zsolt de Harsanyi, published in 1939 and translated into English by Paul Tabor. The title is sometimes also given as *The Star-Gazer (Story of Galileo).*

39. Translated by Charles A. Ward and published in 1940.

40. The various projects were not detailed in any of Heinlein's correspondence, as they seem to have been matters of discussion at face-to-face meetings. A current officer of the International Society for General Semantics, Steven Stockdale, noted that at the 1940 seminar the Heinleins occupied the two "up front and personal" seats on the seating charts and that one of Heinlein's close friends from the Hollywood in-

dustry, Edwin Green, was discussing—Stockdale says "probably more like idle wishing"—with another GS luminary, radio personality Will Kendig, a General Semantics movie "that would be not only entertaining, but educational to the degree that the experience of watching the movie itself would help 'train' the audience in proper evaluation." Steven Stockdale, e-mail to author, 05/30/2002. In any case, nothing seems to have come of this particular project.

41. Leslyn Heinlein, letter to "Miss Kendig" (at Korzybski's office), 10/22/41. Possibly Leslyn is obliquely referring to their involvement with the Colorado Sunshine Club, which had been raided and the attending membership arrested *en masse* as nudists in February 1935, just months after the Heinleins relocated to Los Angeles in August 1934.

42. The exact date was not recorded but was probably July 10 or 11, 1941, from Heinlein's letter to Campbell dated 07/14/41.

43. RAH, letter to John W. Campbell, Jr., 07/14/41.

44. E. E. Smith, letter to RAH, 07/13/41.

45. None of these historic photographs were found among Heinlein's effects; it is likely that either they were destroyed in 1947 by Heinlein himself when clearing out his papers of his life with Leslyn, or else they went with Leslyn in the divorce and were lost or destroyed later.

46. RAH, letter to John W. Campbell, Jr., 08/08/41.

47. Heinlein detailed some of his reasoning about this story to Campbell in a letter dated 09/15/41.

48. RAH, letter to John W. Campbell, Jr., 09/06/41.

49. Submission history handwritten contemporaneously on the original Opus 28 storage folder in the RAH Archive, UCSC.

50. John W. Campbell, Jr., letter to RAH, 08/21/41.

51. Heinlein did not record the sequence of thoughts prompted by Campbell's rejection letter or, indeed, refer to this pivotal moment, except obliquely. However, these oblique references in his correspondence do allow some reconstruction of the principal elements at work. Earlier letters pinpointed the prospect of slipping in his standing and acceptance as a writer as cause for retiring; Campbell's judgment of pointlessness in a story of which Heinlein flatly said:

> [T]he story had a point, a most important point, a most powerful and tragic one. Apparently I expressed the point too subtly, but you and I have rather widely divergent views about the degree of subtlety a story can stand (RAH, letter to John Campbell, 09/06/41)

suggests a reason why Heinlein might consider this "disconnect" an early warning sign of such slippage. He says as much in his letter to Campbell dated 09/15/41.

Thoughts of the inability of humans to connect on any significant level are quite common in such situations among many people, and Heinlein specifically mentioned this subject in several prior letters as a matter of perennial concern to him. Moreover, Campbell and Heinlein had exchanged—and were again to exchange, in a few months—letters dealing specifically with the intellectual and moral connection they had felt each about the other.

The correspondence took up as cordially as ever in the interim before the matter of the rejection of "Creation Took Eight Days" came up again, so Heinlein clearly was exercising a "semantic pause" with regard to a rather major upset to his way of life—a tactic detailed in other correspondence and relating to other matters, such as taking his war news delayed in weekly news magazines.

The sequence of the reconstruction here is governed by what I take to be the relative importance to Heinlein of the personal versus the particular content of the letter, in its context.

52. RAH, letter to John W. Campbell, Jr., 09/06/41.

53. RAH, letter to Robert A. W. Lowndes, 07/18/41.

54. RAH, letter to John W. Campbell, Jr., 09/06/41.

55. RAH, letter to John W. Campbell, Jr., 08/27/41.

56. Virginia Heinlein speculated that Robert Heinlein and Virginia Perdue were more than friendly—"the way he talked about her made me think that there was something between them, or had been." Virginia Heinlein, taped interview with the author, Third Series, Tape A, Side A (March 27, 2001).

57. RAH, letter to Henry Kuttner, 09/11/41.

58. RAH characterizes the title "Lost Legion" as "meaningless" in the Accession Notes, for the donation of papers and manuscripts to the RAH Archives UCSC, written 11/05/68.

59. Robert A. W. Lowndes, letter to "Defenders of the Hein line," 09/08/41.

60. RAH, postscript to Leslyn Heinlein's letter to Robert A. W. Lowndes, 08/15/41.

61. RAH, letter to Robert A. W. Lowndes, 08/23/41.

62. John W. Campbell, Jr., letter to RAH, misdated 09/09/41 but more likely 09/13/41.

63. John W. Campbell, Jr., letter to RAH, 09/13/41.

64. RAH, letter to John W. Campbell, Jr., 09/27/41.

65. RAH, letter to John W. Campbell, Jr., 09/15/41.

66. RAH, letter to John W. Campbell, Jr., 11/21/41.

67. RAH, postscript to Leslyn Heinlein's letter to Robert A. W. Lowndes, 08/15/41.

68. RAH, letter to Robert A. W. Lowndes, 09/17/41.

69. RAH, letter to Robert A. W. Lowndes, 09/17/41.

70.   RAH, letter to Robert A. W. Lowndes, 09/17/41.

71.   RAH, letter to Robert A. W. Lowndes, 09/17/41.

72.   RAH, letter to Robert A. W. Lowndes, 09/17/41.

73.   RAH, letter to John W. Campbell, Jr., 09/25/41.

74.   RAH, letter to John W. Campbell, Jr., 09/25/41.

75.   RAH, letter to Robert A. W. Lowndes, 10/01/41.

76.   Jack Williamson, letter to RAH, 10/03/41.

77.   RAH, letter to John W. Campbell, Jr., 09/28/41.

78.   Willard E. Hawkins, letter to RAH, 10/03/41.

79.   This sixteen-page, staple-bound pamphlet is often cited in book collectors' cir-
      cles as Heinlein's first "book" publication.

80.   RAH, letter to "Vertex Magazine," 11/08/73.

81.   John W. Campbell, Jr., letter to RAH, 10/27/41.

82.   RAH, letter to Mark Hubbard, 10/04/41. I am unable to account for the differ-
      ence in dates between the letters. (Mark Hubbard's letter to which this is a reply
      is dated four days after the reply.) Perhaps this letter is a reply to a telephone
      conversation that was memorialized by Mark Hubbard's letter.

83.   RAH, letter to John W. Campbell, Jr., 10/24/41.

84.   RAH, Accession Notes for Opus 29 file, RAH Archive, UCSC.

85.   RAH, letter to John W. Campbell, Jr.,10/24/41.

86.   John W. Campbell, Jr., letter to RAH, 10/27/41.

87.   RAH, letter to Cal Laning, 11/26/50.

88.   RAH, letter to Bob Bloch, 03/18/49; see also RAH, letter to Bob Bloch,
      04/25/49: " 'Beyond This Horizon' was based on inverting the cultural matrix
      found in my story 'Coventry' and then shaking it to see what would happen."

89.   RAH, letter to John W. Campbell, Jr., 09/25/41.

90.   RAH, letter to John W. Campbell, Jr., 11/15/41.

91.   RAH, letter to John W. Campbell, Jr., 11/15/41.

92.   Jack Wiliamson, *Wonder's Child: My Life in Science Fiction,* 135, detailing a let-
      ter Campbell wrote him dated 11/21/41.

93.   Jack Williamson, letter to RAH, 11/21/41.

94.   Leslyn Heinlein, letter to Jack Williamson, 11/28/41.

95.   Circular dated 11/27/41.

96.   Heinlein probably discussed the trip to New York first in a telephone call
      with Campbell since there is no contemporaneous written record of the dis-
      cussion.

97.   The conversation is recounted in RAH's letter to T. B. Buell, 10/04/73.

98.   The conversation is quoted in RAH's letter to T. B. Buell, 10/04/73.

99. RAH, night letter to John W. Campbell, Jr., 12/05/41.

100. RAH, letter to John W. Campbell, Jr., 12/09/41.

101. RAH, Accession Notes for Opus 29 file, 04/02/67, RAH Archive, UCSC.

102. RAH, letter to John W. Campbell, Jr., 12/02/41.

22. "And put aside childish things . . ."

1. See, for example, RAH's letter to Mr. and Mrs. Collier, 12/08/76; Heinlein seems not to have mentioned the war games incident to Campbell in their contemporary correspondence, which is an important source of information about Heinlein's life at this time (though it might well have been discussed in telephone or in-person discussions).

2. RAH, letter to John W. Campbell, Jr., 01/04/42.

3. Heinlein discussed these matters and others of the early days of the U.S. involvement in World War II with John Campbell in a series of letters from December 1941 through about February 1942. Only a single, misleading fragment of this correspondence is in Virginia Heinlein's selection of her husband's letters, *Grumbles from the Grave;* however, the complete correspondence of John W. Campbell, Jr. and Robert Heinlein is to be published as a volume of the Virginia Edition.

4. Cal Laning wrote a colorful eyewitness account of his experience of the attack on Pearl Harbor. A copy of Laning's original draft is in Heinlein's files in the RAH Archive, UCSC, and available through the online Heinlein archive. It was published posthumously as "Why Don't We Do This More Often?" in *Naval History Annapolis* V: 4 (Winter 1991).

5. RAH, letter to John W. Campbell, Jr., 12/09/41.

6. John W. Campbell, Jr., letter to RAH, 12/08/41.

7. RAH, letter to John W. Campbell, Jr., 12/09/41.

8. RAH, letter to John W. Campbell, Jr., 12/09/41.

9. "Request for Assignment to Duty," RAH naval jacket, folder marked "Re Going Back to Duty," RAH Archive, UCSC.

10. RAH, letter to John W. Campbell, Jr., 12/16/41.

11. RAH, letter to Virginia Perdue, 12/19/41.

12. Information about Heinlein's family immediately after Pearl Harbor is detailed in RAH's letter to John W. Campbell, Jr., 12/21/41.

13. See Leslyn Heinlein, letter to John W. Campbell, Jr., 01/17/42.

14. RAH, letter to John W. Campbell, Jr., 12/23/41.

15. RAH, letter to John W. Campbell, Jr., 12/21/41.

16. RAH, letter to John W. Campbell, Jr., 01/04/42.

17. RAH, letter to John W. Campbell, Jr., dated 12/21/41.

18. Leslyn Heinlein, letter to John W. Campbell, Jr., 01/04/42.

19. RAH, letter to John W. Campbell, Jr., 01/08/42.

20. RAH, letter to John W. Campbell, Jr., 01/08/42.

21. John W. Campbell, Jr., letter to RAH, 01/22/42.

22. John W. Campbell, Jr., letter to RAH, 01/08/42.

23. RAH, letter to John W. Campbell, Jr., 01/17/42.

24. A. B. Scoles, letter to RAH, 01/14/42.

25. RAH, letter to John W. Campbell, Jr., 01/20/42.

26. Leslyn Heinlein, letter to John W. Campbell, Jr., 01/17/42.

27. Leslyn Heinlein, letter to Doña Campbell, 01/23/42.

28. RAH, letter to John and Doña Campbell, 01/26/42.

29. This exchange took place by telephone conversation memorialized in pencil in RAH's hand on two undated scraps of paper in his "Going Back to Duty" folder in the RAH Archive, UCSC.

30. There is nothing in the correspondence that fixes the date with certainty, but John Campbell wrote a letter to Heinlein dated February 13, and the Opus card for "Waldo" indicates he started writing on February 17, 1942, so their arrival in New Jersey must have come between those two dates. Heinlein says in a letter to Cal Laning dated 03/20/42 that he took Leslyn to New Jersey specifically for the operation.

31. RAH, letter to Dr. Schnur, 02/11/59. It has been speculated that Heinlein might have named Waldo after Ted Sturgeon, whose birth name was Edward Hamilton Waldo, but the novella was written before Heinlein met Sturgeon in 1944.

32. L. Sprague de Camp, *Time and Chance: An Autobiography* (Hampton Falls, N.H.: Donald M. Grant, 1996), 172.

33. The meeting is not mentioned in any of Heinlein's correspondence of the period (which may only mean it was arranged by telephone), but is mentioned in L. Sprague de Camp's autobiography, *Time and Chance,* 171.

34. RAH, letter to John W. Campbell, Jr., 01/03/42.

35. Isaac Asimov, *In Memory Yet Green: The Autobiography of Isaac Asimov, 1920–1954* (New York: Doubleday, 1979), 337.

36. Asimov, *In Memory Yet Green,* 337.

37. RAH, letter to Cal Laning, 03/20/42. At that time Laning was at service in the South Pacific in *Conyngham.*

38. Leslyn Heinlein, postcard to William A. P. White, 02/27/42.

39. RAH, letter to Doña (Campbell) Smith, 02/03/52.

40. John W. Campbell, Jr., letter to Robert Swisher, 04/14/42, in *The John W. Campbell Letters with Isaac Asimov & A. E. van Vogt,* ed. Perry Chapdelaine, 80.

41. RAH, letter to Jack Williamson, 03/20/42.

42. See, for example, RAH's letter to Henry and Catherine Kuttner, 04/21/47.

43. Commandant 11th Naval District San Diego to Chief, BuNav, forwarding RAH's request for active duty per questionnaire answered 03/17/42, RAH naval jacket, folder marked "Re Going Back to Duty," RAH Archive, UCSC.

44. RAH, letter to T. B. Buell, 10/03/74, 46–47.

45. A. E. Watson, letter to RAH, 05/02/42.

46. Leslyn Heinlein, postcard to William A. P. White, 05/04/42.

47. RAH, telegram to BuNav, 05/11/42.

23. "Do with thy heart what thy hands find to do . . ."

1. RAH, letter to John W. Campbell, Jr., 07/18/42.

2. Joel Charles, letter to RAH, 04/05/88.

3. de Camp, *Time and Chance.*

4. Virginia Heinlein, e-mail to author, 09/12/02.

5. For further example, see Heinlein's exposition of the political situation in Philadelphia when he arrived, in *Take Back Your Government!*, 236.

6. de Camp, *Time and Chance,* 179.

7. Virginia Heinlein, interview by author, Tape 10, Side A; (March 1, 2000), also Virginia Heinlein, e-mail to author, 09/12/02.

8. Leslyn Heinlein, letter to Phyllis and William A. P. White, 05/18/42.

9. de Camp, *Time and Chance,* 179–80.

10. John W. Campbell, Jr., letter to RAH, 05/13/42.

11. Catherine Kuttner (C. L. Moore), letter to RAH, 07/02/42.

12. RAH, letter to Robert Silverberg, 09/09/61.

13. RAH, letter to Miss Hewey (otherwise unidentified), 12/13/71.

14. J. Hartley Bowen, Jr., "Recalling Robert Anson Heinlein," *Requiem,* ed. Yoji Kondo 260.

15. RAH, letter to John W. Campbell, Jr., 07/18/42.

16. Catherine Crook de Camp, "The Robert A. Heinlein I Knew," *Locus* (July 1988), 38.

17. Catherine Crook de Camp, *Requiem,* ed. Yoji Kondo.

18. de Camp, *Time and Chance,* 177.

19. Asimov, *In Memory Yet Green,* 392–94.

20. Asimov, *In Memory Yet Green,* 392.

21. J. Hartley Bowen, Jr., "Recalling Robert Anson Heinlein," *Requiem,* ed. Yoji Kondo, 258.

22. Virginia Heinlein, IM with author, 02/25/02.

23. Virginia Heinlein, e-mail to author, 09/12/02.

24. Bill Corson, postcard to RAH, 09/28/42.

25. Virginia Heinlein, e-mail to author, 09/12/02.

26. RAH, letter to John Arwine, 11/22/42.

27. RAH, letter to John Arwine, 11/22/42.

28. Forrest J. Ackerman, interview by Robert James, Ph.D., 06/09/2000.

29. Forrest J. Ackerman, interview by Robert James, Ph.D., 06/09/2000.

30. Forrest J. Ackerman, interview by Robert James, Ph.D., 06/09/2000.

31. John W. Campbell, Jr., letter to RAH, 10/09/42.

32. *Rocket to the Morgue* was published in 1942 as by White's standard mystery pseudonym "H. H. Holmes." White created the "Anthony Boucher" pseudonym when Heinlein persuaded him to begin writing fantasy and science fiction. Over the years, White abandoned the Holmes pseudonym and moved everything over to the Boucher pseudonym, so that when *Rocket to the Morgue* was reprinted, starting in the 1970s, it was as by "Anthony Boucher."

33. John W. Campbell, Jr., letter to RAH, 10/09/42.

34. RAH, letter to Phyllis and William A. P. White, 12/06/42.

35. Virginia Heinlein, taped interview by Leon Stover, Tape 2, Side A (October 1988).

36. Anecdote recounted to the author by Rusty Hevelin, 09/01/2002.

37. Philip Wylie, *Generation of Vipers: A Survey of Moral Want and a Philosophical Discourse Suitable Only for the Strong; A Study of American Types and Arche-Types . . . as Well as Certain Homely Hints for the Care of the Human Soul* (New York: Rinehart and Company, 1942), 18.

38. John W. Campbell, Jr., letter to RAH, 02/02/43; see also RAH's undated, handwritten summary of negotiations with Street & Smith in the Campbell-Heinlein correspondence file, compiled sometime in, probably, 1948.

39. RAH, letter to Henry Ralston, 01/28/46.

40. RAH's liner notes for Leonard Nimoy's recording of "The Green Hills of Earth" and "Gentlemen, Be Seated" (New York: Caedmon Audio, 1976).

41. John W. Campbell, Jr., letter to RAH, 01/06/43.

42. Orders dated 06/13/43 in RAH's "Wartime" file, RAH personal papers, RAH Archive, UCSC.

43. Doña Campbell, letter addressed "Dear Heinleins," 05/10/43.

44. Bill Corson, letter to RAH, 02/06[?]/44 (the letter itself is undated, and the postmark is blurred).

45. RAH, letter to Bill Corson, 02/05/44.

46. Bill Corson, letter to RAH, 02/06/44.

47. L. Sprague and Catherine de Camp, letter to Robert and Leslyn Heinlein, 08/13/46.

48. Bill Corson, letter to Leslyn Heinlein, 10/06/43.

49. RAH, letter to John W. Campbell, Jr., 10/17/43.

50. RAH, letter to E. J. "Ted" Carnell, 12/31/43.

51. RAH, letter to John Arwine, 01/08/44.

52. RAH, letter to Garth Danielson, 08/25/76.

53. RAH, letter to John Arwine, 01/08/44.

54. Robert James, Ph.D., citing e-mail interview with Peter Wygle, September 2000, in "Regarding Leslyn," *The Heinlein Journal,* No. 9 (July 2001).

55. Robert James, Ph.D., e-mail interview with Colin Hubbard, June 29, 2001.

56. RAH, letter to H. L. Gold, 10/27/52.

57. RAH, letter to E. J. "Ted" Carnell, 12/31/43.

58. RAH, letter to E. J. "Ted" Carnell, 12/31/43.

59. Bill Corson, postcard to RAH, 12/17/43.

60. RAH, letter to John Arwine, 09/03/44.

61. RAH, letter to Cal Laning, 11/19/44.

62. RAH, letter to Bill Corson, 02/05/44.

63. RAH, letter to Bill Corson, 02/05/44.

24. Keeping On—

1. RAH, letter to John Arwine, 01/08/44.

2. Bill Corson, postcard to Leslyn Heinlein, 02/23/44.

3. RAH, letter to John Arwine, 01/08/44.

4. RAH, letter to John Arwine, 01/08/44.

5. RAH, letter to John Arwine, 01/08/44.

6. RAH, letter to John W. Campbell, Jr., 02/04/44.

7. RAH, letter to John Arwine, 04/15/44.

8. RAH, letter to John W. Campbell, Jr., 10/17/43.

9. RAH, letter to John W. Campbell, Jr., 10/17/43, mentions the query about a review for *Rockets: A Prelude to Space Travel* had been done by postcard (not preserved) "some time ago." There are a multiplicity of completely different titles given for this 1944 book. The *Prelude to Space Travel* title was the one by which Heinlein reviewed the book for *Astounding*. It might have been a pre-publication title, later changed. The Smithsonian National Air and Space Museum Willy Ley collection's chronology (available online at http://www.nasm.si.edu/research/arch/findaids/ley/ley_frames.html) carries the 1944 title as simply *Rockets* (but this is the title of a 1965 book). The 1944 Viking Press publication was actually titled *Rockets: The Future of Travel Beyond the Stratosphere*. This same book was revised and reissued in 1947 as *Rockets and Space Travel* and again in 1952 as *Rockets, Missiles and Space Travel* (all by Viking).

10. RAH, letter to John W. Campbell, Jr., 02/04/44.

11. RAH, letter to John Arwine, 05/25/45.

12. RAH, letter to John Arwine, 05/20/45.

13. RAH, letter to John Arwine, 04/15/44.

14. RAH, letter to Susie Clifton, 11/06/46. Helen Gahagan Douglas (1900–80), wife of actor and political activist Melvyn Douglas, was herself a Broadway actress who gave up acting after a single Hollywood role in *She* (1935), for a career in politics. In 1944 she was the second woman, and the first woman Democrat, elected to Congress. Her political career ended in her 1950 Senate campaign against fellow representative Richard M. Nixon. It was Gahagan Douglas who coined the "Tricky Dick" name for Nixon.

15. Helen Gahagan Douglas, letter to RAH, 12/17/46.

16. RAH, letter to Cal Laning, 01/08/46.

17. RAH, "Agape and Eros: The Art of Theodore Sturgeon," dated September 1985. Published as an introduction to the posthumous publication of Theodore Sturgeon's *Godbody*. Based on passing comments in other places, the project was probably writing technical documentation for radar, the great Allied secret weapon of World War II.

18. RAH naval jacket, attachment to Memo from R. J. H. Conn, Director NAES, to Personnel Relations Officer NAES Subj: Release of R. A. Heinlein for employment by UCDWR, RAH Archive, UCSC.

19. RAH, letter to John Arwine, 09/03/44.

20. RAH, letter to John Arwine, 09/03/44.

21. Bill Corson, letter to RAH, undated but most likely summer of 1944.

22. Heinlein rarely wrote anything at all about this aspect of his marriages, but Leslyn was not so discreet: in later years, she talked in vitriolic terms about Robert's sexual behavior—omitting hers entirely.

23. Asimov, *In Memory Yet Green,* 488.

24. RAH, letter to John Arwine, 01/08/44.

25. Virginia Heinlein, letter to author, 12/11/99.

26. Virginia Heinlein, letter to Leon Stover, 03/29/89.

27. Presumably George Harris, Jr., a lieutenant jg at the time they skated together in Philadelphia. See, for example, "C. C. Hoffner And Miss Waring Win Ice Dance Event," *Lake Placid News* (August 24, 1945), 1.

28. "It was Ian Hay [pseud. of John Hay Beith], I believe, who first discovered that any military administration is divided into three departments—the Fairy Godmother Department, the Practical Joke Department, and the Surprise Party Department. By preparing for Come-What-May I may circumvent and discourage the latter two and be turned over to the benevolence of the first. But I am not optimistic; the resourcefulness of the two larger departments can hardly be

measured." RAH, letter to John W. Campbell, Jr., 09/14/40. He is referring to Ian Hay's *The First Hundred Thousand* (1916).

29.   Virginia Heinlein, letter to Leon Stover, 04/08/89.

30.   Virginia Heinlein, letter to author, 12/11/99.

31.   Bill Patterson, "Virginia Heinlein Biographical Sketch," *The Heinlein Journal*, No. 13 (July 2003), 4.

32.   RAH, letter to T. B. Buell, 10/03/74.

33.   Virginia Heinlein, letter to author, 11/07/99.

34.   See, for example, RAH's letter to Mauricio Nayberg, 07/07/58.

35.   Bill Patterson, "Virginia Heinlein Biographical Sketch," *The Heinlein Journal*, No. 13 (July 2003), 5.

36.   Virginia Gerstenfeld, letter to Leslyn and Robert Heinlein, dated "October something, 1945."

37.   RAH, letter to John W. Campbell, Jr., 01/04/42.

38.   Undated note written by Virginia Gerstenfeld Heinlein for a visit by the author in 2000 or 2001, found among her papers after her death.

39.   See, for example, RAH's letter to John Arwine, 09/15/45.

40.   RAH, letter to Cal Laning, 11/26/50.

41.   Draft letter, RAH to Greg Benford, 11/08/73.

42.   Heinlein expressed this sentiment in a number of letters. As an example, see RAH's letter to Hermann Deutsch, 02/27/57.

43.   RAH dated this to November 1944 in his letter to Ted Carnell, 05/13/45.

44.   Virginia Heinlein, letter to author, 03/04/2000.

45.   See, for example, RAH's letter to Rex Heinlein (his brother), 09/04/64.

46.   Virginia Heinlein, letter to Leon Stover, 04/23/89.

47.   The language used in Laning's Navy Cross citation, attached to Cal Laning's letter to RAH, 04/06/45.

48.   Cal Laning, letter to RAH, 01/15/44.

49.   See, for example, Cal Laning's letter to RAH, 01/15/44.

50.   Quoted in Virginia Heinlein, letter to Bett and Steve Corland, 05/15/75.

51.   RAH, letter to T. B. Buell, 10/03/74, p. 35. Heinlein did not specify the nature of the project, except to say that it involved new kinds of weapons gadgetry, a subject in which Admiral King had an ongoing interest.

52.   I have not been able to identify the office(s) involved in this request or the exact relationships among them. The terms used here are as Heinlein used them.

53.   RAH, letter to E. J. "Ted" Carnell, 10/08/44.

54.   There is no documentation as to the extent and longevity of this project, but Heinlein was still soliciting input on the kamikaze problem in July 1945, and it may be

presumed to have gone on for the entire time he remained in Philadelphia—i.e.,
"for the duration."

55. RAH, letter to T. B. Buell, 10/03/74.

56. Heinlein's "Eros and Agape" introduction to Theodore Sturgeon's posthumous
     novel, *Godbody,* says Hubbard was then on limited duty at Princeton, "attending
     military governor's school." Russell Miller's *Bare-Faced Messiah* says that Hubbard
     applied for the Navy School of Military Government at Princeton on September
     22, 1944, and that he joined the kamikaze think tank on October 4, 1944.

57. Heinlein's impression of Hubbard's war service, derived largely from contempo-
     raneous conversations among his circle, is given in the introduction to *Godbody*:

     The first weekend Sturgeon was there he slept on the hall rug, a choice
     spot, while both L. Ron Hubbard and George O. Smith were in the over-
     flow who had to walk down the street. In retrospect that seems like a
     wrong decision; Hubbard should not have been asked to walk, as both of
     his feet had been broken (drumhead-type injury) when his last ship was
     bombed. Ron had had a busy war—sunk four times and wounded again
     and again—and at that time was on limited duty at Princeton, attending
     military governor's school.

     Russell Miller's *Bare-Faced Messiah,* the first debunking biography of Hub-
     bard, was issued in 1987, the same year this statement was written, though ac-
     cording to Virginia Heinlein, Robert never saw it. Miller gives a great deal of
     information about Hubbard's war service, presumably from official sources
     (Miller was a journalist), but its detail is not sufficient to confirm Heinlein's im-
     pression.

     There are three biographical books about L. Ron Hubbard publicly available,
     all highly antagonistic. A detailed biography is in process, supported by the
     Church of Scientology, but to date there exists no objective, critical biography
     of Hubbard.

58. George Scithers retold this remark in 2001 at the Millennium Philcon Heinlein
     Panel; see also Virginia Heinlein, letter to Leon Stover, 03/28/89; see also Leon
     Stover, letter to Virginia Heinlein, 04/01/89.

59. For many decades, a rumor has circulated to the effect that Hubbard had "bet"
     Heinlein that he could make more money by founding a religion than by writing
     or any other legitimate means, but this rumor is entirely groundless. The very
     most that may have happened is that the subject of the secular power of reli-
     gions in America came up in conversation (it was a matter Heinlein had dealt
     with in several important prewar stories, and it would have been unusual for the

subject *not* to have come up in extended conversations with a colleague, under the circumstances)—and Heinlein may have pointed out that churches in this country are provided with an unusual degree of legal protection. This idea may have lodged under Hubbard's skin and emerged more than ten years later, as Hubbard did casually mention his long friendship with Heinlein on several occasions.

60. RAH, letter to T. B. Buell, 10/03/73, p. 35.

25. Stabilizing, Somewhat

1. Leslyn (Heinlein) Mocabee to Frederik Pohl, 05/08/53.
2. RAH, letter to Ted and Irene Carnell, 10/08/44.
3. RAH, letter to L. Ron Hubbard, 04/24/75.
4. RAH, letter to Arthur C. Clarke, 10/22/69.
5. RAH, letter to Cal Laning, dated "Spring 1945" (possibly never sent).
6. Henry Kuttner, letter to RAH, 09/20/44.
7. Asimov, *In Memory Yet Green,* 416.
8. Henry Kuttner, letter to RAH, 02/08/45.
9. RAH, letter to John Arwine, 02/25/45.
10. Virginia Heinlein, taped interview by Leon Stover (October 1988), Tape 1, Side A; see also Virginia Heinlein, taped interview by author, Third Series, Tape B, Side A (March 27, 2001).
11. RAH, letter to Algis Budrys, 09/06/61.
12. RAH, letter to Sam Moskowitz, 01/25/61.
13. Heinlein did not record the date of this doctor's visit, but in the Moskowitz letter he dates it to "early 1945"—February, possibly, or early March.
14. RAH, letter to Sam Moskowitz, 01/25/61.
15. RAH, letter to T. B. Buell, 10/03/74, p. 48.
16. RAH, letter to Cal Laning, 01/19/46.
17. See, for example, President Harry Truman, letter to Professor James L. Cate, 01/12/53.
18. Cal Laning, letter to RAH, 01/14/45. Both Laning and Heinlein spelled Laning's wife's name *both* as Micky and Mickey. I have not attempted to regularize their variant usages.
19. RAH, letter to Cal Laning, 01/28/45.
20. Ted Carnell, letter to Leslyn and Robert Heinlein, 06/12/45.
21. Leslyn Heinlein, letter to Cal Laning, 03/30/46. Swanson is not further identified. Leslyn cannot mean H. N. Swanson, who functioned for a short time as Heinlein's Hollywood agent in 1940 and 1941: "Swanie," who represented F. Scott

Fitzgerald, William Faulkner, Pearl S. Buck, and Raymond Chandler, among others, died in 1991, aged with the century, ninety-one years old.

22. Calendar leaf for 02/24/45, with penciled notation in RAH's hand, in "Miscellaneous" file of RAH's personal papers, RAH Archive, UCSC.

23. Leslyn Heinlein, letter to Cal Laning, 05/24/45.

24. RAH, letter to *The Saturday Evening Post,* 10/25/46.

25. RAH, liner notes for Nimoy's recording of "The Green Hills of Earth."

26. RAH, liner notes for Nimoy's recording of "The Green Hills of Earth."

27. L. Ron Hubbard's complex relationship with Jack Parsons is covered in most of the biographical writings about either of the men. Russell Miller's treatment of the Parsons-Hubbard matter in *Bare-Faced Messiah,* for a long time the only commonly available writing on the subject, is badly flawed by a lack of understanding of the material—the case also with George Pendle's recent biography of Parsons, *Strange Angel,* which does the rocketry material brilliantly but the magic and science-fiction fandom much less well. There are several sources available for the story, which I have cross-correlated to weigh the versions of the tale.

28. Paul Rydeen, "Brother Jack Parsons: The Magickal Scientist and His Circle," an excerpt of Rydeen's privately published *Jack Parsons and the Fall of Babalon,* at one time widely available on the Internet, but now available on only a few sites. See, for example, http://www.greylodge.org/occultreview/glor_003/magickalscientist.htm.

29. The Alva Rogers memoir published as "Darkhouse" in Terry Carr's fanzine *Lighthouse* V (1962), is quoted extensively in biographies of Parsons, but the narrative is of limited usefulness because Rogers misunderstood—and therefore misrepresented—much of what he was able to observe.

30. RAH, letter to Ted and Irene Carnell, 04/02/52; see also [second] contemporaneous three-by-five-inch notecard, 04/13/45, pencil in RAH's hand, in "Wartime and Snafu Manor" personal file, RAH Archive, UCSC.

31. Eyewitness account by Harry J. Herder, Jr., at www.remember.org/witness/herder.html. A good number of oral histories and eyewitness accounts are being placed online in lieu of print publication and consequently are only available online.

32. RAH, letter to John Arwine, 05/20/45.

33. Clipping from *The Philadelphia Record* (06/25/45), preserved in Heinlein's personal "Wartime and Snafu Manor" personal file, RAH Archive, UCSC.

34. RAH, letter to Ted Carnell, 05/13/45.

35. RAH, letter to Poul Anderson, 09/06/61.

36. RAH, letter to Poul Anderson, 09/06/61.

37. Three-by-five-inch notecard penciled in RAH's hand, "Wartime and Snafu Manor" personal file, RAH Archive, UCSC.

38. RAH, letter to Ted Carnell, 05/13/45.

39. RAH, letter to John and Doña Campbell, 07/03/45.

40. RAH, letter to John S. Arwine, 05/20/45.

41. The expression first occurs quoted back to Heinlein by John Campbell in a fall 1943 letter and recurs periodically through 1945, used by both Robert and Leslyn Heinlein in correspondence with their intimates.

42. Although Heinlein only mentions a "major publisher" contacting him in spring 1945, the first mention in contemporaneous correspondence with Heyliger of what became his first book dated from January 1946. I have chosen to interpret this as the same book project, after a lapse of some time.

43. See, for example, RAH's letter to John W. Campbell, Jr., 09/16/41.

44. RAH, letter to John W. Campbell, Jr., 06/03/45.

45. Joel Charles, letter to RAH, 04/05/88.

46. The text of this report will be given in the first of two volumes of Heinlein's juvenilia and nonfiction writings in the Virginia Edition published by the Heinlein Prize Trust, and is to be made available for download from the online Heinlein Archive, http://www.heinleinarchives.net/.

47. RAH, letter to T. B. Buell, 10/03/74.

48. The only contemporaneous documentation for this assertion is her defense of Robert to Cal Laning in May of 1945.

49. Henry Kuttner, letter to Robert and Leslyn Heinlein, 09/15/45.

50. See, for example, Leslyn Heinlein's postcard to Jack Williamson, 01/09/45.

51. Henry Kuttner, letter to RAH, 09/20/44.

26. Dangerous New World

1. RAH, letter to John Arwine, 02/25/45.

2. In his "Agape and Eros" posthumous tribute to Theodore Sturgeon, Heinlein mentions John Campbell's wartime work on the supersecret radar project and adds, "(And didn't even *think* the word 'uranium,' not even in one's sleep")," implying he knew it was a war secret. In a taped interview with Phillip Homer Owenby conducted in 1994, Virginia Heinlein recalled: "Actually one time we got to talking about uranium and its possibilities and he said, 'We can't talk about this.' So we never mentioned the subject again until the war was over." Clearly Heinlein knew something of what was going on, even if he did not know specific information about the Manhattan Engineer District.

3. Virginia Heinlein, taped interview with Phillip Homer Owenby (1994), Tape 7, Side B.

4. RAH, resignation form letter, 08/15/45, RAH naval jacket, RAH Archive, UCSC.

5. Copy preserved in RAH Archive, UCSC, and first published in the *Robert A. Heinlein Centennial Souvenir Book,* July 7, 2007.

6. The term is Heinlein's and is first recorded in a letter to Cal Laning, dated 09/17/45, where it is used casually and without explanation, suggesting it might already have been in use among the developers of this project for some time.

7. RAH, letter to Cal Laning, 09/17/45.

8. RAH, letter to Henry Ralston, 01/28/46.

9. This is little more than a summary of the case Heinlein made in a series of letters in 1946 through 1948, detailed seriatim in the text, to Campbell and then to Ralston, the "Publications Executive" [Vice President?] of Street & Smith: at the time of the original sale, he had been assured that the purchase of "all rights" was formal only and that rights would be reverted to him on request. Street & Smith then unilaterally changed its policy and would revert only *some* rights, under *some* circumstances. Even worse, as Heinlein observed, the circumstances kept changing.

    It was the dispute over rights, more than any personal disagreement with Campbell, that resulted in Heinlein's refusal to sell to Street & Smith for nearly ten years after the end of World War II ("Gulf" in 1949 was an exception under special circumstances, for which Heinlein waived his usual objections).

10. See, for example, John W. Campbell, Jr.'s letter addressed "Dear Heinleins" and dated 02/06/46, among others.

11. See, for example, RAH's letter to John W. Campbell, Jr., 02/19/41.

12. RAH, letter to John W. Campbell, Jr., 01/28/46.

13. Virginia Heinlein, letter to author, 12/11/99.

14. RAH, letter to Cal Laning, 09/17/45.

15. RAH, letter to Cal Laning, 09/17/45.

16. RAH, letter to John Arwine, 09/15/45.

17. RAH, letter to E. E. Smith, 10/17/45.

18. What is informally known as the Manhattan Project was formally named the Manhattan Engineer District.

19. RAH, letter to Judith Merril, 11/01/67.

20. RAH, letter to Cal Laning, 09/17/45.

21. H. G. Wells, *Phoenix: How to Rebuild the World—A Summary of the Inescapable Conditions of World Reorganization* (Girard, Kans.: E Haldeman-Julius, 1942), 22.

22. RAH, letter to Henry Sang, 09/15/45.

23. RAH, letter to E. E. Smith, 10/17/45; see also RAH's letter to John Arwine, 09/15/45, and similar letters of the same time frame, addressed to others.

24. RAH, letter to Cal Laning, 09/17/45.

25. RAH, letter to the Honorable Jerry Voorhis, 10/04/45.

26. RAH, letter to Henry Sang, 09/15/45.

27. RAH, letter to E. E. Smith, 10/17/45.

28. RAH, letter to E. E. Doc Smith, 10/17/45.

29. RAH, letter to Doña (Cambell) Smith, 02/03/51.

30. RAH, letter to E. J. "Ted" Carnell, 10/18/45.

31. RAH, letter to Cal Laning, 09/17/45.

32. RAH, letter to Henry Sang, 09/15/45.

33. Virginia Heinlein, quoting an expression of Robert's in a letter to George Warren, 03/09/79.

34. RAH, letter to John Arwine, 09/20/45.

35. RAH, letter to Henry Sang, 09/15/45.

36. Cal Laning, memo to RAH, undated, but by context mid- to late September 1945.

37. RAH, letter to John W. Campbell, Jr., 02/16/46; Leon Stover also recorded in a letter to Virginia Heinlein, dated 05/20/89, that Robert Heinlein told him verbally that Susie Clifton was the model for Sally Logan.

38. RAH, letter to Cal Laning, 09/17/45.

39. A recent (2005) biography of Parsons, *Strange Angel: The Otherworldly Life of Rocket Scientist John Whiteside Parsons,* by George Pendle provides the best account of the facts of Parsons's life, without necessarily comprehending Parsons's nonprofessional activities; Pendle's account of Parsons's rocketry, on the other hand, is first-rate.

40. Informally—Scoles organized the Point Mugu naval facility. See, for example, RAH's letter to Cal Laning, 09/17/45.

41. RAH's personal-library copy of the Smyth Report in the RAH Archive, UCSC.
    Perhaps the last line of the dedication was Laning's way of acknowledging the anti-kamikaze think tank Heinlein had set up in Philadelphia in the last months of the war, since as an informal intelligence project it would never otherwise be publicly acknowledged. Laning had criticized Heinlein for not mastering his situation at Snafu Manor; it is possible also that he was thus making amends.

42. RAH, letter to Henry Sang, 09/15/45.

43. RAH, letter to John Kean, 09/20/45.

44. Leslyn Heinlein, letter to John W. Campbell, Jr., 11/27/41.

45. RAH, letter to Cal Laning, 09/27/45.

46. RAH, letter to Willy Ley, 10/15/45.

47. Michael J. Patritch, "One Hour and Fifty Minutes into Forever: A Meeting with Robert Heinlein," *Thrust* XXXIII (Spring 1989), 9.

48. RAH, letter to Willy Ley, 10/15/45.

49. RAH, letter to Armand B. Coign, 10/17/45.

50. RAH, letter to Armand B. Coign, 05/26/46.

51. Possibly "How to Be a Survivor" per RAH's letter to E. E. Smith, 10/17/45.

52. RAH, letter to Ted Carnell, 10/18/45.

53. Virginia Heinlein, taped interview by author, Second Series, Tape A, Side B.

54. "Historical Note" section of the online Finding Guide of the University of Oregon's "Lurton Blassingame Literary Agency Records 1965–1978," http://nwda-db.wsulibs.wsu.edu/ark:/80444/xv82437.

55. Lurton Blassingame, letter to L. Ron Hubbard, 11/05/45.

27. Settling In

1. Heinlein discusses this in "If You Don't See It, Just Ask," an essay originally written for *Playboy* but never marketed.

   Fuller never got into production on the Dymaxion House. The website of the Henry Ford Museum, where the only surviving Dymaxion House has been on exhibit since 2001, says that the partnership fell apart because Fuller would not compromise his design; Heinlein says it could not be sold because there were no housing codes anywhere that would permit it to be erected.

2. RAH, letter to Henry and Catherine Kuttner, 04/21/47.

3. RAH, letter to L. Ron Hubbard, 07/01/45.

4. RAH, letter to John Kean, 11/21/45.

5. Theodore Sturgeon, letter to RAH, 05/13/46.

6. RAH, letter to Theodore Sturgeon, 05/19/46.

7. Theodore Sturgeon, letter to RAH, 05/25/46.

8. RAH, letter to John W. Campbell, Jr., 03/28/53.

9. Cards containing RAH's notes for letter to L. Ron Hubbard, undated but clipped to L. Ron Hubbard's letter to RAH, dated 12/04/46.

10. RAH, letter to Cal Laning, 11/20/45. The University of Chicago Library contains "Minutes of Temporary Steering Committee Meeting, November 15, 1945," which refers to Robert Cornog, but not to John Arwine, in the Cal Tech Athenaeum. Document provided courtesy Author Services, Inc.

11. Edmund Fuller, letter to RAH, 10/23/45.

12. RAH, letter to Richard Pope at Compton's Yearbook, 09/25/74 (for the Paul Dirac article).

13. RAH, letter to John W. Campbell, Jr., 01/17/42.

14. Signed "Rough Draft of Agreement on collaboration on novel, working title *For Us The Living*," between Robert A. Heinlein and L. Ron Hubbard, 12/18/45.

15. Crowley had received *The Book of the Law* by direct dictation from a "preternatural

spirit" in 1904 and founded the religion of Thelema in 1909 based on its revela-
tions. The core principle of Thelema (a Greek word which means "will," in the
sense of the intention precedent to an act) is contained in three precepts. The
first is an adaptation of François Rabelais' maxim: "Do what thou Wilt shall
be the whole of the Law" (Crowley rendered "Will" with an initial capital letter to
indicate the human will in congruence with the divine will). This precept is followed by two others: "Love is the Law, Love under Will" and "Every Person is a
Star"—meaning every human being who self-actualizes is a divine being with a
place in the heavens.

16. Jack Parsons, letter to Aleister Crowley, quoted in Michael Staley, "The Babalon
     Working," at http://user.cyberlink.ch/~koenig/dplanet/staley/staley11.htm; origi-
     nal appearance in *Starfire* I: 3 (1989).

17. Science-fiction fan Alva Rogers was renting a room in Parsons's mansion at the
     time and witnessed enough of the odd goings-on to include them in a memoir
     widely quoted in biographies of Parsons. However, Rogers was not an acute ob-
     server in the first instance, and he interpreted much of what he saw in terms of
     what he thought he *ought* to be seeing (it is not merely "unlikely," for example,
     that he witnessed the summoning of a "demon," it is actually impossible—
     demons not existing within Parsons's well-documented magickal theory and
     practice). Rogers's reports of jealous sexual tension at the dinner table over Hub-
     bard's affair are therefore suspect in view of Parsons's actual behavior in trying,
     almost immediately, to ground an elemental—a fleshly incarnation of one of the
     four elements of classical and medieval science (earth, air, fire, water)—to act as
     his magickal assistant succeeding Sara Northrup (who married Hubbard a little
     later).

18. Leslyn Heinlein, letter to Catherine and L. Sprague de Camp, 08/07/46.

19. RAH, letter to Lurton Blassingame, 06/23/46.

20. RAH, letter to L. Sprague and Catherine de Camp, 02/13/46.

21. RAH, letter to J. Francis McComas, 10/28/68.

22. Undated letter, Cleve Cartmill to William A. P. White, quoted in Robert James's
     e-mail correspondence with Virginia Heinlein, 06/01/2001.

23. Manuscript in Opus 36 file, RAH Archive, UCSC.

24. RAH, letter to Cal Laning, 01/01/46.

25. RAH, letter to John Kean, 11/21/45.

26. RAH, letter to John W. Campbell, Jr., 01/07/46.

27. RAH, "Why Buy a Stone Ax?" manuscript in Opus 38 file, RAH Archive,
     UCSC.

28. RAH, letter to Cal Laning, 02/15/46.

29. RAH, letter to John W. Campbell, Jr., 01/07/46.

30. RAH, letter to Rex Ivar Heinlein, 09/24/64.

31. RAH, letter to Fritz Lang, 05/02/46.

32. RAH, letter to Cal Laning, 01/19/46.

33. Cal Laning, letter to RAH, 03/20/46.

34. RAH, letter to Cal Laning, 02/15/46.

35. RAH, letter to Willy and Olga Ley, 11/23/45.

36. John W. Campbell, Jr., letter to Robert and Leslyn Heinlein, 01/03/46.

37. RAH, letter to John W. Campbell, Jr., 01/07/46.

38. Ultimately published with a change of spelling to "Rhysling" as "The Green Hills of Earth."

39. RAH, letter to John W. Campbell, Jr., 01/07/46.

40. RAH, letter to John W. Campbell, Jr., 01/28/46.

41. Henry W. Ralson, letter to RAH, 02/14/46.

42. RAH, letter to John W. Campbell, Jr., 02/16/46.

43. RAH, letter to L. Sprague de Camp, 02/13/46.

44. RAH, letter to John W. Campbell, Jr., 02/16/46.

45. RAH, letter to L. Sprague de Camp, 02/13/46.

46. RAH, Accession Notes dated 04/02/67 for Opus 42, *Rocket Ship Galileo,* RAH Archive, UCSC; see also RAH, letter to John Arwine, 05/10/46.

47. RAH, letter to Alice Dalgliesh, 02/17/59.

48. Heinlein never specifically detailed Cartmill's advice to him on the subject, but always included him, along with Fritz Lang, as talking him into writing his first juvenile. For example: "I did this one [*Rocket Ship Galileo*] on the advice of Fritz Lang and Cleve Cartmill, advice to the effect that no better field of propaganda existed than that of the adolescent-juvenile." RAH, letter to John S. Arwine, 05/10/46.

49. RAH, letter to Alice Dalgliesh, 02/17/59.

50. RAH, letter to John W. Campbell, Jr., 02/16/46.

51. RAH, letter to John W. Campbell, Jr., 02/16/46.

52. RAH, letter to John W. Campbell, Jr., 02/16/46.

53. RAH, letter to John W. Campbell, Jr., 02/16/46.

54. RAH, letter to Lurton Blassingame, 01/29/46.

55. Lurton Blassingame, telegram to RAH, 02/25/46.

56. Edmund Fuller, letter to RAH, 02/26/46. Fuller wanted to drop several of the early stories entirely and truncate "Methuselah's Children" at the point where the Howard Families take off into interstellar space. Note also that this is before any of the *Post* stories were written or published.

57. RAH, letter addressed to "Ron, Jack, Betty & Co.," 02/23/46.

58. RAH, letter to Lurton Blassingame, 03/16/46.

59. RAH, letter to Lurton Blassingame, 03/16/46.

60.   Wells, *The World of William Clissold*, 358–59.

61.   RAH's Accession Notes dated 04/02/67 for Opus 42, *Rocket Ship Galileo*, RAH
      Archive, UCSC.

62.   RAH, letter to Alice Dalgliesh, 02/17/59.

63.   RAH, letter to Lurton Blassingame, 03/16/46.

64.   Lurton Blassingame, letter to RAH, 03/04/46.

65.   RAH, letter to Lurton Blassingame, 03/16/46.

66.   All of these projects, and his intention to take one of the ideas to Lang, are dis-
      cussed in RAH's letter to Lurton Blassingame, 03/16/46.

67.   RAH, letter to William Holt, 01/15/47.

68.   Henry Kuttner's correspondence with Robert Heinlein covered the entire time
      of his experiment with the Bond-Charteris organization, and he summarized the
      conclusion of the arrangement in a letter to Heinlein dated September 23, 1946:

> On Charteris. Here's the deal, confidentially. You know I did that ghosted
> *Saint* 40,000 worder [in 1945]. He delayed and delayed. Finally he of-
> fered me $100 on account. I said no. He offered $250 on account. I said
> no, he could return the story if he wanted, I wouldn't insist that he buy it.
> That did it. He sent a check for the full amount. It bounced. At that point
> I got mad—I had learned that some of Leslie's previous ghost-writers had
> had unhappy experiences in collecting their dough—and threatened suit.
> And I got another check which was good this time. All of which you may
> find useful to remember in case Charteris wants you to do some more
> work for him. I definitely advise a written contract in advance! I'd feel
> more sympathetic toward him if I hadn't learned that such tactics are, pre-
> sumably, standard business practice with him.

> Heinlein was later (10/26/46) able to tell Kuttner that Charteris had sold
> Kuttner's ghostwritten serial to *Red Book* (a fiction pulp) under the Charteris
> name and for vastly more than he had paid Kuttner—while Kuttner still owned
> the rights to the story, which is why he had paid up. "Sorta like agenting in re-
> verse, with 90% to the agent," Heinlein wryly remarked. He offered to write
> Charteris up in the Authors League bulletin.

> No reply to this matter from Kuttner is preserved in Heinlein's correspon-
> dence.

69.   The magazine had already gone out of business by the spring of 1946, when
      Heinlein recovered the story and sent it to his agent for submission to the other
      mystery pulps. See RAH's letter to Lurton Blassingame, 05/20/46.

70.   Leslyn Heinlein, letter to John W. Campbell, Jr., 03/14/46; see also RAH, letter
      to John W. Campbell, Jr., 03/19/46,

71. RAH, letter to John W. Campbell, Jr., 03/19/46.

72. RAH, letter to John S. Arwine, 05/10/46.

73. RAH, notes for reply attached to L. Ron Hubbard's letter to RAH, 12/04/46.

74. RAH, letter to John Arwine, 05/10/46.

75. Cal Laning, letter to Robert and Leslyn Heinlein, 03/20/46.

76. RAH, letter to John W. Campbell, Jr., 05/23/46.

77. Cal Laning, letter to RAH, 03/20/46.

78. Leslyn Heinlein, letter to Cal Laning, 03/30/46.

79. RAH, letter to Jerry Voorhis, 05/28/46.

80. Leslyn Heinlein, letter to Cal Laning, 03/30/46.

81. Paul Rydeen, "Brother Jack Parsons: The Magickal Scientist and His Circle," http://www.greylodge.org/occultreview/glor_003/magickalscientist.htm.

82. This anecdote is recorded in "Whence Came the Stranger?" by "Adam Walks Between Worlds" (Adam Rostoker), originally in *Green Egg* magazine and republished on the Internet in several places, but see http://pturing.firehead.org/-occult/grok/thelema.htm.

83. RAH, letter to John Arwine, 05/10/46.

84. Leslyn Heinlein, letter to Lurton Blassingame, 03/26/46.

85. Brendan Byrne (editor), letter to Lurton Blassingame, 03/25/46.

86. Owen J. Roberts, letter to Lurton Blassingame, 07/12/46.

87. Rejection letter from William Morrow to Lurton Blassingame, 06/05/46.

88. RAH, letter to John W. Campbell, Jr., 05/23/46.

89. RAH, letter to Ted Carnell, 06/02/46.

90. RAH, letter to John W. Campbell, Jr., 05/23/46.

91. RAH, letter to Ted Carnell, 06/02/46.

92. RAH, letter to Ted Carnell, 06/02/46.

93. Ted Carnell, letter to RAH, 05/25/46.

94. RAH, letter to John Arwine, 05/10/46.

95. Lurton Blassingame, letter to RAH, 07/02/46.

96. RAH, letter to John Arwine, 05/10/46.

97. RAH, letter to John Arwine, 05/10/46.

98. Leslyn Heinlein, supplemental note to RAH's letter to Theodore Sturgeon, 05/19/46.

99. RAH, letter to John W. Campbell, Jr., 05/23/46.

100. RAH, letter to John W. Campbell, Jr., 05/23/46. Since this is the only letter dealing with these events, it is difficult to tell exactly what the mention of a "Sabbat" was intended to convey, combining speechifying with dance and, presumably, a quantity of liquor.

101. RAH, letter to John W. Campbell, Jr., 05/23/46.

102. Leslyn Heinlein, untitled poem dated 06/09/46, in "Poems" file of Robert Heinlein's personal files, RAH Archive, UCSC.

28. Writing Factory

1. Leslyn Heinlein, letter to Lurton Blassingame, 06/11/46.
2. Virginia Gerstenfeld related the occasion of the breakup in a postscript to a letter to the Heinleins, 11/28/45.

> P.S. It's happened. Dammit, Dammit Damn it. George is back. And of course our meeting would be dramatic—right in front of everyone. I was doing a back change of edges, when he tore up with great enthusiasm and said 'Hello Gin.' And wanted to know how long I would be around, and let loose with much gossip, etc. I was very proud of myself, because I took it all very calmly, and when he got hold of a card and handed it to me mostly filled in, and told me that that was my program, I advised him that I wasn't dancing. I am not free skating with much vim, landing Axels in beautiful 3-point landings (two feet and a place not intended for landing jumps on). He asked me to be his partner in group free-skating numbers and I refused. Boy, am I ever doing swell! Expect to take my gold dance test with his pet enemy too. In words of one syllable, I'm through and enjoying it thoroughly.

3. Virginia Gerstenfeld, letter to Robert and Leslyn Heinein, 03/22/46.
4. Virginia Gerstenfeld, letter to Robert and Leslyn Heinlein, 04/22/46.
5. Virginia Gerstenfeld Heinlein, letter to Leon Stover, 03/29/89.
6. Probably Dick Skidmore, one of her protégés in Philadelphia who had come to the West Coast. The Heinleins had known the Skidmores since at least 1937, when an outing on the Skidmores' yacht was reported in the *Los Angeles Times* (July 20, 1937, "Merry Party Takes a Cruise").
7. Virginia Heinlein, e-mail to Robert James, Ph.D., 06/16/2001.
8. RAH, letter to Mary Collin, 07/08/62.
9. Heinlein's copy of "Dance Session," dated "June 1946," is in the "Verse" file of his personal files. Ginny's copy is in her naval jacket. RAH Archive, UCSC.
10. Virginia Gerstenfeld Heinlein, e-mail to Robert James, Ph.D., 06/16/2001.
11. Virginia Gerstenfeld Heinlein, taped interview by author, Second Series, Tape C, Side B (September [9?,] 2000).
12. RAH, letter to John W. Campbell, Jr., 11/05/46.
13. RAH, letter to Virginia Gerstenfeld, 06/26/46.
14. Virginia Gerstenfeld, letter addressed "Dear folks," 06/27/46.

15. RAH, letter to Judith Klein, 12/01/79.

16. Robert and Leslyn Heinlein both published descriptions of their experience. Robert's, from which this and the following quotations are taken, was titled "Journey of Death" but never published; Leslyn's was published in their local newspaper, *The Canyon Crier* (July 19, 1946). Both articles will be republished in the Virginia Edition volumes of Heinlein's nonfiction.

17. Manuscript for Opus 45, "Journey of Death," in the RAH Archive, UCSC.

18. RAH, "Journey of Death."

19. "Altitude Record Set in V-2 Test," *The El Paso Times* front page, Saturday, June 29, 1946, preserved in the Opus 45 manuscript file for "Journey of Death" in the RAH Archive, UCSC.

20. RAH, "Journey of Death."

21. RAH, letter to Lurton Blassingame, 08/09/46.

22. RAH, letter to Lurton Blassingame, 08/09/46.

23. Harvey Rivkins, Lt. Col. Ord Dept. (on War Department Office of the Chief of Ordnance stationery), to Robert Heinlein, 08/15/46, in the Opus 45 manuscript file for "Journey of Death," RAH Archive, UCSC.

24. Both selections are from the manuscript for, Opus 45, "Journey of Death" in the RAH Archive, UCSC.

25. RAH, letter to John W. Campbell, Jr., 08/09/46.

26. Leslyn Heinlein, letter to Lurton Blassingame, 11/29/46.

27. RAH, letter to Ted and Irene Carnell, 02/13/46.

28. In the correspondence, the boy's name is given variously as "Michael" and "Micheal."

29. The project failed to raise sufficient money to bring Carnell to the United States in 1947, but was successful two years later, when Carnell was brought for the 1949 World Science Fiction Convention in Cincinnati. The Big Pond Fund was thereafter dropped, but a campaign to bring Irish fan writer Walter Willis to the United States in 1952 resulted in the founding of the Trans-Atlantic Fan Fund (TAFF), which continues to date.

30. Leslyn Heinlein, letter to Henry and Catherine Kuttner, 10/13/46.

31. Virginia Heinlein, e-mail to Robert James, Ph.D., 06/01/2001.

32. The quotation is taken from RAH's letter to Lurton Blassingame, 03/16/46.

33. Leslyn Heinlein, letter to Catherine and Sprague de Camp, 08/07/46.

34. RAH, letter to John W. Campbell, Jr., 08/09/46.

35. RAH, letter to Cal Laning, 03/30/46.

36. Unpublished draft of a Heinlein biography by Virginia Heinlein, written about 1989, page xv; and Virginia Heinlein, letter to author, 06/04/99.

37. Willy Ley, letter to Robert and Leslyn Heinlein, 08/28/46.

38. The various translations are found with the other manuscript materials in the Opus 48 manuscript file of the RAH Archive, UCSC.

39. RAH, letter to Henry and Catherine Kuttner, 10/26/46.

40. RAH's notes in the Opus 48, "The Green Hills of Earth" file, RAH Archive, UCSC.

41. Lurton Blassingame, letter to RAH, 09/30/46.

42. RAH, letter to Henry and Catherine Kuttner, 10/26/46.

43. RAH, letter to John W. Campbell, Jr., 01/12/47.

44. RAH, letter to Henry and Catherine Kuttner, 10/26/46.

45. Asimov, *In Memory Yet Green,* 489.

46. Robert S. Richardson, letter to RAH, 12/31/46.

47. RAH, letter to Henry and Catherine Kuttner, 10/26/46.

48. Henry Kuttner, letter to RAH, 10/21/46.

49. According to RAH's Accession Notes dated 04/02/67 for the RAH Archive, UCSC "Space Jockey" was sold to the *Post* on October 17, 1946.

50. RAH, letter to Henry and Catherine Kuttner, 10/26/46.

51. Virginia Gerstenfeld, letter to RAH, 11/04/46.

52. The indented points are quoted from Heinlein's letter; the nonindented text summarizes his arguments to Susie Clifton.

53. RAH, letter to Susie Clifton, 11/06/46.

54. Helen Gahagan Douglas, letter to RAH, 12/17/46.

55. This verse is quoted in several letters, but a fair copy is also in the "Verse" file of RAH's personal files, in the RAH Archive, UCSC.

56. RAH, letter to John W. Campbell, Jr., 11/09/46.

57. RAH, letter to John W. Campbell, Jr., 11/15/46.

58. Leslyn Heinlein, letter to Lurton Blassingame, 12/06/46.

59. RAH, Accession Notes dated April 2, 1967, for Opus 48, "The Green Hills of Earth," 11–12, RAH Archive, UCSC.

60. RAH, letter to William Holt, 01/15/47.

61. L. Ron Hubbard, letter to RAH, 12/04/46.

62. RAH, handwritten notes on three-by-five-inch cards attached to a letter from L. Ron Hubbard to RAH dated 12/06/46; there is no indication that Heinlein's letter was ever written or sent—yet Hubbard's letter indicates he knew he was in bad odor with the Heinleins, and Heinlein's note indicates he feels it necessary to explain *why.*

63. RAH, handwritten notecards attached to L. Ron Hubbard's letter to RAH, 12/06/46.

64. Leslyn Heinlein, letter to Catherine and Sprague de Camp, 08/07/46.

65. L. Sprague de Camp, letter to Robert and Leslyn Heinlein (with handwritten P.S. by Catherine de Camp), 08/13/46.

66. Leslyn Heinlein, letter to Catherine and Sprague de Camp, 08/07/46.

29. Separation. Anxiety.

1. RAH, Accession Notes dated 04/02/67 for Opus 48, "The Green Hills of Earth," RAH Archive, UCSC.

2. Robert and Leslyn Heinlein, letter to Virginia Gerstenfeld, 02/28/47.

3. Robert and Leslyn Heinlein, letter to Virginia Gerstenfeld, 03/09/47. Such a sentiment is as close to a direct admission of an extramarital affair as exists in Heinlein's usually discreet correspondence. Such extramarital affairs have been casually alluded to in a number of sources—including particularly Virginia Heinlein's taped interviews for this biography project—but without details. Finding such language in letters written from *both* Heinleins to Ginny (as well as from Ginny, if we may read between the lines of her earlier note to Robert) speaks to Leslyn's acceptance of such arrangement, if not her active complicity (as to which there is no direct testimony). Later assertions from Leslyn's poison-pen letters to Frederik Pohl and William A. P. White, portraying herself as some kind of unwilling victim, must be read with the proverbial grain of salt. In a letter dated only "April 1947," Ginny Gerstenfeld refers to the situation as a "threesome"—which might mean only a social and personal relationship among three people in stable equilibrium, or it might imply a sexual triangle. The discussion in this letter can, admittedly, be read very much like the tactical dilemmas of a junior wife in a three-way marriage.

4. RAH, letter to Jay Stanton, 05/21/47.

5. Cal Laning, letter to RAH, 04/25/47.

6. Virginia Heinlein, taped interview by author, Third Series Tape A, Side B (March 27, 2001).

7. Virginia Heinlein, letter to author, 02/07/00.

8. RAH, letter to Doña and George Smith, 02/03/51.

9. Virginia Heinlein, letter to author, 02/07/2000.

10. The terms of this anecdote are taken directly from Virginia Heinlein's recounting of the incident, in a letter to the author, 02/07/2000, and in an IM, 06/27/2000.

11. Virginia Heinlein, IM with author, 06/27/2000. It is fairly telling that Robert did *not* conclude that the affair with Ginny Gerstenfeld was even marginally involved in the crisis—additional testimony, if testimony of a negative kind, that such extramarital affairs were not a special or exceptional occurrence in the Heinlein marriage—and neither was Leslyn's meltdown.

Possibly corroborating this interpretation is Heinlein's characterization, in much the same terms, of the alcoholic Grace Farnham in *Farnham's Freehold* (1965).

12. Virginia Gerstenfeld, letter to RAH, undated except "Sunday Night" in Virginia Gerstenfeld's hand—but "circa Apr. 46" in RAH's hand. The context seems to refer, rather, to April 1947, as there were no particular emotional crises going on in Robert Heinlein's life in April 1946, and in any case Gerstenfeld was still in New York in April 1946.

13. The discussion of Virginia Gerstenfeld's social life at UCLA is taken from a taped interview of Virginia Heinlein by the author, Tape 2, Side B (February 27, 2000).

14. RAH, letter to Bill and Lucy Corson, 11/10/48.

15. RAH, letter to Henry and Catherine Kuttner, 04/21/47.

16. RAH, letter to Jay Stanton, 05/21/47.

17. RAH, letter to Robert Moore Williams, 05/21/47.

18. RAH, letter to John Arwine, 03/15/47.

19. Lurton Blassingame, letter to RAH, 05/02/47.

20. RAH, letter to Stuart Rose, 05/30/47.

21. From Horatio Winslow, about whom I have not been able to discover any information. Presumably he was one of the magazine editors to whom a Heinlein story was submitted. Lurton Blassingame, letter to RAH, 05/12/47.

   Winslow's recommendation that Heinlein consult Uzzell was a direct observation that Heinlein's stories were not structured like commercial American magazine stories—true enough. Heinlein's stories, from his earliest to his last, showed a wide range of formal experimentation and have more in common with European "art" stories than with American magazine fiction.

22. RAH, letter to Lurton Blassingame, 05/14/47.

23. RAH, letter to Lurton Blassingame, 05/16/47.

24. RAH, letter to Willy Ley, 05/21/47.

25. The details of this situation were not mentioned in any correspondence.

26. RAH, letter to Sprague and Catherine de Camp, 05/03/47.

27. RAH, letter to Lurton Blassingame, 05/16/47.

28. RAH, letter to Lloyd Biggle, 09/30/76.

29. The date and occasion is not recorded, but Heinlein's own statement that he was blocked for about a month makes it roughly coincident with Ginny Gerstenfeld's move to the Studio Club, and so this is a highly probable occasion for the exchange (which he found memorable enough to repeat on several occasions thereafter) to have taken place.

30. Virginia Heinlein, letter to Leon Stover, 03/28/89.

31. RAH, letter to Lloyd Biggle, 09/30/76.
32. RAH, letter to Dona and George Smith, 02/03/51.
33. The symmetry of this precipitate breakup with Heinlein's precipitate proposal fifteen years earlier looks suspiciously story-like, too artful to be quite true, but, as Heinlein remarked elsewhere, "That's the trouble with truth; it lacks the plausibility of fiction." Heinlein habitually did make even life-altering decisions startlingly rapidly—a quality he valorized for his *Homo novis* superman characters in "Gulf" (written in 1949) and again in the television series pilot screenplay he derived from "Gulf," *The Adventure of the Man Who Wasn't There,* in 1963 and 1964.

    It may not be clear why an admission of an attempt to commit suicide would prompt the separation and divorce (and Heinlein never recorded his reasons). Reading between the lines of later correspondence about the breakup, it may be that Heinlein saw himself as having, for three years, turned inward on his marriage, attempting to accommodate Leslyn's evident depression and other psychological problems, trying without success to be the support and help she needed—and to be a shield for her, from outside demands. This is necessarily also a process of giving up the self, pushing one's own needs to the side. This process, by its very nature, is a breaking of the mutual help pattern of a healthy marriage. The attempted suicide might have indicated to Heinlein that this was not a temporary situation from which they could recover and get back to a healthy pattern, but a new and permanent condition from which there was no possibility of recovery.

    In any case, he must have seen some indication in that moment that a transition had happened in the pattern of their marriage, for which the only practical solution was a clean break.
34. Virginia Heinlein, taped interview by author, Second Series, Tape A, Side A (September 6, 2000); see also RAH, letter to Virginia Gerstenfeld, 07/09/47.
35. The evidence about when this incident and the consequent separation took place is contradictory. It is possible—though not likely—that it might have taken place very late in May (after the last mention in one of Robert's letters of Leslyn being bedridden on May 22) or early in June, but the most likely time is mid-June. None of the events definitely consequent to the separation took place before about June 16—the date on which Heinlein withdrew $608.50 from their joint savings account—which argues for the mid-June date. However, a letter dated June 8, 1947, from Cal Laning to RAH indicating that Sprague de Camp had told him about the separation already, and Virginia Heinlein's recollection that it took place while her final exams were going on or the semester was finishing up, suggests the earlier date—that is, in early June at the latest.

I have chosen to regard the Laning letter as casually misdated and probably intended to be dated June 28, 1947—and Virginia Heinlein's recollection as referring to a two-week *time period,* rather than to a precise date on which both her move and her final exams were taking place.

36. RAH, letter to Virginia Gerstenfeld, 05/14/48.
37. Property Settlement Agreement dated 06/26/47, paragraph 6.
38. Virginia Heinlein, taped interview by author, Second Series Tape B, Side A (September [9?], 2000).
39. Virginia Heinlein, taped interview by author, Tape 7, Side A (February [28?,] 2000).
40. RAH, letter to Virginia Gerstenfeld, 08/14/48.
41. Virginia Heinlein, e-mail to Robert James, Ph.D., 06/02/2001.
42. Virginia Heinlein, taped interview by author, Tape 12, Side A (March [3?], 2000).
43. Virginia Heinlein, taped interview by author, Second Series, Tape A, Side B (September 2000).
44. RAH, letter to Virginia Gerstenfeld, 07/07/47.
45. RAH, letter to Virginia Gerstenfeld, 07/08/47.
46. RAH, letter to Virginia Gerstenfeld, 07/08/47.
47. This year's fad was flying saucers—prompted probably by the Roswell flying saucer "crash" that had appeared in the New Mexico papers the day after Heinlein's fortieth birthday.
48. RAH, Accession Notes dated 04/02/67 for the RAH Archive, UCSC.
49. Virginia Gerstenfeld, letter to RAH, 07/09/47.
50. Virginia Heinlein, IM with author, 12/16/2001.
51. Frank D. Morris, *Collier's,* letter to RAH, 07/08/47.
52. RAH, letter to Virginia Gerstenfeld, 07/09/47.
53. Cal Laning, letter to RAH, 06/27/47.
54. RAH, letter to Virginia Gerstenfeld, 07/08/47.
55. RAH, letter to Virginia Gerstenfeld, 07/09/47.
56. See, for example, Virginia Gerstenfeld's letter to RAH, 07/09/47. Over the years, much has been made of the presumed changes Ginny wrought in Robert Heinlein, particularly in terms of political orientation—highly exaggerated, in Robert's opinion:

> I got over my notions about economics slowly. Ginny did a great deal to reeducate me. But I was stubborn about it. The turning point was an article in *US News and World Report*: "The Final Truth About Pearl Harbor" [he means Admiral Theobald's *The Final Secret of Pearl Harbor,* published

in *U.S. News & World Report* (with a slightly differently worded title) and then released as a book in 1954]. That shook me loose of any emotional attachment to FDR, which left me ripe for Goldwater and his *The Conscience of a Conservative*.

Perhaps I would have made the change on my own, without Ginny. But the question is moot. (RAH, letter to Leon Stover, 06/08/86).

But Heinlein wrought changes in Ginny Gerstenfeld, as well, and this burst of domesticity is an indication. Ginny had never before thought of herself as a particularly "nurturing" type, but she found herself buying summer fruits and daydreaming about how she could prepare them for him, to comfort him with peaches. But she found also that she had become politically "activized" by him. Later, when she found a job (at a brassiere manufacturer), she was scandalized by the pay differences she found:

Baby, I was going to sit down and froth at the mouth about some things I've missed in my ivory tower—we made out the payroll at the office, and I discovered that those poor girls who make the bras can't *possibly* manage to live on their salaries. . . . What do you suppose had happened to ILGWU? . . . As a matter of fact, I'm now in a frame of mind where I'd join a union if it would do them any good. . . . You've really opened my eyes, and with this experience, it adds up to a very permanent change. Oh, dear, there I go frothing anyway, but since it's in a cause you approve of, I hope you'll forgive it. (07/16/47)

They changed each other.

57. Virginia Heinlein, taped interview by author, Third Series, Tape B, Side A (March 27, 2001); see also Virginia Heinlein, letter to Leon Stover, 03/28/89. Virginia Heinlein mentioned the social and legal risk involved in cohabiting illegally in several additional places, as well.

58. Virginia Heinlein, taped interview with author, Tape 9, Side A (March [3?], 2000). The context of the remark is that Miss Tarrant was notorious for blue-penciling any writing that was even faintly suggestive. She is said to have remarked once, however, that she could not so edit Heinlein because he had a native tinge of heresy and his writing was "bad clear through." The Heinleins treasured the remark. Other writers tried to sneak off-color remarks through her defenses, the prize of which, passed around the small community of science fiction writers, was a reference to a (male) cat as a "ball-bearing mousetrap." The story was "Rat Race" by George O. Smith, published in *Astounding* in August 1947.

59.   Virginia Heinlein, letter to author, 04/06/2000.

60.   See, for example, Virginia Gerstenfeld, letter to RAH, 07/28/47.

61.   RAH, letter to Virginia Gerstenfeld, 07/15/47.

62.   RAH, letter to Virginia Gerstenfeld, 07/23/47.

63.   RAH, letter to Judith and Dan Merril, 08/28/61.

64.   RAH, letter to Harlan Ellison, 07/27/65, after Ellison rejected "No Bands Playing" for *Dangerous Visions*.

65.   RAH, "On the Writing of Speculative Fiction," in Lloyd A. Eshbach, ed., *Of Worlds Beyond* (Reading, Pa.: Fantasy Press, 1947).

66.   Heinlein made these points for the first time in the "Speculative Fiction" essay but repeated them many times and based the first half of his 1973 James Forrestal lecture on this thesis. The fullest statement of this argument is set out in the original draft of the lecture, which is printed in full in the nonfiction volumes of the Virginia Edition.

67.   Virginia Heinlein, taped interview by author, Tape 7, Side B (February [28?], 2000).

68.   Eric Temple Bell, letter to RAH, 10/14/47.

69.   Allan Gray, letter to RAH, 11/10/47.

70.   Willy Ley, letter to RAH, 07/26/47.

71.   Cartmill's marriage to Jeanne seems to have broken up while the Heinleins were in Philadelphia—probably in 1945, as the interlocutory decree was still in effect in 1947 per a mention in a May 21, 1947, letter to Willy Ley—and the stories the Heinleins got from friends about the divorce were vague and inconsistent. Cartmill had already become, as Heinlein later said in another context, a "mean drunk." RAH, letter to Judith Klein, 12/01/79.

72.   See, for example, Bill Corson's letter to RAH, 09/17/47.

73.   Virginia Heinlein, letter to author, 02/07/2000.

74.   Henry Sang, letter to RAH, 06/30/47.

75.   Cal Laning, letter to RAH, 07/23/47.

76.   RAH, letter to Cal Laning, 08/17/47.

77.   RAH, letter to Cal Laning, 09/13/47.

78.   RAH, letter to Virginia Gerstenfeld, 05/14/48.

79.   Virginia Heinlein, taped interview by author, Tape 5 (February [29?], 2000).

80.   Bill Corson, letter to RAH, 07/10/47.

81.   RAH, letter to Cal Laning, 07/17/47.

82.   RAH, letter to Virginia Gerstenfeld, 07/28/47.

83.   RAH, "A Bathroom of Her Own," *Expanded Universe*.

84.   Lurton Blassingame, letter to RAH, 08/14/47.

85. Complaint in divorce action filed by Zide, Kamens & Zide.

86. Leslyn Heinlein, letter to Jack Williamson, 08/18/47. This letter sounds sane, rational, and mature—and it is almost the only surviving document in her own voice from the period. But many of the cautions about scurrilous stories Leslyn was very indiscreetly retailing came *after* this letter to Jack Williamson, and in fact Cal Laning cautioned Heinlein, almost a month later, not to talk about his affairs because they came indirectly to him across the continent. Heinlein was able to point out that *he* was not talking—the misinformation Laning was getting was coming solely from Leslyn, whose stories were becoming less oriented.

Dr. Robert James, who has carefully researched and unearthed Leslyn Heinlein's correspondence where recipients ultimately placed them in public archives, suggests Leslyn may have been cultivating Williamson in some special way, as her letters to him were unusually centered and oriented; in all her surviving correspondence, for example, Leslyn never admitted to a problem with alcohol—except once, to Jack Williamson, much later.

On this occasion, Williamson took the opportunity to invite Heinlein to drop by if he happened to be in the neighborhood of Williamson's family ranch in Pep, New Mexico (Jack Williamson, letter to RAH, 10/08/47).

30. Also on the Road . . .

1. RAH, letter to Bill Corson, 09/18/47.
2. RAH, letter to Bill Corson, 09/18/47.
3. RAH, letter to E. E. Smith, 03/13/56.
4. RAH, letter to Bill Corson, 09/18/47.
5. Virginia Heinlein, letter to Leon Stover, 03/28/89.
6. RAH, letter to Cal Laning, 09/13/47.
7. The list of appearances and references in the media is taken from Cal Laning's letter to RAH, 08/30/47.
8. RAH, letter to Cal Laning, 09/13/47.
9. Bill Corson, letter to RAH, 09/20/47.
10. RAH, letter to Bill Corson, 10/03/47.
11. Los Angeles County Records, Book 1835, page 297, dated-stamped Sep 22 1947.
12. Virginia Heinlein, letter to Leon Stover, 03/28/89.
13. Virginia Heinlein, letter to Leon Stover, 03/17/89.
14. For Ginny's attitudes at the time, see, for example, Virginia Gerstenfeld's letter to RAH, 08/26/48.
15. The date on which Robert and Ginny left Los Angeles was not recorded, but

they must have reached Flagstaff, Arizona, by no later than September 25, 1947, as that is the date on which Heinlein started his next story, "Gentlemen, Be Seated."

16. Virginia Heinlein, letter to author, 11/07/99.

17. Lurton Blassingame, letter to RAH, 10/03/47.

18. Virginia Heinlein, letter to Leon Stover, 03/29/89.

19. Virginia Heinlein, taped interview by author, Tape 10, Side B (March [2?], 2000).

20. Tombstone City-Marshall Virgil Earp and his two brothers, Wyatt and Morgan, together with friend "Doc" Holliday, had a shoot-out with the "Clanton gang"—local bullies they had been harassing—in 1881. The event had been mythologized by Bat Masterson in his 1907 memoirs, and a highly fictionalized biography of Wyatt Earp in 1928 had put the "Gunfight at the O.K. Corral" firmly into the mythology of the American West.

21. Virginia Heinlein, IM with author, 08/24/01; see also Virginia Heinlein, letter to Leon Stover, 04/19/89.

22. At one point in an IM with the author (12/06/2001), Virginia Heinlein tried to recall one of the Ticky hums for illustrative purposes and came up with a fragment that must have dated from after 1966, as it referenced the deer on Bonny Doon Road, where Robert and Ginny would live from 1966 to 1987.

23. See, for example, Bill Corson's letter to RAH, 09/20/47.

24. As early as his letter to Virginia Fowler, Alice Dalgliesh's assistant, dated 06/29/47, RAH was planning to write the book in the fall of 1947, but he had not started it as late as mid-October.

25. RAH, second set of Accession Notes, 11/05/68, for Opus 59, "Poor Daddy."

26. Virginia Heinlein, letter to author, 11/07/99; see also Virginia Heinlein, taped interview by author, Tape 7, Side B (March [3?], 2000), and RAH's Accession Notes for Opus. 59, "Poor Daddy."

27. RAH, Accession Notes for Opus 59, "Poor Daddy."

28. Lurton Blassingame, postcard to RAH acknowledging receipt of the story, 11/14/47.

29. RAH, second set of Accession Notes, dated 11/05/68, for Opus 59, "Poor Daddy."

30. In some sense, "Our Fair City" may be regarded as the remote ancestor of *The Moon Is a Harsh Mistress,* since both use the device of a practical-joke-playing nonorganic intelligence.

31. Lurton Blassingame, letter to RAH, 12/08/47.

32. Dorothy Heinlein, letter to RAH, 11/20/47.

33. Irving Crump, letter to RAH, 10/22/47.

34. Willy Ley, letter to RAH, 08/28/46.

35. RAH, letter to Cal Laning, 05/01/46. This letter may be misdated by a year (i.e., 1947), as this date in 1946 is bracketed by correspondence to and from Willy Ley about a proposed trip to Southern California.

36. Both the information about Leslyn and the quotation from Bill Corson letter to RAH, 11/10/47.

37. RAH, letter to Bill Corson, 12/01/47.

38. Lurton Blassingame, letter to RAH, 11/06/47.

39. RAH, letter to Bill Corson, 12/01/47.

40. Henry Sang, letter to RAH, 12/19/47.

41. RAH, letter to Cal Laning, 10/26/47.

42. Almost none of Leslyn's letters to Heinlein were preserved, and we know of them and their contents only by passing mentions in letters to others. The single exception is quoted *infra*. Probably they were later moved to a special file Heinlein maintained for her poison-pen letters through about 1953, which file was apparently destroyed when he moved from Colorado back to California in 1967—fourteen years after the last spate of poison-pen letters—and needed to reduce the amount of business and personal material being moved across country.

The destruction of Leslyn's personal voice in Heinlein's files, and the subsequent failure to preserve her own records—on top of Heinlein's friends maintaining a discreet silence in public commentary, to avoid offending Heinlein—has all but obliterated any direct view of Leslyn. For several years, Virginia Heinlein also refused to discuss Leslyn until it became clear that her own memories of Leslyn, and the things Heinlein had told her, were the only historical sources available. She obliged the author and Robert James, Ph.D., by filling in whatever historical lacunae she could, always with the appropriate caution that the source might be prejudiced. Her recollections, properly vetted for consistency with facts derived from other sources, have been an invaluable help.

43. Leslyn Heinlein, letter to RAH, 11/02/47.

44. RAH, letter to Bill Corson, 12/01/47.

45. Bill Corson, letter to RAH, 12/23/47.

46. RAH, letter to Virginia Gerstenfeld, 05/14/48.

47. RAH, letter to Virginia Gerstenfeld, 05/14/48.

48. RAH, letter to Lurton Blassingame, 11/20/47; see also RAH, letter to Lurton Blassingame, 04/17/54. Heinlein notes his stories had not polled well in November 1947, and he must have received this information in direct response to his May 30, 1947, letter to Stuart Rose asking what kind of story the *Post* would like to see next. However, the particular face-to-face conversation with Ben Hibbs,

reported to Blassingame in April 1954, must have taken place in April 1948, as Heinlein noted it took place the "last time" he was in Philadelphia, and in another place he records his most recent prior visit to Philadelphia as between stops in Washington, D.C., and New York before going back to Hollywood to work with Fritz Lang on his speculative Moon rocket film project. RAH, Naval Personal History Statement, 01/31/51.

49.   RAH, letter to Lurton Blassingame, 11/20/47.

50.   RAH, letter to William Corson, 12/01/47; RAH, letter to Dorothy and Clare Heinlein, 12/08/47.

51.   RAH, "The Happy Days Ahead," *Expanded Universe*.

52.   Heinlein made different parts of this observation about his usual working method at many times and in many places; see, for example, RAH's letter to Lurton Blassingame, 03/16/46:

> I suppose you are used to the method of having a writer send in a few chapters and a synopsis. I will do that when requested to, but, unfortunately, once I have gone that far with a novel, that novel will be finished about ten days later, or at least with such speed that only the fastest possible response from the publisher can affect the outcome very much. I am sorry, but it is a concomitant of how I work. I work slowly on a novel for the first few chapters only. As soon as I can hear the characters talk, it then becomes a race to see whether I put down their actions fast enough not to miss any of them. It is more economical in time and money and it results in a better story for me to work straight through to a conclusion, rather than wait for an editor to make up his mind whether or not he likes it. Editors are not likely to like my advance synopses in any case, for it is simply impossible for me to give the flavor of a story not yet written in a synopsis.

53.   Virginia Heinlein, taped interview by author, Tape 6, Side A (February 28/March 1[?], 2000).

54.   Virginia Heinlein, letter to author, 11/07/99b.

55.   RAH, letter to Rex Ivar Heinlein, 10/09/54.

56.   Virginia Heinlein, letter to author, 11/30/2000.

57.   RAH, letter to Betty Jane Babb, 02/04/59.

58.   Virginia Heinlein, IM with author, 02/05/01.

59.   RAH, letter to Betty Jane Babb, 02/04/59.

60.   RAH, letter to Betty Jane Babb, 02/04/59.

61.   On the author's first visit to Virginia Heinlein's Florida home in 2000, she took down the bottle from its display shelf and opened it; a faint odor lingered, after fifty-three years. The bottle was not forwarded to the RAH Archive following

Virginia Heinlein's death and may have been accidentally discarded during the breakup of the house in February 2003.

62. *Methuselah's Children* was not actually published until 1958; his third hardcover book was *Space Cadet*. *Methuselah's Children* was subsumed into Shasta's Future History project as one of five volumes, which would have been published in 1954 or 1955. But the project fell apart after the third volume of short stories and was never completed.

31. Once More, Dear Friends . . .

1. Virginia Heinlein, letter to Leon Stover, 03/17/89.
2. Virginia Heinlein mentioned this fact to the author in an untaped dinner conversation that took place in March 2001. There appears to be no other documentation of the incident, but it is so characteristic of Heinlein that it is highly believable.
3. Edmund Fuller, letter to RAH, 02/26/46.
4. RAH, letter to Lurton Blassingame, 01/31/48.
5. RAH, letter to Ted Carnell, 07/27/61.
6. Lou Schor, letter to RAH, 02/05/48.
7. See, for example, Chesley Bonestell's letter to RAH, 05/02/47.
8. Lou Schor, letter to RAH, 12/01/47.
9. RAH, letter to Lewis Aker, 08/20/51.
10. In 1948, Mardi Gras was on February 10.
11. This quote, and the information about their experience of Mardi Gras in 1948, was taken from RAH's letter to Bill and Lucy Corson, 03/11/48.
12. RAH, letter to Bill Corson, 03/11/48. This letter indicates they stayed in New Orleans through Mardi Gras, but another letter is datelined from Pass Christian three days before Mardi Gras.
13. RAH, letter to Bill Corson, 03/18/48.
14. Virginia Heinlein, letter to Leon Stover, 03/17/89.
15. RAH, letter to Bill Corson, 03/11/48.
16. RAH, letter to Bill Corson, 03/11/48.
17. Alice Dalgliesh, letter to RAH, 02/25/48.
18. Cal Laning, letter to RAH, 02/17/48.
19. RAH, letter to H. L. Gold, 10/25/57.
20. Both observations from Virginia Heinlein, taped interview by author, Second Series, Tape A, Side B.
21. RAH, letter to Bill Corson, 02/20/48.
22. See, for example, Fritz Lang's letter to RAH, 12/17/47, commiserating with him about his state of mind following the divorce.

23. Fritz Lang, letter to RAH, 03/12/48.

24. Fritz Lang, letter to RAH, 03/12/48.

25. RAH, letter to Fritz Lang, 03/18/48.

26. RAH, letter to Fritz Lang, 03/25/48.

27. "System in the Sky" never did sell—a fact Cal Laning, in a February 1, 1990, letter to Ginny Heinlein, attributes to missteps in marketing by Lurton Blassingame. He had shown the manuscript in 1950 to Charlie Horne, then head of the FAA. Horne, Laning said, shook his head and told him, "Had the aviation industry known of this ms. in 1947, we would have forced its widespread publication—or withdrawn our advertising." Considering the enthusiastic reaction to "Flight into the Future," such a reaction is not beyond the realm of possibility.

Heinlein, mentioned a version of the article, retitled "The Billion Dollar Eye," in his 1980 collection *Expanded Universe*.

28. Virginia Heinlein, taped interview by author, Second Series, Tape A, Side B.

29. Gail Morgan Hickman, *The Films of George Pal* (South Brunswick, N.J.: A. S. Barnes & Co., 1977), 36.

30. RAH, letter to Virginia Gerstenfeld, 05/06/48.

31. See especially RAH's letter to Virginia Gerstenfeld, 05/12/48.

32. Miss Hunt's papers are at the de Grummond Collection, McCain Library and Archives, University of Southern Mississippi.

33. "This Trip to Moon Talk Seen as Pretty Serious," *Los Angeles Times* (May 6, 1948, 22).

34. RAH, letter to Virginia Gerstenfeld, 05/14/48. He also took the opportunity to change his California voter registration from the Lookout Mountain address to an address high in the Hollywood Hills, well north of Sunset (though the address is not an obvious one of his connections). Perhaps this may be taken as an acknowledgment on Heinlein's part that the move might well be permanent, if the connection with the film community became long-lasting—though, equally possible, it may simply be that since Leslyn had sold the house before moving to Port Hueneme, he needed to sever all remaining connections with that address and it represented a move of convenience rather than of intention.

35. RAH, letter to Virginia Gerstenfeld, 05/12/48.

36. RAH, letter to Virginia Gerstenfeld, 05/12/48.

37. Irving Crump, letter to RAH, 04/19/48.

38. RAH, letter to Virginia Gerstenfeld, 06/30/48.

39. RAH, letter to Virginia Gerstenfeld, 05/12/48.

40. RAH, letter to Cal Laning, 11/26/50.

41. RAH, letter to Virginia Gerstenfeld, 05/12/48.
42. RAH, letter to Lurton Blassingame, 05/18/48.
43. Fritz Lang, letter to RAH, 05/24/48.
44. Lang recounted his own version of the events of this two-month period—from the correspondence while Heinlein was out of the state to the "let's part friends" letter he sent Heinlein—in a letter to their mutual friend Willy Ley, published as a tiny (thirteen-page) book by Posthumous Press (Rochester, Mich.) in 2005, *Fritz, Willy & Bob and the Summer of '48.* As is to be expected, Lang's intentions and motivations are somewhat clearer than Heinlein was able to discern, and Lang's letter to Ley confirms that the marketing of *Rocket Ship Galileo* was the important deal-breaker Heinlein thought it was. Lang reverts and reexplains his position to Ley so often, in fact (*any* Moon trip story in Hollywood would be alarming to him), that one has to wonder why Lang didn't simply option the property, if not for cash, then as Heinlein's part of the partnership's capitalization—practices as common in Hollywood in 1948 as they are today.

   Lang has remembered the events not quite as the documents say they happened. Not only was Lang's correspondence contemporaneously preserved by Heinlein, but Heinlein memorialized the events as they occurred in letters to Virginia Gerstenfeld, who was in New York at that time, and in conversations with Los Angeles friends such as Bill Corson, so the actual sequence of events and the offers and inducements actually made are fairly well documented—and not quite as Lang has represented them to Ley.

   Lang has, in fact, left out anything that might tend to exculpate Heinlein, and it may well be that Lang's recounting of the incident was tailored to "play" to his friend. Ley was still hurt by Heinlein's withdrawal of support during the period when Ley was "collaborating" (as a journalist) with the Nazi rocket scientists brought to the United States after World War II to become part of Project Paperclip. (Of this, Lang had asked in a March 1948 letter to Heinlein whether they were both still sulking; Heinlein replied that he was not but perhaps Ley was: he had written a cordial letter to Ley in February [about the same time he received a cordial letter from L. Ron Hubbard], but had not heard back from him.)

   In any case, Heinlein's basic conclusion seems sound, that the collaboration—if, indeed, there was ever enough meeting of the minds to justify the term—ran aground when Lang refused to cooperate with Heinlein's agent in working out terms of participation. When an experienced Hollywood figure tries to cut a newbie's agent out of a deal by saying there is "nothing to discuss," it raises a red flag of insurmountable proportions.

   It may well be that Heinlein did not understand the *auteur* stance from which

Lang was operating—and Lang's letter to Willy Ley suggests that Lang had a much more "subordinate" role in mind for Heinlein than Heinlein had—but Lang's lament that Heinlein "has turned out to be a great disappointment to me as a human being" is surely, and at the very least, disingenuous.

32. Fresh Starts

1. RAH, letter to Virginia Gerstenfeld, 08/06/48.
2. RAH, letter to Virginia Gerstenfeld, 05/14/48.
3. See, for example, Virginia Gerstenfeld letter to RAH, 03/22/46.
4. Virginia Heinlein, taped interview by author, Tape 7, Side A (February 28–March 1, 2000).
5. Cartmill had a severe case of polio, which left him disabled: he had to use a string tied to a foot to work the shift key of his typewriter.
6. Virginia Gerstenfeld, letter to RAH, 05/18/48.
7. Virginia Gerstenfeld, letter to RAH, 05/26/48.
8. RAH, letter to Virginia Gerstenfeld, 05/24/48.
9. Virginia Gerstenfeld, letter to RAH, 05/26/48.
10. RAH, letter to Rex Ivar Heinlein, 05/17/48. The split with Rex was caused by what Heinlein took to be extreme inconsiderateness in 1939 when Rex collected belongings stored with Robert and Leslyn Heinlein. Leslyn was upset, so Robert had become very upset on her behalf.
11. Virginia Heinlein, taped interview by Leon Stover (October 1988), Tape 3, Side A (p. 14 of the transcription in the RAH Archive, UCSC). In *The Best of All Possible Worlds* (New York: Ace Books, 1980), 338, Spider Robinson relates that Heinlein called this story one of his "own personal favorites," in private conversation, saying he had the "single specific intention" of making the reader grin and cry at the same time.
12. RAH, cover letter to Lurton Blassingame, 06/30/48.
13. RAH, letter to Lurton Blassingame, 06/30/48.
14. RAH, *Muster Notes* (1949), 43.
15. Irving Crump, letter to RAH, 06/02/48.
16. RAH, letter to Alice Dalgliesh, 09/21/48.
17. The anecdote is told, but the occasion is undated, in Hickman, *The Films of George Pal.*
18. Nowadays we expect major film studios to be managed from Hollywood locations, but periodically, and especially when studios are purchased by other organizations, the go/no-go authority is located in the financial, rather than the technical and administrative, headquarters—which might be anywhere. At this time, the decision makers of Paramount were headquartered in New York City.

19. RAH, letter to Virginia Gerstenfeld, 08/01/48.

20. Virginia Heinlein, letter to Leon Stover, 03/29/89.

21. Undated except "Thursday," but probably July 31, 1948. The copy was preserved among Heinlein's copies of his correspondence with Virginia Gerstenfeld in the summer of 1948, in the RAH Archive, UCSC.

22. The Hollywood film *Men of Honor* (2000), though set in 1962, gives a good look at the diving suits and technology Heinlein was using in 1948.

23. This version of the anecdote, which differs very slightly in some of the details from Ginny Heinlein's taped recollections in interviews with the author, is taken from the formal "Diving Notes" that Heinlein wrote up as a letter to Ginny in New York, dated 08/10/48.

24. RAH, letter to John W. Campbell, Jr., 08/19/48.

25. RAH, letter to Lurton Blassingame, 05/30/49.

26. RAH, letter to Virginia Gerstenfeld, 08/10/48.

27. RAH, letter to Virginia Gerstenfeld, 08/07/48.

28. RAH, letter to Virginia Gerstenfeld, 08/07/48.

29. RAH, letter to Virginia Gerstenfeld, 08/10/48.

30. RAH, letter to Virginia Gerstenfeld, 08/10/48.

31. RAH, letter to Virginia Gerstenfeld, 08/10/48.

32. Virginia Gerstenfeld, letter to RAH, 08/16/48.

33. RAH, letter to Virginia Gerstenfeld, 08/16/48.

34. RAH, letter to Virginia Gerstenfeld, 08/07/48.

35. Virginia Heinlein, IM with author, 08/05/2000.

36. Don Johnstone, letter to Mary Jean Lermer, 09/03/88.

37. Virginia Gerstenfeld, letter to RAH, 08/26/48.

38. RAH, letter to Rip van Ronkel, 10/29/48.

39. RAH, letter to Rip van Ronkel, 10/29/48. For the reference to Eliot, Virginia Heinlein told Dr. Robert James that *Old Possum's Book of Practical Cats* was one of their favorite read-aloud books. Virginia Heinlein, e-mail to Robert James, Ph.D., 01/06/2003.

40. RAH, letter to Alice Dalgliesh, 09/21/48.

41. Alice Dalgliesh, letter to RAH, 10/06/48.

42. Lurton Blassingame, letter to RAH, 09/23/48.

43. RAH, letter to Lurton Blassingame, 09/27/48.

44. Bill Corson, letter to RAH, undated but by context mid-September 1948.

45. Bill Corson, letter to RAH, undated but by context mid-September 1948.

46. RAH, letter to Lurton Blassingame, 09/27/48.

47. Leslyn's life was indeed in a worse state than Robert knew at the time and only got worse over the next few years. Dr. Robert James made a special study of

Leslyn Heinlein's life after the separation and divorce, published in two articles in *The Heinlein Journal*: "Regarding Leslyn," No. 9 (July 2001) and "More Regarding Leslyn," No. 11 (July 2001). Summarizing Dr. James's findings:

After selling the Lookout Mountain house and all its contents (at a tidy profit), Leslyn called on Admiral Scoles, who had moved to Point Mugu, California, after leaving the Air Materials Laboratory in Philadelphia, to establish the missile development and testing facility there. With Scoles's help, she found an administrative secretarial job there, living in nearby Hueneme. Some material about her life in Hueneme appears in letters to and from Heinlein quoted at various points in the text. Her personal and professional life, however, was even more disordered than appears from the testimonial of mutual friends. Leslyn herself indicated, in a 1953 letter to Fred Pohl, that she became fearful—perhaps "paranoid" is not too strong a word—about security and was ultimately forced to resign because of insubordination in that she refused to follow the orders of her superiors with regard to security matters.

Her personal life was even more disordered. From the somewhat confused reports that circulated among Heinlein's friends, it appears that she had a passionate affair with an officer at Mugu whose initials were also R.H. (no attempt at a further identification has been made)—but who was a married man. Then she married another man at Mugu. The marriage did not last long, but Leslyn implied that he dissipated all her savings, including the proceeds of the sale of the Lookout Mountain house, leaving her impoverished. At some point thereafter, she met and married Jules Mocabee, who she said resembled both her father and Cal Laning. The marriage with Mocabee appears to have been stable, though not happy. They lived with Mocabee's father and ran a combination service station and bar in northern California until Leslyn had what she (somewhat disingeniously) called "a series of strokes" in 1950 which hospitalized her. It was during this hospitalization that the last rounds of poison-pen letters went out to Heinlein's professional contacts (matters covered as they occur in the text).

Leslyn eventually recovered both her health and her mental balance and thereafter disappeared from Heinlein's life entirely. She died in Hueneme in 1981.

48. Telegram unsigned but Sam Kamens to Robert A. Heinlein, 10/20/48.
49. Virginia Heinlein, IM with author, 05/04/2000.
50. RAH, letter to Rip van Ronkel, 10/29/48.

Appendix A: Family Background

1. RAH, letter to Werner Heinlein, 02/27/57.
2. Virginia Heinlein, letter to author, 11/16, 17/2000.

3. See, for example, David McCullough, *John Adams* (New York: Simon & Schuster, 2001), especially chapter 2.

4. Heinlein notes that this Lorenz was the "longest-lived" of all the Heinleins in the direct line of descent, but Heinlein's sister Louise Bacchus, who passed away on December 9, 2007, attained the great age of ninety-eight and a bit more than nine months. William I. Bacchus, e-mail to author, 02/15/2009.

5. RAH, *Expanded Universe*, 1–2.

6. RAH, letter to Judith Merril, 05/16/57.

7. Civil War historian Geo Rule researched the enrollment records of Ohio and Illinois and was not able to find a listing for Lawrence Heinlein. He also checked—unsuccessfully—for Samuel Edward's name, out of an abundance of caution.

8. RAH, interview by Alfred Bester, *Publishers Weekly* (July 3, 1973), 44.

9. The dates seem inconsistent, as the 1843 birthdate for Alva Evans Lyle would make him age seventeen in 1860 and therefore an appropriate age for enlistment. However, the Butler Library sources give an 1853 birth year for Dr. Lyle—the same year as Samuel Edward Heinlein—which would make both of them turning twelve in 1865, just barely eligible for the anecdote. The anecdote, as given by Virginia Heinlein in an interview by the author, did not specify which grandfather; however, the peripatetic Lyles could conceivably return to a homestead in Minnesota, whereas it would have had to be Ohio for the Heinleins.

10. The canvas, painted in 1869 and 1870, is now in the collection of the State Historical Society of Missouri at Columbia.

11. Virginia Heinlein, letter to Leon Stover, 05/01/89.

12. A search of President James Monroe's family genealogy going back to England in the sixteenth century fails to reveal any plausible direct connection to the Ohio Monroes from which Adelia Woods was descended.

13. RAH, letter to Alice Dalgliesh, 01/28/52.

14. Virginia Heinlein, e-mail to author, 10/23/2001.

15. Virginia Heinlein, e-mail to author, 10/18/2001.

16. Virginia Heinlein, taped interview by author, Second Series, Tape B, Side A, see also Virginia Heinlein, letter to author, 10/01/2000; Virginia Heinlein, e-mail to author, 10/23/2001.

17. Undated index card in "Misc 3" file of the RAH Archive, UCSC.

18. Notecard found in the manuscript file for *Starship Troopers*. Heinlein kept a card file of ideas and fragments that could be developed into story figures; when he began a book, he would pull out the cards that might be useful for the book and begin shuffling them in his mind. He always finished a book with more cards than he had started with.

Appendix B: Campaign Biography

1. RAH, letter to Cal Laning, 11/26/50, "My next activity was in a councilmanic campaign for James A. Carter, who was later federal attorney and is now, I believe, a federal judge. The L.A. *Times* tried to pin the red label on Jim, using some (faked?) stationery. I don't know whether Jim was ever a commie or not. He did not sound like one, and he did not act like one—but he certainly was in the company of a large number of them at one time or another. I don't think he actually was; his law partner of that period had been Harry Bridges' attorney. Bridges quit him because this partner of Jim's (name escapes me) would not accept the party line—so Jim was probably never a commie."

2. RAH, letter to Cal Laning, 11/26/50, "I seem to have skipped over the '36 elections, in which I was elected to the Democratic County Central Committee and appointed to the state committee. Nothing much about either, as it might relate to communism and me. In the primary I supported Ordean Rockey, a custard-head but firmly anti-communist; in the final I supported John Dockweiler, a devout Catholic. In 1937 I headed up the county committee's investigation of relief agencies and ran into a lot of semi-overt communist activity, a good deal of it run by Pat Callahan, a registered communist and a Workers Alliance organizer. I tangled with him in front of the county committee and tried to get him thrown out. John Anson Ford, county supervisor, then chairman, might remember this."

INDEX

ABC radio, 408
Abolition movement, 15, 21, 486
Ackerman, Forrest J., 237–38, 248, 264, 272, 279, 288, 313, 398–99
Adam Link (Binder brothers), 279
Adams, John (husband of Keith Hubbard), 363
administration, RAH learns, 139
The Adventure of the Man Who Wasn't There, 579n.33
The Adventures of Huckleberry Finn (Twain), 31
Aerojet, 365
aeronautical engineering, RAH's training in, 13, 85
Aeronautical Materials Laboratory (AML), at Naval Aircraft Factory (Philadelphia), 306–19, 325–28
    friction between civilian and Navy-trained personnel, 311–12
African blood in the Lyle family, 485
After Doomsday (proposal), 373
agents, literary, 357, 398–99
agricultural workers, class warfare against, in California, 187–88
Agriculture Adjustment Act, 162
aircraft carriers, 114, 158
Air Force, U.S., and space exploration, 401
airplane motors, RAH's study of, 53
airplane travel in 1948, 470
Air Scoop, 325, 326
alcoholism, RAH's views on, 385–86
Alice in Wonderland (Carroll), 30
"All," 259–60
Allis-Chalmers, 358
All-Story magazine, 30
Alvarez, Luis, 250–51
Amazing Stories, 31, 98, 129, 233, 237, 249, 550n.79
America
    as country of the future, 499n.15

as RAH's religion, 300
    twentieth century, 12
    values of, 16, 239
American Interplanetary Society, 148
American Legion, 428
American liberal movement, radical-socialist wing of, 123
The American Mercury, 388
American populist tradition, 185
American Rocket Society, 345
Americans for Democratic Action, 377
American Zionist Emergency Council, 346
"America's Maginot Line" (article), 375, 388
" '—And He Built a Crooked House—,' " 266, 315
Angelus Temple (Los Angeles), 182
Annapolis, Md., 49
Annapolis (movie), 79
anthologies, 351
antimatter theme, 291
anti-Semitism, RAH's rejection of, 287
antiwar strike by students (1935), 188–89
Appeal to Reason (journal), 125
appendicitis, as cover story for pregnancy, 509n.24
apple selling, 517n.13
Argosy magazine, 30, 416, 447, 448, 455
Aristotle, 225
Arizona, tour through with Ginny, 436–37
Arkansas, USS (battleship), 97–98
arms race, 362
Army, U.S.
    cadets in, 51
    inadequate provisioning of troops in Spanish-American War, 487–88
Army-Navy exercises, in North Atlantic waters, 97
Army-Navy football games
    1926, 80–82
    1927, 93–94
    movie about, 106
Arnold, Elcy, 147, 152

Aronovitz, David, 513n.22
art (painting and drawing), RAH takes classes in, 224
artificial satellites, 356, 377
Arwine, John S., 255, 302, 304, 313, 318, 322, 324, 327, 340, 358–59, 364, 367, 373, 389, 415, 454, 511n.15
Asimov, Gertrude, 310, 334
Asimov, Isaac, 246, 254, 302, 310–11, 312, 325, 326, 334, 340, 346, 379, 402, 429, 532n.47
    "Nightfall," 302
"Assorted Services" project (of Ackerman and Emsheimer), 264
Astonishing, 248, 275
Astounding Science-Fiction, 216, 227, 229, 234, 236, 238, 240, 248, 250, 254–57, 271, 276, 282, 297, 303, 313, 326, 332, 379, 402, 403–4
    "Probability Zero" department of tall tales, 291
    RAH's list of story notes for, 245–46
    reader's popularity poll in (the "Analytical Laboratory"), 246, 265, 268
    writers of, lost to the World War II effort, 296
Astronautics, 345
astronomy
    RAH's interest in, 30, 35, 36–37, 107
    studies at the Naval Academy, 63
atomic bomb, 251, 346–47, 352–55
    international control of, 359–62
atomic physics, 251
atomic power, 253
atomics, Smyth Report on, sent to RAH, 365–66
atomics articles, RAH's, 375–76
atomics theme of stories, 384
Author & Journalist magazine, 281, 288
Authors Guild, 255, 351
    RAH joins, 275
authors' rights, 378–79, 567n.9
Ayers, William Ira (uncle), 20, 484

Bacchus, Louise Heinlein (sister), 593n.4
Bacchus, Wilfred "Bud," 164, 359
    little Bacchi of, 467
"Back of the Moon" (article), 402
Badeau, Frank, 310
Bailey, Luther, 186, 493
Baldwin, Maria Woods (second wife of Samuel Edward Heinlein), 484, 515n.36
Baldwin Locomotive, Standard Steel Division, 358
Ballistic Computer School, 121
Bancroft Hall, Annapolis Naval Academy, 50
banking, 218
Baptists, 21
Barbary Coast, San Francisco, 88–89
Barnes, Arthur K., 253

Barnsdall, Aline, 181
Baruch, Bernard, 388
Bates, William Horatio, sight exercises, 42, 85
"A Bathroom of Her Own," 431–32
Battle of Britain, 262
battleships, 158
    coal-burning, 74
Baum, L. Frank
    Oz books, 30
    Sky Island, 24
Beard, Chester, 152
Beck, Billie (Harriet Helen Gould) (known as Sally Rand), 25, 37. See also Rand, Sally
Bell, Eric Temple (John Taine), 147, 428
Bellamy, Edward, 15, 36, 535n.13
    Equality, 31
    Looking Backward, 2000–1887, 15, 31, 36, 123, 218, 219, 221, 536n.16
Bellamy, Marion, 536n.13
Benét, Stephen Vincent
    John Brown's Body, 280
    Young Adventure, 280
Berlin Wall, 14
Berrien, F. D., 114, 125, 126, 127
Betty Boop comic strip, 122
Beverly Hills, Calif., 206
"Beyond Doubt" (by Elma Wentz, with advice from RAH), 241, 267–68, 275
Beyond This Horizon (book), 423, 464, 516n.9, 536n.14, 537n.17
"Beyond This Horizon" (serial), 290–92, 303, 315, 332–33, 423
Bible Belt Christianity, 111
Bierce, Ambrose, 284–85
Big Pond Fund, 399, 575n.29
Big Secret, 102
"The Billion Dollar Eye" (article), 588n.27
Binder, Earl and Otto (pseudonym Eando),
    Adam Link, 279
Bingham, George Caleb, 487
Black N, 90–91, 505n.18
"The Black Pits of Luna," 443
blacks, 485
Black Tuesday, 117
Blackwood, Algernon, 227
Blakely, Captain, 155–56
Blassingame, Lurton, 370, 376, 378, 382, 384, 387–88, 390, 398–99, 402, 407, 408, 417, 418, 421, 428, 432, 436, 438, 440, 451, 457, 461, 471–72, 588n.27
Bliss, Arthur, 199
blood collection services, 14
"Blowups Happen," 253–54, 265
Blue Book, 230
Boeing F4B fighters, 114

bohemianism, 122–23
Bolsheviks, 499n.35
bombing of civilians, 353
Bond, Ward, 106
Bond-Charteris Enterprises, 351
Bonestell, Chesley, 449
book contracts, morals clause in, 425
The Book of Knowledge (encyclopedia), 30
book publication, RAH thinking of writing for, 348
Borough, Rube, 185
Boucher, Anthony (pseudonym of A. P. White), 283, 559n.32
Bowen, Brita, 152
Bowen, J. Hartley, 311
Bowling, Frank, 43
boys' books, 348, 351, 378–80
Boy Scouts of America, 248
Boys' Life magazine, 438, 456, 461
Brackett, Leigh, 253, 266
Bradbury, Ray, 253, 254
Brady, Franklyn, 280
Brandley, Buck, 149
breastfeeding, 19
Bremerton, Wash., 133–34
Briggs, Mary, 110–11, 113, 146
Britain
    declares war on Germany (1939), 243
    news from, 199
    in World War II, 352
British (Royal) Navy, RAH's description of, 133
"Broken Wings" (alternate title), 440, 443, 452
Bronner (book editor), 315
Broun, Heywood, 179
Brown, John, 486
Brown, Johnny Mack, 79
Browning, Robert, "Pied Piper of Hamelin," 233
Bryan, William Jennings, 36, 490
Bryan, William Jennings, Jr., 176
Buchenwald concentration camp, 346
Buck Rogers (comic strip), 106
Buffalo Bill, 22
Bureau of Investigation (FBI), 39
Bureau of Navigation (Navy), 48
Burroughs, Edgar Rice, 30
    A Princess of Mars, 30
    Warlord of Mars, 30
"A Business Transaction," 241
Butler, Missouri, 17, 496n.6
Butler Academy (Butler, Missouri), 490
"By His Bootstraps," 277, 288

Cabell, James Branch, 103, 220, 279, 332
    Figures of Earth, 303
    Jurgen: A Comedy of Justice, 102–3

Café au lait au sucre "Caffy" (cat), 471
Cagney, James, 179, 180
California
    earthquakes in, 161
    elections of 1934, and governor race, 173–84
    elections of 1936, 194
    elections of 1938, 201–14
    59th Assembly District, 201–11
    immigration into, from the Dust Bowl, 187–88
    oil conservation initiative, Proposition 5, 247
    oil industry in, 239
    party politics in, 174–75
    politics in, RAH's involvement after the war, 364–65
California Newspaper Publishers Association, 177
California Pacific Exposition (San Diego, 1936), 198
California Real Estate Association, 178, 182
Cal Tech, 171
Cameron, Marjorie, 387
Campbell, Doña, 256, 266, 297, 357
Campbell, John W., Jr., 227, 229, 231, 232–33, 234–35, 236, 237, 240, 241–43, 244, 246, 248–50, 253–56, 258–59, 260–61, 263, 264–65, 266, 271, 274, 275–76, 282–83, 284, 285–86, 289–92, 294, 296–99, 301, 302, 303–4, 308, 313–14, 315–16, 328, 332, 335, 345, 349, 357, 376, 378–80, 403–4, 425, 547n.25, 553n.51, 566n.2, 567n.9
    acceptance letter, 241–43
    "All" (collaboration with RAH), 258–59
    confrontation with, over rights, 357
    Heinleins as godparents of child Leslyn, 345
    letter to RAH about contraterrene matter, 275–76
    meets RAH in New York, 256
    misunderstandings of RAH's themes and stories, 249–50
    off-and-on friendly correspondence with, 284, 285–86
    own science fiction writing, 258
    RAH calls, cancelling trip to New York after Pearl Harbor attack, 294
    RAH wish to tell he was retiring from pulp fiction, 264–65
    reactions to long-life series, 274
    rejection letters from, 232–33, 234–35, 237, 282–83, 553n.51
    self-aggrandizing statements of, re wartime research, 379–80
    wartime correspondence with RAH re war, 296–99
Campbell, Leslyn, 345
Campbell, Philinda Duane, 266, 303–4
Camp Goodland, 259

Canadian Douglas Plan, 219–20
Canadian Social Credit Union, 231
"candidatitis," 208–9
Canterbury, Kate, 495n.2 to ch. 1
Cantor, Eddie, 99
Capone, Al, 78, 169, 501n.35
"The Captains and the Priests," 232, 239–43
Captain's Mast, 140–42
carbon-black idea, 377
Carey, Kathleen, 43
Carnell, Michael, 389
Carnell, Ted, 321, 343, 389, 399, 575n.29
Carroll, Lewis, *Alice in Wonderland,* 30
Carter, James M., 187, 489, 594n.1
Cartmill, Cleve, 186, 211, 216–17, 236, 241, 252,
    253, 270, 284, 351, 375, 380, 396, 429,
    582n.71
    "Deadline," 379
    "Oscar," 270
Cartmill, Jeanne, 396, 582n.71
car travel, forbidden to midshipmen, 77
Catholics, 21
Catledge, Turner, 179
CBS, RAH interview on, 13–14
CCC (Civilian Conservation Corps), 162, 230
    a story about, 230–33
Central High School, Kansas City, 33, 40, 43–45
The Centralian high school yearbook, RAH notices
    in, 43–45
Century of Progress World's Fair, Chicago,
    162–63
Chamber of Commerce, California, 182
Chandler, Harry, 189
characters in a story, hearing them talk, 443,
    586n.52
Charles, Joel, 306
Charteris, Leslie, 351, 374–75, 384–85, 572n.68
    The Saint's Choice, 374
Charter of the United Nations, 346
Chase, Stuart, *Tyranny of Words,* 217, 263
Chastain, Dr., 18
Chautauqua circuit, 500n.29
Cherokee Indian blood in the Lyle family, 485
chess, 20
Chesterfield Club (Kansas City), 112, 512n.6
Chicago, Ill.
    Army-Navy game of 1926 in, 80–82
    Bam's short stay in, as child, 489–90
    radicalism in, 490
    RAH studies in, 259–63
    South Side, 262
Chicon (second world science fiction convention),
    263
China, in World War II, 352
Chinatown, San Francisco, 88–89

Christian Church (Disciples of Christ), 21
Christianity, 222
    Bible Belt, 111
    RAH's disbelief in, 238
The Christian Science Monitor, 388
Christmas, Heinlein family's celebration of,
    445–46
Chrysler Building, 121, 449
Churchill, Winston, 256
circus, RAH goes to, and is amused by elephants,
    443
Civic Research League, 194
Civilian Military Training Camp (CMTC), 41,
    46, 58
civilians, bombing of, 353
Civil War, 485–87
Clark, John, 256
Clark, Robert N. S., 112, 114, 130, 134, 137, 152,
    167, 511n.15, 513n.14, 522n.27
Clarke, Arthur C., 13, 336
class warfare, 173, 499n.35
Clifton, Robert, 212, 364–65, 380–81, 530n.29,
    534n.33
Clifton, Susie (Florence G. McChesney), 212–13,
    327, 364–65, 405, 406
Clifton's Cafeteria (Los Angeles), 254
Clingerman, Mildred, 539n.1
Clinton, Clifford, 193
Coca-Cola, 35
codependency theme, 542n.35
cohabitation, illegality of, 424–25
Cohen, Octavus Roy, 304
Coign, Armand, 368–69
Coinage Act of 1873, 168
Cold War, 14, 362
Collier's magazine, 230, 237, 265, 388, 415–18,
    423, 434, 461, 541n.19
Colón, Panama, 88
Colorado silver mine venture, 167–70
Colorado Springs, Colo., RAH's plan to live with
    Ginny in, 469–73
Colorado Sunshine Club, 167, 186–87, 553n.41
Columbian Exposition (1893), 489–90
Columbia Pictures, 117, 143, 145, 540n.13
"Columbus Was a Dope," 416
Combat Information Center (CIC) equipment,
    334
Comet magazine, 279
Comintern, Seventh World Congress of (1935),
    193
command philosophy, 97
commercial space movement, 15
"Common Sense," 288
Common Sense (Paine), 15
communications, RAH's experience in, 116

communism, 173–74
  RAH's opposition to, 257
  as "Red Fascism," 214, 532n.49
  in Russia, 499n.35
Communist International, 191
Communist Party
  infiltration of Democratic Party and EPIC, 197–98, 211–14, 377
  unwelcome endorsement of RAH in 1938 campaign, 205, 214
Comstock, Merrill, 119, 132
Comstock laws, 102
concentration camps, 346
conduct, ranking of, at Naval Academy, 79
Conklin, Groff, 373
conscription, 262
contraterrene matter (CT) theme, 275–76, 291
Conyngham, USS, 293
Coolidge, Calvin, 47
co-op movement, 486
Cornog, Robert, 167, 250–51, 253, 268, 276, 359–60, 365, 377, 525n.35
Coronado, Calif., 158
Corson, Bill, 205, 208, 255, 272, 295, 301, 312, 317–18, 321–22, 324, 384, 408, 429, 435, 437, 439, 441–42, 452, 472
"Cosmic Construction Corps," 230–33
  accepted and renamed "Misfit," 236–37
Cosmopolitan magazine, 461
Coughlin, Charles Edward "Father," 180, 528n.17
Count Basie, 512n.6
counterculture, 15
County Librarians' Association, Los Angeles, RAH's talk to, 455
courts martial (GCM), 341
"Coventry," 253, 258, 264, 265, 290, 546n.11
The Craft (magic), 222
"Creation Took Eight Days," 282, 285
crime, organized, 500n.35
Cronkite, Walter, 13
Crowley, Aleister, 345, 365, 374
  Book of the Law, 374, 569–570n.15
Crown Publishers, 373, 382, 448
Crump, Irving, 438, 456, 461
Cuba, 490–92
Cuba Libres, RAH's favorite drink, 306
Cuppy, Will, 304
currency, value of, in 1930s vs. in 2000s, 514n.33
Curry, Elinor (RAH's first wife), 45, 47, 112–14, 117, 143, 146, 476, 513n.14, 520n.40
  adultery of, during honeymoon with RAH, 114
  divorce from, 128, 129, 131
Curtis, Charles, 98

"Da Capo," 264
Dalgliesh, Alice, 402, 407, 437, 451, 471
  The Silver Pencil, 437
Damico, Tony, 316, 344
dances, in Annapolis, 64, 85
"Dance Session" (poem), 394–95
Dan Patch (horse), 17
Dark Days, 70
Dart, Caryl, 159
Darwin, Charles
  On the Origin of Species, 32, 35
  The Descent of Man, 32, 35
Darwinian thinking, 500n.26
dating, double, in bed, 512n.21
Daugherty, Walter, 278, 288
David, Joseph B., 163
David Lamb (character), 67–68
Davis, Bette, 365
Davis, James, 188
Dawes, Vice President, 81
Deacon, Sergeant, 137
de Camp, Catherine Crook, 302, 310, 318, 334, 410
de Camp, L. Sprague, 253, 256, 301–2, 304, 305, 307, 310, 318, 326, 334, 336, 356, 379–80, 410, 418, 421, 429
  RAH's advice, to tone himself down, 311–12
de Camp, Lyman, 310
Deems, Navigator, 134
Deladrier, Capitaine, 53, 84, 93
Delos Wait (character), 65
del Rey, Lester, "The Luck of Ignatz," 246
demerits, 82–83
Democratic Central Committee (California), 196, 211–14, 493
Democratic National Committee, 176, 493
Democratic National Convention
  1940 (Chicago), 255, 261–63
  1944, 327
Democratic Party, 32
  in 1938 election, 217–18
  in 1946 election, 405–6
  in California, 173–84, 185, 194–98, 201–14, 218
  communist infiltration of, 197–98, 211–14, 377
  Freethinker wing of, 329
  in Kansas City, 21–22
  RAH's post-War involvement with, 380–81
  split in, between EPICs and traditional Democrats, 195–96, 211
Denver, Colo., 164–68, 187, 277–81
  Pendergast men in, 525n.38
Denver Athletic Club, 167
Denver Post, 187
depression, late-onset, 533n.8

Destination Moon (movie), 13
destroyers, 158
Deutsch, Bill, 280
The Devil in the Cheese (play), 102
"The Devil Makes the Law," 265–66
de Weldon, Felix W., 342
Dewey, John, 123–24, 511n.19, 516n.9
    Individualism: Old and New, 521n.11
Diana Productions, 456
Dickens, Charles, *A Tale of Two Cities,* 546n.11
Dirac, Paul, 276
disabled veterans, 373
    Leslyn's work in rehabilitation of, 344, 349–50
discipline, 126, 140–42
diving, 462–63
divorce, 129, 519n.14
    co-respondent in, 519n.14
Dockweiler, John, 194
dog-people theme, 274–75
Doheny, Edward L., 501n.36
double dating in bed, 512n.21
double standard, in the Navy, 142
Douglas, C. H., *Social Credit,* 219–21
Douglas, Helen Gahagan, 327, 405–6, 561n.14
Douglas, Melvyn, 201, 561n.14
Douglas, Myrtle R., 238
Downer, Dick, 152, 156
Downey, Sheridan, 176, 182
Doyle, Sir Arthur Conan, 31
    "The Horror of the Heights," 282
Dreamland Auditorium (Los Angeles), 182
drinking, 136–37
Dugan, Grace "Cats". *See* Sang, Grace Dugan
Duncan, George B., 46
Dunne, J. W., 219, 226
    An Experiment with Time, 103, 147, 234
Dunsany, Lord, 227
Durant, Ariel, 39
Durant, Will, 39, 121
dust devil story, 438
Dymaxion House, 371, 569n.1

Eagle lunar lander, 13
Earp, Wyatt, 584n.20
earthquakes, 161
"Easy Job," 436
Eddy, Nelson, "The Ballad of Rodger Young,"
    348–49
Edgerly, Mira, 225
Edison, Thomas, 106, 449
Edwards, Charles, 358
Edward VII, 199
Einstein-Minkowski space-time, 147
elderly, economic selfishness of, in RAH's view,
    209–10

elections of 1934, in California, 173–84
elections of 1936, in California, 194
elections of 1938, in California, 201–14, 217–18
elections of 1944, Roosevelt's 4th term, and choice
    of Truman as Vice President, 327
elections of 1946, 404–6
    RAH's idea to give the presidency to the
        Republicans, 327
Electrical Experimenter magazine, 30
Electric Park, Kansas City, 37
electric power, cheap, RAH's plan for, 232
elephants, 443
Eleventh Commandment (Thou Shalt Not Get
    Caught), 153
Elite Post Card Co., 24
Elks Magazine, 402, 406
Ellis, Havelock, 37
Elysia (Valley of the Nude) (film), 163
Elysian Fields nudist camp, 163
Emerson, Ralph Waldo, 124
    "Over-Soul," 25
Empire State Building, 121
Emsheimer, Ted, 264
End Poverty in Civilization, 185
End Poverty League, 175, 185, 186, 190, 493
engineering, studies at Naval Academy, 63
Enola Gay, 353
EPIC—"End Poverty in California," 174–84,
    185–98, 201, 203–4, 211–14, 218, 219–20,
    254, 493
    candidates from, 218
    communists in, 211–14
    constitution proposed, to be written by RAH,
        186, 190–91, 493
    continued survival after 1934 defeat, 185–98
    convention (1935), 190–91, 493
    economic plan, 219–20
    fracturing of, into two groups, 185–86
    histories written about, 194
    nominal control of Democratic Party, 201
    political alliances of, 193
    waning power of, 211
EPIC News, 174, 185–86, 201, 203–4, 211, 218,
    219, 254
epistemology, 217, 224
equator, ceremonies when crossing, 135
"Eros and Agape" (introduction to Theodore
    Sturgeon's posthumous novel, *Godbody*),
    563n.56, 566n.2
Eshbach, Lloyd, 423, 428
Esnault-Pelterie, Robert, 148
Esperanto, 36, 238
etiquette, instruction in, at the Naval Academy, 64
Evans, Anna (great-grandmother), 485, 489
Evening News-Standard, 189

evolution, a story about, 230
Ewing, Gen. Thomas, 487
Executive rating, 99–100
extracurricular activities (high school), 35
extramarital affairs, 162, 222

F4B fighters, 114
FAA (Federal Aviation Administration), 588n.27
Facts magazine, 388
Fall, Albert B., 501n.36
"False Dawn" (alternate title), 290
"Fans are Slans" movement, 552n.32
fantasy, 461
The Fantasy Film Works of George Pal (DVD),
    495n.2 (to Introduction)
Fantasy News fanzine, 267
Fantasy Press, 423
fanzines, 254, 267
Farley, James A., 179, 180, 262
Farnham's Freehold, 578n.11
fascism, Popular Front against, 193
fascist governments, 188, 198
    Black and "Red," 214
    United Front against, 191
Fath, E. A., *The Elements of Astronomy,* 107
Fat Man, 352, 354
FBI, 379
feminist theme, 542n.35
fencing and swordplay, RAH's, 28, 53–54, 58, 69,
    73, 77, 79–80, 85, 93
Ferrer Modern Schools, 39
fiction, Victorian vs. Modernist, 12
film industry, opposition to Sinclair, 176–77
film making, packaging deals in, 462
Fink, Dr. David Harold, 413
Finnegan, Joseph, 89–90
Finney, Charles G., *Circus of Dr. Lao,* 199
"Fire Down Below," 264
Fiske, John, 39, 217, 500n.26
Fitts, Burton, 195, 533n.53
Fitzsimmons Army Hospital, Denver, 159–60,
    164–66
    slack treatment at, 165–66
"Flight into the Future" (article collaboration with
    Cal Laning), 434, 588n.27
Flippin, Royce, 66
flying, RAH's unfulfilled love of, 83–85
flying saucers, 580n.47
food, world problem of, 389
football, 80–82
Ford, Henry, 106
Ford, John (movie director), 106
Ford, John Anson, 183, 193–94, 493
Ford Instrument Company, 121, 126–27
"Foreign Policy" (alternate title), 269–70, 271

Forensics (debate) squad, 35
Forman, Edward, 345
Fort, Charles, 282
Fort Clayton, Panama, 137
Fort Leavenworth, Kansas, 46, 58
Fortune magazine, 187
Fort Worth, Texas, 439
For Us, the Living: A Comedy of Customs, 220–23,
    228, 230–33, 240, 243, 248, 249, 250, 258,
    260–61, 283, 290, 374, 536n.17, 537n.19,
    539n.1, 539n.30
    rejected, 231, 237, 253
Fourier, Charles, 219, 536n.15
Fowler, Virginia, 451
Fox Film Corporation, 106
Fox Movietone News, 151–52
Foy, Bryan, 163
France
    invaded by Germany (1940), 256
    mobilizes against Germany (1939), 243
Frank, Raymond, 530n.26
free love, in stories, 260–61
Freemasonry, 222
"Free Men," 390
Freethinker wing of the Democratic Party, 32, 329
French and Spanish companies, at the Naval
    Academy, 51, 59
frenching out (absent without leave), 89–91
Fromm, Erich, 536n.16
frontier, 488
Frontier Exposition (Fort Worth, 1936), 199
Fuller, Buckminster, 371
Fuller, Edmund, 373, 382, 448
fundamentalism, RAH's rejection of, 35
Future, 281, 288
Future History series
    abridged collection proposal, 382
    Future History chart, 276
    hardcover proposal, 448
    notes for, 390
    See also history of the future
Futuria Fantasia, 254
Futurians, 257, 280

GALCIT (the Guggenheim Aeronautical
    Laboratory at Cal Tech), 345, 360, 365
gambling, on board ship, 139
Garmes, Lee, 463
Garrison, John and Alice, 167, 187
gasoline rationing, 306
Gay, Hobart "Hap," 46, 84
Geisel, Theodor Seuss (Dr. Seuss), 455
General Order No. 11, 483
General Semantics, 236, 259, 263, 280–81, 332
General Services company theme, 264–65, 267

General Tire, 365
genetics theme, 287–88, 289–92
"Gentlemen, Be Seated," 447, 455
George, Henry, *Progress and Poverty,* 36
German Rocket Society, 438
German scientists, in American rocketry, 386
Germany
    culture of, need to be destroyed, according to
        RAH, 335
    invasion of France (1940), 256
    invasion of Poland (1939), 243
    invasion of Russia (1941), 278
    Nazi, 193, 198
    prison camps, 254
    superweapons developed by, 347
germ theory, 489–90
Gernsback, Hugo, 30, 31, 117, 215
Gerstenfeld, Virginia "Ginny" (3rd wife), 330–34,
        336–37, 341–42, 357–58, 393–96, 400, 404,
        411–14, 418, 421–26, 431, 435–37, 439–40,
        451–73, 491, 574n.2, 577n.3, 580n.56
    accepted as "family member," 400
    breakup with fiancé George Harris, 393, 574n.2
    considers RAH's marriage proposal, and accepts,
        468–69
    disappears, 404
    emotional handling of separation from RAH,
        459–60
    fiancé George Harris, 330
    flies to Colorado Springs to meet RAH, 470–73
    goes to stay in New York without RAH, 454–70
    goodbye to, at end of WWII, 357–58
    helps RAH move, 421–22
    house guest of the Heinleins, 393–95, 400
    influence on RAH's politics, 580n.56
    kept a secret from close friends during wander
        year in trailer, 439–40, 451–55, 471–73
    love letter to RAH, 413–14
    love of cats, 451–52
    in love with RAH, 424
    marries RAH in New Mexico, 473
    moves West to attend UCLA, 393–96
    notes Leslyn's drinking problem, 412
    pet names for, 425
    poem by, 464–65
    politicization of, 580n.56
    recollections of Leslyn, 158
    relationship with RAH, 431, 435–37
    separation from RAH on his D.C. and L.A.
        trips, 451–55
    sexual relations, 577n.3
    skating prowess, 394–96
    testing dilemma, 341–42
    thyroid deficiency, 414
    typing help to RAH, 423, 426

Gettysburg Address, 220
ghosts, 371, 415
ghostwriting
    by others, not RAH, 351, 374–75, 572n.68
    RAH uneasy about engaging in, 401
GI Bill, 393
Gifford, Jim, *Robert A. Heinlein: A Reader's
        Companion,* 492
Gnostic Mass, 374
God, 73
Goddard, Robert, 355, 377–78
The Gods of Mars (Burroughs), 30
gods owning people theme, 274–75
Golden Age of science fiction, 260
Golden Dawn sex magic, 345
Golden Gate International Exposition (San
        Francisco, 1939), 199
"Goldfish Bowl" (alternate title), 282, 303, 373
Gold N, 90, 93, 505n.18
Goldwater, Barry, *The Conscience of a Conservative,*
        581n.56
Gopher Hole (trailer), 433–34
    sold, 451
Gordon, Pierre, 219
"The Gostak Distims the Doshes," 234
Graf Zeppelin dirigible, 106
Grand Coulee Dam, 249
Grand Olympic Auditorium, EPIC campaign rally
        in, 181–82
Grant, Alan, Anarky graphic-novel series, 511n.19
Grant, Ulysses S., 78
grass-roots campaigns, 180, 206
"gravity gauge" idea, 455
Gray, Allan "Gus," 96, 108–9, 123, 124, 148,
        428–29, 510n.30, 511n.15
Gray, Zane, 546n.11
Great Depression, 13, 117, 143, 174, 178,
        517n.13, 539n.1
Green, Edwin, 553n.40
"The Green Hills of Earth," 394, 402–4, 407,
        411, 449
    title unconsciously appropriated from C. L.
        Moore, 403
Greenwich Village, 121–25
Greenwood Grammar School, Kansas City, 24–26,
        33
Gripsholm Swedish "mercy ship," 320–21
Groves, Leslie, 346, 361, 363
Guam, 293, 295
Guantánamo Bay, Cuba, 74, 75, 89, 98, 121
guided-missile research, 377
"Gulf," 23, 567n.9, 579n.33
gunnery, 126–28, 135
gunnery drills, 76
Gurney, Marshall Barton "Marsh," 67–68, 118

Gymkhana at Naval Academy
  1927, 85
  1928, last year, 95

Haggard, H. Rider, 511n.19
Haight, Raymond, 181, 183
Haiti, 76
Hall Brothers Lithography, 24
Halley's Comet, 22
Hallmark Cards, 24
Halsey, William F. "Bull," 83–84, 91, 514n.28
"Ham and Eggs" old-age pension scheme, 209–10
Hamilton, Edmond, 266, 546n.11
Harding, Murphy & Tucker, 131
Harding, Warren G., 501n.36
Harlow, Jean, 179
Harriman, W. Averell, 346
Harris, George, 330, 333, 357
Harrison, James, 81
Harsanyi, Zsolt de, *The Star Gazer: A Novel of the Life of Galileo*, 280, 552n.38
Hart, William S., 27
Harvard Classics, 31
Hawaii, 148–51
Hawkins, Augustus, 183
Hawkins, Lee (collaborator with E. E. Smith), 98
Hawkins, Willard G., 281, 288
Hay, Ian, *The First Hundred Thousand*, 562n.28
Hayakawa, S. I., 263
Hayland, Mrs. Herbert, 152
Haymarket Riots, 490
Hays, Will, 184
Hayworth Hall (alternate title), 439–40, 443–44
hazing (at the Naval Academy), 65–68, 91–92, 100–101, 508n.13
"Heil!" 254
Heinlein, Alice Lewis (sister-in-law, married to Lawrence Lyle), 523n.6
Heinlein, Alma Ann (great-aunt), 484
Heinlein, Bam (mother). *See* Lyle, Bam
Heinlein, Clare. *See* Heinlein, Jesse Clare "Jay" (brother)
Heinlein, Dorothy (wife of Jesse), 259–60, 262, 296, 438
Heinlein, Dorothy Martin, 502n.52, 520n.40
Heinlein, Edward Ray (nephew), 117, 515n.38
Heinlein, Elinor (RAH's first wife). *See* Curry, Elinor
Heinlein, Francis Marion "Frank" (great-uncle), 482, 483–84
Heinlein, Harvey Wallace (great-uncle), 18, 19, 24, 484
Heinlein, Jesse Clare "Jay" (brother), 19–20, 25, 28, 29–30, 200, 255, 259–60, 271, 296, 367, 479

Heinlein, Jessie (great-aunt), 18
Heinlein, Jessie Clare (aunt), 18, 20, 484
Heinlein, Kitty (aunt), 117
Heinlein, Lawrence (great-grandfather), 482–83
Heinlein, Lawrence (great-uncle), 18
Heinlein, Lawrence Lewis ("Bud") (nephew), 509n.28
Heinlein, Lawrence Lyle (brother), 18, 19, 28–29, 39, 40, 45, 56, 69–70, 104, 143, 159, 273, 296, 367, 479, 509n.28, 523n.6
  enlisting in the Great War, 28–29
  letter to, 56
  marriage of, 40
  and occupation of Japan, 367, 479
  rose to Major General rank, 479
  second marriage of, 159
Heinlein, Lawrence Ray "Ray" (uncle), 117–18, 484, 515n.36
Heinlein, Leonard Smith (great-uncle), 484
Heinlein, Leslyn MacDonald (second wife). *See* MacDonald, Leslyn
Heinlein, Lorenz/Lawrence (great-great-great grandfather), 481
Heinlein, Louise (sister), 19, 164, 359, 467, 593n.4
Heinlein, Mary Alice (great-aunt), 483
Heinlein, Mary Jean (sister), 20, 28, 33, 200, 202, 207, 223, 364, 461, 466–67, 520n.40
Heinlein, Oscar Allen (great-uncle), 18, 484, 495n.2 to ch. 1
Heinlein, Oscar Allen, Jr. (cousin), 91–92, 495n.2 to ch. 1
Heinlein, Rex Ivar (brother), 18, 40, 41, 48, 69, 77–78, 86, 94, 121, 159, 161, 164, 202, 238, 244–45, 466, 496n.9
  appointment to United States Naval Academy, 40
  in the Army in World War II, 296
  childhood rivalry with RAH, 19
  graduation, 86
  joins Army, after graduation from Naval Academy, 94
  at the Naval Academy, 48, 61–62, 83, 85
  parents' favorite, 29, 41, 77–78
  RAH's rivalry with, 69
  reconciliation with, 461
  rejected by RAH, 244–45
  ROTC member, 34
  vision problems, 85
Heinlein, Rex Ivar (father), 17–22, 27, 29, 33, 34, 71–73, 77, 143, 202–3, 490–92, 515n.38
  "brought home on a shutter," 492
  depression of, leading to involutional melancholia, 202–3
  discipline rules, 34

Heinlein, Rex Ivar *(continued)*
   enlisted in the Spanish-American War, 491–92
   family background, 484
   finances of, 27, 29
   funeral of, 515n.38
   gifts from, 118
   gives RAH a hundred dollars, 69
   golden wedding anniversary, 461, 466–67
   house purchase, 33
   occupation, 24, 104
   political connections, 40
   psychologically shattered by Rose Elizabeth's
     death, 72–73, 77
   RAH's letter to, asking to borrow money, 71–72
   visit to Annapolis, 86
Heinlein, Robert Anson
   (1907) birth, 18
   (1907) as child, 18–32
   (1914) enters school in first grade, 24–26
   (1916) first jobs, starting at age nine, 27
   (1919) high school years, 33–45
   (1920–1922) jobs as teen, 39
   (1923) hiking trip to Colorado, 40
   (1923) preparing for college, 40–43, 46–47
   (1924) nominated to Annapolis, 42, 47
   (1925) admitted to Annapolis Naval Academy, 48
   (1925) enters Naval Academy, 49–60
   (1925) Plebe Year, 61–73
   (1926) practice cruise, 74–76
   (1926) Youngster Year, 74–86
   (1927) Frenching Out incident, demerits, loss of
     leave, time in the brig, and aftermath, 89–92
   (1927) named CPO of regiment, 93
   (1927) practice cruise, 87–90
   (1927) Second Class Year, 87–96
   (1927) trip home to Kansas City, 92
   (1928) First Class Year, 97–109
   (1928) practice cruise, 97–98
   (1928) rated midshipman 2PO, 99
   (1929) rated midshipman 1PO, 104
   (1929) applies for Rhodes Scholarship, 107–8
   (1929) graduation from Naval Academy, 108
   (1929) receives commission, 109
   (1929) post-graduation return to Kansas City,
     110–14
   (1929) marriage to Elinor Curry, 113–14, 115
   (1929) on the *Lexington,* 114–56
   (1930) divorce from Elinor Curry, 128,
     129, 131
   (1932) meets Leslyn MacDonald, and proposes
     marriage, 146–48
   (1932) weds Leslyn MacDonald, 152
   (1932) promoted to lieutenant, j.g., 155, 159
   (1932) on the *Roper,* 156–57, 158–63
   (1933) tuberculosis treatment, 159–66

   (1934) forced retirement from Navy for medical
     reasons, 167, 170
   (1934) visit to family in Kansas City, 169
   (1934) advanced degree work, 171–72
   (1934) volunteering for EPIC campaign,
     177–78
   (1935) with the EPIC movement, 185–98
   (1935) lecture to West Hollywood Democratic
     Club, 188–90
   (1935) letter in *Hollywood Citizen-News,* signed
     "Lieut., U.S. Navy," 189–90, 191–92, 305,
     530n.15
   (1935) purchase of house on Lookout Mountain
     in Los Angeles, 192–93
   (1936–1937) allegiances during EPIC
     fracturing, 185–97
   (1936) work in unifying the Democratic Party
     in California, 196–98, 200
   (1938–1939) esoteric studies and first writings,
     219–42
   (1938) runs for California 59th Assembly
     District seat, 201–11
   (1938) Democratic Party organizing, 203,
     214–15
   (1938) loses Democratic primary to a
     Republican, 211
   (1938) political disillusionment of, giving up on
     the Democratic Party, 214–15
   (1938) first steps getting into SF writing,
     215–18
   (1939) memo re start of World War II,
     243–44
   (1939) fight with and rejection of brother Rex
     Ivar, 244–45
   (1939) consultantship on oil conservation
     initiative, 247
   (1940) pays off mortgage on Lookout Mountain
     house on proceeds of sales from writing, 254
   (1940) road trip across country to New York,
     256
   (1940) meets fans in New York, 257
   (1940) politics at Democratic National
     Convention of 1940, 262–63
   (1940) buys used car from Doc Smith, 265
   (1940) Christmas gifts to and from Leslyn, 270
   (1941) remodeling Lookout Mountain house,
     with studio, 271–73
   (1941) speech at Denver WorldCon, 279,
     531n.40
   (1941) considers retiring from writing for pulps,
     283, 286
   (1941) support of Leslyn's mother, 289
   (1941) possible recall into Navy service, 292
   (1941) asks for active duty assignment after Pearl
     Harbor attack, 293–305

(1941) personal preparation for wartime duty, 295

(1941) seeks Naval Reserve commission, 295–97

(1942) offer of job at Aeronautical Materials Laboratory in Philadelphia, 299–305

(1942) rents out Los Angeles house, 301, 304, 364

(1942) wartime civilian employment for Naval Aircraft Factory, Philadelphia, 305–19

(1942) dislikes conditions at AML wartime job, 309

(1943) evaluation and promotion at AML, 316

(1943) wartime strains on marriage, 317

(1943) interest in joining merchant marines, 318–19

(1943) on medical leave in hospital without pay, 319–21, 324–25

(1944) realization of own unfitness for combat, 324–25

(1944) considers resuming writing, 325–26

(1945) thinks seriously about going back to writing, 348

(1945) reaction to Hiroshima, 353–54

(1945) resigns from NAES at war's end, 354

(1945) moon rocket project, 354–70, 376, 377–78, 386

(1945) final satisfactory year of wartime work, 350–51

(1945) cross-country drive home to Los Angeles, 358–63

(1945) return to Los Angeles after the war, 363–65

(1945) relaxation in Murrieta Hot Springs Hotel, Murrieta, California, 367–70

(1945) return to Hollywood house after renter vacated, 371

(1946) work at Naval Aircraft Factory portrayed as boondoggle, in a Philadelphia paper exposé postwar, 379–80

(1946) bans liquor from house and stops drinking, 385

(1946) Ginny comes as house guest, 393–95

(1947) copes with Leslyn's drinking, 412–13

(1947) divorce from Leslyn proposed, 419–21

(1947) burning of personal papers, 421

(1947) divorce from Leslyn not final, 424–25

(1947) leaves Lookout Mountain house, 421–22

(1947) trailer sought by, 424–25, 433–34

(1947) plans post-divorce, 430–31

(1947) divorce from Leslyn finalized, 432, 435, 473

(1947) trailer living with Ginny, 435–37

(1948) New Orleans and Mardi Gras with Ginny, 453

(1948) trip to D.C. without Ginny, 453–54

(1948) trip to L.A. without Ginny, to discuss film projects, 454–70

(1948) change of California voter registration address, 588n.34

(1948) relationship with parents and siblings in Los Angeles, 461, 466–67

(1948) collaboration with van Ronkel on film script, 462–66

(1948) proposes marriage to Ginny in a letter, 468

(1948) arrives in Colorado Springs to meet Ginny, 470–73

(1948) marries Ginny in New Mexico, 473

(1950) attempt to get security clearance, 532n.49

(1988) worldwide grief at death of, 11

advice to himself, 57–58

anti-racist upbringing, 21, 33

art classes taken by, 224

athletic abilities and preferences at Annapolis, 53–54

on authors' sale of rights to own work, 315–16, 351, 356–57, 378–79, 567n.9

award for fencing, 86

books as presents for his birthday given at WorldCon, 280

boxing and wrestling requirement at Naval Academy, 53, 503n.16

burning of papers (1947), 421

burning of papers (1987), 537n.24

calm presentation of self to outside world during times of personal trouble, 414–15

campaign biography for 1938 campaign, 493–94

cats and dogs, attitude toward, 451–52

a character in a *roman à clef*, 314

character strength of, 84–85

childhood memories, 22–23

childlessness, reasons for, 266–67

communism, attitude toward, 198, 214, 257, 532n49

considers becoming a Republican, 389

dating (and hypnotizing dates), 104

dating at Annapolis, 82

dating in high school, 44–45

decision making, speed of, 579n.33

demerits at Naval Academy, 95, 98

discipline problem (political letter published in local paper) preventing wartime service, 300–305

disciplining of, as child, 34

divorce from Leslyn, emotions and stress from, 434–35, 458–60

divorce from Leslyn, friends' responses to, 428–30

Heinlein, Robert Anson (*continued*)
  emotional nature of, 55
  extracurricular activities at Naval Academy, 70
  extramarital affairs, 538n.28, 577n.11
  fascination with the stars, 22
  feminist, anti-sexist, and women's rights
    advocate, 308, 373
  on fencing team at Annapolis, 28, 53, 54, 58,
    69, 73, 77, 79, 85, 86, 93
  film project ideas, 382
  financial straits after divorce from Leslyn,
    443–46
  financial straits after forced retirement, 170, 197
  financial straits at Naval Academy, 71–72,
    103–4
  financial straits during World War II, 335
  in fire control assignment, 97, 98
  flight qualifying exams, fails, 84, 115
  gallantry, attitude toward, 102–3
  getting out of science fiction, according to
    Leslyn's rumor-mongering, 439
  grades and class standing at Naval Academy, 70,
    78–79, 86, 93–94, 96, 99–100, 104
  graduate degree pursuit, rethought and rejected,
    172
  haircuts, 448, 508n.13
  as hazer or discipliner, 91–92, 100
  hero worship tendency, 84
  in high school, not liked, 43
  high school subjects, 34–35
  honesty of, in not hiding falsified test results,
    328
  house guests of, 317, 372, 384, 400
  house in Los Angeles. *See* Los Angeles
  hypocrisy, attitude toward, 102–3
  ice skating hobby, 395–96, 400, 412, 462
  illumination of, when researching new ideas,
    226
  independent attitude of, as child, 29
  as intellectual father to readers worldwide,
    11–12
  internationalism of, 388–89
  interviews with, 13–14, 326
  learns about justice, discipline, and punishment
    on board ship, 139–42
  legal counsel for accused seamen, 156–57
  and Leslyn, post-divorce, 441–43
  and Leslyn's drinking, obliviousness to, 385–86
  letters to and from home while at Annapolis, 54
  letter to father about financial straits at Naval
    Academy, 71–72
  life modeling by, 104
  and marriage, attitude toward, 114, 329
  medal for Expert Rifleman and Expert Pistol
    Shot, 167

medical career wished for, by parents, 40
meeting people and getting to know them, 208
mid-life self-assessment, 467–68
military interests and involvement, 36, 45–47
military pay in retirement, 170–71
mining venture in Colorado, 168–70
monetary theory of, 283
monikers "Bobby" vs. "Bob" vs. "Robert," 98,
  425
moral and legal issues re cohabitation with
  Ginny, 424–25
as moralist, 12
motion picture contract conflict, 418–19
mystical experiences starting in childhood,
  25–26
Navy service number (0-62624), 108
nudist activity, 163, 167, 259
odd jobs and money-raising schemes as teen,
  38–39
one-track mind of, when writing, 387
open marriage of, with Leslyn, 162, 329
outsider status, coping with, 55–58, 101
painting hobby, 122
philosophy of, expressed in letters to Armand
  Coign, 368–69
photography club membership, 161–62
as platoon leader at Annapolis, 56
political activities of, post-War, 364–65, 368,
  373, 377, 380–81, 388
political campaigning, 194–95
political involvement, attitudes and psychological
  constitution toward, 196
political leanings of, as radical liberal, 176,
  532n.47
political leanings of, not a conservative or
  rightist, 532n.47, 581n.56
political platform, 204
politicized by class warfare in Southern
  California, 187–88
post-war world, view of, 354–55
pragmatic socialist outlook, 212
prejudice lacking in, 33, 279
progressive and unorthodox ideas of,
  development of in teen years, 35–39
as a public figure, 12–16
public speaking by, 35, 188
reading, love of, 24, 29–32, 314–15
reading habits of, 314–15
as real estate salesman, 194, 197, 528n.12
recognition of own oddity, 92
relationship with Ginny, 425, 431
relationship with Mary Briggs, 110–11
relationship with mother, 29, 55
religious background and upbringing, 21
religious disbelief and skepticism, 111, 238, 300

research of new subjects, 223
rifle and pistol practice, 137
roommate's write-up of, for the Naval Academy
  class yearbook, 105
science fiction reading, 117, 129, 215
as a science fiction writer, with aspirations to be
  more than that, 15–16
sculpture hobby, 122, 124, 517n.12
self-assessment, 467–68
self-discipline of, 141
self-presentation, problems with, 56–58
sexual attitudes, 147, 162
sexual relations, 110–11, 521n.10, 561n.22,
  577n.3
social movements influenced by, 15
social outsider at Annapolis, 55–57, 101
social skills training at Annapolis, 85
spirituality of, 238–39
stammering problem, 19, 35, 188, 197, 199,
  227, 496n.9
theater endeavours at Annapolis, 70, 102
theater endeavours in high school, 35, 37–38
tooth knocked out by an irate husband, 98
travel lust, 40
typing skills, self-taught, 223
virginity, lost to a grandmother, 46
volunteerism of, 14
writing career, as business, 223, 535n.10
writing course at Naval Academy (Major-
  Browning class), 78
writing methods, 443–44, 543n.12, 586n.52
Heinlein, Robert Anson, health
  bladder cysts, 166
  cold, influenza, and sinus infection, 185
  deterioration in wartime job, 340–41
  exercise prescribed, 412
  eye and vision problems, 65, 84–85, 93, 95
  eyesight poor, 42
  gains weight and muscle after Plebe summer, 60
  gonorrhea, suspected but disproved, 165
  hemorrhoids and operation, 319–21, 324–25
  kidney ailment, 400
  medical problems impeding wartime active duty,
    295
  mental stress, medical attention for, 341–42
  physical, mental, spiritual deterioration as result
    of wartime overwork, 340–41
  physical examination before entering Naval
    Academy, 48–49
  prostatitis, 185
  pulmonary tuberculosis, 159–66, 295, 319,
    526n.59
  removed from high-altitude testing, 308
  seasickness, 159, 295
  sedative prescribed for, 341

sinusitis, 185, 348, 385
underweight, 48–49, 58
unfitness for combat, 324–25
urethral infection, 137–38, 143, 160, 165
weakness, while at UCLA, 172
wrist problem, affecting his ability to stay on the
  fencing team, 93, 95
Heinlein, Robert Anson, writings of
  agents for, moving away from Campbell and
    Street & Smith, 357
  atomics articles, 369
  bad, hack editing of, 284–85, 286
  "bad clear through" editor's remark, 425,
    581n.58
  boys' books, 348, 351, 378–80, 425, 432, 439,
    443–44, 455
  class yearbook at Naval Academy, 85
  difficulty with, post-Leslyn, 440–47
  evolving past pulp writing, 255, 264
  fantasy stories, 461
  fiction vs. articles, RAH's feelings about,
    376–77
  first fiction by (1929), 118–19
  first full-length book manuscript, 218–23
  first sale, 230–31
  first steps getting into SF writing, 215–18
  girls' books, 437–38
  irony in, 228
  juvenile writing, 348, 351, 378–80, 381–84,
    425, 432, 437–38, 439, 443–44, 455
  notes on first writings, and ideas for, 227–29
  pay rate from pulps, 248
  plot deficiency and need for coaching, claimed,
    417–19
  poetry and doggerel, 406
  popularity post-war, 373–74
  pseudonyms used, 233–34, 248, 303
  public influence of, 15
  pulps vs. slicks vs. book publication, RAH's aim,
    348
  puns in titles of, 229
  quotations from writings, 12, 397–98
  rejections, effect on RAH, 249–50
  remain in print, 15
  reviews by RAH, 291–92, 313, 326
  for shipboard newspaper, sample of, 132–33
  story structure, 546n.11, 578n.21
  story theme dilemma, 248–50
  story written for Ginny, 426–27
  "world-saver" articles, 406
Heinlein, Rose Elizabeth (sister), 20, 33, 55, 143
  accidental death of, 72–73, 77, 202
Heinlein, Samuel Edward (grandfather), 17, 18,
  19, 24, 483, 484, 488, 515n.36, 593n.9
  death of, 33

Heinlein, Virginia (third wife). *See* Gerstenfeld, Virginia "Ginny"
Heinlein Brothers, Agricultural Implements, 19, 24
"the Heinlein effect" (inspiring technological ideas), 377
Heinlein family, 475–76
  background and genealogies, 479–92
  disciplining of children, 34
  expectations of children's grades, 25
  finances of, 26
  German roots of, 479
  in Kansas City, 17
  love of reading, 29–30
  meaning of the surname, 480
  military tradition, 479
  move to Hollywood, Calif., 202
  political affiliations, 21–22
  religious observance, 21
  in World War II, 296
Heinlein Family Association, 479
Heinlein grid, 431
Heinlein-Hurst, Mina Ladine (aunt), 484, 515n.36
Heinlein-Pemberton, Alice Irene (aunt), 484, 515n.36
Heinlein Prize for Accomplishments in Commercial Space Activities, 14, 477
Henie, Sonja, 333
Henlein, Konrad, 205, 211
Henning, Carl, 95
Henry Holt & Company, 237, 271
Hepburn, Katharine, 179
Herbster, V. D., 140, 151
Herndon Monument climb, 73
Hevelin, Rusty, 315
Heyliger, William, 348, 382, 384
Hibbs, Ben, 411, 443, 585n.48
Hindu sacred writing, 25
Hinton, C. H., *A New Era of Thought,* 95–96, 103
Hirohito, Emperor of Japan, 100
Hiroshima, bombing of, 353
history of the future, 230, 238, 240, 249, 250, 258, 268, 378
  chart of, published, 276
  See also Future History series
Hitler, Adolf, 214, 278, 295, 347
  assassination attempt (July 20, 1944), 326
Hitler-Stalin pact, 243
Hollywood, Calif., 206, 363–64, 366, 418
Hollywood Citizen-News, 189–90, 305, 493
Hollywood High, 224
Hollywood Independent Citizens Committee of Arts, Sciences, and Professions, 365
Hollywood New Economics Group, 231
The Hollywood Reporter, 418

Holmes, H. H. (pseudonym of A. P. White), 252, 559n.32. *See also* Boucher, Anthony
Holt, William, 407
Holystone, 75
homesickness, 51, 54–56
Hong Kong, 295
honor code, 153–54
honor system, 83
Hoover, Herbert, 94, 98, 149, 162
Hoover, J. Edgar, 39
Hoover, John H., 115–16, 119, 128, 132, 134, 136, 138–39
Hoover Dam, 249
Horace Mann Elementary School, 24, 26–27
Horatio Alger books, 30, 31, 34, 383
Horne, Charlie, 588n.27
Horoshem, Isidore, 35
"The Horse That Could Not Fly," 394
Hough, Emerson, 546n.11
Hour of the Knife (proposal), 373
Howard, Dr., 166, 384
"How To, in Four Tricky Lessons," 428
How to Be a Politician, 180, 373, 387–88, 527n.1, 528n.16
"How to Be a Survivor" (article), 369, 390
"How to Write a Story" (humor article), 267, 288, 540n.17
Hubbard, Keith MacDonald (Leslyn's sister, Mark's wife), 295, 312, 320–22, 335, 348, 363, 384, 409
Hubbard, L. Ron, 253, 256–57, 308, 334, 335, 336, 339, 345, 369–70, 371–74, 382, 387, 390, 409–10, 438, 538n.28, 563n.57, 563n.59, 565n.27, 570n.17
  biographies of, 563n.57, 565n.27
  "Final Blackout," 256
  founding a religion, 563n.59
  RAH rejection of, 409–10
  RAH writing project with, 374
Hubbard, Mark, 289, 295, 312, 335
  death as Japanese captive, 338, 347–48
Hubbard, Matt and Colin, 384
Hubbard, Polly, 369, 409
Huddick, John, 341–42
Hughes, Howard, 449, 464
humanities, studies at the Naval Academy, 64
human race, future of, in space, 13–14
Hunt, Mabel Leigh, 455
The Huntington Park Signal, 177
Hutchins, USS (destroyer), 333–34, 343
Huxley, Aldous, *Brave New World,* 287
Huxley, T. H., 32, 35, 37
hypnosis, 125, 343
  of dates, 512n.21
hypocrisy, RAH's disgust for, 42

Icaromenippus, 432
ice skating, 394–96
ice skating story, 437–38
"If This Goes On—," 254, 256, 257
illumination, 226
Imperial Valley, 187
Incredible, 248
index cards, use in campaigning, 206
Indianapolis, USS (aircraft carrier), 352
Infantry Journal, 388
Ingalls, Roscoe, 188
Ingram, Bill, 80
injustice, RAH unforgiving of, 90
inspections, 138–39
Institute of General Semantics, 226
insubordination, 341
international control
    of atomic weapons, 359–62, 377
    of rocketry, 376
International Harvester, 24, 104
interplanetary travel theme, 382
involutional melancholia, 202–3, 533n.8
Ira Johnson, Dr. (character), 20, 35
Irvine, Jeanne, 284
Isip, M., 240
isolationism, 205, 295
Italy, Fascist, 198
" 'It's Great to Be Back!' " 407, 427
"It's Impossible!" (alternate title), 276
I Will Fear No Evil, 506n.10
Iwo Jima, battle for, 342–43

Jack (a Catholic boy), 33
Jacobs, Edward "Jake," 462–63
Jacobs, Sylvia, 462–63
Jameson, Malcolm, 390
Jameson, Vida, 400, 401, 403, 406, 411, 429
    house guest of the Heinleins, 390
    "The Thirteenth Trunk" (radio play), 408
Japan
    atrocities, 347
    attack on Pearl Harbor, and declaration of war,
        293–95
    battles with (1944), 333–34
    conquest of home islands, estimate of Allied
        casualties to accomplish, 343, 347, 352–53
    culture of, need to be destroyed, according to
        RAH, 335
    exports of oil and iron to, 239
    invasion of China (1932), 149
    militarized, 259
    occupation of, 367, 475
    peace overtures at end of War, thought to be
        buying time, 352–53
    RAH's hatred of, after Pearl Harbor attack, 294

    relations with U.S., war "inevitable," 100
    resistance strategy (1944), 326
    surprise attacks by, 149–51
    unconditional surrender, 354
Japanese midshipmen, visit from (1927), 79
Jazz Age, 13, 122
Jenkins, Will F., 304
Jerome, Jerome K., *Three Men in a Boat,* 31
"Jerry Was a Man," 394
Jet Propulsion Laboratory, 360, 365
Jewish coworkers at AML, 312
Jews, relocation in Palestine, 346
Johnson, Elizabeth (great-grandmother), 20, 482
Johnson, Mr. (in Technocracy movement), 254,
    547n.32
Johnstone, Don, 38, 301, 469
"Journey of Death" (article), 397–98
The Jungle (Sinclair), 15
Junior Literary Guild, 407
juvenile books
    for boys and girls, 437
    conventions and taboos of, 383, 425

Kamens, Sam, 366, 419–20, 440, 472–73
kamikaze (suicide pilots), 334, 335–36, 350
"kamikaze" think tank of science-fiction writers
    started by RAH, 335–36, 394, 438, 568n.41
Kansas, history of, 485–87
Kansas Border War, 486
Kansas City, Missouri, 111–14, 496n.6, 500n.35
    adult entertainment in, 506n.12
    Democratic politics in, 168–70
    gangsters in, 169–70
    history of, 485, 487
    midshipmen from, in RAH's classes, 69, 77, 86,
        99, 112
    politics in, 97–98, 327
    RAH's early days in, 13, 20–47
    RAH's later visits to, 108, 256, 359
    See also Pendergast political machine
The Kansas City Journal, 30
Kansas City Junior College, 46–47
Kansas City Public Library, RAH's part-time job
    at, 39, 41
The Kansas City Star, 27, 48, 86
Kansas-Moline Plow Company, 18
Kansas-Nebraska Act of 1854, 486
Kant, Immanuel, 147
Kaplan, Joseph, 172
Kean, John, 354, 358, 364, 367, 379
Keeping Posted, 407
Keith, Leslie (pseudonym), 286
Kellar, Harry, 498n.17
Kelvin Club, 35
Kemp, Earl, 552n.32

Kendig, Will, 553n.40
Kimmel, Admiral Husband, 293, 388
King, Ernest J., 125, 133–36, 138–42, 148,
    150–52, 154–56
  appointed to high rank by Roosevelt, 304–5
  RAH serving under on *Lexington* aircraft carrier,
    126–32
  RAH's secret wartime projects for, 335–37
  relieved of duty and career supposedly over,
    155–56
King, Martha, 518n.7
Kingsbury Ordnance, 358
Kingsley, Charles, *The Water Babies,* 24
Kinsey, Alfred, *Sexual Behavior in the Human
    Male,* 448
Kipling, Rudyard, 30, 332
  Mary Gloster, RAH memorizes, 68
  verse of, 118
Kitchin, Elizabeth (grandmother), 484
Klein, Alfred M., 379
Klein, Saul, 186, 493
Klyce, Scudder, *Universe: A Verifiable Solution to
    the "Riddle of the Universe,"* 511n.19, 521n.11
Knepper, Max, 187
Korda, Alexander, 199
Korshak, Erle, 446–47, 448
Korzybski, Alfred, 224–26, 236, 255, 259, 278,
    279, 283
  General Semantics seminar, 236, 259, 263,
    280–81
  *Manhood of Humanity: The Science and Art of
    Human Engineering,* 225
  *Science and Sanity: An Introduction to Non-
    Aristotelian Systems and General Semantics,*
    224, 225–26, 236
Kriegspiel game, played by RAH, 256
Kuttner, Catherine "Kat" (C. L. Moore), 301, 304,
    340, 369, 403, 545n.1. *See also* Moore, C. L.
Kuttner, Henry, 252, 253, 301, 304, 340, 351,
    369, 371, 374–75, 385, 401, 414, 572n.68
  "Hollywood on the Moon," 402

Labor movement, 490
Labor Temple (Los Angeles), 190
Laguna Beach, Calif., 363–64
Lang, Fritz, 286, 368, 377, 380, 382, 384, 406,
    454–57
  collaboration with RAH on trip-to-the-moon
    film story, 452–57, 589n.44
  Fritz, Willy & Bob and the Summer of '48,
    589n.44
Langley, USS, 135
Laning, Caleb Barrett "Cal," 66, 96, 99, 102,
    108–9, 112, 113–14, 123, 124, 129, 143–46,
    148, 152, 222, 233–34, 293, 295, 303,
    333–34, 343–44, 350, 356, 364, 365–66, 368,
    375–76, 386, 396, 401, 410, 429, 451, 454,
    457, 510n.15, 511n.19, 513n.20, 513n.22
  collaborative articles written with RAH,
    411–12, 415–18, 423–24, 431, 434, 440, 462
  "System in the Sky," 451, 454
Laning, Mickey, 343, 451
"The Last Adventure" (high school verse by RAH),
    44
"The Last Days of the United States," 376
Las Vegas, Nevada, 284
Lawrence, Kansas, 487
Lazia, Johnny, 78, 169–70
League of Nations, 36
Leahy, Admiral, admonishment of RAH, 191–92
Lee, Sunrise, 273
left-wingers, toleration of Soviet totalitarianism,
    329
Leighton's Cafeteria (Los Angeles), 191
Lepper, G. H., *From Nebula to Nebula,* 37
Lermer, Andy, 224, 421, 520n.40
Lermer, Mary Jean, 421, 513n.15
" 'Let There Be Light,' " 237, 248, 256, 541n.25
Lewis, C. S., *Screwtape Letters,* 314
Lewis, Samuel L., 231
  Glory Roads, 231
Lewis, Sinclair, 217, 240, 543n.12
Lexington, USS (aircraft carrier), 110, 114–56
  aircraft aboard, 130–31
  fire on, 130
  rotating duty on, 116
  in war games, 135–36, 149–51
Ley, Olga, 391, 429
Ley, Willy, 253, 254, 256, 286, 289, 304, 356,
    368, 378, 386–87, 391, 401, 406, 429,
    589n.44
  association with von Braun alters relationship
    with RAH, 438–39
  The Days of Creation, 291, 292
  RAH's reviews of books by, 291–92, 303, 326,
    561n.9
  Rockets: A Prelude to Space Travel, 326, 560n.9
  Shells and Shooting, 313–14
Leyte Gulf, Battle for, 333
liberalism, 123, 173, 329
  collapse of, 193
libertarianism, 14, 15
Liberty Bell, tour of the country in the Great War,
    28
liberty card incident, 115–16
Liberty Memorial (Kansas City), 46–47
life after death, 109
life-drawing class (high school), 35
"Life-Line" (RAH's first sale), 228–31, 236, 238,
    246, 315, 351, 357, 541n.18, 541n.19

Life magazine, 449
life-modeling jobs, RAH's, 104
The Lighthouse Annapolis student manual, 50, 61
Lincoln, Abraham, 183, 220
Lindsey, Judge, *Companionate Marriage,* 113
liquor, on board ship, 138
Literary Guild, 411
Little Boy, 352, 353
"Little Boy Lost" (alternate title), 416, 443
"little Oklahomas," 187
Loesser, Frank, "The Ballad of Rodger Young," 349
The Log (Naval Academy news magazine), 61
"Logic of Empire," 267
London, Jack, 31, 36, 546n.11
Long Beach, Calif., 128
   earthquake, 161, 524n.8
longhand writing, RAH's, 375
Long Island City, N.Y., 121
long-lifer theme, 264, 273–74
Longshoremen's Union, 175
Lookout Mountain. *See* Los Angeles, RAH
   house in
Lord & Taylor, 179
Los Alamos, N.M., 469–70
Los Angeles, Calif.
   overcrowding in, after the war, 363–64, 454
   RAH goes to live in, 171
   RAH house in (Lookout Mountain address),
      192–93, 254, 271–73, 364, 414–15, 421–22,
      588n.34, 592n.47
The Los Angeles Examiner, 434
Los Angeles Junior College, 188
Los Angeles Science Fiction League (later, Los
   Angeles Science Fantasy Society—LASFS),
   238, 269
The Los Angeles Times, 175, 177, 178, 179, 184,
   189, 190, 345, 455
"Lost Legacy," 234, 241, 245, 247–48, 249,
   267–68, 283, 284–85, 286, 303, 544n.32
"Lost Legion" (alternate title), 283, 284–85
love stories, essential in commercial fiction, 232
Low Countries, German invasion of (1940), 256
Lowell, Percival, 30, 436
Lowndes, Robert A. W. "Doc," 257, 281–82,
   284–85, 286, 288, 531n.39
Lucian, *True History,* 432
Lucky Bag yearbook, 85, 100, 104–5
Ludekens, Fred, 407
Luzon, Philippines, Japanese attack on, 293
lyceum bureaus, 500n.29
Lyle, Anna (aunt), 17, 488
Lyle, Bam ("Aunt"), 488
Lyle, Bam (mother), 17–21, 33, 86, 224, 238, 421,
   438, 488, 491
   golden wedding anniversary, 461, 466–67

letter to, 55
move to Hollywood, 202
not nurturing to RAH, 29
Lyle, Dr. Alva Evans (grandfather), 17–18, 19, 20,
   35, 161, 484, 485, 488–90, 593n.9
death of, 20, 26
Lyle, Park (uncle), 17, 29, 489
Lyle, Robert (great-grandfather), 485
Lyle, Robert (great-great-grandfather), 18
Lyle family, 17
   Irish roots of, 475, 485
   meaning of surname, 485
Lyon, Charles W., 194, 201, 205, 214

MacArthur, Douglas, 295
MacDonald, Anson (pseudonym), 259, 266, 275,
   276, 286, 303
MacDonald, Colin, 222, 520n.3, 538n.26
MacDonald, Florence Gleason "Skipper" (Leslyn's
   mother), 222, 289, 322, 335, 537n.24,
   538n.25
death of, 338
MacDonald, Leslyn (second wife), 144–48,
   152–54, 158–60, 164–71, 176, 196–97, 203,
   216–18, 221–22, 226, 227, 244–45, 254,
   271, 275, 279, 295–98, 300–303, 310, 312,
   313, 317, 320–23, 325, 329–30, 334–36,
   338–41, 343, 344, 349–51, 366–67, 369–71,
   381, 385–86, 391–92, 398, 400, 406, 408,
   411–13, 415, 419–21, 430, 432, 433,
   440–42, 451, 452, 458, 472, 493, 513n.14,
   522n.27, 523n.3, 524n.16, 531n.45,
   537n.24, 538n.28, 539n.28, 540n.13,
   548n.35, 561n.22, 577n.3, 577n.11,
   579n.33, 583n.86, 585n.42, 591n.47
affairs, 369–70
alcoholic deterioration, 442
alcoholism developing in, 385–86, 411–13,
   538n.28
article by, on V-2 rocket firing, 398
badmouthing of RAH, pre-divorce, 421,
   430
balance in relationship with RAH, 322–23
bouts of rage, 338–39
communication with RAH after the divorce,
   440–41
"Communists are Religious Fanatics," 197,
   531n.45
cooking of, 523n.3, 548n.35
depression of, 303
disappearance of records concerning, and
   consequent obliteration of direct view of,
   585n.42
dissatisfaction with marriage with RAH,
   539n.28

MacDonald, Leslyn (*continued*)
  divorce proposed, 419–21
  downhill life of, after divorce, 591n.47
  extramarital affairs, 524n.16, 538n.28, 577n.11
  fight with RAH's brother Rex Ivar, 244–45
  files for divorce, 432
  final satisfactory year of wartime work, 350–51
  fired from Point Mugu job, and joins AA, 472
  friends who took her side in split, 451
  gallstone problem and operation, 300–303
  health improving (1946), 385
  health problems, 203, 218, 591n.47
  ill health from war work, 325
  instability of, 330
  jealousy of Ginny, 413
  lack of support from friends during breakup,
    430
  learns of release of relatives from Japanese prison
    camp, 320–21
  literary agentry of, 408
  magical practices of, 343
  marriage to Jules Mocabee, 592n.47
  marriage to RAH, 152, 513n.14, 522n.27
  personality changes after three years of marriage,
    197
  pet name for, 420, 433
  physical, mental, spiritual deterioration in
    wartime job, 340–41
  poems for publication, 254, 271, 523n.3
  poem to RAH, "Little Miss Hitter-Skitter,"
    391–92
  poison-pen letters, 537n.24, 538n.28, 583n.86,
    585n.42
  political campaigning by, 493
  political leanings of, as radical liberal, 176, 329
  political work for the Democratic Party in
    California, 196–97, 493
  post-divorce dealings with RAH, 452
  psychological background of, 222
  psychotic episodes, 221–22, 350, 415, 537n.24
  RAH's appreciation of, 329–30
  recipe published in *Sunset Magazine,* 523n.3
  recovering from stress, ordered confined to bed,
    371, 381
  rehabilitation of disabled veterans, 344, 349–50
  relationship with RAH during World War II, 350
  resistence to psychological help, 537n.24
  science fiction stories writing plan, 296–97
  sexual relations, 561n.22, 577n.3
  sister's family trapped in the Philippines, 298,
    312
  state of RAH's marriage with, after six years,
    221–22
  stress from homelessness on post-war return to
    Hollywood, 366–67

  studying Korzybski's semantics, 226
  suicide attempt, 419, 579n.33
  supporting and mentoring role of, 413
  supportive of RAH's science fiction writing
    ideas, 216–17, 221, 227, 275, 296
  tachycardia, 381
  wartime strains on marriage, 317
  war work, 310, 313
  weakened physical and emotional state, from
    wartime strain, 322–23, 338
  wishes to see RAH post-divorce, 458
  at WorldCon, 279
  as writing "coach" (story doctor), 400, 406,
    540n.13
Macmillan Company, 223, 231
"Madcap Enterprises" (L. Ron Hubbard's), 391
magazine subscriptions, RAH's selling, at age nine,
    27
magic, 222
"Magic, Incorporated," 255, 365
magic tricks, RAH's fascination with, 28
Maginot Line, 256, 375
Maine, 75
Maine, USS, explosion on, 491
Major-Browning class, 78
Malina, Frank, 345, 360
Malzberg, Barry, 261
Managua, Nicaragua, earthquake at, 138
Mañana Literary Society (MLS), 252–53, 255,
    266, 284, 291, 314, 378, 391, 408
Manchuria, 354
Mandelkorn, Dick, 100, 172
Manhattan Engineer District ("Manhattan
    Project"), 346–47, 352, 360, 567n.18
  scientists of, 360–63
"Man in the Moon" (article), 369–70, 406
"The Man Who Sold the Moon," 416
  prediction of Moon landing in, 13
"The Man Who Traveled in Elephants," 461
"The Man Who Was Too Lazy to Fail," 65
Marais des Cygnes, Missouri, 486
Mardi Gras, 449–51
Marie, Queen of Romania, 79
marijuana, 89
Maritime Strike (San Francisco), 175
marriage
  forbidden to midshipmen, 101
  open, 222, 329, 539n.28
marriage-reform movements, 123
Mars, 30
Mars Hill observatory, Flagstaff, Ariz., 436
Martin T4M torpedo bombers, 114, 130–31
Marvel magazine, 542n.34
Marx, Karl, 36, 173, 536n.15
Marxism, 499n.35

Maskeraders (Naval Academy's drama society), 102
Masons, 112
Massey, Raymond, 199
mathematical symbology, 225
mathematics
    academic courses in, 92–93
    RAH's private study of, 95–96
Matz, Dr. Philip B., 94
Mayer, Louis B., 179, 184
McBee, Alice, 45, 78, 82, 89, 92, 113, 508n.8
    death of, 94, 509n.24
McCauley, Clayton, 130
McClurg's Book News, 432
McComas, Annette, 252
McComas, J. Francis, 252
McHugh, Vincent, 314–15
    Caleb Catlum's America, 199, 233, 314, 332,
        533n.52
    I Am Thinking of My Darling, 315
McKinley, William, 490
McPherson, Aimee Semple, 181, 182
medicine and doctoring, when RAH was growing
    up, 20
Meitner, Lise, 251, 373
Mencken, H. L., 181
"Men in the Moon," 375, 376, 388
merchant marines, 318–19
Mercury Artists Agency, 449
Merriam, Frank, 173, 175, 201
    won California governor's race, 183–84
Merriam for Governor organization, 178
"Merriam Tax" (anti-Sinclair fundraising
    organization), 179
Meteor Crater, Arizona, 363
Methodist Episcopal Church (MEC), 21
Methuselah's Children
    book project, 448, 451
    publication, 587n.62
"Methuselah's Children" (story), 275, 286, 290,
    446–47, 571n.56
Metropolitan Water District Strike, 493
Mexico, agricultural workers from (braceros), 187
MGM studios, 179, 184
Michelson, Albert Abraham, 107, 504n.3
Midland Manufacturing Company (Midland
    Implements), 18, 19
migrant farm workers, 187–88
military service
    Heinlein family tradition of, 34
    romance of, 43
Millay, Edna St. Vincent, 122
Miller, Russell, Bare-Faced Messiah, 563n.57,
    565n.27
mining, financial backing for, 168–70
"Misfit," 236–37, 248, 254

missile research, 365
Missouri
    history of, before and after the Civil War,
        485–88
    religious denominations in, 21
    volunteer infantry, inadequate provisioning of,
        491–92
Missouri Compromise of 1820, 21, 486
Missouri National Guard, 45–47
Missouri Synod Lutherans, 21
Mitchell, Greg, Campaign of the Century, 194
Mocabee, Jules, 592n.47
Modernism, 12
Moise, Stanley, 40
mokusatsu (kill with silence), 352
money, 220
money game, RAH's plans to write about, 283
monopolies, 218
Monroe, James, 484, 593n.12
Monroe, K. (Sophia) (great-grandmother), 488
Monroe, Lyle (pseudonym), 234, 248, 254, 256,
    283, 286, 531n.39
Moon, trip to, film story, 452
The Moon Is a Harsh Mistress, 14, 23
Moon landing
    Air Force announces intent (1946), 401
    RAH's yearning and planning for, 13–14, 148
moon rocket project, 376, 386
    discussed in Truman's cabinet, 401
    impetus from Navy research, 377–78
    RAH's, 354–70
Moore, C. L. "Cat" (pseudonym of Catherine
        Kuttner), 252, 253, 545n.1
    "Shambleau," 403
    See also Kuttner, Catherine
Morrison, Marion (John Wayne), 106
Moskowitz, Sam, 257
Moten, Benny, 99
Motor Boys series, 30
Moulton, F. R., 63
Mount Suribachi, raising of U.S. flag on, 342–43
movies, selling stories to, 379, 384
municipal utility ownership, 218
Munson, Gorham, 231, 233, 237, 240, 248, 253
Murrieta Hot Springs Hotel, Murrieta, California,
    367
Mussolini, Benito, 214, 347
Muster Notes (Naval Academy Class of 1929
    reunion book), 461
Mutual Assured Destruction, 14
"'My Object All Sublime,'" 236, 237, 248, 281,
    284, 286, 288, 541n.19
mystery writing
    not interesting to RAH, 351, 384–85
    RAH tries hand at, 374–75

Nagasaki, bombing of, 354
nakedness, RAH's fondness of, 20–21, 137, 163
National Club movement, 15
National Defense Act of 1920, 41
National Defense Research Committee, 328
National Fantasy Fan Federation (N3F), 552n.32
National Geographic, 40
National Guard, 175
Naval Aircraft Factory (Philadelphia), 75
  Aeronautical Materials Laboratory, 299–305,
    306–19, 325–28
  dysfunction in, 342
  exposé of wartime work in, 379–80
  RAH's memo at end of WWII, proposing
    future projects, 354–56
Naval Air Experimental Station (NAES), 325,
  345–46
  Materials Laboratory, 328–31
Naval Air Materials Center, RAH's memo to, of
  August 14, 1945, proposing future projects,
  354–56, 401
naval aviation, RAH's yearning to join, 83–85, 91
naval history, study of, 78
Naval Hospital, San Diego, 163
Naval War College, 149
navigation, 75, 119, 132, 134
Navy, U.S.
  airpower in, 114
  bureaucracy of, 375
  Bureau of Aeronautics, 386
  dysfunction in, clear to RAH as civilian, 339,
    342
  officer ranks in, 51
  peacetime, 100
  secret gadget derived from a RAH story, 256,
    547n.24
  social life, 128–29
  and space exploration, 401
Navy Regulations (The Book), 126–27
Nazi scientists, in American rocketry, 386, 439,
  589n.44
Negative Debate Team, 35, 45
Nehemiah Scudder (character), 232
Neill, John R., 24
Nelson, Harriet, 462
New Deal, 162, 175–76, 184, 211, 217–18
New Orleans, La., 438, 449–51
Newport, R.I., 75
The New Republic, 123
Newton Club, 35
New Worlds, 399
New York, N.Y., 75, 121–25
New Yorker, 379
New York Post, 434
The New York Times, 81, 179

The New York World-Telegram, 179
Nineteenth Amendment, 36
Nixie (dog), 158
Nixon, Richard, 404, 561n.14
"No More Rivers to Cross" (song), 100
Norden bombsight, 336
Norfolk, Virginia, Naval shipyards, 106
Normandy invasion (1944), 326
Northrup, Helen, 365
Northrup, Sara "Betty," 365, 374, 387, 390,
  570n.17
Northrup Aircraft, 377
Norton, Alden, 284–85
Nostradamus, *Oracles* of, 280
Novacious publication, 288
Novak, Frank, 49, 58
Nowlan, Philip Francis, 106
NRA (National Recovery Administration),
  162, 178
nude photography, 272–73
nudism, 163, 167, 259, 538n.28
  arrests for, 553n.41
  shows of, 199
  in stories, 260–61
Nulton, Superintendent, 59

O. A. Heinlein Mercantile, 18
O'Brien, George, 106
The Observer ship newspaper, 132, 186
Ocean Rancher (alternate title), 471
Ocean Rancher project with Scribner's
  (alternate title), 462, 465
Of Worlds Beyond (book of essays on writing,
  published by Fantasy Press), 428
Ogden and Richards, *The Meaning of Meaning,*
  217, 224
oil industry, 239
Ojai, Calif., RAH move to, 422–23
"Okies," 187, 230
Okinawa, battle for, 343
Oklahoma, U.S.S., 87–90, 112
  sunk, 293
Oklahoma Dust Bowl, 187
Old, Edward H. H., 95
old-age pension schemes, 209
The Oleanders (house), 450
Olson, Culbert, governor of California, 183, 185,
  201, 218, 247
Olson, Floyd, governor of Minnesota, 174
One World, 224
"On the Slopes of Vesuvius," 437
"On the Themes of Speculative Fiction"
  (article idea), 427, 428
open marriage, 222, 329, 539n.28
Operation Downfall, 353

Operation: Moon (collaboration with van Ronkel), 463–66
"Ordeal in Space," 452, 455
orders
  getting them in writing, 342
  obeying, 150
orders, military, Naval Academy class in, 78
Ordo Templi Orientis (OTO), 365, 374
Orpheum Theatre (Los Angeles), 99
Osborn, Donald R., 92
"other-endness" (of an earthworm), 26
Otto, Richard, 183, 184, 185, 190, 197
"Our Fair City," 336, 438, 463
Ouspensky, P. D., 315
  A New Model of the Universe, 226, 511n.19
  Tertium Organum, 147–48, 234, 511n.19
Oz books, 24, 30

Pacific Fleet, 149
Pacific Theater of Operations (PTO), 350
packaging deal in films, Schor's interest in, 462
paganism, 222
Paine, Thomas, 15
Pal, George, 462, 463–65, 469
Palestine, 346
Palmer, Harlan, 195, 489, 533n.53
Palmer, Kyle, 179
Palmer, Raymond A., 233, 249, 268, 550n.79
Panama Canal, 88, 119–20, 128
Panama City, 136–37
Panama Pacific International Exhibition (1915), 89
Panic of 1893, 168, 490
Panic of 1907, 18
Pannessa, Alfred, 435
Paramount, 464
Parker, Dorothy, 122, 180
Parsons, Jack, 339, 345, 360, 365, 374, 382, 387, 390, 408, 469, 565n.27, 565n.28, 565n.29, 568n.39
Pasadena Civic Auditorium, 181
Pass Christian, Miss., 451–52
past-life memories, 219
patriotism, 34, 36
  phony, 178
"Patterns of Possibility" (alternate title), 234, 236, 237, 249, 276
Pauley, Ed, 247
pax americana, 359
Paxton, Johnny, 364, 366, 371
Pearl Harbor
  anticipation of surprise attack upon, in 1932, 149–51
  Japanese surprise attack upon, in 1941, 293–95, 581n.56
Peenemünde, V-2 scientists from, 386

Peirce, C. S., 516n.9
Pendergast, Jim, 22, 180, 500n.35, 528n.16
Pendergast, Tom, 22, 111, 168–70, 327, 500n.35, 528n.16
Pendergast political machine, 21–22, 42, 77–78, 111–12, 168–70, 327, 500n.35
Pendle, George, *Strange Angel,* 565n.27, 568n.39
Pendray, George Edward, 304
Penn, William, 480
Perdue, Virginia, 284, 538n.28, 554n.56
Perreault, Seraphin Bach, 58, 62, 77, 99, 510n.15
  RAH's write-up of, for the Naval Academy class yearbook, 104–5
petroleum reserves issue, 239
phalansteries, 219, 536n.15
Philadelphia, Pa.
  graft in, 307, 438
  immigration through, 480
  RAH in, for war work, 305–19, 325–28
  RAH's travel to, to look for wartime assignment, 299–305
  sesquicentennial celebration, 75
The Philadelphia Record, 379
Philippines, Japanese attack on, 293, 295
photography
  nude, by RAH, 272–73, 313
  RAH hobby of, 272–73
"Pied Piper," 233, 284
"Pie from the Sky" (article), 376
pioneers, 487
Pittsburgh, Pa., 317
Pixie (cat), 451–52
Pixie II (Ethelrude Pixilated Colorado) (cat), 471
Plan Orange, 149
Platte City, Missouri, 113
Plebes
  life of, 49–60
  tormented by Youngsters, 76
The Plebe's Log section of *The Log,* 61
Plexiglas aircraft canopies, 328, 350
pneumothorax procedure, 164
The Pocket Book of Science Fiction, 316
pocket book publishers, 379
  interest in science fiction, 351
Pohl, Frederik, 248, 267–68, 283, 284–85
Point Mugu, Calif., 365
  Leslyn working at, after the divorce, 441, 592n.47
policy think tanks, 15
political campaigns
  how to run them, 204–11
  person-to-person, 206–8
  RAH's running of own, 205–11
political reform, topic in RAH's first writings, 220–21

politics
    RAH's early lesson in, 42
    RAH's how-to book for politicians, 384, 387
poll watchers, 182–83
"Poor Daddy," 437–38
Popular Detective, 416
Popular/Fictioneers, 284–85
Popular Front, 193
Popular Mechanics, 301
Populist movement, 15, 490
"Potemkin Village" (alternate title), 258
Potsdam Declaration, 352
Pottenger, Francis, 160–61, 163
power politics theme, 384
practice cruises, 74–76
Practice Squadron, 62
Pratt, Fletcher, 256, 297–98, 304
pregnancy, in unmarried women, and appendicitis,
    509n.24
"Problem Child" (alternate title), 290
producers, film, 463–64
Production-for-Use, 174, 185
progressivism, 31–32, 173–74, 193
Prohibition, 134, 138, 165, 168, 517n.13
Project Paperclip, 589n.44
"Prometheus 'Carries the Torch,'" 232, 233,
    234–35, 236, 237
propaganda, RAH's seeking a Naval assignment in,
    551n.2
psychic experiments, 343
public policy, science fiction's contribution to, 12
publishers, hardcover, interest in science fiction,
    351
pulp genre, 12
pulp magazines, 30–31, 40, 351, 542n.34
    pay rate of, 229
    RAH's last period with them, 283, 348
    search for new writers, 216
Pure Food and Drug Act, 15, 492
PWA (Public Works Administration), 162

Quantrill's Raiders, 486
quarterly fitness reports, 115
Queen, Ellery, 304
Queens Science Fiction League, 257
The Quest, 102, 109, 123, 148, 511n.19,
    512n.30

Rabbits (Kansas City), 496n.22
Rabelais, François, 570n.15
racism in science fiction, 260
radar, 336, 377, 451, 561n.17, 566n.2
radar proximity fuses, 336
radical liberal movements, of the late nineteenth
    and early twentieth century, 15

radio
    projects for, discussed in L.A., 418
    selling stories to, 379
radioactive dust weapon theme, 268
radomes, 336, 350
Railway Mail Service, 47
Ralston, Henry, 357, 378–79, 425, 448, 567n.9
Rancho Amelia (Ojai, Calif.), 422–23
Rand, Sally, 25, 37, 99, 163, 198–99, 221,
    510n.5, 532n.50, 538n.28
Random House, 232, 233, 237
rationing, wartime, 389
Raton, N.M., 473
reading, RAH's love of, 29–32
real estate, RAH possible career in, 178, 528n.12
reality, RAH's quest for, 102
Red Book pulp magazine, 572n.68
Red Cross, 320
Reed, James A., 42, 111, 168
Reina Mercedes (ship, and Naval Academy brig),
    83, 90–91, 98, 505n.18
Reinsberg, Mark, 446–47
reprints, 351, 357, 373
Republican Party
    1928 National Convention, 98
    1946 election, 405–6
    in California, 174–75
    freethinkers in, 332
    in Missouri, 21
    origin of, 183
    RAH considers joining, 388–89
"Requiem," 243, 250, 543n.17, 545n.39
resource salvage drives, 498n.19
Revolutionary War, 15
Rhoads, August, 484
Rhodes, Cecil John, 106
Rhodes Scholarship, 106–8, 110
    RAH disqualifies himself for, by marrying, 115,
    514n.27
Rhysling, blind singer of the spaceways (character),
    344, 401–2
Richardson, Robert S., 402–3, 452
Riefenstahl, Leni, *Triumph of the Will,* 199
Rifle Club (high school), 34
"Risling story" project, 378
Riverside, John (pseudonym), 303, 312
road city stories, 249
"The Roads Must Roll," 253, 258
"Road-Town" (later called "The Roads
    Must Roll"), 249–50, 253
Roaring Twenties, 16, 113
Robert A. Heinlein Archive, 491
Roberts, Owen J., 388
Roberts, Sammy, 92, 112, 113
Robeson, Paul, 457

Rob Wagner's Script, 197, 531n.45
rocketry, 345, 360
   American, 589n.44
   of the Navy, 377–78, 386
   Nazi, 589n.44
Rocket Ship Galileo, 407, 432, 437, 451, 463,
   465, 469
   film interest in, 449, 456, 458, 462, 589n.44
   success of, 438
Rocket Story (film project with Lang), 454
Rockey, Ordean, 194–95, 212, 493, 533n.53
Rockey-for-Congress Ball, 194
Rockwood, Roy, Great Marvel series: *Through*
   Space to Mars and *Lost on the Moon,* 24
Rogers, Alva, 345, 565n.29, 570n.17
Rogers, Hubert, 254, 302, 304
Rohm & Haas, 350
romance story structure, 546n.11
Rommel, Erwin, 326
Roosevelt, Eleanor, 345
Roosevelt, Franklin, 162, 175–76, 179, 217, 239,
   255, 304–5, 333, 346, 581n.56
   3rd term presidency, 262
   4th term presidency, 327
   death of, 345–46
   Fireside Chats, 178, 180
Roosevelt, Theodore, 15, 41
Roper, USS (destroyer), 156–59
Rose, Ralph, 271, 273
Rose, Stuart, 416, 585n.48
Rosicrucianism, 222, 542n.6
Ross (Pendergast man in Kansas City), 169
Rostoker, Adam, 573n.82
Roswell, N.M., flying saucers, 580n.47
ROTC (Reserve Officers' Training Corps), 34, 43
Rover Boys series, 30
Royce, Rosita, 199
Russell, Bertrand, 225
Rydeen, Paul, 565n.28

sadism, at Naval Academy, 66–68
The Saint's Choice, 374, 375–76, 384
Saint-Simon, Henri de, 261
Saipan, 326
Salute! (movie), 106
Salute magazine, 388
Sandburg, Carl
   The People, Yes, 280
   The Prairie Years, 280
Sanders (Coon-Sanders), 99
San Diego, Calif., 88
San Francisco, Calif., 133–34
   bridges at, 249
   RAH's diversions in, on a practice cruise,
     88–89

Sang, Grace Dugan "Cats," 371, 391, 413, 429,
   442, 545n.1
Sang, Henry, 316–17, 329, 336, 366, 369,
   371–72, 384, 391, 408, 413, 429, 440, 442
sanity gap, 225
San Jacinto tunnel, 494
San Joaquin Valley, 187
San Pedro, Calif., 89, 117, 291
Santa Fe, N.M., 359, 396
Santa Fe Trail, 487
Santa Monica Democratic Club, 173–74
Saratoga, USS (aircraft carrier), 149
The Saturday Evening Post, 265, 284, 411, 440,
   449, 461, 585n.48
   Heinlein stories published in, 13, 402–4,
     406–10, 416–17, 427, 443
Saul and Solomon (Jewish twins), 33
Saunders, Caleb (pseudonym), 233, 241,
   276, 286
Schenck, Joe, 184
Schmidt, Chief Yeoman, 116, 142
Schofield, Admiral, 151
Schor, Lou, 418, 432, 449, 456–58, 461–64, 469
Science and Invention magazine, 40
science and invention pulps, 31, 40
science clubs (high school), 35
science fiction
   anthologies, 315–16, 351
   conventions. *See* World Science Fiction
     Conventions (WorldCon)
   cutting-edge issues explored by, 12–13
   flourishing of, during World War II, 348
   Golden Age of, 260
   interest in, after the Bomb, 427
   off-color language in, 581n.58
   publishers of, 423
   in pulp magazines, 31, 117, 227
   RAH's boyhood reading, 40
   source of ideas for the war effort, 334
   transformed from a pulp genre to a public policy
     dialogue partner, 12
   writing of, 215–18
science fiction fans, 253, 254, 257, 268–69
   clubs, 215–16
   communists among, 257
   outcast status of, 279–80
   rude and malicious ones, 280, 398–99, 552n.35
   youthful, 278
Science-Fiction League, 215–16
Science Fiction magazine, 281
science fiction writers
   regular meetings of, in Los Angeles, 252–53
   think tank of, started and led by RAH, 335–36,
     394, 438, 568n.41
   value of, to war effort, 326, 334

Science Wonder Stories, 147
scientific method, applied to life problems, 225
Scoles, Albert "Buddy," 69, 77, 82–83, 86, 130, 136, 148, 299–305, 312, 365, 441, 462, 592n.47
Scopes trial broadcast on the radio, 54
screenwriting, 463
Scribner's, 402, 407, 411, 427, 432, 437, 439, 461, 462, 465
Script magazine, 253
Scully, Frank, 179
scurvy, 76
seamanship, 53
seasickness, 159
Seattle, Wash., 134–35, 153–55
Second American Revolution, 232, 238
security clearance, RAH's, for atomics articles, 375–76
self-discipline, 34
self-help and self-improvement movements, 500n.29
semantic pause, 226–27
semantics, RAH's research in, 224–27
serial-time theories, 219, 226
sex
    RAH's attitudes toward, 147, 222
    selling books with, 375
sex magic, 345
sexology, 37
sexual freedom, 222
sexual revolution, in the 1920s, 113, 122–23, 135
sexual triangles, 577n.3
"The Shadow of Death," 264
Shakespeare, William, *The Tempest,* 546n.11
Shakespeare Club, 35
Shannon, Joseph B., 111, 496n.22
Shasta Press, 446–47
Shaver, Richard, 550n.79
Shaw, Frank, 530n.26
Shep's Shop (Hollywood), 237
Sherlock Holmes stories, 31
shirking (malingering), 98
Shrine Auditorium (Los Angeles), 181
Shrine Circus, 443
shudder pulps, 542n.34
Simpson, Wallis, 199
Sinclair, Mary Craig, 125, 186
Sinclair, Upton, 15, 36, 173–84, 190–91, 197, 203, 212, 220
    California governor's race, 183–84, 489
    Depression Island, 184
    I, Candidate for Governor, and How I Got Licked, 184
    The Jungle, 125
    Mental Radio, 125
    power vacuum after retirement of, 185–86
    The Profits of Religion, 177

propaganda campaign against, 177–79, 180–81
    RAH meets, 186
Singapore, 295
Single Tax idea, 36
Siodmak, Curt, *Donovan's Brain,* 296
"Six Against the Empire," 263
"Sixth Column," 263, 271, 273–74, 275
sketchbook teaching method, 87–88, 131–32
Skidmore, Dick, 574n.6
Skylark IV (car), 265, 453, 461
slans and mundanes, 552n.32
slavery, and the Civil War, 485–87
slick magazines
    RAH's first sale to, 402
    RAH thinking of writing for, 348, 389–90, 427
Sloane, William, 237
Smith, Captain, 166
Smith, E. E. "Doc," 98–99, 258–59, 263, 265, 266, 273, 281, 308, 358–59
    The Skylark of Space, 99, 129
    Skylark series, 129, 237
Smith, Freddie, 518n.7
Smith, George O., 335, 340
    "Rat Race," 582n.58
Smith, Harry A., 46
Smith, Jeanne, 265, 266
Smith, Verna, 265
Smyth Report, 365–66
"Snafu Manor" (AML), 316, 339
social activities, in Annapolis, 64
social conventions, in science fiction stories, 260–61
Social Credit, 219–21, 290, 333, 536n.17
    RAH's book about (*For Us, the Living*), 230–33
Social Credit Union, 231, 233, 237, 240
Social Darwinism, 32
social engineering, 32, 225
socialism, 39, 123–24, 173–74
    American radical, 536n.16
    Marxist/communist, 173–74, 499n.35
    utopian, 32, 36, 219, 536n.15
Socialist Party, 173
Social Security account numbers, 247
sociology, as social engineering, 225
solar power, 218
Soldier Field, Chicago, 80–82
solipsism, 25–26, 497n.6
"Solution Unsatisfactory," 271, 276, 362, 373, 384, 545n.39
Sophie and Shively Lodes, 168
Southern California, 193
South Pacific, war in, 326
Soviet Union, 14, 198
    and the atomic bomb, 361–62
    invasion of Manchuria, 354
    propaganda against, 373

Space Cadet, 77, 444, 448, 451, 461, 469, 502n.8, 587n.62

space cadet idea, 427, 439

space flight, RAH's early interest in, 30, 83

"Space Jockey," 403

"A Spaceship Navy" (article), 411–12, 423–24

space stations, 377

Spaceways fanzine, 267

Spanish-American War, 17, 490–92

Spanish influenza epidemic, 29

Speer, Albert, 199

Spence, Herbert, 261

spooning (at the Naval Academy), 68–69

SRBP (Short Range Battle Practice), 76

Stalin, 278, 346

stammering, 496n.9

Stanton, L. Jerome, 335

Stapledon, Olaf
  Last and First Men, 287
  Odd John, 234

Starship Troopers, 23, 492

Startling Stories, 227, 416

Stassen, Harold, 389

Steele, Isobel, 254

Steinbeck, John, *The Grapes of Wrath,* 187, 529n.4

Sterne, Laurence, *Tristram Shandy,* 199

Stevenson, Ian, *Twenty Cases Suggestive of Reincarnation,* 25

Steward, Ron, 117

Stewart, Captain, 300–301

Stiles, Art, 65

Stimson, Henry, 346, 388

stock market
  crash of 1929, 117, 514n.33
  pre-crash, 105–6

Stone Acres incident, 153–55

Stover, Leon, 513n.22, 530n.29
  Before the Writing Began, 476, 493, 532n.49

Stowe, Harriet Beecher, 15

Stranger in a Strange Land, 13, 14, 23, 539n.30

Street & Smith, 227, 232, 258, 315, 351, 356–57, 378–79, 448, 567n.9
  acceptance of "Life-Line" story, 230
  RAH's rights problems with, 403–4

Streit, Clarence, *Union Now,* 224

student antiwar strike (1935), 188–89

Sturgeon, Theodore, 335, 557n.31
  Godbody, 563n.56

submarine operations, 92

"Successful Operation" (also called "Heil!"), 254

Sudetenland, 205

sugar, rationing, 306

suit diving, 462–63, 471
  almost fatal accident while, 465–66

Super Science Stories, 255–56, 283

Surigao Strait, Battle of, 334

Swanson, H. N. "Swanny," 271, 418–19

Swanson (unidentified victim of Leslyn's magic), 343

Sweetser, Lt. j.g., 126–27

Swink, Robert A., 178

Swope Park, Kansas City, 20
  train accident in, 22–23

Sykora, Will, 267

"System in the Sky" (article collaboration with Cal Laning), 588n.27

Tacoma, Wash., 118–19

Tacoma Narrows Bridge, 128

Taine, John, *The Time Stream,* 147

Take Back Your Government! 527n.1, 528n.16

"The Tale of the Man Who Was Too Lazy to Fail," 503n.20, 511n.17

The Tales of Hoffmann, 28, 53

Tarrant, Katie, 425

Tatnall, Frank, 358

Tat tvam asi (Thou art That), 25

Teague, Elwood "Woody," 65, 105, 194, 286–87, 511n.15

Teal, Quintus, 371

Teapot Dome scandal, 42, 501n.36

Technocracy, 254, 268–69, 280, 282, 548n.32

technological change
  dominant issue of the future, 12
  social effects of, 278

technology of language, 224

teleology and pattern-making, 32

telepathy, 124–25

Tennessee Valley Authority, 249

Terrill, Rogers, 416

tesseract theme, 259, 266

test results, falsifying, 341

Thalberg, Irving, 176

Thelema, 345, 365, 374, 570n.15

Thelma (daughter of Anna Lyle), 17

Theobald, Admiral, *The Final Secret of Pearl Harbor,* 581n.56

Theosophy, 222

"They," 258, 275, 282, 303, 497n.9

"They Do It with Mirrors," 375, 384

Things to Come (movie), 443

This Week magazine, 456

Thompson, T. B., 131–32

Thrilling Wonder Stories, 215–16, 229, 233, 237

"Thunder over California" leaflet, 181

Thurston, Howard (Thurston the Magician), 28, 498n.17

"Ticky hums" (jargony poems), 437

time
    and fourth dimension, 147
    serial, 219, 226
    theories of, 219
time binding, 225–26, 279
Time Enough for Love, 20, 65, 67–68, 505n.14,
    533n.52, 537n.17
Time magazine, 174, 179
Tinian Island, 352
Titanic sinking (1912), 22
Tombstone, Ariz., 436–37, 584n.20
Tommy gun, RAH learns to use from brother
    Larry, 39
"Tomorrow, the Moon" (article), 432
Tom Swift series, 30, 382
To Sail Beyond the Sunset, 20
totalitarianism, 193
Town and Country magazine, 452, 455, 456
Townsend Plan, 209
tramp (character), 23
Trans-Atlantic Fan Fund (TAFF), 575n.29
travel, in the 1920s, 62–63
Trinitite (mineral created by atomic bomb),
    362–63, 367
Trinity, N.M., 396
    test of atomic bomb, 352, 362–63
trip-to-the-moon film story, 452
Truman, Harry S., 168, 205, 345, 352–53, 388
    discusses moon rocket project in a Cabinet
        meeting, 401
    RAH's approval of, 327
    RAH's proposal that he resign and run again in
        1948, 405–6
Tsien Hsue-shen, 360
tuberculosis, treatment of, 159–66
Turchinsky, Flora, 189
Turner, Lieutenant Colonel, 397
Twain, Mark, 89
    1601 (play), 102
    The Adventures of Huckleberry Finn, 31
    as intellectual father, 11, 99
    "Mental Telegraphy" essays, 125
    as moralist, 12
    The Mysterious Stranger, 31
    A Tramp Abroad, 93
    What Is Man? 31
    worldwide grief at news of death of, 11
Twentieth Century Pictures, 184
typewriting, RAH's, 375

UCLA, 393
Uncle Tom's Cabin (Stowe), 15
Union Army, devastation of Missouri by, 486–87
Union Station Massacre, Kansas City, 500n.35
United for California, 178–79, 180–81, 182

United Front, 191, 193
United Nations Conference on International
    Organization, 346
United Progressive News, 185, 186, 216, 252
United States, role of, after World War II, 359
United States Naval Academy, Annapolis, Md.,
    49–109
    academic studies at, 63–64
    appointments to, 40–43
    Class of '29 (RAH's), 80, 348, 461
    class size, 64, 80
    daily regimen, 51–53
    degrees not given by, in RAH's time, 171
    fire in Isherwood Hall, 59–60
    Heinlein entering, 12
    midshipmen leaving or washing out, reasons for,
        64–65, 73, 79
    RAH's feelings at, as basis of a story, 230
    report cards, 64
    Ring Committee, 95, 510n.29
    roommates at, 49, 58
United States Naval Institute *Proceedings,*
    388, 431
United States Naval Observatory, 40, 107
"Universe," 268, 276, 373
    sequel to, 278
University of California, Los Angeles, 171–72
University of Chicago, 262
Unknown magazine (later called *Unknown Worlds*),
    227, 229, 237, 249, 253, 254–56, 258, 265,
    270, 275, 297, 303, 312
    RAH's list of story notes for, 245–46
"The Unpleasant Profession of Jonathan Hoag,"
    303, 312, 368
uranium, 353, 566n.2
Utah (BB-31), practice cruise on, 74–76
utility companies, 218
" 'Utopia' Means 'Nowhere' " (alternate title), 290
utopias, 218–19, 288, 291, 536n.15
Uzzell, Thomas, *Narrative Technique,* 417–19

V-1 buzz-bomb rockets, 326
V-2 rockets, 355, 360, 386–87, 391
    German development of, 438
    RAH views launching of one from White Sands,
        396–98
Vandenberg, Arthur, 405
Vanderbilt, Cornelius, 75
Vanderbilt, Gertrude Whitney, 122
Vandervort & Teague, 194
van Ronkel, Alford "Rip," 462–64, 469
V-E day, 347
venereal disease, 137
Verne, Jules, 30
veterans, disabled, 373

Veterans Division of the National Committee
(California), 196
veteran-with-TB story, 427–28
Victorianism, 12
"—Vine and Fig Tree—," 240, 241–43, 244
V-J Day, 354
voice of command, 127
von Braun, Werner, 386, 438–39
von Kármán, Theodore, 360
Voorhis, Jerry, 183, 191, 194, 218, 241, 248, 258,
262, 368, 377, 380–81, 386–87
loses congressional race to Richard Nixon
(1946), 404
voter registrations, fraudulent, claimed, 180–81

Wagner, Rob, 253
Wait, Delos, 101, 503n.20, 510n.15
Wake Island, 293, 295
"Waldo," 303
Waldo (character), 301
war, 225
war games, 149
War Mother' National Memorial Home, 164, 167
Warner, Harry, Jr., 267
Warner, Jack, 176
War of the Worlds broadcast, 535n.9
Washington, D.C., 453
Washington, George, farewell address, 240
Washington Naval Treaty, 114, 149
The Watchtower Society, 542n.6
The Water Babies (Kingsley), 24
water bed, RAH's invention of, 165, 525n.27
"Water Is for Washing," 416
WAVES (Women Accepted for Volunteer
Emergency Service), 331
Wayne, John, 106
" 'We Also Walk Dogs,' " 273
weapons, conventional vs. atomic, RAH's views,
375–76
"Weekend Watch" (RAH's first story), 118–19
Weems, P. V. H., 101–2
Weird Tales, 227, 271, 403, 463
Welles, Orson, 535n.9
Wells, H. G., 12, 29, 31–32, 36, 39, 83, 103,
123–24, 147, 173, 178, 199, 202, 218, 221,
225, 249, 250, 267, 278–80, 282, 301, 315,
360, 382, 443, 499n.15, 499n.35, 516n.10,
517n.10, 525n.27, 528n.12, 535n.9, 546n.11
"The Discovery of the Future" (speech), 278
Experiment in Autobiography, 280
First Men in the Moon, 282
In the Days of the Comet, 315
A Modern Utopia, 218, 250, 546n.11
The Open Conspiracy (What Are We to Do with
Our Lives?), 517n.10

Open Conspiracy concept of, 279, 360, 516n.10
Outline of History, 39
Phoenix (pamphlet), 360
RAH meets and gets book autograph, 267
Things to Come (film), 199, 218
"The Truth About Pyecraft," 301
War of the Worlds, 535n.9
The Way the World Is Going, 103
When the Sleeper Wakes, 31, 83, 218, 267,
525n.27
"Wings Over the World," 443
The World of William Clissold, 225, 360,
516n.10
Wentz, Elma, 186, 203, 216–17, 223, 240–41,
275, 429
"Beyond Doubt" (with advice from RAH), 241,
267–68, 275
Wentz, Roby, 186, 203–4, 211, 241, 255, 351,
375, 429
West Hollywood, Calif., 171
West Hollywood Democratic Club, 179–80, 181,
188–90, 493
West Hollywood EPIC Club, 191
Westinghouse Works, Philadelphia, 75
Westminster Press, 348, 378–80, 381–84
West Point, appointments to, 41
Westport High, Kansas City, 45
"While the Evil Days Come Not" (alternate title),
273–74, 275
whiskey, rationing, 306
White, William Anthony Parker "A.P.," 252, 283,
285, 375
Rocket to the Morgue, 314
Whitehead, Alfred North, 225
White Sands, N.M., 386
trip to see V-2 rocket shot, 396–98
white witchcraft, 222, 343
"Why Buy a Stone Ax?" (article), 376, 388
wife swapping, 538n.28
Wigelius, Frank, 100–101
Wilder, Thornton, Theophilus North, 75
William Morrow (publisher), 388
Williams, Yeoman Second Class, 142
Williamson, Jack, 253, 266, 275, 288, 291, 334,
336, 369, 396, 432, 583n.86
Willis, Walter, 575n.29
Willkie, Wendell, 262
Wilson, Woodrow, 36
Windsor, House of, 199
Winslow, Horatio, 578n.21
Winston (publisher), 384, 388
Wise, Stephen, 346
"Wise Choice" (poem to Ginny about separation),
453–54
witchcraft, 222

Wollheim, Donald A., 315–16
Wonder Stories, 215
Wood, Anson S. (great-great-grandfather), 18, 488
Wood, Rose Althea Adelia (grandmother), 20, 488, 593n.12
Woodford, Jack
  RAH's repackaging of advice of, 428
  Trial and Error, 223, 232, 250, 375, 417, 419
Woodrow Wilson "Lazarus Long" Smith (character), 273
world peace, 405
World Press, 281
World Science Fiction Conventions (WorldCon)
  1940 (Chicago), 263
  1941 (Denver), 277–81, 531n.40
  1947, 399, 575n.29
  1949, 575n.29
World War I (the Great War), 26, 28–29, 498n.19
World War II, 83, 278
  Allied gains (1944), 326
  end of, 354
  German gains (1940), 256
  German reverses (1944), 326, 337
  imminence of, and recall of retired Naval officers, 291–92
  Japan in, 295
  keeping America out of, 262
  Pacific Theater, 347, 350, 354
  post-war agreements, 346
  RAH's predictions about development of, in a memo for his own file, 243–44
  start of, 243–44

United States in, 293–354
U.S. declares war on Japan and Germany, 295
V-E Day, 347
World War III, 373, 384
WPA (Works Progress Administration), 162, 193, 493, 539n.1
Wright, Frank Lloyd, 205
Writer's Markets & Methods, interview in, 288
writing
  business end of, 223
  commercial, RAH's five rules for, 428
  creative end of, 400
writing of military orders, Naval Academy class in, 78
Wygle, Peter, 320
Wylie, Philip, *Generation of Vipers,* 315, 339
Wysocki, Ed, 547n.24

Yalta Conference, 346
Yarnell, Admiral, 149–51
Yellow Peril pulps, 260
Yerke, Bruce, 268–69
  The Damn Thing, 550n.86
Yom Kippur, 312
York, Simon (pseudonym), 375
Young, J. U., 84
Young, Rodger, 348–49
The Young Atomic Engineers and the Conquest of the Moon, 382–84, 388, 411–12
Youngblood Hawke, 122

Zagat, Arthur Leo, 255